TO ERICH LINDEMANN, M.D., Ph.D. (1900–1970)

A prophetic social psychiatrist,
inspired educator, and dedicated humanist,
whose teachings and writings have provided the
guiding spirit for our work

CONTENTS

CONTRIBUTORS

PETER N. ALEVIZOS, Ph.D.
Research Specialist, Camarillo-Neuropsychiatric Institute,
UCLA Research Center, Camarillo State Hospital, California

JEAN ALLGEYER, M.S.W.
Assistant Director, Venice Division of the Didi Hirsch
Community Mental Health Center, Venice, California

MORTON BARD, Ph.D.
Professor of Psychology, Graduate School, City University
of New York, New York

JOHN B. BAREN, M.S.W.
Assistant Clinical Professor of Social Work, Department
of Psychiatry, University of California, Davis, California

ROGER BARON, M.A.
Consultant, Center on Administration of Criminal Justice,
University of California, Davis, California

EARL J. BEATT, M.S.W.
Executive Director, Family and Children's Service,
Minneapolis, Minnesota

WILLEM G. A. BOSMA, M.D.
Director, Division of Alcoholism and Drug Abuse,
University of Maryland Medical Center, Baltimore, Maryland

A. NICHOLAS BRAUCHT, Ph.D.
Associate Professor of Psychology, University of
Denver, Colorado

BRYAN D. BROOK, D.S.W.
Manager of Community Alternatives, Southwest Denver
Community Mental Health Services, Inc., Denver, Colorado

SAUL L. BROWN, M.D.

Director, Department of Psychiatry, Cedars-Sinai Medical Center, Los Angeles, California

VIVIAN BARNETT BROWN, Ph.D.

Deputy Director, Didi Hirsch Community Mental Health Center, Culver City, California

GERALD CAPLAN, M.D.

Director, Laboratory of Community Psychiatry; Professor, Department of Psychiatry, Harvard Medical School, Boston, Massachusetts

RAQUEL E. COHEN, M.D.

Associate Director, Laboratory of Community Psychiatry; Associate Professor, Department of Psychiatry, Harvard Medical School, Boston, Massachusetts

RUSSELL R. DYNES, Ph.D.

Professor, Department of Sociology; Co-Director, Disaster Research Center, Ohio State University, Columbus, Ohio

DONALD J. EGAN, M.D.

Director, Drug Treatment Unit, Veterans Administration Hospital, Denver, Colorado

NORMAN L. FARBEROW, Ph.D.

Co-Director, Suicide Prevention Center, Los Angeles, California

FLOYD FEENEY, LL.B.

Executive Director, Center on Administration of Criminal Justice, University of California, Davis, California

JOEL FOXMAN, Ph.D.

Senior Coordinator, San Pedro Mental Health Service, San Pedro, California

NANCY K. GRAHAM, B.A.

Social Work Assistant, St. Francis Hospital, Lynwood, California

NORRIS HANSELL, M.D.

Professor, Department of Psychiatry, Northwestern University, Chicago, Illinois

CARL A. HANSSEN, M.D., M.S.P.

Chief Physician, El Monte Health District, El Monte, California

DWIGHT HARSHBARGER, Ph.D.

Associate Professor, Department of Psychology, West Virginia University, Morgantown, West Virginia

DON M. HARTSOUGH, Ph.D.

Associate Professor, Department of Psychological Sciences, Purdue University, West Lafayette, Indiana

EDWARD F. HEFFRON, Ed. D. M.S.W.

Deputy Center Director, Hazelton–Nanticoke MH/MR Center, Nanticoke, Pennsylvania

MARDI J. HOROWITZ, M.D.

Director, Stress Research Unit, Langley Porter Neuropsychiatric Institute, San Francisco, California

RUTH E. INGHAM, M.S.W.

Assistant Director, Benjamin Rush Center; Didi Hirsch Community Mental Health Center, Culver City, California

GERALD F. JACOBSON, M.D.

Executive Director, Didi Hirsch Community Mental Health Center, Culver City, California

FREDERIC T. KAPP, M.D.

Professor, Department of Psychiatry, University of
Cincinnati Medical Center, Cincinnati, Ohio

MICHAEL W. KIRBY, JR., Ph.D.

Research Director, Polydrug Treatment Center, Denver
General Hospital, Denver, Colorado

GERALD L. KLERMAN, M.D.

Professor, Department of Psychiatry, Harvard Medical
School; Deputy Chief, Psychiatric Service, Massachusetts
General Hospital, Boston, Massachusetts

ANN S. KLIMAN, M.A.

Director, Situational Crisis Service, Center for Preventive
Psychiatry, White Plains, New York

ALAINE KRIM, M.S.W.

Special Project Director, Child Development Center of the
Jewish Board of Guardians, New York, New York

DONALD G. LANGSLEY, M.D.

Professor and Chairman, Department of Psychiatry,
University of California, Davis, California

ROBERT PAUL LIBERMAN, M.D.

Director, Program in Clinical Research, Camarillo-
Neuropsychiatric Institute, UCLA Research Center,
Camarillo State Hospital, California

ROBERT J. LIFTON, M.D.

Foundations' Fund Research Professor of Psychiatry,
Yale University, New Haven, Connecticut

ROBERT E. LITMAN, M.D.

Co-Director, Suicide Prevention Center, Los Angeles,
California

RICHARD K. McGEE, Ph.D.
Professor, Department of Clinical Psychology, University
of Florida, Gainesville, Florida

ERIC OLSON
Research Associate, Program in Clinical Psychology and
Public Practice, Harvard University, Boston, Massachusetts

DONALD R. OTTINGER, Ph.D.
Professor and Director of Clinical Training, Department of
Psychological Sciences, Purdue University, West Lafayette,
Indiana

HOWARD J. PARAD, D.S.W.
Professor, School of Social Work, University of Southern
California; Educational Consultant, Center for Training in
Community Psychiatry, Los Angeles, California

LIBBIE G. PARAD, D.S.W.
Lecturer, Department of Sociology; California State
University, Northridge, California

TERRY L. PAULSON, Ph.D.
Psychological Assistant, Assertion Training Institute,
North Hollywood, California

PAUL R. POLAK, M.D.
Executive Director, Southwest Denver Community Mental
Health Services, Denver, Colorado

STEPHEN H. PORTUGES, Ph.D.
Associate Director of Research, Didi Hirsch Community
Mental Health Center, Culver City, California

E. L. QUARANTELLI, Ph.D.
Professor, Department of Sociology; Co-Director, Disaster
Research Center, Ohio State University, Columbus, Ohio

HELEN REID, M.S.W.
Coordinator, Pre-School and Infant Parenting Service,
Cedars-Sinai Medical Center, Los Angeles, California

H. L. P. RESNIK, M.D.
Clinical Professor of Psychiatry, School of Medicine,
George Washington University, Washington, DC;
Lecturer, Department of Psychiatry, School of Medicine,
The Johns Hopkins University, Baltimore, Maryland

DAVID K. REYNOLDS, Ph.D.
Assistant Professor, Department of Human Behavior,
University of Southern California, Los Angeles, California

ELAINE ROSE, M.S.W.
Clinical Coordinator, Crisis Clinic, Cedars-Sinai Medical
Center, Los Angeles, California

CHARLES R. ROSEWALL, M.D.
Chief Psychiatrist, Los Angeles County Crisis Evaluation
Unit, Norwalk, California

JAMES SELKIN, Ph.D.
Director, Violence Research Unit, Department of Psychiatry,
Denver General Hospital, Denver, Colorado

MAX SIPORIN, D.S.W.
Professor, School of Social Welfare, State University of
New York, Albany, New York

JOHN P. SPIEGEL, M.D.
Professor, Florence Heller Graduate School for Advanced
Studies in Social Welfare, Brandeis University, Waltham,
Massachusetts

JAMES L. TITCHENER, M.D.
Professor, Department of Psychiatry, University of
Cincinnati Medical Center, Cincinnati, Ohio

RICHARD L. VANDENBERGH, M.D.
Chief, Psychosomatic Division, University of Colorado
Medical Center, Denver, Colorado

RITA R. VOLLMAN, Ph.D.
Clinical Psychologist, Fort Logan Mental Health Center,
Denver, Colorado

GERALD WEINBERGER, Ph.D.
Associate Professor, Clinical Psychology Program, Teachers
College, Columbia University, New York, New York

VAIL WILLIAMS, Ph.D.
Chief of Research, Bereavement Project, Fort Logan Mental
Health Center, Denver, Colorado

CAROLYN WINGET, M.A.
Senior Research Associate, Department of Psychiatry,
University of Cincinnati Medical Center, Cincinnati, Ohio

CARL I. WOLD, Ph.D.
Director of Clinical Services, Suicide Prevention Center,
Los Angeles, California

RICHARD M. YARVIS, M.D.
Clinical Director, Division of Mental Health, Sacramento
Medical Center, University of California, Davis, California

THOMAS H. ZARLE, Ph.D.
Associate Director, Psychological Services Center, Purdue
University, West Lafayette, Indiana

JACK ZUSMAN, M.D.

Medical Director, Gateways Hospital and Community
Mental Health Center, Los Angeles, California

FOREWORD

The crisis model, in one form or another, underlies most of the work described in this book. The essential elements of the model that seem to me to have stood the test of time are that: *a*) it advocates immediate short-term interventions; *b*) it emphasizes increased receptivity and susceptibility to influence in individuals, groups, populations, and institutions during periods of temporary upset precipitated by a sudden significant situational change, and *c*) it draws attention to the arousal of motivation to intervene among "third parties," i.e., potentially influential people who become actively involved although they were initially not centrally affected by the situation (see Chapter 9).

The last point is of special significance, particularly since we have become aware of the pressing and widespread unmet needs for human services in our communities as well as of our inevitable shortages of resources. I believe that one reason for the recent popularity of crisis intervention is that crisis mobilizes interest and altruistic energy (see Chapter 19) among bystanders, and this encourages them to volunteer their help. Fundamental questions about the efficacy of crisis intervention have not been answered, in this book or elsewhere, and there is a clear and urgent need for evaluative research. But even though we do not know whether such intervention is in fact successful in the short or long run; the crisis intervention model does provide a point of leverage that makes sense, and it breaks down the vast overall community service delivery problem into manageable bits.

Since one characteristic of crisis is that the upset usually settles down spontaneously after a while, we must be careful not to overestimate the intervenor's contribution to what would have occurred in any case. Moreover, intervenors, irrespective of the benefits they may confer on people in crisis, are likely to be personally gratified by satisfying their own need to intervene that has been aroused in them by the crisis situation. They must, therefore, make a special effort to avoid complacently losing sight of the overall community service delivery problem, vast and frustrating as this is. They must constantly seek ways, in addition to crisis intervention, of fulfilling their mission to prevent and shorten human suffering and to improve the quality of life in the total population.

Such thoughts have guided me over the years, and while continually striving to exploit to the full the benefits of the classic crisis model in developing intervention strategies and techniques, I have also taken an interest in its limitations and searched for additional models to guide my planning and service efforts. I have warned against reliance on a single model, however powerful, and advocated a multi-model approach, likening myself as a user of conceptual models to a professional photographer who uses a number of cameras; each with its special mix of alternative lens systems, in order that he may invariably take high quality photographs, whatever the nature of his subject and the prevailing light conditions.*

Two examples come to mind that may alert readers of *EMERGENCY AND DISASTER MANAGEMENT* to themes they may find in a number of its chapters. First, I have encountered in my community mental health practice many situations, from bereavement to community disaster, which I originally conceptualized as pure crisis because they were characterized by upset precipitated by a sudden dramatic situational change and the obvious need for rapid intervention. (This often led to apparently good results in mobilizing useful resources.) Eventually, I discovered valuable additional dimensions when I realized that the *initial* crisis upset was usually followed by a *prolonged* period of adjustment during the adaptation to a radically new pattern of life. During this lengthy adaptation period there was an increased susceptibility to crisis (see Chapter 36), each of which might be helped by my usual crisis intervention techniques. But the issues involved in the long-term changes in life situations demanded that I continue supportive contact or that I supply such follow-up from other sources. I also had to come to grips with the realization that all problems in life are *not* "soluble," even if a person successfully accomplishes his "worry-work" and "grief work" in line with the prescriptions of crisis theory, and even if we help him deal entirely rationally with his predicaments by making the unconscious conscious. For instance, a widow who loved her husband never really *recovers* from his death—and certainly not within the period of a few weeks of the initial bereavement crisis—as we once used to think. The most we can usually hope for is that over a period of two or three years she will learn to live with her loss, and in spite of it to build other relationships and get other life satisfactions. If we really want to help her, we must do more than provide initial short-term crisis intervention.

Second, and related to this, I have begun to pay more attention to a particular element in our original crisis model (one that my colleagues and I at Harvard have now developed into a major model in its own right, which we have termed *support systems*). We have long realized the importance of the social surround, i.e., family, friends, neighbors, formal and informal caregivers, in modifying for good or ill the behavior of persons in crisis (see Chapter 2). Most contributions to this book can be interpreted as techniques for directly or indirectly improving the influence of the social surround to promote successful crisis coping. When we analyze the nature of the cog-

---

*Caplan, Gerald: Support Systems and Community Mental Health: Lectures in Concept Development. New York, Behavioral Publications, 1974)

nitive and affective elements in this influence, we may begin to conceptualize the social surround as a supportive factor of great potential importance that may not only help deal with the short-term aspects of time-limited crisis upset, but may also augment the capacity of individuals and groups to master the long-term challenges and burdens of enduring life changes. This support comes from continuing or repeated interactions with significant others—individuals, groups, and organizations—and it comes also from values and belief systems that have been internalized as a consequence of such interactions.

As my colleagues and I elaborated on this model, we began to appreciate the ubiquitous examples of its operation in nature, particularly in the form of religious denominations and person-to-person mutual help groups and networks. The latter are mainly nonprofessional, and until recently we professionals did not pay serious attention to them (apart from such obtrusive examples as Alcoholics Anonymous and Synanon). As we begin to focus on them, however, it becomes clear that they represent a field of powerful may rightly begin to ask how we may make use of them, or better, how we may develop some form of collaboration or partnership with them, in achieving our own mission.

The support systems model does not supplant the crisis model, but complements it, and also acts as a bridge between the crisis model and what might be called "the model of adjustment to long-term life changes." Together, the three models offer us more fruitful guidance than we have had in the past in achieving our human services mission of catering to the needs of people on a population-wide scale.

Gerald Caplan, M.D.
Director, Laboratory of Community
Psychiatry; Professor, Department of
Psychiatry, Harvard Medical School,
Boston, Massachusetts

PREFACE

What is a *mental health emergency*, and just how does it differ from a *crisis* or a *problem in everyday living?* Despite the wealth of literature on these topics,* the struggle to define and categorize these terms continues. One frequently quoted definition of a mental health emergency, which states that "all patients whose condition warrants prompt psychiatric treatment, for whatever reason, are designated emergencies," borders on tautology.† Some professionals, opting for a more specific definition, limit their usage of the term to those who might harm themselves or others or who are temporarily unable to feed, clothe or otherwise care for themselves. Then again, there are the pragmatists: if any individual has to be seen immediately, it's an emergency; if he can wait a day or two, it's a crisis; anyone settling for an appointment more than two days in advance has a problem in everyday living. The editors view a mental health emergency as resulting from "some unforeseen, isolated incident, which, if unresponded to, will result in life-threatening or psychologically damaging consequences."‡

A number of interrelated factors provided the impetus for *EMERGENCY AND DISASTER MANAGEMENT: A Mental Health Sourcebook,* and are focused upon and discussed by the contributors. These include: 1) the current depopulation of our mental hospitals, signaling a trend away from institutional and toward community care; 2) a negative result of that trend, i.e., the discharge of many crisis-prone persons, vulnerable to personal and social stresses, into often inadequate or virtually nonexistent community care support systems in many areas of the country; 3) the proliferation of easy access, walk-in crisis clinics and hot-line suicide prevention centers; 4) the growing interest of mental health professionals and paraprofessionals in preventive and remedial care in time of disaster (i.e., floods, tornadoes, earthquakes, fires, airplane crashes or train wrecks); 5) increased federal legislative activity promoting emergency mental health programs. (*The Community Mental Health Centers Act* [PL-88-174] requiring 24-hour emergency care; *The Emergency Medical Services System Act of 1973* [PL-93-154], which provides guidelines for medical and psychological

---

*Bloom BL: Definitional aspects of the crisis concept. *In* Crisis Intervention: Selected Readings. Edited by HJ Parad. New York, Family Service Association of America, 1965

†Ungerleider JT: The psychiatric emergency: Analysis of six months' experiences of a university hospital's consultation service. Arch Gen Psychiatry 3:593-609, 1960

‡Parad HJ, Resnik HLP: A crisis intervention framework. *In* Emergency Psychiatry Care. Edited by HLP Resnik, HL Ruben. Bowie, Md., Charles Press, 1975

emergencies, and the Counseling Assistance and Training Section of the *Disaster Relief Act of 1974* [42-USC-5183]), and 6) the ongoing professional commitment to improve the coping repertories of individuals, families, and groups during periods of stress-induced disequilibrium.

A continuing education seminar on emergency mental health, sponsored by the National Institute of Mental Health in Washington, D.C. (June, 1973) brought together a number of professionals whose talents had focused on these subjects. With these six major factors as a basis for the discussions, new perspectives on suicide prevention, crisis intervention, urban violence, disaster aid, and other aspects of emergency mental health care were presented. Contributors to the seminar evaluated experimental programs that had been initiated utilizing brief therapy and continuing care on a community level. The emphasis was not only on treating the problems of the individual, but on involving significant others in responding to those problems, thus offering constructive support to the person in need. Also emphasized was the need for immediate response to an individual in crisis through the establishment of mental health teams in community outreach services and hospital emergency rooms where, after initial treatment, patients are referred to community services for follow-up. In the aftermath of a disaster, the needs of a community in crisis are met by teams of crisis professionals who seek out persons in need and direct them through the stages of immediate and long-range care.

EMERGENCY AND DISASTER MANAGEMENT: A Mental Health Sourcebook is a compilation of the material presented at that June 1973 seminar, supplemented by additional contributions from other leading professionals specializing in these areas. The material herein is relevant to the needs and concerns of mental health administrators, practitioners, students, researchers, and other human service professionals in assisting individuals, families, or communities in crisis situations.

Many persons and organizations have encouraged our endeavors. We express our deep appreciation to Dr. Bertram Brown, Director of the National Institute of Mental Health; Dr. Arnold Beisser, Director of the Center for Training Community Psychiatry, Los Angeles (where the senior editor has served as a consultant on emergency mental health), and Dr. Norman Farberow, Co-Director of the Suicide Prevention Center of Los Angeles. Of course, we owe a special debt of gratitude to Dr. Gerald Caplan and to the many mental health professionals and social scientists who gave so generously of their time in preparing the chapters of this volume.

If this sourcebook stimulates further practive innovation and study, resulting in cumulative knowledge-building in the field of emergency mental health, our efforts will be abundantly rewarded.

H.J.P.
H.L.P.R.
L.G.P.

EMERGENCY
and
DISASTER
MANAGEMENT

Emergency Mental Health Services

I

program designs and perspectives

The papers in this section present a range of innovative approaches, reflecting how mental health professionals struggle with implementing community care programs, meeting emergency needs, and coping with the problems created by current policies of dehospitalization.

Describing the advantages and pitfalls of providing emergency mental health services within a general hospital setting, Klerman stresses the importance of a three-way linkage between the community mental health center, the general hospital, and the state hospital if the goals of accessibility, comprehensive treatment, continuity of treatment, and avoidance of hospitalization are to be met.

In Hansell's design the convening of a cluster, or group, provides a social context which counteracts the fragmenting of our social networks and enhances adaptational work by the person in distress. Hansell argues that the person should enter a helping system that has the flexibility to offer whatever service is needed—rather than force the hapless person to route himself through the mental health maze.

Langsley and Yarvis describe the translation of the Denver pilot project (a controlled experiment in offering alternatives to hospitalization) into a countywide community mental health program despite problems of population size, resource constraints, geography, and staffing.

While Hansell's model brings persons to an agency which then moves back to community, and Langley and Yarvis mention the desirability of home visits, Foxman's psychiatric emergency team moves out of the clinic to provide emergency services in the home. The team's focus on alternatives to

1

hospitalization stimulates a comprehensive program of community consultation, especially for the police.

Another use of home visits is discussed by Selkin and Braucht in their chapter on Home Treatment of Suicidal Persons. *They evaluate the effectiveness of treatment in the home by visiting nurses who have received a minimum of special training and support through consultation. Their experimental–control group design, utilizing a variety of measuring instruments, is illustrative of the type of study needed to measure differential program effectiveness.*

The Continuing Relationship Maintenance Program *described by Litman, Wold, and Graham in their progress report, is aimed at the population at highest risk, i.e., chronically suicidal persons with high lethality ratings. It describes a novel postcrisis intervention service delivered by volunteers under the leadership of paraprofessionals.*

The community is again the locus of treatment for another high-risk group at the Fort Logan Mental Health Center, which has used a group home as an alternative to hospitalization in an acute psychiatric ward. The negatives, including staff anxiety, as well as impact and effectiveness, are candidly presented.

An ancient ward proved a serendipitous setting for the Crisis Evaluation Unit, a county unit established to screen patients who had arrived for admission at a state hospital. Although located at the hospital, this gatekeeping unit has been using crisis intervention techniques focused on alternatives to hospitalization.

The chapters in Part I show a variety of administrative arrangements to 1) maximize the use of mental health manpower, 2) emphasize accessibility, reaching out, and follow-up, 3) stress avoidance of hospitalization, and 4) reflect the current concern for accountability in terms of program effectiveness and cost.

LINKING COMMUNITY HEALTH PROGRAMS TO HOSPITAL EMERGENCY SERVICES

Gerald L. Klerman

The rational development of emergency medical services, including emergency mental health services, is a pressing national concern. Currently, there is widespread conviction that available professional skills and therapeutic techniques are not being utilized effectively, in large part because of the poor organization and lack of coordination characteristic of the American health delivery system.

In this chapter the development of emergency psychiatric services is approached as an organizational and administrative problem: *How does the current system operate? Can a systems approach offer insights for new designs?* Specifically, the focus is on the linkages between psychiatric emergency services in general hospitals and community mental health center programs. Although formal data are not available, my impression is that such linkage for provision of emergency services is frequent. It has historic precedents; one of the stated goals of the NIMH program, enunciated after the Kennedy message in 1963, was to offer priority to mental health centers developed in close relationship to general hospitals as part of the stated desire to bring the care and treatment of the mentally ill back into the mainstream of medicine.

This linkage has important functional strengths. Over the past two decades, utilization and scope of the general hospital emergency service have increased rapidly. It is seen by the community and its agencies as a major portal of entry into the health care system. The available evidence indicates that utilization of psychiatric emergency services has increased more rapidly in the past two decades than has the urban population or the use of emergency services in general (453). The reasons for this increase are multiple, but whatever their source, the trend demonstrates increased public awareness, accessibility, and acceptance of mental health services within the total health model.

Since emergency services in general hospitals are seldom mandated or organized to provide continuing care or definitive treatment, alternative resources must be readily available. Here the community mental health center provides a functional, complementary linkage, since its mandate calls for a range of services (inpatient, outpatient, partial hospitalization) for coordinated programing and continuity of care. Thus, historically and functionally, the linkage between the general hospital emergency services and the community mental health center program has society's sanction and support. Before reviewing the experiences of two urban settings, it is desirable to describe the theoretical orientation we have used in planning, operating, and evaluating these services.

Our theoretical approach derives in large part from the trenchant analyses by Goffman (147), Parsons (317), and other social scientists who have pointed out the highly structured nature of the mental health system and its multiple barriers to the patients seeking treatment.

In the experiences reported here, a systems approach was utilized to understand the relationship of the two components of the mental health system: the general hospital and the mental health center. These observations are interpreted by approaches developed in the operations research area and applied by the Tavistock group (288) to health care systems. This approach offers a model by which institutions may compare entry systems with each other and within their own structure when reorganizations occur.

A community's mental health system may be regarded as a *throughput* system, taking patients and processing them through various administrative practices and intake, evaluation, and treatment programs with the goal of discharging them back into the community as "nonpatients."

THE ENTRY PROCESS

Processes of entry can be described in systems language and terminology. In an attempt to conceptualize these entry processes in a systematic fashion, we have subdivided *entry* into five major phases, which are by no means rigidly demarcated but are interrelated.

Epidemiology

Important here are the processes within the population at risk which results in persons developing symptoms and behaviors of mental illness. These community processes are usually measured by indices which are related to the potential incidence and prevalence of disorders in the community. Such indices include measures of social disorganization, economic welfare, and current admission rates to mental health facilities, as well as of the standard social–demographic characteristics of the population.

The Decision to Seek Health Care

Epidemiologic and sociologic research indicates that the incidence of health problems is high, but that only a fraction of persons define these as health problems and decide to seek assistance from the formally designated health institutions such as general hospitals or community mental health centers.

Entry

This phase involves transactions by which the individual is taken into the clinical facility, e.g., the organizational and administrative policies of the hospital or center, its staffing and service patterns, its training and research activities.

Evaluation

This phase includes the activities by which the staff members of the hospital and center bring their expertise to bear on understanding the patient's illness and planning a suitable treatment program. Various professional activities are usually brought into play during the evaluation phase; these include diagnostic interviewing; medical procedures such as physical examination, laboratory tests, x ray, and EEG; psychological testing, including projective tests and intelligence testing; and interviewing families. In addition to specific professional procedures, these activities involve the subtle social psychological transactional processes between clinicians and patients.

Allocation to Treatment Resources

The evaluation phase leads to some assessment of need (the diagnosis in medical settings) and of disposition (the treatment). In the case of emergency services, it is most likely that the treatment resources will lie elsewhere than in the general hospital emergency service ("elsewhere" meaning in a different geographic architectural setting, under different administrative and fiscal auspices and direction, and carried out by different persons).

PROBLEMS

From this simple analysis, it is evident that major discontinuities exist in the processes whereby emergency mental health services are provided. It is the task of the planners and the administrative executives to identify these discontinuities and to develop mechanisms for minimizing their impact on the patient in a mental health emergency.

When we focus on the entry process as a crucial decision point, we see that this process involves a complicated set of transactions between the applicant and one or more clinicians and other staff. At the end of the entry process, services are either offered or not, and they are either accepted or they are not. The extremes of these decisions are clear: 1) if no applicants are offered treatment, then something is amiss in the understanding of the applicants or in the understanding of their referral sources about the nature of services being offered; 2) if treatment is being offered to everyone, then there is either a lack of discrimination or an elaborate and effective (formal or informal) screening process occurring before the applicant is seen by a clinician; 3) similarly, if a high proportion of patients drop out after being recommended for treatment, there is a need for a closer review and alteration of either the evaluation proper or barriers within the institutions which make it difficult for patients to begin treatment.

THE NEW HAVEN EXPERIENCE

The entry process for emergency services in greater New Haven and in the Harbor area of Boston was studied and detailed attention given to linkages between the emergency service of a general hospital and the community mental health centers within both communities. These two facilities represented the predominant sources of public mental health care. The decision points and outcomes of the entry process for emergency care are particularly important. A sizable component not studied involves the private practitioners of psychiatry and psychology. Although both cities have a higher percentage of such practitioners than the national average, informal evidence indicates that the general hospital and the community mental health center provide the largest volume of mental health services.

The author's observations about New Haven are derived from personal experience as Director of the Connecticut Mental Health Center, and from a number of formal research studies on emergency mental health services (453, 454).

This extensively studied community was the site of a major epidemiologic study by Hollingshead and Redlich (180) in the early 1950s. While the city of New Haven proper has declined slightly in population in the last decade, the larger region, including the suburbs, has grown in total population. Its ethnic. racial, and social composition is representative of many Northern urban communities.

Since the Hollingshead-Redlich study (180), the community's mental health services have undergone extensive evolution. New Haven is now served by a full range of facilities including a mental health center, a Veterans Administration hospital, a state mental hospital, two child guidance clinics, psychiatric units of two general hospitals, and a sizable number of private practitioners.

The Facilities Available

Clinical experience and previous research had indicated that the greatest proportion of adult outpatient care was provided by two community facilities, the Yale–New Haven Hospital and the Connecticut Mental Health Center (CMHC). The Yale–New Haven Hospital is a prestigious facility with major university teaching and research involvement. During the period of our study, a large volume of psychiatric care was provided within the hospital's Emergency Service (ES) which, like other facilities in large urban general hospitals, has had an increased volume of patients seeking care. [This service has been studied extensively in the past two decades by Errera, Wyshak, and Jarecki (113); Coleman (81); Schwartz (375); and Tischler (406).]

The CMHC is a relatively new institution, jointly operated by Yale University and the State of Connecticut. It is conveniently located and has a modern building with a wide range of facilities. Opened in 1966, it was intended to serve as a model of a university-affiliated community mental health center. While patients were admitted from the greater New Haven region, the major commitment was to a specific catchment area of about 72,000 persons (the Hill–West Haven area), and a separate clinical administrative service was organized for this area (219, 345).

For the Hill–West Haven service, there was a major effort to provide psychiatric services to the lower socioeconomic groups. The therapeutic orientation emphasized increasing accessibility to lower income patients, and group therapy was combined with individual psychotherapy.

Acquiring Data to Evaluate the Programs

The data reported here were derived from samples of patients taken at the two institutions. In 1968–1969, a random sample of one third of all patients who kept their first appointments at the CMHC were interviewed, and data were collected on expectations, symptomatology, and social background. During a comparable period, samples were also taken of patients coming to the ES, and information on social background, clinical symptoms, and patient expectations were collected by interview and questionnaire. Only those data relative to immediate outcome are reported here. Data from a 10-year review of operations of Yale–New Haven Hospital ES were used as a comparison along with extensive analyses of mental health center programs developed under the Psychiatric Utilization Review and Evaluation program (PURE) (349).

Defining Patient Needs

The Yale–New Haven Hospital and CMHC shared administrative and clinical responsibilities for all emergency psychiatric services. The ES was located in the general medical hospital, and therefore physically separate from CMHC. It was staffed 24 hours a day, 7 days a week, by second–year psychiatric residents who were in training with the Yale Department of Psychiatry. The psychiatrists on duty saw patients with psychiatric complaints, as well as many who presented surgical, medical, and neurologic problems. Those psychiatric patients who came to CMHC, and were in need of immediate medical or surgical services were sent or taken directly to ES. This category included alcoholics in withdrawal states and patients attempting suicide. Usually, an evaluation interview was completed in such a single visit, but took up to 15 hours for an appropriate treatment plan to be reached. In 1969–1970, 2485 persons were seen in the psychiatric component of the ES for a total of 3401 visits. The majority (75%) were seen for only one visit.

Although the number of patients seen at the CMHC and at the ES are roughly comparable, the attitudes of the patients are often different. Many patients who come to the ES have not defined their conditions as psychiatric or considered them under the rubric of mental illness.

Factors to Consider in Arranging Treatment.   The initial triaging, performed by the senior nurse, is an important decision point. The task for the psychiatrist on duty, usually a resident in training, involves this decision—to determine that the sorting has been appropriate and that the condition needing immediate attention really is psychiatric. Often, consultations with internists, pediatricians, neurologists, and other medical specialists were needed before definitive decisions could be made. Some patients must receive medical or surgical attention before they can be seen by a psychiatrist. These include persons with injuries or drug problems, and persons attempting suicide. Of these latter groups, a sizable proportion are hospitalized.

Evaluating the Data

The dominant activities of the psychiatric ES in a general hospital involve evaluation to determine whether the patient is in need of psychiatric or medical evaluation and disposition and a decision on psychiatric treatment allocation. Such decisions include hospitalization versus nonhospitalization, designation for outpatient treatment and referral, and consultation and crisis treatment. Most decisions are made immediately and involve diverse dispositions.

From the data collected on these patients, a number of observations emerged.

Effect on Emergency Services.   A review by Zonana et al. (453) of 10 years of emergency services indicates that no decrease occurred in the use of psychiatric emergency services, at least up through 1972. The early expectation that the opening of a community mental health center would provide an alternative treatment resource and thus reduce utilization of the ES was not realized, at least not within the first 3–4 years after the opening of the CMHC. Nor was this reduction achieved for the specific Hill–West Haven catchment area which was served by the federally supported comprehensive service. If anything, there was a high degree of new cases and increased use of all mental health facilities. As we later indicate, data from the Boston experience suggest that there may be a time lag and that increased availability of facilities ultimately may reduce use of emergency services, particularly if community-based neighborhood or outreach facilities are developed.

Facilities Used by Patients.   There was a high degree of utilization of both facilities. Over 50% of the patients used both the mental health center and emergency room. This was particularly true for patients of the lower socioeconomic groups, who regarded the two facilities as interchangeable and often presented themselves during periods of crises at both facilities.

Effect on Hospital Admissions.   There was no immediate reduction in admissions to the Connecticut Valley State Hospital. In fact, the analysis done by Klerman and Missett (220) indicates that decreased admission to the state hospital due to the number of psychotic patients treated by the CMHC was more than offset by an increase in patients being treated at the state hospital for alcoholism and for problems with drug abuse and drug dependence.

Finding the Weak Links.   Continuous efforts were required to develop closer clinical and administrative relations between the CMHC and the ES of the general hospital. The ES saw a large volume of patients, but only a small fraction were referred for treatment within the resources of the general hospital. The two major "outflows" from the ES of the general hospital were to the CMHC (30%) and to the state hospital (25%). While considerable work was done to develop the linkages between ES at the general hospital and the CMHC, relatively little effort was made, at least up through 1970, to develop the linkages to the state hospital, which continued to receive a sizable number of admissions from the greater New Haven area. Subsequently, in 1972–1973, efforts were made to develop and improve administrative and clinical relations with the Connecticut Valley State Hospital which had undergone its own internal metamorphosis, including development of a unit specifically designated to serve the New Haven area. The development of unitization at the state hospital provided an administrative basis for later forging of linkages with the ES–CMHM complex in New Haven proper.

Problem Areas.   These arrangements, constituting a partial system, were characterized by dissatisfaction by all concerned. The ES of the general hospital was a frequent object of public criticism and citizens' complaints, particularly by lower income patients and by representatives of the Black and Puerto Rican communities and other minority groups. The consumer dissatisfaction was mirrored by the sense of frustration and impotence of the professional staff who felt that they were faced with increasing numbers of patients, only a fraction of whom they considered to be experiencing true emergencies. The prospect of an ever-increasing number of patients with multiple problems, coupled with limited community resources, produced more frustration and irritation, not only by the clinical staff assigned to the ES, but also by the administrative staff who felt the administrative and fiscal burden of the ever-increasing demand on the ES in general and its psychiatric component in particular.

Problems in Staff Approach.   These contentions were reflected in conflicts among the faculty and staff of the Yale Department of Psychiatry at the Yale–New Haven Hospital and the CMHC, as well as among the many trainees. In part, this was due to a lack of definition of commonly shared goals and, in part due to differences in ideology and commitment to various aspects of training for specific psychiatric skills, such as individual psychotherapy and development of community-based services (50).

These trends are illustrative of the rapid changes within the mental health care system in the late 1960s and the pressures on health centers caused by changes within the system itself and from the marked socioeconomic changes, particularly in cities like New Haven with large proportions of minority group patients living in inner city ghettos. For these patients, the psychiatric emergency services of the general hospital and university health center complex are crucial as visible and accessible resources for assisting them in meeting the multiple problems which beset their families. Health-seeking behavior at a time of crisis has, at least until recently, been the predominant form of urban minorities' relationship to the mental health system.

The New Haven experiences were valuable when planning began for the comprehensive community mental health services for the Harbor catchment area in the Greater Boston area.

THE MASSACHUSETTS EXPERIENCE

In 1966, Massachusetts had been divided into 39 mental health and mental retardation areas, with the mandate that the full range of mental health services, including emergency services, be provided in each of these areas.

The Massachusetts plan also provided for a citizens' advisory and consultative board to be appointed within each of the 39 areas. Moreover, there was a provision in the law that if a medical school or general hospital facility was located within the area, it should be involved in the selection of leadership and in program planning.

The Erich Lindemann
Mental Health Center

The Erich Lindemann Mental Health Center is a large, architecturally innovative, impressive structure located in the Government Center urban renewal area of downtown Boston. The structure was completed in 1970, and staffing began soon after. It was intended to be the major mental health facility for the Harbor mental health and mental retardation area, a complex grouping of seven separate ethnic and geopolitical communities (the North End, West End, Beacon Hill, Charlestown, East Boston, and the adjacent municipalities of Chelsea, Winthrop, and Revere). Planning for this facility had begun in the mid-1950s when the late Dr. Erich Lindemann (to whose memory the present volume is dedicated) was Chief of Psychiatry at Massachusetts General Hospital and Dr. Jack Ewalt was Commissioner of Mental Health. The original plans were modified following the development of the federal program, and the commitment to a catchment area was crystallized in the late 1960s.

The Erich Lindemann Center is located within walking distance of Massachusetts General Hospital. From the very beginning, program planning was undertaken with the understanding that major professional and administrative linkages would be developed between the Massachusetts General Hospital and the new mental health center. These linkages have been forged from the beginning and continued with the involvement of Dr. Eisenberg, Chief of Psychiatry at the Massachusetts General Hospital, in the selection of the Superintendent and the joint appointment of all members of the professional staff of the two institutions.

Emergency Psychiatric Services

One major component of the joint planning has been for provision of emergency psychiatric services. It was decided early that no separate 24-hour emergency services would be developed at the Lindemann Center because of the high quality and high volume of services in existence at the Massachusetts General Hospital through the Acute Psychiatric Service (or as it is known locally, the APS). The APS at the Massachusetts General Hospital evolved in the late 1950s and early 1960s to meet the growing volume of psychiatric emergencies seen in the hospital emergency service and because of staff concern with the theory and techniques of crisis intervention (239). Building on the teachings of Dr. Erich Lindemann concerning crisis intervention (260) and community relations with the West

End project (138), the psychiatric and social service staffs of the Massachusetts General Hospital had developed extensive experience in emergency services. They were able to relate to both the general hospital as a community in itself, as well as to the adjacent neighborhoods of the West End, North End, and Beacon Hill. These activities have been documented in the writings of Lindemann, the clinical descriptions of Chafetz and Frankel (134) and the extensive and insightful social science studies of the adjacent neighborhoods conducted by Whyte (434), Gans (145), and Fried (139).

As in New Haven, the volume of patients seen at the emergency service of the Massachusetts General Hospital has consistently run high. However, the specific proportion of Harbor area patients being served has averaged about 25% of those seen. Thus, of approximately 1000 psychiatric emergency service patients seen per month, about 250 (25%) come from the Harbor area, the catchment area served by the Erich Lindemann Mental Health Center. Attempts are made to give priority to this group.

Changing the Approach to Treatment

Based on the experience in New Haven, two significant decisions were made in regard to the design of the system for catchment services that have had major impact on the provision for psychiatric emergency care.

One innovation was to limit radically the role of the state hospital. Starting in 1970, the Department of Mental Health's policy has been to decrease admissions to the state hospital and to insist that community mental health centers be truly comprehensive. Applied to the Harbor area and the Erich Lindemann Mental Health Center, this policy has brought about a progressive closing of the back door, so that since 1971, it has no longer been possible for patients from Harbor area communities to go directly to any of the state hospitals in Massachusetts. This administrative move put pressure on the Lindemann Center and Massachusetts General Hospital to develop 1) alternatives to hospitalization and 2) community placement for chronically disabled patients. This administrative decision has had profound clinical impact on the provision of emergency services. Admissions to the state hospitals have declined to almost nil. Within the past year less than a half dozen patients from the Harbor area went to a state hospital, and this was only after special negotiations and review of alternatives. A recent analysis of state hospital admissions and resident populations by the Department of Mental Health documented that between 1970 and 1972 there had been a 73% reduction in the number of Harbor area patients residing in Massachusetts state hospitals and that this reduction was the highest among the 39 mental health areas within the state.

Walk-In Clinics.   This "closing of the back door" was related to a second systems design—the development of four community-based, comprehensive, ambulatory clinics. The total catchment area of over 170,000 persons has been divided into four subareas, and within each area, a locally based, community-oriented clinical team operates, providing outpatient services to children and adults as well as consultative services to community agencies. Recently, day treatment programs have begun in two communities, and it is expected that each of these four community clinics will soon have its own partial hospitalization program, including a day hospital, community residences, and halfway houses.

This network of four community-based clinics provides walk-in services on weekdays, 9 AM to 5 PM. More significantly, the system provides for continuity of care, so that the cycle of revolving door readmissions and recurrent use of the emergency room for crises is expected to decrease. Some evidence is beginning to appear that this systems design is having the desired impact. Since July 1972 there has been a 20% decrease in the psychiatric utilization of the APS; this decrease has been overall, but most apparent in the Harbor area. This marks the first decrease in APS utilization in over a decade.

Patients coming to the general hospital do not necessarily define themselves initially as psychiatrically ill; the labeling process is accomplished through the diagnostic and consultative services of the institution, particularly the triage officer and psychiatric and medical staffs. In contrast, patients coming to the mental health center have already defined themselves as psychiatric cases and usually do not see themselves as immediately requiring hospitalization. Thus, there are differences in the initial definition of the problem, the severity of illness, and the need for immediate institutional disposition.

The nature of the responsibility differs in different components of the system. In the general hospital ES, it is essential to clarify the patient's condition diagnostically and to determine the need for hospitalization. Treatment efforts in the ES may be considerable, with the emphasis on clarifying and subsequently deflating what is making the situation an emergency. The responsibility usually ends following the crisis intervention and referral to the appropriate facility.

PROGRAM IMPLICATIONS

These observations elucidate further the sorting process by which different patients are referred to and treated in different components of the mental health system. Under modern urban conditions, a wide range of facilities is available for the treatment of mental illness, and these facilities vary as to their level of intramural care and degree of accessibility to the patient. There are a number of factors operating, including severity of illness, institutional practices, and need for immediate hospitalization. Where hospitalization is needed and medical evaluation required, the psychiatric unit of the general hospital seems to be the facility most used.

Since the passage of Federal legislation providing for the construction and staffing of community mental health centers, there has been a rapid expansion of community programs across the country. Hopefully these programs provide services for a wider segment of the population (especially the lower socioeconomic classes) and change the destructive aspects of the large, custodial state hospital system. In this chapter, we have described the system for conceptualizing and studying the entry process whereby persons in need of emergency services within a community apply for, and are evaluated and allocated, the treatment resources of the mental health system.

However, before we completely accept the efficacy of these systems design innovations, further evaluation research is called for. How does the creation of such new facilities alter the patterns and rates of utilization of different facilities within a community? What types of individuals come to what types of facilities? To what extent do patients of lower socioeconomic status and of minority groups in urban ghettos make use of these new facilities? Does the creation of these new neighborhood facilities reduce the demand on the overcrowded and poorly staffed emergency rooms of general hospitals? Is there greater client satisfaction with these innovations than with existing programs such as child guidance clinics and mental health centers? Is there reduction in the amount of time needed for evaluation and an increase in the percentage of patients entering treatment? Can community facilities meet the needs of persons previously served by state hospitals? These questions can only be answered by systematic research. Studies are needed to assess the effectiveness and utilization of the system and its components so that comparisons *between* programs, as well as *within* programs, can be made in response to organizational and administrative changes.

2

RECEPTION SERVICE IN EMERGENCY CONTEXTS

facilitating adaptational work

Norris Hansell

SITUATION AT RECEPTION

A reception service is a place where people in trouble come into contact with resources which may become helpful. It has been given surprisingly little attention in our strategic reflections. We have used terms such as *intake* to refer to it, and sometimes described it as a trivial event occurring before the *real* service begins. Yet reception service is where people *arrive* for help; it is where service *begins*. People arrive in distress. They show the "whir and blur," a loss of distinct personal identity and of a sense of direction, and reductions in recent role performance (167, 416, 424). They enter reception service at a time when they are particularly ready to pursue adaptive work (41, 76, 260, 380, 420) because they are especially ready psychologically to meet a challenge. But because we have not envisioned reception work as a productive interval in service, we have sometimes wasted its potential. We have taken the valuable, flexible moments of the adaptational interval and spent them making an entry on a waiting list. We have studied a person in ritual detail. We take a *social history*; we try to find out *why* the person is troubled the way he is; we examine the *background*. Our distraction with these elusive mysteries has often resulted in our losing the fleeting readiness for personal reorganization that was present initially.

In the past decade reception activity has emerged as a powerful part of the helping service in and of itself. Much of the value of reception work lies in its opportune placement in the flow of events, which allows it to harness the flexibility of crisis. Practices which embody a "rubber band-like focus" on the task of initiating the process of coping, and on helping a person figure out what is going on, lie at the center of this work. Reception work formulates the strategic questions in a service episode: What is the person trying to do with his life? Where does he want to go? What kind of person does he want to be?

Identifying Services the Patient Will Need

Frequently, in the reception service setting, we come upon a person who has been showing deteriorative role behavior; his usual behavior patterns are decaying. The vigor and clarity of his attachments to friends and to life projects are declining, and he is somehow excluded from his social network—family, friends, and job. These fairly common aspects of the presenting predicament at crisis form the background for one basic element of the reception services—the efforts to convene fragmenting social networks. Bringing together an individual's ordinary social contacts supplies an essential component of adaptive work—a regulative context. Similarly, practices which draw together several types of service staff at the time of reception generously repay the added cost.

Several agencies can usefully become involved, because heavy users of service need several types or "packages" of services. Such persons may need job training, counseling, or phenothiazine medication for the biochemical component of schizophrenia. These parts of the service package often can best be assembled at reception. Reception practices also can respond to the fact that several members of the family may be requiring services at the same time. Convening members of the family and the agency networks makes possible a power and speed that was missing in earlier practices. For instance, previously, a person had to go to agency A to become entered into that agency's type of service. Then, often past the time of crisis, he would be referred to agency B to enter a complementary component of service. Changing the design of reception services from "sectoral reception" to "system reception" creates possibilities in timing and cooperation that were formerly unavailable.

Seeing the Patient as an Individual

An attempt is made at reception to detect an individual's personality and identity through the distress that he displays during the period of challenge. A flurry of kicking, biting, sucking, and clinging may distract people who do not know him well and prevent them from noticing his identity, interests, and capacities. But these distracting displays are a type of "plumage" regularly offered at crisis. If professionals focus narrowly on such ordinary signaling plumage—describing it, classifying it, trying to decide whether the person is primarily suspicious or primarily sad, primarily using alcohol or primarily relinquishing role duties—they may overlook the more productive task of discovering the person beneath the distress. Changing the focus of interest allows professionals to *look through* the package of distress behavior and more quickly find out "who is there." An individual's characteristics as a unique person and his basic goals make up a "signal" of first-order importance, often buried in the ordinary noise of adaptational signaling. When professionals set themselves to detect this signal, they may greatly speed up an individual's ability to envision a future, make decisions, and take action. Experiencing a sense of identity and direction ordinarily precedes any activities aimed at deciding what the problems are and what is obstructing the business of life.

Helping the Patient Find Help

Another salient activity at reception is conduct of the entrance procedures. In many communities, residents face the prospect of tedious determinations before they qualify to enter a mental health service. Each agency in a community may have its own rules, its own way of assessing people in distress, and each agency may use different methods of classifying troubled people. An individual may have the twin problems of qualifying himself for help and also finding his way through the system so as to receive proper help from several agencies. He may have to try to negotiate a complex maze at the very time when he is least able to make speedy decisions. In this context, significant expediting and ombudsman functions are emerging in settings where reception has become a substantial discrete service (163, 164, 168).

ARRANGING THE SOCIAL CONTEXT

All persons need a group for certain phases of the work of problem solving (61, 380, 420). The group helps to identify the presenting problem and to advance the person from "offering a laundry list of complaints" toward "specifying the tasks to be done." The social surrounding appears to offer a set of semiautomatic actions which have the regulatory effect of advancing the person from describing troubles toward deciding on a course and taking action. These and other regulatory actions by a cluster of *other* persons are intrinsic to ordinary adaptational work. Arranging for the availability of such a cluster constitutes a central activity of the reception service.

Somewhat surprisingly, these semiautomatic regulatory functions may be carried on by any one of several types of small groups or *clusters*. The cluster may comprise kin, friends, or persons with a religious or situational affiliation. It may be an *ad hoc* self-help group or, quite often, a set of persons who happen to be passing through the agency at the same time. Formerly, professionals sometimes themselves provided the corporate substrate for the adapting individual by offering "a personal relationship" to the challenged person. There is a long tradition in which a *therapist* assisted an individual in figuring out who he was, where he was going, and what problems obstructed the way. Over the past several decades the limitations of trying to conduct problem-solving work in social isolation have been recognized with increasing clarity (227, 228, 274). But also, the earlier approach of correcting isolation by arranging social encounters with professionals has revealed the intrinsic hazard of creating solutions dependent on continuing contact with professionals (465). These practices, termed *recruitatory*, are likely to result in highly convoluted but resilient links between formerly serviced clients and professional persons. The resilience of these crisis-wrought links in the face of later *discharge* efforts has proved considerable. The majority of such links remain active and promote a lifestyle with continuing patienthood and reduced adaptational flexibility. Consequently, current designs for service are moving to employ a *crisis strategy*, a strategy which gives more attention to these long-term problems. These strategies have in common the objective of providing a social substrate based on new linkages rather than on an invitation to sanctuary. The effort is based on attempts to enhance adaptational work by creating new links for isolated persons without linking them to professional helpers. For example, a set of persons successfully linked at reception service may each demonstrate prior isolation but also the currently increased affiliational behavior intrinsic to the crisis interval. Although each person is an isolate, the set can become a cluster because the affiliational possibilities for each person are activated by passage through the adaptational state at the same time. This practice of convening at reception is acquiring a dominance and usefulness that few would have predicted several decades ago. Underlying the dramatic usefulness of convening is the basic adaptational requisite for a corporate context within which to conduct the work of coping.

SPACE AND PROCEDURES

Physical Space

Reception service activities have space requirements somewhat different from the activities for which many service spaces were conceived earlier. A brief look at some of these problems suggests the nature of the remedies in process. Reception work increasingly involves emphasis on a reliable space for convening assemblies of people for time-limited tasks. Bringing together a group of 10 to 15 people is more satisfactory if there is space of an appropriate size and comfortable furnishings. Because service space often has been designed for a two-person format, some local efforts at reception work have been hampered. In some places, reception efforts have been squeezed into hallways and small waiting rooms. Physical space organized to receive a whole family in a dignified manner and draw them into task work around a table distinctly advances the convening efforts. The ability to hold a directive discussion in a room offering privacy and dignity is intrinsic to the task.

Conventions

Similarly useful is a comfortable set of conventions for the businesslike conduct of reception work. Precise conventions can apply a task-centering structure to the turbulence ordinarily present in an emergency. Professionals working in reception settings appear better able to detect the personality and identity underlying an episode of distress if there is a problem-framing logic to their procedures and inquiry. A step-by-step pattern in the conduct of the work of receiving, assessing, and planning also adds a surge of task-directness to the efforts of clients and families.

One regularly sees a constructive attitudinal change as an individual, entering in turbulence, anguished and suspicious, moves into a designated space and discovers that he is in the presence of several people who seem to know what they are doing. They meet him with informative instructions. "Glad you're here . . . . Let's get started by selecting a schedule for our tasks . . . . Who's with you? . . . . Let's move into the planning room and see if we can figure out a line of action which offers promise for you in handling this situation."

When the process of receiving persons in distress is conducted with familiar and attractive conventions, the onset and pace of adaptive work are accelerated. The scale of the increments is sufficiently important to warrant professional interest in regularizing the formats as basic tools.

ASPECTS OF SERVICE

Mobile Reception Service

Reception work is notably advanced by the capacity to move the site of the work to a variety of places within the community. Mobility can add significantly to the accessibility and speed of reception activities. If the reception staff can go to the jail, to a hospital receiving room, to a nursing home, or to an individual's residence, surprising additions are made to the list of persons who may be convened. Many otherwise unavailable facts can be assessed. The more surely a presenting individual is known to be a heavy user of services, the more useful it may be to assess him in a setting other than a hospital or clinic. The behavior that such an individual ordinarily offers in a hospital-based or clinic-based reception setting may represent the most disorganized, atypical view available. For instance, at several reception services it has been found that reception conducted by using a home visit noticeably increased the opportunities to use home care or other noninstitutional treatment settings. In any community, reception and assessment practices tightly restricted to hospital settings appear to narrow the range of settings selected for the subsequent services. Perhaps this situation exists because any individual in sufficient distress will present whatever behavior he discovers will generate access to service. Distressed persons appear exquisitely attuned to cues which suggest the signals for entrance. They are engaged in whatever signaling will gain the helpful services of these nice people in this place. Mobile reception and home visiting practices can set aside the need for much of this signaling, because a reaching out, inviting message has already been established.

Types of Service

The more reception procedures signify that they have passed beyond a determination of *whether* the individual qualifies for service, the more information they can yield about *what kind*. The earlier term, *intake service*, has probably accurately profiled the access-qualifying activities conducted, because the question under review has been, "Is this person going to enter service here?" The most competent response of a deeply distressed person, and the one most often made, is the selection of adaptational plumage which stimulates the answer, "Yes, an intake will occur here." The more reception practices unambiguously shift the focus toward questions of what our best beginning service is, the more the individual will be free to relinquish the display of intake plumage.

Procedural Style

Other features of reception procedures can encourage an individual to start coping. Practices which quickly define and signal a set of outcome possibilities are particularly basic to full usage of the adaptational state. For instance, the individual may be a multiple user and may have acquired a set of habits about how to act in a mental health service. Such ideas of what it is like to be a patient may instruct him to desist from his efforts to cope. They may instruct him to try to discover what is wrong with himself. They may foreshadow a period of life in a cloistered environment (212, 213). These sentiments are residues of an earlier sanctuarial style of helping and seem to interfere significantly with the conduct of the current work of adaptation (166, 270).

A general posture which endorses decisive, earnest work on problems can be signaled quite efficiently via procedural style. For example, it is useful to set target dates for the accomplishment of tasks: *This is what we are going to have done by tonight. . . . This is what you are likely to have completed within 3 weeks.* The description of a series of steps, with a schedule for the pace, is most regulative when it is offered without diffidence. There is usually more than enough uncertainty in the mix, and a schedule can begin the work which will later resolve some of the unknowns. At reception, family members are asking strategic questions, often silently: "Are we bringing George here for 15 minutes or 15 years?" The turbulence of reception holds open a measure of flexibility about whether the family will disengage or stay and work. The person in distress remains flexible about whether he will seek sanctuary and wait for some medication or open himself to the rediscovery of his life objectives.

To implement such outcome signaling interests, consider the impact of informative declarations such as, "We're glad to have you here (because very likely some good things are going to happen). . . . This is our job (and we like it and do it pretty well). . . . This is the schedule (for the satisfying work you will accomplish with our help). . . . In 7 days we will all get together (and take satisfaction in our efforts)."

Reception practices which arrive at, and declare, specific purposes, with a schedule and pace, regularly elevate the expectations of all participants. It becomes easier for a group of people to coordinate their activities. Conversely, reception practices which do not yield a specific plan and schedule tend to suppress active progress in problem solving.

Scheduling.   A word should be said about the strategy of forecasting a schedule when there is incomplete information. The workers at reception never have complete information, and they seldom can be sure that any initial suggestion is going to work out. But the basic purpose is to start the suspended adaptational work within the fleeting interval of its blossoming, and the clear fact is that established plans can always change. Purpose and pace can be redefined and often are. Seldom is anything lost by setting dates and allocating responsibilities. Getting started yields a momentum which changes the context of all subsequent efforts.

Pacing.   The task of converting calls of distress into problem-solving work is further facilitated at reception by professional helpers who take action to stabilize the pace. They arrange at each contact for the subsequent occasion when they can assess the process under way. The pace is cemented by a set of scheduled convenings. Reception practices which set before a group a pace for the future are as helpful to the family as they are to the person in trouble. When a member of one's family is "coming apart at the seams," it is a reassuring experience to come into a place where the people *hear* one's troubles and confidently move to an outline of purposes and pace. A format which socially regulates the pace seems to generate a decision to get started, a feeling that this is the place and the time, "Let us get started!" If professional helpers demonstrate such a style for pacing adaptational work, families pick it up. Then there is a network of allies for the tasks. Families also appear to notice when a staff does not carry peculiar ideologic burdens. They take notice when their helpers are not looking for scapegoats, for example, schizophrenogenic mothers or depriving husbands. If the staff says they can confer at a certain time, for example Tuesday evening, the family will hear that they are being called to duty. They detect when they will be expected to make contributions intrinsic to the outcome, and they can get excited about meaningful work.

SOME RESULTS OF MODERN RECEPTION PRACTICES

Because reception activities exert powerful effects on the outcome of the later assistance given to each person passing through service, such work takes on an organizing role in local affairs. Reception practices have a general effect on the design of other local services. The residents of the community quickly begin to use less inpatient service and more outpatient service (91, 109, 157, 238, 284, 400). Community agencies develop an increased knowledge of each other's practices from participating in multiagency reception formats. They tend to accelerate their volume of joint programing. A multiagency format for the clinical record often develops (165). There may also develop a type of interagency service agreement promoting additive "packages" of service or a symmetric, nondecline service agreement. In such an agreement each of two or more agencies which have been taking care of some of the same people in the same territory agree to service all referrals from the other agency. Perhaps one agency has been serving adult male alcoholics from the east side of town while another has been serving those on the west side of town, or perhaps one agency services referrals by doctors, while the other receives referrals from social welfare agencies. Agencies which discover a shared category of clientele can agree to assess individuals *on behalf of the services of their combined capacity*. Clients referred by each are accepted by the other, and the personnel agree to meet periodically and resolve any imprecision in their referral habits. Such agreements transfer difficulties in entering the service system from the circumstance of the patient at the front door in the middle of the night to an interagency administrative conference. These agreements also make the staff hours spent in assessment activities distinctly more productive.

Reception service offers a convenient place for citizens to express their concerns about local mental health services. To the extent that a reception facility gradually comes to function as a principal point of entrance into many different services within a community, it develops an increasingly effective linkage with the goals of the citizens of that community. Then the citizens come to exercise a closer and more confident scrutiny of the practices and purposes of the facility. For example, they may decide to make sure that individuals' rights and values are protected as they enter and move into service. The citizens often decide that an ombudsmanlike activity is intrinsic to the work of the reception facility. Citizens regularly indicate concern that the style and values expressed in the operations of the facility are generally in keeping with local sentiments.

NOAH AND THE ARK: AN ANALOGY

The more a reception facility applies itself to commencing the adaptational work of those presenting with the difficulties attendant on the emergency, the more that reception facility will become an entry point to brief services. To the extent that a reception service sets itself up to offer sanctuary, or chemical relief of distress, or to promote *tolerance* of prolonged displays of symptoms, it will inhibit the growth of persons who present in distress. Consider the story of Noah and the Ark. Reflect on how it would have been if Noah had presented in a reception facility with his "emergency."

The story of Noah was passed along by word of mouth through many generations before being put into print. It can be regarded as a "folk journalism" story of the way a man faced a major problem. The problem was the Flood; the coping device was the Ark. The adaptational work was successful, and the man survived. Many societies have a story with a flood, an ark, and other common characteristics—perhaps such a persisting story expresses concepts which remain valuable through the ages.

The first thing that happened in the story of Noah was a lot of begetting. This prelude may be a way of saying that there was a steady state of ordinary life before the trouble. Next, God told Noah there was going to be a flood. This step denotes the *recognition of impending hazard;* it marks the cognitive state of a warning. After Noah heard about the flood, he felt "distressed," and experienced a feeling that "God didn't love him." He wondered if he might be bad. He envisioned that he might drown as punishment for his sins. These reports are of behavior that is quite common to the crisis-in-transit state. Feelings of unworthiness, of not being able to manage, are frequent findings at a time of crisis.

After wrestling with his awareness of the hazard for a while, Noah thought of several things that he could do. He could pray, but he didn't believe that would help enough. He considered trying to get away from the flood, but God had told him, "The Waters will cover the entire Earth and all the mountains thereof." There could be no escape. After a period of consideration, Noah decided on his best option. He would build a three-deck ark, 300 cubits long. The background of this specific decision is illuminating. Noah had decided that the ark would have be able to carry forward all that was of value from his past life, namely, his "wife and sons and two of every living thing upon the Earth." He was careful to recollect his cherished past so that his solution could carry him into a future sufficiently attractive to maintain his identity and provide a comprehensive system of meaning (167). After deciding on his plan, he built the ark, thus *taking action*. Then Noah tested the ark to see that it would float. The actions depicted are not careless or frivolous. After Noah had two of every living thing aboard, "The Waters did rise." They came up all around the ark; the winds were strong; the waves were high; the ark began rocking. This part of the account indicates that Noah's experience in passing through the crisis-in-transit interval is painful, fearful and distressingly turbulent. One does not know whether he is going to make it. Noah reported that the "Waters were upon the Earth 40 days and 40 nights," and during the worst it seemed, "They would never end." But as he reviewed the experience subsequently, he wanted us to know that it had a beginning, a middle, and an end, and that it lasted about 6 weeks.

Finally, the ark came to rest on Mount Ararat and Noah sent out a dove. This report marked Noah's determination to test whether his adaptational efforts had been effective. He did not leap out assuming that all was well. The first dove came back quickly. Noah decided that the dove could find no landing. He would continue with the ark a little longer. He sent out another dove which returned with an olive leaf. Noah decided that if the bird could have landed and stayed, it would have. Perhaps only the treetops were uncovered. Later he sent another dove which did not return. Noah was reporting how important it can be to determine whether one's adaptational work is successful before desisting one's efforts.

The story does not end here. Noah reported further that he, his family, and the two of every living thing had survived. They all felt a sense of joy and pride. They thanked God. Here Noah was reporting the joy attendant on the experience of facing and solving problems. The self esteem, earlier lost, has now returned. And Noah reported that they returned to their begetting. After these events, Noah lived for 900 years and proceeded to repopulate the earth. The story has a before, an onset, a during, and an end, thus showing that there is a period of life after the crisis. The story offers a particular kind of happy ending: Noah took a considered, precise action to solve a problem. He tested it, and it worked. The story is of continuing interest because it reviews the basics of a quite general model for problem solving.

The professionals working in a reception service can help individuals in distress identify the flood, decide on the dimensions of the ark, proceed with the work of the chosen action, and test the results of such action. Modern reception practices are allowing many to rediscover the ancient observation that the satisfactions of adaptational accomplishment may outlast the relief of sanctuary.

3

CRISIS INTERVENTION PREVENTS HOSPITALIZATION

pilot program to service project

Donald G. Langsley
Richard M. Yarvis

The community mental health movement was developed to try to answer the need for treatment of the mentally disordered and to contribute to prevention of mental illness. Although the movement is still young, it has already had major impact in the organization of mental health services; it has given an indication of the ability to provide direct and preventive services to large populations, including the poor and minority groups, and in regions which lack mental health manpower. The goal of providing comprehensive, coordinated, and accessible mental health services with continuity of care for all citizens has not yet been achieved. The sought-after partnership between consumers and providers is not always evident. Nevertheless there are many indications that the community mental health approach is effective and can meet these goals. In California, for example, the entire state program for the mentally ill has been oriented toward community mental health.

ESTABLISHING SERVICES IN SACRAMENTO COUNTY

Sacramento County has been especially successful in demonstrating the potential for developing community treatment and prevention. State hospital admissions have dropped from over 1000 a year to almost zero. The resident inpatient population of chronic mental patients has dropped 99% from that of 5 years ago. This has not been accomplished by simply closing the doors to the state hospital. It is the result of the development of community treatment.

In 1968 the Department of Psychiatry at the University of California, Davis (UCD), a new medical school, accepted responsibility for organizing and implementing the mental health program in a county which had lacked community treatment. The Chairman of Psychiatry at the Medical School became the Director of Mental Health Services for the county. Mental health services were organized along catchment area lines in an urban–suburban area. The county included five catchment areas.

Organization of Crisis Teams

Services for the residents of two catchment areas were arranged by contract with mental health centers developed in community general hospitals. The UCD Department of Psychiatry took responsibility for services to the other three, with each area serviced by a multidisciplinary team consisting of faculty and staff recruited by the University. Involvement by the School of Medicine made it possible to staff these teams with quality professionals and to establish community mental health oriented training programs in psychiatry, psychology, social work, and nursing. Paraprofessionals were also involved in staff or contract funded positions. Each team was responsible for offering comprehensive mental health services to the catchment area population (approximately 150,000 at the time of implementation). Continuity of care was assured by training almost all staff to be primary therapists. In each case appropriate psychiatric involvement and backup occurred. Each team developed a neighborhood clinic facility with daytime crisis intervention, outpatient services, partial hospitalization, and mental health consultation. Inpatient services were centralized in a cooperative unit operated by the three teams. The team member treating the patient continued to be responsible for treatment at the inpatient setting.

Method of Operation

A key factor in the success of the program was that crisis intervention and emergency services were given first priority. The fourth team was a crisis–emergency team based in the county hospital emergency room (at that time the only 24-hour emergency service in the county). The crisis team related to all three University catchment area teams and the two contract catchment area services. Staffed in an interdisciplinary fashion, it provided night and weekend emergency service coverage for the entire county and served as the intake unit for the catchment area teams. All new patients (emergency or elective) were seen by the crisis team. Contacts were by 24-hour telephone service or by walk in. Crisis team staff were on duty around the clock. Psychiatric residents were assigned to this service to supplement crisis team staff nights and weekends. New patients were seen immediately, and if rapid evaluation indicated that the patient could be treated by brief (up to six visits) outpatient crisis intervention, or could improve with a stay in the crisis unit for up to 72 hours, the patient was the responsibility of a crisis team. If the patient (from the beginning or after a trial of crisis intervention) required more intensive or prolonged treatment, he was assigned to the catchment area team where he resided. All teams treated children, adults, and families.

There were no additional specialized clinics or services. (The goal of comprehensive mental health services avoids separate and isolated specialized treatment programs.) The crisis team was also responsible for coordinating various kinds of mental health consultation, including services for the nonpsychiatric units in the general hospital, and work with human service programs which crossed catchment area lines. The crisis team, the front door of the mental health service, was the most visible and, as it needed to be, the most responsive unit of the program. The degree of community support was often related to the responsiveness of the crisis–emergency service.

PILOT STUDY USING CRISIS INTERVENTION TO AVOID HOSPITALIZATION

Denver Pilot Project

In 1964, Langsley and Kaplan (236) undertook a 5-year study at the Colorado Psychiatric Hospital, Denver, to determine whether family crisis intervention could provide an effective alternative to hospitalization. The University Psychiatric Inpatient Service treated patients in both the Denver Metropolitan area and all of Colorado.

The Denver project attracted an exceptionally high caliber of staff, well trained, dedicated, committed to the project, and with an interest comparable to that of the researcher. The project had a definite beginning and a definite end, was limited by a set number of cases and hence not plagued by the unending assault of patients every day with which a service-oriented crisis team must cope.

Procedure

After a pilot year in which treatment and measurement techniques were developed, a fulltime team (psychiatrists, psychologists, social worker, and nurse) treated 150 families. Each family included a member considered in need of immediate hospitalization. All patients in the sample were members of families who lived within an hour's travel of the hospital, representing 70% of those admitted to the Colorado Psychiatric Hospital. When one of these patients came to the emergency room, the psychiatric resident would call the family crisis team. A random selection system determined who fell into the Family Crisis Therapy (FCT) sample. If the patient did not fall into the sample to be immediately treated by FCT, he was admitted to the hospital. The study also included a randomly selected comparison group of 150 families with a member who was a hospitalized patient. FCT included approximately five conjoint family visits, a home visit, and several telephone contacts, and lasted approximately 21 days. Hospital treatment consisted of an average stay of 28 days.

The goals of FCT (and hospitalization) were *a*) to return a patient to the previous level of adjustment, *b*) to refer appropriate cases for treatment of long-term maladaptive patterns (about one third of each group), and *c*) to obtain follow-up information on the adaptation of each patient and his family and their subsequent use of mental health services. Other measures were designed to compare the effectiveness of hospital versus crisis treatment.

The two groups were indistinguishable by chi-square on 25 different characteristics. Baseline data were collected from FCT and hospital groups, and follow-up data were collected at 6 and 18 months in all cases. A 30-month followup is also available on approximately one third of the families in both groups. The project is reported in detail in a book (236) and in a number of articles (237, 238). Perhaps it is sufficient to summarize the results by saying that the crisis cases were as well adapted as the hospital cases and had no greater degree of psychiatric symptomatology in the follow-up ratings. The patients treated by hospitalization were far more likely to be readmitted and those cases had an average stay far in excess of that of the small number of crisis cases hospitalized *after* the crisis treatment. The crisis treatment cases showed greater effectiveness in solving family crises than did the patients treated by hospitalization. In short, FCT was demonstrated to be an effective alternative to hospitalization.

Denver as a Model for Sacramento County

The Denver pilot project experience was the basis for assigning first priority to the development of crisis services for the Sacramento County mental health program. It gave us the hard evidence, as well as the conviction, that crisis intervention could be accomplished with even the most seriously ill. Nevertheless in Denver we were clearly dealing with a demonstration and pilot project. The staff was a group of fully trained and highly dedicated mental health professionals. The Denver group took great pride in the fact that they kept all 150 crisis intervention cases out of the hospital. However, the Denver client group did not include patients who lived alone, and it did not include patients who lived far from the treatment facilities.

TABLE 3.1 Crisis Team Visits by Diagnosis and Age (1971)

Category	Age						Totals*
	0–12	13–18	19–35	36–45	46–65	66–	
No diagnosis	1	28	107	27	19	10	192 (2.92)
Schizophrenia	1	67	892	305	231	10	1506 (22.94)
Depression	0	52	387	184	147	15	785 (11.95)
Depression (psychotic)	0	3	40	33	47	4	127 (1.93)
Personality disorder	1	76	644	159	103	1	984 (14.99)
Psychoneurosis	0	9	134	31	26	0	200 (3.04)
Adjustment reaction	10	210	518	87	72	7	904 (13.77)
Childhood/adolescent behavior disorder	13	84	0	0	0	0	97 (1.47)
OBS	0	14	59	33	95	50	251 (3.82)
Other	9	191	784	254	257	23	1518 (23.12)
Totals within age categories	35	734	3565	1113	997	120	6564 (99.96)
	(0.53)	(11.18)	(54.31)	(16.95)	(15.18)	(1.82)	

* Numbers in parentheses are percentages.

(See discussion on page 30)

TABLE 3.2   County Population by Age

Age	Males	Females	Totals	Totals within age categories*
0–12	81,148	77,240	158,388	35 (0.53)
13–18	39,457	38,489	77,946	734 (11.18)
19–35	69,452	75,652	145,104	3565 (54.31)
36–45	38,145	40,232	78,377	1113 (16.95)
46–65	62,668	64,274	126,942	997 (15.18)
≥66	19,152	25,589	44,741	120 (1.82)
Totals	*310,022*	*321,476*	*631,498*	*6564 (99.96)*

* Numbers in parentheses are percentages.

The translation of a pilot program into a working model, especially in a large urban–suburban county, represents no small feat. Table 3.1 analyzes data available for calendar year 1971, and illustrates the magnitude of the task. In all, 6564 cases were seen that year by the Sacramento crisis team. In Table 3.2 a breakdown by age of the total county population is provided to permit comparisons with the number of patients seen in each age group. From this it can be seen that young adults were overrepresented and children and the elderly were underrepresented among patients seen. The data were accumulated from a protocol taken at the first visit.

In California the State Department of Health, which provides up to 90% of the funds utilized by community mental health programs, requires that all cases be categorized into one or more target groupings. Table 3.3 does this with that same patient population. Since a patient can be assigned to more than one target group, the total exceeds 6564. Tables 3.1–3.3 together demonstrate not only the large number of patients seen, but the wide range of problems requiring assistance as well. What then are the problems encountered in the provision of such services?

TABLE 3.3   Target Problems Enumerated in Patients Seen by the Crisis Team in 1971

Target category	Patients (No.)	(%)
Mental disease	4001	63.4
Mental retardation	110	1.7
Alcoholism	731	11.6
Drug abuse	1014	16.1
Life crisis	2521	39.9

Operational Problems

A research project such as the Denver experiment may select for its scrutiny any segment of any population defined as being within the purview of its interests. Moreover, within the bounds of a good research design it can limit the overall size of that population. A community-based mental health program may do neither of these things. It must take any and all patients and must provide for those patients' needs as best it can. The Denver project, as has already been mentioned, limited its study population to 150 control and 150 study patients from families who lived within an hour's drive of the hospital.

Four general categories of problems have to be considered: 1) the problem of numbers; 2) the problem of geography; 3) problems relating to the nature of the patient population, in terms of impairments and of family resources; and 4) problems relating to the nature, capabilities, and training of the staff and the effects on them of the kind of work they do.

Number of Patients. In 1971 the Sacramento Mental Health Services crisis team saw just under 550 new cases per month. Since then case loads have increased. In any given month then the crisis team sees more than 3 times the number of new cases that were seen in the whole of the Denver project. With about 30 staff members who must man 3 shifts, 7 days a week, the patient–staff ratios faced by the crisis team do not remotely begin to compare favorably with those of the Denver project. In terms of numbers alone, replication of the Denver project on a community basis becomes an impossible task. In lieu of such replication, several things happen. For some patients, family crisis treatment along the lines of the Denver project is provided. For others, some of the principles of treatment proved efficacious by the Denver project are utilized (i.e., minimal use of hospitalization, the family as the unit of intervention) when the whole concept of the Denver approach cannot be. In many instances, patients who might profitably have benefited from crisis team intervention are referred to other sources of help within and/or outside the mental health services area. In these other settings, family crisis intervention is not often furnished. An ongoing attempt by the mental health services to broaden the clinical base from which crisis treatment is provided will, in the long run, improve this situation.

Geography. Sacramento County has an area of 980 square miles, within which the crisis team provides the *only* 24-hour-a-day, 7-days-a-week source of mental health crisis intervention. Supplementary resources do exist on a very limited basis during weekday daytime hours within the rest of the mental health services, but the rest of the time the crisis team is it. The southernmost communities in the county are actually much closer to the San Francisco Bay area than they are to Sacramento Medical Center out of which the crisis team operates. The relative geographic isolation of such communities presents access problems to the team. The Denver project chose its population from people who were able to get to the hospital. The crisis team must view all persons in the county in need of crisis services as its population of responsibility, not simply those who are able to reach the hospital. Many of the patients who turn to mental health services for care are indigent and, in general, have less than adequate access to private transportation. The county, moreover, does not have an adequate public transportation system. The Denver project defined away the geography problem. The Sacramento crisis team can afford no such luxury (See section on *The Future of the Crisis Team*).

Make-Up of Patient Population. We have no data with which to compare readily the nature of the patient population seen at the University of Colorado in 1971 with that seen by Sacramento County Mental Health Services the same year. In spite of that it is fairly safe to presume that there is considerable overlapping of the two populations as well as some difference in the proportions of certain kinds of cases treated at one or the other of those facilities. Sacramento Medical Center is the facility to which Sacramento city and county police bring any and all problems. The Mental Health Services patients include a significant proportion of individuals and families who have within their grasp few family resources, if any at all. Many come quite suspicious and quite leery of all kinds of psychotherapeutic intervention, including crisis intervention. *Acting out* frequently takes precedence over *talking out* problems. Many patients are brought to the attention of the crisis team not because they feel themselves to be in crisis but because some private third party or some public agent considers them to be in crisis or to be some sort of bother or danger to the community.

In essence then, while the crisis team does see patients who are indistinguishable from those seen in the Denver project, it also sees many patients with far less motivation and far fewer resources than those seen in Denver. Indeed, the service-oriented community program must face the task of dealing with many totally isolated individuals without any family resources whatever, another task that the Denver project simply defined away. It requires greater ingenuity on the part of the staff to cope with this. In addition, the term *family* must often be defined in very broad terms so as to include welfare workers, probation officers, and the like in order to supplement inadequate family resources, and at times to supplant nonexistent ones. Needless to say, the task of providing adequate treatment intervention with such a patient population becomes a much harder proposition than that originally faced by the Denver project staff.

Staff Problems. As stated earlier the Denver project was staffed by a highly dedicated and sophisticated group of people who were engaged in a joint research endeavor that showed great promise and was of vital interest to all of them. They had, with a relatively limited patient population, an opportunity to work out, develop, and test a particular therapeutic strategy. To suggest, however, that overall the Sacramento County crisis team is as well trained or as sophisticated as the Denver project staff would be misleading. Persons with skills in crisis intervention techniques are relatively rare and hard to come by. Most staff members are recruited without such specific skills and are given as much on the job training as possible. While efforts to augment the entry level skills of the crisis team staff continues unceasingly, the sheer volume of the work load makes that effort, to say the least, difficult at times. What we are able to provide is clearly not enough, and the constant struggle to provide more goes on.

The crisis team has been labeled by some of us "the meat grinder." Even staff members who are adapted for and skilled in crisis work find, in the unending succession of crisis situations, stresses that tax all of their skills and personal resources. Working with the crisis team is a wearing and grueling experience which takes its toll on even the most capable personnel over a period of time, and requires relief and a change of pace for staff members.

Many of the concepts that came out of the Denver project have been incredibly useful in working with hundreds of patients in Sacramento. We point out the problems only to suggest that it is a long way from pilot project to service-oriented program and that the transition is not an easy one.

The Future of the Crisis Team

There are a number of future directions the crisis team could take. The first aim is self evident: The team must continue to grow in order to meet the community's need for crisis intervention services more adequately. Given the geographic problems suggested above, that growth must include not only the continued development of the crisis team itself, but provision for an increasing volume of crisis services by other elements of the mental health services as well. This begins to meet the geographic problem, since these elements are decentralized throughout the county.

The mobile crisis team concept is another way we hope to meet this problem. So far this concept has been put into operation on a very limited basis. Home visits have been made in the course of family crisis treatment or to see new patients. Inability of the patient to reach our services has been the motivating force behind this concept. Both diagnostic determinations and treatment have been provided in the home. We see this, however, as an area which ought to be expanded significantly. We feel that use of multidisciplinary teams operating in the community may help us better understand and treat the dynamics of family conflict. Moreover, the sterile and uninviting quality of many hospital settings makes crisis team intervention in the home desirable. Visits where "home" is a nursing home or convalescent facility will enable us not only to provide for the needs of specific patients quickly but to provide consultation and training for nursing home staff in crisis intervention as well. A team that could respond soon after, or simultaneously with, police to the scene of a violent family argument, an attempt at suicide, or other such crisis problem could provide services at the source of the problems without delay and without recourse to the hospital setting.

Finally, our recently initiated Crisis Observation Unit requires further development to maximize its treatment potential. Such a unit provides for several needs. It affords hours of relief for a family which has been coping with a crisis problem without sleep for several days. It serves as a substitute family setting for patients who come to us without family resources. It offers an opportunity to observe family interactions in other than the interview setting itself. We have encouraged families to spend several hours in the unit while a family member is being treated there. The unit also provides a setting in which more intensive intervention can be accomplished than is possible in a traditional outpatient setting, especially for that group of patients who would otherwise have been hospitalized for a longer time and in a more institutional setting but who can actually be pulled together with neither. Finally, the unit provides us with a safety valve for staff who, at times, hesitate to treat particular patients on an ambulatory basis, and yet hesitate to hospitalize them. The Crisis Observation Unit buys some time, time in which to make further observations of the patient and come to further conclusions (see Chapter 8) about the most appropriate mode of treatment.

4

THE MOBILE PSYCHIATRIC
EMERGENCY TEAM

Joel Foxman

In July 1969 the Lanterman-Petris-Short Act was passed in the state of California. The law increased the percentage of monies that the state allocated to the counties for community mental health programs, established new priorities and services for community mental health centers, and prescribed a new code of conduct and procedures to protect the civil rights of mental patients. In addition, it designated the community mental health clinics of the counties as the key agencies to evaluate persons for possible involuntary hospitalization. The Director of the Department of Mental Health of Los Angeles County, in conjunction with the Board of Supervisors, decided that mobile Psychiatric Emergency Teams (PET) would play a key role in the assessment for hospitalization.

Heretofore, the use of home-visiting teams had not been attempted in such a geographically dispersed and heavily populated area (66), and none had been established in response to a mandate by mental health legislation. Moreover, none of the efforts to prevent psychiatric hospitalizations by such teams had become a primary part of a community mental health treatment program, such as the one described in this chapter.

In order to safeguard the civil rights of the citizens of California, the law changed the acceptable criteria for involuntary hospitalization. Only if a person were suicidal, homicidal, or gravely disabled owing to mental illness (later alcoholism was included) could he or she be hospitalized. Therefore, being mentally ill was not sufficient reason for hospitalization. Second, the length of time that a person could be held against his will in a mental hospital was carefully specified. The team has the authority to hospitalize someone for a maximum of 72 hours for a period of observation and evaluation. If it is necessary, the patient can then be certified for a maximum of 14 days. Before the 14 days pass, he must be reevaluated or discharged. According to the Crisis Evaluation Unit at Metropolitan State Hospital, approximately 98% of the clients are not held longer than this period, regardless of the reason for which the person was originally admitted.

Since a person would be held a very short time and the treatment offered in the hospital was minimal, hospitalization often accomplished nothing and, in fact, may have done considerable harm. Nationwide, the recidivism rate is approximately 55% (452). Thus once an individual is hospitalized, he is likely to return again and again—the phenomenon of the "revolving door." The hospitalized person begins to view himself as being "sick," and once he accepts this label and sees hospitalization as an escape, he is likely to use it when future stresses arise. Also the family can avoid responsibility by entering the disturbed person into the hospital whenever a crisis occurs. The creation of the PET program has provided an alternative for the different parties involved.

PSYCHIATRIC EMERGENCY TEAMS

Procedures

Each of the regional mental health offices in Los Angeles County was given an automobile to be used for the emergency calls. The disturbed individual was to be evaluated as close to his residence as possible, within his own community, instead of being sent 40–50 miles to the state hospital for observation. Obviously, evaluation *per se* did not constitute community-oriented treatment. The teams needed to learn how to do crisis intervention work in the field under potentially hazardous conditions. However, other than a brief paper on dealing with acutely disturbed clients (131) and a single presentation at each of the 12 regional offices by the author regarding the handling of the dangerous client, little training was offered. The teams in the county were in a state of crisis themselves. The majority of the teams were not functioning well and requests were being made for karate lessons, soft restraints (which are illegal), and for mattresses to be used to pin clients against the wall if team members were attacked. The phrase *Psychiatric Emergency Team* engendered fear, not confidence. No one felt prepared to do emergency work in the community.

Problems

Specific problems which became apparent included the following.

1. Making an evaluation is generally a waste of time and effort and can be very dangerous if no other intervention is planned. Almost one-quarter of police fatalities and half of police injuries occur when policemen are assessing a family conflict situation (469).
2. If a person was hospitalized, no program was established for follow-up, and if he was not hospitalized, only given a general invitation to come to the clinic, nothing happened. This invitation was rarely accepted.
3. The staffs needed to learn how to work in the community, where they were often viewed as the intruder or stranger. In San Pedro, only 8% of the calls are from the identified client, and therefore the team is an uninvited guest.
4. Most clinicians are not accustomed to viewing the individual in the context of his community, including family, friends, neighbors, employers, or other agencies.
5. Family therapy and consultation play an important role in the rate of admissions to the hospital (358). If the individual is to remain in or return to a particular living arrangement, the family needs to be worked with so that it changes or at least is able to cope more effectively with the person in crisis.
6. Cross-cultural differences are another area of concern. Many minority group members do not receive or seek service until a crisis period occurs, and then the values of the particular ethnic group are important to the treatment program.

THE SAN PEDRO EXPERIENCE

Over a 3-year period, the San Pedro Mental Health Service has developed some expertise in dealing with these problems (131, 337); basic facets of progress are described here.

The Community

The San Pedro Mental Health Service is situated in the Harbor area of south Los Angeles County, which includes San Pedro, Wilmington, and most of Palos Verdes Peninsula, an area of approximately 50 square miles with a population of about 250,000. Forty-nine percent of Wilmington is Mexican–American, and there is a sizable number of Blacks, Samoans, Filipinos, and other minorities. San Pedro has a variety of ethnic enclaves including Italian, Yugoslav, and Mexican–American. The Palos Verdes Peninsula is affluent, and only in the most extreme situations would its residents contact the San Pedro Mental Health Service. The population of the entire catchment area is younger than average, and there are many family groups. In addition, there is considerable stability, as many persons live permanently in the area.

Despite many serious problems there are relatively few services in the area. Drugs and alcohol are critical problems; unemployment and poor housing are so extreme that many persons have used the state mental hospital as their vacation spot. Metropolitan State Hospital is about 40 miles from San Pedro. A general hospital in the area has few psychiatric programs for the community and limited emergency capabilities.

The PET Structure

The San Pedro Mental Health Service is responsible for direct service, including the treatment of children and adults with emotional problems or psychiatric disorders. In addition there is a strong emphasis on indirect services and the prevention of emotional problems through crisis intervention and community mental health consultation and education programs. To provide counseling and psychotherapy for 300–400 clients, consultations to schools, welfare, police, probation, free clinics, and community education programs, and man the mobile emergency service, there are 8 fulltime staff. The mental health professionals include 2 psychologists, 3 social workers, 2 nurses, and one psychiatric technician. One M.D. position is shared by 5 physicians who primarily write prescriptions.

Although originally only 3 members of the staff chose to work on PET, the entire staff has gradually become involved. It is very important that participation be voluntary; otherwise the staff may procrastinate in responding to calls, or if a response is made no commitment is made to the client.

After 3 years of working together, many of the initial problems have been resolved. The philosophy behind PET had to be established: choices had to be made regarding crisis intervention therapy versus long-term treatment, viewing the client as having problems in living versus being mentally ill, and outpatient treatment versus inpatient treatment. An internal support system was established to decrease staff fears and to give staff an opportunity to talk about issues and philosophy, as well as to focus on positive and successful aspects of the work.

How PET Operates.   Each call is immediately evaluated by the intake worker, who records the relevant information and attempts to have the person with a problem brought into the clinic. If the person walks into the clinic, he is seen by the worker on duty, who is a regular member of the staff. If the individual cannot come in or is in crisis, or the situation is an emergency, the team is given the pertinent information. The precipitating event, important collateral people in the patient's life, availability of weapons, history of hospitalization, and other information are recorded on a special form. The team (consisting of two mental health workers) also fills out a similar form in the field. When the two forms are compared, it is easy to evaluate whether a good assessment was done over the phone or whether the situation in the field differs from that presented to the team by the intake worker. After scrutinizing the data the team can call to gather more information if they feel it is necessary. A careful assessment must be made, as the team accepts the responsibility for care of the person in crisis until the emergency situation is resolved whether the actual predicament is a psychiatric emergency or a family conflict. (Since staff time is limited, nonemergency problems are handled through the clinic's regular channels.) Careful assessment is also important to anticipate potentially dangerous situations and prepare strategies in advance of the face-to-face contact.

Attempts are made to contact the identified client to make him aware of our plans to visit him. If possible, an invitation is elicited from the person. Otherwise the team can expect to be met with a certain amount of hostility. If collateral people can be of help, they are asked to gain the invitation for the team or at least to be present when the team attempts to make the intervention. Moreover, the identified client may not really be the one in crisis. It may be only the caller who is in crisis, and it is always assumed, regardless of the circumstances, that the caller is in crisis. He will be given some assistance, but the next task is to determine whether the identified client is also in crisis, and this can be assessed by talking to the individual himself.

The PET is always composed of a male and a female therapist. Emphasis is placed on making a successful crisis intervention with the individual and/or his family and in engaging them in treatment. The treatment might be a series of home visits, telephone contacts, a clinic appointment, or even hospitalization.

Results

Only the more important statistics for the first 2 years of PET at San Pedro Mental Health Service are reviewed here. In 450 field contacts, no therapist or client has been physically injured, and no client has committed a homicide or suicide as a result of a decision made by PET. Two clients later attempted suicide, but neither attempt was completed. Fifteen percent of the identified clients were hospitalized, one third being homicidal, one third gravely disabled, and one third physically disabled because of medical problems. Thus 91% of the persons with functional disorders were maintained in the community. Only 2% of the clients were hospitalized 2 or more times by PET. The major precipitating factors were family conflict (32%), paranoid ideation (24%), separation (15%), drug/alcohol episode (10%), loss of job (7%), terminal illness of self or relative

(5%), organic reaction (5%), and birth of a child (2%). Approximately 25% of the calls involved the threat of suicide, 14% involved the threat of homicide, 10% were from persons gravely disabled owing to psychosis or physical disability, and the remainder involved acting out or bizarre behavior. Only 8% of the clients were self-referred, about half being referred through families and friends and the remainder from other agencies. However, about 90% of the clients have become involved in a therapeutic program. After the intervention about 80% of the crisis situations were evaluated as improved or resolved.

INNOVATIVE PROGRAMS

Consultation was an unanticipated role for PET. Many agencies called to request that someone be hospitalized immediately. When they learned that finding alternatives other than hospitalization was a goal of the team, the agencies began asking for consultation rather than for direct service. At first the agencies were quite resentful that PET questioned their decisions when hospitalization was required. After being informed regarding the philosophy of community psychology and PET, agencies began to ask pertinent questions regarding appropriate interventions that they might make with their own clients. Instead of viewing PET as a hospitalization service they began to see it as a crisis intervention and consultation service. The staffs of agencies that use the consultation service are expressing satisfaction and considerably more confidence in their work.

Through telephone consultation or actual joint collaboration in the field, PET developed a reputation for expertise in emergency service. Soon consultations and training sessions were given at the Department of Public Social Services, the Harbor Free Clinic, the Harbor Division of the Los Angeles Police Department, the Fire Department, and the Rescue Squad.

If a client was referred by an agency where the person was in counseling or psychotherapy, PET required that the ongoing therapist be at the residence while the evaluation was being made. The team thus had an opportunity to watch the therapist perform so that *a*) constructive feedback could be given, and *b*) to make clear that responsibility for the case remained with the referring agency.

Unfortunately, the PET office hours of 8 AM to 5 PM Monday–Friday, imply that only crises between these hours are worth answering and that during the other hours no crises will be permitted, or at least no one will attend to them. The few agencies available at other times of the day are often not viewed by the community or by themselves as treatment agencies. The police are one of the main examples. Since the formation of PET the Los Angeles Police Department, Harbor Division, has become a significant consumer of crisis consultation services, and over the past 1½ years, training and consultation have been periodically provided to the supervisors. Generally speaking, the police are responsible for the mental health needs of the community for about two-thirds of the day. The clinic provides 24-hour telephone consultation service to them. Referrals from the police and the interventions that they can make can help alleviate serious personal crises occurring in the community. The role of the police in any psychiatric emergency program should not be minimized. The police can also provide critical support for PET when a potentially hazardous call is being made. However, careful consideration is made before police support is requested.

Results

As was previously mentioned, the team has been very effective in engaging clients in some treatment program. However, the therapeutic programs in the clinic are not adequate to handle the needs of all of the clients. Two special programs were therefore begun as an adjunct to the team. First, a Home Visiting Unit (HVU) of 7 volunteers from the community was started. These volunteers were trained to make home visits to persons who have been seen by PET or whose situations could develop into a crisis unless they had additional resources..They were to be friends, not therapists. The volunteers can help by talking to the clients, many of whom are extremely depressed and isolated, or by providing concrete help such as transportation for appointments and shopping. Their training basically consisted of presentations from the staff including such topics as reality therapy, transactional analysis, psychoanalysis, the battering parent, depression, and parent effectiveness training. Once the home visiting began, time was made available for the volunteers to talk about their experiences in the field. An example of the HVU is given in the following report.

CASE REPORT 1

A young woman, promiscuous and very depressed, had recently had her child removed by Protective Services because of neglect. She would be asleep most of the day on sleeping pills given to her by her doctor. Owing to several recent suicidal attempts, scars covered both her arms. The volunteer, a mother of three, visited 4–5 hours, usually twice a week, and they talked about child rearing and other things that they had in common. She helped the woman find a suitable apartment and provided transportation to doctor appointments and to the welfare office. The volunteer was an excellent model for the client, the only person she knew who "had her head straight." Soon they became friends, and when the client needed someone to talk with, she would call the volunteer.

The second program was the Social Club formed to provide the clinic clients with some minimal social life and human contact. Many PET clients have a history of social isolation and alienation. People are often avoided, and the thought of talking with other people generates considerable fear. The Club is a safe and well-structured vehicle for them to develop social relationships and social skills. The Club has its own officers, and the clients are gradually accepting more responsibility for its growth. Activities of this group serve not only as an excellent treatment program but as a means of preventing problems from developing.

Attempts are made to visit the hospitalized client. If distance makes visitations impossible, telephone contact is maintained. For many chronic institutionalized clients, going to the hospital is like returning home. The individual with a history of psychiatric hospitalizations is well prepared for the journey to the hospital, the entrance and evaluation, the restraints, the electric shocks, and the injections of tranquilizers. For the newcomer it is usually a traumatic event, and the concern shown for the client by the team at this time provides vital support.

PET appears to be an effective alternative to hospitalization as well as a useful means for developing consultation relationships and supportive follow-up services. Establishment of a halfway house, a crisis-oriented day treatment center, and a vocational rehabilitation work program might further reduce hospitalization. However, until these additional services are provided, PET will continue to be a service for only the most acutely disturbed individual or family.

The therapist must be very aggressive in establishing and maintaining the therapeutic relationship. The stereotype passive and aloof therapist is not able to work successfully on the team. Often it is the ability to become quickly involved by caring and sharing of oneself that makes for a successful intervention. The following case report illustrates many of the PET treatment principles already described.

CASE REPORT 2

Pamela is an exceptionally tall young woman in her mid-30s, mother of two girls, ages 5 and 8. The 5-year-old had some damage to her spinal cord, resulting in problems with motor coordination and difficulty in bowel and urine retention. Protective Services had been called by neighbors because of the very strange behavior that Pamela was exhibiting. This was her first acute psychotic episode, precipitated by her boyfriend's departure. She would stand in the middle of the room, moaning and groaning, become rigid, and then fall to the floor. Her conversation was difficult to follow, but it was clear that the Devil was trying to tear her heart out and she was fighting him. She kept saying that she had to tell the truth. There was much symbolic placement of dishes, scissors, vases, and pictures which had special meaning to her. If she moved a particular part of her body, she felt that this could cause changes in other parts of the world. However, during all her difficulty, she would still ask where the girls were and if they were safe.

I asked the Protective Services worker to take the children into the other room and entertain them while I talked with their mother. She did not want them to leave her sight, but I told her that seeing her upset was not good for the children and that we both were most concerned about her children. As I tried to unravel the story of her boyfriend's departure and reflect back the feelings that she had about the boyfriend, the children, witchcraft, and so on, she would arch her back, lean backward looking at the ceiling, and fall to the floor. After having spoken to her for about half an hour, I grabbed her as she fell and held her in my arms and spoke very gently to her. It was clear that she could not be treated on an outpatient basis, and I spent a great deal of time preparing her for the hospitalization, which meant leaving the children. She questioned my sincerity and whether I was trustworthy. I told her to look into my eyes as deep as possible to find out. She said that she couldn't tell, and I told her that she would have to test me to find out.

Eventually, she accepted the decision that hospitalization was needed and was able to play a key role in making the contract to go to the hospital. Even though she was struggling with her psychosis, she locked the windows in the house, gathered up the toys in the children's room, and took a few articles, and then I walked her down the stairs, holding her hand as we went to the ambulance.

When she was at the hospital, I visited her. Within just 3 days she was in control but decided to stay at the hospital for a longer time. In part, this was in response to the hospital staff, who had frightened her about the consequences of leaving too early. On her return home I visited her, and we agreed that it would take her a few days to get prepared for the return of the children. The kids were soon returned to her, and she took excellent care of them. Every 2 or 3 days, I would stop over, and we would talk about her "rebirth" and the stages through which she felt she was passing. Soon we were discussing her boyfriend, her poor choice of men, and her dependency. I tried to prepare her for any crisis that might arise so that she would never feel so hopeless that she would "flip out" again. Since she considered herself a strong woman, a competent person, she did not want to come to the clinic, for that would only indicate how weak she was. We met a total of 8 times. This was 2 years ago. About once every 6 months she calls to "touch base." Sometimes it is a minor crisis, and sometimes it is simply to let me know how she is doing. At the time of the original crisis it was possible to develop a close and lasting relationship and to have a meaningful and constructive impact on her life.

SUMMARY

Until the formation of PET the San Pedro Mental Health Service was a fairly traditional clinic. Even though there was a worker on duty to handle any walk-in crisis and a 24-hour telephone service for emergency calls from the clinic's clients, the clinic operated on a long-term, analytic, medically oriented philosophy. Almost all the clients in the clinic were called patients, and each was on a number of medications. The patient would be in a group psychotherapy program for an indefinite length of time, and the turnover of patients was small. The therapists worked in their offices; a home visit was an unusual occurrence. The consultations provided to the community were very rare and typically were treatment programs in the school, the therapist leading a group while one school person might observe but not participate. The use of labels and analytic terms permeated the agency, but rarely did one use any behavioral or reality-oriented descriptions. No attempt was made to evaluate the impact on the community of its direct service program, and in fact, no research was done.

Now the clinic is a community mental health facility and a crisis center. The total philosophy of the clinic has changed. Long-term individual and group psychotherapy have been reduced; short-term modalities are being emphasized, especially those approaches that focus on the present problems; the use of medications has been reduced as well as the use of mental illness as a label; the community is viewed as the therapist; consultations have become a component critical to the emergency services programs as well as to the other programs in the clinic; and preventive programs are much more strongly emphasized. Outreach and home-visiting services are now offered. These changes did not occur abruptly, but very gradually, only after some confrontations among the staff and as PET began to prove itself. More than anything else, success of the mobile psychiatric emergency team seems to be related to the new attitudes of the staff toward the clients and an aggressive stance toward therapy and consultation.

5

HOME TREATMENT OF SUICIDAL PERSONS

James Selkin
A. Nicholas Braucht

THE DENVER EXPERIENCE

In October 1966, Denver General Hospital opened an Emergency Room Psychiatric Service to provide helping services to medical Emergency Room (ER) patients whose reasons for coming to the ER were behavioral or emotional rather than medical. Prior study of ER records revealed that as many as 10% of the ER patients (nearly 5,000 of 50,000 a year) had asked for help for essentially emotional problems.

Emergency Room Psychiatric Service

The ER psychiatric service was initially staffed by psychiatric nurses with a psychologist as director. The main function of the service was dispositional, consisting mainly of routing patients in a humane and efficient manner to appropriate sources of care. Later, greater emphasis was placed upon brief on-site psychotherapy and a crisis telephone line for suicidal persons was established.

Shortly after the ER psychiatric service was established, it became apparent that many problems impaired the efficiency of the system. The primary difficulty was that many of the patients never arrived at the source of care to which they were referred. Others arrived at the source of care,

This program was supported by National Institute of Mental Health grant No. RO1=MH18164 made one or two visits, and then failed to follow through. A number of random samples were drawn from the referred population, and in every sample it was found that initial appointments were not completed by at least half of the sample. Of those who did follow through, about half completed more than one appointment with the outpatient team to which they had been referred. Thus, effectiveness (defined as two completed interviews at the source of care) hovered around the 20% level.

Large numbers of suicidal patients were seen at the ER psychiatric service because Denver General Hospital was the only publicly operated, centrally located hospital designed specifically to serve the health needs of Denver's poor. In 1971, 1469 individuals came to the ER psychiatric service following a suicide attempt. Hundreds of others came with varied symptoms of emotional distress, including suidical ideation. When interviewed, many of these patients denied their suicidal thoughts and feelings. Others were so heavily drugged or so ill that they could not be interviewed while they were in the emergency room. Intensive medical care was required for these patients, and they were soon transferred to the medical wards. Of those suicidal patients who were interviewed and referred to mental health clinics for follow-up care, the usual small percentage followed through.

Home Treatment

This then was the situation which stimulated the development of the Home Treatment Project: a large number of patients, obviously in serious distress but rejecting available services, constituting a high-risk population for completed suicide, alcoholism, and other forms of deviant behavior.

The Department of Psychiatry at Denver General Hospital works closely with Denver's Visiting Nurse Service (VNS). The VNS provides follow-up care for some discharged patients, and their personnel are frequently asked to check on a patient who has stopped coming to his therapy program. As personnel in the ER psychiatric service became increasingly aware of the high dropout rates of suicidal patients referred by the ER, the idea emerged of asking visiting nurses to treat these patients in their homes. Some initial exploratory work brought forth very positive responses from the VNS, which was anxious to expand its knowledge about and competence with psychiatric patients. Since the prospective program did not conflict with already established treatment modalities and the target population was available and not previously assigned to any treatment facility, it proved possible to establish this program without any interagency conflict.

The nurses' initial visits to the attempted suicides brought forth reassuring and positive statements from the patients but anxiety and fear from the nurses who visited them. When the nurses first began making home visits to suicidal patients, the major question in their minds was whether they would say the wrong thing and trigger a suicide. This question was related to the unresolved fantasies of omnipotence characteristic of young professional workers in the helping services. To cope with these fears, project personnel quickly established a consultation group to which nurses involved in the project were invited on a weekly basis. This group featured the presentation of case material and discussion of this material in a nonchallenging, supportive atmosphere. Reassurance and reality interpretation were the major techniques employed. The nurses responded positively to the group meetings, which were held regularly for over a year.

The home treatment research project was funded in June 1970. The essential purpose of the project was to evaluate the effectiveness of home treatment as therapy for those who attempt suicide by using the experimental group-control group method.

THE HOME TREATMENT RESEARCH PROJECT

Subjects

The subjects for this study were male and female adolescents and adults living in a large area surrounding Denver General Hospital. All the subjects were volunteers. The number in each category and mean ages are given in Table 5.1.

The subjects were assigned to one of two groups. The home treatment group (N = 37; 27 females, 10 males) received treatment for at least five sessions from a visiting nurse. The control group (N = 40; 26 females, 14 males) received no treatment from visiting nurses. Only subjects who did *not* require psychiatric hospitalization following their suicide attempts were included in the study.

TABLE 5.1 Data for 77 Subjects in the Study Group

	Number	Age
Adults		
females	27	33.1
males	14	30.8
Adolescents		
females	26	17.7
males	10	17.8

Measurement Studies

All subjects were tested twice, a day or two after the suicide attempt and again about 8 weeks later. The measures used were *a*) the 190-item Social Analysis Questionnaire (SAQ), *b*) the Miskimins Self-Goal-Other Scale (MSGO), (291) and *c*) a lethality questionnaire.* All items in the SAQ were administered to subjects within 1 or 2 days after the suicide attempt, and about one third of the items on the questionnaire (those items subject to change) were readministered an average of 8 weeks after the attempt. The changes evident between the initial administration and the later administration of the test constituted a major portion of the dependent (criterion) variables in the study analysis.

A revised form of the MSGO scale was also administered to the subject 1 or 2 days after and again about 8 weeks after the suicide attempt.

In addition, the psychiatric ER nurse who saw each subject after the suicide attempt completed a lethality questionnaire, assessing on a scale from 1 to 7 the adequacy of planning, effectiveness of method, and provision for rescue.

Procedure

All subjects were obtained from the psychiatric ER of Denver General Hospital after an initial screening procedure. It is hospital policy that all persons admitted as a result of attempted suicide are first examined in the medical ER, and then, if they are physically fit, they are referred to the ER psychiatric service for further care.

If the patient lived in the target research area and agreed to participate in the study, within 24 to 48 hours a researcher from the hospital would visit the patient's home to administer a questionnaire. The researcher would make a return visit in about 8 weeks. Some questionnaires were administered in the hospital if the researcher was there at the same time as the patient.

Those subjects who were seen first, while the study was in progress, were selected as the VN-treated group. If the subject agreed to have a VN (visiting nurse) visit him at home at least 5 times within the subsequent 8 weeks, the psychiatric nurse would make a VN referral. The visiting nurse always made the initial contact with the patient within the first 24 hours after the suicide attempt.

There were 23 visiting nurses involved in the home treatment of patients who had attempted suicide. All these nurses had completed college

---

* Copies of the Social Analysis Questionnaire and the lethality scale are available from the authors on request.

training. In their visits the nurses were asked to *a*) establish a supportive relationship with the patient, *b*) talk with the patient about his life situation, and *c*) evaluate his family situation. Supportive, cathartic, and advisory techniques were most commonly employed. At the end of the five project-supported visits, the nurse decided whether to continue or cease her visits, or to refer the patient to another agency for further care.

Thirteen 1-hour case conferences were scheduled with the psychiatrist who was team leader of the ER psychiatric service. He provided both consultation and medical direction for the nurse following a study patient. Nurses were encouraged to attend the case conferences for assistance with their patients. Initially, nursing attendance at these meetings was high, perhaps because of their anxiety level. But the nurses responded readily to the support and guidance from the consultation sessions, and in time, attendance at the weekly meetings became more selective in relation to the nurses' needs.

Suicide attempters seen by the psychiatric ER staff after the home treatment group had been selected were assigned to the control (nontreatment) group. These subjects were also told about the initial questionnaire and the fact that it would be readministered. Control subjects were matched with treatment subjects on age, sex, and length of time that had elapsed between the first and second administrations of the questionnaire.

Results

It was hypothesized that visiting nurse treatment would produce favorable changes in 17 personality constructs measured by the MSGO (self-concept) and SAQ.* Each of the 17 personality variables was assessed at two time points: 1) within 2 days of the suicide attempt, and 2) after 6 to 8 weeks. The difference between the second assessment and the first was calculated for each of the 78 suicide attempters for each of the 17 variables. The resulting change score for each subject was then treated by a 2 (adult vs adolescent) by 2 (VN-treated condition vs no VN treatment) analysis of variance.

Of the 17 analyses, 7 produced significant *F* ratios pertaining to the differential effectiveness of visiting nurse treatment. Three significant main effects of treatment versus no treatment were observed:

1. VN-treated attempters became more optimistic and hopeful about their chances of attaining life goals (life chances disjunction score: $F = 6.70$; $df = 1.69$; $P < .025$).

2. VN-treated attempters became less alienated (change in alienation score: $F = 3.32$; $df = 1.69$; $P < .10$).

---

* Data regarding the internal consistency and reliability of SAQ measures are available on request. The MSGO scale has been extensively employed in suicide research.

3. VN-treated attempters changed more in the direction of feeling that others were more supportive and understanding (change in the perceived social support score: $F = 6.82$; $df = 1.69$; $P < .025$).

On four other change measures the influence of VN treatment was shown to be moderated by the effects of age or sex of the attempter or by a combination of these two variables. In general, VN treatment seemed to be of greater value for adults attempting suicide than for adolescents. The interaction of the treatment condition and age variables achieved statistical significance on two measures. The Mosher hostility-guilt scale scores showed that VN-treated adults changed in the direction of expressing less guilt about their own feelings of hostility. They were more accepting of their angry feelings. In contrast, VN-treated adolescents showed the reverse effect. They were more guilty about their anger. This interaction between treatment condition and age of attempter was significant at the .001 ($F = 12.85$; $df = 1.69$).

The Buss-Durkee assaultiveness scale revealed similar changes. Adults treated by visiting nurses more easily expressed their angry feelings than did adolescents. Untreated adults continued to feel that they could not express angry feelings. Untreated adolescents saw themselves as being more expressive. This interaction effect was significant ($P < .025$; $F = 5.70$; $df = 1.69$).

Two significant triple interaction effects reinforced the impression that adults responded more favorably to visiting nurse treatment than did adolescents. Results for the variable *alcohol consumption* revealed that adult men treated by visiting nurses reduced their alcohol consumption, while untreated men did not change in this respect. Adolescent boys treated by visiting nurses did not significantly change their pattern of alcohol consumption. Untreated adolescent boys, however, drank less. This interaction was significant ($P < .011$; $F = 21.06$; $df = 1.66$).

A similar pattern emerged on the self-concept disjunction scale (discrepancy between actual and ideal self). Adolescent males felt more inadequate when they were seen by visiting nurses. Self-concept did not change among untreated adolescents. Adult men, on the other hand, became more hopeful and more confident when they had been visited by the nurse. Untreated adult men felt more hopeless about their situation on retest. Thus, here again, treatment elicited a favorable response in adult men and an unfavorable response in adolescent boys.

With females who attempted suicide this self-concept variable manifested a pattern almost diametrically opposite to that of the males. Adolescent females became more hopeful when seen by the visiting nurses and less hopeful when untreated. Adult females responded unfavorably to visiting nurse treatment, but self-concept improved among the untreated subjects. This interaction was significant at the .005 level.

The results may be summarized as follows:

1. For all subjects, visiting nurse treatment reinforced optimistic and hopeful attitudes about the future. It improved confidence and enabled the recipients to feel a sense of community concern and interest in their unique situation.
2. In general, visiting nurse treatment was more successful with adults than with adolescents. Adults treated by the visiting nurses felt less guilty about their angry feelings and expressed them more easily. The opposite was true for adolescent subjects.
3. Study of significant triple interaction effects showed that adult men responded most positively to visiting nurse treatment, while adolescent males responded least positively and even showed some regression. Adult men were more hopeful and reported that they drank less. The opposite was true for the adolescent male population. This effect was reversed for females. Adolescent girls responded more favorably to visiting nurse treatment, as evidenced by improved self-concept, than did adult women.

CONCLUSIONS

The concept of the helper who visits the sick and elderly and brings warmth as well as professional care and concern is not new in Western civilization. The *Assistante Sociale* on the streets of Paris is as familiar as the Good Samaritan of Great Britain. In our own country, nineteenth and early twentieth century doctors spent much of their time visiting the sick. Today, in rural areas and in many urban areas as well, the public health nurse is a major source of health care delivery. Thus, the tradition of the home visitor is an old, well-established one, extending back to a time when the distinctions between medical illness and emotional turmoil were less sharp and not as well understood as they are at present.

The results presented herein strongly support the usefulness of the visiting nurse tradition. In general, our VN-treated population showed very positive response in reviewing the effects of their experiences with the visiting nurse. These results are striking when viewed in light of the fact that the control or base rate population is known to show improvement without any treatment at all. Both our previous work (374) and that of Batchelor and Napier (27) indicated that untreated suicide attempters showed marked relief from depression, anxiety, and somatic symptoms within 1 month of their suicide attempts. Accordingly, our results can be interpreted to indicate that the untreated group showed *mild* improvement, while the treated group showed *marked* improvement on the particular variables noted.

Many authors have noted the relationship between object loss and suicidal behavior. Recently, Jacobs (191) showed very vividly how suicidal behavior in adolescence is related to both recent and remote object loss. In this context the VN can be viewed as a replacement or substitute object for the bereaved suicide attempter. Her visits can be interpreted psychologically as providing a new source of nourishment and support for the dependent bereaved individuals who attempt suicide. This point of view is supported by the results mentioned previously.

There are many reasons why those who attempt suicide fail to follow through on referrals to mental health clinics. Some have tried psychological counseling and found it wanting. Others are fearful of close human relationships, and still others do not possess the drive, organization, and resources required to complete an appointment in a place outside of their daily environment. For whatever reason the referral is rejected, a visiting nurse brings to these patients a source of help not otherwise available. She offers to people who, if left unaided, would continue as high suicide risks an opportunity to explore the meaning behind their suicide attempts. Accordingly, a unique result of this project is that it reached a hitherto untreated population.

A most intriguing aspect of the results is the age and sex differences in response to VN treatment. Adult men responded most positively. Adolescent girls also responded well to the VN therapy. Adolescent boys, on the other hand, reacted quite poorly to the VN, as did adult women.

Since all of the visiting nurses were females and in uniform, these differential reactions to them can be tentatively interpreted in terms of sex role attitudes. Our subject population consisted largely of ghetto residents. Most of our subjects were poor, and many were identified with Denver's large minority of Hispano residents. The adolescent boys in the study were frequently school dropouts. Drinking, truancy, and deliquency histories were common among them. This is the group that responded least favorably to the visiting nurses. We suspect that their uniforms were seen as signs of official prestige and power and conveyed to these youths a punitive meaning. Visiting nurse uniforms were seen as similar to police uniforms, as well as to the suits and ties of school principals, judges, and probation officers. These youths interpreted their suicide attempts as "bad acts" and anticipated censure or punishment from the nurse. They reacted to her visits with increased defiant feeling but less open expression. Acting out in the form of alcohol abuse remained unchanged from an originally high level.

Adult men responded most favorably to the visiting nurse. Alcohol consumption decreased markedly, and self-concept measures showed distinct improvement. It is suspected that the adult men in the study were pleased and flattered by visits from attractive young women. Their sense of masculine prowess was strengthened, and their fantasy life was enriched. Many of the men contacted had serious problems with alcohol, and these in turn reflected a lifelong overdependency on female figures. They were preconditioned, as it were, to respond positively to the presence of an attractive, nourishing, nondemanding female in their lives.

The young girls in the study did well with the visiting nurses. Positive identification with a successful same-sex adult would account, at least in part, for the development of these positive relationships. Loya (267) has written about the inadequate preparation of the adolescent Chicano for life in America's urban areas. The VNs had many observations and suggestions to share with these girls about growing up in the big city. In addition, they could well have served as role models.

On the other hand, adult females who attempted suicide seemed to feel that they had already exhausted many of life's options: it was too late for them to choose a good husband, finish high school, or develop a successful career. Saddled with too many children and too many bills, thay had little or no financial or psychological support in their lives. For them the VN contact may have underlined the contrast between rich and poor, between success and failure. Visits from visiting nurses seemed to increase their sense of inadequacy and hopelessness as they viewed the gap between their own place in the world and that of the VN therapist. This gap was seen as an unbridgeable chasm.

This speculative explanation of differential response to VN treatment is, of course, testable. According to the viewpoint presented, male visitors in street dress would do better with adolescent boys. Older women from a similar socioeconomic background would do better with adult women suicide attempters. Further research on this issue is in order.

Suicide Prevention Centers have yet to establish themselves firmly as actually influencing the suicide rate in their communities. One of the reasons for this state of affairs is that the centers have not been able to reach out to important segments of the population who are highly lethal. In this chapter we have described a new technique for reaching out to suicidal persons, and further, we have been able to show positive response to the treatment from the clientele treated and from the community agencies employed in delivering the service.

6

BEYOND EMERGENCY SERVICES

the continuing relationship maintenance program

Robert E. Litman, Carl I. Wold
Nancy K. Graham

Since December 1971 the Los Angeles Suicide Prevention Center (SPC) has been providing certain high suicide risk clients with a long-term program of continuing relationship maintenance. This report describes the rationale, objectives, and operations of this program, together with the research design for evaluating its effectiveness.

RATIONALE

The principal activity in emergency counseling services and suicide prevention centers is not *prevention* in a public health epidemiologic sense. Strictly speaking, we engage in suicide *intervention* according to a crisis therapy model. Most observers agree there is great deal of short-term benefit and that probably some lives are saved. However, nowhere in the United States is this saving of lives reflected in dramatically reduced suicide rates. Of course, there are many well-known problems associated with using suicide rates as a standard of effectiveness, since criteria for certification as presently reported are variable, uncontrolled, and virtually unstudied. Still a really dramatic response to crisis intervention, the development of antidepressant drugs, or the development of new health care facilities has not been noted in suicide rates.

An explanation of this may emerge from follow-up studies of SPC clients. According to Litman (264) a majority of patients interviewed 2 years after their first contact with the SPC said that they had tried to follow the counsel of the SPC workers. In general, those patients in touch with the SPC because of acute situational stress and acute suicidal problems had received considerable help through crisis intervention and made a good recovery. People who were chronically suicidal and had no special acute situational stress at the first contact tended to have further difficulties, and a number of them continued to be suicidal after the contact with the SPC was discontinued.

The following hypotheses have been offered: About half the people who commit suicide are acutely suicidal, or they have acute situational stress. Suicide prevention centers can help such people and should make strong efforts to reach more of them. About half the people who commit suicide are chronically suicidal or have chronic situational stress. There is some question about the effectiveness of the suicide prevention center crisis intervention in preventing the eventual suicide of such people. Apparently, crisis intervention is appropriate for suicidal patients who conform to the theoretical model for crisis therapy in that they have had a previous period of stable adjustment and have fallen into disequilibrium because of some acute stress. For suicidal patients who do not conform to the crisis model, supplementary types of intervention are indicated.

Wold and Litman (442) reached a similar conclusion after investigating 8 suicides by persons who had been in contact with the SPC. The time lapse between last contact with the SPC and death ranged from 1 day to 28 months, the median time lapse being 6 months. A crisis model of suicide could not adequately describe the subjects. All of the deaths resulted from their life styles and were relatively independent of the emergency or crisis which had existed at the time when they were in touch with the SPC. Suicide was associated more with gradual exhaustion of resources than with sudden stress or loss.

Only 40% of the SPC clients conformed to the classical descriptions of people in crisis states. For many of the long range, highest risk, suicidal persons the potential danger of suicide can be projected ahead for several years as a problem ameliorated by crisis intervention but tending to recur. Perhaps the SPC interventions are postponing suicides in these persons rather than preventing them.

CONTINUING RELATIONSHIP MAINTENANCE PROGRAM (CRM)

These research findings led us to develop the Continuing Relationship Maintenance (CRM) Program. High-risk suicidal individuals, recognized through the "call-for-help" telephone service and evaluated as being high risk by the lethality rating indicators, are assigned to the program for a 24-month period. The program is not referred to as therapy, nor is it conducted by "therapists." Rather the program is based on *relationship*, and is conducted by paraprofessionals and volunteers with supervision by professional staff. Each subject in the program receives at least one telephone call during the week; for most there are additional relationship activities. The program emphasizes home visits, befriending contacts on the Good Samaritan model, and individual and group meetings at the SPC and other meeting places. Subjects are encouraged to use all available community and personal resources. This intervention model is based on rehabilitation rather than crisis intervention, the goals being to develop increased competence in the subject and increased resources in the community over an extended period of time during which team effort and innovative thinking are focused on maintaining the continuity of the relationship process.

Additional rationale for this program is provided by social scientists who have pointed out that suicide is most likely to occur when individuals feel isolated and alienated, and does occur when in fact they are alone. According to sociological theorists the higher the degree of social relationships, the less the susceptibility to suicide. For example, Maris (275) advances the concept of external constraint provided by relationships as a major postulate in a developing theory of suicide. Living alone is one of the leading indicators of high potential for suicide (411, 440). Aloneness may be by personal choice (as in psychological depression) or because of a hostile interaction between a subject and his environment (as in divorce). A variety of helping groups, from the Salvation Army to the Good Samaritans (130), have emphasized that extended personal relationships are the most potent of antisuicide remedies.

In summary, we advance the hypothesis that the combination of an emergency counseling service with an organized relationship maintenance outreach program extended over a period of time offers the greatest opportunity for preventing suicides.

CRM is an innovative, inexpensive, antisuicide program for high risk, chronically suicidal persons based on recent advances in theory and practice and new developments in the training and employment of paraprofessionals and volunteers. In addition, the program is designed to yield a direct evaluation of results in comparison to costs.

CONTROLLED STUDY OF AN ANTISUICIDE PROGRAM

Although there is general worldwide interest and much activity directed toward the diagnosis and management of suicidal behaviors, we conclude, as did Haughton (171) that on the basis of the present evidence one could not answer with any objective certainty the difficult question, "Do suicide prevention, crisis intervention, and emergency mental health programs save lives?"

There are no classic studies evaluating suicide prevention. The basic problem is how does one measure events which did not happen, e.g., a prevented suicide? The classic answer is a controlled experiment. The difficulties in doing a controlled experiment concerning suicide are many, and include the selection of subjects, the ethical issues involved in experiments on human beings, the problem of providing an antisuicide impact to large numbers of subjects at low cost, and the unmet need for standardized measuring instruments. Motto (298) reported a controlled study in which patients discharged from hospitals after suicide attempts who received no other treatment were divided into two subgroups: "contact" and "no contact." Those in contact group received regular communication from the staff member who interviewed them when they were in the hospital. Contact was by telephone, or, more often, by a brief letter. The content of the message was simply an expression of concern that the person's life situation was reasonably satisfactory and invited a reply if the person desired to respond. An effort was made to personalize the letters as much as possible to avoid the impression of a form letter. At the end of an 18-month follow-up period the suicide rate in the two groups was the same (1.5%). Motto felt that possibly the length and frequency of contacts had been too small to generate a feeling of attachment and relationship.

Research Design

Our research design is similar to that of Motto, (298) though it provides relationship contact with more intensity and frequency than in his program. As in Motto's study, it is important for our investigation to use as subjects individuals who are considered high risk. As Diggory (94) demonstrated, the more suicidal the subjects, the less wasteful and the less costly the intervention program.

Among people referred to suicide prevention centers or who call in themselves, the suicide rate is approximately 1% a year for the next 2 years according to follow-up studies (264, 436, 439). This is comparable to the suicide rate for those seen at a general hospital. Indeed, the populations are similar in that half of the callers to the Los Angeles SPC reported prior suicide attempts, and about 30% had been in mental hospitals at some time.

A special and entirely unique feature of this program is that the patients are screened three times for high suicide risk through the use of prediction scales which have been developed at the SPC (246, 263, 266). The important result is that only the highest risk subgroup has been selected for the antisuicide effort. This makes it possible to have a group for study in which a large enough number of suicides can be anticipated so that valid comparisons between the intervention group and the comparison group can be made.

Impact on Subjects

A word should be said about the protection of human rights in a study such as this. Although the on-going relationship of the CRM was not offered to the high-risk subjects in the control group, there was no factual evidence that they would be missing anything of value. Until the program was tried and tested, no one could say that the control subjects were being deprived. They did, of course, receive the best available help from the crisis intervention service of the Los Angeles SPC. All existing forms of help other than the CRM program were still available to them.

Concerning the rights of subjects in the intervention group, it should be noted at the outset that all the subjects originally contacted the SPC voluntarily. Because this was a new type of service, it was necessary to obtain the informed consent of all those participating in CRM. If the continuing relationship was by telephone only, verbal consent was accepted as being adequate, since the subject could terminate the relationship at any point by hanging up the telephone. If relationship contacts were by other means, then written consent was required. A few CRM subjects (4%) had decided to discontinue contacts with the program. Efforts were made to determine why, and to persuade the subject to remain in contact, for example, by changing the worker or by discussion with a senior member of the staff. If the subjects still rejected the relationship, we accepted their decisions, leaving the door open for them to reactivate the relationship with ease.

In evaluating possible risk to the subjects, it is important to keep in mind the goals and limitations of the services. Most of the workers had had no professional training, although the leader of each team is a paraprofessional with considerable mental health experience. The workers did not represent themselves as offering a treatment program; rather, their role was to maintain a concerned relationship facilitating use of the complete range of community agencies and resources. Will there be risks to experimental subjects in a relationship program when the investigation is terminated? Perhaps our volunteer workers would become, in 2 years time, "significant others" to the research subjects, and the termination of that relationship could be an important loss for those subjects. The answer is that we attempted to make every effort to see that the relationship program continued after the study was completed. It was hoped that most subjects would be ready to phase out of the relationship program, having achieved enough supporting relationships elsewhere in the community. For others who showed a continued need for the service, it was made available. If the program proved successful in that it offers needed and effective help, funding of the program (approximately $250/client/year) could easily be sustained by local resources.

Methodology

Subjects for the study were selected from among suicidal callers to the Los Angeles SPC. We identified a subgroup of those SPC callers as high risk. Prior research led us to estimate that this group will have a 5% yearly mortality rate from suicide (263). At the current level of assessment of suicide risk, it would not be possible to assemble a group of people with a much higher risk potential, given the best known identifying criteria.

Clinical associates on the crisis service, those volunteers who answer calls from suicidal people in the community, make one page of notes on each call and a judgment of suicide risk based on clinical assessment. All of these notes on each caller are reviewed during a first screening to select high-risk subjects. When signs of high suicide risk were apparent, the person was called back about a week later. This call-back interview was structured in such a way as to provide answers to some 68 items which collectively provided an assessment of suicide risk, and selectively helped to identify the subject for later follow-up. Our earlier follow-up studies (264, 439) taught us the importance of obtaining varied and thorough identification such as names of relatives and friends, professionals, date of birth, social security number, and driver's license number. This information, ascertained initially, made it possible to relocate these people, many of whom lead unstable lives. Two other measures of suicide risk were also taken, one developed by Brown and the other by Lettieri (246, 263, 266).

During the final screening all information was reviewed by the senior research psychologist and an experienced paraprofessional for final selection. Subjects identified as high risk were assigned either to the CRM group or to a comparison group, using a table of random numbers. From the beginning of the study in January 1972, assignments continued on a monthly basis until we had assembled 200 subjects in each of the two groups. As soon as a subject was assigned to the CRM group, a trained volunteer worker began to establish an on-going relationship.

An effort was made to select and train a group of volunteers most representative of the Los Angeles community from which they come. The group was heterogeneous, both men and women, with varied ethnic and socioeconomic representation. Volunteers with a history of a prior suicidal episode from which they were currently distant in both time and feeling states were not automatically rejected. After initial screening interviews with senior staff members, potential workers were offered an 8-week training program. This training aided in selection of volunteer workers by providing our staff the opportunity to become familiar with the volunteers and, most importantly, by providing volunteers the opportunity to anticipate the work and discontinue if they felt that it was not suited to them. About 80% of the volunteers initially selected and screened went on to complete the training and begin to offer service. The training program itself combined didactic presentations by the senior staff and direct experiences with clinical materials using role playing and actual case examples.

Volunteer workers were able to regulate the level of time and energy which they invest in the program by the number of high-risk subjects with whom they chose to establish relationships. Our experience has shown that volunteers, on the average, remained in contact with five subjects, spending about an hour per week with each. Approximately 40 volunteer workers were responsible for about 200 CRM subjects. A subject generally remained in a relationship with his worker for about 22 months. Subjects in the comparison group had not been assigned a worker, and no effort was made to engage them in an on-going relationship. Nevertheless, some of them received the regular crisis service, which continues to be available to them. Comparison subjects will be contacted again at the end of the relationship program offered to CRM subjects. At that time, group comparisons will be made between CRM and comparison subjects on the issues of suicide risk and life adjustment, as well as determinations on how many subjects in each group committed suicide.

Characteristics of the Subject Groups

In order to emphasize the special characteristics of the high-risk subjects, some comparisons were made with the general population of SPC callers (Table 6.1). As was anticipated, male sex and older age were important factors which discriminate high-risk subjects from unselected SPC callers. As shown in Table 6.1, 45% of the high-risk subjects were male, while only 31% of the total population of SPC callers were male. The median age of high-risk subjects was 40 years compared with a median age of 34 years among SPC callers generally.

An examination of Table 6.1 reveals that suicidal problems were chronic and repetitive among high-risk callers. Over 75% of the high-risk subjects had attempted suicide at some time prior to their contact with the SPC. This contrasts with an incidence of 56% among SPC callers in general. It is noteworthy that over half of the high-risk subjects have a suicidal history going back more than 5 years.

Alcoholism is a special indicator of high risk—45% of the high-risk subjects had been identified as alcoholic at some time in their history. Many had become increasingly isolated and experienced few meaningful contacts with other people. Of these people, 34% were living alone during the time of their contact with the SPC, and 44% were not working and therefore were without that social interaction as well.

The severity of their sense of hopelessness about the future was expressed by an inability to conceptualize alternatives to suicide and to feel

TABLE 6.1 **Characteristics of Subjects at High Risk for Suicide Compared with Unselected Suicidal Callers to the SPC**[*]

Category	All SPC Callers[†]	High-Risk Subjects[†]
Males	31%	45%
Median age	34 yrs	40 yrs
Suicidal history		
One prior attempt	26%	19%
Two or more prior attempts	30%	58%
Suicidal more than 5 years	Not currently available	54%
Suicide risk		
High	25%	100%
Low	75%	0%
Special risk indicators		
Alcoholism	28%	45%
Not working	19%	44%
Living alone	Not currently available	34%
Prior professional help		
Psychiatric hospitalization	37%	55%
Future orientation		
Feels future is hopeless	Not currently available	20%
Sees no alternative to suicide	Not currently available	9%
Says eventual suicide is most probable	Not currently available	18%

[*] Based on data from an accidental sample of 7900 callers to the SPC from 1970 to 1972.

[†] Where total of all SPC callers = 129; high-risk subjects = 128.

that their eventual suicide was most probable. Although such responses characterized only a small subgroup of high-risk subjects, it will be informative to correlate these people who identify themselves as being painfully depressed about the future with those subjects who go on to commit suicide.

The CRM Program

The CRM program is flexible, and client-centered contact is primarily by telephone; meetings at the SPC or at the subject's home are arranged when possible and appropriate. Workers are trained to keep their expectations for the clients low keyed, not to expect miraculous improvements but to set limited and realistic goals. In their weekly contacts with subjects, workers are sensitive to their clients' needs, varying the form and content of the relationship accordingly. Some clients benefit from relatively intense involvement. Others can sustain only a brief or superficial contact. Many clients are cautious at first, gaining trust in the worker eventually. Some fluctuate from an enthusiastic response to calls, to suspicion, withdrawal, or overt hostility. Others find it so difficult to communicate by telephone that they prefer to write to the worker.

The CRM relationship is not seen as therapy in the formal sense. However, the relationship between worker and client has its therapeutic aspects. The suicidal person learns that he can discuss his hopelessness, anxieties, suicidal fantasies and acts, and even delusions and hallucinations without alienating his CRM worker. The worker tries to empathize with those feelings rather than to negate them or to conspire with the patient in masking or repressing them. Often it seems appropriate for the worker to refer his client to other community resources. In this way, volunteers can help their patients tolerate the anxieties they might feel when venturing into therapy, rehabilitation training, a new job, or feared social and sexual relationships.

Once each week the volunteers meet in small groups of six or eight with the staff for the purpose of consultation and ongoing training. At these weekly clinical meetings, individual cases are discussed, ideas are exchanged, and responsibility for the patients is shared by the group as a whole, including supervisory personnel.

Experience has shown that chronically suicidal persons are so needy, dependent, and demanding that they easily exhaust the energy and goodwill of friends, family, and therapists. It was recognized in the design of the CRM program that in order to maintain a relationship with these distressed and chaotic people for a prolonged period, workers would have to pace themselves, not for a sprint but for a long-distance run. Therefore new workers are cautioned to conserve their energies and not to become depleted by responding to each new situation as if it were an isolated crisis. At first, CRM volunteers find it difficult not to respond to the client's sense of constant emergency. In a way this is natural because of their experience in crisis intervention. However, this is one area in which the support of the group, and particularly of the experienced antisuicide worker, can be of help to the new CRM worker.

In the weekly antisuicide meetings, workers discuss the anxieties that they have in their relationships with clients, and also report on trends which suggest improvement. Very often a client who is beginning to throw off his depression expects too much from himself and is easily devastated by even moderate disappointments. Workers report that it seems to be quite therapeutic for the client to be reminded that there are still other avenues of approach to his problems, that there is always tomorrow, and that someone is still with him and understands his painful feelings of defeat and frustration.

As of June 1973 there were about 200 suicidal clients in the CRM program, and we had no *completed suicides*. However, there had been several suicide attempts, some of high lethal potential.

CASE REPORT

A high-risk client, Mrs. J, was assigned to an antisuicide worker, Mrs. B, in January 1972. Mrs. J was at that time a 32-year-old married woman with a history of severe depression dating back to 1956. She had become highly suicidal while in college in 1958 and had to be hospitalized following an attempt at that time. Things failed to improve at home owing in large part to the fact that Mrs. J had never had a good relationship with her mother, who was herself extremely disturbed and is reported by the client to have beaten her severely when she was a child. The client's depressions became worse and she was hospitalized in 1960 for almost a year. At that time she was treated by Dr. M, who was then a psychiatric resident and who has since treated Mrs. J on an outpatient basis. During the next several years the patient enjoyed periods of relative stability. She completed training to become a dietician and worked in that capacity for a local college. In 1964 she married Mr. J, a geologist, and in 1968 gave birth to a daughter. In 1970 Mrs. J became pregnant again, but this was an unplanned pregnancy, and she reacted to it with intense depression. She made a suicide attempt with pills and was hospitalized for 2 months. The baby's birth several months later brought about many unwanted changes in Mrs. J's life. The J's had to move from their apartment to a house in a new neighborhood, and Mrs. J felt isolated from her former friends, alone, neglected, and trapped with two preschool age children. She again became highly depressed and suicidal. Soon after this she began calling the SPC, telling workers that she couldn't bear to go on living and would have to kill herself. Because of her long history of depression and the number and seriousness of her suicide attempts, Mrs. J was evaluated as a high risk and assigned to the antisuicide program.

At first, Mrs. J's response to her worker's calls was negative. She told Mrs. B that she had never been able to trust an older woman because when she needed them they always let her down. Mrs. B told the client that she did not want to relate to her as an older woman to a younger one but instead as one contemporary to another.

At this time, Mrs. J was almost totally immobilized by her depression. On January 6 she said, "There's no hope. . .I can't do anything. . .not even the dishes. I'm such a burden." She was haunted by memories of her own childhood, and her greatest fear was that her children would grow up and see her as crazy and incompetent. She wept as she told Mrs. B her fears that she would never really be well and be a "normal mother."

On April 2 she went to a motel room and ingested 70 nonprescription sleeping pills. She telephoned the SPC and asked for Mrs. B. She said she had to die because she was hurting everyone else and because she was so lonely and miserable. "No one likes me," she said. "No one wants to talk to me." She would not tell Mrs. B or her husband where she was but agreed to call Dr. M. He was able to persuade her to go to the hospital, and he sent the ambulance for her. Mrs. J's condition was serious, and she required lavage, cardiac massage, and 4 days of hospitalization.

When she returned home, she still suffered from temporary neurologic dysfunction and required nursing care for 2 weeks. After the nurse left, Mrs. J became depressed and agitated and begged to be hospitalized indefinitely. Although she was convinced of her total inability to cope with life, Dr. M took a different view and opposed any further regression on her part. He also urged Mr. J and Mrs. B to encourage her to take some responsibility for herself and the children.

The next several months were agonizing for Mrs. J, and she leaned heavily on the SPC for support. She called in almost daily and in the middle of the night as well, frequently threatening to overdose or stab herself to death. Sleep was impossible because she worried over the financial and emotional burden she had become to Mr. J. On June 9 she reported, "I can't take it any more. It is so lonely to be awake when everyone else is sleeping." During the day she was tearful and lethargic and spent most of her time in bed, sometimes drinking and usually self-medicating. Her daughter was at nursery school, and she took her son out of the playpen only to feed and diaper him.

Meanwhile she eagerly accepted the contact with her worker. She confided in Mrs. B that she had been having a love affair with a married man. He was, however, about to terminate the affair and Mrs. J was again feeling abandoned and rejected. Mrs. B asked the patient if she had discussed this problem with Dr. M, and Mrs. J said she was not able to tell Dr. M about the man. She was afraid he would be angry with her and then he would reject her too. There were other things that she was unable to discuss with Dr. M, also for fear of disappointing and losing him. She told Mrs. B, for example, that at times, when she was bathing her son, she had fantasies of drowning him or that if she killed herself, perhaps she would kill the children as well.

Mrs. B was deeply concerned about these revelations and strongly encouraged Mrs. J to discuss this material with her psychiatrist. She pointed out to the client that Dr. M had been actively involved in her case and at no time had he expressed a desire to terminate therapy. Encouraged by Mrs. B's continued acceptance of her after hearing her secrets Mrs. J was gradually able to discuss this material in therapy. There followed a period of productive work with Dr. M, and the client reported to Mrs. B that thanks to this closer communication with her therapist and a new regimen of medication, she was feeling much improved.

During the course of her relationship with the client, Mrs. B has discussed her case frequently in the Wednesday clinical meetings. In this way other workers shared the responsibility for Mrs. J and were also able to coordinate their helping efforts when they had occasion to talk with the client.

It was agreed that when Mrs. J called in, workers should help her to realize her strengths and encourage her in constructive activities. In this way it was felt that she could be helped to abandon her helpless little-girl image. When Mrs. J was very depressed or disoriented, she would be encouraged to do some small task like fix herself a cup of tea or take a warm bath. Other times when she was feeling better, Mrs. B would suggest that she take the children to the park or out for lunch.

Over a period of several months Mrs. J came to feel that she could manage a little better and even began to think of going back to work. Mrs. B encouraged her in this plan but let the client know that she would not be critical or rejecting if working proved too stressful for her.

In late October, Mrs. J was hired as a part-time dietician by the college where she had worked formerly. She has been working regularly since then and has had good relationships with her co-workers and supervisors. In January she increased the number of hours she worked and made appropriate arrangements for the children's day care. She continues in therapy with Dr. M and is still telephoned weekly by Mrs. B. She enjoys reporting her new activities and recently told Mrs. B that she joined an exercise group and has been steadily losing the excess weight she gained during her pregnancy 2 years ago. Moreover, she can now sleep without pills for the first time in several years.

Mrs. J still has anxiety over her capabilities as a mother, and if the children are ill or injured, she becomes depressed and panicky. However, she has not felt acutely suicidal for approximately 6 months. She feels warmly toward the SPC as a helping resource but rarely calls in now. SPC records indicate that Mrs. J telephoned the SPC 97 times in 1972. She called just twice in 1973.

SUMMARY

We have presented a preliminary report of an inexpensive antisuicide program for high-risk, chronically suicidal persons. This program, called "Continuing Relationship Maintenance," is based on recent advances in theory and practice, including new developments in the training and employment of paraprofessionals and volunteer workers. In addition, this experimental program is being carried out within a methodologic framework designed to yield a direct evaluation of results in comparison to costs.

7

CRISIS HOSTEL

an alternative to the
acute psychiatric ward

Bryan D. Brook, Michael W. Kirby
Paul R. Polak, Rita Vollman

A number of models (114, 285, 318) of alternatives to hospitalization for intermediate to chronic psychiatric patients have been described. Very few models exist, however, for community based alternatives to acute psychiatric hospitalization when patients require more than home treatment (140) and family crisis therapy (340).

In 1970 the Crisis Intervention Division at the Fort Logan Mental Health Center replaced its inpatient service with a crisis hostel located in the community. A follow-up study of patients admitted to the crisis hostel compared with patients previously admitted to the crisis inpatient service was carried out. Social systems assessment and intervention (123, 326) were used in the actual life setting of both crisis hostel and hospital patients. It was anticipated that involvement of significant persons in treatment would be strengthened when the patient was admitted to a community setting. The crisis hostel also offered a unique opportunity during its 5-month operation to enlighten neighborhood residents about emotional problems.

ESTABLISHING THE CRISIS HOSTEL

Newspaper articles, radio spot announcements, and staff participation in television talk shows resulted in offers of several potential community hostel sites. An older home, in a multiple unit-zoned area of Denver, owned by a young registered nurse was selected. The nurse, who once was hospitalized for over a year with asthma, together with some of her former inpatient friends now living nearby, agreed to be a natural neighborhood support group for the crisis hostel.

The hostel was licensed by the Colorado State Department of Health as a residential care facility and provided four beds with a two-bed back-up apartment down the block. Since the nurse worked weekdays, several of her neighborhood friends agreed to prepare lunch and supervise residents as needed.

Procedures

While neighborhood young adults provided a warm homelike atmosphere, the physical structure, unfortunately, tended to be depressing and crowded when it was full. Guests often helped with meal preparation and shopping at a neighborhood store, while others did housekeeping chores. Two men or two women could stay in each of the two separate upstairs bedrooms, social interaction being centered in the kitchen and living room areas. Several residents continued working during the day and returned in the evening. This worked well, since the daytime atmosphere tended to be boring. The absence of group therapy or other structured activities seemed to motivate some to organize their own lives again, while it discouraged others.

When the woman next door found out about the crisis hostel, she told several neighbors that this halfway house for psychopaths might subject her 6-year-old daughter to the risk of sexual assault. The psychiatrist visited these concerned residents, explained the actual program, and enlisted their support.

Maximum stay at the community hostel and Fort Logan's crisis inpatient setting was 7 days. Primary reasons for entry into the hostel included stabilization on medication and resolution of acute suicidal or homicidal crises. The psychiatrist evaluated each resident, and an appointment for a physical examination and laboratory work was made at Fort Logan's outpatient medical clinic. The owner of the home unlocked the medicine closet at regular times, giving the residents access to their daily prescribed medications.

Staff nurses living 5 minutes from the hostel were on 24-hour back-up via a bellboy system. The crisis unit psychiatrist and Fort Logan's medical on-call system provided 24- hour medical back-up. One hospital bed at Fort Logan was available for initial 6-hour rapid tranquilization procedures (327) covering 10 PM to 8 AM admissions.

During the 5 months, 49 individuals ranging in age from 18 to 62 and spanning the diagnostic spectrum, stayed at the hostel. Half of the residents were moderate to high suicidal risks, but none made suicide attempts during their stay. One man required rapid tranquilization during an acute suicidal episode and slept while his wife stayed with him for support and security. The community setting conveyed the expectation that residents use their personal strengths instead of feeling like mental patients.

Problems

Several staff members were very anxious about placing persons in the hostel. The structured setting of the hospital had provided a degree of security that was difficult to leave. Some nurses were uncomfortable with the shift from medicine nurse–therapist to fulltime therapist. A major limitation of the hostel was the lack of a consistent natural social structure during the day. In addition, several residents required more supervision and longer treatment than the hostel offered and were transferred to longer term psychiatric services at Fort Logan. Cost for room, board, and laundry at the hostel was $5.00 per resident per day, which was much less expensive than maintaining a 24-hour inpatient hospital unit and nursing rotation in the state mental hospital. Thus the hostel demonstrated real advantages in cost and social setting.

FOLLOW-UP AND RESULTS

Throughout the crisis hostel project a controlled study research design assessed various measures of outcome. The same staff delivered systems interventive therapy for both hospitalized and community-treated patients. Thus evaluative procedures were geared to determining the impact of the treatment setting.

The 49 patients treated in the crisis hostel constituted the experimental group, while the comparison group comprised the last 49 patients admitted to the crisis inpatient hospital service before it closed. Thus the study involved two 24-hour care groups of 49 patients each, one group receiving crisis treatment in the traditional hospital unit and the other in the crisis hostel.

Staff ratings of patient improvement as a result of treatment were obtained for all 98 subjects at the point of discharge or transfer to outpatient care. Six to eight months after this data collection, letters were mailed to these same subjects requesting a follow-up interview for the purpose of evaluating their satisfaction with the crisis treatment. This interview usually took place in the home of the expatient.

Test Results

An analysis of salient demographic variables was conducted in order to determine the comparability of the two groups. The t test analyses revealed no significant differences between the groups in terms of age, sex, marital status, socioeconomic status, or admission diagnosis. Similarly, there was no difference in the average length of stay in the hospital or hostel.

The first set of research measures consisted of staff ratings on nine dimensions of treatment outcome taken when the patient left the hospital or hostel. These ratings were routine procedure for staff members and required no familiarization. Table 7.1 presents the mean staff ratings for both groups on these nine dimensions.

TABLE 7.1 Average Discharge Staff Ratings of Patients on Outcome Dimensions for Hostel and Hospital Groups*

Outcome dimension	Hospital	Hostel	*t* Value
Family relationships	4.10	3.86	1.34
Community relationships	3.72	3.75	0.09
Self-confidence and self-reliance	3.76	3.89	0.66
Antisocial activities	3.82	3.88	0.15
Use of leisure time	3.79	3.94	0.68
Individual problems	3.68	3.98	1.27
General symptom improvement	3.17	3.69	2.27†
Self-maintenance	3.52	3.80	0.92
Work (or academic) improvement	3.68	4.09	1.40

* Each group was composed of 49 subjects. The rating scale was *1*, recovered; *2*, markedly improved; *3*, moderately improved; *4*, slightly improved; *5*, unimproved; and *6*, regressed.

† Exceeds the 0.05 level of significance.

Inspection of Table 7.1 reveals a trend toward slightly higher means for the crisis hostel sample, although only one dimension is statistically significant. The outcome of treatment was rated by staff as being different for hostel patients in a negative direction in the area of general symptom improvement, this difference exceeding the 0.05 probability level of significance.

The next set of data consisted of interview information taken at follow-up, the interview occurring anywhere from 8 to 10 months after the subject left the protective setting. For each sample (hospital and hostel) 20 interviews were obtained, representing 40.8% of the total. Whenever it was possible, interviews were also conducted with family members and friends of expatients.

Both hospital and hostel patients received crisis treatment while they were in a 24-hour care setting. Such treatment typically involved systems intervention with family members and friends of the designated patient. It was hypothesized that treatment in the crisis hostel setting conveyed a more positive message to the patient and his family about the difficulties that they were experiencing and allowed for easier transition back into the home and community. Thus it was predicted that the hostel would result in significantly better outcome in community adjustment, family functioning, and the patient's perceived satisfaction with changes in himself and in his interpersonal relations.

Accordingly, outcome measures selected for the follow-up packet included an abbreviated form of Journard's Self-Disclosure Questionnaire, intended to assess the degree of self-disclosure and to serve as an individual index of family interaction (44) as suggested by Bodin; an abbreviated version of a community adaptation schedule; the Treatment Effectiveness Scale (30), which measures perceived changes in satisfaction with self, interpersonal relations, and the outcome of treatment itself; and the Mini-Mult (211), a brief form of the MMPI intended as a measure of symptomatology.

When t tests were conducted on the interview data, no significant differences emerged between hospital and hostel groups on the self-disclosure scale ($t = 0.47$) and the community adjustment scale ($t = 0.19$). Similarly, scale scores on the Mini-Mult were not notably different.

The t values for the two groups on the Treatment Effectiveness Scale did reach significance ($t = 2.12$ and $P < 0.05$). The mean scores for the hospital and hostel groups were 82.59 and 73.05, respectively, a higher score being indicative of greater satisfaction with changes in the self and interpersonal relations and with the outcome of treatment.

Evaluation

Finally, the initial data on readmission rates at 6-month follow-up suggested that crisis hostel clients were readmitted less frequently than patients who were hospitalized. Six persons from the inpatient hospital group had been to Fort Logan, three of them twice (nine total readmissions). During this same time only one of the crisis hostel residents required readmission. Readmission to other facilities was not recorded, so that this finding can only be viewed as being suggestive of any readmission patterns which occurred.

DISCUSSION

To summarize, the results from staff ratings at discharge and follow-up interviews with patients indicated significant differences between the two groups on "general symptom improvement" at discharge and a broad scale of treatment effectiveness at follow-up. On the remaining eight outcome dimensions rated by staff at discharge and the three other outcome scales included in the follow-up interview, no differences between the groups were revealed.

It would seem that, contrary to the experimental hypotheses, results point toward a trend in favor of the hospital over the hostel as a setting for 24-hour acute crisis treatment. However, the finding of significantly greater symptom improvement as rated by staff may have been a reflection of restraint on the part of staff to medicate hostel patients to the same degree as hospital patients. With this speculation in mind, a chi-square test was calculated on the amount of tranquilization for each group; as was expected, the hospital group received significantly more tranquilization than did the hostel group ($\chi^2 = 4.40; P < 0.05$). This finding may account for the difference in staff ratings for general symptom improvement, as tranquilization is often the major factor affecting symptoms in acutely agitated crisis patients. It could also account in part for the observed differences at follow-up on the treatment effectiveness measure.

The results of the crisis hostel project were used as the basis of a more comprehensive inpatient alternative system currently in use at Southwest Denver Community Mental Health Services, Inc. Medication is more carefully monitored, while rapid tranquilization, when needed, takes place in an apartment coordinated by a live-in college couple. Five host families each provide a more therapeutic social system than was available in the crisis hostel. Preliminary results indicate more positive measures of family communication and satisfaction with treatment at 6-month follow-up for persons in alternative homes than for those hospitalized at Fort Logan. Significant findings on these measures occurred only from the point of view of the client. Ratings by staff and persons important in the client's life were not significant. These findings have been particularly notable in new clients rather than in patients with histories of chronic hospital use.

In any study of social innovation, one cannot fully ascertain to what extent the particular innovation approximates the ideal or model on which it is based. The implementation of any given alternative to the mental hospital involves a number of variables which taken singly or in combination may considerably affect the efficacy of the alternative. In concluding that the particular hostel investigated in this study may have been slightly less effective than the hospital, it does not follow that any similar alternative is likewise less effective. In many respects, such as patient feedback and *per diem* costs, the hostel proved significantly better than the hospital; this study focused only on the treatment outcome aspects, and it is difficult to generalize from these results.

Nevertheless, it is important to attempt to gain some understanding of those factors related to this particular hostel which could potentially have affected the outcome. Staff questionnaires, completed at the termination of the study, revealed a negative impression with regard to staff morale during the trial period in which the hostel was operative. While staff members appeared highly favorable to the concept of an inpatient hostel, they perceived quite clearly the operational problems which occurred.

These problems as described by the staff generally fell into two categories: 1) neighbors who had committed themselves to helping at the hostel during the day did not follow through, and 2) the hostel was sometimes over-crowded, resulting in a less than desirable social atmosphere.

CRITICAL EVALUATION

The crisis hostel experimental project points to the need for critical management of several key areas in the implementation of any alternative models to hospitalization. Provision of a specific and responsive social structure using community resources is pertinent to quality care and staff morale. Size of the patient group needs to be limited for a positive living atmosphere to evolve. An effective and flexible medication system is undoubtedly a primary necessity for community treatment of many acute psychiatric conditions. In addition, staff anxiety concerning new commun-ity approaches needs to be acknowledged and continually monitored with respect to the implementation of the program. Thus, with all its varied strengths and limitations the community crisis hostel offers some useful operational ideas for future community models alternative to the acute psychiatric ward. Southwest Denver Community Mental Health Services, Inc., continues to assess the relative merits of such alternative community approaches.

8

THE CRISIS EVALUATION UNIT

a ripple in the pond

Carl A. Hanssen
Charles R. Rosewall

THE PURPOSE OF THE
CRISIS EVALUATION UNIT

The Crisis Evaluation Unit (CEU) was established at Metropolitan Hospital, Norwalk, California, in April 1971 as a "gatekeeping plan" to monitor the flow of patients into and out of the state hospitals, and to build up a system of alternative treatment resources in the community. Although the CEU is located on the grounds of the state hospital, it is a Los Angeles County operated mental health facility, designated for the care and handling of voluntary and involuntary patients.

The underlying premise of the CEU operation is that whenever possible the patient should not be hospitalized; the patient should receive definitive treatment in his own community as close to his own natural resources as possible. Thus the CEU proposes to deal with each patient from a holistic point of view. Crisis intervention is the major instrument, but it is applied with a broad objective. The whole individual is dealt with as well as his interrelating systems—social, economic, or familial. Precipitating stresses are viewed against the backdrop of the individual's unique personality organization.

The immediate goal in the initial contact is to deal with the crisis situation which the patient presents and then provide an appropriate treatment resource for follow-up care and ultimate resolution. The long-term goal involves the de-emphasis of inpatient care as the treatment of choice in acute psychiatric disorder. Instead, we offer a range of specifically designed, individually oriented, acute treatment programs for the care of the patient where he lives. Traditionally, "inpatientism" and sequestration in some out-of-the-community setting has only tended to compound the initial difficulty by adding the problem of reentry. It seems bizarre to try to rationalize treatment in a vacuum when the acute disorganization did not derive from a vacuum. The patient should be treated in as close contact with the disequilibrating stresses as possible, the better to learn to cope with them.

LOGISTICS OF THE CEU

Basically the CEU is an emgency walk-in and screening clinic. Its clients include all of those patients who would ordinarily present at the Metropolitan State Hospital for admission whether voluntary or involuntary. They might be self-referred, brought in by the police in custody, or transferred from other hospitals because of lack of space or determination of chronicity. It was decided to initiate the CEU concept at Metropolitan State Hospital because it had been shown that 88% of the applicants were presenting for admission unscreened by any element of the county mental health system.

Physically, the CEU is located on one of the State Hospital wards under a formal county lease agreement. One-half of the unit's staff are state employees and are also under county contract. This latter arrangement differentiates the CEU from other mental health clinics in that its staff is from two separate and distinct systems. Other features, however, make this unit unique: its treatment philosophy and method, and the flexibility of the program with its close ties to the follow-up links of the treatment chain. Nevertheless, although the CEU is unique as implemented, the basic idea is not new. In Southern California alone there are two noteworthy precedents. The first was established at the Los Angeles County–University of Southern California Medical Center–Unit III in the middle 1960s (286); following this an Emergency Admitting Unit was opened at the Orange County Medical Center (371). The latter is the closest analogue to the CEU as it was originally conceived.

The ward in which the CEU operates is adjacent to the State Hospital's acute admitting suite. Ironically, this ancient high ceilinged concrete building—with large rooms, open sleeping bays, an enormous dayroom accommodating a piano, ping-pong table, television, bookcases, writing tables, and several clusters of chairs and sofas—lends itself to the goal of relaxed informality and freedom of movement. This physical setting is much more suitable than the typical mental health clinic atmosphere with endless cubical offices opening onto narrow corridors.

PROBLEMS AND CONSIDERATIONS IN STAFFING

Staffing the unit was a special problem. The primary objective was to establish a team concept of operation, the physician acting essentially in an advisory capacity to the staff. Staffing needs had to be met quickly. When the project was announced, it was described as an innovative and challenging opportunity. Personnel from both Metropolitan State Hospital and the County Mental Health Service were invited to investigate the program. The subsequent applicants were an already sympathetic, largely superior group of professionals who wished to do something more with their training than past experience had allowed. A mature, stable, warm personality and a desire to stretch one's mind and personal horizons were considered as important as training and experience or past performance in traditional professional roles.

The mechanics of staffing a 24-hour, 365-day clinic are formidable. However, after some early adjustments a staffing structure was established which provided optimal coverage for the admission pattern which emerged. On each shift each of the mental health disciplines was represented, except on the night shift—from 12 midnight to 8 AM—generally a time of lessened activity.

A typical staffing problem concerned the number of psychiatric technicians needed on the night shift. Two were sufficient except that in an emergency two males were usually required for safety measures; however, the lack of a female staff member was both legally and therapeutically unsound. The result was a staff of three technicians, one of whom was a woman, in addition to the psychiatrist.

The ethnic and social backgrounds of the staff is another important concern, since the presenting patient population represents a broad mix. At the time of this writing the day shift included three Blacks, two Mexican-Americans, one Filipino, and one Asian-Indian. Seven of the eleven staff members were female. The Black and Mexican-American staff members were particularly important to the therapeutic effort. Some middle-class white professionals (e.g., the authors) are not fully aware of the limits of their effectiveness in dealing with members of a different ethnic group. Working alongside colleagues from these ethnic subcultures increases this awareness and offers a unique learning experience. Furthermore, in Southern California there is a large population of Mexican-Americans who do not speak English, making it essential to have some Spanish-speaking staff members.

SELECTING CLIENTS

The clients of the clinic represent a wide range of presenting problems. Most suffer from psychotic illnesses, usually with a history of chronicity. Many viewed Metropolitan State Hospital as the only place of refuge (often arriving with a packed suitcase) when they were in emotional difficulty. This population is composed largely of persons at marginal levels of social, economic, and educational adjustment. In addition, they tend to have a simplistic view of mental illness versus mental health. Many of these chronically mentally ill persons who have been seen at the CEU seem to operate within a special system of paralogism: "If I am not in the state hospital, then I am well [and don't need outpatient therapy or medications]; if I begin feeling ill again, then I must enter the state hospital."

Thus for many of these persons there is no middle ground between hospital and home. Attempts to get them started in outpatient therapy or a day treatment center in lieu of admission to the hospital are interpreted as rejection, callous disregard for their needs, and failure to understand that they are ill. Not only are they from a world which equates *illness* with *hospital*, but those with previous hospitalizations tend to identify themselves, as do their families, as *mentally ill*. They carry with them a passive hopeless sense of futility about attempting to alter this destructive demoralizing identification. They are particularly vulnerable to life stresses because they see themselves as being unable to cope even before trying to do so.

Criteria for Selection

Predictably, since the CEU opened, the problems of the presenting patient population to Metropolitan have become increasingly more serious. This is largely due to the screening process which occurred as stricter criteria for admission were employed. Basically those defined by the Lanterman-Petris-Short Act (LPS) for involuntary hospitalization, the criteria include: 1) danger to oneself (suicidal), 2) danger to others (homicidal), and 3) gravely disabled (threat to survival). The conditions for voluntary hospitalization closely approximated these.

Prior to the opening of the CEU, virtually everyone (96%) who applied for hospital admission was accepted. Thus, a significant number of patients were admitted for whom, with some effort, other dispositions might have been made, e.g., board and care placement, referral to an outpatient clinic, or partial hospitalization. The goal of the CEU effort was to find alternative treatment resources for 25% of these patients who, although they were less disabled, had become habituated to recycling through the state hospital when conditions became adverse for them. For another 15%, truly marginal cases, arrangements and placements were made as well, but because conditions in many sectors of the alternative resource system are less than adequate (board and care placements are often custodial at best, and the tracking mechanism is such that patients frequently get lost between the time of referral and the appointment), many of these began to recycle back. In fact, the return rate at the CEU has climbed steadily, approaching an average of about 33% of the applicants seen each month.

Identifying Client Needs

How sick are those who are seen? Some patients are hospitalized simply because there is no adequate alternative and their capacity to cope is severely diminished—they are gravely disabled by ordinary standards. Nevertheless, the CEU staff strives to find alternatives for them, as most of these patients are deeply mired in a psychotic episode or a severely handicapping, often dangerous neurotic condition. For these patients there is no alternative to hospitalization except for the treatment focus and energy of those who staff the CEU. A careful screening process is carried out, and if there is any reasonable doubt, the patient is kept on the ward for observation and treatment for up to 20 hours (the treatment period has been extended beyond 20 hours in some cases). The primary consideration is the crisis condition. The diagnostic process is aimed at the current and precipitating stresses, the predisposing personality constellation, the absence (or presence) and character of the interrelational support system, and other relevant social and economic factors. These elements are sorted out, and a beginning attempt is made to work out a more feasible matrix for resolution of the problem outside of the hospital; family counseling is instituted during the diagnostic and treatment period; social and treatment agencies are alerted, and a linkage is made for support back in the community.

It is only when all of the above efforts have been exhausted with no appreciable improvement in the situation that the patient is considered for hospitalization. Whether the hospitalization will be on a voluntary or involuntary basis is a decision based on the conclusions of the foregoing evaluation. This decision can have significant implications for the patient, since it involves the question of choice and the capacity for reality testing. If he can choose to commit himself voluntarily, then ultimately he might decide to choose to get well. He has taken some responsibility for himself.

There is a tendency to define crisis intervention as short-term therapy for the "normal" person who is temporarily overwhelmed by an overload of external stresses and who returns to his former level of coping after treatment. However, at the CEU we have found that this definition and the corresponding treatment plan are equally appropriate to the chronically psychotic person who is decompensating during a life crisis of his own. For him to reachieve a compensated, reasonably well-functioning state is a legitimate goal of our crisis intervention effort. An important part of learning for the CEU staff, therefore, has been to resist the tendency to assume that a person already labeled psychotic when he appears in the clinic, is simply suffering an exacerbation of his psychotic process, even though he is exhibiting no increase in psychotic symptoms. Since his best level of functioning is marginal, the psychotic person is often not granted the right to have a life crisis by some professionals; he is only allowed a deeper deterioration into his psychosis.

CEU METHODOLOGY

How does the CEU treatment method differ from that of other mental health clinics? Basic to the design of the CEU has been the purposeful reeducation of each of the professional disciplines to a generalist orientation. It was felt that each member of the team should be able to carry out virtually every aspect of the unit's operation (except prescribing medication): nurse, social worker, psychiatric technician, and psychiatrist should be able to perform evaluations, do therapy, make community referrals, and decide on hospital admissions, as well as carry out the attendant administrative procedures and complete the paper work. Furthermore, each staff member would stand ready to lend his particular professional expertise and experience to the training of his colleagues when assistance from his area of specialization was required. This method provided an atmosphere of sharing.

A natural consequence has been a blurring of interdisciplinary lines. The goal has been to expand professional capabilities, to have multiple practitioners for each function where before there were but few.

Involving the Psychiatric Technician

The most dramatic effect of this principle has been the expansion of the role definition of the psychiatric technician. The psychiatric technicians comprise approximately 50% of the full-time staff. They all come from the state hospital system, their experience ranging anywhere from 3 to 15 years. A description of the psychiatric technician's function prior to working on the CEU might be that he had "supplied the muscle" and "emptied the bedpans." This role description has been altered substantially, however, by emphasizing the concept of total case management. Each patient is assigned to a psychiatric technician (or other mental health worker) who assumes full responsibility for that patient until the case is closed or until, at shift's end, the case is specifically reassigned to another therapist coming on shift. This process ensures treatment continuity for the patient. The responsibility for the case includes *a)* doing the diagnostic workup, *b)* involving the patient, his family, and/or significant others, and *c)* rendering treatment either through medication (under medical supervision), or by one-to-one or family therapy, or by any combination of these. In addition, when disposition and referral are at issue, this therapist must make the contacts, arrange for the community placements and appointments, and fill out all necessary documentation. With this method the physician's time is used most economically and to the best advantage for the entire operation.

The Role of the Staff Psychiatrist

There is only one psychiatrist on each shift. To expect him to accomplish a complete work-up on each patient would be time consuming and impractical. Nor would this permit any time for the important task of supervising the treatment of other patients on the ward. Accordingly, the psychiatrist "floats." As each staff member completes his initial evaluation, the case is discussed with the psychiatrist. The staff member and the psychiatrist then interview the patient and family briefly and together arrive at a treatment decision or disposition.

The psychiatrist is used by the staff as a consultant and teacher. In this way the psychiatrist maintains an overview of what is going on at all times and is always available for emergencies. The case discussion and subsequent supervision of therapy is the vehicle for teaching. Learning by doing, the heart of the clinic's training program, has resulted in developing increasingly effective, better-equipped crisis therapists.

A treatment plan is developed for each patient; it includes a description of the disease entity, a differential diagnosis, the key dynamics, treatment criteria and priorities, indications of potential behavioral patterns, and suggestions for alternative courses of treatment, including medications. This plan, under the supervision of the attending psychiatrist, serves as a mechanism for treatment orientation for the therapist to insure that all patients will *not* be treated alike, as they now are in many facilities. It also serves as a framework for systematized learning.

Since the CEU can work with patients for up to 20 hours, the individual-centered treatment plan is especially advantageous because it provides a more uniform treatment capability. Although the working shifts are only 8 hours long, the objective of a longer term treatment design may be achieved since each assigned therapist, in turn, is fully informed of the basic condition and the plan of operation. This allows for maximum communication among staff and ample opportunity for periodic evaluation of progress, with the option of changing the therapeutic course if that is indicated. Each individual therapist is free to practice his unique skills and talents in dealing with the patient, but all of the involved therapists cooperate in carrying out a specific plan.

Importance of Milieu

In the CEU the sacrosanct concept of the "therapy chamber" has been eschewed; private offices are not used for consultation with patients. Working space was defined as that space around the therapist, wherever he might happen to be—in the dayroom, the kitchen, the reception room, the dining room, or outside. The effect of this decision has been beneficial. First, the entire unit has developed an open, friendly atmosphere. There is always activity, and groups of people are seen conversing in a relaxed way, drinking coffee. Patients are seen with their families or alone by the simple expedient of moving just a few feet away. Also the patient feels less threatened. He can see what is going on. There are no closed doors beyond which lie he knows not what.

CASE REPORT

At 5:30 in the afternoon a 39-year-old widow, mother of four children, was brought to the CEU by her cousin. She was unable to walk without assistance and was intermittently sobbing, sometimes hysterically, and canting about the Devil and Death. She was confused, markedly depressed, apparently delusional, and withdrawn. Her dress and hair were disheveled although she was basically clean. She was brought to the clinic because of increasing withdrawal and inappropriate behavior over the past 2 weeks. That afternoon, 2 hours prior to admission, her behavior had become so bizarre that her children were frightened. Her cousin had interceded, and she was brought to the hospital.

Past history revealed a 2-week hospitalization for a similar event 2 years earlier. Subsequently, she had been in outpatient therapy for 6 months with gradual withdrawal of antidepressant medication; she had done well until the present episode.

During the initial phase of the interview the cousin was the chief informant. The patient continued to weep and act in a generally unintelligible manner. But by the gentle persuasions and ministerings of the interviewer–therapist (psychiatric technician) the patient began to respond by joining in the interview process. The story which emerged showed the patient to be under severe stress; her emotional reserves were depleted to the point where she could no longer sustain herself or her children. In addition, she was markedly fatigued due to lack of sleep over the past several nights.

The mental status examination showed indefinite orientation except as to place, with blunted affect and marked depression. Her sensorium was intact, but her thought content was skewed by some delusional material, as indicated before. Her intelligence seemed unimpaired, but her judgment and insight were virtually nonoperative. The initial diagnostic impression was that of a severe depressive reaction, the specific character of which was as yet undetermined.

At this point the psychiatrist was brought into the case. The technician outlined the case to him and gave her impressions. The psychiatrist probed the presenting circumstances and suggested some alternative considerations before proceeding further. Then the psychiatrist and the technician saw the patient together.

From the short, intensive interview which followed, it was decided that the core problem was not one of psychosis. Instead a very definite hysterical component was detected which, when admixed with confusion and the fear of isolation, presented more bizarrely than might ordinarily be anticipated.

The decision was made to maintain the patient on the CEU for observation and treatment; formerly, she would unquestionably have been hospitalized. A treatment plan was decided upon. Since the presenting problem was one of depression, the plan was constructed around the fundamental dynamics of depression with a caution to be aware of differential considerations.

The basic tool to be used in the management of this patient was that of therapeutic relationship and a plan was developed which promoted both contact and interaction. The approach was to be gentle but firm and directed toward loosening up the tightly bound internal pressure. After some careful approaches on the part of the technician, the patient began to open up. She first related the story of the death of her husband some 9 years earlier, which she was still reliving. The degree of detail was phenomenal. Slowly, affect began to emerge as the tale unfolded, tightly bound anger derived from the requirement to maintain a facade of strength and support. The patient visibly began to change. By 11 PM she was ready for sleep. The next morning, refreshed and rested, she arose and ate with the other patients. After breakfast the therapy was resumed and finally completed by another technician who, following the case plan and the verbal and written comments of the preceding therapists, and in consultation with the staff psychiatrist, arrived at and arranged for an optimal disposition. The patient was also involved in the disposition process. A call was made to an outpatient clinic close to her home. The entire therapeutic transaction, as well as the recommendations, were communicated to the referral clinic, and a specific appointment was made for the patient.*

The cousin was called, and the patient was released to return home once more to her children. She left at 11 AM barely 18 hours after her arrival at the CEU. Both she and the CEU staff felt satisfied that a significant reconstitution had occurred during even that brief period.

---

* The referral process involves, in addition, two forms: 1) *The Transfer Form*, sent separately to the referral clinic, recapitulating all of the relevant clinical data communicated during the referral phone call, and 2) *The Transfer Follow-Up Form*, to be completed and returned by the referral clinic to indicate resultant treatment and ultimate disposition.

ISSUES IN TRACKING

Because of the problems identified in the tracking of patients and the need to interconnect the links of the alternative treatment system, a reliable clinical data base was imperative. Often the patient's first point of contact with the mental health system, the CEU, was the logical place for initiating research. A design was developed for the collection and processing of pertinent clinical and social data concerning the patient.

For an effective tracking system each element of the treatment chain, past, present, and future, must be informed as to the patient's movement. The first task then, from the evaluation standpoint, is to develop an instrument that can be applied widely and that will permit the dissemination of maximum information. Confidentiality is not an issue, since information is passed only between the various elements of our own system and once the patient is admitted for treatment, he becomes a patient of the entire system, not of any single unit or solitary practitioner. When referrals are accomplished, feedback information is necessary for the referring agent so that he can complete his own records. These problem areas have been broached with some success, and the beginnings of an operative system of transfer and transfer follow-up have been established.

RESULTS

The disposition of the 7988 persons seen in the first full year of operation (April 1, 1972, through March 31, 1973) was as follows: Of the total number of patients presenting, 37% arrived on involuntary status, and 14% of these were released to community resources after an initial treatment period on the CEU. For these, hospitalization was avoided. Of the 63% who presented for voluntary admission, only slightly more than half (54%) were admitted to the state hospital wards. The rest were referred to the local mental health clinics, the county hospitals for medical complications, or to board and care facilities and the social service elements of the county system.

The sources of referrals were self-referred, 47%; law enforcement (police, probation, and/or courts), 22%; County General Hospital, 20%; county mental health clinics, 9%; and board and care, private hospitals, and private MDs, 2%.

A general breakdown of the presenting population according to target groups showed 80%, mentally ill (all categories, with a predominance of psychotic states); 13%, family crisis (mainly transient situational reactions); 6%, drug and alcohol abusers;* and 1%, mentally retarded. Of these

---

* The drug and alcohol patients are handled under another mechanism by closely related centers and are, therefore, a small percentage of those seen by the CEU.

totals, 7% were children (under 18); 90%, adults (18–64); and 3%, geriatric (65 and over).

The ethnic distribution was 64% white, 22% black, 11% Mexican-American, and 3% miscellaneous.

SUMMARY

In 1971 the Los Angeles County Mental Health Service established the Crisis Evaluation Unit, a psychiatric emergency center, located on the grounds of a state hospital. Its purpose was to implement a county screening mechanism for all patients presenting to the state hospital for admission. Another more important focus was to provide a resource for crisis intervention.

Accordingly, the architecture of the program, the staff development methodology, and the underlying research premise were oriented toward developing the clinic as an integrated part of a larger system. The clinic itself was specifically linked with the other elements of the mental health care delivery system, the staff members were trained as integral members of a team, and the patient was treated by reviewing past therapy efforts, assessing present strengths, and preparing a case management plan for future crisis resolution. A continuum-of-care concept set the theme.

The result has been an ongoing, innovative crisis treatment service effective in stimulating other community programs in the direction of cooperatively offering a comprehensive mental health care delivery system.

II

Crisis Intervention with Individuals, Families, and Groups

macro- and microtechniques and issues

The chapters in this section focus on understanding and dealing with diverse crisis phenomena experienced by individuals, families, small nonkinship groups, and communities. Focusing on the behaviors of crisis intervenors in community conflict situations, Spiegel analyzes the intervenor's varied roles of advocate, conciliator, mediator, arbitrator, and research evaluator. The latter role, especially as it may be assumed by a participant observer, is an especially important but usually neglected aspect of community conflict, hence the lack of systematic research on the efficacy of third party intervention. On the assumption that community conflict is ubiquitous and rarely completely resolved, Spiegel argues cogently for the use of the concept of conflict management *to replace the fanciful term* conflict resolution. *He also argues that one way of reducing the escalation of violence in community crises is through the process of* conventionalization, *providing ritualized outlets for the otherwise destructive aggressiveness often accompanying urban crises.*

Also directing attention to the application of crisis approaches to the social life of collectivities, Brown views the crisis concept within an ecologic framework, linking multifactorial systems in population-oriented change efforts. Of special significance are the opportunities triggered by community crisis incidents for moving minority groups and other hitherto disenfranchized citizens from powerlessness toward constructive environmental change.

The next two contributions underscore the special role that can be played by law enforcement and correctional personnel in family crisis intervention.

In discussing the crucial ingredients of immediacy and authority in crisis counseling, Bard (confirming Foxman's observations in Part I on the importance of work with police in relation to the mobile psychiatric emergency team) reminds us that the half-million police officers in the United States represent "an untapped natural resource" for managing unpredictable domestic crises and such other catastrophic events as rape or natural disasters that challenge "the mental health institutional capability." The need for greater collaboration between police personnel and mental health professionals is reinforced by Bard's persuasive presentation on the role of police in the delivery of human services.

Describing the Sacramento 601 Diversion Project, Baron and Feeney offer another contribution to the application of crisis counseling in the correctional system. They document how a diversionary project, using the techniques of time-limited family crisis intervention, can keep the child out of the juvenile detention center by involving the child and his family in new coping methods. In their experimental effort, an impressive number of children were actually kept out of the correctional trap—and many stayed out during a 12-month follow-up period.

The chapters by Alevizos and Liberman, and by Weinberger, provide additional creative examples of family-oriented crisis intervention in community settings. Alevizos and Liberman give a clear and detailed account of behavioral modification techniques in working with families under stress, and Weinberger spiritedly demonstrates the need for and the value of time-structuring if crisis intervention is to meaningfully meet the needs of populations-at-risk in communities where the demand for immediate help far exceeds available mental health resources.

Allgeyer and Farberow, each from a different vantage point, attend to a little-used crisis modality, namely, group crisis counseling. From her richly eclectic perspective, Allgeyer shows how transactional analysis and Gestalt techniques can facilitate the recovery efforts of group members as they grapple with novel coping skills and support each other in the process. And Farberow, sharpening our understanding of the importance of postcrisis intervention, elaborates on a series of responsive therapeutic procedures for self-destructive persons, including long-term, intermediate, and drop-in group therapies. Farberow concludes with a fruitful comparative analysis of the key dimensions in each of these group approaches, basing his conceptualization on Yalom's ten "curative factors."

The crisis modality, earlier hammered out by Caplan in Israel and elsewhere, is further developed for transcultural use by Ingham. She gives a step-by-step account of the flexible consultation process she employed in diverse societies, and in doing so makes a strong case for the relevance of crisis intervention in emergency care programs in widely different sociocultural settings.

No sourcebook on emergency mental health would be complete without reference to one of the nation's major health problems, alcoholism. So we conclude this section with Bosma's chapter on alcoholic crises, which alerts health professionals to the often lost opportunities for intervention in the medical emergency room.

9

THIRD PARTY INTERVENTION IN COMMUNITY CONFLICTS

John P. Spiegel

There is a direct and relevant reason for considering intervention in social conflicts in the general context of the crises which ordinarily require emergency health services. This has to do with the broad implications of human conflict as a process potentially subject to technical intervention, no matter at what level and in what context. Conflicts can be prevented, accelerated, or resolved through the various techniques of intervention. In particular, the symptoms generated at the crisis stage of a conflict invite or demand intervention. For example, although levels of collective violence characteristic of the 1967-1970 period (463, 464) are currently much reduced, the principles of third party intervention developed during that time are now being successfully applied in such intense confrontations as occurred at Wounded Knee, South Dakota.

THIRD PARTY INTERVENTION DEFINED

Third party intervention consists of a series of conflict-shaping and conflict-reducing inputs that have emerged in recent years from efforts to cope with the wildly escalating, chaotic events of naturally occurring disorders. Intervention of this sort is largely unreported and is therefore relatively unknown, both to laymen and to scientific groups. The procedures involved are not well understood even by those who practice them,

This article appeared previously in Vol. 52 of the proceedings of the Association for Research in Nervous and Mental Disease, Inc., New York.

because they are too new, too subject to change, too much a response to intense practical needs growing out of evanescent circumstances. To capture and report the circumstances of the kaleidoscopic, emotionally heated events of a disorder is a triumph in itself. Therefore, codification of these practices is just getting underway.

But there is another reason for the lack of reporting of intervention procedures. As crisis workers who become involved in domestic conflicts well know, it is dangerous to intervene in a fight between two other people. They can easily both turn on the third person. Accordingly, the intervenors are reluctant to present themselves as experts, feeling, especially at this early stage, that they might elicit more hostility than acceptance, more doubt than credibility. In the tenuous, delicate situation in which intervention takes place, credibility depends more on word-of-mouth reports of past behavior than on scientific reputation or professional standing.

This chapter represents an attempt to organize and codify a set of social procedures—social engineering, if you will—which promise to be helpful in the reduction of levels of collective violence. Although varying in some respects, it is derived from the previous work of Dr. James Laue and his associates at the Community Crisis Intervention Project, Social Science Institute, Washington University, St. Louis (77).

Some of the issues relevant to the topic will not be dealt with. First, the general theory of conflict behavior is not included, because it is too diffuse and in any event needs to be specified for system levels, such as personality, small group, wider community, the state, national, or international system (38, 45, 83, 93, 277). Second, neither the remote or underlying causes of civil disorders, nor theories of the riot process and the escalation of violence will be discussed. These are currently matters for vigorous debate (47, 122, 387). Because it is necessary to impose some sort of time frame on the phenomena of community conflict in order to explain third party interventions, an *ad hoc* set of states-of-conflict which may characterize the community situation at any one moment of time will be proposed.

COMMUNITY CONFLICT

Let us assume that conflict in the community occurs between two parties. The first group consists of a set of aggrieved groups such as racial or minority, student or political protesters, who believe their concerns have not been met, or even listened to, and that they do not have the power to effect change through the ordinary political process. The second group consists of local authorities who have three responsibilities that are not always compatible: to deal with the demands of the protesters, to keep the

peace, and to punish wrongdoing. It is generally assumed that the authorities always have the power, if not necessarily the inclination nor the
capacity, to meet these responsibilities.

In the context of this two-party conflict, there is always the possibility of
intervention by a third or outside party. What can be done, however,
depends on the state of the conflict at the time. The relevant states are the
following. The conflict may be: 1) *dormant*, that is, not only quiescent, but
unrecognized or its symptoms denied by the authorities; 2) *escalating*, that
is, giving rise to demonstrations, protest meetings, confrontations or minor
scuffles whose significance can no longer be denied; 3) *in crisis*, that is,
characterized by intense confrontations in streets, school buildings, prison
yards, and other localities where the conflict threatens to or actually
becomes violent; 4) *stalemated*, that is, unresolved and characterized by
alternating periods of quiescence and flare-up, a chronic state that leaves
no one's mind really at rest; 5) *resolving*, where the issues at conflict are
being solved through compromise by means of negotiation or the use of
normal political channels; and 6) *relapsed*, that is, after a course of
apparent resolution, the whole structure of compromise breaks down and
the situation returns to escalating or crisis states.

USING THIRD PARTY INTERVENTION

Third party intervenors enter the situation and perform roles or functions
adapted to the prevalent state-of-conflict. A question must be raised about
the use of the word "role." In standard usage, *role* describes a conventionalized behavior pattern associated with the function, position, or title a
person holds within a group or organization. The behavior patterns to be
described are not yet sufficiently conventionalized, nor is there complete
agreement on what role term to assign to the various functions (124). There
are other reasons for questioning this usage, such as lack of clear
differentiation in behavior patterns (250), but role terms (like names for
hurricanes) remain convenient devices. The conflict between protesters
and authorities during the Democratic and Republican Conventions in
Miami Beach in the summer of 1971 will be used to illustrate the
application of the roles to concrete situations. The staff of the Lemberg
Center had the opportunity to study the entire sequence of events from
June through September, including the prior planning for the confrontations and the aftermath of the violence on the last day of the Republican
Convention. Since this represented what collective violence researchers
call a *scheduled event*—as opposed to an unexpected, spontaneous
disorder—it was possible to collect more systematic data on the planning
and the outcome of plans than is usually the case.

The Advocate

The first of the intervenor roles is that of *the advocate*. He represents a person or group entering a conflict situation during the dormant state or when escalation is just beginning, as an advisor or consultant to the aggrieved group. Unlike all other intervenors to be discussed, he is unabashedly *not* neutral, being pledged to support and facilitate the goals of just one party to the conflict (448). He lends his skills as an organizer to the group, helping it to create a structure capable of taking action, and advises the group on the formulation of its demands and on sources of financial or political support. Since he is not a part of the group but enters from the outside, he is presumably cooler and more objective, more capable of creating an effective strategy of protests, demonstrations, and confrontations, than indigenous members of the group. He may be committed to nonviolent techniques or he may be willing to risk violence in pursuit of the groups' goals, depending on his moral values and his previous strategic experience.

A decade ago, the advocate would probably have been called an outside agitator, and he may still receive this label in some parts of the country. To be sure, his function is to awaken a dormant conflict or to escalate one in progress in order to bring the issues to a head and to achieve change. But, as a result of the disorders of the 1960s, public attitudes toward collective violence have become more sophisticated. In metropolitan areas especially the focus is on conflict management in order to avoid violence while preserving the possibility of peaceful change. There is a general consensus that the more highly organized and successfully led the protest group, the greater the opportunity to avoid the irrationality and chaos that breed violence. Since the advocate would usually prefer change without violence if this is possible, he is increasingly perceived as playing a part in the complex maneuvers involved in conflict management.

The Conciliator

Although the advocate contributes to conflict regulation, human relations in extreme and emotionally laden circumstances are inevitably unpredictable, and the conflict may still mount to the crisis stage. Crowds assemble on the streets, hostages are taken in prisons, face-offs occur in which the atmosphere of impending violence is reinforced by rapid physical motion, confusion, and the possibility of an impulsive, aggressive act. The prime characteristic of a community disorder in the crisis stage is the possibility of surprise—the unexpected act which precipitates the violence. It is at this stage that the second intervenor role, *the conciliator*, makes its appearance. The conciliator attempts to cool inflamed tempers by creating physical and emotional distance between adversaries and by suggesting temporary expedients to resolve the crisis.

For example, the reader may recall the incident at the Washington DC jail, Wednesday, October 11, 1972, when the largely black inmate population seized Corrections Director Kenneth Hardy as a hostage and were ready to die when told that 100 riot-equipped police were prepared to rush Cell Block 1 which they were holding. Aggression arousal was so high that they were scarcely able to articulate the demands or grievances underlying their uprising. Washington lawyers Julian Tepper and Ronald Goldfarb appeared, and, reinforced by the presence of Representative Shirley Chisholm, managed to calm the inmates and obtain Director Hardy's release by arranging for the inmates to appear in court to plead their case before Judge Bryant (73,306).

The actions of the conciliators in this case were impromptu. If they had not happened to show up after hearing about the incident on the radio, another Attica might well have occurred, and this illustrates the lack of conventionalization of intervenor roles. But in other instances, specifically at Miami Beach for the political conventions, conciliator roles were planned months ahead. An organization called Religious and Community Leaders Concerned (with the Conventions), RCLC, arranged to bear witness to nonviolent confrontation for the Greater Miami Community by training neutral observers, setting up a rumor control and reporting service, and by offering to serve as go-betweens for the authorities and the protestors. For example, they negotiated a campsite at Flamingo Park for the nondelegates, as the protestors were called. Another organization, the National YMCA Outreach Program, arranged for medical and legal services for the nondelegates and provided communications equipment for the not always congenial groups: the Yippies, the Zippies, the SDS, women's rights groups, the gay organizations, and the Viet Nam Veterans Against the War, to name a few who planned to participate in street theater, sit-downs, and demonstrations against the policies of the Nixon administration.

The actions of conciliators are distinguished from the functions of the advocates because they are taken only after consultation with the authorities, or at least with their sanction. Conciliators represent the interests of both sides in an emergency situation. Although they may be closer to one side than another, they cannot function unless they have credibility with both sides. For example, during the boycott of the John Wilson Junior High School in the Canarsie section of Brooklyn by a group of white parents protesting the transfer of black students from the Brownsville area, street confrontations took place, rocks and eggs hurled and racial epithets exchanged. From October 31 to November 8, 1972, violence was averted in this tinderbox situation to a large extent by on-the-spot conciliation attempts conducted by the Community Relations Service, an official arm of the Federal Justice Department. That a government agency could obtain credibility with both racial groups during this crisis is testimony to the careful cultivation of human relations on the part of the CRS with individuals and groups residing in the area far in advance of the crisis itself. This is only one example of the many crisis events in which the Community Relations Service has been quietly involved. But since it sedulously avoids publicity, its activities are relatively unknown and unappreciated.

The Mediator

The third type of intervenor is *the mediator*. The Community Crisis Intervention Project at Washington University in St. Louis has defined the functions of mediators in this fashion: *Mediation is the process by which a third party who is acceptable to all conflicting parties in a dispute helps them in reaching a mutually satisfactory settlement of their differences.* One might also say that if advocates generate a situation in which mediation may be necessary to avoid violence, conciliators produce the situation, in the midst of crisis, in which mediation is possible. However, it is important to point out that if mediators enter the conflict situation during escalation and before a crisis occurs, the crisis may be altogether avoided.

Mediators not only have to be acceptable to both sides, but may also have to do a great deal of legwork and perform psychological feats of interpretation in order to get each side to agree to sit down and talk together. For this reason, mediators are sometimes called negotiators. As I said previously, there is some disagreement about role terms. However, there is a growing consensus that negotiations can only take place between the two parties, the adversaries, who are in direct conflict with each other. Mediators can prepare the way for negotiations 1) by offering neutral ground for a meeting place, 2) by interpreting each side's position to the other, 3) by carrying messages back and forth and, above all, 4) through their steady and optimistic attitudes that compromise and peace are possible. A noncontroversial, anxiety-reducing, problem-solving and yet realistic and tough orientation is an essential part of the mediator's equipment.

In Miami Beach, because it was a well advertised event and because both the protestors and the police (plus other local authorities) had indicated well in advance their desire to avoid violence, would-be mediators offered their services by the dozens. However, only a few groups managed to obtain the confidence of both sides. Their activity, particularly during the planning processes before and between conventions, generated a spirit of trust between the police and the protestors which was instrumental in avoiding violence until the last day of the Republican Convention. On that day, the carefully nurtured trust broke down. Unfortunately, time is too short to review here the reasons for the breakdown of trust and the resulting teargassing, injuries, and arrests that marred the otherwise successful conflict management.

The Arbitrator

The fourth intervenor role is that of *the arbitrator*. This is the newest and perhaps the most promising of all the community conflict intervenor roles. In many neighborhood conflicts (e.g., tenants versus landlords or housing authorities, or hospital boards and administrators on one side, and patient groups or health care consumers on the other) specialists who have had much experience in mediation are now being given legal authority by the courts to settle the dispute. The arbitrator must, of course, again be acceptable to both sides. Arbitrators can also function without such formal, legal authorization. In Miami Beach a mediator representing the Religious and Community Leaders Concerned organization was given responsibility, for the Republican Convention, of obtaining a park permit on behalf of the protestors, enabling them to occupy Flamingo Park as a campsite. The City Council was not willing to give the Park directly to the protestors because the various groups were too antagonistic toward each other to be responsible for governing the campsite. As the responsible holder of the permit, this mediator then had to arbitrate the various disputes that erupted on the campsite between the rival groups of nondelegates. If this sounds like an impossible assignment, it should be considered that the arbitrator has the advantage (or disadvantage, depending on one's view) of being blamed by each side for the settlement he imposes. To be sure, he would rather obtain an agreement than impose a settlement. But if he is forced to be arbitrary, the leaders of the various factions can minimize the disappointment and resentment of their followers by blaming the arbitrator. This enables them to preserve their leadership position. Rapid leadership turnover, which is characteristic of most dissident groups, is dysfunctional from the point of view of conflict management.

The Research Evaluator

The fifth and final intervenor role is that of *the research evaluator*. This is the role that staff persons of the Lemberg Center assumed in Miami Beach. As with the other roles, the researcher must be acceptable to all sides or he will not be permitted access to the data he needs. If he is not careful, he may even be chased off the premises, as most participants easily adopt the attitude, "Who needs research?" Protestors resent the money that goes to research rather than to their needs, while authorities fear that they will be portrayed in a damaging light. Therefore, the researcher does his best to behave in an impartial, objective, and helpful way while minimizing any direct intervention in the event he is observing, lest he influence the very process he is studying. At the same time, the researcher makes clear his own sympathies, attitudes, and values and is prepared to articulate them if requested. His direct effect on the conflict should thus be minimal, subject only to the possibility that people may behave differently if they know they are being observed. However, the ultimate impact of his work on future conflicts through the writing and dissemination of his research reports may be more substantial.

SUMMARY

In conclusion, it is our impression that these intervenor roles represent a valid contribution to the reduction of collective violence. Only future events and the study of more cases will determine whether this impression will stand up over time and be supported by firmer empirical evidence than is now available. In the meantime, however, the effectiveness of such intervention is dependent on two concepts which have been introduced into this chapter without the extended discussion they deserve: conflict management and conventionalization. Conflict management (121) is proposed as an alternative to the expression "conflict resolution" on the grounds that conflict over important social issues is seldom completely resolved. It can, nevertheless, be made manageable, that is, violence within the community can be averted, through the process of conventionalization, or, as the anthropologists would suggest, ritualization (302). Given the innate aggressiveness of human beings, it would appear that conflict management through ritualization of hostile encounters accompanied by problem-solving procedures offers the best hope of keeping levels of intergroup violence within acceptable limits of tolerance.

10

COMMUNITY CRISIS INTERVENTION

the dangers of and opportunities for change

Vivian Barnett Brown

Crisis intervention not only provides a theoretical basis for direct treatment in the office, but also provides a basis for training paraprofessionals and gives them an opportunity to get out of the office and into the community to the place of crisis, as well as to get involved in prevention programs to ward off crises in high-risk populations and/or situations. Crisis theory is an ecologic theory, allowing us to view man as a system suspended in multiple systems.

THE CRISIS INTERVENOR

In order to meet the mental health needs of the community, the crisis intervenor must move through a continuum from individual treatment through community intervention. The levels of treatment as seen by the author are as follows: individual treatment, conjoint, family, extended family (particularly important with Spanish-speaking patients), multiple family, group, and community. While, in individual crisis intervention, the focus is often on intrapsychic variables and the immediate life space of the individual, with family crises there is a shift from the individual equilibrium to the dynamic state of the family as a social system. Kalis (200) states that both "the disruption of equilibrium and the intervention at any point in any system have implications and reverberations at all levels and for all interlocking systems." Thus, the community crisis intervenor must be aware of all the systems involved.

General systems theory construction allows the crisis intervenor to link therapeutic and community processes. One of the constructs from general systems theory that is used in discussing community process is power. Defining power as the ability to produce some change or bring about some event, Ullman (415) states "Community process is intimately linked to the deployment, accumulation, and operation of power along both formal and informal lines." Two years earlier, Ryan (365) had suggested that, since a mentally healthy person must be able to perceive himself as at least minimally powerful or capable of influencing his environment to his own benefit, a "program of mental health enhancement and emotional disorder prevention, therefore, can meaningfully address itself to the issue of personal and community power."

As we move into a broader social frame of reference, the crisis intervenor can use his skills to assess and evaluate the interfaces at each level of the continuum from individual to community; to study the distribution of power and its uses, misuses and abuses; and to help the community move toward a model of equal sharing of power in decision making and problem solving. The crisis on an individual level is defined by Caplan and his followers (63) as a state provoked when "a person faces an obstacle to important life goals that is, for a time, insurmountable through the utilization of customary methods of problem-solving." This upset in the individual's equilibrium or steady state leads to an experience of power-lessness and inadequacy. The precipitant of the state of crisis is labeled a hazard, an external situation in which there is a sudden alteration in the field of social forces.

On the community level the disruption of the dynamic equilibrium has a radiating effect. While on an individual level, hazards may involve a loss or threatened loss of a significant relationship or a transition in social status and role relationship, hazards for the community involve losses or shifts in power structure which involve a number of interlocking systems, such as a major change in the racial composition of a school or redevelopment and relocation of a community. Individual hazards, such as death and premature births, have been studied extensively; community hazards have not received widespread attention. Only in the case of disasters (see Part III) have there been large-scale studies.

COMMUNITY HAZARDS

It is important for crisis theory and practice to expand the study of hazardous events and adaptive behavior to the community level. Most community hazards can be conceptualized as loss or shift of power. Specific events include loss of community leader, loss of community program, homicide of community member, changing racial balance of

so
ni
ti
al
de
in
cc

R

Tl
Fı
m
hε
di
si
in
aı
st
cł
cł
tł

cı
sε
oı

A
P
fı
oı
tı
q
c
v
a
sı
s
tl
a
lı
c

school, urban redevelopment and relocation, or allocation of funds to one group over another.

Loss of Community Leader

Community equilibrium is upset when a leader leaves voluntarily for promotion or because of dissatisfaction, involuntarily due to loss of job, illness or death. For example, an administrator of a large community social service agency might leave the agency and community to take a position in another state. The radiating effect of this event may involve the demoralization and subsequent resignations of staff who are mainly community residents, demoralization of clients and subsequent loss of client utilization of agency and subsequent cutback of program, and an increase in unemployment of community residents due to resignations and cutbacks. If there are few alternative employment opportunities for the community residents, there would follow further demoralization of the population.

The disruptive effects of this type of hazard must be taken into consideration. Intervention should involve consultation with management and various levels of staff, as well as providing technical assistance in organizing the community. Management needs to understand the significance to staff and community of the loss of a leader and to take steps to include both groups in future planning for the agency. Staff members need to ventilate their grief at losing an important role model and to feel a part of reorganizing the program. Staff and community need help in understanding their feelings of loss in order to work through the separation and accept a new leader. Community involvement by means of advisory boards and committees helps to decrease the feeling that "they are doing it to us" and increase feelings of control and competency.

Loss of Community Program

The previous situation, if carried to increasing crisis proportions, could lead to loss of the agency. However, losses of community agencies, particularly grassroots organizations, may occur due to loss of funding or to a need to move the program to another community. This event involves not only loss of services but also demoralization of staff and community residents. Loss of funding is an extremely hazardous event, particularly for low-income communities in which there is always a fear of money (power) being cut off by the wealthy power structure.

When this happens, community groups are more likely to use disruptive and confrontative strategies to demonstrate some degree of remaining power. Intervention should include management consultation, community organization, technical assistance, provision of possible funding resources, and development of replacement services. It is possible in this situation to prevent extensive loss by organizing community resources to fill the gap in

services and provide employment for those residents who would find themselves without jobs. These steps should be taken well in advance of the loss of the agency.

Homicide of Community Member

When a community member is deeply imbedded in the community, i.e., he and his family have been residents for a number of generations, his loss could have considerable impact, particularly when his death was due to homicide by a representative of a powerful system. For example, a member of the community is shot to death by a police officer; the event appears to be victim-precipitated, i.e., the community member has provoked the officer to kill him. In this situation, the radiating effect involves intense anger on the part of the family and the other community residents toward the powerful system (police). If the police officer and the victim are of different ethnic backgrounds, the rage will be directed toward the police on racial grounds and could escalate to a riot.

Intervention in this event should include fact-finding, interpretation, consultation to both police and community, confrontation, and training. In this highly sensitive event, community members need to feel that the crisis intervenor will be able to secure information and clarify the tragedy as well as to understand their feelings of rage. The intervenor must also be able to help the community and police understand the concept of "victim-precipitated homicide"; training in alternative methods of handling such events on the part of the police system needs to be provided. In addition, ongoing consultation to police and community groups needs to be established in order to prevent future tragedies.

Changing Racial Balance in Schools

Another hazard occurring with more frequency is the change, sometimes planned and often not planned, in the racial composition of the student body in schools within the community. This change is often accompanied by hostilities, fears, and misunderstandings. Walton and his colleagues (425) described a crisis team intervention in this type of school-community unrest. In one of the communities the population consisted mainly of semiskilled and unskilled workers. The white members of the community were upset by the recent influx of black residents. Some of the school personnel contributed to the increasingly tense atmosphere by calling white parents and telling them to come to school because their children were being menaced. Many parents used the children to act out their own conflicts and frustrations, which led to a breakdown in discipline and control within the school. There were incidents of teachers being attacked.

The crisis team organized and developed an ongoing committee of administrators, teachers, community representatives, and resource persons to provide a channel of communication between school and community and to plan an educational program for the school. The crisis intervention in this case helped establish some community control of the school and allowed parents and residents to share in the decision-making that determined the educational program and its implementation. Thus, this intervention allowed for more equal sharing of power between school and community residents.

Redevelopment and Relocation

The loss of power is strongly evidenced in cases of imposed relocation. Fried (138) has documented the increased crisis potential of an imposed move as distinguished from one that is actively sought. The community hazard in this case usually involves a sense of impotence, grief, and disenfranchisement. Two groups which are particularly vulnerable to this situation are low-income/minority residents and senior citizens. Low-income/minority communities are frequently scheduled for redevelopment, and residents experience their loss of power as a punishment by the power structure rather than an opportunity for constructive environmental change. In the case of elderly people, their decreasing ability to cope with change and their increasing dependence on familiar surroundings make them extremely vulnerable to the crises associated with relocation.

Intervention should include educating the community residents and community planners about research and findings on mental health consequences of redevelopment and relocation, consultation to individuals and organizations, confrontation, and community organizing.

Allocation of Funds

Particularly in low-income and minority communities, the allocation of funds is an extremely sensitive, hazardous event. If funds are awarded to one minority group, a shift in power occurs within the community and often triggers acting-out destructive behaviors in the other groups. The consequences of this situation may lead to funds being taken back because "that community can't get itself together," sabotage of the funded program, and violent confrontations between community groups.

Intervention methods should include community organizing, technical assistance, management consultation, provision of additional funding sources, training, and mediation. The funded group needs help in understanding the potential hazard and in developing an equal-sharing model for the program; the groups not funded need to ventilate their feelings of anger, fear, and powerlessness and to begin developing activities and leadership roles for themselves. In addition, political strategies aimed at changing funding policies need to be instituted.

HIGH-RISK INTERFACES

There are a number of interfaces within communities which provide the potential for crises. Two brief examples were described previously: police-community and school-community.

The police-community interface involves a variety of possible hazardous events including the sudden appearance of an external police squad to carry out a widespread arrest, a planned attack on a specific criminal activity such as "wiping out the drug pusher," the changing of police personnel in the community, or the handling of street gangs which hang out in the community.

School-community systems often come in conflict over situations such as the desegregation issue, community control over educational policies, the rate of dropouts and suspensions of minority students, the placement of minority students in mentally retarded or educationally handicapped classes, and university control of community health care delivery systems.

Other conflicts may arise between landlords and tenants, merchants and consumers, clients and agencies, management and labor, and different racial groups. The Community Crisis Intervention Center has described some of the uses of mediation and advocacy in these conflict situations (77). Mediation is used when there are identifiable parties with recognized leadership who agree to participate in face-to-face bargaining, and when both sides are willing to reach a settlement which is less than a total victory for either party. The advocate, unlike the mediator, openly favors one party's demands over the other's, and may even espouse its goals as his own.

Low-Income and Minority Communities

Most low-income and minority communities feel powerless, and therefore tend to use coping methods symptomatic of apathy or cynicism such as withdrawal, violence, drugs, and other antisocial behaviors. At times of crisis, the community attempts to use its usual coping methods, but these behaviors usually either fail or bring drastic consequences. The riots in our low-income and minority communities demonstrate the use of violence as the means of expression and redress in order to change the system by those who suffer the frustrations of powerlessness. The crisis intervenor in the community must therefore play a number of roles—therapist, intervenor, consultant, educator, and social action agent. He or she must have not only a commitment to the community but also to risk-taking for the community. He or she must be extremely sensitive to potentially hazardous events and able to move quickly in helping community groups reduce the crisis potential. Strategies include: 1) community organization; 2) educating the community about research and findings on mental health consequences of such institutions as welfare; 3) consultation to individuals and organizations representing the power structure of the community with the aim of changing their policies; 4) political strategies such as using confrontation methods and establishing political alliances; 5) encouraging activity and leadership roles for the "powerless"; 6) mediation; 7) advocacy; 8) provision of financial resources, and 9) lobbying and/or drafting legislation (77, 359).

CRISIS CENTERS

The Los Angeles Psychiatric Service/Benjamin Rush Centers, after establishing the first walk-in, non-hospital-based crisis center in the West, established its second crisis center in Venice, California, designed to provide crisis intervention services to a low-income and minority community. Venice is a small multiracial, multigeneration community. The area has dilapidated housing, low-income families, unemployment, school dropouts, and inadequate health care. It is the "drug center by the sea." Estimates run as high as 40% for the use of hard drugs in the barrio and ghetto areas. Venice is also surrounded by newly established high-income developments such as Marina del Rey, which occupies land once farmed by Chicano families living in Venice. There is a constant threat of the high-rise development forcing low-income families out of the community. In summary, Venice, California, is a crisis community, with characteristics representative of low-income and minority communities across the country.

Intervention Following Homicide

Two specific situations illustrate the types of crisis interventions which can be carried out by community mental health professionals. At the time of the first event, the assassination of Martin Luther King, only a small number of mental health professionals were actively involved in community work. Immediately after the assassination, word spread rapidly through the community that there were threats of rioting, and many Venice residents were afraid of this possible aftermath. An emergency meeting was set up at the Venice State Service Center (at that time considered neutral territory) by a number of the mental health workers and indigenous workers. Both community residents and police were invited. The major goal of the meeting was to stop the impending crisis situation, and two subgoals were used to accomplish this: 1) to help the police understand the dangers and accept the community's help in handling the hazard, and 2) to help the community feel that they had the ability to change the situation (that they had *power*) and that there were coping methods other than rioting.

By means of some rather heated discussions several positive results were obtained. The community representatives, after expressing fears of violence, asked police cooperation in handling the potential danger (residents feared that sending additional police into the community would trigger the violence). Then the community representatives formulated a constructive plan of action as follows:

1. They asked the police not to increase the number of officers in Venice and particularly not to have officers "walking the beat."
2. They asked police permission to "man" their own streets.
3. They established a community cadre of troubleshooters to drive through the streets in marked vehicles throughout the weekend.
4. They requested the use of the marked vehicles of the Venice State Service Center.
5. They asked professionals to be on hand by phone should they be needed.

The plan was successful in preventing a crisis situation.

Intervention in a Drug Crisis

A less dramatic situation occurred during a drug crisis in the community. Four community workers involved in a street program were unable to continue functioning because of their own increased heroin addiction. They spoke to their supervisor who contacted a community psychiatrist on the staff of the Los Angeles Psychiatric Service and UCLA Neuropsychiatric Institute to ask for help with this crisis.

The first step was to put the four workers in the hospital for detoxification. However, as has been stated in crisis literature many times, crisis is both a danger and an opportunity. This situation gave some of the professionals in the community an opportunity to begin a massive attack on the drug problem which had caused 60 deaths from overdoses that year.

The second step was for the supervisor to contact a number of mental health professionals who were active both in Venice and in the drug abuse area to plan a joint effort of all professionals, agencies, grassroots organizations, and community residents to establish the Venice Drug Coalition. This organization not only became an umbrella organization through which the separate subgroups could maximize coordination and create new drug programs, but also established a spirit of cooperation and working relations among ethnic groups as well as between professional and nonprofessional groups.

Since the formation of the Drug Coalition, the UCLA/Venice partnership was formalized by the awarding of the California Council of Criminal Justice (CCCJ) Grant. Three community components were established: *Tuum Est*, a drug-free therapeutic community directed by an ex-addict program director; *Via Avanta*, a methadone maintenance therapeutic community sponsored by Los Angeles Psychiatric Service/Benjamin Rush Centers and directed by both a mental health professional and an ex-addict program director; and *Vita*, a prevention, referral, and counseling center sponsored by the Neighborhood Youth Association and directed by a mental health professional and two ex-addict program directors. In addition, the following task forces were formed: Crisis House, Community Out-Reach, Education and Social Action. A new grant proposal was submitted to NIMH by the UCLA Venice Drug Coalition. This crisis intervention demonstrates the potential not only for professionals to help community groups resolve crises, but also the potential for evolving new forms of caretaking in the community.

11

IMMEDIACY AND AUTHORITY IN CRISIS MANAGEMENT

the role of the police

Morton Bard

During the past three decades crisis intervention has occupied an increasingly important place in mental health practice. Lindemann (260), an early contributor to crisis theory, posited that early skillful and authoritative intervention in disruptively stressful life experiences offered the prospect of forestalling the long-term maladaptive consequences of such events. The logic of this formulation was subsequently supported by others (22, 63, 86), mostly in settings that lent themselves to his approach, i.e., in hospitals and clinics.

But applications based on emerging crisis theory posed a great challenge to mental health institutional practices. Long accustomed to a model requiring people to come for help, professionals have found, and continue to find, difficulty in developing methods to enable therapeutic intervention at times of crisis when people are "more susceptible to being influenced by others than at times of relative psychological equilibrium" (19). A variety of efforts has been tried to achieve institutional flexibility with some outreach capability, including 24-hour walk-in clinics, telephone hot-lines, mobile crisis units, and local store-front clinics. These methods, intended to reduce the time interval between the crisis event and the "laying on of hands," have brought to light some inherent flaws. For one thing, crisis services were usually ancillary to the more central concerns of the mental health enterprise. Traditional diagnostic, treatment, and training demands on mental health institutions precluded anything more than peripheral attention to crisis intervention as a preventive strategy. (This phenomenon is no different essentially from the fate of preventive medicine in the priority system of the parent profession.) Indeed, with the law of congruity operating, it became increasingly difficult to distinguish crisis as anything but a state synonymous with an acute psychiatric emergency. And so, consistent with the shaping effects of organizations on theory as well as on practice, crisis intervention was something new added to the armamentarium; but only apparently, since its ultimate effect was tantamount to putting old wine into new bottles.

Early efforts to deliver crisis services brought out other difficulties as well. Often, the use of the service was determined by the sophistication of the person in crisis; that is, by his recognition of need for the service or even by his knowledge of the service's existence. In many cases, proximity of location played a role. Most important, perhaps, the methods typically employed rarely reached those unsophisticates who, by virtue of education and social class, were unlikely to recognize their need and to reach out for help at the time of crisis. Further, since crisis services usually are a part of mental health facilities they are not positioned to be naturalistically proximal to psychologically stressful events. Finally, even when in crisis, many people are apprehensive about the implications of any psychiatric contact.

Since there is reason to believe that applications of crisis theory have been constrained by a variety of institutional and social forces, have we reason to be optimistic about the future of crisis intervention? Yes, but only if some fundamental reconsideration is given to the most basic elements of theory, and only if real alternatives to existing methods of implementation are found. Immediacy and authority are factors that offer leverage prospects in the application of crisis theory.

IMMEDIACY

Those who have worked with the crisis concept have emphasized the importance of the *earliness* of the intervention in taking advantage of the accessibility which disruption of defense affords. However, the most crucial variable affecting immediacy of crisis intervention as a preventive strategy may be that of predictability. As McGee (283) has suggested, crises fall on a continuum of predictability; there are those that can be seen coming, so to speak. They range from the normal developmental crisis to such events as a new job, a school examination, or elective surgery. And then there are those crises precipitated by wholly unforseen events such as natural disasters, serious accidents, or crimes. It would seem logical that the crises which can be anticipated lend themselves to planning, and that therefore earliness of intervention can be assured. But the unanticipated or sudden crisis event presents an extraordinary challenge. Since it cannot be predicted, how is it possible to plan for immediacy of intervention?

AUTHORITY

Leaving that question for the moment, let us consider the importance of authority. The perceived power of the caregiver has always been the secret weapon of the helping system. Its significance is only partly demonstrated by the placebo effect and by iatrogenesis in the field of medicine. Indeed, it is quite difficult frequently to distinguish the technical effects from those occasioned by "operator" effects in clinical medicine. This phenomenon is crucially important in the management of people in crisis—particularly those under the impact of a sudden unanticipated crisis. The crisis has a chaotic effect; coping mechanisms are severely taxed and a sense of helplessness ensues. In a sense the individual is, to a lesser or greater extent, so reduced in adaptive effectiveness that his state may be regarded as regressed. Facilitative help or direction is sought either actively or passively, and those in the environment who are perceived as powerful are likely to be seen as the source of order and stability in an otherwise suddenly chaotic world.

For the surgical patient undergoing the crisis of a sudden change in body form or function, only the surgeon is seen as having almost magical powers to order, to restore, to facilitate adaptation (20). What he says and does and how he says and does it may be endowed with significance far beyond the real. But seeking the helpful power of authority is very real when a person is in a crisis-induced regressed emotional state.

THE ROLE OF THE POLICE

Recognizing the significance of authority provides a context for returning to our earlier question about planning for immediacy of intervention in crisis. Clearly, it is not possible to plan for the sudden, unpredictable, and arbitrary stressful event. But it is possible to enlist the participation of an existing service delivery system whose domain is crisis, whose mode is immediacy, and whose very essence is authority. These attributes are singularly congruent with the essentials of crisis theory. The irony is that they should be absolutely unique to an agency not usually identified as part of the helping system, the police (197). Police officers usually are the first summoned when a sudden crisis occurs (appeal for help); they have a highly organized mobile response capability (immediacy); and they have the legal and symbolic power to do something (authority). The crises with which they commonly deal include natural disasters, crimes, and serious accidents—events that can have shattering impact. These factors, taken together, persuasively attest to the unique potential of the police as a primary crisis intervention resource.

In effect, then, the half-million police officers in this country constitute an untapped natural resource for the management of the unpredictable crisis event that so defies the mental health institutional capability. Indeed, it can be argued that this group is already delivering crisis services but grudgingly and ineptly in most instances. However, this grossly inadequate service delivery is only the natural consequence of the paradoxical role the police occupy in society. As the instruments of power, the police are encouraged to view themselves simplistically as "dirty workers" whose essential mission is to clean up or control the human flotsam and jetsam of industrial society. At the same time, they have increasingly fallen heir to a vast array of helping functions (estimated as 80% to 90% of total manhours). In effect, police role definition is achieved manifestly along the control dimension and latently along the helping dimension. Police institutional reinforcing myths, incentives, and rewards almost entirely disown helping functions and emphasize controlling ones. This disparity between the manifest and the latent is reflected in the expression "We are not social workers; our only job is crime control." This persistent self-characterization as unskilled watchmen or armed guards is an ultimately self-destructive adherence to the manifest aspects of police work. The latent aspects of police work are emphatically denied, when in truth they have become the largest portion of work and require a high degree of ego-satisfying skill and competence.

Clearly, there is need for a rational juxtapositioning of the manifest and the latent. In fact, it can be argued that acquiring the competence defined by the latent enhances the achievement defined by the manifest. That is, there is evidence that enabling the police to deliver complex helping services with skill and competence has a positive effect on their performance of the more traditionally valued law enforcement functions (450).

Crisis intervention, then, may serve as an ideal point of intersection of the interests of both institutions: mental health and law enforcement. Each can contribute elements that the other is unable to deliver; the former through providing skills training and back-up support, the latter through the attributes of immediacy and authority. But in acknowledging the communality of purpose, there is a danger of overlooking the pitfalls in the way of effective collaboration.

EFFECTIVE COLLABORATION

Barriers to collaboration exist on both sides. The word *collaboration* is carefully chosen in contradistinction to the word *cooperation*. In organizational terms, the former connotes an *active process between coaccountable equals;* the latter implies a passive process between unequals with accountability assumed by the *superior* system. Cooperative programs may be quite successful in the short-term but have little effect on the long-term functioning of either system. For each, the program is a temporary "marriage of convenience" with little investment in the ultimate outcome and with little expectation of long-term commitment. To date, almost all programs that bring together mental health and law enforcement have this quality about them. A collaborative program, however, may be generated by one or the other system but its design and ultimate responsibility for outcome is equally shared. With such arrangements it is difficult to frustrate a lasting effect.

While the underlying basis for mutual distrust and negative perceptions by both systems are quite complex, some of the difficulty must rest on discrepant class-linked values. Any collaborative relationship, as a first principle, should recognize that differences exist and should seek to reduce the tensions generated by them. Unless acknowledged, the clash between the essentially working-class values of the police system and the middle-class values of the mental health system can have a destructive effect.

There are dysfunctional elements in that system. The failure to appreciate the special knowledge of police officers is one such factor. Police officers have special knowledge that must be valued and identities that must be respected. Mental health professionals must recognize the policeman's knowledge and preserve his identity, while resisting the temptation to coerce the kind of "cooperation" that could occur in the process. Of course, this implies that in no way will there be an attempt to make the police officer over in the image of the mental health professional. Subtle forms of proselytizing can be among the silent factors that contribute to difficulties in collaborative programs.

Another element that may interfere with the mental health system's collaborative effectiveness is failure to fully appreciate the ramifying effects of the police function on the broad sense of security in society. The term *security* need not be limited to crime. Rather, security in an otherwise alienated and technologically depersonalizing environment is a sense that flows from being "connected" to others. A critical dimension of "connectedness" is the assurance that there are predictable sources of help and caring immediately available when needed. In that they are the only immediately available helping resource, the police stand virtually alone in engendering a sense of security in any community. A recent community survey indicated that in low-cost housing projects where the police were specially trained in conflict management techniques, the residents felt safer despite an actual increase in crime during the year studied (450). This suggests that feeling safer may have to do with the quality of the responsiveness and competence of those whose functions are so closely linked with a sense of security.

CASE REPORT

The dynamics of a representative crisis situation are shown here in order to illustrate the significance of *immediacy* and *authority* in affecting outcome.

> An 11-year-old girl was accosted in the elevator of a high-rise apartment building by a 16-year-old male, taken at knifepoint to the top floor and raped. In apparent shock and pain, the child returned to the street level, went to the playground to retrieve her paddle tennis racket, related the event in a dull unemotional manner to friends, and then went to her own apartment to tell her mother about it. The police were called and arrived promptly. They advised immediate hospital examination and treatment and interviewed the child to ascertain the basic facts. The police informed the parents that detectives would be visiting shortly to make a more thorough investigation. Their interest, clearly consistent with their self-concept, was to acquire those facts necessary to apprehend the rapist. The subsequent visit by the detectives later that afternoon was also devoted to determining investigative facts, albeit with concern and sympathy. However, the victim and her family (mother, father and 15-year-old brother) were left with the enormous task of adapting to this shattering occurrence.
>
> Three weeks after the event, the parents sought treatment for the child because of her acute insomnia and phobic reactions.

Discussion

Forcible rape is an event that can have catastrophic impact on the victim and her family (57). The traumatic consequences can reverberate for years. Rape is also a crime that appears to be on the increase but which may, because of changing attitudes, be reported more often. In any case, it is a situation that presents much potential for the application of crisis theory.

If, in the case described, the officers who responded had training equal to their task, might the subsequent need for treatment been averted?

The responding officers, and certainly the detectives, were in a position to be of incalculable assistance to the family in weathering the crisis. In so doing, they might also have enhanced their ability to acquire significant information necessary to the successful completion of their investigation.

Rape as Crisis

The effects of forcible rape need to be seen in relation to the basic tenets of crisis theory. Rape can be said to be the ultimate violation. Most crimes against the person as well as crimes against personal property are experienced as violations. Assault and robbery, burglary or armed robbery are usually experienced as a personal defilement. In each instance the individual has lost autonomy or control and has suffered either physical or financial loss. The victim of a burglary returns home to find the "nest"—

the physical extension of himself—befouled. The victim of an armed robbery finds himself helpless to prevent a valued part of himself from being taken. The victim of an assault and robbery suffers the dual indignity of being unable to prevent loss of a part of himself and, additionally, to prevent his external space (external body) from being violated. The rape victim, however, suffers the violation of external space but, more importantly, also the violation of inner space. Through body orifices, the rapist intrudes to the very locus of the private, ultimately controllable "self". To overlook the ego's autonomous functions compromised by rape and to concentrate entirely on the sexual is to fail to understand why rape can constitute a trauma of such profound proportions. Rape can, and often does, severely disrupt basic ego functions.

For the family, regardless of the age of the victim, empathetic anxiety approaching panic often ensues. There is a sense of not knowing what to do, no previous experience to call upon, no special knowledge to muster. Most commonly, there is irrational guilt as well, born of the conviction that somehow they have failed to protect the victim. The guilt and anxiety, sometimes further complicated by highly symbolic factors originating in normal family life, can lead to deep depressions and other psychopathologic sequelae.

Police in the Helping Role

Police officers have more experience with rape victims and their families than do any mental health professionals. Their primary responsibility is the apprehension of the rapist since experience has shown that this crime is committed repeatedly by the same individuals. In order to successfully complete an investigation, police officers are dependent on the victim and the family for the specific information necessary to establish the rapist's habitual patterns. Police officers should know that knowledge of crisis intervention theory and skills could make this information more readily available. Why? Simply because repression operates quickly to expunge the traumatic event, and the immediately available authority could serve to prevent that process from taking place. Repression not only threatens long-term functioning of the victim but also hides facts that may be crucial to the conduct of the investigation. Since most investigating police officers are male, their very maleness can serve as a barrier to open communication unless care is taken to further the relationship with the victim. The investigating officers, in accord with these considerations, would be best advised to approach the assignment as crisis counselors. I believe in that role the ultimate mission of apprehending the rapist would be best realized.

In the case described, the detectives could have established a relationship with the child and encouraged her to express her feelings with freedom. The parents could have been advised of their natural tendency to suppress the child's efforts to tell and retell the details of the experience. In their greater wisdom born of experience and knowledge, the officers could have alerted the parents to *a*) the advisability of allowing the child to speak repeatedly, and *b)* restrain their (the parent's) equally natural tendency to dissuade the child by saying, "Don't talk about it; if you don't, you will soon forget it." The officers might even, within the context of a counseling relationship, describe to the parents how guilt functions and explain its role in suppressing the victim's ventilation. They might enlist the parents' help in noting new facts as they emerged in retelling the incident.

In this same situation, the police officers are presented as being in a strategic position to deliver a preventive mental health service. Immediacy in time and place as well as their authority demonstrate the advantages that could be gained for police officers if crisis counseling skills were to be learned and applied. This concept shows how crisis intervention as a skill might facilitate achievement of their primary mission.

POLICE RESPONSE TO OTHER CRISES

The range of unpredictable crisis events that come within the purview of the police is almost infinite. Members of that service delivery system are positioned in time and place for an array of crisis intervention roles. In addition to crime victimization as described in the illustration, the following typify the kinds of events that lend themselves to skillful crisis intervention as a preventive strategy by police officers:

Natural Disaster. In this category are included such events as fire, flood, explosion, earthquake, or tornado. The suddeness and impact of the event lead to a *disaster syndrome* whose dimensions must be understood, and in relation to which specific techniques of intervention could be helpfully employed by the police, (see Part III).

Notification. This is a frequent police activity that is little recognized by laymen. Notification involves informing the family or next of kin of the death or injury of a family member. In this circumstance the police officer himself is the crisis stimulus.

Accident. Personal accidents range from vehicular homicides to injury from falling objects. These events differ somewhat from the disaster syndrome in that the chaos is personal and exists in an otherwise ordered and intact environment.

Psychotic Reactions. Police are called to attend to interpersonal problems often unrelated to specific identifiable stresses. Psychotic reactions have profound effects on others, particularly on family members.

Suicides and Attempted Suicides. As with psychotic reactions, suicide attempts have a profound impact on others. Skillful intervention by police affords significant preventive opportunities.

THE POTENTIAL FOR SERVICE

Even a cursory examination of the events briefly described shows that there are unique potentials for crisis intervention in the police service delivery system. However, present role conceptions in that field militate against effectiveness in that connection. It would seem that the preventive mental health objectives of crisis intervention theory are, given institutional constraints, unlikely to be realized by existing mental health operations. Ultimately, it may be more rational, and indeed more economical, to utilize the police system for the achievement of the desirable objectives of crisis intervention. I am suggesting that the kind of immediacy in time and place that can be achieved by the police cannot be achieved by any other group of caregivers in the helping system. It really remains for the mental health professions to acknowledge that fact and to develop means by which the police may work naturalistically in an outreach capacity. The acceptance of such a strategy will require new ways of conceptualizing functions in mental health and new ways of sharing knowledge with those who are in a position to be more effective than the primary professionals themselves. If there is a commitment to prevention (see Part IV), then there is a challenge inherent in developing means for making use of the immediacy and authority of the police system.

12

CRISIS INTERVENTION AND THE JUVENILE COURT

one project's approach

Roger Baron
Floyd Feeney

The teenage years are often a time of crisis for both children and parents. Many youths attempt to deal with this crisis period by running away from home or by standing their ground within the family in such a way that they are beyond parental control. For many thousands of youths around the country this kind of crisis ultimately results in conflict with the law, arrest, and referral to juvenile court. The laws of nearly every state stipulate that children who run away from home or who are beyond the control of their parents are subject to the jurisdiction of the juvenile court.

Youths in these two categories are among the most common in the juvenile court. In California, for example, in 1969, these kinds of cases constituted about 30% of all cases reaching intake and over 40% of all juvenile hall admissions (460). They are known as *601 Cases* because they are brought within the jurisdiction of the juvenile court by Section 601 of the Welfare and Institutions Code of the state of California.

The conflict and lack of communication in these cases is often quite intense. The child involved will be adamant that he doesn't want to go home, while one or both parents will declare that they wouldn't allow him to return even if he wished. In many cases the family is one in which a divorce has occurred and so there exists some continuing disagreement or lack of communication which exacerbates the conflict and allows the youth involved to play one set of parents against the other.

In juvenile court this kind of case has traditionally been handled in much the same way as criminal cases involving juveniles. If the offense is a relatively minor one, and is the first or sometimes the second time the situation has arisen, the child is sent home to his parents and does not go to court. If there is intense disagreement or the situation has occurred before, however, the case is generally viewed more seriously and is referred to court. In California the time between referral and the actual hearing will generally be 2 to 3 weeks, and the youth will often be detained in juvenile hall during this period. After the court hearing the youth will most often be placed on probation and a probation officer is assigned to him. Generally the probation officer will see the youth and sometimes the parents for counseling about once a month.

This probationary system has only a limited capacity in helping with crisis situations. It is geared to making factual determinations which are fair to all parties but not to respond rapidly to intense human needs. The help that the system does provide comes, not at once, but usually 4 to 6 weeks after the hearing.

The Sacramento 601 Diversion Project was an experiment designed to test whether juveniles in this kind of situation could be handled more successfully through short-term family crisis therapy than through the traditional procedures of the juvenile court.

The objective of the project was to demonstrate the validity of the diversion concept of delinquency prevention by showing that:

1. Runaway, beyond control, and other types of 601 cases can be diverted from the present system of juvenile justice and court adjudication.
2. Detention can be avoided in most 601-type situations through counseling and alternative placements that are both temporary and voluntary.
3. Young people who are diverted have fewer subsequent brushes with the law and a better general adjustment to life than those not diverted.
4. This diversion can be accomplished within existing resources available for handling this kind of case.

The intent of the project was to keep the child out of the juvenile hall, keep family difficulties out of the court, and still offer counseling and help to the family.

Entering into the development of the project was the growing body of evidence that crisis counseling and short-term casework are two of the most effective ways of dealing with problems arising out of family situations.

For example, one recent study (348) showed that:

Planned, short-term treatment yields results at least as good as, and possibly better than, open-ended treatment of longer duration.

Improvement associated with short-term treatment lasts just as long as that produced by long-term services.

Short-term treatment can be used successfully under most conditions if its objectives are appropriately limited.

The report indicated that "extended casework was three times as costly as short-term, with no better results to show for it." In explaining these results the report stated that the brevity of the service period may have "mobilized the caseworker's energies and caused a more active, efficient, and focused approach" while at the same time calling forth "an extra effort from the client, producing a better outcome."

A highly successful program in Denver, Colorado, demonstrated the potential of brief family crisis therapy as an effective alternative to psychiatric hospitalization (236).

Projects such as the family crisis counseling program developed for police officers by the Psychology Department of the City College of New York have demonstrated the usefulness of these techniques at the first level of contact in the criminal justice system (21, 22).

PROJECT OPERATION

The 601 Diversion Project began handling cases on October 26, 1970. For purposes of the experiment the project handled cases 4 days a week, with the regular intake unit handling the other 3 days. Days were rotated monthly.

On project days when a 601 referral came in, whether from police, school, parents, or someone else, the project staff arranged a family session to discuss the problem. Every effort was made to ensure that this session was held as soon as possible; most were held within the first hour or two after referral. Through the use of family counseling techniques, the project counselor tried to develop the idea that the problem was one that should be addressed by the family as a whole. Locking up the youth as a method of solving the problem was discouraged, and a return home with a commitment by all to try to work through the problem was encouraged. If the underlying emotions were too strong to permit the youth's return home immediately, an attempt was made to locate an alternative place for the youth to stay temporarily. This is a voluntary procedure which requires consent from both the parents and the youth.

Families were encouraged to return for a second discussion with the counselor and, depending on the nature of the problem, for a third, fourth, or fifth session. Normally, the maximum number of sessions is five. Sessions rarely last less than 1 hour and often go as long as 2–2½ hours. First sessions take place when the problem arises. Since the project staff remains on duty until 2:00 AM, a few begin after midnight. Crisis line service after project closing hours is handled through referral by the probation department switchboard to the home of the probation counselor. This service has not been used a great deal, but its availability is important in conveying the counselor's concern to the family.

Staff

The unit staff consists of a supervisor and six deputy probation officers. The unit supervisor has approximately 10 years' experience and his assistant 7 years' experience. The deputies range from no experience in a probation setting to approximately 4 years of experience. There are 3 male and 3 female deputies. The 3 deputies without probation experience all have some previous experience in a social service agency.

Family Crisis Counseling

The techniques of crisis intervention and family crisis counseling are crucial to the concept of the project. The central ideas of family crisis counseling are two: 1) that problems should be dealt with immediately as they occur, and 2) that problems are best dealt with in the context of the whole family rather than in the context of the individual person whose conduct is the immediate cause of the problem. The reasons for dealing with the problem in the context of the whole family are well set forth by Langsley and Kaplan (236):

> The family is not only the source of stress in many cases but has been a major resource in the resolution of stress. The family is the one social unit through which the troubles of all members usually filter. Each person brings home his problems, and he hopes for the understanding and support which will help him master life's struggles. The family is a potential source of strength for individuals who are bruised in the course of everyday living. When the family is functioning well as a stress mediating system, it is a source of enormous comfort and strength to its members. When the family fails in this function, it often adds to the burdens which individual family members are already experiencing.

The principles of intervention are perhaps most clearly stated by Satir (366):

> Those of us who have studied family interaction as it affects behavior in children cannot help wondering why the therapy professions have so long overlooked the family as the critical intervening variable between the society and the individual.
>
> The family system is the main learning context for individual behavior, thoughts, feelings.

How parents teach a child is just as important as *what* they teach.

Also, since two parents are teaching the child, we must study family interaction if we are going to understand what the family learning context is like.

The attempt of the project is to get the family to approach the situation not as a question of blame, involving a child to be dealt with by some external agency, but rather as a situation involving the whole family and to which the whole family must respond. The attempt is to unblock the family communication processes and help the family achieve both the desire and the capability of dealing with the problem.

Training

Family crisis counseling is normally a technique employed by therapists who have undergone long periods of training. In addition, the application of this technique at the intake point of probation presents some novel and difficult questions. The training portion of the project was therefore one of its most crucial aspects. Project training involved two phases: initial training and ongoing training.

Initial training was conducted during a one-week period. This included demonstrations of actual family counseling by a number of different therapists, intensive discussion, and role-playing of the kinds of problems which counselors were expected to face.

The ongoing portion of the training is built around weekly consultations with the project psychiatrists and the project psychologist.

In these sessions the project counselors have opportunities to observe, discuss, and work with the project consultants. Other training sessions have focused on the role that other agencies play in helping to deal with family situations.

RESULTS

Diversion from Court

One important objective of the project was to test the idea that 601 cases could be diverted from the juvenile court. Data for the first 12 months of the project indicated rather clearly that this objective was being accomplished. During this period the project handled 977 referrals to the probation department involving opportunities for diversion, but filed only 36 petitions. Court processing was consequently necessary in only 3.7% of these referrals as opposed to 19.8% of the referrals handled in the control group. Because a youth may be referred to the probation department two, three, or more times before a petition is filed, or without a petition being filed, the number of referrals handled exceeds the number of individuals handled.

Referrals and Petitions. Table 12.1 shows the number of petitions filed while there was an opportunity for diversion from court rather than petitions filed as a result of recidivism. Consequently, if a petition was filed on a youth handled by either the project or the control group, and that person subsequently returned on another 601 matter and an additional petition was filed, the additional petition is not included in the totals in this table. Similarly, if a youth handled on a 601 matter by either the project or control group subsequently returned for some kind of 602 behavior and a 602 petition was filed, that petition also is not included.

If these kinds of petitions were included, as well as those resulting from referrals involving opportunities for diversion, project data indicate that during a 12-month follow-up period, 41% of all control group youths and 20% of all project group youths ultimately went to court. The total number of petitions filed for 526 youths handled in the control group was 401, while the total for 674 project group youths in the same period was 219.

TABLE 12.1 Referrals and Petitions in the First 12 Project Months

	No. of referrals	No. of petitions	(%)
Control	612	121	19.8
Project	977	36	3.7

Informal Probation. In California a second entry point from intake into the juvenile justice system is through informal probation. Informal probation is provided for by Welfare and Institutions Code, Section 654, and is a voluntary procedure entered into when the probation intake officer believes that the matter can be handled without going to court but that some probation supervision is required. During the first 12 months of the project, a total of 117 control cases were placed under informal supervision as a result of initial handling, as opposed to 22 project cases under informal supervision (Table 12.2).

TABLE 12.2 Use of Informal Probation During the First 12 Project Months

	No. of referrals	No. of informal probations	(%)
Control	612	117	19.1
Project	977	22	2.3

Taking both petitions and informal supervision together, the number of cases going forward in the system from intake was 38.9% of control cases but only 6.0% of project cases (Table 12.3).

**TABLE 12.3   Petitions Filed and Informal Proba-
tion Given During First 12 Project
Months**

	No. of cases	Petitions & informal probation	(%)
Control	612	238	38.9
Project	977	58	6.0

Detention

A second major project concern was that of detention. A great deal of evidence suggests that detention is itself a harmful factor which serves on the one hand as a school for crime and on the other as an embittering factor which makes the family reconciliations necessary for the resolution of 601 cases more difficult. Table 12.4 shows the extent of overnight detention in juvenile hall resulting from initial arrests. Under California law all cases involving detention longer than 48 hours (not including weekends and other

**TABLE 12.4   Detention in Juvenile Hall as a Result of Initial
Referral or of Initial or Subsequent Arrest During
12-Month Follow-up***

Detention	Control (%)	Project (%)
Result of initial referral		
No overnight detention	44.5	86.1
1 night	20.7	9.9
2–4 nights	19.2	3.0
5–39 nights	14.4	0.7
40–100 nights	1.2	0.3
Result of initial or subsequent arrest		
No overnight detention	30.6	57.6
1 night	14.8	12.8
2–4 nights	17.2	12.4
5–39 nights	24.5	10.4
40–100 nights	11.2	6.1
Over 100 nights	1.7	0.7

* Youths referred October 25, 1970 to October 25, 1971

nonjudicial days) must be brought before the juvenile court judge or referee for approval. The figures in Table 12.4 indicate that more than 55% of all control group youths spent at least one night in juvenile hall as compared with 14% for youths handled by the project. These initial differences in the length of detention are also reflected in the average number of nights each youth spent in detention. Thus, while project group youths had an average of 0.5 nights in detention as a result of initial handling, control group youths spent an average of 4.6 nights in detention. In addition to spending more nights in detention as a result of initial referral, control group youths also spent more nights in detention during a 12-month follow-up period.

These figures (Table 12.4) indicate that, considering both initial arrest and subsequent case history, more than 69% of the youths handled by control spent at least one night in juvenile hall as compared with 42.3% of the project youths. Stated another way, project youths averaged 6.7 nights per case in juvenile hall as compared with 14.5 nights per case for control youths.

Repeat Offenses

For many persons the true test of the project was whether it discouraged repetition of behavior that might bring the youth back into juvenile court. To determine the rate of recidivism, all project and control cases which were handled during the first year were followed for a period of 12 months from the date of initial handling.

In both groups, the rate of recidivism was high. Project youths, however, did noticeably better than did control youths. Thus, while at the end of the 1-year period 54.2% of the control group youths had been booked again for either a 601 offense or for a violation of the penal code (Section 602 of the California Welfare and Institutions Code), the comparable figure for the project group was 46.3%. This represents a reduction of almost 8% in the rate of repeat offenses. If we consider only those offenses committed after initial handling which involved criminal conduct (Section 602), we again note improvement for the project group (Table 12.5).

TABLE 12.5   Percent of Juveniles Booked Again Within 12 Months

	601 or 602 violation	602 violation only
Control (N = 526)	54.2	29.8
Project (N = 674)	46.3	22.4

There were also substantially fewer project youths who were "rebooked," 24.6% compared with 31.6% of controls for two or more rebookings of any kind; 7.4% as compared with 12.2% for two or more 602 rebookings, and 3.6% of project youths versus 5.9% of controls for two or more rebookings for felony or drug offenses.

The figures just cited reflect the differences in the number of youths booked again for an offense within the 12-month period. Since each youth who was rebooked for a new offense might be rebooked more than one time, the previous figures do not, however, show the total number of new offenses committed. Therefore, this aspect of the problem was examined separately; results are indicated in Table 12.6. For these data, a youth who was rebooked once was counted as one, and a youth rebooked four times was counted as four. In Table 12.5 each youth was counted as one.

Table 12.6 shows that for each 100 youths initially handled, the control group had 71 subsequent bookings for 601 offenses, 49 subsequent bookings for 602 offenses, and a total of 120 subsequent bookings. This compared with totals of 64, 35, and 99, respectively, for project youths. These figures indicate that for each 100 project youths there were 17.5% fewer new bookings than for the same number of control youths, 9.9% fewer 601 new bookings and 28.6% fewer 602 bookings.

TABLE 12.6 Number of Bookings for a New Offense Within 12 Months per 100 Youths Initially Handled

	Repeat for 601	Repeat for 602	Total
Control youths (N= 526)	71	49	120
Project youths (N = 674)	64	35	99

These and other figures suggest that most of the project impact comes early in the process. Given the project emphasis on providing immediate help to youth and families this was to be expected. In addition, the fact that the difference in the number of repeat bookings persists over a period as long as a year suggests strongly that the improvement is of relatively long duration and not simply temporary.

CONCLUSION

The concept of crisis intervention is relatively new to the juvenile court. For a substantial number of cases, however, it offers an important alternative to adjudication and traditional court processing. Many youths who become involved in the juvenile justice system need immediate rather than deferred help. Family counseling at the time of intake is one promising method of accomplishing that end.

13

BEHAVIORAL APPROACHES TO FAMILY CRISIS INTERVENTION

Peter N. Alevizos
Robert Paul Liberman

The community mental health movement has tried a variety of treatment strategies for families in crisis. Problems in the development, applicability, and delivery of traditional therapeutic services to crisis situations prompted a search for viable alternative interventions (148). A relatively untapped resource in the further development of crisis treatment is behavior therapy with its emphasis on the environmental determinants of behavior (201). Such an emphasis is compatible with the theory and practice of community-based crisis intervention, since from its inception the community mental health movement has focused on the broad social and environmental forces which both influence and prevent deviant behavior. This chapter, therefore, formulates a behavioral approach to crisis theory and reviews the relevance and use of behavior modification for treating families in crisis.

A BEHAVIORAL FORMULATION OF CRISIS THEORY

Much of the early work in crisis theory by Lindemann (260), Caplan (63), and others (236) served to identify *a*) stressful precipitating events, *b*) individual factors, and *c*) family interactions as the determinants of the course of a crisis and the maladaptive behaviors which lead to crisis referral (310). It is assumed that these three factors interact to produce crisis behavior. For example, particularly stressful life events disrupt an individual's or a family's (189) emotional homeostasis. The precipitating event intensifies certain maladaptive behaviors in the individual or family and overtaxes their capacity to solve the problem and cope with the stress. Such stressful events can include psychiatric emergencies (such as new manifestations or acute exacerbations of psychiatric disorders), accidental situational demands (including medical illness or accidents, death, divorce, job loss or change), and transitional developmental demands (including entering school or college, getting married, or becoming a parent) (373).

Traditionally, the term crisis has referred to an individual's emotional reaction to a stressful event and not to the event itself (88). However, a behavioral analysis focuses on the response excesses, deficits, and strengths which are elicited by the crisis situation, on the particular antecedent stimuli which trigger the behaviors, and on the consequences which serve as "secondary gain" in reinforcing them. These behaviors and their controlling environmental antecedents and consequences form the basis of the treatment procedures to be described in later sections of this article.

Retirement, loss, separations, and similar events would be defined behaviorally as the withdrawal of relatively powerful reinforcers which lead to the disintegration of important behavioral patterns. Progressive or sudden declines in the rate of positive reinforcement have been shown to precede depressive behaviors (249, 253) or to trigger other emotional reactions during a process of extinction (12, 364). Individuals often lack the social skills to deal with the withdrawal of reinforcement (254), and families which are initially sympathetic and reinforcing often become frustrated and increasingly punitive. Transitional demands such as marriage and promotions require an increased level of individual or family skill and performance if previous reward levels (schedules of reinforcement) are to be maintained. Psychiatric emergencies can also result from a sudden change in reinforcement and the withdrawal of family supports. Separations, runaways, or behaviors with legal consequences generate strong emotional reactions, and family members often resort to negative or coercive means in an attempt to solve the problem.

RECIPROCITY, COERCION, AND FAMILY CRISIS BEHAVIOR

Jackson (190) suggested that the therapist must analyze certain redundancies or typical repetitive patterns of interaction which characterize the family group. Metaphorically, these are described as family rules because the family behaves as if it were restricted to certain interaction patterns. Behaviorally, such covert rules can be observed as a system of *quid pro quo* interactions in which family members exchange a limited range and amount of reinforcement.

Patterson and Reid (322) have directly studied the reinforcement exchange systems in families with child behavior problems. Their research identified two major patterns, reciprocity and coercion, which characterize problem family interactions. Reciprocity refers to the equitable rates of reinforcement exchanged between individuals. Reciprocal interaction in families is characterized by their responsiveness to one another's requests and by their mutual reinforcement of one another's behavior. Coercion refers to interactions in which aversive stimuli control the behavior of one person and positive reinforcers maintain the behavior of the other. Coercion can be observed when requests from one family member take the form of strong demands. Noncompliance is punished by that member's escalating his aversive behaviors (for example, threats, tantrums, criticism, or withdrawal) and compliance is (positively) reinforced by submission to the demand and (negatively) reinforced by terminating the aversive behavioral stimuli following the expected response.

In the clinic, couples and families often present themselves as having lost the rewards or satisfactions necessary for participating in family life. As Patterson (319) and others (107) have observed, there are few positive rewards dispensed, and reciprocal positive reinforcement as a strategy for influencing a spouse or family member is replaced with coercion and negative reinforcement. Thus, when confronted with the additional stresses of financial problems, loss, separations, or runaways, these families are crisis prone; they lack the mutual supports necessary for working together to cope with the crisis. Often such families resort to their most common coercive control strategies, escalating them in an attempt to deal with the stressful event. In escalating aversive control, they usually alienate one another and prevent any attempts to solve their problems.

Behavior therapists have found that when the amount and balance of mutual positive reinforcement is made more equitable between couples or family members, the marital problems of couples or disruptive crises of their children can be significantly reduced (322, 399). Thus, for behavior therapists a crisis amplifies problem interactions which helps identify them to the family and the therapist; it serves as a problem-solving focus in treatment since reciprocity must be increased if the interactions which predispose them to a crisis and maintain their undesirable behaviors are to change. In identifying maladaptive behavior, a crisis offers a well-defined behavioral criterion which can be measured to determine the efficacy of treatment.

Crisis intervention has had particular significance as the basis for secondary prevention whereby relatively small investments of time can have a high payoff, defined either negatively through averting disastrous consequences or positively in building new strengths and adaptive resources (84). Behaviorally, new repertoires are more easily taught to individuals when their previous response patterns fail to elicit expected or desirable consequences. Crisis intervention, however, encompasses a broad variety of treatment procedures. Many of these approaches emphasize working with the family or social system surrounding individuals in crisis (174, 237, 290, 326, 340, 366). While crisis theory is composed of a rather coherent set of assumptions, the clinical techniques used are relatively unstructured and unsystematic. They include maintaining an explicit focus on the crisis, facilitating the expression and management of emotions, providing information, and confronting the mutual problems and roles of system members. Crisis treatment procedures also lack the specificity necessary to assess the adequacy of interventions made at points of crisis. Behavioral approaches, however, offer a greater delineation of techniques which can be useful in training crisis therapists and evaluating the effectiveness of the crisis interventions.

BEHAVIOR MODIFICATION AND FAMILY CRISIS INTERVENTION

Behavior therapists have developed numerous techniques which may be used to focus directly on the environmental variables precipitating and controlling family crisis behavior. While behavioral approaches to family and couple therapy have been the subject of much recent attention (241, 251, 398), there have as yet been few actual demonstrations of the effectiveness of behavioral principles for crisis intervention (16, 107).

DIFFERENTIATING BEHAVIORAL METHODS

Behavioral methods of family crisis therapy are distinguishable from other approaches by their emphasis on specifying both problems and goals in concrete behavioral terms, on measuring change in behavior from the problematic to the desirable, and on using principles of learning and conditioning to facilitate behavior change. Specification of the problem leads to an elaboration of therapeutic goals which are a mutual, collaborative effort between the therapist and his patients. The development of a simple but reliable recording or measurement system for monitoring the targeted behavior provides an opportunity to evaluate therapeutic progress. The therapist and clients should frequently review the record of progress as a guide to making decisions about changing goals and interventions. Principles of learning such as positive and negative reinforcement, modeling, shaping, extinction, punishment, satiation, time out from reinforcement, stimulus control, and counterconditioning form the basis for formulating family treatment tactics and strategies.

A thorough understanding of behavioral principles of human interaction permits the crisis therapist to gather information with which to make tentative hypotheses about the environmental influences that maintain the problem behaviors and make it difficult for patients to function more adaptively. The most important feature of a behavioral crisis therapy, however, is its inextricable bond with empirical values. As in other sciences, the science of human behavior relies utterly on measurement. The implication for clinicians is that they should not use a technique for its own sake, but only for its effective impact on behavior.

In summary, a behavioral approach to family crisis treatment involves the following procedures:

1. Identify the precipitating crisis events and the behavioral excesses, deficits, and strengths which they have elicited.
2. Identify the critical patterns of family interaction which are hypothesized to maintain the maladaptive behavior(s).
3. Since crises often generate extremely negative emotional reactions which accelerate deviant interaction, train family members to express noncoercive negative affects (frustration, fears, regret, grief, hurt) in amounts which are appropriate to the eliciting crisis situation.
4. In place of coercive controls, develop cooperative problem-solving behaviors in the family through a directed program of reciprocal positive reinforcement.
5. Whenever feasible, measure the critical interactive behaviors, both positive and negative, to determine the effectiveness of behavioral interventions.
6. Finally, direct family members in applying (generalizing) their newly acquired coping skills to other areas of family conflict.

Specific behavioral treatment techniques can be applied to family crisis therapy, and case examples are given here to illustrate their use. Demonstration of the effectiveness of behavioral approaches to crisis intervention, however, must await further controlled investigation.

Feedback and Instructions

Providing feedback to families and instructing them in alternative interactions is hardly unique to behavior therapy. Dynamic family therapists, including Haley (159), Framo (132), and Zuk (455), describe the need for active therapeutic intervention which provides feedback to family members regarding the consequences of their present behaviors. In behavior therapy, feedback has been used to change a variety of behaviors.

However, it is rarely used in isolation. Thomas, Carter, and Gambrill (404) showed that feedback could be combined with instructions in controlling the problem verbal behavior of a married couple. Bernal (37) used closed-circuit television and videotaped playbacks to provide feedback and instructions to mothers who were learning to modify the "brat" behaviors of their children. She held seven instruction sessions during which the mothers' management of their children was shaped toward providing more appropriate contingencies of responsiveness. These and other controlled studies (422, 451) suggest that, while instructions or feedback are important cues controlling behavior, clients are more likely to follow instructions which are accompanied by and result in positive reinforcement. In behavioral crisis therapy, it has often been suggested that immediate feedback on a family's characteristic patterns of interaction may be a prerequisite to changing them (107). Feedback can be used to point out confused or discrepant communications and to show the family, as a unit, its difficulties in effective problem-solving behavior. Some families so avoid conflict that they discuss anything but their most difficult problems. Other families prevent problem-solving attempts when so much excess emotion is aroused that effective discussion is impossible. Still other families blame the family problem on a particular individual (usually the identified patient) instead of sharing the responsibility among all members.

The following case illustrates how instructions and feedback can be used to train reciprocity in family interaction.

CASE REPORT 1

Mrs. G., a 27-year-old mother of three young children, had been in psychotherapy for 4 years. She complained of frequent, severe depressions during which she felt suicidal, and occasionally hysterically out of control. Antidepressant medication and other tranquilizers were ineffective. Before deciding to hospitalize the patient, the current therapist referred her to the Day Treatment Center of the Oxnard Mental Health Center, where the authors are consultants.

A family session (which included the patient, her husband, and her parents) plus a detailed history-taking effort, led to a behavioral analysis of the problem. Mrs. G.'s husband, a taciturn, conscientious, hard-working man, spent little time talking with her except when she seemed depressed. At these times, he became exquisitely sensitive to her, responding with solicitude and concern even to her nonverbal signals of unhappiness and moodiness. To compound the reinforcement that Mrs. G. received for her depressions and expressed helplessness, her parents immediately would come to her side whenever she intimated a need for them. Mrs. G. spoke with her parents on the phone several times a day and saw them daily. Her parents would take off from their jobs to rush to her side when she called in crisis saying, "I can't go on by myself." The elicitors of her depression were mainly recurrent bouts of pyelonephritis and cystitis, which were painful and debilitating. But the primary element in the depression was the bountiful and constant social reinforcement Mrs. G. received from her husband and parents for the sick role.

A behavior modification approach was formulated and implemented by a nurse at the Day Treatment Center. Mrs. G., her husband, and her parents participated in framing the details of the program and agreed to carry it out. Mrs. G.'s parents were instructed to completely ignore her complaints (she agreed to this and urged them to follow through, after understanding the rationale), and were reassured that, by so doing, they would be assisting her growth toward a position of strength and confidence. They were also told to converse with their daughter at least once a day, and to focus on reality issues and on her successful coping efforts at home. Their conversations on the phone and personally were to terminate as soon as she began complaining about symptoms or helplessness. Mr. G. was instructed to do the same but in addition was provided with a more tangible means of reinforcing his wife's adaptive behavior. The behavioral analysis revealed that the chain of complaining and depressive behaviors lasting most of the evening began at the moment that Mr. G. returned home from work. A frown, downcast look, or tearful eyes cued Mr. G. that something was wrong and then began the spiral of his reinforcing her depression with concern (or impatience and annoyance), her showing even more depressive features, his reinforcement, etc.

We decided to reverse the chain at its beginning by having Mr. G. reinforce any nondepressive behavior shown at the time of his arrival with the giving of a poker chip to his wife. She would have to return the poker chip to him if she exhibited any depressive behavior that evening. She could exchange the poker chips earned thereby in the following manner: individual "therapy" chats with her nurse-therapist at the Day Treatment Center during which Mrs. G. was free to discuss anything, including her complaints, one chip for 15 minutes; complaining time with husband, one chip for 15 minutes; lunch out with mother, five chips; and evening out with husband for dinner and show, ten chips.

Mrs. G. accumulated chips quickly; rarely an evening passed without her earning and keeping a chip. She initially spent her chips for complaint sessions with her therapist and, less often, with her husband. These occurred three times the first week, twice the second week, and only once the third week. She then began spending her chips for "fun" outings. The spiral was reversed and she continued receiving social reinforcement from husband, parents, and people at the Day Treatment Center for her improved verbal and task-oriented behavior. During the fifth week of the program, she traveled 100 miles by herself to a university medical center for a diagnostic work-up of her renal disease, an accomplishment that was new to her and that netted much additional recognition of her functional capacity. Two months later, Mrs. G. was no longer coming to the mental health center. Her husband, however, who was the critical agent for change, continues to visit the nurse-therapist at increasing intervals for booster sessions to keep his reinforcement flowing contingent upon his wife's adaptive behavior.

Assertive Training and Behavioral Rehearsal

Assertive training is a generic term covering any structured therapy situation that facilitates the acquisition of emotionally expressive behaviors. The therapist prescribes and supervises the practice of more desirable responses to interpersonal conflict situations. Behavioral goals can include learning how to assert oneself: saying "no" to family members or others rather than be exploited, or expressing affection, tenderness, or sadness, as well as anger. Theoretically, any affective dimension of behavior can be taught (6, 445). Case reports (119, 444) and empirical investigations (281) both show the effective use of this relatively new behavioral technique.

In applying the technique, behavioral clinicians assume that once the appropriate overt expressions of emotion are practiced in family sessions, the inward or subjective feelings will eventually be experienced. The process of assertive training with families involves a series of steps:

1. Identify the problems in expressing feelings, and specify the "where, when, how, what, and with whom" of the problem.
2. Target the goals of training, which may consist of new behaviors that rectify deficits in family interaction or may modulate their excessive or overly intense emotional expressiveness.
3. Simulate certain crisis situations using family members to role play or rehearse the relevant scenes.
4. Model the appropriate behaviors for the family and shape (reinforce successive approximations to) appropriate expressive behaviors (the elements are added one by one: facial expression, vocal tone and loudness, posture, appropriate body gestures, eye contact, speech fluency, and content).
5. Provide positive reinforcement for improvements rather than confront failure.
6. Give the family members assignments to practice the behaviors outside the session with other individuals as well, using the family group approval to reinforce success.

Modeling and the Role of the Therapist

The particular behaviors taught in assertion training or behavioral rehearsal can initially be presented to a family via modeling procedures. In family crisis intervention, modeling or *imitative learning* refers to the use of the therapist or a family member as a model to demonstrate alternative, desirable, and adaptive behaviors which are appropriate to family interaction. The extent to which behavior can be learned is governed by a family member's ability to spot the modeling cues, his opportunity to process and rehearse the cues, and his possession of the necessary components in his behavioral experience which can be combined to reproduce the more complex modeled behavior (17, 18). Behavior therapists use imitative learning with instructions and feedback to enable an individual to short circuit the tedious and lengthy process of trial-and-error (or reward) learning while incorporating complex chains of behavior into his repertoire.

When modeling techniques are used in assertive training and behavior rehearsal, the family crisis therapist must actively interrupt nonproductive response patterns (for example, overreactivity, withdrawal, continual faultfinding, or other limited or rigid patterns of verbal interaction). The therapist models and instructs family members in explicit verbal and nonverbal alternatives to the behaviors which characterized their crisis referral. With practice, adaptive behaviors soon elicit desirable responses and family members become motivated to progress further.

The behavioral therapist is concerned with creating and maintaining a positive alliance between himself and the family unit. The active working alliance is the lever which stimulates change in successful interventions. Behaviorally, the positive relationship between therapist and client(s) permits the therapist to serve as a model and social reinforcer for shaping adaptive behavior. However they are specified, the behavioral attributes of a therapist that lead clients to value his feedback and regard him warmly also determine his effectiveness as a model and reinforcer. Case Report 2 illustrates the use of modeling techniques with instructions and feedback.

CASE REPORT 2

Mr. E. came to an outpatient crisis service complaining of suicidal feelings and extreme frustrations resulting from his inability to deal with his wife and 3-year-old child. During the course of a brief history-taking, Mr. E., a 30-year-old machinist, related that he had received previous therapy which terminated successfully over a year ago. In the past year his wife had frequently and resentfully refused him sex, complained of his lack of affection, and cried profusely at their slightest disagreement. When called, she refused to accompany him for therapy. Their child manifested severe tantrums with a mean frequency of four per day. Mr. E. felt that his interactions with his wife and his depression should be the initial focus of treatment. He was assigned to keep records of his interactions with his spouse, recording the antecedent behaviors and consequences of their patterns of interaction, and to record the time he spent with her. The assignment revealed the following typical patterns: affectionate greeting and approach to wife, wife disgustedly shrugs shoulders and accuses husband of solely sexual impulses, husband becomes confused and angered, wife cries and later complains that he isn't affectionate. The frequency of such interactions averaged between 4 and 5 per week. A behavioral analysis of Mr. E.'s problem indicated that his confusion and anger served as a reinforcing consequence to the typical interaction pattern. The therapist then role played the situations demonstrating an assertive and yet paradoxical response which would not reinforce the wife's refusal, yet communicate affection. Essentially the class of responses which were modeled involved:

1. Accepting the wife's refusal openly and briefly, "That's O.K. Fran, you must be tired."
2. Providing a paradoxical response, "You know, dear, I really like the way you stand up for yourself," smiling, and leaving the room.
3. Working with the strategy that both spouses needed help and that their verbal patterns of interaction often prevented other positive behaviors.

Mr. E. soon developed his own successful repertoire of responses. His wife, he announced, "was dumbfounded but really began to turn on." These responses gave the client the opportunity to observe and influence situations in which he had previously felt hopeless. A parallel program of increasing their time spent together and providing genuine positive support for the wife's appropriate behaviors evidenced significant gains. After 8 weekly sessions, their frequency of intercourse had increased to approximately 4 times per week and Mr. E. spent over 100% more time with his wife. At this point the spouse became interested in therapy and in ways she could deal with her son's tantrums. A simple behavioral program was initiated. The parents were given a standard parent training manual in which they recorded the interactions and the frequency of the tantrums. Within 2 weeks they had markedly reduced the tantrums from two or three per day to one during the second week. During a 3-month follow-up Mr. E. reported no depression and a substantial satisfaction with his family relationships. Mrs. E. reported that she had identified some infantlike behaviors in herself that she, with her husband's help, had successfully changed.

Direct Family Intervention and Parent Training

When dealing with deviant child behavior, the family crisis therapist may sometimes function most effectively in the role of educator and consultant to other more useful change agents, the parents. A pioneer in the scientific behavioral analysis of deviant child behavior has been Patterson (319). He and his colleagues (320) researched a family treatment approach that takes place in the home. Moving the treatment focus from the clinic to the home represents an important departure, since behavior change in both the parents and their children will be more likely to survive if the initial change occurs in a natural setting.

In Patterson's approach, baseline observations of family interactions are made for at least two weeks, with the focus on the ways in which parents maintain deviant behavior in their children by inadvertently reinforcing it. The parents are required to work through a programmed manual containing illustrations of principles of reinforcement, extinction, and methods of specifying and recording behavior. The parents are helped to specify which problem behavior in their child they wish to modify and what goals they wish to accomplish. In some cases the child is given the same opportunity to alter parental behavior. The parents are then asked to record the frequency of these behaviors during a particular hour of the day or sampled throughout the day. They must also record the consequences that the desired and undesired behaviors engender in themselves. In the final phase, the parents are taught through demonstration and supervised practice to change their reinforcement contingencies from maladaptive to adaptive behaviors.

Another method taught is termed "time out" from positive reinforcement; this consists of putting the child in isolation for a brief period for severe misbehavior (e.g., tantrums or aggression). Besides serving as a mild punishment, it removes the child from a situation where he might inadvertently be reinforced in his deviant behavior. In this stepwise fashion, family problems are modified one at a time. When indicated, similar reinforcement practices are also introduced in the school and peer group settings.

The direct training of parents as (behavior) therapists for their children has resulted in over 34 published reports (35). An increasingly popular and more efficient approach to treating families of deviant children is within a parent class (160) or multiparent training group (423). These groups can be offered by local mental health centers as an initial treatment service for the parents in crisis families. Such groups often follow Patterson's training format utilizing programmed behavior modification manuals designed specifically for parents (32, 321). While the child's behavior is usually the criterion of interest, further evaluation of leader and parent trainee behaviors is crucial to determining the effectiveness of multiparent training groups.

Contingency Contracting

In accelerating coercive control strategies, crises can also intensify feelings of distrust to a point where effective communication appears impossible. In such instances, behavioral contracts have been used to provide immediate positive consequences for constructive problem-solving or other desired behaviors. A contingency contract is a negotiated written agreement which details the conditions under which two or more individuals will exchange positively reinforcing and desired behaviors in order to promote change in one another. Changing one's behavior is made with the anticipation of a positive consequence, a desired change in the behavior of others. In establishing a contract the therapist organizes a monitoring or record-keeping system to enable the family and the therapist to assess the reciprocal fulfillment of its terms.

The development and use of family contracts has been described by Patterson (319). Written contracts have been used to treat child behavior problems (403), and adolescent delinquency (398), and to increase reciprocity between married couples (399). Contracts often make use of points or tokens that are earned when the behaviors specified are performed and that are later exchangeable for previously determined reinforcers. Contract negotiation is a family learning experience. Family members can be taught reciprocity and compromise in detailing the elements of the agreement. The process of negotiation and the use of contracts can provide the therapist with the means to maintain a problem focus and teach problem-solving skills. In so doing, coercive verbal interactions can be curtailed, reciprocity reinforced, and feelings of trust increased. The following case outlines the application of contingency contracting to family discord.

CASE REPORT 3

The crisis that brought the family to the mental health center was the pregnancy and recent abortion of the 15-year-old unmarried daughter, Jill. Although the parents had helped their daughter in obtaining the abortion, they were, nonetheless, upset and angry about her pregnancy. They showed their anger in several ways. They refused to allow Jill to go out in the evening, were verbally abusive to her, and pointed out how she had let them down despite the many things that they had done for her. Jill responded with stony silence and withdrawal from family interaction.

After a discussion of family problems, the contingency contracting procedure was introduced as a means of alleviating the problems by spelling out in detail the expectations of each party as to responsibilities and privileges. It was also explained that the role of the therapist was that of mediator, helping to ensure the rights of both Jill and her parents to a balanced, fair contract which would be reciprocally implemented and honored.

At the first session Jill agreed to complete routine chores around the home in exchange for the privileges of date nights, visiting her friends, and going to the beach. In a later session, Jill requested that she be given money for refreshments and for bus fare to a local shopping center. Although the amount of money that Jill requested was small, it was significant since the father was out of work at the time. Jill's request for an addition to the contract permitted a chance for the family to negotiate responsibilities and privileges of the contract without the active intervention of the therapist. The family successfully did this, arriving at a sum of 50 cents for Jill in return for an added chore of cleaning the family bathrooms.

The last addition to the contract was for Jill to approach her parents and voluntarily describe her out-of-home activities, in return the mother would not interrogate her regarding her whereabouts. After trying this exchange for a week, the family reported no success. At this point, an electronic prompting device ("bug-in-the-ear") was used by the therapist to direct the family members' discussions with one another about Jill's activities. After this session, the family reported more success in their conversations.

When the contract was initiated, Jill completed all the chores that were her responsibility. The parents complied by allowing her to engage in her earned privileges. The last exchange in the contract was not as well met, but the parents reported that Jill was approaching them more often and talking for longer periods of time.

An important byproduct of the contingency contracting procedure was the family's ability to focus attention on goals and accomplishments. By formalizing their mutual expectations into behaviors and giving recognition for achievements, the family became more positive in their interactions. The economy of the contingency contracting procedure is also noteworthy. The family was seen weekly for five sessions, then four biweekly sessions, and the final session at a 1-month interval.

Although this case represents a good example of how contingency contracting can be used successfully in crisis family therapy, it would be a mistake to attribute the success solely to the technique of contingency contracting. Other factors must also be considered. A family's attendance and follow-through on assignments is partially a function of the positive therapeutic alliance developed with the family. One means of achieving this is to judge which family member has the weakest motivation for therapy and offer reassurance and support to this person. The therapist should conceive of his task as that of shaping or successively approximating desired goals through the use of his therapeutic alliance with the family. As is frequently the case, all the conditions of a contract may not be met the first time the contract is tried. However, a generally successful strategy is to draw attention to accomplishments, however small, and use failure as a possible index that initial goals were set too high.

Groups for Married Couples

Most approaches to the treatment of married couples have involved conventional, open-ended, spontaneous and nondirective styles reminiscent of psychodynamic group therapy, or in the encounter, humanistic tradition. Behavior therapists have been developing experimental approaches which rely heavily on an educational format (252). Crisis couples groups can be developed for a set number of sessions (usually 6–10) with a two-phase design. During the first phase, couples use modeling and behavior rehearsal to learn interpersonal communication skills—listening, empathy, expressing feelings directly, admitting feelings, expressing anger without being accusative, and expressing and receiving affection. Both therapists and patients serve as models for each other, and conscious use is made of behavioral specification, reinforcing gradually improving performance, ignoring or suppressing—by ground rules—nonproductive complaining, and the dragging out of old skeletons from closets (226, 251).

Some couples obtain sufficient benefit from this corrective emotional learning experience to resolve the crisis and terminate therapy. The remaining couples, usually with more chronic and severe strains in their marriage, move into a second phase that makes use of contingency contracts. As a first step in the contracting procedure, a husband and wife are helped by answering the question, "How would you like your spouse to be different from the way he/she is now?" The following lists were constructed as the first step in building a contract for one married couple.

Wife Wants From Husband
1. To get up early on weekend mornings
2. To spend time together at least four evenings each week
3. To get home in time for supper during weekday evenings
4. To refrain from hostility or withdrawal when wife is not in the mood for sexual relations

Husband Wants From Wife
1. To keep husband company during breakfast
2. To do a better job of keeping the living room clean
3. To dress in a more appealing way
4. To initiate affection such as kisses, handholding, hugs

The terms of the contract were mediated by mutual contingencies of reinforcement. For each time one of the partners fulfilled a commitment in the contract, he or she received a receipt. The receipt, a conventional form purchased in a dime store, was initialed by the receiver of the desired response. Subsequently, the receipt could be exchanged for a response desired from the other partner. Each week, at the married couples' group, the receipts exchanged were tallied and reported to the members and the therapist. In the therapy group, married couples are taught reciprocal exchange and bargaining skills. Bargaining and negotiating are used as a means of crisis conflict resolution, taking the place of accusation and withdrawal.

One critical aspect of such groups is the assessment of the kinds of crisis problems which can be effectively treated in groups (see Chapters 15 and 16). Because of the behavioral techniques used, sexual dysfunction and sexual deviancy are treated in individual or conjoint sessions. However, further research is necessary to assess the efficiency of behavioral counseling methods for the treatment of marital discord through a conjoint or group format.

CONCLUSION

The behavioral approach to family crisis therapy offers a greater specificity in clarifying the relationship between precipitating events, the individual's strengths and deficits, and family interaction. Stressful events often elicit crisis reactions in deficit or crisis-prone individuals and the family system which incorporates them. The system is characterized by coercive strategies of interpersonal control and a paucity of reciprocal positive support. Although widespread in popularity, the basic assumptions of crisis theory and the concept of family systems lack the specificity necessary for defining particular therapeutic techniques. Behavioral approaches furnish a functional utility by specifying the crisis in ways which have direct implications for treatment. It should be emphasized, however, that the behavioral approach does not simplistically reduce the family system or family interaction to individualistic or dyadic mechanisms of reinforcement. The richness and complexity of family interaction has been described as an interdependent system where the behaviors of an individual or dyad is often determined by the behaviors of other members within the family complex. A systems view of the family also influences behavior therapists to go beyond the here-and-now of the therapy to collaborate with and involve schools, rehabilitation services, and the home as the natural systems where behavior change must be sustained.

The advantages of behavioral approaches to family crisis intervention outlined in this chapter remain to be proven by systematic research. However, such specificity of technique lends itself to better therapist training and to a more rigorous evaluation of crisis intervention. Crisis research should investigate family crisis interaction as essentially behavioral sequences which can be specified and measured with a fair degree of accuracy. It is hoped that behavioral techniques and the active role of the behavior therapist may stimulate traditional crisis therapists to specify more clearly their interventions, their goals, and their empirical results.

14

BRIEF THERAPY IN A CHILD GUIDANCE SETTING

development, delivery system and theoretical rationale

Gerald Weinberger

The Children's Psychiatric Center (CPC) has been using a brief therapy model since 1965, and about 6000 cases were seen between 1965 and 1975. The current interest in and openness about brief therapy in a child guidance setting is relatively new (25, 360, 378). It is hoped that a careful description of the evolution and operation of the CPC brief therapy delivery system for children and adolescents and delineation of the underlying theory and rationale that was painstakingly developed, will arouse interest in and facilitate the development of similar services elsewhere (110, 428, 429).

Before 1965, the Children's Psychiatric Center had used the traditional, analytic theoretical model and team delivery system, as did virtually all other child guidance clinics at that time. The analytic model involved routine use of long-term therapy and such concepts as reconstruction of the past, resolution of transference, and postulation of hypothetical underlying and unconscious conflicts that were inferred from their overt expression in behavior and affect. These were called *symptoms*, and it was felt that before meaningful change could occur one had to develop insight into the source and nature of the unconscious conflicts. Essentially we all functioned under an *illness* model.

The delivery system included a lengthy and elaborate diagnostic work-up which took up to 3 months to complete. Treatment, when offered, was delivered by a team among whom the family was divided. Most clinics with delivery systems that operate on this model had long waiting lists.

By mid-1964 a number of the staff, all of whom had been trained in the traditional approach, began to question the delivery system. They questioned the fact that they were applying a treatment and a conceptual model universally for all clients when they were not even sure they accepted the model any longer. In the summer of 1964, as an experiment, the first 12 people on the waiting list were called, and a brief time-limited therapy of 4 weeks was arranged. To our surprise it turned out that some of the clients seemed to derive noticeable benefit from the brief treatment. At the very least nobody became worse and they had all received some form of help. The staff then began to restructure the entire delivery system. The changes in service preceded conceptual development; that is, the ideas did not come first with implementation following. Rather, the staff wanted to do things differently, and as they began to do so they also began to discuss and try to understand. The staff began to meet with a consultant every week for 2 hours to go over cases, talk about issues and problems, and begin developing a theoretical rationale for what they were doing.

The delivery system that was developed in the first 2 years (1965-1967) has remained virtually intact. What was developed in the beginning still seems to work. To give some idea of numbers, about 1500 new cases a year are currently handled on an outpatient basis. About 150 new patients a month apply during the school year with a smaller number during the summer. This is a reasonably high turnover, especially since it includes emergency cases and juvenile court-referred cases. When the brief therapy system started, the clinic was accepting 30 new patients a month; within 3 months the application rate doubled. This was not expected, and when referral sources were contacted and asked what had happened, they replied that they finally felt the clinic was providing meaningful service to the families they had referred.

THE BRIEF THERAPY DELIVERY SYSTEM

The basic notion underlying a brief therapy delivery system is that one tries simple therapeutic interventions before trying complex ones. One does not start with a service that may be suitable to only 5% of one's cases; one starts with services suitable for 50%-75% of cases, and provisions are then made, at increasingly refined stages along the way, for people who need more.

Elimination of Evaluation

The first step, therefore, was to eliminate all formal diagnostic evaluations. The only place in the spectrum of clinic services from which any kind of discrete assessment is provided is in the Center's day school for autistic children. Occasionally, emergency evaluations are done as part of CPC's contract with juvenile court. Our intent was to end the artificial dichotomy between assessment and therapy. Therapy and assessment are seen as inextricably entwined for any therapist constantly assesses what he is doing. He uses what he knows about his clients to modify what he does, and much of his information occurs as a result of the interventions that he tries out.

The Six-Week Therapy Plan

It was planned that all clients would immediately enter into a brief therapy period of 6 weeks. The 6-week period was chosen in 1965 because, based on the rate of application and number of staff, everyone could be seen within a week or two of applying. (In brief therapy programs *six* seems to be the magic number.) The other reason 6 weeks was selected is that 5-6 interviews is the national average. It was also decided that the model number of sessions per week would be 2, thus providing a 6 × 2 model. One session per week would be spent with the parents, and one session with the child (the Center was still operating on old notions). Thus, there would be 12 sessions in a 6-week period, about twice the national average of interviews but in a condensed period of time, providing intense and concentrated treatment.

About 20% of all brief treatment occurs in 6-week groups which meet for 2-hour sessions and contain 4 or 5 sets of parents. The children are seen concurrently either in a parallel group (which may join the parent group for a session or two) or individually by the same therapists who meet with the parent group. Due to the complexity of multiple family group treatment, two cotherapists are generally used. The groups' focus is on behavior management, and they are more workable if the children are about the same age and have similar presenting problems. This helps the parents to quickly form a common bond and increases their interest and investment in the other parents. The goals and objectives set in the brief groups are the same as if the parents were seen individually, and we found the dispositions at the conclusion comparable to those relating to an individual family unit.

Single Therapist Versus Team Concept

The next step was the decision to formally discard the team concept, as the staff felt it impaired rather than facilitated case management and communication. Therefore, it was decided to use a *private practice model* in the clinic; that is, one therapist saw the whole family and was responsible for managing the case. He had available as consultants anybody else in the clinic, and, in fact, the staff made free use of their colleagues. For example, one might ask for a psychological or speech evaluation, or to have a colleague sit in on a session and give an opinion. When consultants are asked for help, the emphasis is on rapid feedback to the therapist. When the therapist has only 6 weeks, he cannot wait 3 weeks for a report.

Family-Centered Therapy

Another change made was that the family became the unit of assignment rather than the child. That did not mean that all cases would be seen in family therapy but that the *conceptual* unit was the family. In fact the staff did a good deal of family treatment. A separate determination was made for each case as to how best to work with the family, and during the 6 weeks they were seen in a variety of modalities. Generally, with young children the emphasis was on work with the parents on management issues, under the assumption that the child would respond quickly to changes in parental handling. In cases concerning children approximately 8 to 13 years of age, the child and the parents were generally seen about equally in all modalities, with family meetings increasing as the child got older. In adolescence two modalities predominated. Either the adolescent was seen alone (or in a group) with relatively little effort concentrated on the parents, or the entire family was seen together as a unit. With all cases there was an emphasis on *flexibility*, and on devising the most appropriate strategic approaches for that particular family.

Treatment Beyond Six Weeks

A further step was to deal with a perfectly obvious fact—not all cases could be treated within 6 weeks. When brief treatment is begun the therapist makes an explicit contract with the family in which he offers to meet with them for up to 6 weeks, during which he would try to understand what was going on and help them with their problem. At the end of brief treatment they would all evaluate together what had been accomplished, what still remained to be done, and how they should proceed. The family was very much a part of these discussions and decisions.

At the conclusion of brief therapy there are a number of options. One option is to terminate. During each of the past 10 years, about 40%-50% of the cases were terminated within the initial 6-week period. Another option exercised in about 20% of the cases was referral for nonpsychotherapeutic services such as vocational rehabilitation, remedial education, or residential placement. About 30% to 40% of the patients continued into time-unlimited (long-term) therapy. With the 40% to 50% of cases that were terminated, extensive use was made of planned follow-up sessions. Follow-ups were especially useful with "shaky" families who had made some gains but were not sure (nor was the therapist) if these could be maintained. Some families may have thought that therapy was a magic amulet and without it everything would collapse again, but their anxiety dropped sharply as soon as they knew they could call for help at any time.

(This was reassuring because many people think that once they have left they can never get back.) Often the therapist, using what is almost a pediatric model, suggested that the family return in 4 or 6 weeks to evaluate their progress, thus gradually phasing out therapy and maintaining a monitoring check on whether gains were maintained. Clients were encouraged to stay in touch, for example, "When the report arrives for the next marking period, would you call and let me know how Junior did?", and some families did. There was one final option available, although rarely used, and that was to go immediately into another round of brief therapy for 6 more weeks.

When families did go on to long-term therapy the wait was anywhere from 1 day to about 3 months. When possible, the same therapist continued with the family, thus maintaining continuity of care. While a break in treatment was not desirable, at least the family already had 6 weeks of help directed toward the problem for which they came. Hopefully there had been some alleviation of conflict and anxiety, and perhaps most important, the knowledge that they had somebody to call while they waited. This was encouraged. Most of the long-term cases tended to be poor, disorganized, and severely disturbed. What had been done, quite deliberately, was to reverse traditional clinic procedures to filter out the very kinds of serious and chronic cases that CPC now keeps. The traditional long-term case, i.e., the middle-class, verbal, insight-oriented, psychologically sophisticated, and (in most cases) white client, is completed as soon as possible. In addition, the staff encourages them to be less psychologically searching and less prone to examine every bit of behavior for hidden meanings. Families with delimited problems who pick up principles quickly, who are generally healthier at the start, and who come prepared to work, tend to improve more in brief treatment and not to return after its completion.

Emergency Treatment

The brief therapy delivery system meets the needs and concerns of families with chronic, nonacute problems of all degrees of severity. However, the brief therapy model as described here is also applicable to crisis and emergency care in a child guidance setting.

Essentially, crisis treatment at CPC is viewed as forming one end of a spectrum of services, with 6-week brief therapy in the middle and long-term (or time-unlimited) therapy at the other end. A family may finish, or depart, treatment at any point on this continuum. When parents call to apply, they are told what the current wait for treatment is. If they feel they cannot wait that long, a telephone evaluation is made by a staff therapist to see if crisis treatment is warranted. Most families applying are in a state of disequilibrium, and some are dealing with more urgent problems than others. If an emergency is judged to exist, the family will be seen as quickly as within the hour and generally no later than the next day.

Families viewed as in crisis are dealing with such diverse behaviors as suicide threats or attempts, acute depression or psychotic behavior (but not chronic states of either—someone who has been delusional for 5 years can usually wait just a little longer), acute drug episodes, assaultive behavior (but not routine fights), running away from home (usually seen on return when the entire family is most upset and uncertain as to what to do), school phobia (not necessarily life-threatening but requiring rapid intervention to prevent stabilization of avoidance behaviors), traumatic events to a child such as parental separation, divorce or death, or sexual molestation.

Families seen for emergency treatment are seen for no more than two sessions, with the focus on delineating the nature of the crisis, its development within the family, how it is perceived by the various family members, and how they each have tried to resolve and handle the crisis. As in brief treatment, the therapist tries to rapidly assess the situation, focusing on the narrowly defined crisis of the moment, and utilizing the strengths and coping behaviors of all family members. He is very active and directive as he tries to develop a temporary solution acceptable to all participants that will reduce some of the intense affect usually associated with crisis-induced helplessness and rage. By the end of the first session a contract should be made, one that will help the family terminate their ineffective and often repetitive ways of dealing with the crisis and will also suggest new ways of relating to each other which are less conflict-arousing. When the family leaves, they should feel in better control of the situation and more optimistic about the future.

The second session, if held, serves to evaluate how things have gone, revises the arrangements made so as to consolidate the resolution of the crisis, and may, if appropriate, look at some of the more characteristic expectations and patterns of behavior that led to the development of the crisis. This is not always necessary, as the crisis itself may "explode" these old patterns and permit the rapid development of new behaviors. At this point the therapist has several dispositional options: termination (especially if the family seems unmotivated to pursue the problem further and/or are satisified with the resolution of the crisis); continuation into 6 weeks of brief treatment (if the crisis continues or to consolidate gains and more extensively alter the behavioral issues and expectations which led to the crisis); or referral elsewhere (if other services are now more appropriate, e.g., an abortion clinic for a pregnant girl). No matter which disposition is selected, the therapist can and often does suggest a follow-up session in a specified period of time so that the family's progress can be evaluated.

Evaluation of Effectiveness

The final step in the development of a brief therapy service was the extensive use of data collection and feedback to the staff as a means of constantly monitoring the rapid handling of many cases by many different staff members. The data collection starts with a set of three questionnaires given to all clients when they apply. (The withdrawal rate before and after the use of the questionnaires was unchanged despite the fact that almost half of our families are poor; obviously literacy has not been a factor.) They are asked to fill out two forms which ask for basic demographic, educational, and developmental information; one form is a 237-item problem checklist. After the first interview the therapist fills out a pathology rating scale. They are also asked to make an estimate, using the same scale, of the changes that they expect to occur over the 6 weeks. At the end of the 6 weeks, therapists are again asked to rate the family members. Depending on what other questions are being asked at a particular moment, the family may again fill out the problem checklist or a variety of other instruments, such as a "satisfaction with treatment" form.

Approximately every 3 months these data, plus a variety of demographic descriptive data, are reported to the staff who have found this regular, ongoing feedback crucial for evaluating the clinic's functioning and effectiveness. To give an example, a satellite clinic was recently opened in a rural area. In the next 3-month period the initial pathology ratings rose sharply (they are usually highly consistent from one period to another). In trying to account for this it was clear that the new clinic had provided the bulk of the higher ratings. Since the staff there were not new to the brief therapy system, it seemed likely that clients were now being seen who had not been coming previously in any substantial numbers. In fact, they turned out to be very poor rural people, many of whom were migrants, or in New Jersey parlance "piney woods people" (most were kin to people who live in the hollows of Appalachia). The data feedback then enabled the staff to focus on this new problem and to talk about ways to intervene with these clients so as to be helpful to them.

There are four evaluation statistics which relate to the receptivity to and effectiveness of the brief therapy program.

Drop-Out Rate.   The first is that from the onset of the brief therapy model the drop-out rate, once treatment begins, has been consistently under 10% for the past several years. That is a remarkable statistic because the withdrawal rate from traditional child guidance services is closer to 60%-80%, between diagnostic evaluation and initiation of treatment. That is, once people are told that they will only have to invest 6 weeks of their time, they tend to remain for the entire CPC program. We were concerned when we started the 6-week treatment program that clients, having bought the New Yorker cartoon image of psychotherapy which involves a couch and long-term therapy, would resist brief therapy. The opposite was true. The notion of setting explicit time limits on therapy made sense to clients. They expect therapists to know what they are doing and how long it should take. When a client asks about length of treatment and receives a vague or uncertain response, it does not inspire confidence in the therapist's knowledge or skill. Those clients who were apprehensive about whether 6 weeks would be sufficient were reassured by the promise to reevaluate at the close of brief treatment. Ironically, the main opposition to the brief therapy approach has come from private practitioners—especially psychiatrists—in the community, who felt that the Center was doing only superficial symptom removal.

Return Rate. The second set of statistics involves the return rate after the close of treatment. This rate has also stayed around 10%. Clients are not going elsewhere for service because there is only one other clinic in the county which refers former CPC cases back to the Center. In addition, because of extensive consultation involvement with many schools, it is possible to keep close contact with old cases. Not only is the return rate reasonably low, but therapists tend not to be upset if clients return. It is not considered a failure if people have to come back occasionally, and some cases are seen two or three times in a period of several years.

Satisfaction With Treatment. Because the county's population is not very mobile and follow-up studies (247) are possible, our retrieval rate (with some diligent persistence) has gone as high as about 68%. Before starting these studies, which dealt with satisfaction with treatment, we became curious about how much clients knew about the Center and about their therapist. During a 24-hour period when the Center was busiest, every client who had an appointment was given a questionnaire asking such questions as the name of the agency, name of the therapist, amount of fee, and where clients thought the money went. We found that many clients either did not know the name of their therapist or had distorted it; some did not know the name of the Center; and some were not even sure how much their fee was. In fact some already involved in treatment were not quite sure what they were doing there in the first place! As a result of this study an information fact sheet was developed which was routinely given to all clients when they applied.

A satisfaction-with-treatment questionnaire was also developed, and given at the close of brief treatment, then given again during a follow-up period of between 6 to 18 months. The questionnaire (given separately to each parent) included queries such as: Did the therapist see you on time? Did you think you were treated with respect? Did he help you? To what degree were you helped by therapy? (ranging from "things got worse" to "a great deal"); To what degree were you satisfied with the help you received?

The results indicated that about 90% felt they had benefited from treatment; a 6-month follow-up showed a drop to about 75% in rating themselves as "slightly" to "considerably" improved. Clients were also asked whether, if they returned for help, they would want to see the same therapist. An astounding 97% responded positively. These figures must be viewed skeptically, for despite assurances that their therapist would not see the results, many clients may have feared he would. Perhaps the most revealing statistic about satisfaction with brief therapy occurred in response to whether clients had referred anyone else to the Center for help; 45% indicated that they had. Clients were also asked if they had gone elsewhere for help (in the follow-up studies) and only 2% had done so; most said they would return to CPC if they needed further help. The application rate over the past few years has grown about 15% a year, a rate far exceeding the rate of population growth in the county.

The Problem Checklist. Finally, we used our lengthy Problem Checklist in evaluating the results of treatment. All clients filled this out at the time of application and then again, depending on the specific study, after the close of treatment. The decrease in the number of problems checked is highly significant, although this undoubtedly reflects both a change in behavior of the child and a shift in attitude of the parents (whereby they became less anxious and concerned about the child's behavior, which may not have changed at all). At one point we compared clients' subjective ratings of improvement with the number of items checked off as being of concern on the Problem Checklist. We came across some parents who insisted that therapy had been of no help to them but who checked significantly fewer problems. Obviously the change that had occurred was not a personally felt change. There were a high number of clients in this group who had been forced into treatment (by juvenile court or the schools) but who did not want to be there. The therapist felt that therapy had been helpful to them, but the clients accepted this grudgingly, and as soon as they could leave treatment, they did so.

THEORETICAL RATIONALE

First and foremost, brief therapy is a "health" model for the delivery of services to children, adolescents, and their parents. Pathology is viewed as the discrepancy between a child's behavior and the expectations of others (be they parents, teachers, or a judge), *and* the effect of this discrepancy upon self-attitudes, self-concept, and self-worth. This triangular model (Figure 14.1) permits intervention at any point along that system, or

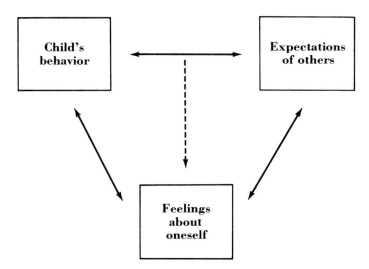

FIGURE 14.1 Triangular model showing opportunities for intervention.

between any two points in the system, or the interaction among all three points. Thus one can talk about expectations, about behavior, about the internalization of attitudes, or any combination of these.

Brief therapy at CPC rejects the notion that people who seek help are "sick." It raises questions about why people seek help in the first place and tries to clarify what brought them to the point of applying. Families often come because of the pressures of other systems with which they or their children are involved. Such pressures, which often involve labeling children as disturbed, may have more to do with problems, perceptions, and expectations of the referring source (especially true of schools) than with any real problem that the child or family is experiencing. Brief therapy programs assume that clients have capabilities within themselves and within their families to bring to bear on solving their problems and changing the ways they relate to each other.

Inherent in a health model is the awareness that normality is a very broad and highly relative concept. Normality is tied not only to specific behaviors but to the congruence of behavior to cultural expectations, to social systems and values, to family rules, expectations and goals, and finally to individual standards and expectations. There is no behavior or affect that is normal or abnormal in an absolute sense. Normality not only encompasses an extremely broad range of behaviors, but these in turn are significantly related to anxiety and subjective distress.

If normality is relative, and anxiety is in part related to the expectations of others and oneself, then therapists who do brief therapy need to know a great deal about normal child and family development. Concepts of pathology make sense only when viewed against a backdrop of normal behavior and not when developed from a selected sample of malfunctioning youngsters and parents. One ought to know, for example, that parents make more mistakes, and are significantly more uncertain and anxious with firstborns than with those born later. Moreover, being a brief therapist means knowing that 7-year-old boys play comfortably with girls, so that when a mother comes in and expresses concern that her 7-year-old son may be turning into a homosexual because he plays with the girl next door, the therapist can tell an overanxious mother that her son's behavior is perfectly normal and foretells nothing about his future sexual identification. Child clinicians ideally should have strong backgrounds in developmental psychology as well as experience in working with children and adolescents in nonclinical settings.

Brief therapy is an approach that rejects the use of inferences as much as possible. It especially rejects the use of hypothetical constructs which are inferred from overt behavior which, I would suggest, are often the projections of the clinician, and thus can vary from therapist to therapist. Brief therapy focuses on and emphasizes *overt, explicit behaviors, and cognition*. At the same time, brief therapy makes major use of common sense ideas and terminology; it is a pragmatic approach. As such, nothing is taken for granted; jargon (therapist's or client's) is avoided; global omnibus terms are rejected. The brief therapist tries to be very precise when clients offer vague and overgeneralized statements such as "I'm depressed"; he tries to define the problem by asking questions. "What do you mean by depressed? Under what circumstances? What elicits it? How do you handle these feelings? When are you not depressed? Are you ever happy?"

Brief therapy is a *problem-oriented* approach which focuses upon *current behaviors*, starting (and often ending) with those problems for which the client seeks help. Somehow it seems to be a radical notion that when clients come with a problem one should pay attention to what *they* are concerned about rather than shifting as rapidly as possible to what the clinician infers might be the underlying causes and conflicts (429). The brief therapist works with the present reality, with what is going on right now. Clients are asked about why they are concerned about certain behaviors (a fascinating question in itself, and one which includes querying why they came and what they expect to happen). The approach is essentially a *descriptive* one, so that when explanations or interpretations are offered to clients, the therapist talks in common sense language rather than using diagnostic labels or hypothetical constructs. That means too that brief therapy is an *ahistoric* approach. When one does take history, it is generally of the current behavior with which clients are concerned. For example, when parents describe their son as fighting with other kids in school and getting poor grades, the brief therapist would inquire about the way the parents have tried to handle the problem, and the results. Parents generally come to child guidance clinics as a last resort after all else has failed, and the brief therapist needs to know what has already been tried and the response to these unsuccessful attempts.

Brief therapy primarily utilizes *conscious attitudes*, although it recognizes that people are not always aware of what they do or why they behave in a certain way. It is an approach which inquires into clients' explanations of their own behavior and into their goals for themselves. Major therapeutic use is made of concepts such as coping, mastery, and responsibility— especially the latter. Complaining about their child's behavior, many parents are really saying they would like him to be more responsible. The brief therapist then tries to help the child become more responsible by emphasizing the *consequences* of behavior rather than the origins. Brief therapy assumes that most people operate volitionally and with some awareness of what they are doing; the notion that people are helpless and cannot control themselves is rejected.

Brief therapy tries to set *precise behavioral goals* as quickly as possible. Most clients are reasonably explicit about what they want help for, and when they are unclear it is up to the brief therapist to help the client focus on his goals. In 6 weeks one obviously cannot work on all problems, so that the therapist must decide with the client which areas are to be worked on. One tries to select target behaviors or conflicts which, if altered, will permit more adaptive responses to emerge in the client's real world outside of therapy. For example, if communication can be opened within a family which has withdrawn from each other into hurt silence, then hopefully their beginning to talk to each other will set off other changes. It will permit new responses to each other to emerge. Brief therapy assumes that if people change their behavior towards each other they will not only feel differently about each other, but also feel differently about themselves. However, the brief therapist also tries to help clients become more realistic about their own goals and expectations (of themselves and others). It helps to be a little philosophic, to realize and to convey to clients that not all problems are solvable, that life is difficult, that anxiety and conflict are sometimes unavoidable, and that often, as a therapist, the best one can do is help clients cope with and tolerate very difficult life situations (e.g., a child who is truly unwanted and is given up for foster home placement).

On the part of the brief therapist there is a clear expectation of change in accordance with client goals and concerns. More important, there is an *active monitoring* of change during the course of treatment. For example, if a problem to be worked on involves getting a child to sleep at night instead of letting him run around the house for hours, the therapist will suggest a management plan to be tried for a week and then evaluated at the next session. When the parents return the therapist will ask, "How did it go? Did it work?" If the answer is positive, "Great!" If negative, then the reasons need to be explored. Was the plan incorrect or were the parents unable to carry it out successfully because of their own anxieties? A suggestion is followed through to successful completion or it is revised or discarded. One actively sees what works and what doesn't. Generally, less sophisticated, less well educated clients are the most receptive to authority. They expect the therapist to be the expert and if told what to do, many of them will comply. They may not understand *why* they are behaving differently, but neither are they particularly interested in understanding. More sophisticated clients want to know why problems have occurred and why they should behave differently. They are less receptive to authority and more in need of cognitive maps. Where possible in brief treatment, one tries to provide these for all clients; that is, one tries to sketch for them an understanding of the connections between attitudes and behavior, expectations and behavior, and the contingencies between behavior and outcome. Clients can modify what they do far better when they understand these relationships than if the therapist just manipulates behavior. Then they can generalize too, and handle new situations more appropriately in the future.

A clear and explicit value of brief treatment is in learning by *active doing* rather than by *passive discussion*. Therapy is an artificial situation and the payoff is in what clients do outside of therapy and not what they do in the therapy session itself. The notion that clients have developed real insight into their problems is meaningless unless it is translated into effective living outside of therapy. Consequently there is a deemphasis on the magic of the therapy hour. Perhaps a good brief therapist needs to be skeptical about the effects of therapy. At the very least it is seen as simply one way of changing people, and it becomes even more effective when it is used in conjunction with community resources. In about one-half to two-thirds of CPC cases a visit is made to the school during the brief therapy period. The purpose of the visit is not only to gather information, but to develop with the teacher and related school personnel more satisfactory ways of handling the child in the school setting. The notion is that the hours the child spends there are much more important generally than the hour or so a week in therapy, and intervention directly into the arena of conflict is much more effective than merely talking about it in a far removed setting.

The role of the brief therapist is quite different from the traditional analytic picture of the detached, neutral therapist who views his function as aiding the "patient" in developing insight into his difficulties. The therapist's role in brief therapy is a combination of consultant, educator, problem-solver, and behavioral programmer and manager. The brief therapist develops contracts with his clients, treats them as collaborators, and makes them an active participant in what happens. Not every clinician is temperamentally or philosophically suited to be an effective brief therapist. One must not only work within an arbitrarily selected and limited time period, but one must be comfortable with a therapeutic style that is active, open, directive, and involved. The brief therapist must be a *strategic planner* who will plunge right into the family system, give advice and directions, make suggestions, and do them all very quickly.

The brief therapist also has to be a *confronter*, not in the encounter group sense where the therapist says, "I'm going to really hit you in the face with gut feelings," but confrontation in the sense of very rapid and sometimes intense feedback. Clients are really not as fragile as has been supposed and they can handle a great deal of direct information. As quickly as possible, the brief therapist tries to tell them what he thinks is the problem. The brief therapist does not wait until he is 100% sure before he intervenes, but rather works with hypotheses which are confirmed, negated, or revised as a function of the client's reactions. The brief therapist can say to the client that he is not sure about what is going on but that he would like to try out a formulation. Obviously he can be wrong, but if he never presumes to be infallible then he and the client can learn from the therapist's mistakes.

The brief therapist is humble in the sense that he must be open and realistic about his own limitations and those imposed by the time limit of treatment. On the other hand, he knows a great deal about the interaction between behavior and attitudes, and he can change the former so that feedback can change the latter. The brief therapist *assumes and accepts the responsibility* for making things happen (perhaps the most anxiety-arousing aspect for new brief therapists). He does not wait until the client develops "elegant insight." The brief therapist clarifies, articulates, focuses, maximizes, and intensifies. In training brief therapists, the supervisor will ask after the very first session, "What's going on and what are your goals? Where are you going to be 6 weeks from now? What are you going to do to get there?"

During every step of the way, the effective brief therapist is thinking and planning along these dimensions, and he always enters a session with a plan of action, even though it can be discarded if necessary. The brief therapist learns as he goes along, fed by the results of his interventions and reinforced both by the changes which he directly observes and by the clients' reports of satisfaction or dissatisfaction. When the goals of treatment are clear, overt, and measurable (at least experientially), then brief therapy is the best modality in which a therapist can assess his own effectiveness—the only criterion that matters to clients who wish help!

15

RESOLVING INDIVIDUAL CRISES THROUGH GROUP METHODS

Jean Allgeyer

Crisis groups have been used at the Benjamin Rush Center in Los Angeles since 1965. In 1965 a pilot study on the crisis group was conducted, and the results were promising enough to warrant ongoing use of this new modality (396). Combining crisis intervention with group process seemed a natural mating based on our observations that crisis is a leveling phenomenon, and that people in crisis relate to one another with empathy and helpful support (297).

The literature on crisis groups is sparse. Peck and Kaplan (323) make brief mention of the use of crises occurring in ongoing therapy groups, but do not deal with groups composed of patients already in crisis. The article by Strickler and Allgeyer (396) was the first to report on a group formed specifically to treat patients in crisis. Relatively long-term crisis groups for the poor are described by Bloch (42). In addition, three California programs incorporate a crisis group approach (Warren Jones at the Psychiatric Clinic of the Huntington Hospital, Pasadena; Hyman Weiland at the San Fernando Child Guidance Center; and Henriette Groot at the Veterans Administration Domiciliary in Los Angeles), but to the best of my knowledge these programs have not been described in the literature.

THE TREATMENT PROCESS

Initial Contact

The initial contact for a consultee at the Benjamin Rush Center is usually with a volunteer receptionist who greets him and helps him fill out a form on which the consultee describes his problem. Often these forms are enlightening for the therapist in giving a quick sense of the degree of personal upheaval being experienced by the consultee. The Center Coordinator then sees the consultee for a brief interview to evaluate the severity of the crisis, possible need for hospitalization, and appropriateness for the crisis group. Consultees are excluded if they exhibit 1) serious suicidal or homicidal risk that might not be adequately controlled in a group, 2) psychotic process so severe that it might make the person noncommunicative or seriously disruptive in a group, or 3) inability to speak English. The consultee can choose individual treatment if he prefers. However, the merits of the group are explained to him lest he refuse to join a group out of lack of knowledge.

Initial Interview

The crisis group therapist sees the consultee as soon as possible for a pregroup interview. The clinic uses the pregroup interview for the specific task of formulating the crisis before the consultee enters the group. However, as an experiment in a pilot project, the author eliminated the pregroup interview and formulated the crisis in the first group session. Contrary to expectations the group did not seem to make crisis delineation more difficult. Instead, the group was helpful in identifying the precipitating events leading to the crisis, and in some instances in overcoming resistance to sharing information. Furthermore, it seemed that more empathy developed among group members who were present at the early, crisis-defining stage of each other's treatment than developed when the first contact was exclusively with the therapist. Early entry into the group seemed to increase consultee interaction and lessen competition for the therapist's attention. This experience leads to the possibility that a pregroup interview could be eliminated under certain circumstances.

In the first hour, whether individually or in the group, the therapist helps the consultee identify the precipitating event that upset the individual's psychic equilibrium and led to the state of crisis. In addition, it is necessary to clarify why the old ways of coping are no longer effective and to help the consultee clearly delineate the nature of his dilemma. This may require highly individualized *detective* work, involving active exploration of the client's current life situation, to uncover actual or anticipated losses of important life roles or significant others, points of marked change in affect, and the stirring of memories of analogous stressful events. The therapist formulates the dynamics of the current crisis against the background of personal history offered by the consultee. Finally, it is crucial to define the hazardous situation in a clear manner to the consultee so he can understand what has gone wrong and why his habitual ways of coping are not working, hence plummeting him into crisis. If the crisis has been accurately defined by the therapist, there should be a noticeable lowering of tension and the patient's ego should be revived for the important task of crisis resolution.

Within the Group

On entering the group (whether before or after a pregroup session), the consultee is asked to tell the group why he is there and, with the therapist's assistance, to clarify the precipitating event, the ensuing crisis, and the habitual coping which is no longer effective. The group is then challenged to work with the new member in helping him explore alternate coping mechanisms leading toward crisis resolution.

The special function of the crisis group requires a radical departure from usual group treatment models. In crisis groups, it is vital to structure the group to lend itself to the characteristic phases of crisis resolution, thereby facilitating working through of the crisis. Because the crisis experience is time-limited, persons in the crisis group must be afforded an opportunity to work on their problems at each group session. The sequence of 1) bringing both the crisis and former coping mechanisms into cognitive awareness, 2) suggestions for problem-solving, and 3) support for new ways of coping, must be followed. Because of the focus on individual crisis resolution, the group must be problem-centered and task-oriented. To accomplish this, the group leader assumes an active role, keeping each person focused on the resolution of his particular crisis. This necessity for a highly focused approach may limit the free flow of group process, since the group leader must intervene to limit content that does not promote crisis resolution. Moreover, without an accurate focus on each individual's major task—to resolve his crisis—the group would fail in its primary responsibility. In a group model that allows only 6 sessions per member, any straying by the group into the ongoing character problems of its members will detract from the effectiveness of the group and divert vital time and energy from its central task.

GROUP METHODS USEFUL IN CRISIS RESOLUTION

The following discussion of group methods represents only the view of the author and may not reflect general practice at the Benjamin Rush Center.

In a crisis group, the group process should not overshadow the emphasis on crisis resolution. However, group process is a powerful tool to enhance the clarification of the crisis and to move the consultee towards resolution. As previously stated, group members can be skillful in helping the person delineate why he is feeling stressed: what event or events upset his former equilibrium? As the consultee examines his old ways of coping, he often reacts with this same pattern in the group, making this behavior open to examination in the here and now of group experience. In the process of group interaction, multiple opportunities for desensitization and corrective emotional experiences take place (297). In crisis resolution, regression is to be avoided in favor of increasing a person's sense of adulthood and competence. The group process of helping others toward problem-solving counteracts the typical feelings associated with crisis—helplessness, hopelessness, and a sense of failure. Finally, the intangible quality of hope is generated when members see others risking new ways of coping and changing.

CASE REPORT 1

Mrs. W., the mother of 2 young girls and a baby, went into crisis when she discovered her husband nude in her daughters' room one night. Her husband's history of arrest for sexual involvement with a young girl made this client fear for her daughters' welfare. The hazard of finding her nude husband in the room of her sleeping children late at night triggered an intense reaction of fear in Mrs. W. She found herself immobilized and unable to cope with her husband's inappropriate behavior. She felt herself to be reacting in a helpless childlike way, frightened of future consequences for her daughters but unable to mobilize herself on their behalf. Her behavior in the here and now of group interaction clearly demonstrated her "child ego-state," reactivated by the recent threat. In the group, she acted excessively frightened, tearful, overwhelmed, and pessimistic about her ability to cope with her husband's behavior.

The group pointed out her inappropriate childlike reaction, that is, her fearfulness of the current situation as if she were the child involved rather than an angry, indignant mother. At this group confrontation, she recalled an analogous childhood experience with her stepfather who had abused her sexually. She had been terrified, but unable to protest against this powerful threatening man. Following this memory, she recognized that her husband's actions had stirred up these old fears and that she was again reacting as a child caught in a trap, unable to free herself without suffering mortal danger. Hence her feelings of being frozen and unable to move. The group helped her see that she was no longer a defenseless child and that her fears would be reduced by taking appropriate action. In the group, she role-played her intended conversation with her husband and practiced her decision to put a stop to his "night walks." Her success in doing this was followed by a change in her behavior in the group—from that of a helpless terrorized child to that of a concerned mother determined to protect her daughters.

In this case, the group's movement from an awareness of Mrs. W.'s childish ego-state reaction to confronting her with its inappropriateness led to her memory of the analogous event in her early life that had been unresolved and had left her vulnerable. With group support, she worked through her unresolved fears from her past and mobilized herself for appropriate action to deal with her current dilemma. Her inappropriate affect and behavior in the here and now of group interaction provided the decisive clue to understanding her inability to cope with her crisis. This is a clear instance of the use of group process to diagnose and treat a crisis situation.

Different therapeutic schools with widely divergent points of view have developed ways of working with people that are applicable to crisis intervention. A brief review of their contributions and usefulness in the crisis group modality is given here.

Transactional Analysis

Transactional analysis gives us a unique way of clarifying the consultee's past life experiences that are likely to be still affecting his current coping. In transactional analysis, importance is placed on early parental injunctions to the child which lead to childhood decisions that may still be affecting current behavior in a destructive way. These early decisions that have not been modified in the light of adult knowledge often are of critical importance at times of crisis.

This can be illustrated by consideration of the suicidal person. Often a suicidal urge follows a disappointing life experience which reminds the person of earlier and deeper disappointments, usually in connection with his parents. If the parents' early injunction was the powerful message, "Don't exist!" based on their own pathology and resentment of the child, and the child's early decision was, "OK, I won't!" he remains vulnerable to suicide until he makes a redecision. If a crisis is caused, for example, by the current loss of a loved one or of a valued life role, old feelings of being a born loser may be reactivated, and the person may turn to suicide as a way to cope with feelings of inevitable rejection and nothingness.

When the therapist senses that a current crisis is reactivating an early decision, it is very useful to help the person get in touch with the old injunction and early decision and to work toward a redecision—a new decision based on current information about himself. Times of crisis usually stir up old poorly resolved problems, often revolving around a low sense of self-worth. Old parental messages of depreciation and disapproval are reactivated by new crisis situations, leaving the person vulnerable to early self-depreciatory decisions. Helping the person recall and reevaluate (in his adult ego state) old injunctions and early decisions can free him to choose new and more adult solutions for current crisis situations.

A fascinating example of the use of the transactional analysis approach with a suicidal person occurred following the Los Angeles earthquake of 1971.

CASE REPORT 2

A young woman living in the San Fernando Valley near the earthquake epicenter witnessed severe destruction all around her, but her home survived. She sought professional help following an argument with her neighbor; the neighbor had refused to share in rebuilding a fence destroyed in the earthquake. The patient described herself as feeling "wiped out" and suicidal. She expressed intense feelings about the earthquake, viewing it as a catastrophic event in which God might be punishing certain people. She wondered why she had been spared, as if she had expected to be destroyed along with the physical destruction that surrounded her. The triggering event that focused her catastrophic feelings was the argument in which her neighbor would not grant her any rights. Her old method of coping was to try to always be right and to argue for doing the "right thing" in each situation. In this instance, her neighbor would not listen to or acknowledge her rights, and her husband would not back her up. She reacted by feeling despondent and suicidal. This intense reaction to a relatively mild rebuff cued the group leader that the current crisis might be reactivating an old script with a powerful "Don't exist" message.

The young woman told the following life story: She was the illegitimate child of a Mexican mother who felt shamed by her birth. Her father left her mother shortly thereafter, giving the impression he wanted nothing to do with this "unblessed" event. She described herself as always having been "one big mistake" and of feeling that the only way she could make it up to her mother (for the shame and pain she caused her) was to not exist. Clearly, from both parents, this young woman received a "Don't exist" message, to which she had responded with an early decision: "I don't have the right to be here, I'll try to justify my existence by always doing everything right, and if I can't do it right [hence the need to always be right], I will kill myself."

She viewed the earthquake as a catastrophic event in which God might be seeking to punish and destroy certain people, perhaps people like herself who lived an unsanctioned existence. Thus the earthquake, and the threat to her life that it represented, reactivated old childhood fears of being, as she stated "X'd out." The incident with her neighbor reinforced the feeling of not counting. Her intrapsychic response was to feel despondent and hopeless and begin thinking of the solution that her "Don't exist" script called for, namely suicide.

This depressed woman was treated by reviewing her script with her, getting her in touch with the "Don't exist" parental injunction and with the part of her that agreed with that early message which she called the "X who crosses me out." Fortunately, this woman also had a strong wish to live and to fight the "X" part of her. She was then invited (and encouraged by the group) to have a dialogue between the two warring parts of herself, the X-who-crossed-her out and the I-who-wanted-to-live-a-normal-life. During this dialogue, the "I" argued with the "X" that she did not want to be crossed out, and finally that she was not going to allow this to happen.

At this point she was ready for a redecision. The leader then reminded her of her own early decision to go along with the "Don't exist" message by agreeing that she didn't have a right to exist, but would try to justify her life by always doing everything right, and if she failed, she would kill herself.

Now, fully in touch with her old script, aware of its lifelong destructiveness, she made a redecision in her adult ego state. In her redecision, she granted herself the right to live unconditionally, regardless of her inability to perform perfectly or to be confirmed in her rights by others. Following her redecision, she no longer had to spend her life justifying her existence to others or trying to rectify the mistake of her birth (196).

Gestalt Methods

From a different perspective, i.e., Gestalt therapy, we can gain skills for putting people in touch with the affective side of a crisis. People in crisis commonly are in a dilemma because they are experiencing acute conflict reflected in "internal splits." The aim of Gestalt therapy is to help people become whole, to integrate their fragmented parts. Gestalt therapists have evolved methods which are helpful in working with people in crisis. Often during a crisis, a person is experiencing such a painful reality that he splits off the affect and thus does not experience his pain fully nor can he resolve it effectively. This is a frequent occurrence in unresolved grief work. The Gestalt method of role-playing, which emphasizes the person's imagining and acting out all the parts in his personal drama, is a way of venting repressed feelings and confronting others in fantasy in preparation for real-life confronting and coping (324). It is also a way of completing unfinished business with persons living or dead, which can be essential in successful grief work. Other useful Gestalt methods include the use of fantasy to put a person in touch with walled-off feelings; exaggeration of symptoms or behavior to inform the person of the impact and meaning of the behavior; emphasis on staying with the immediate moment, that is, "being in the now"—especially for the person who wants to cope by escaping to the past; becoming aware of the meaning of body language; and learning to *stay with* important feelings until they are understood and integrated. Gestalt methods focus on gaining emotional insight and thus are most useful when crisis resolution hinges on working through a refusal to feel, such as is typified by unresolved grief.

CASE REPORT 3

A mother who lost a son in the war was seen a year later, still unable to overcome her grief and move back into the mainstream of life. The anniversary of her son's death provoked a crisis for her, hence her participation in a crisis group. She was invited to retell the story of his death. As she did so, it became clear that she had not yet said goodbye to her dead son, that she was still holding on to him in fantasy and preventing the emotional separation from taking place. The Gestalt method of role-playing was used. The mother was asked to confront the son as she last saw him, dead, and to tell him her feelings about losing him. At first she was unwilling to do so, sensing perhaps that she would no longer be able to hold on to the fantasy of his existence if she participated. Supported by the group, she began to tell him of her anguish, her longings for him, and her terrible pain at his death. The therapist then encouraged her to say goodbye to him, in her own way, as soon as she was ready. Her struggle in doing this, clearly mirrored her reluctance to let go and to face this grim reality. The group participated in her sadness and her tears in a community sharing of her leave-taking.

Following this, she was asked to go around the group and tell each member how she was going to begin to pick up the threads of her own life. She began by saying she did not think she ever wanted to begin again, but as she moved around the group, her reluctance gave way to some small hope and then beginning conviction that she could go on and badly needed to do so. When she came to the final person, she found herself assuring him that she would now be all right. She knew what she needed to do and that saying goodbye to her son—and to that grief-filled phase of her recent life—would make emotional room for new beginnings. Her affect changed markedly in the session, from a beginning point of sadness and despair, to one of some relief at having faced the unfaceable and surviving, to feeling more alive again.

The Gestalt role-playing method affords an opportunity for the person to reexperience in fantasy, with appropriate affect, the situation that is unfinished and to have another chance at integration. Traumatic events, such as unforeseen death, are often handled by splitting the affect off to reduce the pain. These feelings must be reintegrated into the personality if the individual is to feel whole and alive again. Finally, working with unfinished business such as saying goodbye is often important in grief work where the person handles the loss by keeping the person alive in fantasy. This prevents the necessary phase of active grieving that will eventually free the person from his ties to the lost person and allow him to reinvest in new relationships.

COMMENTS

In working to resolve an individual's crisis within a group setting, a variety of techniques are useful to facilitate the treatment process. Stressful events that may lead to a crisis occur in everyone's life, but whether a crisis develops depends ultimately on the characterological stability of the person and the appropriateness of his coping repertoire in dealing with the impact of the hazardous event or stress. Every person has unresolved characterological problems which can be triggered off by stressful events, thus making him vulnerable to crisis. If an internal state of crisis does occur, some regression will follow and with it some degree of reactivation of old personality problems. Thus, during crisis, an individual is given another chance to work through some of these unresolved problem areas, and in this sense crisis intervention can be viewed as a growth modality.

In our experience, crisis groups offer a highly effective way of treating the person in crisis. The group helps the individual articulate and understand his crisis, as well as offering multiple resources for ideas, stimulation, and support. Using a variety of therapeutic methods seems to offer the therapist the greatest flexibility in his approach and encourages him to creatively choose the ways in which he will individualize and relate to the person in crisis.

16

GROUP PSYCHOTHERAPY FOR SELF-DESTRUCTIVE PERSONS

Norman L. Farberow

Group therapy as a therapeutic procedure for self-destructive persons has been singularly neglected. Reports of programs in this area have been few despite the general impression of positive impact and almost specific usefulness of the group format for suicidal people. Several authors (7, 115, 158, 188, 350) have described group psychotherapy experiences for self-destructive patients, some in hospital settings and others in community agencies. Others (48, 209, 214, 280, 289) have described reactions in a psychotherapy group to the suicidal (sometimes equivocal) death of one of its members. Frederick and Farberow (135) compared group psychotherapy of suicidal patients with group treatment of other kinds of patients. More recently, Motto and colleagues presented two papers at the 1972 American Association of Suicidology meeting in Detroit on group psychotherapy with patients recently admitted for attempted suicide, and Farberow and colleagues presented progress reports on the Los Angeles Suicide Prevention Center (LASPC) group treatment programs at the American Association of Suicidology meetings in Denver in 1972 and Houston in 1973.

The impetus for the development of the group therapy program at LASPC lies in the changing demands for effective suicide prevention. It is well substantiated (392, 441) that most of those persons using the facilities of a suicide prevention center are chronically disturbed, tenuously adjusted individuals in whom the current suicidal crisis is an exacerbation of ongoing conflicts and problems. While the procedures for crisis resolution are appropriate and effective not only for them but for the one-third acutely suicidal persons in the population, the chronically suicidal patients need much more. Essentially the *more* is the development of a relationship in which the primary feature is continuing evidence of caring, interest, and concern. The needs of the crisis and postcrisis period (considered in varying lengths) are hopefully met, at least in part by the several models of group therapy that have been developed. These are in addition to the hot-line services and the experimental relationship maintenance program conducted at the Center (see Chapter 6).

The group therapy program at LASPC now includes two long-term insight-oriented groups (once a week), a postcrisis-oriented, time-limited group (twice a week for a specified period of 8 weeks), a drop-in group (5 days a week), a creative expression group (using nonverbal expressive procedures, meeting once a week), a socialization group focusing on interaction relationships (meeting once a week), and four drug rehabilitation groups (once a week). This report focuses on the three modalities—long-term, intermediate, and drop-in groups—presenting the progress and problems in these three.

LONG-TERM GROUPS

One of the two long-term groups had been in operation approximately 3 years, and the other about 1 year at the time of this report. In the first group, three of its six members were in the group since it started; the others entered at varying intervals. In the second group, two of the six members were with the group from its start, while the others arrived at different times. Patients are generally received on referral from the intermediate group or from the clinical associates who provide the hot-line telephone services. The therapists have been one male professional and one female certified group therapist.

The primary focus of the long-term groups is the social and interpersonal relationships of the patients, with the interaction within the group used to highlight the character of the relationships experienced outside. Insight into dynamics is sought but only when it helps to identify behaviors and to clarify assumptions. Depression, anxiety, and suicidal behavior are the most frequent themes, or at least they are for the newer patients in both groups. For all patients, the most common concern is self-concept and self-esteem—who am I? and am I worthy of love? In their explorations of these questions, they reveal both their inadequate defenses against being exposed and their vulnerability to anticipated rejection. Depression or suicidal feelings are readily brought in. The patients know the topic is acceptable, that others have been there, and that understanding and tolerance are available. The group usually rallies to the help of the depressed person at such times, offering help which frequently extends beyond the time of the meeting, for social contacts outside are encouraged. The patients also know that the Center is always available for additional help at any hour if needed.

Some of the patients have individual therapy outside the Center in addition to our group therapy. Since we do not offer individual therapy ourselves, this is encouraged because of the usefulness of increased sources of support, the dilution of the transference which can become intense, and the sharing of the dependency demands, which may also become extreme.

The newer long-term group has displayed the usual procession of themes found in intensive work with suicidal persons. One early, almost basic, theme in the new group has been identified as "victimology." Almost everyone describes behaviors which have put him into untenable positions where he will be hurt, rejected or disapproved, and thus be able to verify his feelings of worthlessness. Mrs. J., for example, an extremely bright, divorced woman, works as a file clerk at night in a hospital, a job she cannot tolerate but cannot leave because of her financial situation. She continually gets into trouble because she ventures beyond the confines of her job, seeking contact with the patients in whom she senses the loneliness of the severely ill. Before entering the group, she was completely unable to protest when her best friend took her lover away, declaring she wasn't really worthy of the relationship in the first place. Mrs. L. had the same thing happen, losing her husband to another woman, and feeling that she deserved it for the other woman would be so much better for her husband than she. Mrs. M. was still involved after prior years of work in a psychoanalytic group, with trying to see how her marriage had failed when she had made so many efforts to be a good wife, living up to all the preestablished standards which she had set up and could not possibly achieve. Mr. W., too, had divorced his wife and given her everything, convinced that he was worthless. He was unable to see how his rigid, compulsive, mechanical approach to life made all his efforts at a relationship unsuccessful.

In the older group, the victim theme appears in the more recently added group members. Some of the older members have shown remarkable changes in behavior. For example, two addictive personalities have changed, one a little, the other a lot. Mrs. S. a former alcoholic, has given up her need to victimize both herself and her brain-damaged child by keeping him home as a constant source of responsibility and guilt. She permitted herself to improve her appearance by fixing her teeth, has even started a business of her own, and most recently has given up regular use of tranquilizers. Mrs. C. has transferred her addiction from Seconal to pot. While she still needs to get stoned every day, she has also moved toward stabilization of her stormy relationship with her younger common-law husband and to acceptance of a remarkable talent in tapestry sewing. Mrs. J. has relinquished her suicide attempts as a way of controlling her relationship with her schizophrenic husband and has learned to accept her competency in her nursing profession. One of the newer members in this old group provokes more concern, however. Totally convinced of his inherent worthlessness, he is resentful of his obligations and disparaging of his achievements (he is a lawyer in a local government agency). In his 3 months in the group, his pervasive depression has already led him to one serious suicide attempt. Yet, as so often happens, he can be extremely helpful and reassuring to others, building their esteem and substantiating their worth.

On reflection, the type of person who has not benefited from the long-term groups has been one unable to stand the slower pace, impatient with the demands of others for inexhaustible support, and the necessary pause in the group work to provide concentrated, all-out support when the suicidal impulse breaks out. Mr. H., in the old long-term group, broke away because he felt there was not enough confrontation and challenge. He was a member of encounter groups, worked at one of the local self-development centers, and demanded more touch, more feeling, more movement in the group. In the newer group, Mrs. J.J. dropped out because of impatience. She found the abrasive self-exposure demanded in an encounter-type patient-at-patient relationship gave her a much greater feeling of progress.

INTERMEDIATE GROUP

Another form of group therapy has been a postcrisis-oriented, time-limited intermediate group, set up to treat suicidal patients within an arbitrarily established time period of 8 weeks. This group consists of a maximum of eight patients and meets twice weekly for 1½ hours each session. The group is open-ended, with new patients admitted to it whenever a vacancy occurs. Patients are referred primarily from the drop-in group in the Center and by the Center's telephone-answering clinical associates. Two certified group therapists, both women, have served as the group's therapists since its inception about 8 months ago. Recently, one therapist-in-training, drawn from the clinical associates conducting the drop-in groups, has been added.

An intake interview is held with each patient for the usual purposes of evaluation of the suitability of the patient and to determine the nature of the presenting stress. The primary emphasis of the intermediate group work is explained as focusing on and helping him to resolve his immediate life-crisis situation. The 8-week time limit is stated to be inflexible as a way of putting pressure on both patient and therapist to achieve the mutually established objectives by a concentration on the here-and-now postcrisis problems amenable to resolution.

Although many sources of conflict may be identified during the group situation, the therapeutic emphasis is placed on relieving the oppressive suicidal symptoms and assisting the patient in reconstituting himself to at least a preemergency level of functioning. The patient is directed toward assessment of his ego strengths as well as his problems. Although the patients frequently use the threat of suicide as a defense against being confronted with maladaptive life patterns, the therapists respond to these threats without anxiety and with an empathic acceptance of the validity of the patient's distress. This permits the patient, often for the first time, to ventilate his frustrations, fears, and needs, as well as his omnipotent wishes, and so obtain much needed relief. The fact that other group members speak directly about their own suicidal feelings, breaking the taboo of silence around the subject of suicide, is helpful.

Despite the short-term aspects of the treatment program, dependence develops rapidly and with great intensity. The dependence on the group has been in many ways the most ego-supportive and therapeutically effective factor, although it has also presented the greatest problems, especially toward the latter part of the 8-week period when the imminence of termination begins to be felt. Their separation anxiety reactions are interpreted in the further working through of their problems, particularly of their reactions to loss, their dependency needs, and their fears of change. Actually, their separation anxieties are buffered by the fact that all of the patients have the option of continued participation in drop-in groups and/or of availing themselves of our 24-hour answering service. Thus, the patients find there is always someone available if an emergency arises.

For the therapists, having a cotherapist not only permits a sharing of the considerable responsibility involved in the care of these seriously ill patients, but also serves to divide the transference affects and to offer an opportunity for shared evaluation and discussion of the group dynamics after each session. Most importantly, there are weekly supervisory sessions with an experienced senior therapist, and these provide ongoing guidelines and enable the group leaders to handle their responsibilities with security and a sense of shared responsibility. Two clinical vignettes illustrate the way in which the intermediate group has worked.

CASE REPORT 1

Mrs. A., a 32-year-old Caucasian woman in the process of getting a divorce, came to the center after two suicidal attempts within 2 months following the breakup of her marriage. To compensate for her feelings of rejection, she was running around frantically with a succession of different men and had so neglected her work that she was on the verge of adding to her sense of rejection by provoking a dismissal from her job. Mrs. A., who had initially presented herself to the group as a compassionate, understanding, and loving partner, began to face her inner rage and jealousy at the woman who had displaced her in her husband's affection. As she became more able to accept these previously unacceptable feelings in herself, the self-destructive suicidal impulses with which she had been struggling were lessened.

CASE REPORT 2

Mrs. B. was a 33-year-old Caucasian woman with a history of several schizophrenic breakdowns, for one of which she had been hospitalized over a year. She was an extremely secretive, highly intelligent person who had completed all of her requirements for a PhD in science at a prestigious eastern university but who had decompensated when she was unable to complete her thesis. She had just broken with the psychoanalyst who had treated her for 17 years and was now clinic-hopping to get her phenothiazine medications. She lived with two guns and three dogs for companionship and security, but nevertheless she was holding down a responsible job which she was in marked danger of losing.

In working with her, we focused primarily on her dependence-independence conflict, buttressed by a major emphasis on her essential strengths and unique qualities. Her delicate and volatile balance is illustrated by an incident in one of the sessions when she became upset with another member who was monopolizing the group's attention. In a fit of anger, Mrs. B. left the room. Her distress was obviously so intense that one therapist followed her out and found her standing in the parking lot. Her initial impulse had been to harm herself by hitting her head with the jack handle in her car, but she had become distracted by a nearby pigeon and was now attempting to tame it. She was asked to return to the group. She replied that she would do so only if she could succeed in taming the pigeon and bringing it in with her. The therapist reported this to the group and a few moments later Mrs. B. entered with the pigeon in her hands and sat on the floor in a corner of the room. The group accepted her, and a lively discussion then ensued, focusing on the issue of sibling rivalry, and the anger that it provoked. Although at the end of the 8-week period she had great difficulty in coping with the process of separation, she made liberal use of the Center's emergency telephone service while she gradually was integrated into the open-end group. To date she is continuing to maintain her emotional equilibrium and to function effectively on her job, which is the central stable element in her life situation. Mrs. B. is the type of patient with whom the goal is primarily restoration, at some level, of homeostatic functioning. On the other hand, Mrs. A. is the kind of patient with whom, once the emergency stresses have been resolved, efforts at additional changes can be made by referral to a more insight-oriented therapy program.

In the 8 months after this program began, all 26 patients treated had attended the entire 16 group sessions. At the end of each patient's 8-week period, the acute impulses toward suicide had subsided, and it was possible to refer them to other appropriate services where further therapeutic change could be pursued.

DROP-IN GROUPS

Drop-in groups vary more from the traditional than the other groups described here, and a more detailed description is in order. The drop-in groups were conceived especially to meet the needs of chronically emotionally disturbed persons suffering a temporary stress situation that for them was a valid crisis. What seemed most needed for these patients, all of whom were feeling lonely, unwanted, unloved, and unlovable, and not welcome in most agencies in the community, was a resource that could provide feelings of caring and concern. The groups were planned to meet every day, but until enough trained personnel were available the meetings started out on a twice-a-week basis. At this writing the groups are meeting every week day, with plans to hold similar groups on weekends and evenings as additional personnel are trained. The demand has been great enough to require it.

Membership Procedures

There is no waiting period for the drop-in groups. The patient can come in to a group meeting the same day he calls. If more than ten patients appear, the group is split, and two simultaneous meetings are held. Patients are also invited to "drop-in" as many times as they wish, but there is no seeking of a commitment for continuing attendance. They are informed that there may be unfamiliar members when they return to future meetings and that there are different therapists at each session. The group provides the patient with a place to come at the same time each day, where he can meet with other members and staff, and where he may share experiences and feelings in a supportive, accepting atmosphere.

Many of the patients attending have been found to be in treatment with a therapist elsewhere. The patient is asked to tell his therapist about his coming to the drop-in group. When possible, a consultation is held with the patient's therapist so that he will be aware of any activities engaged in by the patient related to therapeutic goals. To date, only one therapist has forbidden a patient to use the intermediate group but did encourage her to use the drop-in group.

Patients are referred to the drop-in sessions by the clinical associates receiving incoming calls, by workers in the Continuing Maintenance Relationship Program (see Chapter 6) who deal with high-risk suicidal patients, and by therapists in the community. The patients attending include both sexes and all races, and have ranged in age from 17 to 70 years, with most in the 40-50 year age group. The most prevalent stress situations have been loss of a loved one, recent divorce or separation, loss of a job, forced retirement, and progressively deteriorating life activities. The chronic, lonely, isolated, depressed patient used the group most often. Patients who did not seem to benefit from the drop-in groups were *a*) alcoholics (although many former alcoholics have attended) and *b*) intensely dependent persons who find themselves frustrated by the lack of commitment and the changing personnel. For many participants, however, the nongroup concept has been a primary attraction, especially for those intensely suicidal and isolated patients for whom it provided a welcoming place to come, something to do, and people to be with.

Profile of Staff

The coordinator of the drop-in program was a certified group therapist, and the remaining staff was made up of clinical associates, i.e., persons originally trained as volunteer telephone counselors. The clinical associates have been selected because of their experience and skill as well as their high level of interest in learning something new. The drop-in groups have fulfilled the need of the well-trained clinical associates who have outgrown the telephone work after a year or so and wished to go on to new areas. The group work gives them an opportunity for face-to-face contact with patients.

Techniques in Training.   From this group of trainees, six of the most experienced were selected to be therapists in charge, usually one for each session, with primary responsibility for conducting the session. In addition, there may be from one to three trainees and a professional consultant. The therapists are all scheduled to participate in one group session per week. Students and nurses from various universities who are in training at the Center may also attend assigned sessions as observers.

Following each group session, a conference for the therapists and observers is held with the professional consultant. Education and training are provided by exploring the dynamics of the group process and discussing the significance of patient behavior.

Capsule notes are formulated for the patients' files and also distributed to all the therapists who participate in the drop-in group program. When a group includes a high-risk patient who is thought to need further interaction, a follow-up is requested. Follow-ups are usually performed that same day by telephone workers assigned to the evening shift.

Once a week there is a group therapy seminar in which administrative problems, theoretical questions, and differential procedures within the groups are discussed. Guest speakers are occasionally invited. All persons working in the group program are required to attend the seminars, and they are also available to all personnel at the Center.

Attendance Patterns

During the period from February 1972 to January 1973, 155 patients attended drop-in groups, each one choosing his own attendance pattern. Table 16.1 illustrates the varied attendance patterns.

Although the majority of patients used the group during a crisis, attending from one to nine sessions, 20 patients attending between 10 and 89 sessions, have become known as "regulars," some of them attending each day, while others have attended from time to time.

It has been interesting to note that in spite of the deliberate avoidance of traditional group procedures and absence of group commitment, there have been strong tendencies toward group formation. Participants often strike up quick, sympathetic friendships with each other, and there are endless examples of self-help and assistance to each other among members of the groups. We had not anticipated that so many patients would continue to return after the crisis had passed, or that they would drop out after a few visits, only to return, sometimes months later when another crisis developed, or simply because they felt lonely and remembered the drop-in group as a comfortable, friendly place.

Although many patients who attend were extremely depressed and difficult to manage, the therapists have not felt overburdened because the responsibility and transference are shared by all. A small follow-up study has disclosed that only one person who had attended drop-in sessions committed suicide. She was a chronically depressed person with many previous hospitalizations for suicide attempts, and had attended the group only once.

TABLE 16.1 Attendance at Drop-in Groups from February 1972 to January 1973

Sessions	Patients	Sessions	Patients
1	86	15–19	2
2	16	20–29	3
3	13	30–39	2
4	5	40–49	2
5	5	50–59	2
6–9	10	60–69	2
10–14	8	70–89	1

The Drop-In Group at Work

Three examples of use of the drop-in group during and after a crisis are given here. The first illustrates the original conceptualization of the service, and the other two illustrate its use as an unexpected but valuable resource for those patients who find the loose structure so helpful.

CASE REPORT 1

A 56-year-old divorced Caucasian woman lost a job as accountant that she had held for 20 years. She took an overdose of drugs once and was in severe crisis when she came to the drop-in group. She attended eight sessions, reporting extreme anxiety and painful somatic symptoms. In addition, she called the Center several times each day. She was encouraged to go out on job interviews in spite of her anxiety and pain. After 2 weeks, she found an excellent job as a comptroller, and all her symptoms subsided, making it no longer necessary to use the group.

CASE REPORT 2

A former patient of the Center called to ask if he could return to the long-term group which he had attended more than 6 years previously. He was a 43-year-old, single Caucasian male, highly intelligent, with the capacity to work on an insight level. He had done well in his original group at the Center, and after he left that group he became successful professionally and functioned well for several years. When he called, he was again unemployed and felt himself slipping into the kind of depression that he remembered so well. Because there was no room for him in the long-term groups at the Center at the time he called, he was referred to the drop-in group. He has participated in the drop-in group as he felt the need.

CASE REPORT 3

A 53-year-old single Caucasion male had called the Center frequently over a period of several years, usually when drunk. He was often seriously suicidal. He was known at the Center as a repeater who was alcoholic, abusive, and difficult. He had refused all referrals to Alcoholics Anonymous. He had attended a community treatment center but because he had behaved in a threatening and violent manner, he was asked not to return to that facility. When he was invited to attend the drop-in group, he was told that he could return as often as he wished so long as he was not drunk while attending. He came to 85 sessions in all, 80 of them consecutively, and remained sober throughout. He improved steadily, his suicidal ideation diminished, and he gradually took on the role of patient cotherapist. In general, he was helpful and interested in group participation. When other members of the group questioned him about his need to be in group, he said that he enjoyed the contact with people and found the supportive atmosphere pleasant. He left the group after he found a job, the first in many years.

Evaluation

The group therapy programs involving the drop-in and intermediate groups are still too new to report any investigations, although one is currently in process for those attending the drop-in meetings. A recent study (287) investigated the value of group therapy to members of the group program from March 1968 to July 1972. During this time, there were 52 persons attending groups, and this included all the suicidal people who had attended the crisis-oriented group between March 1968 and December 1969 (N = 30) and the long-term group (N = 22) from December 1969 to July 1972. (*Note:* December 1969 marked a change in the character of the group from crisis-oriented to long-term, insight-oriented group psychotherapy.) Eighteen subjects were located for the study, 8 in the crisis group and 10 in the long-term group. Five had died: 2 by suicide, 2 from natural causes, and 1 from undetermined causes. Four of the deaths occurred among the crisis group members; 4 of the subjects who were located refused to participate; the remainder (N = 25) could not be located.

Interviewer ratings of lethality showed a slight change (on a nine-point scale) before group participation at the time of follow-up, with the rating for the crisis group subjects increasing from 4.1 to 4.6 after group participation, the rating for the long-term group decreased from 4.1 before to 3.3 after participation. However, subjective reports from the persons interviewed indicated an overwhelmingly positive reaction to the group experiences, e.g., 17 out of 18 felt "cared about" by the therapist and 16 out of 18 felt, "They wanted to help me a lot." Self-perceptions of suicidal feelings indicated a significant decrease in lethality, especially among the long-term patients. Fifteen of the 18 interviewed stated the strong possibility that their contact with the Center and treatment in the group saved their lives.

Along with feelings of enthusiasm for the drop-in and intermediate group programs, there is good clinical evidence of benefit for the patient. As indicated previously, a number of patients, ordinarily seen as poor therapy risks, showed considerable improvement. This occurred despite the use of widely varying formats, structures, procedures, and objectives.

Operative Factors. It is informative to note how the curative factors as outlined by Yalom in his comprehensive book *The Theory and Practice of Group Psychotherapy* (447) are operative in the three major programs. A chart has been prepared, with comments on the relationship of Yalom's ten factors to each of the programs (Table 16.2).

Most of these factors appeared in all three kinds of groups. *Imparting information* takes place relatively rarely in the long-term groups but does occur rather often in the intermediate and drop-in groups; the *corrective recapitulation of the primary family group* is rarely a factor in the drop-in groups but may appear in the intermediate and long-term groups; and *group cohesiveness* is not specifically fostered in the drop-in group, although it tends to play a frequently significant role. Group cohesiveness is most important in the long-term groups and was moderately achieved in the intermediate group. Probably the most important factors for all three groups are the *instillation of hope, universality,* and *interpersonal learning.*

TABLE 16.2 Comparison of Yalom's Curative Factors for Long-Term, Intermediate, and Drop-In Groups

Curative factors	Long-term group	Intermediate group	Drop-in group
Imparting information	Occurs rarely or infrequently as part of group process	Moderate amount may be given, role playing may be used to avert anxiety about an impending event	Occurs often, frequently used for basic needs, e.g., to find shelter, food, or a job, or to handle interpersonal stresses with employer and fellow employees
Instillation of hope	Patients see progress in others, infrequently expressed openly by therapists; sometimes expressed indirectly by patients	Imparted often by therapists and new patients; also expressed implicitly by interest and concern	Many direct expressions, intellectualizations used as handle for depressive feelings; other patients used as examples
Universality	Patients receive strong sense of support from recognition of common suicidal feelings and bases for them (most often interpersonal alienation and convictions of basic inadequacy)	Sense of sharing feelings of self-destruction without shame. Recognition others have gone through the same trials. Sharing of posterisis problems	Most useful for restoring "self" concept, awareness of similar feelings in others reduces anxiety about inability to be helped
Altruism	Appears often in both emotional and practical support	Occurs fairly frequently, patients receive sense of worth from many opportunities and occasions to offer help to others	Extremely helpful to learn that their experiences can be valuable for others; spurs self-esteem
Corrective recapitulation of primary family group	Probably plays a role for most patients who react to therapists and to each other; being together a long time permits historical material to appear on which the group members can work	Modified form of family experience may appear; both therapists may appear; a few patients may be women; a few patients appear, but often together the entire time, but often new patients appear; focus on here-and-now and on problem solving, so transference has relatively little chance to grow, even though relationships may become intense	Infrequent or absent; with two to four therapists plus an observer (usually female), transference does not have opportunity to develop

TABLE 16.2 *(Continued)*

Curative factors	Long-term group	Intermediate group	Drop-in group
Development of socializing techniques	Confrontations on ways of behaving, thinking, and feeling frequent; objective to improve social interaction skills	Focus may be on a personal manner which produces conflicts, an important area for relieving problems of immediate postcrisis period	Practical social behavior may be a frequent focus; many patients have few or no social skills
Imitative behavior	Therapists serve as role models; direct imitative behavior infrequent	Some imitative behavior through role-playing or direct suggestion to adopt someone else's more successful mode of coping with a specific problem	Little or no opportunity for imitative behavior except when patient directly questions staff or other members
Interpersonal learning	Change may occur through transference, corrective emotional experience, insight; patients learn new ways of thinking, feeling, and behaving; may receive insight at many levels	Intensive focus on specific areas leading to and ensuing from suicidal behavior; insight gained on some levels	Valuable interpersonal experience; some possibility for self-esteem seen from interactions
Group cohesiveness	Very marked, close feeling; high level of sharing, much evidence of caring; this context sought and fostered	Moderate aspect; affected by frequent addition and loss of members; stability in continuity of therapists	Not fostered or consciously sought, but feelings of relatedness often appear; object for relatedness is often the Center
Catharsis	Important factor in early phases; sharing of "bad" aspects may appear infrequently in later phases	Occurs moderately often; held to lesser level by shift to and focus on realistic problems	Useful in self-exposure which, in tolerant environments, allows relief; frequent occurrence in this group

Speculations on Improvement in the Drop-In Groups

At the beginning of the program, the drop-in group was an experimental procedure, and we were concerned about its usefulness for seriously disturbed self-destructive people. In the course of a year and a half, a number of persons seem to have improved considerably, even though many were among those judged to have the poorest prognosis. To repeat, most of the people who have come to drop-in have been borderline, chronically disturbed people in emotional crisis who have found difficulty in making an adequate adjustment to the demands of society. They showed the usual irregular employment record, low socioeconomic status, few or no close relationships, alcoholism, drug abuse, and similar indications of chronic maladjustment. Many of them have been hospitalized repeatedly for emotional difficulties. For most, their use of our Center was but one, often the last, of a long succession of visits to a wide variety of community resources. They were well known and often unwelcome to the welfare network, for they seemed not to profit at all from what was done for or offered to them. Their capabilities allowed them to use the help they received only temporarily, not to integrate it and to progress from there. Nevertheless, these persons returned to the group each time it met, apparently making an attachment to the group process rather than to the people involved, since they often met new people whom they had not seen the day before, including the group leaders. True, as the number of people who returned continued to increase, they began to form tentative relationships with each other in the sessions. Some even began to socialize, a process encouraged by the group leaders.

Why did some of the patients improve? The people improving in this kind of setting had been unable to profit from any of the other kinds of therapeutic experiences they had had. We feel that it is specifically the loose, undemanding nature of the drop-in group which was the facilitator. The drop-in group asks nothing from those who attend; it makes no demands on them other than that they restrain any aggressive impulses, and that they allow others to talk. They are not asked to commit themselves to attend; they are not asked to assume any responsibility for any of the other persons. The therapists might ask one member to help another by recounting his own experiences, but he can refuse or postpone by stating he is not ready, which is perfectly acceptable. The first attachment, if any at all occurs, is to the agency, the Center, and not to staff or to other patients. In other words, focus on self is not only permitted but encouraged, and the implicit message is that their relationships with others in the group, whether staff or patients, are to be used to help themselves. Such a situation is novel for them. Even in previous hospital stays, demands were made for them to get better as quickly as possible, e.g., the bed was needed. In the Center, they could come as often as they wished without accounting for themselves and their time. It is not quite total acceptance, for both the implicit and explicit attitude is always that it is much better to be healthy than ill, to be mature rather than immature, and to be responsible rather than childish. But the level of tolerance is high, and behavior which is often regressive, insensitive, and demanding is rather readily absorbed. Some of the most difficult, irritating, childish patients have come repeatedly and improved. The absence of demand by the therapists and the lack of responsible individual commitment at first is tested, and then seems to be used positively. It's as if a child tests out the limits of acceptance, finds they always include acceptance of him as a person, and then is able to integrate some of the positive elements from his group experience into his life style. From this he can then go on to grow.

This process is impossible on an individual face-to-face basis or even in traditional group therapy programs. The demand on the therapists and on the other patients is too draining and therefore too difficult to tolerate. It is because the therapeutic personnel shift daily that the demand can be tolerated. The patients, too, are not expected to assume any responsibility for meeting the needs of the others, and so are able to relate on the basis of their capabilities of the moment, which includes not relating at that moment if they cannot.

SPECIAL PROBLEMS

Two problems brought to focus by the group therapy program in the Center are of special interest—the impact of the program on the Center, and labeling.

Program Changes

With the advent of the group therapy program, the Suicide Prevention Center had to undergo a radical change in its self-image, the result of a basic change of philosophy and a reformulation of objectives. Heretofore, the focus had been on the development of crisis therapy, prevention procedures, and emergency techniques. We recognize now, however, that to prevent suicide adequately, the concept of prevention must extend beyond the immediate crisis. Previously the procedure had been to establish adequate liaison with community agencies to continue the required treatment process once the emergency was handled. However, the agencies are often neither trained nor willing to handle the suicidal person, especially the chronically suicidal person. Such patients are hard to transfer—no one else wants them—so the Center must continue to treat them.

Additional Changes

The Center had to undergo both physical and operational changes. Telephones are not enough; there must be room for patients to be treated in groups, often several at a time. There must be a waiting room where patients can assemble, with a sensitive, tactful receptionist who can handle inquiries, demands, and requests of all kinds. There must be toilet facilities to meet the increased needs. There must be enough clinical associates interested and willing to work in face-to-face situations, either to talk with an emergency walk-in patient before the group meeting, or to the hanger-on who is reluctant to leave afterwards. The administrative staff is taxed with greatly increased paper work.

Assigning Responsibility

Most of all, for the Center there is the problem of responsibility for the patient. Often, the patient is in treatment elsewhere. Sometimes he comes in without the therapist's knowledge; at other times it is at the therapist's urging. If he is in treatment elsewhere, our policy has been to consider the therapist as the primary treatment resource and to collaborate with him when possible. When the patient comes in without the therapist's knowledge or approval, are we to notify his therapist? What about confidentiality? Can the patient trust us if we insist on telling his therapist? Can he trust us if we do not? Our policy has been that the therapist must know, but that when possible the patient's cooperation is to be obtained. The patient must understand the need for the trust to be mutual in his relationships to all his treatment agents. We have called a therapist without the patient's consent, but only in emergencies. The guiding principle at all times is the welfare of the patient.

Labeling

The problem of labeling refers to the identity problem of the suicidal patient as he engages in his treatment. At least two sources for the labeling exist. The first is from the patient himself and the second is from the treatment agency. The process of labeling is initiated immediately once the patient decides to call the Center, and this has both advantages and disadvantages for the patient and his treatment resource. By calling the LASPC, the patient has labeled himself as a person intending to kill himself, and as such he has established his means of obtaining help, marshaling of resources, evoking responses which are designed to help him. To the extent to which he has expressed openly his need for help, the labeling process is an advantage to all concerned—the patient, the agency, and the significant others involved. However, in many cases the labeling is dangerous. The patient, for example, may label his identity as worthless and inadequate. It makes no difference how much evidence of accomplishment exists, the patient is convinced that everything achieved has no real value when seen within the emptiness and lack of meaning of his inner core. It is exactly such persons for whom the group process is best suited. The implicit, yet denied, demands for reassurance and love are so great that no single therapist could possibly supply them. At times they tax the group, but at least there are seven or eight additional people available to lend the support required. The process of change for such persons is slow. It requires change in deeply entrenched self-concepts. It may be accomplished by massive support, gradual confrontation of resistances, and reintegration based on the accompanying emotional experience of acceptance, valuation, and love.

The identification imposed by an agency is the other side of the labeling coin. We are well aware from research and other reports of the impact of the institutional label as shown by the studies of Caudill (70), Weitz (432), and Reynolds and Farberow (353). Our Suicide Prevention Center, by its very name, imposes a pejorative label on the users of its facilities. To some it implies a haven for help and understanding. Such dependency can become extreme, as in the case of Mr. W. who has used the services of the Center in every imaginable way: long-term group, drop-in (almost every day), creative expression group, continuing relationship maintenance group, and frequent calls on the telephone. While excessive, for Mr. W. this dependency is necessary and one which is probably saving his life. His internal struggles as he works to change his whole life pattern are open for all to see. On the other hand, Mr. R., an ex-alcoholic who presents his problem of impotency as a ticket of admission to the group, seems content to come regularly and to sit. No change in his behavior has been observed. The focus for him in the drop-in group has been a concerted push to seek a job and commit himself to some active program for self-support.

In general, I do not feel we can escape the process of labeling. It is part of our society. Indeed, our efforts to reduce the stigma of shame associated with suicide are really a part of our efforts to influence the process of labeling. To the extent to which it has brought support and attention to a prominent public health problem, the labeling process has been highly useful; and to the extent to which it has brought crisis intervention and emergency mental health to a higher level of development and maturity, it has been a positive force.

17

TRANSCULTURAL CONSULTATION ON CRISIS INTERVENTION

Ruth E. Ingham

UNIVERSALITY OF CRISIS INTERVENTION

Out of a conviction that crisis intervention is needed in mental health facilities where resources are limited and the population unsophisticated, the writer has sought to teach the method in unusual settings. Crisis intervention is a favorable model for societies where patients are unfamiliar with the entire pattern of modern psychotherapy and unused to revealing their emotional lives to strangers. It is also a favorable model to present because it can be simplified and codified more readily than other forms of psychotherapy. A further advantage is that the activities of therapist and patient are more nearly like the behaviors they find familiar and comfortable.

One frequently discovers that introducing the principles of psychoanalysis or sensitivity training has confused and angered mental health personnel of other societies. These approaches are one step away from our own cultural attitudes, and three steps away from theirs. Indignation does not lead to learning no matter how important or correct the concepts that cause it may be. Crisis intervention can bring new life into psychiatric consultation for the developing countries throughout the world.

Minority groups and subcultures within the United States can also benefit from education in crisis principles. Isolated rural populations, immigrant groups, and peoples of urban ghettos are familiar examples that illustrate the cultural barrier to traditional mental health services regarded as outlandish by the majority. Wherever a sense of separateness and difference from the surrounding society exists, a ladder is needed to scale the barrier. Such a condition often exists in unexpected circumstances: among the students admitted to a university under an outreach plan for underprivileged youth, among recipients of workmen's compensation, and among teachers on strike. When a smaller group becomes categorized and fears that an outer group may criticize, despise, or misunderstand its position, acute insecurity gives rise to defensiveness. The defensive attitude makes the smaller group less approachable, and thus unresponsive to help from outside. Members of the group become a population-at-risk, vulnerable to a high rate of emotional emergencies and yet resistant to help. If crisis intervention were available, it would contribute an ideal ladder to scale the barrier and prevent extended damage.

CONSULTATIVE METHOD

Consultation must be tailored to fit the special attributes and requirements of the consultees. There are many common elements in disparate cultures, and the course of consultation is similar in each. Three basic phases through which the consultative process moves are prior learning, location learning, and action.

Phase I: Prior Learning

The consultant may choose an assignment out of a deep empathic interest in a group well known to him, or he may discover a teaching opportunity in a society with which he is unfamiliar. In either case, but particularly the latter, he should study in depth all aspects of the community and its mental health services. He is thus involved in the first phase of consultation which takes place before reaching the selected location. By reading literature on the group, and learning at least a few words of the language or dialect, he prepares for his entry. He can also search out people related to the group and, insofar as is possible, attempt to gain a feeling for the life of the people with whom he will seek to share experience.

Phase II: Location Learning

When he arrives at his destination, he enters the second phase whereby he must gain acceptance and trust and, simultaneously, design a strategy for consultation. The developing societies, with roots deep in the past, tend to live in a more formal manner and preserve traditional protocols. The consultant may want to dress and speak more conservatively than at home. On the contrary, when a consultant enters a "hippie" culture or a disadvantaged group in the United States, he may decide to discard formality in favor of an easygoing manner. Gifts often carry a meaning of warmth and generosity. When the consultant offers books, journals, or reprints at the beginning, he not only fulfills custom but also meets a vital need of isolated facilities to have current literature in the English language.

It is very important that the consultant meet the mental health staff with an open, friendly attitude. He interacts by welcoming questions as well as asking them. If he can share his own feelings, thoughts, and experiences freely, he will open the door for confidences from others at a later time. But if such openness is uncomfortable for him, he would be wiser to hold back rather than to fall into the disadvantage of a defensive position. He is on safe ground when he talks about his own life interests, or the recreation or art that interest him in the new community; he will find kindred spirits to pursue these interests with him.

As work begins, an impressive nonverbal way of demonstrating involvement is to faithfully give every 8-hour day of the week to the task. With such concentrated attention, however, the staff is usually fearful of judgments or unfavorable comparisons, even more than the usual facility would be when under inspection. The consultant therefore verbalizes his positive responses and praises the favorable aspects of the program. For example, the hospitals in Teheran afforded abundant kindness and affection to patients without the artificial effort that we in the traditional hospitals almost have to enforce when we want to establish a favorable milieu. As this quality may well be essential to the patients' recovery, it is natural and sincere to express strong admiration. If he can honestly do so, the consultant also actively expresses acceptance of striking differences in culture (for example, belief in magic) and how they can affect approach toward treatment.

In order to gain an understanding of the staff's orientation and methods of psychiatric treatment, keen observation is required at the beginning. Visits to other facilities in the community and to mental health training centers place the methods in perspective. The consultant asks himself how the crisis model can supplement the services that are already in operation. He plans a tentative strategy based on his observations without denying his intuition about what will work. His strategy relates to both expressed and self-evident needs, to the level of local knowledge, and to the interfaces of the culture that can accept new concepts.

Phase III: Action

Now the consultant is ready to engage in the third phase of his work. He avails himself of opportunities for spontaneous case discussion during ward rounds, in staff meetings, and after observation of interviews. He plans talks that present the background and the specific methodology of crisis intervention. Increasingly, staff members will invite small group discussions relating to particular questions or problems. The consultant becomes more assertive in these activities. As he speaks, he consciously attempts to convey his thoughts slowly, clearly, and definitely. He tries to use simple language because the newness of the concepts creates enough complication in itself. Definitions of terms may assume an unexpected challenge when they have been reassessed within the context of the culture. (Even the word *crisis* was sharply questioned in Iran.) Clear definitions and repetition of major points are further aids to communication. When an interpreter is necessary, additional discussions involve him in the subject and hopefully lead him to become enthusiastic. Visual aids, even of the simplest kind, are positive reinforcers of the model that can reach through the language barrier. Diagrams, role playing, and demonstrations enhance learning. Cases from practice at home and from the immediate environment illustrate the universality of the approach.

Trust grows slowly, and feedback usually is delayed. One must be prepared to sustain tension and discouragement during much of the involvement in the consultative process.

CONSULTATION IN IRAN

Phase I: Prior Learning

The invitation to consult in Teheran was offered to the writer by a professor of psychiatry who recently retired as director of psychiatric services of Roozbeh Psychiatric Hospital. Extensive reading during 6 months' preparation provided background knowledge of the Iranian culture. In addition to sociologic studies, novels helped to create a picture of the day-to-day life of the people.

Phase II: Location Learning

Strategy must be closely related to the mental health setting in which consultation takes place. Under the sponsorship of the medical school of the University of Teheran, Iran, the Roozbeh Psychiatric Hospital operates as an emergency center with limited volume and duration of inpatient admissions and with active outpatient clinics.

Not only is the hospital established on a medical model, closely related to the medical school and with doctors having the highest status, but it also reflects the basic structure of Iranian society in that it favors a heirarchical, authoritarian organization. Without clear cut lines of authority and carefully defined status, Persian people would feel disconcerted. To this consultant, the mental health staff of Roozbeh Hospital appeared unlike both the majority of the Iranian people and the incoming patients. They are members of the élite, highly trained in their professions; they move in intellectual circles, and live in a more sophisticated mode than most professional Americans. While they dedicate themselves to service and teaching, they may find human relations with their underpriviliged and uneducated clients somewhat perplexing. This is exactly the kind of gap that the crisis model can bridge.

Strategy.   Consultation strategy, therefore, had to take into account the medical model, a strict hierarchy, the pride of status, and the training objectives of the hospital. A variety of problems in communication could be anticipated also; staff members adhered to different theories from diverse sources of training outside of Iran, and experienced distance from their own uneducated people.

Another factor requiring careful thought was the attitudes of the patients who were to receive the mental health services. They were for the most part people who feared the stigma of the hospital and whose pride led them to prefer visible physical symptoms to weaknesses of an emotional kind (90). Awed and frightened by the unusual attention, women covered their faces and waited for their husbands to speak for them. Men resorted to the pattern of their everyday experiences where safety lay in secrecy and silence. When patients were free enough or disturbed enough to talk, their stories were filled with genies and evil spirits. Out of long training anger was restrained, allowing only sadness to escape.

Phase III: Action

Active consultation gained momentum when I presented my first "lecture" to the total staff. I modified my description of crisis intervention for the purpose of gaining acceptance in this particular environment. (It might have surprised colleagues in the United States.)

The crisis model, accordingly, was presented as a therapeutic approach that was a practical combination of concepts already known, but reassembled to construct an efficient and speedy method of treatment. There was to be no attempt to alter personality patterns, and individual history was to be explored only when past events applied to the current disability. This method was most valuable *a*) for patients who had suffered an environmental life stress, and *b*) when used very soon after the event. It could also apply, however, at a later date, and even with patients who evidenced endogenous illness.

Defining "Crisis."   Questions about the word "crisis" were answered by simply defining it as a disturbance in the usual life balance of an individual. A further explanation was that the word refers to an emergency—usually a sudden and confusing one—and also serves to differentiate between external stress and a more complicated disturbance within the personality. A crisis occurs when a loss threatens the individual's usual means of maintaining psychological balance and self-respect, or when a loss results in severe conflict about choices of alternative actions. The therapist's major question about the crisis is why the patient is immobilized by this particular loss when he has surmounted many other stresses, disappointments, and problems throughout his life span. Consideration of three factors is likely to supply the answer: *a*) if a life role essential to the person is, or may be, destroyed; *b*) when a series of losses has depleted the person's emotional reserves, and *c*) when the reaction is doubled because it is the repetition of a similar loss in earlier life that was never mastered. A diagram (Figure 17.1) can be used to represent an individual's life balance, marked by events and losses, until it reaches the crisis where a disruption breaks the line. From that point of crisis, dotted lines portray the possible outcome at a higher level of functioning, a far lower level, or a resumption of the previous adjustment.

LIFE BALANCE

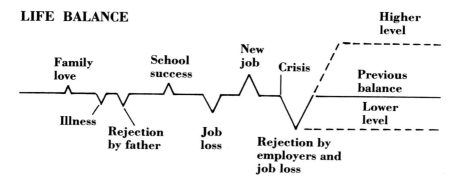

FIGURE 17.1 A diagram of critical events affecting a person's life balance.

Intervention Steps. After a crisis affecting life balance, five steps in crisis intervention can be carried out:

1. Pinpoint the life event or stress.
2. Find out its meaning. How is it a loss? Why can't the person recover?
3. Explain to the patient the connection between the event and its meaning, and delineate the reasons he cannot manage it.
4. Work with the patient to find useful ways to manage.
5. Encourage and support his new efforts and plans.

CASE REPORT 1

This example of a crisis situation contains universal elements related to aging, loneliness, and family conflict. The patient was a hospital nurse. When she encountered what she felt was an unfair attitude by the administration in relation to her position, she lost her job by reverting to the childhood hostility she had felt toward the rejection by her father, who had favored her identical twin. When the elements of her crisis became clear to her, she experienced relief from anxiety and was able to find new ways to adapt to her profession. A startling question arose during staff discussion of the case: "How is it that you seek insight in a first interview?" It was explained that comparable experiences from the past move easily into the memory at a time of high anxiety or crisis confusion. They can then be viewed rationally rather than emotionally and used to help solve the current dilemma.

CASE REPORT 2

An Iranian patient, Sohila, had been disturbed for 5 days, using ugly language, bursting into anger, and complaining that djinns were forcing sexual advances on her at night. She had married at age 12 and had 7 children, all girls. Seven years previously she had succumbed temporarily to a postpartum psychosis after the birth of her fourth child. She had managed very well in the interim until this event, precipitated by criticism from her husband's sister at a time when, because of a physical illness, the patient had turned to her eldest daughter for help in the household.

With the current stress in mind, the crisis intervenor was able to inquire easily about circumstances 7 years ago. She learned that her mother had severely criticized Sohila about the care of her home and children. Sohila had been helpless to defend herself in any way other than to protest through confusion and collapse. At that time, and in this instance as well, her husband had appeared to agree with the criticism. We explained to the patient that she became upset because her role of mother and homemaker was sacred to her. She could not bear criticism by women she respected, especially if her husband seemed to be influenced by them. Next, in support of her woman's role, it was confirmed that she really was a fine mother and housekeeper. It was suggested to her that she ask her husband to stand by her, and that they should speak to his sister together. Sohila thought she could try. In this case, again, the patient felt more normal and found a direction leading toward pride and dignity.

CONSULTATION IN AN AMERICAN INDIAN HOSPITAL

Phase I: Prior Learning

Arrangements for consultation to the Navajo Indians were made by the psychiatrist who directs the mental health and inpatient services of the United States Public Health Service Hospital for the Navajo Indians in Gallup, New Mexico. In this case, the relative closeness of those on the reservation permitted more personal communications than are available when preparing for work in a distant country. Discussions, in addition to intensive reading (222, 416, 449), provided increased understanding of the *Dinéh*, the Chosen People, who, to a considerable extent, have retained their ancient social patterns in the face of twentieth century pressures.

Phase II: Location Learning

As one would expect, mental health services are a recent introduction to Navajo society. No Navajo psychiatrist existed at the time of this consultation. For Dinéh to compete and succeed in medical training would be contrary to their belief that a person should act modestly, never exceeding others in a way that would display pride and selfishness. Therefore, for this as well as other reasons, Navajo personnel are paraprofessionals, social workers, or nurses rather than psychiatrists. Traditionally, emotional disturbances have been treated at home by the medicine man, who was well versed in ancient rituals. Even now, when religious sings arranged by the family do not cure the patient, witchcraft is feared.

Ward 4 East, the psychiatric inpatient service of the Gallup Public Health Hospital for Indians, furthers the ideal of community-based care by protecting the Indian context—including native medicine—while it seeks to retain fully the Indian democratic spirit. As many as 50 patients live in the ward's accepting atmosphere, where others speak their language, and where they can retain close contact with home and relatives.

Psychotherapy of the usual one-to-one variety is not meted out to them; the standard psychotherapeutic interview is almost nonexistent. Rather, the patients talk with staff members and one another freely when they are ready and form supportive relationships as they choose. A patient often selects a role model from among the staff and turns to him most easily, yet concurrently discusses specific kinds of problems with others. Correspondingly, the staff talk readily and relate openly to the patients in their desire to be available as therapeutic influences. Not only are the staff free with one another in presenting suggestions about the goals and therapy for each patient, but they also welcome patients' ideas about how to help others.

The Author's Strategy: A Personal Account

In the setting of Ward 4 East, I considered factors that would affect the form consultation should take. During the prior learning phase I had focused sharply on clues that would facilitate communication. I knew that I must expect important conversations to be lengthy and indirect. If possible, I would use metaphors in preference to terms denoting emotional states for which the Navajo language has no words. Though I expected to have many interpreters, I would attempt to reach through the language barrier by understanding at least some of the natural folkways from which communication springs.

Effects of Cultural Differences on Staff.   I wanted to take into account the combination of people on the staff and more importantly their various roles. The most obvious differentiation lay between Indian and Anglo personnel. All were conscious of the difference and most were active in working through feelings about it by sustained open talk. At the same moment in the same conference, when both were communicating thoughts to one another to the best of their ability, blocks of which they often were unaware rose between them. The blocks consisted of inbuilt habits and style of speech. As a single example, the Anglo personnel spoke rapidly, loquaciously, and used more complicated verbiage; the Indians spoke simply and slowly, with long pauses for thought. As in any group, the active speakers appeared to dominate the more meditative members who waited and sought response from the others. In spite of every effort on the part of each group, the Navajo felt depreciated at times, while the others felt defensive or hurt.

Bringing the Program to the Community.   Beyond the hospital, Ward 4 East relates to the central mental health office in Window Rock, Arizona, capital of the Navajo nation, where staff attend meetings to participate in overall planning for the entire reservation. The ward personnel also carry responsibility in varying degrees for outposts of mental health care that are widely scattered and sometimes best reached by airplane. A network of communications must be sustained. In turn, this network relates to the development of a sound relationship to the Indian community outside the hospital. Patients and their families need reassurance about the strange Anglo form of treatment. Outreach aspects of the work are essential to its success.

After outstanding features of the setting had been observed and formulated in relation to strategy, the first rule of consultation became simply, "Always find out the Indian way." The rule emphasized not only my own desire but also the need and hope of the Anglo staff to become more adroit in learning from the Navajo their reactions and interpretations around each event as it took place.

Phase III: Action

The active phase of consultation came into being slowly, almost imperceptibly. It took time to absorb the diffuse therapeutic influence carried out through a democratic milieu, reflecting faith in people's capacity to decide and to grow.

A major portion of the two-way learning took place in the morning gatherings of staff with patients, sometimes held outdoors. This was experiential learning at its best. Crisis intervention methods were applied spontaneously when a patient was ready and was searching for such help.

In the afternoons when staff alone met, still informally, to review cases and discuss theory and problems, other aspects of consultation emerged. At times the staff wished to examine themselves in quest of truth, identity, and open communication. Sometimes they were overly critical of themselves and needed support. Reassurance was appropriate, too, when relations with the outlying facilities or community became confusing and arduous. Teaching of the crisis model fitted well into both case review and discussion of theory, the central themes of this conference.

I accompanied Navajo personnel to other hospital wards, to the central outpatient clinic, and to small distant clinics; at times we also visited homes.

The most formal talk I presented was at Window Rock, to representatives from many centers. As in Iran, I first described briefly the background and rationale for the crisis intervention model, but I defined "crisis" more simply as a shock to the usual life balance. I drew a similar diagram to illustrate the crisis view of a person's equilibrium in life. A hypothetical Navajo boy was used as the hero, and his story was traced through ordinary problems and frustration, identifying who helped him and how he coped, and finally specifying the crisis which had incapacitated him. It was briefly explained that first the helping person must analyze how the crisis is different from the patient's usual life and what special meaning the situation has for the patient, after which he can assist the patient in understanding what has happened.

The case of a Navajo patient whom we helped is illustrative of the process.

CASE REPORT 3

Lillian, a Navajo woman who had entered the medical emergency ward after an intentional overdose of drugs, was interviewed by both the consultant and the Navajo social worker to determine whether psychiatric hospitalization was required. Lillian's normally sweet, bright face was sad and tear-stained, but she had put on her silver brooch, bracelet, and necklace. She talked for a very long time about pains around her heart combined with trouble in breathing. She also said that although she felt eager to weave she had been much too tired. She had not been well enough to have sex relations for a long time. She confessed her husband had grown weary of hearing her complaints; he also feared that he might lose his job because she took up so much of his time. Recently, he indicated that he would leave her. During all this trouble, she said, "My family just sits there." The overdose occurred on Lillian's thirtieth birthday.

When she talked about her 4 children, she began to cry as she related that a 12-year-old daughter had died 2 years previously. Since then, Lillian had had a hysterectomy and the menopause had begun. All of her present pains had started then and had grown worse and worse. She had to begin taking pills. We asked her to tell us what had happened to lead her to swallow too many pills the previous night. After having shared her hurts and her sadness, she felt trustful and could reveal that 3 days before she had seen her husband with another woman, and this had made her sick to her stomach. No one seemed to notice or care. She tried to ignore the shock and forget the image of what she had seen. The trouble was that all her pains and memories had become so unbearable she only wanted to die and thus find peace.

Presentation to Personnel. In discussing this case before hospital staff and representatives from the point of view of crisis intervention, I wrote key words on a poster and pointed out the ingredients of the patient's story that fitted each step of the treatment process. As in Iran, my object was to simplify the terms for those not fluent in the English language. Table 17.1 shows the analysis of the case.

This lecture seemed to be sufficiently graphic to engage the interest of the audience. The positive responses might have been out of Navajo politeness, but later I felt assured that the ideas had been useful as I saw them applied. In the matrix of the Indian mental health setting, I believed that day-by-day interaction of personnel was of the first importance and would not have been surprised if a lecture had had little impact.

TABLE 17.1   Use of Crisis Intervention Technique With a Female Patient on Ward 4 East, Gallup Public Health Hospital for Indians

1. *The Latest Trouble*
   She saw her husband with another woman
   She then attempted suicide

2. *The Meaning to Her*
   Her husband might leave (fear of loss)
   She is hurt in her woman-role, as wife, mother, and weaver
   She recalls losses 2 years previously—this increases her fear and grief

3. *Explain It to Her*
   Make clear the reason for pain and sadness

4. *How Can She Cope?*
   She needs ways to rebuild her woman's role
   Possible ways are
   a) talking to her husband
   b) having sex relations again
   c) weaving
   d) taking care of her children

5. *Help Her Try New Ways*
   Gain husband's cooperation
   Praise the healthy efforts

SUMMARY

The crisis intervention model offers a useful therapeutic tool to mental health personnel in societies different from our own and resistant to outside influences. As an immediate short-term method, it fits especially well with emergency mental health services. These services are often a priority in developing communities in the United States or elsewhere.

The crisis approach applies universally because it can be explained simply and lends itself readily to modifications that relate it to other cultural systems and mental health settings. It provides definite guidelines to workers at various levels in training. For these reasons, consultation can result in assimilation of the crisis concept into an existing structure.

The consultant is unpretentious in his approach. He is ready to learn as well as teach, and he knows that he must create a positive atmosphere in order to be effective. He proceeds through three distinct phases: 1) *Prior learning*, involving preparation through study of the literature and personal contacts in relation to the cultural background. 2) *Location learning*, characterized by *a*) sensitive, on-the-spot *observation* of the functioning of the society and the staff, and *b*) *adjustment* of the consultant's style and plans within a strategy designed to fit into existing culture, practices, and staff preferences to supplement the services. Too often the transfer of technical material from one location to another fails because it is not relevant for the receivers. 3) *Action*, which means involvement in active teaching that follows the plan and uses every available opportunity.

The writer's experience in two diverse societies, illustrating the phases of consultation in detail, serves to describe factors that must be taken into account in relation to plans and presentation anywhere.

In Iran, the situation was authoritarian, and the medical model reigned. Patients there were subjects of medical treatment that provided kind and expert care. In an American Indian hospital, the organization was informal, the procedures democratic, and the staff largely paraprofessional. Patients were highly respected as people and given as much opportunity for self-direction as could be arranged. In both settings, and presumably in many others, the fundamentals of crisis intervention could provide a viable addition to established mental health practices.

18

ALCOHOLIC CRISES
IN THE EMERGENCY ROOM

Willem G. A. Bosma

Personnel who do emergency medical work are in a position to be at the forefront of a nationwide effort to bring under control our second largest medical problem, the disease of alcoholism (456). Emergency care affords an opportunity to reach two discrete populations of alcoholics—those who are beginning to have problems and those who are established alcoholics.

ALCOHOLISM—A DISEASE

Traditionally, the medical profession has tried to ignore the existence of alcoholism, which has the distinction of being the only malady to be *officially* declared a disease by professional medical organizations (199). This step was taken to counteract the negative attitude of medical care personnel. In 1956 the American Medical Association first declared alcoholism a disease, and more recently the Board of Regents of the American College of Physicians published a similar statement. Their statement itself indicates the lack of interest among physicians toward the diagnosis and treatment of alcoholism, the fourth most common cause of adult deaths in the country.

Attitudes Toward Alcoholism

In the emergency room, a great number of alcoholic patients have their first encounter with a treatment facility. This is their first exposure to experts who can diagnose their disease and direct them to appropriate treatment facilities. Thus, the emergency transport system, the treatment facility itself, and, above all, the emergency personnel, are extremely important to the alcoholic (307). Knowledgeable emergency room personnel with a positive attitude towards diagnosing and treating the alcoholic can mean his entry into a helping system. However, merely treating the patient's medical problems without recognizing his underlying alcoholism dooms the individual to returning many times for alcohol-related medical problems.

Alcoholism is a complex disease. If one sees it only as a physical–medical problem causing body injuries, e.g., liver disease and the complications of withdrawal, one's perspective is limited to a great degree. There are many diseases that are associated with alcoholism. However, if the alcoholism is not arrested, these related diseases will occur much more frequently than in other population groups. Straus discusses the *clustering phenomenon* in alcoholics, which means that the alcoholic is hospitalized three times more frequently than the nonalcoholic (394). In general hospitals about 30% of the adult patients have a drinking problem (199). This figure supports Straus' estimate, since approximately 9%–10% of all adults have a drinking problem.

Most emergency room personnel seem to consider the alcoholic an impossible nuisance. At best, their attitude can be described as negative. At worst it can be characterized as negligent. We encountered these same attitudes in setting up a comprehensive treatment program for alcoholics at the University of Maryland Hospital.

Role of the Alcoholism Counselor

An important aspect of that program involved placing alcoholism counselors in the emergency department from 7:00 AM to 11:00 PM daily. This schedule was instituted because alcoholics returned again and again to be treated only for their immediate medical needs. It was reasoned that such counseling support would help resolve the revolving door phenomenon.

These patients would have access to people particularly interested in their disease who, at the same time, would educate the emergency treatment professional staff. Too frequently during their education physicians and nurses have been given little or no preparation for diagnosing or treating alcoholics.

Problems In The Program

As soon as the alcoholism counselors started working in the emergency room, certain unforeseen problems arose. Emergency Department personnel tended to refer the alcoholic from the reception desk to the willing and eager counselor *without* making a medical evaluation first. If the counselor recognized medical complications and brought them to the attention of the physician in charge, the latter reacted with hostility. Before long, the counselors, of whom about 50% were themselves sober alcoholics, were overwhelmed by the hostility of the emergency room personnel—a hostility they were frequently neither able to cope with nor change. This resulted in increasing isolation of the counselor from the rest of the staff.

At present, we are reevaluating these services in the hope that we can discuss attitudes and their influence on the performance of medical duties towards patients with this chronic disease of alcoholism.

Effects of Attitudes on Diagnosis

What can be done to change these negative attitudes which so many of the helping professions have toward alcoholism? Lisansky points out in his perceptive article that "learning what there is to know about the disease" is only part of the defense against this negativism (262). The physician must learn something about the *alcoholic*. Only then will this field of intellectual and emotional understanding and acceptance enlarge, and only then will he be able to effectively implement what he "learns about this disease."

Too often the physician has hidden behind his professionalism in treating the alcoholic because he does not want to recognize the sociologic and psychological aspects of alcoholism. He is troubled by the attitudes of a society that sees the alcoholic as a moral degenerate, a will-less person. *In casu*, the physician denies problems with alcohol and treats the alcoholic for his direct physical problem, be it a broken leg, acute pancreatitis, a stomach ulcer, or upper respiratory infections. He avoids the underlying diagnosis and recognition, and in many cases codes the patient's records without mentioning the causative factor, namely alcoholism. In most cases, this is caused by the life experience of the physician himself, the imprinted attitudes that he has received from society, of which he is an exponent, plus his own personal and family experiences with alcohol. His own prejudices and his own alcohol consumption bias his opinion of other people's use of alcohol.

Chafetz (262), surveyed the treatment of alcoholics in the Massachusetts General Hospital emergency room, and he found that if the alcoholic came from the same socioeconomic background as the physician, if he appeared in a business suit with shirt and tie, if he had a similar standing in society as the physician, then he was unlikely to be diagnosed as an alcoholic. On the other hand, if the person who came into the emergency room was obviously from a lower socioeconomic background, if he was sloppily dressed and ill-kempt, if it was difficult for the physician to establish rapport, then the chance of this person's being diagnosed as an alcoholic was much higher. In our emergency room, the poor, unkempt, black person is sometimes incorrectly diagnosed as an alcoholic; and even though he might not have any problems with alcohol, he may be referred to a treatment modality for alcoholism.

Lisansky attempts to correlate the patient's physical status and the attitude of the physician toward him (Table 18.1).

TABLE 18.1   The Physician's Concept of a Patient Presenting With Alcoholism as a Possible Diagnosis*

Patient's status	
Alcoholism (without cirrhosis)	Alcoholism (with cirrhosis)
Physician's concept of patient *An emotional disorder (psychopathology), the sick role not sanctioned*	Physician's concept of patient *A medical–surgical disorder (pathophysiology), the sick role sanctioned*
Physician's reaction *Hostile, rejection of patient*	Physician's reaction *Acceptance, care for the patient*

* Lisansky ET: The avoided diagnosis—alcoholism. Bull Am Coll Physicians, March 1974

TREATING THE ALCOHOLIC

Clues to Recognizing the Potential Alcoholic

The alcoholic patient's lifestyle, as well as related syndromes, can reveal a great deal to the health care professional. Major points in making an assessment are given in Table 18.2.

In taking case histories, it is important to learn to listen with "the third ear." Frequently, a word or phrase can give a clue as to a hidden drinking problem. For instance, beware of the patient who says, "Who me? Drink too much? I can take it or leave it." A nonalcoholic rarely thinks about whether he can take it or leave it.

Emergency Treatment

The following symptoms call for definitive and immediate medical treatment.

1. Acute psychosis with or without hallucinations
2. Cardiac arrhythmias—even a few extra systoles
3. Extreme agitation
4. Tachycardia of 120 beats/min or over
5. Temperature of 101°F or over

Alcoholic patients who come into the emergency room with other problems such as panic or anxiety, upper respiratory infections, or appendicitis, may have withdrawal symptoms shortly after their admission.

Recognizing Withdrawal Symptoms

It is vitally important to recognize these symptoms during this period of withdrawal. Early care and appropriate medication can prevent the more severe stages of withdrawal, which account for 5% to 30% of alcoholic deaths.

TABLE 18.2 Clues to Possible Alcoholism

From life history
1. Alcoholism in the family, especially a parent
2. Living alone—divorce, separation
3. Job absenteeism or frequent job changes

From medical history
1. Frequent hospitalizations; accidents; tuberculosis
2. Pancreatitis, gastritis, peptic ulcers, gastrectomy
3. Frequent upper respiratory infections
4. Impotency
5. Transient and repeated episodes of amnesia, blackouts, or seizures
6. Amenorrhea in the female
7. Recurrent periodontal disease
8. Episodes of atopic dermatitis
9. Depression

Physical findings
1. Many scars, tattoos
2. Looks older than actual age
3. Telangiectasis and liver palms
4. Frequent instances of unexplained bruises (frequently lower extremities, especially women)
5. Enlarged liver, tenderness in the abdomen
6. Posttraumatic shock or infection and fever; may cause hypoglycemic episode (liver disease)
7. Red beefy tongue, cheilosis
8. "Blurry-eyed," edema of lids and face, blood-shot eyes
9. Unexplained multiple rib fractures
10. Any form of liver or pancreatic disease

The extent of the alcohol withdrawal syndrome is dependent on the amount of alcohol intake and attendant tolerance, the length of drinking prior to the examination, and the patient's physical condition. The various syndromes are easily recognized, but their severity is often underestimated and treated incorrectly. The severity of withdrawal is dependent on the duration of intake, the amount of alcohol ingested, the abruptness of cessation, and individual susceptibility.

Etiology of the withdrawal syndrome is unclear, but it is thought by most investigators to truly represent withdrawal from alcohol. The condition may even develop while the alcoholic is drinking if the blood–alcohol level is decreasing, as in "tapering off," or it may occur after complete cessation of alcohol intake.

Alcohol withdrawal effects may be separated into several syndromes which simply reflect degrees of severity.

1. *Uneasiness.* This symptom is not of itself a criterion of alcoholism, but in conjunction with certain aspects of the history and of the patient's

general appearance, it should lead to a suspicion of alcoholism and further inquiry.

2. The *tremulous stage*. "The fidgets" is the mildest form of withdrawal. The most common signs and symptoms are tremors, insomnia, anorexia, anxiety, depression, nausea, vomiting, flushed facies, injected conjunctive tachycardia, and agitation. This state often subsides in several days with abstinence, with another drink, or with mild sedation; or it may progress to delirium tremens.

3. The *acute hallucinosis stage*. This usually includes the signs and symptoms of the tremulous stage; but in addition, visual, auditory, or tactile, hallucinations are present. Characteristically, the hallucinations are threatening and unpleasant. Usually they are transitory, as in the tremulous stage, but occasionally they may last for several months. Chronic hallucinosis in the alcoholic may appear schizophrenia-like, but frequently, the advanced age at onset makes this diagnosis doubtful.

4. *Delirium tremens*. This is a medical emergency requiring immediate hospitalization and treatment. The mortality rate ranges from 5% to 30%, with death resulting from peripheral vascular collapse, cardiac arrythmias, hyperthermia, associated infection, or head trauma. Delirium tremens should not be diagnosed unless there is evidence of the tremulous stage, hallucinations, disorientation (at least intermittent), and delirium. Autonomic activity is extreme, with frequent fever, profuse perspiration, tachycardia, tachypnea, and severe agitation. Convulsions (rum fits) are not uncommon in patients without previous history of convulsive disorder. They only occur within 3 days after total withdrawal from alcohol. If this fact were recognized, fewer patients would be taking Dilantin and Phenobarbital without real medical indication.

The patient may present himself at the Emergency Department in any of the aforementioned stages. Alcohol withdrawal extends over the 10 days following the cessation of drinking. The most severe symptoms occur on the second and third day. If the patient is properly medicated within the first 48 hours, only the first stage or perhaps a partial second stage at most, would be seen: the third or fourth stages would not be reached. The amount of medication can be decreased rapidly without severe withdrawal symptoms.

Variables Influencing Medication

The appropriate amount of medication needed for prevention of severe withdrawal symptoms depends on several questions.

1. Are there severe medical complications, especially central nervous system damage resulting in impaired consciousness?

2. Is extensive supervision for medical care needed other than for his withdrawal?
3. Can we keep the patient basically responsible for himself?

Treating a patient with the withdrawal syndrome to maintain consciousness requires that the patient be under continuous supervision. He needs medication that has a short serum half-life. Although paraldehyde has the shortest half-life (90 minutes), it is not a preferred drug in the treatment of alcoholism. Paraldehyde is more addictive than alcohol itself and, although it does take care of the withdrawal syndrome, withdrawal from it thereafter is often just as severe. Paraldehyde has to be given very regularly because of its short half-life, thus creating the need for intensive nursing care. As a result, paraldehyde is indicated on very few occasions. Hydroxazine (Vistrail) and Diazepam (Valium) which have a half-life of 12–14 hours are more useful. Chlordiazepoxide which has a half-life of 30 hours is the drug of choice if the patient is being treated on an ambulatory basis. Of the group of patients who come with alcoholism to the emergency room at the University of Maryland Hospital, about 1 out of 12 have convulsions. Rarely is it the first time they have had convulsions connected with withdrawal. If a careful history is taken, the patient will explain that he has had them before when he has tried to stop his drinking. If we suspect convulsions might develop or the patient has had convulsions before, we treat the patient with Valium and Dilantin, usually for about 5 days.

Although the treatment of the withdrawal syndrome is relatively easy, sufficient medication must be given. Many physicians believe that the doses they give to their patients with neurotic or other mental disorders are adequate for alcoholics who have withdrawal. This is not so. Not only does alcohol cause cross-tolerance for these drugs, the withdrawal syndrome itself can only be controlled by unusually large doses. The accepted treatment in the more severe withdrawal syndrome is intramuscular Vistaril or Librium, 100 mg, or Valium, 20–30 mg, to be repeated every hour until the patient is slightly drowsy and calm. It is quite common for the patient to require 300–800 mg Librium in the first 24 hours. Fortunately, one need not worry about withdrawal from these high doses of medication. At University of Maryland Hospital this medication is given in the emergency room where the patient stays for approximately 6 to 24 hours. Then he is sent to a secondary detoxification center where he is placed on 25 mg Librium po, qid, for another 5 days.

Specific Guidelines

During the acute stage of detoxification, the patient is extremely sensitive to sensory stimuli. Any sound is amplified many times. Because of the noise in an emergency room, it is easier to provide a regular sound level, for instance by letting a radio play. Lights may also be very upsetting; as a result, the light intensity and the noise level have to be kept low and comfortable. All lights should be on because frequently shadows in the room make the patient anxious.

Intravenous procedures should also be avoided as much as possible since they make the patient afraid and anxious. The patient should not be tied down, as this greatly increases his fears. A mattress on the floor prevents his hurting himself by falling out of bed.

During the withdrawal stage the alcoholic may be dehydrated but more often he has retained excess water and salt. Intravenous solutions are more frequently contraindicated than indicated. Another concern of many physicians is electrolyte imbalance; however, imbalance requiring correction is rare. Only when there is a rhythm disorder of the heart is it prudent to investigate further and initiate corrective measures as indicated.

Needless to say, the alcoholic, frequently still anesthetized by alcohol and in distress from withdrawal, is not the best patient to give an adequate history or pinpoint physical distress to the examining physician. Therefore, a thorough physical examination is indicated in the majority of cases.

At this point, the physician should not forget that a part of treatment is to confront the patient with the cause of his distress *and to refer him to a treatment modality for alcoholics!* This is necessary not only for the patient with a primary diagnosis of alcoholism, but also for the patient with a secondary diagnosis or one suspected of developing an alcoholism problem. This may take a little time from the extremely busy schedule of the emergency room, but it is time well spent.

A word of caution is necessary. The words "alcoholism" and "alcoholic" still have strong moral connotations. They carry with them a stigma which the patient and his family often feel most acutely. This is particularly true if the patient is a woman. Any such problem will be vehemently denied, and infinite tact and finesse are required to get the facts straight. Thus, use of the words "alcoholic" and "alcoholism" are often sufficient to end all further discussion and therefore should be avoided. It is advisable to talk in terms of drinking problems, or a problem with drinking.

MAKING THE REFERRAL

The helping person must have the same empathy for the alcoholic that he would have for any suffering person; furthermore, he should show it. A very matter-of-fact tone is helpful, along with the assurance that alcoholism is a disease that can be helped. The entire discussion should be carried on in the same context as if a purely physical disease were being explained.

The alcoholic is accustomed to being rebuffed and treated with hostility. He is frequently filled with guilt and feelings of worthlessness. These cause him to vehemently deny his problem and at the same time become defensive. This is usually perceived as hostility. Thus, anyone who would be

III

Disaster Aid Phenomena
and
Mental Health Emergencies

New information about disasters may emerge from hypothesis testing in the scientific model, systematic individual case studies in the patient care model, or day-by-day experience in the real world model. Drawing on all three approaches, Siporin's chapter on altruism and disaster affords a broad perspective for viewing the later chapters in this section. Also comprehensive in scope, Horowitz's contribution offers an impressive conceptualization, at once insightful in theoretical terms and practical in assisting clinicians to develop phase-specific intervention strategies.

Many of the authors of the chapters in this section grapple with complex and elusive cause-and-effect relationships.

Do natural disasters "cause" or precipitate mental health emergencies and/or serious posttrauma aftereffects? If so, what stress magnitude (e.g., in terms of loss of life and property) is required for a disaster to induce such effects? If there are such mental health sequelae, do they affect a significant number of disaster victims? And what proportion of the population-at-risk would be considered "significant"?

The literature on natural disasters (as contrasted to man-made) has been devoid of practical well conceived studies based on long-term follow-up to delineate psychological morbidity. Zusman reminds us of the epidemiologic perspective and the need for total population studies, using predisaster mental health baseline measures. Until Hurricane Agnes descended on the East Coast in June 1972, clinicians who were called on to work in natural disasters could draw on relatively limited observations. A few long-term follow-up studies of the effects of man-made disasters on people did exist—relating, for example, to concentration camps, military combat, or atomic bomb victims. Of course, man-made disasters may awaken more social conscience (guilt?) and more available funds to carry out such studies, and survivors may offer a clearly circumscribed accessible population. In actuality, formalized mental health intervention *did not exist in any of the training or operational programs of the key caregivers in disasters, including the Office of Emergency Preparedness in the White House, the military disaster response system in the Department of Defense, or the American Red Cross.*

Thanks to Hartsough's initiative, we have assembled a list of the services more or less available to the bewildered survivor in the "disaster shopping center" that may be immediately set up on site. What is missing, of course, from any such inventory is the sense of frustration, humiliation, and uprooted territoriality that virtually all survivors experience.

The contribution by the Codirectors of the Disaster Research Center at Ohio State University, Dynes and Quarantelli, represents their first detailed consideration of the emotional effects of disasters on the individual. It is invaluable because of the wealth of data drawn from their long experience with more disasters than any other researchers in this country. Their chapter indicates that individuals in disaster situations exhibit more adaptive than maladaptive behavior. However, the authors' limit their observations to the aftermath of natural agents, and their focus is on the family and community as mediating structures, without systematic detailed psychiatric histories of individuals.

Although many of the chapters relate primarily to two disasters— Hurricane Agnes' effect on northeastern Pennsylvania (Zusman, McGee and Heffron) and southeastern New York state (Kliman), and the slag dam breakdowns in the Buffalo Creek Valley of West Virginia (Harshbarger, Lifton and Olson, Titchener, Kapp and Winget)—the issues they consider and the clinical syndromes they report are the first in-depth and long-term follow-up analyses of the mental health of natural disaster survivors. Harshbarger approaches the Buffalo Creek disaster from a multidimensional ecologic perspective. His model for all disaster first aid planning proposes to relate at-risk groups to coping processes and various social organizations that facilitate healthy adaptation. Lifton's classic work on Hiroshima, delineating the survivor syndrome and its core concept of the death imprint, is unforgettably etched in the clinical histories he and his associate, Olson, report in a series of visits to Buffalo Creek. With the same population, Titchener and his colleagues from the Department of Psychiatry at the University of Cincinnati, report follow-up data based on structured, yet sensitive clinical interviews and testing of 625 Buffalo Creek residents, including 250 children. This inquiry evolved from a legal suit that claimed mental health damages against the coal company which the victims held responsible. There was an out-of-court settlement resulting in approximately

$10,000 per survivor, thus avoiding the question of legal and moral responsibility as well as the adjudication of definitive responsibility for the emotional sequelae of such disaster events.

The Wilkes-Barre program developed in a relatively organized way. The National Institutes of Mental Health, after an on-the-scene report by its Mental Health Emergencies Section, funded a comprehensive study of "natural" or community based paraprofessional crisis intervenors. The project brought together diverse but complementary groups in instant fashion. An experienced group of crisis intervention trainers, headed by McGee, was asked to adapt techniques derived from hot-line and suicide prevention programs to postdisaster phenomena. Although they often faced complex bureaucratic and other political problems, they set up crash training programs for community workers who were organized into an outreach effort coordinated by Heffron and his associates. Subsequently, the project was evaluated by Zusman's community psychiatry group from Buffalo. Their mutual endeavor, although handicapped by the suddenness of their association, produced much information about therapeutic interventions for the local residents that later would become useful for other communities in distress. Simultaneously, in Corning, N.Y., Kliman was developing a comprehensive local support system based on exemplary community organization.

At the time a midwest tornado demolished Xenia, Ohio, and Monticello, Indiana, there existed a body of crisis intervention experience that immediately was made available to Hartsough, Zarle, and Ottinger at Purdue University, and they were able to intervene both rapidly and effectively in Monticello. Cohen's unique experience in Managua, Nicaragua, following the earthquake there, afforded an opportunity to apply knowledge gathered in the United States in a crosscultural context. Her paper is a clear exposition of the effects of good community organization and on-site professional education in a country where adequate mental health services were not readily available. Perhaps this is a common finding—disasters do not usually strike in localities where there is a plethora of mental health service available. Furthermore, when this does happen, the professionals involved have rarely been exposed in their training or experience to the clinical problems that occur. From a mental health standpoint, disaster aid preparedness is still shockingly underdeveloped.*

Emotional first aid in urban disasters can be marshalled under a variety of circumstances. Baren reports a clinical response to the aftermath of an airplane crash into a Sacramento ice cream parlor, and Krim details disaster

---

* *Fortunately, an NIMH Contract (NIMH-SM-75-0018), recently awarded to Dr. Norman Farberow and his colleagues at the Los Angeles Suicide Prevention Center, is supporting the development of a model program to train indigenous professional and paraprofessional personnel to be available for crisis intervention as part of a mental health support system, before as well as when disaster occurs.*

aid services for the victims of large fires in New York City. Their chapters represent impressive attempts to mount effective clinical programs under extraordinarily difficult conditions. Documenting the traumatic difficulties experienced by children in disaster situations, they both point out that family and social support systems are the prime vehicles for coping.

The theme pervading the chapters in this section—whether overtly or covertly expressed—is that psychological first aid is exhausting work. One can never forget the mental health of the intervenors, and that ongoing group meetings to share the burdens of stress, scheduled relief periods, and strong adaptable leaders are all necessary to make such efforts successful. These chapters on disaster phenomena are the products of flexible, imaginative, and courageous mental health professionals; their successful efforts rest in the hearts of those who taught them through their pain and suffering.

19

ALTRUISM, DISASTER, AND CRISIS INTERVENTION

Max Siporin

In the current state of crisis on the mental health scene, we appear to be turning toward new directions and tasks to serve people in need more effectively. We are being asked to do so with far fewer resources than have been available to us in the past. This applies particularly to the delivery systems and practices of crisis intervention, to which there has been a major commitment, as a basic helping method, in the rapidly expanding system of community mental health centers and in the social welfare agencies.

For a time, and for some of us, crisis intervention represented a symbolic crusade, encompassing certain welfare ideals in relation to community care of the mentally ill. By using its theoretical rationale and helping principles, much has been accomplished in changing the climate of public opinion about mental illness, in beginning to empty out the huge, isolated mental hospitals, in developing new structures of comprehensive community care, and in relating treatment orientations to the context of social living within natural human communities. But there has been public criticism of certain practices of mental health professionals. A number of grandiose plans for preventive care have not been implemented. One senses now, on the part of helping professionals, many feelings of self-questioning, frustration, and uncertainty.

This state of affairs comes at a time when our help is needed more urgently than ever. In recent years, for example, there has been a plethora of natural disasters—floods, earthquakes, hurricanes, and tornadoes. Spring floods of the Mississippi and other rivers constituted one of the greatest disasters in our national history, creating billions of dollars worth of damage and loss and affecting millions of people. Mental health workers have been and continue to be involved in helping people who are disaster victims—individuals, family groups, and the general population—to cope with the effects of adversity.

We explore here the subject of altruism as it relates to crisis intervention and disaster aid. Crisis intervention theory is examined to clarify the role of altruism as a needed value and ingredient in our helping systems. The role of altruism in the helping processes and among helping professionals is considered, particularly in relation to the negative views of social work students about their own altruism. Several tasks are identified for us in maximizing altruism as a norm and value in our society, and in the development of new service systems emphasizing natural, informal, altruistic helping and self-help networks of mutual aid.

CRISIS INTERVENTION

During the 1960s, crisis intervention theory had a rapid and widespread development and acceptance in the mental health field as well as in social welfare agencies generally. Certain features of crisis intervention (63, 309, 338) provided a needed and convincing rationale and a set of operating procedures for the brief service efforts that were all that was available from helping professionals in short supply.

The focus on the precipitating stressful event, the current reality, and their meanings to the client; the deemphasis on pathology and the use of ego psychology in building on personality and family strengths; the emphasis on social functioning improvement, to be achieved within limited goals and treatment time; the quick intensive aid for crisis-phased tasks; the accessibility and availability of material resources; the environmental stress-reduction and change; the active, direct advice giving and educational approaches—all these features were attractive as a theoretical framework for practice theory. Crisis intervention helped get us out of the bind of traditional psychoanalytically oriented procedures, enabled us to move toward a more sociocultural orientation, particularly in work with the poor, and spurred development of indigenous workers and paraprofessionals. Pragmatically, crisis intervention has worked, as the effectiveness of its results demonstrate (236, 348).

Application to Individuals and Families

In more recent years, the emotional crises of individuals have been included as part of a wider concern with the social crisis situations of families, groups, and communities (65, 202, 340, 396). Some effort was made to develop the cognitive theoretical aspects of crisis intervention (401). But major work has gone into the move to use group, milieu, social network, and ecologic approaches, and to encompass as well the modification of social institutional structures in educational, legal, health, and social welfare systems. The present concern is to provide social support systems, the social services and caregivers needed by individuals and families to negotiate life-cycle tasks and life-cycle-stage transitions (64). An important extension of crisis intervention theory has been in work with normal as well as clinically disturbed populations, to aid people to cope with community conflicts, with such normal crises as school entrance or widowhood, and with the effects of natural disasters.

In the course of these developments, some limitations and difficulties in crisis intervention theory and practice have also emerged. Many individuals and families appear to be involved in chronic crisis situations, to need more than the time-limited treatment of crisis therapy. For example, in the Denver crisis intervention project (125), it was found that 50% of the patients required long-term treatment, and therefore required referral to long-term treatment agencies. The thrust to use social action activities to provide and increase the supply of needed resources has raised questions about the appropriateness and effectiveness of such activities. The free-floating nature of crisis therapy has proved too unstructured and uncontrolled for certain clients as well as agencies to accept. One result has been a growing predilection for "planned short-term treatment" as a treatment modality, in which a contract for specific services and goals could be established and implemented. Within social work practice, as the Parads (311, 312) have pointed out, crisis intervention now takes its place as one aspect of a lengthy tradition of short-term casework treatment.

The Clinical Model of Crisis Intervention

A larger set of difficulties relates to the clinical model of crisis intervention. Problems are still defined and located as internal to the individual or family who are sufferers and subject to unusual emotional distress. In recent extensions of crisis intervention, from work with the mentally ill to work with disaster victims, therapeutic teams have reached out to help victims, especially traumatized children, to recover from the shock reactions of earthquakes, hurricanes, and floods (40). In conscious and well-intentioned efforts to provide needed social supports and a "therapeutic community," members of helping teams, including volunteers, are encouraged to become "therapists," in order to aid the sufferers and victims. Mothers and fathers are helped to assume role obligations and role identities as therapeutic helpers, rather than as parents. Also, the team therapists, including the indigenous workers, are paid for their services. The quality of help given takes on a therapist-to-patient relationship rather than the normal relationship among friends, neighbors, and fellow-citizens. It has been suggested that this aspect, as part of the increasing professionalization and bureaucratization of the American Red Cross, (see Chapter 26 for a positive view of the American Red Cross) has led to reactive resentment by victims they have helped (129, 393). In addition, the volunteers and nonprofessionals assume secondary and lower-status helping roles. There is a general atmosphere of depreciation or neglect for the natural, altruistic, helping impulses of friends and neighbors, who play very subordinate roles in the therapeutic scenarios and rituals which are established by helping professionals. Even the current efforts being made to revive voluntary service programs seem to be oriented to the clinical helping model, with its use of therapeutic teams and its hierarchy of mental health professionals.

These difficulties are particularly regrettable because the numbers of professionals or trained therapists presently available, or who could be made available, are grossly inadequate for the enormous number of sufferers and the magnitude of tasks involved in helping them. The mental health and human service professionals cannot begin to meet such potential service needs even with optimal expansion in the supply of indigenous workers and paraprofessional helping agents. (See Chapter 26 for a discussion of the role of the paid indigenous worker in disaster aid.) It therefore seems not only logical but necessary that we turn toward the tremendous reservoir of potent helping forces and manpower that is associated with natural, informal helping systems, with self-help programs and organizations.

DISASTER AID AND ALTRUISM

Disaster aid is defined as the system of formal and informal welfare services and benefits that help individuals, families, and groups to resolve personal, social, and economic problems caused by disasters (382). In this system, a basic element is the arrangement for mutual aid and self-help among survivors of a disaster. But natural disasters (48 officially declared disasters occurred in 1972, a record number) have been causing enormously costly damage. As a result, vast government programs have been developed, and nearly 50 federal agencies alone are now involved in disaster aid activities. Formal and informal responses consist of both rehabilitative and preventive aid programs.

Disaster as Crisis

A disaster is an extreme social crisis situation in which individuals and their social systems become dysfunctional and disorganized, sustain personal, collective, and public hardships, and also become a "community of sufferers." Like other crises, a disaster involves a stressor event, a "roller-coaster" process to recovery, and a time-limited progression of phased tasks. The recovery process is influenced by a number of psychosocial, internal, and environmental influences: the nature and extent of damage and loss sustained; the positive or negative definition of the event; the age, sex, and social status of the participants; the social resources and supports available; and successful problem-solving experience and competence.

Three aspects of this recovery process merit our further attention. One is the "disaster culture," consisting of informal and formal programs and a climate of preparatory attitudes and beliefs about the meanings of disasters and how best to survive them (293). Norms of mutual aid and social responsibility are strongly prescribed and given very high value and sanctions. Plans and preparations may include the establishment of warning, communication, and coordinating programs; the rehearsal of clearly defined disaster roles and tasks; the practice of disaster operating procedures for individuals, families, work organizations, and community associations; the allocation and warehousing of needed facilities and provisions; the sense of a collective and cohesive group ready to cope with the problems and tasks of a disaster.

The personal and collective definitions of a disaster strongly influence the response to it by the victims as well as by outsiders (175). The attribution of causality and responsibility which defines the disaster as externally caused rather than the fault of the participants or victims (98), generally leads to a positive coping effort and to positive welfare giving and therapeutic responses from others. The personal reactions are generally constructive and only temporarily disorganized. Many people are observed to act rather calmly, although in severe situations there is a transient disaster syndrome of shock and staring, apathetic, confused behavior (198). Most people recover fairly quickly from these reactions, and this is related in great part to the active participation of individuals in supportive family and primary groups, and their own competence in having needed skills which can contribute to aiding other disaster victims, although they themselves may be injured.

The Altruistic Community

A further aspect is the development of an "altruistic community," of an emergency welfare and self-help system that comes into being after a disaster (26). This is activated during the phase of the mass assault, in the immediate postimpact period, when informal community resources and emergency first-aid and rescue services are mobilized and provided. People give of themselves, even sacrificially, in a tremendous self-help effort, characterized by much chaotic collective behavior, by inefficient but effective mutual aid. This effort is made individually, and mostly as part of family groups or local community organizations. A strong sense of community and solidarity emerges, a postdisaster utopia, in which altruistic generous feelings and behavior are predominant. This is not to deny the occurrence of negative kinds of reactions and behaviors such as looting, but these are minor in degree. Rather, there is much affectionate, democratic openness and genuineness, a sense of shared heroic and tragic experience, mutual helpfulness in emotional support and in the provision of personal possessions for material aid. (See Chapter 20 for a discussion of community adaptive behavior.) It is suggested that a crucial element in the activation of this postdisaster "utopia" is the empathic ability of individuals to extend their personal identities into a shared community identity (402). There is also a convergence of helping people and resources that pour in from the outside.

But as the need for the emergency welfare services and mutual aid declines, so does the altruistic community. The formal and external disaster relief organizations take over to provide the more substantial emergency mass care and the rehabilitation services that are needed.

The altruistic community serves important problem-solving as well as therapeutic functions for the victims, the survivors, and the helpers. It makes available direct, emergency, helping services to people in urgent need. It increases self-esteem and self-worth through social confirmations and self-reinforcements for positive self-images associated with the enactment of competent, virtuous behavior. It is anxiety resolving and guilt relieving; it creates and reasserts valued social bonds, identities, and memberships; it enhances the sense of internal power and the recuperative forces based on consensual motivations and collective striving. It enables individuals and groups to reconstitute and reorganize themselves, often at a better level of functioning than prior to the disaster.

In its response to natural disaster, the altruistic community is a prime example of a natural, informal system of mutual aid. Barton (26) who has analyzed the components of such altruistic communities, has suggested that a number of mechanisms help to produce them: activation of formal and informal communication systems; willingness of victims to talk about their deprivation; a knowledge of the extent of deprivation gained by community members; sympathetic identification with, rather than blaming of, victims; a better understanding of one's own relative deprivation (in social comparison processes); the operation of normative helping standards; and the presence of situational and motivational determinants (such as personal contact with victims and observation of models helping victims).

Barton gives much emphasis to the salience of altruistic, equalitarian, or collectivist values, norms, and ideology. He declares that the altruistic community can be made a permanent feature of our society through organized societal arrangements, that "mutual aid can be bureaucratized, routinized, and made reliable in spite of the ups and down of mass emotions." He further suggests that altruistic relationships and behavior patterns, and the motivation of "ordinary people to play appropriate helping roles" in everyday life can be stabilized by developing clearly defined norms and mutual role expectations for such helping relationships.

THE CONCEPT AND CORRELATES OF ALTRUISM

Altruism is defined in the dictionary as selflessness, or "unselfish regard for or devotion to the welfare of others." It is also defined (271, 446) as behavior which is primarily beneficial to another person who is in need or distress, which places the interests of others above one's own, and which is motivated by a desire to help the other person. The concept is a complex and ambiguous one; its connotations and usage vary a great deal; and it is difficult to operationalize, observe, and measure. Altruism refers to *a*) a general personality trait, *b*) an element of moral character, *c*) a basic innate need, *d*) an attitude, motive, or value, and/or *e*) a behavioral habit. It also refers to behavior that is moral and ethical, prosocial, and virtuous, i.e., giving to and helping others. The altruistic person is a Good Samaritan, responsible, giving, a "do-gooder." These qualities of altruism are difficult to measure because they are self-reported (varying greatly from actual behavior), or they need to be inferred from overt behavior (with varying degrees of objectivity or evidence as reported by observers).

Durkheim (102) and Sorokin (385) have emphasized that altruism consists of action that does not have expectation of rewarding consequences for the actor. However, it is recognized that altruism is not a pure motive but part of the mixed motives and attitudes that determine human behavior. There may be reinforcing consequences for the actor, although not in direct, explicit terms. For example, an act of generosity may result in a self-reinforcement of heightened self-esteem. It may involve the reduction of variously expressed distress; or represent the ventilation, avoidance of, or compensation for guilt feelings; or express a felt obligation to restore equity in interpersonal relations; or be a meeting of the needs of others as an extension of oneself; or be a disguised kind of self-seeking. Altruistic behavior may also mean a disinterested, problem-centered and creative response to the logic of a situation. Some people may

> dispassionately assess a situation, conclude that the rational and fitting solution to the problem requires from them an action of a certain sort, and then go ahead and do it. The fact that the action is one that others would label unselfish does not enter into their considerations. Their attention is wholly focused upon the realization of a general value (that is, not a self-orientated one) such as the increase of health or justice in a community, the efficient and humane running of an institution, or the

creation of knowledge. This kind of altruism has been almost entirely neglected by psychologists . . . (446, p 150)

Altruistic, benevolent motives and norms are increasingly required in our society, in which people are more and more interdependent on each other for social exchange and reciprocal services with which to accomplish life tasks. Titmuss (408) stressed that altruism, expressed in gift-giving, fosters social integration and a sense of community and discourages social alienation and isolation through the creation of bonds of mutual obligation.

Since the brutal murder in 1964 of Kitty Genovese in New York City (361), which took place without intervention from any of 38 spectators, and the countless repetition of such incidents, there has been a revival of academic interest in and research on altruism. Much of this research has been narrowly conceived. Researchers have largely used experimental designs in laboratory settings with students as subjects and have found much difficulty developing valid measures of altruism as a motive. Recent research has been of a debunking variety, for example, declaring that altruistic norms are *explanatory fictions* to rationalize prior helping or nonhelping behavior (89); or that altruism is really motivated by selfish reasons, by feelings of shame or guilt, or by striving for status and power (230).

Altruism has been found to depend on such factors as attachment to one's in-group, social learning and reinforcement, empathic mental processes, utility values in relation to costs and risks, pressures to conform to social responsibility norms, and on situational contingencies (229, 446). Dependent variables may be categorized in terms of attributes of the benefactor (resources, competence, social status), and of the recipient (attractiveness, dependency); on the nature of their relationship, (friendship); or on the moral norms in operation (social responsibility) (229). Altruism is positively correlated with such personality attributes as self-esteem, self-control, resistance to temptation, greater age, maturity, and with ethnocentric, self-actualizing and particularly with empathic tendencies. A preoccupation with self-worth and self-actualization, however, is found to be related to a tendency toward the kind of self-concern than inhibits altruism (36). People who are given to, learn to give, and tend to give to others; there is much emphasis on the influence of parental and other helping models for behavior learning and norm-internalization, as well as for direct situational influence on actors in helping situations (9, 206, 229).

Environmental influences, through socialization and norm-setting processes, may reinforce or discourage altruistic standards and behavior, both for individuals and for collectivities. Titmuss compared the voluntary and effective blood donor program in Great Britain with the commercialized and ineffective blood supply programs in the United States. He found the latter to repress the expression of altruism, erode a sense of community, lower scientific standards, limit professional and personal freedoms, and place immense social costs on the poor, inept, and sick. He generalized that

> . . . ways in which society organizes and structures its social institutions . . . can encourage or discourage the altruistic in man; such systems can allow 'the theme of the gift'. . . . of generosity toward strangers to spread between social groups and generations (408).

There are three interdependent attitudinal elements of altruism that seem to be highly related to helping behavior. These are the attitudes or feelings of caritas (or love), caring, and responsibility. They express the humanistic value-orientation of the helping professions.

Caritas, or *agape*, or charity, is held to be the highest form of love. The ancient Hebrew *Zedakah* (for charity) had connotations of an obligatory act of justice and also of alms-giving; the wider *Gemilut Chasadim* or *Chesed*, meaning loving kindness, refers to the voluntary surplus of benefaction, including generosity and personal service which "spring from emotions of compassion and human kinship (141)." May (278) speaks of *caritas* as devotion to the welfare of the other. Tillich (405) holds that a basic aspect of the philosophy of social work is that of a "listening love," or

> *Caritas*—the love which descends to misery and ugliness and guilt in order to elevate. This love is critical as well as accepting, and is able to transform what it loves.

May gives much emphasis to caring as compassion and ultimate concern, as meaning "to wish someone well," and to be a source of both love and will (278). Erikson (112) associates the many forms of selfless caring with the psychosexual stage of generativity. Sennett (377) suggests that caring about people means knowing and accepting people in all their unique "differentness" and specificity.

Mayeroff (279), in his lucid and inspiring book, *On Caring*, explains that,

> To care for another person, in the most significant sense, is to help him grow and actualize himself. . . . By helping the other grow, I actualize myself. . . . 'Being with' characterizes the process of caring itself; in caring for another person, we can be said to be basically with him in his world; in contrast to simply knowing about him from outside. . . . I can only fulfill myself by serving someone or something apart from myself, and if I am unable to care for anyone or anything separate from me, I am unable to care for myself . . .

Caring, as Mayeroff sees it, is a mutual act involving a process of mutual trust, development and actualization of one's self and of the self of the other.

Although the caring may activate a return caring, he considers that it may not be reciprocated, may be made dispensible, and is not to be considered a "trade."

A sense of responsibility refers to one's feeling that one is a causal agent of one's own actions, that one is obligated to act in terms of certain ethical principles, and that one is accountable for the consequences of one's behavior. This sense of responsibility is also a generalized expectation that one has some significant measure of control over one's life, that self-initiated behavior will realize one's intentions, and that such behavior will be rewarded. It also is related to a sense of personal autonomy, in feeling able to make responsible decisions and choices in life. It further includes a sense of social responsibility, of felt obligations to give to and help others, of some accountability for the welfare of others and for not harming others. The acceptance and attribution of responsibility, relating to one's self and to others, are central concerns in the construction of one's life and identity, and in interpersonal behavior and relationships.

Altruism thus appears to be of fundamental importance in the development, functioning, and behavior of individuals and of society. With its components of love, care, and responsibility, in relation to one's self and to others, altruism is a basic value and ethical principle by which to live. It is a basic norm and standard of what is good and worthy in people and in society. It is also a fundamental objective and ideal for all individuals and collectivities to achieve in growth and also in therapeutic processes.

> A morale-enhancing feature unique to therapy groups is the incentive and opportunity they afford for members to help one another. Altruism combats morbid self-centeredness, enhances the individual's feelings of kinship with others, and strengthens his sense of personal worth and power (133).

Altruism and Professional Helping

Altruism is the basic value and ethical principle of the helping professions, in what we call "the service ideal." This means that the helping person gives priority to meeting the needs of the client over those of his own, even at some cost to the helper. According to Goode (150) the service ideal is "a collectivity orientation," and a "norm that the technical solutions which the professional arrives at should be based on the client's needs. . . ." Society believes that a profession obligates itself to follow this ideal, and it rewards the practitioner who lives by this ideal, so that virtue pays. The service ideal is also a feature of the welfare ideology, in which the central idea of welfare is humanitarian regard for our fellow man (259)."

A very similar notion is that of a personal–service ideology, described by Halmos (161) as a set of beliefs developed by the helping and personal–service professions. It is characterized by a faith in the technically skilled use of love for helping purposes and by an ethic of social responsibility and care. Halmos presents this ideology as a potent social and moral force in our society and indicates that its ideals have created a moral reformation of leadership and a moral renewal in our society.

We, therefore, assume that those in the helping professions are essentially altruistic and committed to the service idea. We further assume that these attitudes and feelings are what activates them to enter the helping occupations, or that they take on these attitudes and feelings by virtue of their socialization into these professions.

Yet there are questions about the helping professional's sincerity in the commitment to the service ideal. In a study (418) of the values of social workers, it was found that such a commitment increased with professional education but remained at a moderately strong level. Perhaps the level should be higher. But it has also been found that bureaucratic organizations (in which most social workers are employed) tend to weaken professional service orientations (435).

In my own current research on altruism, and in my own effort to develop a measure of altruistic attitudes and behavior, I have found a surprising rejection by social work students of their own altruism. They reported some moderate altruistic helping behavior on their own part, in terms of visiting the sick, donating blood, or helping people in disaster situations. It should be recognized that most of these students are young and relatively inexperienced in life. Yet, in discussing the subject they explained that they did not feel altruistic, because they were helping people with an expectation of reward for their services, if not from clients directly, then indirectly through their employing organizations or through self-reinforcements for being*good* people. Some students thought that they were not altruistic in the sense of being selfless and because they felt unwilling to submerge their own personal selves in helping encounters with people in need. Some thought they could grant an altruistic component in their motives, in their being drawn into this field. And there were a number of students who spoke of the feeling of hypocrisy they associated with the term altruism. There was some cynicism about the self-seeking and self-aggrandizement seen to be involved in what people, including helping professionals, alleged to be their altruistic behavior. They were willing to admit that in applying for admission to the profession and to the schools of social work they had emphasized their desire to help and their concern for the welfare of people in need, but some stated that they did so because they knew this motive was expected of them.

These are surprising and troubling reactions. There is evident a lack of understanding about altruism and a denigration of their own altruistic inclinations by these students. One can expect that this would be a handicap in helping clients. Certainly there are questions to be raised about their actual feelings. Perhaps these students are insufficiently socialized.

Perhaps there is a need to be realistic and unpretentious about the valid and genuine kind of altruism they would admit to feeling.

Official and Unofficial Helping

Such responses by fledgling professional helpers about their altruistic feelings can help us begin to explore differences between professional (or official) and natural (or unofficial) types of helping. This does not mean that we support the current misguided attacks on professionalism, nor does it mean that professional helpers ought to be friends with clients. Long before the recent assault on professionalism and credentialism, Jane Addams (4) expressed sharp criticism of organized charity work, and spoke of how estranged the charity workers were from poor people's normal worries and desperate struggles for existence. She argued that direct, personal assistance is best given within friendly and neighborly relationships, and that the "natural rule of giving . . . is bounded only by the need of the recipient and the resources of the giver." Allport (8) later observed that there is much tension between professional and friendship approaches in the helping of people through social services, and that this tension needs to be better resolved. There is another position, that psychotherapy is a "professional friendship," purchased by people who need and want the love and intimacy of a relationship with a close friend (368).

Yet professional helping is not friendship, and no make-believe can obliterate the different qualities of help given by a friend and by an altruistic stranger. To help people work through their crippled feelings in transference relationships, however intense and intimate such relationships may be, requires a different quality of giving, of reciprocity, status inequality, distance, authority, and acceptance of difference, than occurs in friendship. The love of *philia* is different from the love of *agape* or *caritas*. And as Titmuss clarified, the welfare ideal means giving love to and meeting the need of the stranger.

There is another aspect to be considered, namely, the needs of people for more than official, professional types of help. An early principle of helping, as formulated in social work by Mary Richmond, was that "We should seek the most natural and least official sources of relief, bearing in mind the ties of kinship, friendship, and neighborliness . . ." (357, p 153). She gave much value to safeguarding and strengthening the direct, personal devotion of natural helping relationships, in contrast to the politically-oriented, inflexible, impersonal character of public relief, against which she was prejudiced. In more recent years, this principle has been restated in the increasing sentiment that people who are in social–emotional need, and who deviate from societal rules of conduct, should be aided as much as possible outside of official, stigmatizing channels and rehabilitative, correctional agencies (369, 469).

We need to recognize that helping professionals are community agents; they are designated and licensed to represent the community, to facilitate social change and social control processes in society. They serve as social parents and community caretakers, as well as mediators, brokers, rule-enforcers and rule-benders (383). There is a valid brief to be made in support of the constructive and necessary use by helping professionals, of labeling (see Chapter 16), social typing and stigmatization procedures, as part of the resocialization, therapeutic, and conversion processes for deviants in our society. However, we can also recognize that these procedures may be unnecessary and harmful for certain people in particular situations, because they make harder the tasks of social reconnection and reintegration, and of the reconstitution of valued social and self-identities. But professional treatment alone cannot do the job of reversing deviant careers, of helping people recover from their "madness."

Professional helping needs to be yoked to the natural, unofficial helping systems of altruistic and mutual aid evolved by society as part of our everyday activity in communal life (232). Through the subcultures and the bonds of group and communal fellowship, powerful and essential healing and helping forces are made available to people in need. These forces provide motivation, support, inclusion, and confirmation on which are based the esteemed, worthy character and identity of the individual and the moral and social order.

Mutual benefit and protective societies, voluntary, "friendly," and benevolent associations, cooperatives and self-help groups of many kinds, in secular and religious terms, have long been a part of the social fabric of a well-ordered community. They gained great importance in response to the ills of the urban, industrial cities, in which older forms of family and community associations were fragmented, particularly from the beginning of the nineteenth century. In recent years there has been a rapid growth of voluntary service programs and of self-help groups for deviant individuals (24, 187, 205, 419). The voluntary programs, such as Vista, Peace Corps, hot-lines, and crisis clinics, have been much stimulated by federal support. The self-help groups include former mental hospital patients, exconvicts, divorcees, single parents, alcoholics, mental retardates and their parents, recipients of public welfare, homosexuals, and drug abusers. In the form of rural and urban *communes*, self-help groups for normal as well as for deviant individuals, have proliferated in recent years. These self-help groups and arrangements, in addition to those provided by family and kinship associations, are a major resource for natural, informal, and unofficial helping processes. Along with their mutual benefit features, they represent altruistic impulses and activities made available to strangers with a common need.

The public welfare systems, including government programs, voluntary agencies, and private professional helping services, back up and supplement the unofficial informal system of mutual aid. The disaster aid system described earlier comprises such a mixture of unofficial and official, voluntary and governmental arrangements and programs. Professional helpers intervene when the natural helping processes are inadequate or require the powerful resources and expertise that professionals can supply; they supplement the natural helping processes and then return the deviant or the problem to the ministrations of the natural helpers, of the families and communities involved. Both professional and natural helpers realize altruistic impulses, albeit of somewhat different kinds and in somewhat different ways. We know little about these differences. But both these expressions are particularly valuable today.

New Directions and Tasks

We should take note here of the charge that in our society a general decline of altruistic feelings and behavior has taken place. There also appears to be a serious increase in levels of alienation and mistrust in our society, especially among the college student population (362). The public media report an increasing volume of incidents of violence, of the Kitty Genovese type. There are reports of such incidents as the suicide of a 23-year-old male motorist, stranded on a highway in midwinter, who after 11 hours of unsuccessfully attempting to get passing cars to stop and assist him, killed himself in desperation (New York Times, February 7, 1973). Good Samaritans who try to intervene in order to halt violence on a person are themselves sometimes killed.

There are even indications that there has been a decline in the incidence of the postdisaster altruistic community. A recent study (300) suggests that there is not a significant increase in the number of people who perform altruistic acts during disasters, as compared to their predisaster helping behavior. One can question whether a decline in altruism is also reflected in the hostile aggressiveness of flood and hurricane disaster victims who demand help from the American Red Cross and demand repayment of their losses from the federal government rather than seeking help according to their needs.

If these trends are true, there are wider questions that emerge for our inquiry. Is the erosion of altruistic feelings related to the decline of communities in the United States? To the extreme individualism that characterizes our lives? To our preoccupation with contractual, *quid pro quo* and adversary relations in marriage, in family and community life, and even in the therapeutic relations between professional helpers and their clients or patients? To a general process of social alienation, conflict, *anomie*, and disorganization?

From a more optimistic perspective, we can identify certain countertrends in operation that seek to reestablish altruism as a basic principle in our daily lives and relations, as a basis for new forms of family and community structure, of morality and culture. The development of official welfare and therapeutic systems, such as community mental health centers and neighborhood service centers, of voluntary service programs, such as Vista, of the self-help group and commune movements—all these represent an institutionalization of many of the features we have described as part of postdisaster altruistic communities. This is a new social movement to which we need consciously to contribute. We can do so by a more explicit attention and effort to help reinvigorate and maximize altruistic values, norms, and behavior within professional helping systems, as well as within the everyday lives of people generally.

There is need for us to clarify the value orientations of professional helpers and members of the human service professions, especially as they relate to altruism as a valid value and norm for professional and ethical behavior. Attention should be given within educational programs, and within service agencies, to the provision of relevant moral training, to help students and practitioners sort out their feelings and come to terms with the moral dilemmas involved in being altruistic as a helping professional.

There is also need to learn much more about the altruistic communities that emerge in response to natural disasters, and the extension of their principles to other kinds of crisis situations. We should have more knowledge about natural helping networks of people, within extended family groups, self-help groups, and in informal community processes between neighbors and friends (1, 85, 381, 402). Because of the interrelation of altruism and empathy, high priority needs to be given to education and human relations programs that aim to enhance and strengthen empathic capacities and skills, including programs in the public schools and universities. Research is very much needed on the subject of altruism, in real life rather than in laboratory situations, preferably using participant–observation methods to study altruistic feelings and behavior.

The self-help movement deserves much support, and we need to encourage as well as study these "friendly societies," built around common problems and needs. Instead of going along with a denigration of professional helping contributions, indications for professional contributions can be identified, and positive value given to informal altruistic motives and activities. Optimal use should be made of natural helpers, without coopting them into clinical helping programs, but rather keeping them related to natural helping networks, in families and work and neighborhood associations. A prime example is the work being done to stimulate the development of informal helping networks for the day care of children (82).

Of course, there is a basic need for the development of viable and well-functioning communities, capable of evoking the identifications and solidarity people seem to want so much today. Community development approaches need to be fashioned and applied directly to encourage and maintain such communities, based on an altruistic ethos. It would seem helpful to apply principles and procedures learned from models of natural family and communal groups in other societies and cultures, where individuals and families cope with their predicaments, using normal problem-solving rituals, as in calling together a clan or a village. *We also need to develop and institutionalize a predisaster culture of norms, procedures, and clearly-defined role responsibilities, that can prepare people as individuals, families, and communities, to cope well with disasters and other kinds of crisis situations.*

Further, we need to find ways to again give credit to people for being virtuous, to reward giving and helping behavior, now sorely lacking in our society, which rewards and reinforces other kinds of values and behavior. This type of urgently needed culture should bind us to our collectivities in ways that will enhance and integrate personal and social identities, as well as encourage a mutuality of personal and social development and living. Crisis intervention delivery systems need to emphasize such community development approaches. (See Chapters 9 and 10 for further discussion of community perspectives.)

There is a need to move away from community development approaches that exacerbate conflict and polarize people under the slogans of confrontation and redistribution of community power, and to eliminate a clinical subculture that tends to define ordinary human events as crises and disasters, and reactions to them as pathology and sickness. One of the insights we have gained from crisis intervention theory is that crisis-proneness consists, in part, in a tendency to define hardship events as crises.

It behooves us to move toward integrative, consensual strategies for helping people, and to use ways of helping that can contribute to an increased level of hopefulness, of collective morale, of valid, genuine joyousness in human affairs. We need to provide public joyous occasions and celebrations so that people can mobilize and exercise their resources and common humanity through altruistic sharing of food, and of themselves.

There is an urgent task for us to relinquish our preoccupations with an unrealistic individualism and false equality to which we presently give so much value, but which appear to increase social conflict and frustrate our needs for social belonging and solidarity. This means reexamining and modifying the currently popular acceptance of consumerism, and of contractual and adversary approaches to family living and human relations. Our experiences and relationships require collaborative, collectivist, synergistic orientations and the pursuit of common interests.

There is again in this country an era of exploration in and experimentation with utopias. Sennett (377) presents an appealing vision of utopian "survival communities" in our urban cities. They would replace anarchic alienation with pluralistic group living based on a new social ethic of caring about people. Caring about men and women in society means caring about social issues and reforms. The altruistic impulse awakens in helpers that kind of empathic identification with people in need that activates not only direct helping activities, but also the inclinations and efforts toward a wider social reform. In seeking to establish altruistic communities, we shall also be seeking to establish a new moral and social order that can better enable us to achieve both collective and self-realization.

20

THE FAMILY AND COMMUNITY
CONTEXT OF INDIVIDUAL
REACTIONS TO DISASTER

Russell R. Dynes
E. L. Quarantelli

Disaster events by their very nature are not everyday occurrences. For most people, therefore, the experiential dimension concerning disaster behavior tends to be mediated through others, generally through the mass media. Mass media accounts generally emphasize stories of individual reactions which are dramatic and traumatic. The extensiveness of the individual trauma is often used as the primary measure of newsworthiness: the greater the trauma, the greater the newsworthiness. Consequently, the *experiences* that most persons have with disaster effects are focused on individual trauma. Such reportage, in addition, often implies a causal sequence somewhat as follows:

1. Disaster agents create effects which produce extensive individual disorganization.
2. Aggregate individual disorganization, in turn, creates family disorganization.
3. Aggregate family disorganization creates community disorganization.

In such a causal sequence, psychological stress is seen as additive, and when some *optimum* number of individuals are affected by stress, the entire community can be characterized as disorganized. Since such

The research on which this paper was based was supported in part by PHS Grant 5 RO1 MH-15399-04 from the Center for Studies of Mental Health and Social Problems, Applied Research Branch, National Institutes of Mental Health.

linkages are consistent with certain individualistic assumptions common in American society, and since few people have extensive experience in a variety of disaster situations, such causal linkages seem very logical.

This set of interrelated assumptions about disorganized behavior is often central to initiating remedial actions in disaster situations. The assumptions about widespread disorganization, for example, are often used to justify urgency in providing outside assistance for disaster areas. A variety of assistance programs are then established, based on the assumed needs for such programs within such impacted areas. However, the effectiveness of such programs is seldom evaluated. If they are evaluated, it is usually done by involved staff members who usually attribute their lack of success to the absence of prior planning, the lack of rapid mobilization, or some other convenient bureaucratic targets. Such efforts at assistance tend to be reinvented and repeated over and over again in every major disaster, primarily because few persons have any cumulative experience in disaster aid.

There is, however, a major source of cumulative experience about disasters available that is found in research dealing with the human aspects of disaster (104), the result of the work of many individual scholars and research organizations in many different nations (26, 103, 129, 276, 295). Without reviewing it here, we will utilize this information in investigating the common assumptions just set forth, as it implies a quite different causal chain. It suggests that, as a result of disaster, individual disorganization is somewhat minimal because the potential effects are mediated through various social structures within which individuals play roles. We are particularly concerned with the family and the larger community as mediating structures. The consequences of such structural mediation are that, in most disaster situations, individuals are able to exhibit situationally adaptive behavior. Rather than being characterized by widespread maladaptive behavior, disaster situations are, in many ways, characterized by a greater proportion of adaptive, goal-oriented behavior than may be true in so-called normal situations. In addition, the trauma which is inherent in such situations is probably handled more effectively and has fewer long-term consequences than does "normal" trauma.

Unfortunately, *disaster* is one of those sponge terms in the English language which encompasses almost any phenomena one dislikes. Here we restrict the meaning to *social disruption* that is the consequence of physical damage created by natural agents such as tornadoes and earthquakes. More narrowly, we are concerned with agents that are characterized by sudden impact, creating a diffuse damage pattern within an urban community, and with the immediate pre-impact and post-impact setting.

Four areas of concern are 1) the warning process in which an interpretation of danger has to be made by aggregates of people; 2) the actions, preventive and otherwise, that persons take when danger is imminent; 3) the reactions of persons in the immediate post-impact situations, and 4) the handling of loss of persons or of property.

WARNING OF THREAT

Three assumptions are frequently made about warnings of impending disasters. It is assumed that *a*) official warning messages will go directly to individuals; *b*) these individuals will primarily respond directly to the content of that message, and *c*) the message acting as a stimulus will evoke a response which may be maladaptive unless great care is taken in the wording of the message. These assumptions, in the main, are incorrect. As Charles Fritz (142) has noted, "Many of the difficulties in obtaining the desired responses to warning stem from an oversimplified conception held by persons issuing warning information. They often conceive of warning as a direct stimulus–response type of communication, in which the person issuing the warning gives the signal *danger* and people automatically respond as though danger were imminent."

Receiving the Warning

In actual fact, most people typically get warnings indirectly through other people and assess the possible validity of the message through perceiving the actions of others as well as interacting with them. They act on the basis of their interpretation of the warning messages, as this is mediated by the groups of which they are a part.

It is true that most people in most American disasters typically get their first or initial warnings from the mass media. Thus, 91% of the households first heard of Hurricane Carla (295) from either radio, television, or newspapers, although a more typical example is the situation in Denver, Colorado (96), where only about half of the households got an initial flood warning from mass media sources. But generally even this first warning is received in the presence of known others. Thus it was in one systematic field study (96), that while 52% of 278 families studied received their initial flood warning from either radio or television, two thirds of those families received the warning in the presence of other family members. Equally important, persons typically get additional warnings from persons outside of their own households, sometimes in place of warnings from media, but far more often in addition to the initial warning. For example, almost all studies (such as that of Hurricane Camille and those of tornado situations where warning was possible) indicate that after the initial warning people receive information on the threat from multiple other sources, especially relatives. (Drabek (99) reported that 26% got their first indication of possible flood danger from friends, neighbors, or relatives.) Put very simply, where it is possible, people generally learn of danger through and/or with others known to them, especially family members.

Response to Context

Given the social and group context in which warnings are received, it is not surprising that the *context* rather than the *content* of the message is the important factor in influencing the response. That is, instead of responding directly to the warning message, there is an attempt to assess its validity on the basis of how known others react to it. One study (99) reported that "Friends, relatives, and neighbors served as an important confirmation mechanism. As might be expected, interaction with neighbors was largely face-to-face, whereas friends and relatives were usually contacted via telephone." Interestingly, authorities are seldom contacted. In the study just alluded to, only 9% of the households attempted to check with officials in the community. Put another way, most families warned of danger looked to see how others were interpreting the warning message. The validity of its content was filtered through a context of activities of personally known others.

Nature of Response

Even when confirmation of danger is obtained, there is no automatic bolting to get away from the supposed threat. Time is usually taken to assess what others, whose opinions are of value, are doing and what the consequences for the family will be if the threat materializes. When those others decide to leave or stay, the family follows suit. It is particularly noticeable that in situations where there is a disaster subculture (i.e., a tradition of response to emergencies partly derived from earlier community disaster experiences), there is a strong tendency to minimize the possible impact of the danger. Not only prior experiences but collective assessments of possible consequences for selves and property through discussion among family members influence if and how a response is made to warnings. In short, even when warnings of danger are accepted, a variety of alternate responses are probable because the actual response is derived from the social context.

IMMEDIATE REACTIONS TO THREAT

Certain assumptions are often made about the typical range of immediate reactions of individuals to disaster situations. It is assumed that disaster victims behave in disorganized or dysfunctional ways. This supposition rests on the notion that typical patterns of response take the form of *a*) panic, *b*) shock, or *c*) passivity. Although this view is widespread, even among personnel of disaster organizations, it is generally a misconception according to almost all systematic disaster studies conducted. Disaster victims do not break into panic flight or otherwise markedly engage in behaviors characterized by irrational decisions, illogical actions, and an antisocial disregard for others. Likewise, persons involved in disasters are seldom so stunned or shocked that they can not adaptively respond. Nor do victims lack initiative, become docile, or wait childlike for relief workers or the authorities to command them and to tell them what to do in the emergency. Instead, disaster victims generally assess with others the demands of the immediate situation facing them, move collectively to deal as best as they can with the perceived problems, and otherwise actively attack the emergency with their fellow victims.

Disaster studies show that people do not flee wildly from a disaster area. Solo or collective panic flight, in fact, is so rare as to be an insignificant practical problem. Despite stories of thousands abandoning their communities under some threat, most people remain, letting the tourists and the transients flee. Even in the highly atypical, largest evacuation in American history when more than a half million persons left coastal areas of Texas and Louisiana in the face of Hurricane Carla, and despite 4 days of warning, 55% of the population remained in their own area (295). Together with their fellow citizens, most residents stay and make decisions such as where to build levees or when to go to tornado shelters, or they join together with friends, relatives, and neighbors in boarding up houses or removing store stocks to upper floors of buildings. And when there is evacuation from some location, such movement tends to be orderly, logical, and adaptive, with predisaster social ties being maintained. Thus, one disaster researcher after another has reported that evacuation is almost always by family units, not solitary individuals (e.g., in one flood situation studied (99), of the families which were together prior to evacuation, 92% left together). Even when evacuation is very sudden, as one study of a dam break threat showed, 23% of those fleeing assisted community members other than those who were in their own original fleeing groups (87). So, far from individualistic panic flight, although flight might be necessary, there usually is a collective and reasonable response to an immediate threat.

There is some limited evidence of what has been called a *disaster syndrome* (i.e., a state of shock leading to regression in normal cognitive processes). However, it appears only in the more traumatic and sudden kinds of catastrophes, is confined to the post-impact period, lasts only a short time (minutes or hours), and does not occur on a large scale (329). In one disaster study (143), for example, using an area probability sample, it was found that, at most, only 14% of all respondents manifested some of the initial stages of the syndrome. Nor do disasters generally have disabling emotional consequences or leave numbing severe mental health problems among any large numbers of their victims. It is true that a majority of the population in the disaster struck areas will often show varying degrees of stress reactions in the aftermath of a major emergency (e.g., anxiety, nausea). But what is important is that such reactions do not basically affect the willingness and ability of people to take the initiative and to respond well, especially in the emergency period. In one tornado study, the victim and fringe population (with almost no aid from formal agencies) was able within 3–4 hours to take from two-thirds to three-fourths of the 927 casualties to nearby hospitals (129). Isolated cases of shock and inability to act with others can be found in some disasters, but such a response is not a typical disaster response pattern.

Disaster victims react in an active manner, not passively. They do not wait around for offers of aid by organizations or outsiders. They act on their own. On a large scale, once they have started to react to the crisis, victims show personal initiative and a pattern of self-help and informal mutual aid. The National Opinion Research Center (276) in one of its disaster studies found that 43% of all males in the impact area searched for the missing and 21% engaged in rescue efforts in the 6 hours after tornado impact. Available evidence indicated that at least 55% of this activity was not oriented solely to kin or to intimates. Similarly, when victims evacuate they do not usually go to public or institutional shelters but instead seek refuge with friends and relatives. Thus, Drabek and Boggs (97) found in a flood situation that only 3.5% of the families studied went to any type of organizational shelter, and Moore (295) noted that 58% of the families fleeing Hurricane Carla moved into other private quarters. In the recent San Fernando earthquake fewer than 7% of 70,000 persons evacuated below a weakened dam sought housing aid from public agencies. It has become a rather consistent finding among disaster researchers that disaster victims turn first to kin, co-workers, and known others for aid. Only after exhausting other sources do they attempt to get assistance from formal organizations. In an immediate emergency, victims do not stand and wait for "Big Brother" to tell them what to do; instead they usually work with others to tackle the problems they see, be they digging out trapped victims from under debris or obtaining temporary shelter for the night. In short, even under very severe stress, people do not become completely irresponsible or totally impotent; rather they seek, in conjunction with others, to solve their emergency problems in those ways that seem reasonable to them as they view the situation. Generally the same can be said of them that has been said of combat soldiers, "Under the most harrowing circumstances, they are able to control fear and anxiety, to think clearly, and to make appropriate decisions with rapidity" (155).

IMMEDIATE REACTIONS TO IMPACT

One concern that is often expressed is the possibility that those survivors in the immediate impact period would be faced with agonizing choices as to the direction of their attention and efforts. In particular, there is concern about the consequences and effects of role conflict in disaster situations. This concern was often derived from an influential article published by Lewis Killian entitled "The Significance of Multiple Group Membership in Disaster" (210). Killian's stated intent was to develop a typology of role conflict that might generalize to situations other than disaster, since multiple group membership was an integral characteristic of all modern societies. While he identified four different types of possible conflict, he devoted most attention to the possible conflict between the family and other groups, principally the employment group or the larger community. In subsequent years, a particular section of Killian's paper was quoted widely in the popular social science literature.

> The great majority of persons interviewed who were involved in such dilemma resolved them in favor of the family, or, in some cases, to friendship groups. Much of the initial confusion, disorder, and seemingly complete disorganization reported in disaster communities was the result of the rush of families to find and rejoin their families.

Most of those who use the quote, however, drop off Killian's next line, "Yet in none of the four communities studied did the disastrous consequences contemplated above seem to have materialized."

Such social science findings, of course, would have important practical implications. If persons in crisis situations resolved their role conflicts in terms of family loyalties, any coherent organized emergency activity would be difficult if not impossible to achieve and would make outside assistance essential. The expectation that such a *familial retreat* was a usual consequence was of considerable concern to those charged with emergency planning.

Our own research on disaster was initiated in 1963 and, since we were specifically focused on organizational involvement in disaster, we were aware of the usual interpretation and conclusions given to the Killian article. We had initially contemplated that the behavioral consequences of role conflict might be a major problem confronting emergency organization so we were sensitive to indicators of it. In our experience over the years, in over 100 disasters and in the course of interviewing over 2500 different organizational officials, we found that role conflict was *not* a serious problem which created a significant loss of manpower. (On the contrary, a case could be made that a major problem is the presence of excess potential personnel who are motivated to help but who have no relevant roles available to them within the emergency system.) In fact, we have had difficulty in finding any illustrations of the phenomenon described, let alone documenting the pervasiveness of it. In looking carefully we could not find a clear case of role abandonment of persons occupying positions in key emergency organizations as a result of their anxiety to play *protective* familial roles. A study of Hurricane Audrey supports this general observation (28).

There are a number of reasons for this. While verbalization of possible contradictory demands might be, for a specific individual, some measure of anxiety levels, it is not an accurate predictor of the direction of behavior when persons are actually confronted with choices. The role conflict literature often states *obligations* in oppositional form, e.g., family versus work. But this oversimplifies reality, since there is greater continuity among and between role expectations of particular individuals. For example, successful occupational performance is an integral part of the expectations of the husband and father role.

A better understanding of the lack of role problems is achieved when the analytic focus is shifted from the dilemma of individuals attempting to make allocative decisions to the community role systems themselves and the consequences of disaster for these role systems. One can argue that the malintegration of role systems is universal, and consequently, types of role strain and/or conflict are a normal state for most actors. Since this is a *normal* state for all actors, there are certain institutionalized mechanisms which allow the actors to reduce or avoid the potential strain, e.g., compartmentalization, sequential role playing, delegation, or elimination of certain role relationships. However, the ability of any actor to minimize role strain is both limited by and determined by certain structural features, primarily those which deal with the integration of various role systems. While there may be factors which create or increase role strain during the emergency period, it is suggested that the aggregate scope and intensity of role strain is perhaps less in disaster situations than it is during normal times. Consequently, this facilitates rather than hinders the fulfillment of specific role obligations during the emergency period. In fact, some of the changes which occur in emergencies provide for the positive reinforcement of relevant emergency roles. These factors can be discussed in terms of a) the total community role system, b) the role structures of emergency relevant organizations, and c) the family as a facilitating *role budget* center.

THE COMMUNITY ROLE SYSTEM

Role obligations are ultimately based on values, and any community system can be viewed as the collective attempt to achieve many different values. Thus in a normal state, time, energy and other resources are normally available to achieve multiple values, even when some of these values are potentially contradictory. To some extent, therefore, a free market state exists which allows the achievement of multiple but often conflicting values. But a disaster event changes this. No longer can the community assume that the resources will be plentiful so that all values can be achieved. Choices have to be made. Certain values become more critical than others in the survival of the community and therefore are more important in the allocation of resources. This means that certain norms and roles become important while others become less important. This set of value priorities has elsewhere been called an "emergency consensus" (103). Its highest priority is care for disaster victims, both medical care and provision of basic necessities. Somewhat lower in the priority system are those tasks which are directly relevant to achievement of core values, such as restoration of and maintenance of essential community services, and maintenance of public order. Other traditional roles within the community, however, are drastically altered. For example, roles related to production, distribution, and consumption of goods and those related to socialization and to social participation are in large part irrelevant to the key values within the emergency context, so while the emergency consensus makes certain roles more critical, it makes other role obligations completely irrelevant. The net result, from the viewpoint of the individual, is to reduce the scope of the total role obligations and as a consequence to minimize the probabilities of role strain for individuals. At the same time, this insures more adequate performance on the part of individuals in those critical roles which remain. The total role structure, thus, becomes more coherently organized around a set of value priorities and, at the same time, irrelevant roles which could produce strain are eliminated until the emergency is over.

Role Structure of Emergency Relevant Organizations

From the viewpoint of the total community system, a relatively small number of roles are essential for the immediate tasks created by disaster impact. The more obvious problems, and therefore the best known problems, are those which involve search and rescue of victims, provision of medical attention, and protection against continuing threat. These tasks are usually assumed by various community organizations in which there is a high probability that persons will occupy the positions and perform the roles with competence. Such organizations—police and fire departments, hospitals, ambulance services, segments of public works departments—are structured with such emergency tasks as a part of their organizational domain. They build into their organizational roles certain explicit expectations about emergency behavior as well as other implicit understandings about emergency obligations. These involve the expectations to stay on the job, if on duty, when the emergency occurs or to report to duty when knowledge is received that an emergency has taken place. These expectations may be generally understood and/or they may be institutionalized into organizational notification schemes such as fan-out systems.

Such emergency organizations generally operate around the clock. With multiple shifts, they have between two and three times the personnel necessary to maintain the normal operations at any one time. The possibilities of expansion of organizational activities to compensate for overloads also allows for a surplus to compensate for any potential loss of personnel from injury or from absence from role conflict. Because of the assurance that these organizational members on duty will remain, other organizational members not on duty have the reassurance that they have time to check personal and familial damage and also to engage in limited amounts of nonoccupational role behavior before reporting. In addition, the built-in guarantees of multiple persons to fill specific roles minimizes the loss of any one person in a specific role.

With the exception of a relatively small number of individuals who have immediate responsibilities in relevant emergency organizations, most other occupational roles within the community system become irrelevant. This frees individuals to perform familial roles or to perform more informal altruistic, neighboring, helping roles. For example, most of what is called search and rescue operations are conducted by unattached persons in the impact area. The initial actions of these individuals are often supplemented later by more organized activity. While this activity is sometimes viewed by outsiders as being disorganized, it is a situation where individual and small informal groupings become involved in similar activities. The individuals who participate usually have no other specific role responsibilities in the emergency or, if they do, their initial actions are considered by themselves and by others to be within the scope of their occupational involvement, e.g., a policeman or a fireman becoming involved in search and rescue activity. Search behavior for family members, neighbors, and any others is seen as a legitimate role-expectation for those without explicit emergency role obligations since it is consistent with the core values which have become critical in the emergency.

The Family as a Role Budget Center

With the simplification of the role structures within a disaster-impacted community, existing family units can make internal allocative decisions which facilitate the assumption of various emergency roles on the part of various family members.

In one major earthquake, a man who had had previous volunteer experience with civil defense (CD) assumed the responsibility of keeping the local CD office open so that the CD director could deal with field operations. His wife came with him and assumed clerical and secretarial responsibilities, and his teenage daughter who was no longer in school played an important role as messenger from local CD to other offices. In this case, an entire family unit assumed a major portion of the expanded role responsibilities of the local CD director.

In another situation, an employee of a public works department experienced heavy damage to his own house. He moved his family over to a relative's house and the two families combined to make the best of the emergency situation. There was sufficient personnel within the two families to allow his release from family activities and to concentrate on his increased occupational responsibilities during the emergency. In these situations, there were persons released from other obligations who picked up disaster responsibilities, or there were persons who picked up familial responsibilities so that others could be released for participation within the emergency system. This suggests that family units are able to consider the aggregate responsibilities of their members and make internal allocative decisions as to family resources (328). This allows the allocation of resources from these family units which, in turn, becomes a major part of the larger community mobilization. All of this suggests that both communities and family units within communities facilitate emergency actions rather than provide a set of barriers which present individuals with agonizing choices and psychologically debilitating consequences.

Coping With Loss

Of course, one of the major reasons for concern about the resultant psychological effects of disaster is that disaster has the potential for creating widespread loss of life and property. The potentialities, however, are seldom realized. In most American disasters, there is an initial tendency to provide very high estimates of casualties. Immediately after impact there are inadequate conditions for collecting accurate information about its consequences. On the other hand, there is a very high demand for news. News, then, is derived from estimates created in the absence of information. Public officials generally guess high. These initial estimates are usually the figures that are subsequently remembered. By contrast, the ratio of casualties to the total number of persons involved has been quite low in every major disaster in recent American history. The largest death toll in any American disaster was in Galveston, Texas in 1900 where more than 5000 persons perished in a hurricane. Aside from maritime disasters, only three other American disasters have resulted in over 1000 fatalities. In fact, Red Cross figures show that in a 4-year period from mid-1966 to mid-1970 major disasters claimed only 779 lives (334). We cite these figures not to minimize the potential suffering but to emphasize that disasters in

American society tend to involve primarily property damage.

Even given a situation where there is widespread loss of life and property, there are several reasons which suggest that such losses have minimal traumatic psychologic effects. "Ordinary" losses, such as the death of a family member or the destruction of valued property, are often difficult to bear since they raise questions for those suffering the loss as to why the tragedy happened to them, rather than to someone else. In addition, "random" or idiosyncratic events have an isolating and nonsharable quality to them. It is difficult for others to become aware of random tragic events, and it is difficult for others to empathize and to provide sympathy for circumstances with which they are only tangentially familiar. In those disasters which do produce massive losses, two factors seem to be particularly important in making such losses easier to accept. These are a) the loss has to be evaluated in the context of relative deprivation and b) the bereavement process occurs within the context of increased social cohesion.

Suffering in the Context of Relative Deprivation

In most disaster-impacted communities, there is considerable communication about the extent and nature of suffering. The daily life of most persons in most American communities is characterized by rather routinized existence. Disaster events, however, are rather dramatic events which evoke extensive communication about their consequences. One residue of such intensive communication is that American communities often date their collective histories by disaster events, e.g., "That was before the flood." Sudden suffering, as opposed to chronic or gradual suffering, tends to evoke more concern and communication. Also in situations where the victims tend to be blameless, compared to situations where it is their fault, communication and concern are increased. Since disaster tends to have somewhat random effects within the community, all social groups may be affected and become concerned with the consequences of disaster. Those who have suffered from the disaster become salient as a reference or an identification group for others within the community. By contrast, for example, blacks whose poverty is chronic (their "own fault") and who are isolated from the rest of the community and are the responsibility of the welfare department, are unlikely to evoke the same attention and concern.

While those who suffer in a disaster become an important reference group in the community, they often view their own losses as being relatively less traumatic when, as a consequence of increased communication, they learn about others who have suffered greater losses. The person who lost 2 family members is *luckier* than the person who lost 4 family members. The person whose house was damaged is *better off* than the person whose house was totally destroyed. The collective communications process tends to focus on luck and providence rather than selectivity and suffering.

In essence, then, disaster tends to provide optimum conditions for the acceptance of suffering. Natural disasters tend to be free of those ideologic disputes about cause and blame. Such conditions reduce the barrier to communication and knowledge about suffering within the community. This makes for greater saliency of sufferers as a common reference group and creates conditions whereby those who suffer have to evaluate their own experience, not in terms of absolute deprivation, but always in terms of relative deprivation.

Increased Cohesiveness Within the Disaster-Impacted Community

One of the major reasons why suffering is easier to bear is that within the social networks in the disaster-impacted community cohesiveness is heightened. This is due to a number of factors. Opportunities for community members to participate in activities that are for the good of the community are increased. The emergency consensus places a high value on those activities that benefit the whole community and low value on selfish interests. The disaster also creates needs that are obvious and solutions that are amenable to action which give immediate results. Previous social distinctions tend to be minimized since all groups and statuses within the community are affected. The democratization of social life is created by the fact that danger, loss, and suffering become public phenomena. Community identification is enhanced by the dramatic event itself and one's participation in it.

These changes provide major gratifications for the survivors. People are able to confirm that others are basically like themselves. That people respond to disasters in somewhat similar ways provides reassurance for those who had previously felt isolated, detached, or like outsiders. They are able to see with a clarity never before possible that there are certain underlying universal values and that these common values provide a feeling of belonging and a sense of unity which is almost impossible to achieve in normal circumstances. Social relationships take on a primary group quality. As Fritz has suggested (142), "The quality of interaction within these groups and in the entire community of survivors approximates more closely the characteristics of intimate, personal, informal, sympathetic, direct, spontaneous and sentimental interaction set forth in the concept of the primary group."

Obviously, there are many unique variables which cannot be considered here which would ultimately affect the acceptance of loss, but, in general, disasters which create massive suffering also create the conditions in which relative deprivation also operates. Too, the increased cohesiveness which occurs moves the community toward a qualitative difference in social relationships which are precisely the types of support which have always been critical for adjusting to bereavement and in coping with grief in a socially productive manner.

SUMMARY AND CONCLUSIONS

Most widespread images of disaster behavior are based on a concept of the weakness of the average individual and the fragility of typical social organization in being able to cope with crises. Research, however, has revealed the resilience of individuals and social structures under conditions of great adversity. Four different behavioral contexts have been examined here: reactions to warning, reactions to threat, reactions to impact, and coping with loss. In all of these situations, the family and the community context provided mechanisms which tended to reduce, deflect, and soften the potential consequences of a disaster event.

21

MEETING MENTAL HEALTH NEEDS IN A DISASTER

a public health view

Jack Zusman

The title of this chapter summarizes very briefly the general subject. However, it probably implies the existence of more knowledge about some of the crucial issues of disaster situations than we actually have. An appropriate subtitle for the chapter might be, *What Are the Implications, for Disaster Services and Rescue Workers, of the Good Deal We Know and the Great Deal We Suspect About Human Reactions in Disaster, and What Do We Need to Do to Find Out More?*

Among the leading competitors for the title of "World's Oldest Profession" surely must be rescue workers. There can be little doubt that when man was still living in caves, children got their hands caught in crevices, families became trapped under landslides, forest fires destroyed villages, and flash floods wiped out dwellings and food and clothing supplies. It seems reasonable to assume also that even at that time some persons became adept at helping the victims while some of the more reflective members of the group noticed that being exposed to a situation involving great threat or great loss resulted in great emotional distress. Whatever means there were available then to restore calm and soothe jagged nerves were no doubt applied.

How far have we come since then and what are we doing to take advantage of our superior knowledge? Not too far and not too much, unfortunately.

Psychiatric case studies of individuals who have gone through disasters of one sort or another abound and are too numerous to list here. However, the interested reader may wish to review Weil and Dunsworth (427), Adler (5), Moore and Friedsam (294), Fogleman and Parenton (126), and also the many reports of the total aspects of individual disasters published by the National Academy of Sciences, National Research Council, Washington, DC, and the extensive bibliography in the Office of Emergency Preparedness (467). Some reports assemble data for a few individuals, others for hundreds. Most of our beliefs about disaster reactions are based on case studies. Yet most of these studies lack a crucial perspective which would help us to understand their significance and determine exactly how much of a problem exists with psychological reactions to disaster. This perspective might be called the epidemiologic one.

EPIDEMIOLOGIC PERSPECTIVE

Epidemiology is concerned with total populations, not just treated cases, and with natural history, not just brief segments of individuals' lives. The authors of the conventional case studies have not told us how their cases compare with the individuals they did not see. Does each reported case represent a hundred untreated cases with similar or worse symptoms, or is each case an isolated event? Since, as far as we know, every human group—whether residing in the Garden of Eden or in a concentration camp—contains some individuals with mild symptoms and some individuals with serious symptoms of mental illness, do these observed postdisaster cases simply represent the expected natural incidence of mental illness which happened to occur after the disaster or do they represent additional unexpected cases reacting to the stress of disaster?

Does each reported case represent a brief response to severe stress in which recovery is quite likely without intervention, leaving no sequelae, or is it the beginning of a downhill course unless there is effective intervention?

Of the population exposed to the stress of disaster, which persons develop symptoms and which do not? What predisaster experiences and traits *immunize* a person against stress and what experiences increase susceptibility?

Such questions can be answered only by total population studies and a lifetime point of view.

Before considering the epidemiologic perspective any further, it will be useful to summarize the information provided by case studies.

Case Study Findings

In general those who have examined groups of persons exposed to disaster report findings which may be remembered easily as "three-by-three." Tyhurst's work (412) is typical. Cases can be divided into three categories and the reactions to the disaster fall into three phases. (Of course, no situation conforms exactly to general principles and the nature, magnitude, and length of the disaster process, as well as the predisaster state of the population, significantly influence the reaction.)

From case studies it seems that in a population exposed to disaster, somewhat less than one fourth of the persons may operate efficiently and effectively (cool and collected) to get rescue operations under way and begin restoring normal conditions. Another one fourth of the population or less will show grossly inappropriate responses to the situation: confusion, paralysis, hysterical reactions, and sometimes psychosis. More than one half of the individuals will show behavior characterized as stunned and bewildered but only for a short period of time. They will then begin operating effectively to deal with the disaster.

With regard to the phases, the first phase of postdisaster reaction (*impact*) consists of random movement, isolated rescue efforts by individuals, and generally ineffective responses. In the second phase (*recoil*), people begin to get together, search for leadership, and respond very readily to suggestions for action. There is a good deal of dependency but also altruism (see Chapter 19) and concern for the welfare of others. In the last stage (*posttraumatic period*), before return to normal behavior, there is mild euphoria, high group morale, and a good deal of optimism. This response probably occurs in large part because of the effective group behavior which often appears out of the second phase. However, for some individuals this period is marked by the development of chronic symptoms.

Most of the postdisaster case studies are relatively short-term. They involve days, weeks, or at most, months and therefore tell us relatively little about the effect of major disaster over the course of a lifetime. Moore and Friedsam (294), for example, did a 4-month follow-up and considered that long-term.

Long-Term Effects of Severe Environmental Stress

In order to obtain information about long-term effects, we must turn to studies of other kinds of severely stressful situations which usually are not thought of in connection with disaster studies. Nevertheless, these provide us with a good deal of information if we are willing to make the assumption that the forces operating are similar to those in disaster.

Examples of long-term studies are those of concentration camp survivors by Krystal and Niederland (234), atomic bombing survivors by Lifton (256), and psychological casualties of military service by Lidz (255). Among the prominent themes of these reports are long-term psychological (and often physical) disability in some survivors, including nightmares, fears, difficulty in concentrating, and general loss of interest in life. There is also a frequent feeling of guilt at having survived when others in exactly the same situation perished. Occasionally there is a special social status accorded to survivors: for example, the *Hibakusha*, the atomic bomb survivors (256), and this has both negative and positive aspects although the negative ones may predominate.

Military studies are particularly useful in that they involve *the distillate* of extremely large numbers of individuals who have been exposed to stress of many different degrees, while the rescue service (i.e., the military medical service) remains fairly uniform and tends not to be disrupted by disaster. Military psychiatrists have developed a good deal of experience in diagnosis and effective treatment of psychiatric casualties (146).

Military experience indicates quite definitely that severe stress can cause long-term mental disability. It is also clear that the mixture of etiological factors is complex. The status of the individual soldier's group and his ties to that group influence his susceptibility to symptom development, and the physical environment influences the nature of his symptoms. The location and nature of treatment influences his recovery, as does (surprisingly) the social integration of the psychiatrist who treats him (146). Finally, the existence of a vast network of treatment facilities and disability compensation through the Veterans Administration must have an effect.

Long-term studies, although they complement the more numerous short-term studies, still do not provide the entire picture. To fill the gap, the epidemiologic approach should be considered.

EPIDEMIOLOGY

Epidemiology involves the study of total populations, not just of individuals who are manifestly ill or who happen to enter treatment. In this way it is possible to learn about the entire spectrum of disease, starting with those who have no disease at all, going on to those whose symptoms are minimal and usually not recognized, and finally on to those whose symptoms are so severe and disabling that they may not be able to make them known and therefore may not receive treatment. In the middle group are the many individuals who do receive treatment and who are typically the subjects of case studies.

A psychiatric epidemiologic study of disaster should tell whether there are more individuals disabled following the disaster than would normally be expected from the same population *had there been no disaster*. It should also tell what proportion of the group exposed to the disaster are affected in any way and what are the specific characteristics of the group which is affected in contrast to the group which is unaffected.

There are few, if any, adequate epidemiologic studies of disaster situations, and there are good reasons for this because epidemiologic research usually requires comparisons in the status of a population for at least two points in time. This means that typically there is a pre-event baseline study and then a study of the same population following exposure to some noxious agent.

Disasters by their very nature are unexpected. Usually when disaster strikes, preparations have been minimal and certainly little thought has been given to carrying out a baseline epidemiologic investigation to lay the groundwork for the follow-up study. Therefore, the basis for comparison is usually missing.

Secondly, epidemiology requires that the subject of the study be a defined population. It must be possible to know with certainty who falls into the counted group and who does not and to be able to locate all of the members of the group to be counted. Yet in disasters the population is usually disrupted. In a serious disaster of large magnitude, many individuals will leave the area and cannot be traced. Even in a smaller disaster there is likely to be a significant amount of moving, particularly if one effect of the disaster is destruction of homes. Since one of the most frequent means of characterizing a population is that of geographic location—particularly by home address—the boundaries of the population are lost and a study is impossible.

Finally, many epidemiologic studies depend on existing service agencies to provide a significant element of the study, i.e., classification and diagnosis of affected individuals. It is extremely expensive and often impossible for the researchers themselves to examine every member of a population or even an adequate population sample. Instead, the assumption may be made that cases treated by agencies represent the actual number of symptomatic individuals in the population and that those individuals who do not receive treatment are not in need of it. (It has already been pointed out that this is a doubtful assumption.) However, if the questionableness of this assumption is put aside for a moment, the problem still remains that in a disaster the treatment services themselves are often disrupted. Even if not disrupted, they are significantly changed and, in fact, are likely to be shifting during the very period of study.

Immediately following a disaster there is likely to be a shortage of treatment services. This will affect agency intake, diagnosis, and treatment policies so that the cases treated at that point cannot properly be compared with cases in treatment before the disaster. As treatment resources pour into the disaster area, the service shortage abates, and eventually there may be a surplus. At that point individuals whose symptoms probably do not warrant treatment and who certainly would not have been treated earlier in the rescue operation may be invited to come in for treatment and will be counted on the epidemiologic rolls.

Therefore, the researcher who finds an increased number of treated cases or who finds a cycle of changing frequency of cases cannot know whether this change represents a true change in the population or simply is based on changing admission policies in the treatment agencies.

A less serious problem, but one nevertheless frequently present, is that under the stress of disaster the agencies tend to neglect their record keeping which in any case often has not been very useful for research. Information thus becomes even less accessible.

THE 1972 WILKES-BARRE FLOOD

A typical range of the problems mentioned previously was encountered in the Wilkes-Barre, Pennsylvania, area where an epidemiologic type of study was carried out after the serious flood in the spring of 1972.

Results of the Flooding

On June 23, 1972, following Hurricane Agnes, the Susquehanna River began breaking protective dikes and flooding sections of Luzerne and Wyoming Counties in the Wilkes-Barre metropolitan area in northeastern Pennsylvania. By June 26, more than 72,000 of the 342,000 residents of the area had been dislocated, and the total economic loss was estimated at as much as $500,000,000 (see Chapter 26).

Rescue efforts began immediately but, as is to be expected, they were relatively uncoordinated at the beginning. Mental health professionals were involved in flood-related activities as soon as the flood danger was announced. Unfortunately, this announcement came only about a day before the flood and caught the service agencies relatively unprepared. In part, this was because several previous severe river floods had not reached the top of the dikes at Wilkes-Barre. Preflood efforts by mental health professionals were simply to evacuate files and assist in building up the dikes. After the flood (in which the homes of approximately 50% of the staff of the Wilkes-Barre Mental Health Center were washed out), professionals at first helped with rescue and evacuation but soon began to organize to assist flood victims in need of psychiatric care. A number of teams were set up, radio communications were established, and volunteer workers from outside the area were assimilated.

Crisis Intervention Operation

Federal funding for establishing a group of outreach crisis intervention workers became available in August. Evaluation of this outreach program was the responsibility of the State University of New York at Buffalo, Division of Community Psychiatry, which began partial operation in the area in late August, weeks after the event. Although efforts were made to reconstruct data for the period during which no researchers were on the scene, the data were, of course, far from satisfactory.

The epidemiologic information which could be obtained is sketchy. Few good baseline data were available. The most important thing which can be said for the information is that it is the best that was available.

Epidemiologic Data

Mental Health Center 1 in Wilkes-Barre, which served much of the affected population, admitted 260 patients between June 24 and August 28, 1970, and 283 patients between June 24 and August 24, 1971. In 1972, the postflood period, 343 patients were admitted, an increase of 21%.

Of the patients admitted in 1971, 33 were classified as having "thought and affective disorder." In 1972, 102 cases were in that category, an increase of 208% and far beyond the increase in number of cases. In 1971, 25 patients classified as having "disturbance of social relationship" were admitted, in comparison to 9 cases in 1972 after the flood—a decrease of 64%.

At state hospitals serving the two-county area the admissions in July 1972 were higher than for any month of the previous 4 years. Death statistics showed a sharp increase in Luzerne County in June, July, August, and September, 1972, in comparison with the same months in previous years. In June 1972 there were more suicides than in any month since January 1969. Total statistics for 1972 showed 38 suicides in comparison with 23 in 1971. There were also large increases in deaths due to heart disease in July, August, and September of 1972. Between July 1, 1971, and June 30, 1972, the local drug abuse treatment agency received 522 referrals. From July 1, 1972, to March 30, 1973, a postflood period of only 9 months, there were 932 referrals. All of these data, although admittedly inadequate and probably somewhat inaccurate, suggest that there have indeed been long-term, unfortunate psychological (as well as physical) effects of the disaster. Our study is not yet completed and we hope eventually to have more details.

PREPARATION FOR MENTAL HEALTH SERVICES IN DISASTER RELIEF

In the absence of more definitive information, policy proposals and decisions must be made based on the best available working assumptions. Before turning to a consideration of suggested policies and an examination of present operations, these working assumptions should be stated.

1. Immediately following a disaster a significant proportion of the involved population will exhibit symptoms of psychological stress, and a few of these individuals will show very serious symptoms.

2. Any individual who shows symptoms is at risk of developing long-term disability.
3. Appropriate intervention will relieve many symptomatic individuals and therefore reduce the risk of disability.
4. Susceptibility to development of symptoms after a disaster can be reduced by appropriate preparation of individuals prior to the disaster.

The current commonly accepted approach to disaster rescue operations in the United States is seriously deficient in dealing with the psychological aspects of disaster. In three fundamental phases of disaster work—predisaster preparation, training of disaster workers, and actual disaster operations—this deficiency is pervasive and almost complete. In instance after instance, highly trained, competent disaster workers at all levels of professional responsibility can be seen functioning as if their patient–clients had no psychological needs and were simply physical beings. Disaster victims can be seen time and time again with every tiny cut neatly bandaged, every possible fracture splinted, paper work nicely completed, and serious psychological symptoms completely neglected.

Training

Most front-line rescue workers in the United States come from two groups: regular fulltime government employees such as policemen, firemen, and ambulance attendants whose day-to-day duties involve a good portion of "rescue" work although often on a very small scale; and volunteers (some of whom, e.g., volunteer firemen, are highly trained and experienced), and temporarily-assigned government employees. A second echelon of rescue workers consists of physicians, nurses, other medical personnel, and social workers who participate as part of their regular fulltime duties but who are usually (incorrectly) not considered to be rescue workers because they frequently operate at some distance from the scene of the disaster.

Many of these workers start out ill prepared to deal with problems of psychosocial stress. Training front-line rescue workers such as policemen and volunteers to meet the mental and physical needs of disaster victims is usually through formal short-term courses, often taught by individuals who are themselves volunteers or at least not fulltime teachers of rescue work. The system of standardized first aid courses and loosely supervised instructors established by the American Red Cross, one of the most widely used teaching operations, serves as an example. Other organizations have established similar teaching systems. In every case these depend heavily on use of a textbook, a canned curriculum, and a predetermined set of exercises. Because of this standardization, it is possible to know the nature of the training of rescue workers on a national scale.

Examination of a number of the texts in common use reveals that they are generally uniform in their approach to psychological problems. Examples are: Grant and Murray (153); Committee on Injuries, American Academy of Orthopaedic Surgeons (461); and American Red Cross (457). These usually contain a page or two on how to restrain an individual who is acting in a very bizarre or dangerous manner; how to recognize the acute effects of alcohol and intoxicating drugs; and sometimes a discussion of the legal rights and responsibilities of first aid workers in restraining individuals. No text could be found which considered such issues as the psychological effects of physical injury; the psychological effects of disaster upon injured and uninjured victims alike; and the psychological effects on rescue workers of having to operate in the midst of disaster conditions.

Physicians and other second-line professionals are similarly ill prepared to deal with these kinds of problems. Most medical professionals now take psychiatry as part of their basic training program. Many members of related mental health professions (e.g., social work, psychology) also take such courses. However, psychiatry is usually taught as a formal academic discipline with great emphasis on theory and major illness. There is usually little consideration of minor problems such as the impact of current stress and what to do about it.

The personal characteristics of rescue workers often pose a problem. The newly recruited policeman, fireman, or volunteer (and with the rapid expansion of services in recent years, many workers *are* new) is often barely out of his teens. His interests are likely to center on girls, cars, his career, and perhaps his new marriage. How can he spontaneously empathize with a bereaved family, a seriously injured victim, a depressed and senile grandparent? Too often, expressing feelings of concern, pity, or even fear is considered a lack of toughness or manhood.

Operations

In view of these deficiencies, from which most rescue workers suffer, it is not surprising that in operation they commonly neglect the emotional needs of their patients. A number of workers have pointed out that policemen (who are probably the prototypical rescue workers) tend to be uncomfortable or even apparently unconcerned when called upon to intervene in psychosocial crisis situations such as domestic disputes. This is despite the fact that a significant proportion of police calls involve such problems and that such calls are generally considered among the most dangerous which policemen face. Our own observations of one police department and associated rescue units over a period of several years support these observations. Bard (21) has established a widely recognized training program in domestic crisis intervention for policemen in order to deal with one aspect of this problem. (See Chapter 11 for further discussion of the role of police in disaster aid.)

In the police agency which we studied, approximately 26% of all calls were related to psychosocial crises. Yet the training which policemen receive both through the Police Academy and through American Red Cross first aid courses does not cover assisting persons in psychosocial crises. The firemen who participate with police in rescue work similarly receive no training in this area although they all take Red Cross courses and, more recently, a New York State emergency medical technician course.

In the agency studied, policemen tended to ignore the emotional reactions of persons they were dealing with. When they cannot ignore such reactions, policemen carry out whatever maneuvers they believe will quickly quiet the individual. This may include a superficial emotional closeness, expressions of sympathy, or encouragement of ventilation. When the individual does not respond to these maneuvers, the policeman typically becomes increasingly uncomfortable and attempts to leave the situation as rapidly as possible or to exert his authority to enforce quiet when he can appropriately do so.

Firemen, on the other hand, seem to maintain an emotional distance while they work quietly and efficiently to minister to the physical needs of the individual. As soon as immediate first aid measures are completed, the individual is whisked as rapidly as possible to the hospital, often without the presence of a family member or even communication with a family member which would in itself act as a soothing element during a stressful period.

Starr (391) has reported on a neglected aspect of psychological situations in disasters—that of the rescue worker himself. In a recent night club fire in Montreal in which 37 people died and more than 50 were injured, the majority of those injured were treated at a few nearby hospitals where nurses worked for many hours. The stress on workers who must deal hour after hour with dead and seriously injured victims, often under primitive and confusing conditions, is difficult to appreciate. Our own observations substantiate this. A physician who is accustomed to working in a brightly lighted hospital room with proper equipment at hand, the necessary personnel assisting him, and a chair and a cup of coffee to relax with between tasks cannot appreciate the chaotic conditions under which rescue workers must often provide service. One can only admire the policemen or firemen who, at a nighttime bus disaster, for example, can find their way amidst a maze of parked cars and emergency vehicles, highway flares, leaking fire hoses, crowds of onlookers, hidden clumps of mud and sand, and highway ditches, all illuminated by headlights and flashing red lights, to find the injured and minister to their needs. What is the emotional cost to these workers to exert the self control, the drive, and the efficiency to work for hours without any emotional outlet or even any recognition that an emotional outlet would be helpful? The "professional armor" that develops through such situations must be thick indeed. Hence the emotional distance between worker and client.

Importance of Predisaster Training

A third deficient phase is predisaster preparation. Although good evidence is lacking, theoretical indications are strong that much of the negative effect of disaster and other kinds of psychosocial stress can be minimized through activities carried out before the stress occurs. Caplan (63) has discussed anticipatory guidance, through which individuals are told about what to expect in a crisis and encouraged to prepare themselves for what they will encounter. The military services have found that by strengthening a group and keeping the group together through the stressful situation, the rate of psychiatric casualties can be reduced. The success of programs such as Outward Bound and military survival schools suggest that by exposing individuals gradually to increasingly stressful situations which push them almost to the point of disorganization, individuals can learn to operate effectively in stressful situations and develop confidence in their ability to do so.

However, these principles have rarely been applied outside unique situations such as military or Peace Corps training. Although disasters are not rare in the United States, community drills and even less elaborate discussions about how to cope with disaster are unpopular and rare. Rescue workers do commonly engage in drills, but usually these drills are not under stressful conditions, and many elements of the drill are in the *pretend* category which is a far cry from the real thing. Even more striking is the fact that the fulltime workers are the ones who commonly receive no training at all beyond their original introductory or basic professional training, which may be many years in the past by the time it is called on in a major disaster. In many municipalities, policemen, firemen, and ambulance attendants are so occupied with carrying out their day-to-day duties that no time is allocated for practice to prepare for the unusual overwhelming emergencies and psychosocial crises triggered by disasters.

The result is, of course, that when disaster occurs, the victims are more vulnerable to stress than they need be, and the workers are less equipped to operate under stress than they should be.

Implications of Studies

The implications of these findings fall into three categories—training and predisaster preparation, rescue operations, and research.

Training. Training must be increased at all levels, beginning with average citizens (the potential victims of disaster) and including all elements of the rescue system up to highly trained professionals such as physicians. Admittedly such additional drill and training is costly in terms of time and effort. Although much of the data that could demonstrate unequivocally the value of good preparation is lacking, there is enough to suggest strongly that preparation in advance reduces later problems.

Predisaster Preparation. Individuals residing in disaster-prone areas (e.g., areas subject to flood, tropical storms, or earthquakes) should devote more attention to discussing preparations for disaster, working together in groups, assisting each other in an organized way, and possibly even having drills where they can experience the effects of controlled amounts of stress. Of course, such a proposal is likely to be politically unpopular. Nevertheless, it is our responsibility as professionals to make known what we know and to attempt to convince those who are in need of this knowledge to accept it. For the average citizen, preparation to face a crisis is likely to pay off not only in case of disaster but also in facing the routine developmental crises of life.

Rescue workers must receive greatly strengthened training in mental health aspects of disaster work. This can be accomplished through rewriting of standard texts (or supplementation of these texts) and preparation of related teaching materials. There must be a much greater emphasis in regular first aid courses on the general emotional climate in which first aid activities take place and a recognition that every individual has emotional needs, not only the individual who appears mentally ill. The rescue worker's own emotional needs must be considered, both through drills which apply some of the stress which he will face in the actual disaster situation, and through postdisaster discussions in which he can express his feelings and examine them in a supportive setting. Mental health professionals interested in emergency work lag far behind their colleagues in such fields as orthopedics or cardiology where national organizations have sponsored training programs to translate the latest medical knowledge into terms meaningful and useful for rescue workers.

All service professionals, medical and social welfare, must also be trained in the psychological aspects of disaster. They, too, have important roles to play which can ameliorate or exacerbate the psychiatric casualty incidence following disaster. They, too, have their own emotional needs which require some consideration when they are working under disaster conditions.

In planning disaster rescue operations, increased consideration must be given to methods of dealing with the immediate mental health needs of the population involved. It must be recognized that a small fraction of the population will suffer from long-term symptoms and require continued involvement.

Rescue workers who are adept at recognizing emotional problems and dealing with them must be rewarded for their skill. Much as contests are now held and awards given to those who are proficient at extricating victims from smashed cars or splinting long-bone fractures, encouragement must also be given to the good mental health first aid worker. On a professional level, the surgeon who recognizes the emotional needs of his patients must be credited with an effective skill in healing, much as the man who is effective in use of instruments and sutures already is.

Research. The final area is research. As has already been pointed out, there are probably enough case studies of victims of disaster. Although it is enticing when faced with a good number of clinical cases to begin categorizing and describing them for publication, the research need is in other areas. A high priority should be given to epidemiologic research— that is, studies of total populations exposed to disaster with intensive efforts made to find out about those who customarily are lost to follow-up or who do not apply for help. Comparisons must be made between the condition of these populations before and after disaster. This means increased attention to carrying out baseline studies in disaster-prone areas and to moving quickly to follow up disasters in areas where good baseline information is already available. Long term follow-up of disaster victims must be carried out despite the fact that this is difficult and expensive work. In fact, it is probably no more expensive to do a limited number of good postdisaster studies than to do a large number of mediocre studies as is now being done.

A second important area of research is what might be called operations research applied to disaster operations. We need to investigate delivery of services in order to answer a variety of questions: What kinds of persons make good disaster workers? What kinds of training are useful and what kinds useless? How many staff are likely to be needed for disasters of varying severity? And, most important, are present concepts of disaster work correct and useful? Evaluation studies, a small but essential part of operations research, must be extensively supported. The history of social welfare services is that testimonials can be generated for just about any kind of service, even when subsequent, more objective studies may demonstrate that the testimonials have been incorrect. For far too long rescue operations have been guided mainly by the anecdotes and impressions of experienced workers, rather than by the careful observations of trained analysts. This situation must be changed.

22

DIAGNOSIS AND TREATMENT OF STRESS RESPONSE SYNDROMES

general principles

Mardi J. Horowitz

Stress response syndromes generally include signs and symptoms of two distinct, seemingly opposite but actually interlocking, clusters which can be labeled as "denials" and "intrusions." These clusters of experience often occur in phases, and treatment should be oriented toward recognition of these phases.

BACKGROUND

Clinical, field, and experimental investigations are in agreement in finding denial and intrusion as general stress response tendencies. Conglomerates of these signs and symptoms comprise the semiofficial diagnosis of "traumatic neurosis" as defined in psychiatric (177) and psychoanalytic (292) dictionaries although this diagnosis has been dropped from the official nomenclature (DSM-II, 1968). These indications of denial and intrusion are found in such types of stress response syndromes as:

1. Immediate patterns of psychological response to a stress event. This roughly correlates with the diagnostic terms *acute traumatic neurosis, gross stress reaction,* and *transient situational disturbance.*

The research on which this paper is based has been supported in part by grants from the USPHS (NIMH 2-444949-24744) and the Academic Senate of the University of California (504903-19900).

2. Extended (subacute or chronic) patterns of response to the stress event. This roughly correlates with common usage of the term *traumatic neurosis* when the symptoms or signs are relatively severe.

3. The precipitation of latent and idiosyncratic psychological conflicts and reactions by external events which may or may not be stressful to the average person. This category correlates with the general idea of precipitating stress, crisis, and psychoneurosis that follows trauma.

4. Changes in personality as a consequence of stress events and items 1–3 above. This category would perhaps correlate with special syndromes such as the *survivor syndrome* (233, 303).

Clinical studies, anchored by the early work of Breuer and Freud (51), reveal the compulsive repetitiousness that characterizes the intrusive phase and the avoidance maneuvers, such as repression, which characterize the denial–numbing phase of responses to an external stress event (137, 144, 182, 370). Field studies indicate the generality of such responses across populations of divergent personalities (75, 162, 197, 198). Experimental studies confirm that these tendencies occur in most persons after a variety of stress events (184, 185, 240).

PHASES

General stress response tendencies can be distinguished by phases although individuals and situations vary. The degree and time for anticipation before an external stress event will alter the nature of responses after the event. Individual history and character patterns will affect the order of entry into phases, time in each phase, and the clinical manifestations within a phase. The usual pattern, in spite of these variances, is an initial response of outcry, followed by denial, then intrusion, then working through, and finally, completion. As shown in Figure 22.1, the initial outcry

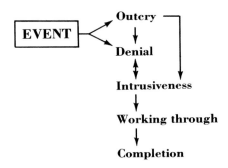

FIGURE 22.1 Phases of response after a stressful event.

may not occur and the person may enter directly into the denial period or even into the intrusive phase.

Outcry

Outcry is a term for an almost reflexive emotional expression upon first impact of unexpected new information. The expression may take the form of weeping, panic, moaning, screaming, or fainting. For example, a woman told that her husband has just died in a work accident may sob in anguish.

Denial

Denial is the term given a phase relevant to the implications of the stressful event in which there is some combination of emotional numbing, ideational avoidance, and behavioral constriction. Detailed signs and symptoms of this state are grouped by cognitive systems in Table 22.1 (183). The widow alluded to previously might enter this phase after a day or so. For example, relatives might come to join her both to help out and to participate in the funeral services. Since they are probably not as deeply affected by the loss, they may have already entered the intrusive and repetitive phase. They would have many thoughts of the deceased, cry episodically, and experience feelings of sadness and painful loss.

The widow, in contrast, might be numb, fearless, and even involved in hyperactive planning and "entertaining" of the relatives. If the relatives are charitable, but ignorant of stress response tendencies, they may say, "She is very strong," or, "She is doing very well." If they are less charitable, they will say, "She didn't really care for him."

Intrusion

Intrusion is a descriptive label for the period of unbidden ideas and pangs of feeling which are difficult to dispel and are of direct or symbolic behavioral reenactments of the stress event complex—a complex which is an amalgam of internal and external components of meaning. Intrusions include nightmares of the stress event, recurrent unbidden images, and startle reactions with perceptual or associational reminders. This variety of intrusive signs and symptoms is listed in Table 22.1 where contrasts can be drawn with roughly equivalent denial signs and symptoms.

The widow mentioned earlier might enter an intrusive–repetitive phase after a period of denial. But this phase might not begin until after her relatives have left. Then, 6 weeks or 6 months later, she might begin to oscillate between periods of denial and numbing and episodes in which she experienced waves of searing grief, ideas about the emptiness of her life, and even an hallucinatory sense of the presence of her lost husband.

TABLE 22.1 Tabulation of Common Stress Responses

Systems	Intrusive–repetitive phase	Denial–numbness phase
Perception and attention	Hypervigilance; startle reactions	Blunting of perception and attention Dazed appearance Selective inattention
Conscious represen-tation	Intrusive–repetitive thoughts and behaviors illusions pseudohallucinations nightmares reenactments (direct or symbolic) ruminations	Amnesia (complete or partial); nonexperience
Ideational processing (sequential and simultaneous organ-ization of representa-tions)	Overgeneralization; inabil-ity to concentrate on other topics; preoccupation; con-fusion and disorganization	Denial; loss of reality ap-propriacy; constriction of associational width; inflex-ibility of organization of thought
Emotional	Emotional attacks or "pangs" (fear, guilt, rage, shame, sorrow)	Numbness
Somatic	Symptomatic sequelae of chronic fight or flight readi-ness (or of exhaustion of such responses)	Tension–inhibition type
Control	If direct controls are insufficient, other control systems may be activated leading to symptoms such as with-drawal, substitutive or counterphobic behaviors, altera-tion of state of consciousness, or regression. Flight into overactivity is common in the denial phase.	

* Horowitz MJ: Phase-oriented treatment of stress response syndromes. Am J Psy-chother 27: 506–515, 1973

Order of Phases

Persons may enter the abstract sequence of phases (shown in Figure 22.1) at any point and go through sequence in any order. Take, as an example, the instance of a couple in a car that suddenly veers off a mountain road and descends a steep slope strewn with boulders and trees. The driver stays cool, skillfully maneuvering the car past obstructions while the passenger thinks of the destructive possibilities, is terribly frightened, and faints. As the car comes to a safe halt the driver relaxes, considers the same shattering possibilities, and only then feels fear or faints. When action is possible, alert perception, planning, and execution top the hierarchy of claims on cognition. Fearsome images of possible bodily damage are warded off. When passivity is possible, with relaxation of warding-off operations, then recognition of possibly disastrous outcomes and emotional flooding may occur.

Theory

The phases of denial and intrusion, which seem antithetic at a phenomenologic level, are linked at a theoretical level. Were it not for warding-off maneuvers, repetitions would not be experienced as intrusive.

The intrusions are continuations of cognitive and emotional processes that may lead to assimilation of the stressful event. Such completion would include the revision of pre-stress event schematas of self, others, and the world so that these cognitive structures were aligned to new realities. With completion, memory of the stress event would be integrated into long-term storage, and a kind of dynamic or active memory, with an intrinsic tendency to repetition, could be erased.

Before such completion, each repetition is discrepant with enduring schemata, and this incongruity evokes responses, including felt emotions. The threat of painful affect, with repetitions, can be averted by inhibitory controls. Such defensive operations produce the state of denial and numbing by preventing representation and associational linkages or facilitating oppositional ideas and feelings (185).

Intrusion and denial phases are, then, phenomenologic manifestations of a dynamic conflict. The tendency toward repetition-until-completion is opposed by controls aimed at avoidance of the painful emotions evoked by the new information. Since the balance between operants varies, the technique of treatment should also vary according to the phase of stress response of the patient.

PHASE-ORIENTED TREATMENT

In the past there has been a tendency to determine treatment techniques by schools or "brand names." For example, psychoanalytically oriented psychiatrists in World War II tended toward abreactive–cathartic treatments, and so-called directive–organic psychiatrists tended toward sedation, support, and rest. Combinations of treatment were used by many, of course, and, in general, treatment was revised during the Korean and Vietnamese wars (46, 155, 186).

General Application

The central aims of the two broad categories of treatment can be stated at a very general level. Suppose the same person goes through phases of response after a stress event. These phases are determined, to a large extent, by the current degree of control over a tendency to repetition. In general, rest and support treatment is an effort to supplement relatively weak controls. The treatment staff takes over some aspects of control operations, and they reduce the likelihood of emotional and ideational triggers to repeated representations. In contrast, the abreactive–cathartic methods reduce controls through suggestion, social pressure, hypnosis, or hypnotic drugs. The long-range goal of the abreactive–cathartic treatment

TABLE 22.2 A Classification of Treatments for Stress Response Syndromes*

Systems	Denial–numbing phase	Intrusive–repetitive phase
To change controlling processes	Reduce controls; interpret defenses; use hypnosis & narcohypnosis suggestion; introduce social pressure and evocative situations (e.g., psychodrama); change attitudes that make controls necessary; uncover interpretations	Supply controls externally; structure time and events for patient; take over ego functions (e.g., organize information); reduce external demands & stimulus levels; encourage rest; provide identification models, group membership, good leadership, orienting values; behavior modification with reward and punishment
To change information processing	Encourage the following: abreaction, association, speech, use of images rather than just words in recollection and fantasy enactments (e.g., role playing, psychodramas, art therapy), reconstructions (to prime memory and associations), maintenance of environmental reminders	Work through and reorganize by clarifying and educative interpretive work; reinforce contrasting ideas (e.g., simple occupational therapy, moral persuasion); remove environmental reminders and triggers; suppress or dissociate thinking (e.g., sedation, tranquilizers, meditation)
To change emotional processing	Encourage catharsis and emotional relationships (to counteract numbness); supply objects	Support; evoke other emotions (e.g., benevolent environment); suppress emotion (e.g., sedation or tranquilizers); desensitization procedures; relaxation and biofeedback

* Horowitz MJ: Phase-oriented treatment of stress response syndromes. Am J Psychother 27: 506–515, 1973

is not to reduce controls, however, but to reduce the need for controls by helping the patient to complete the cycle of ideational and emotional responses to a stress event.

Individual Treatment

Such generalities orient understanding but do not help in the decisions for specific treatments. Any individual treatment is constructed by selection of many specific maneuvers from the repertoire of available techniques. This selection is based on clinical inference about the patient's immediate state and guided by theory. Unfortunately, the contemporary repertoire of techniques is poorly classified. A rudimentary attempt at phase-specific technique is presented in Table 22.2. The goal is to convey a general idea, not to recommend particular treatment forms. Chemical, social, Gestalt, and behavior therapy techniques have been included, along with psychoanalytically oriented focal psychotherapy techniques.

Treatment Goals

Completion of integration of the meanings of an event and development of adaptational responses are the goals of treatment of a stress response syndrome. One knows this end point is near when the person is able to freely think about, and freely *not* think about the event. These goals can be broken down according to immediate aims that depend on the patient's current state. When the stress event is on-going, aims may center on fairly direct support. When the external aspects of the event are over, but the person swings between *paralyzing* denial and *intolerable* attacks of ideas and feelings, then the immediate aim is to reduce the amplitude of these swings. Similarly, if the patient is frozen in a state of inhibition of cognitive-emotional processing, then the therapist must both induce further thought *and* help package responses into tolerable doses. These injunctions to "be careful" can also be tabulated, as in Table 22.3.

Variation in Individuals

Any person has characteristic modes for solving problems or warding off threatening ideas and feelings. These character styles will affect both response to general stress tendencies and response to therapeutic intervention. Also, any stress event will activate many lines of associational response, some more conflicted or harder to accept than others. At any given time, one complex of ideational and affective responses may be functionally intrusive, another complex may be latent, warded-off, and functionally in a denial phase. At that time the therapist would probably deal with the active complex and remain alert to evidence that other lines of response are inhibited from awareness. Thus, the individual therapy would be a far more complex situation than suggested by the foregoing generalizations.

TABLE 22.3 Priorities of Treatment Determined by Patient's Current State*

Priority	Patient's current state	Treatment goal
First	Under continuing impact of external stress event	Terminate external event or remove patient from continuity with it; provide temporary relationship; help with decisions, plans, or working through
Second	Swings to intolerable levels—ideational–emotional attacks; paralyzing denial and numbness	Reduce amplitude of oscillations to swings of tolerable intensity of ideation and emotion; continue emotional and ideational support; select techniques from *Intrusive–Repetitive Phases* (Table 22.2)
Third	Frozen in overcontrol state of denial and numbness (with or without intrusive repetitions)	Help patient "dose" reexperience of event and implications (i.e., help to remember for a time, put out of mind for a time, remember for a time, and so on); during periods of recollection, help patient organize as well as express experience; increase sense of safety in therapeutic relationship so patient can resume processing the event
Fourth	Able to experience and tolerate episodes of ideation and waves of emotion	Help patient work through associations (conceptual, emotional, object-relations, and self-image implications) of the stress event; help patient relate stress event to prior threats, relationship models, and self-concepts, as well as to future plans
Fifth	Able to work through ideas and emotions on his own	Work through loss of therapeutic relationship; terminate treatment

*Horowitz, MJ: Phase-oriented treatment of stress response syndromes. Am J Psychother 27:506–515, 1973

Decision Points

Each transition between phases becomes a decision point within the treatment contract. Not infrequently, the act of establishing a therapeutic contact may reduce pressure enough so that the patient can enter or regain a state of denial and numbing. If he was upset prior to this phase, he will feel much better.

As the patient feels less upset, he or she may be motivated to avoid discussing the stress event and its implications and want to withdraw from the therapeutic relationship. This change is manifested in a gut reaction of the therapist: the patient is boring, the curiosity of the therapist diminishes, and his enthusiasm wanes. The first therapy hours during the initial upset only begin to disclose information. The therapist wants to know much more, the patient, feeling less, discloses less. At this point, there is a danger of premature termination or overzealous pursuit of "material" or emotionality.

The denial is not an unhealthy defense to be removed, cracked, or even interpreted. It is an adaptive movement that allows the patient to resume control and will later allow him to dose the amount of reaction within tolerable limits. An appropriate therapeutic tactic is to simply continue or to make another appointment later on, in order to see when the patient enters a repetitive phase, and resume work then. Eventually the therapist can counteract denial even when it seems frozen or resistant to adaptation. Although both are characterized by low upset, the difference between denial and completion can be noted clearly. During denial, the implications of the event are not conscious, and the person does not have sufficient control over the stress event, memories, and responses, to discuss them freely.

KEY DECISION POINTS IN THE MIDDLE PHASE OF THERAPY

Recent stress events bring character traits and pathology into sharp relief. They activate latent conflicts and memories of past stress events. These observations have led to various positions on what direction therapy should take. To sharpen the issue, two divergent extremes can be stated:

1. States of stress are ideal times to work on character pathology, neurotic conflicts, and previous unintegrated stress events because change is necessary, static positions are disrupted, and the issues are unusually clear.
2. In spite of activation of traits, conflicts, and past memories, the main aim in treatment of stress response syndromes should be to

work through *that* syndrome to a point of relative completion. At that point the traits and conflicts will subside to latent status, and earlier traumas will be less emergent.

The divergence of views indicates a decision point rather than a controversy. This decision point can be located during the repetitive phase when the patient is bringing up the event and the associative contents and reactions to it. One route is toward character or *core neurotic conflict* analysis, the other toward working through the stress event to completion (Figure 22.2). There are, of course, many intervening choices. Note that the route that focuses on completion of the stress event in Figure 22.2 is diagrammed as shorter in time and is followed by a decision point at which character or conflict analysis can be recommended.

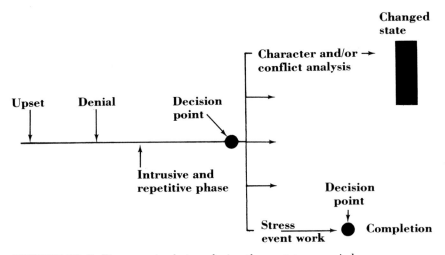

FIGURE 22.2   Therapeutic choices during the poststress period.

The direction at either decision point is followed, on the basis of multiple factors, by the informed patient working with the therapist's recommendations. It is unlikely that the stress event work can proceed without some work on relevant character traits, activated conflicts, and memories. The decision as to how far to go in this direction includes consideration of the degree to which traits, conflicts, and compulsive repetition of past traumas contribute to:

a) the occurrence of the recent stress event;

b) present reactions to the recent stress event; and

c) difficulties in working through the recent events or difficulties in the therapeutic relationship.

Other concerns in this decision include:

a) the general maladaption of the patient;

b) the readiness and capacity of the patient to change;

c) a kind of ratio consideration between the objective magnitude of the stress event and the degree of reaction of the patient;

d) cost and sufficiency factors.

SUMMARY

Clinical assessment of persons exposed to external stress events requires careful inquiry into both kinds of deflection from a homeostatic (or homeokinetic) state: extreme warding-off of the stress event and its implications, resulting in ideational denial and emotional numbing; and intrusive repetitiousness of memories and associations to the stress event, with pangs of painful feeling. Across groups of persons, there is a general tendency to denial first and then intrusion, in a progression of phasic responses to stress. Individuals will vary in the order of entry into such phases, time spent in a phase, degree of oscillation between phases, and specific manifestations during any phase. Treatment, in addition to orientation according to individual personality, should be phase-specific.

23

AN ECOLOGIC PERSPECTIVE
ON DISASTER INTERVENTION

Dwight Harshbarger

THE DISASTER

In the coal mining regions of the Appalachian Mountains, the expression *gob pile* refers to a refuse pile of slate and shale, often as large as a 3- to 5-story building, that is left as a byproduct in the deep mining of coal. The creation of gob piles has been virtually unregulated, and coal companies have been subject to few, if any, restrictions in dumping their refuse. In Abfervan, Wales, it was a gob pile that buried an elementary school a few years ago. In the southern West Virginia coal fields, gob piles are omnipresent—silent testimony to the region's single economic base.

Some gob piles catch fire and slowly smolder for years. Others when placed across ravines act as dams, with a single gob pile sometimes impounding hundreds of thousands of gallons of water. Historically, gob piles which have impounded water have not been classified as dams, and therefore have not been subject to state or federal controls on dam construction.

In February 1972 three gob pile dams traversed a ravine near the head of Buffalo Creek Valley, a narrow valley containing an 8-mile long series of communities, paralleling Buffalo Creek in the heart of southern West Virginia's Logan County. These dams were sequentially arranged, with the

The preparation of this report was supported by a research contract between the Bureau of Community Environmental Management, Department of Health, Education and Welfare; and West Virginia University (RFPEPAR 71-NEG-155), *A Survey and Analysis of Human Ecosystems and Human Service Systems in Appalachia.*

second and third dams resembling stair steps behind the first. Collectively they impounded over a million gallons of water.

At 8:05 AM on February 26, 1972, following weeks of winter rains, the uppermost of these dams broke, causing the other two gob pile dams to burst. A wall of 1.4 million gallons of water poured through the Buffalo Creek Valley, a valley that is sometimes no more than 100 yards wide. The force of the wall of water virtually leveled the entire communities of Lorado, Lundale, Craneco, and Sanders. Other communities suffered the loss of up to half of their homes. In 20 minutes 118 persons died, 4000 people were left homeless, and $50 million in property damage was done.

Unlike that in other flood disasters, this devastation more resembled the destruction of a tornado or earthquake than a flood. It was a rapid and "total loss" disaster, more like the Alaskan or San Francisco earthquakes than, for example, the 1972 floods of Hurricane Agnes.

INTERVENTION IN THE AFTERMATH

Immediately after the flood, mobile medical units from nearby hospitals, health agencies, and the Red Cross moved into the valley and began to provide services. The familiar images of friends and relatives searching for one another while warily watching the posting of the deceased list; of the human experiences in the temporary shelter of the local high school gymnasium; of the National Guard regulating entry and exit to the disaster area, were all present in the immediate aftermath of the Buffalo Creek flood.

Two functions were given highest priority immediately after the flood: 1) clearing debris, and 2) locating quasipermanent shelter for persons who lost their homes. Both have become subject of debate and hard feelings among residents of the valley and intervenors, and with the clarity afforded by hindsight, both raise a number of questions about the structure of intervention efforts in Buffalo Creek.

Role of National Guard

Immediately after the flood, the National Guard allowed no residents to return to their homes, and during this time National Guardsmen placed an "X" on all buildings which were to be destroyed. According to some residents, the X was frequently placed on a home without adequate inspection by Guardsmen. Further, some allege, this activity afforded Guardsmen themselves an opportunity to loot homes. While there is no clear evidence to support either of these claims, these beliefs existed, and they may have grown out of the nature of the intervention efforts. Clearly the continuation of the destruction of communities through governmental intervention deserves more careful consideration than it has received.

Role of HUD

The function of locating quasipermanent shelter for residents was largely carried out by the Department of Housing and Urban Development (HUD). In Buffalo Creek, as later in Wilkes-Barre, the basic strategy of HUD was to resettle survivors in mobile homes; 483 trailers were located on 14 sites in or near the valley. Residents were offered 1-year free trailer occupancy with an option to then purchase the trailer at a reduced cost. But, while HUD was rapid and efficient in responding to the immediate housing needs of Buffalo Creek residents, its policies raised serious and as yet unresolved problems.

Problems During the Aftermath

The first problematic policy concerned the procedure for assigning people to mobile home parks, and to their specific trailers. Assignment was made on a virtually first-come, first-serve basis. Little or no attempt was made to group in the same trailer park those residents who had lived in the same community before the flood. Survivors who had already lost their familiar personal possessions, found themselves further removed from the familiar. The social groupings which might facilitate the regeneration of community social structure, and thus lend socioemotional supports, were made almost impossible through this policy of assignment.

A second problem was created by the far higher density of residential units in the HUD trailer parks than in the home communities of flood survivors. Thus, added to the stress of the disaster, the problems of grief management among survivors, and the decimation of the potential for rapid recreation of community social structure, was the adjustment to high density residential living.

It is difficult to avoid speculation on the long-range consequences of these policies. The work of Selye (375, 376) on the general adaptation syndrome and stress; Cassel (67, 68, 69) on the relation between stability of social structures and health disorders; the Dohrnwends (95), on social mobility and mental disorder; Levy and Rowitz (248) on mental health and ecological characteristics of communities; and Rahe and Holmes (335) on the relations between life crises and disease onset have strongly suggested that community and individual life changes, and factors facilitating adaptation to change, may be major variables in producing physical and mental health problems.

Of particular interest is Cassel's research, in which he attempts to relate the individual's biological coping potential with tolerance for changes and disruptions in surrounding social systems, and the research of Rahe and Holmes which has quantified change and empirically related these measures to the probability of disease onset. Their work strongly suggests that reliable statistical probabilities for the onset of pathology among stressed individuals or populations can be developed.

All of the preceding research clearly indicates that increases in the unpredictable or the removal of familiar benchmarks in life, whether people or objects, increases the level of stress. When combined with the absence of a community social system and further complicated by the additional stresses of living under conditions of high density, one can only speculate on the long-term physical and mental health problems likely to emerge among flood survivors.

Presently, informal data has suggested that one of the largest HUD trailer parks in the valley is the site of a very high frequency of drug and alcohol abuse, family dismemberment, and other problem behaviors that might have been predicted from the ecological models developed in the research cited earlier.

Positive Aspects of the Intervention

On a more positive note, some mental health program development efforts were helpful in the months following the disaster. The nearby Logan–Mingo Comprehensive Community Mental Health Center, in cooperation with the West Virginia Department of Mental Health, established a mental health outpost in the valley, and organized a program of trailer visits which facilitated the management of grief among survivors. However, problems of staffing and program design have hampered the development of this effort. Similar grief management programs were developed by area ministers trained in clinical pastoral care. (See *TIME*, Oct. 29, 1972 for further discussion of these programs.) Both programs have been constrained by their limited resource base, as well as by the stresses and demands placed on their staffs. The latter problem will be discussed more fully later in this chapter.

LONG-TERM INTERVENTION

The Red Cross and the Office of Emergency Preparedness have made some $7 million in relief funds and $5.4 million in loans available to residents of Buffalo Creek Valley. The mining company which constructed the gob pile dam is slowly paying claims for property loss although it has not acknowledged formal responsibility for the disaster (see Chapter 24).

Various state and federal agencies which responded immediately after the disaster by setting up offices in and nearby the community had, by midsummer of 1972, closed their offices. Organized volunteer efforts subsided at about the same time, or shortly thereafter. While the mental health programs mentioned have continued, although with very limited resources, there has been no significant increase in other health services or health programs for residents of the valley.

A state–federal redevelopment plan for the valley has been developed. This document, while necessary for federal redevelopment aid, has had a highly controversial history, and it can be anticipated that its future is likely to be stormy. Among its controversial proposals is a highway, the construction of which would use large quantities of the scarce flat land on the valley floor, thus placing major constraints on future community development in certain parts of the Valley. While in other places or under other circumstances this might not be a major community problem, in Buffalo Creek the highway plan is seen by many survivors as further denying them the familiar, or a sense of place; in a sense it may be interpreted as an organized continuation of the flood damage.

PROBLEMS OF GROUPS AT RISK AFTER THE DISASTER

Three groups at risk, survivors, intervenors, and agencies, were clearly visible following the Buffalo Creek Disaster. While each group experienced some problems unique to the Appalachian Region, it is probable that many of their problems are experienced in other community disasters.

The Survivors

Virtually no one who lived in the Valley was untouched by the disaster. Many persons lost close friends, family, and personal possessions; some lost either family or possessions; many lost neither, but experienced the feelings, usually guilt feelings, associated with survival when all around them others were experiencing major loss. Workers in the disaster area during the first 24 hours after the flood have estimated that 88% of the 4000 persons displaced by the water exhibited shock and incoherent thinking. During these 24 hours, workers reported, there was little crying or manifestations of grief, rather, behavior was silent, emotions were numbed.

Later, anger among some, guilt among many, and grief among all were commonplace. Intervenors such as HUD, the Red Cross, and various state agencies were the frequent targets of anger stemming from feelings about personal losses. Anger seemed to be typical in persons who had lost property rather than in persons who suffered the loss of those with whom they had close social ties.

Now, over a year after the flood, two principal behavior problems remained. The first of these might be best described as phobic responses to rain, particularly among children. On rainy days many children became tense, clung to parents, and otherwise displayed behavior suggesting that they were emotionally distraught. While some kind of desensitization therapy seemed appropriate, the manpower to carry out such a task at the community level was unlikely to be available in the professionally under-manned environment of the southern West Virginian coal fields.

A second and much more pervasive problem is the hesitancy of many residents to engage in behaviors that allow them to "talk out" their feelings about losses experienced in the flood. This problem is a very complicated one, stemming both from the religious fundamentalism of the region and from cultural norms regarding the stolidity of mountaineers.

Many survivors believe that the flood was truly an Act of God. To be critical or even angry would be to blaspheme against the Lord. Hence, whatever feelings of rage might be present are internally censored and contribute to continuing tensions.

Complicating matters further is a view of life, both in mining towns and more generally in the mountains, that life is tough, and to survive one must accept hardship and continue on with life's tasks. In this way of thinking, to grieve is to belabor what cannot be undone, and in that sense human folly. Further, this behavioral norm is quite congruent with the fundamentalist religion of the region and is thus maintained by these parallel systems of support.

It should be noted that the traditional stolidity of mountaineers has probably been a very functional behavior, facilitating survival under very difficult social and economic conditions. The preceding is not intended as a criticism of that cultural characteristic. Rather the point is that this functional survival characteristic has certain dysfunctional qualities following major loss, in that it prevents the active processes of grief management regarded as so significant in the grief-crisis intervention literature [e.g., Lindemann (260), Caplan (63), Parkes (314), and Silverman (381)].

It also seems likely that feelings of loss and anomie which persons might have felt in the weeks and months following the flood were only intensified by the HUD policies previously described. In fact, it might be argued that if a deranged social scientist were to design a system of disaster intervention that would maximize pathology, it is likely that he would do precisely what was done.

The Intervenors

The provision of emergency services following disasters is typically focused on the survivor, rightly regarding survivors as in need of tremendous amounts of aid and support. However, such a point of view often overlooks the socioemotional needs of the intervenors themselves. These persons, whether Red Cross professionals or community volunteers, are expected to give inordinately of their energies, and to receive little in return for their efforts. And their casualty rate in Buffalo Creek, and probably in other disaster intervention efforts in general, has been high. For example, the mental health clinic established in the Valley had 3 directors in 7 months. Other agencies experienced similar problems. One lawyer, proud of his volunteer work in helping the valley's flood victims file claims for property loss, confided that he had to leave after two 12-hour work days, "I just couldn't take it," he said, referring to his own problems in managing the grief of his clients, not the long hours.

If intervention efforts are to reduce the rate of turnover among staff and increase the longevity of both personal and agency involvement in disaster intervention, careful attention must be given to socioemotional support systems for intervenors. This problem contributes to the rapid rate with which intervention agencies often organizationally disengage after disasters. Moreover, ineffective stress management among intervenors is also likely to reduce the quality and efficacy of problem solving among persons who have been delegated important responsibilities for both individual and community decision making.

The Agencies

Few agencies get an opportunity to practice disaster intervention, particularly following disasters in which entire communities are destroyed. Those agencies which do have some practice in the functional behaviors required of intervenors, agencies such as the Red Cross, are themselves commonly attacked as too bureaucratic and professionally aloof. ("They even charged 10¢ for a cup of coffee!") But beyond the problems of making agencies that are typically associated with disaster intervention a little more human in their efforts, it would seem that at least two problems in the agency organization of disaster intervention should be dealt with.

First is the problem of a conceptual framework for intervention efforts. Perhaps the logic of many agencies is expressed in the following excerpts from a letter from the Director of the Office of Emergency Preparedness (OEP) in the Executive Office of the President. The letter was written to a congressman who had relayed my criticism of federal intervention efforts in Buffalo Creek.

> Dr. Harshbarger raises some important considerations in providing temporary housing assistance following a major disaster. There is no question that psychological, sociological and ecological factors should be taken into consideration after a disaster strikes. However, these factors cannot, in our judgment, have the same priority as the physical necessity of providing shelter for disaster victims.
> When a disaster strikes, it is necessary to use the resources which are immediately available. The selection of trailer sites is done to provide the

immediate need of temporary and emergency housing. The land which is available is, of necessity, the land which is used. It is in the later phases of recovery that psychological and sociological principles enter into planning.

During the first phase of a disaster operation, the focus of the relief effort is on the immediate needs of the victims—housing, food, and clothing.

The second phase of a disaster operation involves short range rehabilitation of the affected area. During this phase, such things as the repair of water and sewage lines, the compensation of disaster losses, and the restoration of essential public facilities and services takes place.

The third phase of a disaster operation involves long range planning for the rehabilitation of the affected area. During this phase the psychological, sociological, and ecological aspects of planning cited by Dr. Harshbarger are given greater emphasis.—*G.A. Lincoln, Director, Office of Emergency Preparedness, to Congressman Ken Hechler, September 15, 1972*

The OEP conceptual framework is a linear model, projecting a rational series of stages of problem solution. While it would be foolish to question the immediate human needs for shelter and emergency medical care, it seems equally foolish to build a model for the structuring of intervention efforts that assumes the suspension of socioemotional problems of survivors until the final phase of its operation. Assuming that intervention efforts in Buffalo Creek have reflected this model, then after a year of work agencies are still in the midst of Phase 2. Unfortunately, psychological, sociological, and ecological problems were not suspended awaiting the completion of Phase 2.

Linear models may be appropriate for many problems. However, their usefulness in the organization of disaster intervention is questionable. In fact such a model may be actively harmful to survivors, in that critically needed services which are likely to be maximally effective if used early in the crisis period, such as mental health services, are delayed by the model until after the community's physical needs are met.

In general, human behavior only occasionally, perhaps even rarely, conforms to the demands of a linear model. It seems particularly inappropriate that such a model should be applied to such nonlinear events and human processes as those occurring in the aftermath of a disaster.

Perhaps related to the preceding analysis, are the many difficulties experienced by agencies in their disaster intervention efforts that can be almost directly traced to a lack of planning, both in relation to internal programs and to external interagency programs and relationships. For example, prior to the Buffalo Creek disaster, the Department of Mental Health in West Virginia had no plans for disaster intervention. The story is told that in Wilkes Barre, in the HUD trailer parks which were similar to those in Buffalo Creek, there was a policy that no nonresident was to be allowed in unless specifically invited into the park by a resident. At the same time, HEW was funding a paraprofessional mental health outreach program aimed at persons displaced by the flood. However, these workers could not visit the trailer parks because there were no invitations, and residents did not invite workers in because they were not aware of them. It was with some interagency embarrassment that the problem was resolved.

Perhaps the all too common lack of true understanding between agencies and the individuals eligible for their services is typified by the elderly lady who, after the West Virginia flood, was told by an HUD representative that she would receive a trailer to live in. The lady declined the offer, indicating that she didn't regard her home as uninhabitable and would continue to live there. The HUD representative insisted, however, that since she was eligible for a trailer she would receive one. Over the lady's protests a trailer was moved into her backyard. The lady staunchly refused to live in the trailer, but in the months following the flood her physical problem of cataracts worsened. A local welfare case worker strongly suggested an operation on her cataracts to improve her vision. Replied the lady, "Not until you get that damn trailer out of my yard."

ECOLOGIC CONSIDERATIONS IN ORGANIZING EMERGENCY MENTAL HEALTH SERVICES

The devastation of the Buffalo Creek disaster has gone. The valley floor has been cleared and rebuilding has begun. But the tragedy lingers. This is due in part to the intense and pervasive character of the disaster. Unfortunately, it may also be due in part to the inadequacy and lack of organization of intervention efforts.

As a first step in examining the adequacy and organization of human services, particularly mental health services, following disasters, I would suggest that our methods for assessment of services at the community level be examined. Further, these services should be systematically examined within the context of a limited but multidimensional ecological model.

In an earlier paper (169), I proposed such a model for the assessment and design of community-level human intervention throughout the lifespan. In the present chapter I would propose a somewhat similar model as indicated in Figure 23.1.

The model proposed here attempts to systematically relate groups at risk to both coping processes and forms of social organization which will further facilitate those coping processes. For example, a mental health program planner might assess programmatic ways in which families (survivor groups) are being assisted with a) grief management (stress management), both through formal intervention efforts and through being systematically linked with informal caregivers in the community such as other families

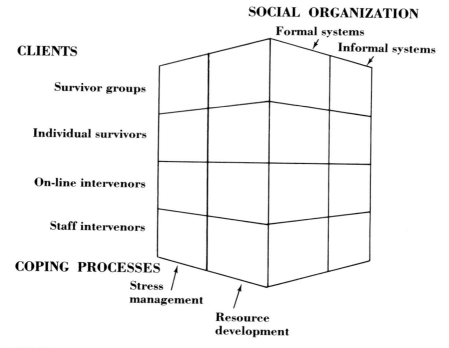

FIGURE 23.1   An ecologic model for the assessment and design of mental health
services following disasters.

who can aid in grief management; and *b*) resource-developing formal
systems such as legal aid, welfare or business assistance agencies, as well
as informal resource development systems such as efforts to link former
neighbors and reestablish social support systems.

Typically, the organization and assessment of disaster intervention
programs, as well as the planning of these programs, has been largely
restricted to formal system resource development for individual, and to a
lesser degree collective survivors. This proposed model for assessment and
design of services attempts to extend these considerations through some
additional dimensions, hopefully generating a more complete ecologic
structure for the re-creation of community life.

Of particular interest is the consideration the model would give to formal
and informal support and resource development systems for line and staff
intervenors, groups which have been too long ignored in the delivery of
human services following disasters. In this ecologic model these groups
would be included from the outset in the planning, organization, and
assessment of services.

Human behavior has a long history of repeating itself. Disordered, minimally effective, or even potentially destructive intervention efforts following disasters are, in all probability, no exception to this observation. Perhaps the observations and suggestions in this chapter will act as a deterrent in repeating our more disastrous disaster intervention efforts of the past. The lessons of the Buffalo Creek tragedy can act as constructive guides for future disaster intervention programs.

24

THE BUFFALO CREEK SYNDROME

symptoms and character change after a major disaster

James L. Titchener, Frederic T. Kapp,
and Carolyn Winget

On February 26, 1972, a dam formed by the Buffalo Mining Company's "gob piles" gave way, unleashing over a million gallons of water and black mud to rush down the Buffalo Creek Valley destroying everything in its path, killing 118 persons and leaving 4000 homeless. This Appalachian tidal wave, carrying houses, human bodies, trailers, cars, and all sorts of debris, completed its devastation on the 18 mile valley in no more than 15 minutes, and within 3 hours everything had washed into the Guyandotte River (see also Chapter 23). Some of the survivors eventually instituted legal action against the Pittston Company, a conglomerate that owned the mining operation.

PURPOSE AND FORM OF THE STUDY

A group of 65 psychiatrists, social workers, and psychologists from the Department of Psychiatry, University of Cincinnati, visited Buffalo Creek in June 1973, and in April and May 1974, to prepare the psychiatric studies for attorneys of the 625 plaintiffs, including 250 children.

This chapter contains an analysis of the disaster as we learned about it both from official accounts and from the stories of our respondents who lived all the way from Saunders (just below the fateful dam), to Kistler, near Man, West Virginia (where Buffalo Creek ends). The actual events must be understood in order to understand the acute and prolonged stresses they imposed. This chapter also describes the psychiatric findings from our case reports and then presents an explanation of the persistence of symptoms and the appearance of actual change in character and lifestyle stemming from the 1972 experience and still manifest in follow-up as late as October 1974.

Our psychiatric teams examined the survivor litigants in their homes in the Buffalo Creek area. Confronted by an imposing task, we devised a technique for gaining data from the survivors which would indicate the psychodynamic connections between the disaster experience and the symptoms and character changes that resulted. The studies began with a conjoint interview with team members and all family members present. The family was asked to tell us about their particular experiences during the disaster. The mode of interaction and behavior of each family was noted. In the culture of Buffalo Creek, where reticence with regard to individual expression of feelings is strong, especially to outsiders, the family interview was highly effective, because the interaction within the family brought out feelings which the individual would keep hidden. With the emotions thus exposed in the context of family interaction, team members then conducted one-to-one interviews with each survivor, including the children.

In July 1974, just before the case was to come to trial, a settlement of 13.5 million dollars was agreed on, more than 6 million of which was for *psychic impairment*. This was the term the attorneys devised for social, vocational, and personal disability from psychological causes springing from the disaster and its aftermath. A team of raters assessed every litigant's record on a scale of 0 to 4 for the degree of psychic impairment: 0 = no impairment; 1 = minimal; 2 = moderate; 3 = severe; and 4 = total disability. On the basis of this scale, fewer than 2% (less than 10 individuals) had no psychic impairment; 20% had minimal ratings; 70% were moderately or severely impaired; and 1% (5 persons) were considered totally disabled. These ratings, abstracted from the individual psychiatric reports, indicate that significant psychological problems were nearly universal as a result of the Buffalo Creek disaster, and that they were still affecting the survivors 24 to 30 months after the original trauma.

ANALYSIS OF THE DISASTER

From a psychological point of view the tidal wave of black mud had these characteristics: it was visually and aurally terrifying, unimagineable except to those who witnessed it; it was tremendously threatening to life and to all manmade structures in its path; nearly everyone saw the dead, or the dying, and many saw relatives, friends and neighbors killed; all of the survivors were somehow involved in strenuous efforts to escape the wave and the black water; many were caught by it, and some helped, or failed to help, others to safety; there was in most cases loss or damage to the home, and these losses were painful, partly because of the intrinsic value but also because of sentimental and symbolic value as mementos evoking their own past or that shared with loved ones (304).

Kai Erikson has discussed the destruction wrought on the community structure and on the sense of communality in an area lacking the formal governmental structure of other parts of the United States. He showed how the sense of community, although tenuous and not institutionalized, was essential to the mountaineers' personalities.*

PSYCHIATRIC FINDINGS IN SURVIVORS

Psychiatric findings in the overwhelming majority of the survivor litigants appeared in three ways: *a*) the acute effects of the disaster's impact, its immediate and short-term aftermath, *b*) symptoms persisting months and years later, and *c*) pervasive changes in character, in attitudes to self and others, and in style of life (see also Chapter 25).

Acute Effects of the Disaster

After the flood, when survivors were trying to locate friends and relatives, bury the dead, and secure temporary housing, they suffered disturbances in memory and cognition, insomnia, nightmares, irritability, startle reactions, occasional panic, transient hallucinations and delusions, withdrawal from others, and interferences in daily activities. These effects and reactions were consequences of the disruption of the stimulus barrier and the damage to psychic structure by the massive overload and continuing excitation beyond the capacity of the individual to integrate it. The psychological shock of the event, with its complex meaning to the person, his family, and his community, inflicted on the individual mind a devastation comparable to the physical devastation which can be seen in newspaper photographs. However, the mind and its integrating functions are capable of recoil and reconstitution.

Symptoms of the Chronic Stage

After the phase of reconstitution and the wearing away of the acute effects, and with the process of reorganization, the chronic stages of the syndrome began. In that stage we observed in 80% of the survivor litigants the following symptom groups:

1. Continuing anxiety; obsessions and phobias concerned with water, rain, certain noises, and wind; apprehension about conditions of dams and slag heaps

---

* Kai Erikson. Unpublished data, 1974.

2. Depression from loss, guilt and shame, anger, resentment, and the "death imprint" (256)
3. Increased smoking and drinking in many persons, as well as changes in eating patterns
4. Loss of interest and enjoyment in sex relations, socializing, and hunting and fishing

Chronic Changes Observed

In addition to the persisting symptoms already described, we found changes in character and patterns of behavior and social adjustment.

Isolation as a feeling in relation with others became a way of behaving in the community and neighborhood. This isolation in feeling and behavior was accompanied by a sense of loss of the value of the self and a diminished trust in others. Nearly every adult survivor reported a reduced interest in conversing or visiting with neighbors. They described "a wall" between themselves and others, erected as though each drew protectively into his own shell. "He's got his own things to worry about and he don't care anymore," they would say. At the same time we observed a clinging vigilance in families, a need to know where each family member was. It was as though physical closeness was needed to maintain family stability in the absence of a mature feeling of family closeness.

Survivor's guilt and shame was a common manifestation, sometimes overt, sometimes concealed. It was integrated into character and lifestyle changes in many ways. For example, ambivalence toward the litigation was expressed, sometimes angrily, in terms of feeling accused of symptoms or adjustment difficulties, thus reviving the guilt: Characteristically, many seemed to be saying, "You are trying to prove I have symptoms. I'm not guilty, for to admit that would be to admit guilt over being alive." These irrational feelings in many cases were traced to self-blame for not doing more to rescue people and a guilty joy at having survived. An important aspect of this survivor's guilt was its expression in decreased skills, ineptness, absenteeism, and violations of rules in daily work activities.

Impotent rage and dismay over the senseless destruction of life and property was another persisting symptom. It was an anger that had insufficient outlet and only contributed to the idea of the ineffectiveness of the self and the weakness of the community. For some survivors, the litigation was an expression of ego strength, reducing the sense of impotence.

Unresolved grief over the loss of family, friends, and acquaintances, as well as grief over the loss of the sense of community, of their way of life, and of the valley the way it was before, became a pervasive affect, coloring almost all behavior and communication, including patterns of movement, tone of voice, mood, facial expression, and view of life. It was an aspect of changed character and lifestyle because it was ingrained, a matter of attitude, influencing total behavior more than a circumscribed symptom like depression or phobia. Like some other changes in character and lifestyle, unresolved grief was as strong in those who moved away from the valley as in those who stayed. It was a factor that weighed heavily in favor of the argument that moving out would not have a curative action.

A sense of meaninglessness developed in the Buffalo Creek survivors—in their feelings and attitudes toward life, the present, the future and the human condition. It had its origin and associations first with the unforgettable visual and auditory impression of the great black wave as it rolled and crashed down the valley. There was no meaningful answer, for anyone who was there, to the question of why anyone would do something or fail to do something to have prevented its occurrence, and yet no one could deny that it could have been prevented, that no one should have taken the risks with lives and property that were taken.

Also contributing in a gruesome way to the sense of meaninglessness in the Buffalo Crek syndrome was the concrete memory of the tumbled, slimy, black, muddy devastation, with television sets, cars, and houses mingled with human bodies and bridges, a sight we can only conceive of through photographs, and the suddenness of it all—occurring in 15 minutes. This view of the disaster was volunteered by nearly all of the survivors, "Nothing seems to matter anymore, there just isn't any point to anything, no fun, no drive." It was not just an ennui, an affective or depressive state, but loss of a sense of the reliability and continuity of life—life had become a brittle thread to be fractionated, snapped off, and was therefore empty of meaning at any moment. Generally there is less of a future orientation in Appalachian culture than in the rest of the United States (223) so that we could not expect the usual investment in the future, but we found a loss of meaningfulness in our respondents with regard to the *present* and the *past;* for instance, mementos, photographs, and the material goods one had worked for were swept away.

A feeling of helplessness was seen in most of our respondents, related to the acute moments of the water's impact. We also found varying degrees of unconscious resistance to the memories of this feeling of helplessness, and these resistances took many forms which are discussed as one of the pathogenic factors in the next section of this chapter.

The resistance that many psychiatrists warned us to expect, and the one which some who were readying themselves for the trip to Buffalo Creek predicted, was that of *secondary gain*, i.e., symptoms and suffering for the purpose of dependency, sympathy, and monetary gain. This particular resistance did not appear frequently even though we were examining plaintiffs in a suit, and in fact there is evidence from some of our studies that the symptoms which would indicate this form of resistance were more frequent in nonplaintiffs.

A process of entrenchment was also observed, an acceptance of symptoms as a way of life, while mild tranquilizers to alleviate the depression and anxiety were becoming a fixture of the lifestyle. The anxiety and vigilance to ward off a recurrence of the trauma led to Librium and Valium dosage, and the tranquilizers and the symptoms became necessary to each other. Further, there appeared to be an *entrenchment of character changes* too. The unresolved grief, impotent rage and dismay, the sense of meaninglessness as a view of life and the self, and the feeling of isolation in relations with others and the community as a whole, were all hardening and showing signs of permanence. Evidence for the entrenchment phenomenon comes from the serial observations we have had in nearly 50 cases, as well as retrospective reports by subjects on themselves and family members observing each other.

Analysis of Dreams and Early Memories

The individual psychiatric records of 63 litigants were randomly selected, and dreams and early memories were abstracted. As indicated in Table 24.1, dreams had been recorded from 53 persons and early memory was present in 41. These protocols were content analyzed using the Gottschalk–Gleser (152) technique of verbal behavior analysis. Because of its relevance, anxiety was the focus of the analysis in this preliminary work. Since the protocols were usually brief, they were scored only for the presence or absence of any given subcategory of the anxiety scale. This was true also of the comparison normative sample reported by Winget, Kramer, and Whitman (438) referred to in Table 24.1. The most notable

TABLE 24.1 Comparison of Types of Anxiety in Dreams and Early Memories: Buffalo Creek Sample vs Normative Sample

	Dreams		*Early memories*	
	Buffalo Creek	Normative sample	Buffalo Creek	Normative sample
Type of anxiety	(%)	(%)	(%)	(%)
Death	79	29	20	10
Mutilation	11	11	24	20
Separation	26	18	24	18
Guilt	17	3	22	9
Shame	9	3	7	9
Diffuse	26	14	7	3
One or more types	92	61	76	51
None	8	39	24	49
Total Sample	*53*	*182*	*41*	*259*

findings regarding dreams are the following: 1) Some type of anxiety was present in 92% of the dreams of Buffalo Creek subjects and in only 61% of the normative sample. 2) There was more than twice as much death anxiety in Buffalo Creek dreams as was found in the normative sample. 3) Separation anxiety and diffuse anxiety showed higher trends in Buffalo Creek dreams than in those of the normative sample.

The comparison of the anxiety in the early memories for the two samples indicated similar tendencies. Overall, more Buffalo Creek early memories showed the presence of some kind of anxiety than was true of the normative sample. Compared to the normative group, guilt anxiety, as defined by the Gottschalk–Gleser scale, was markedly higher in the Buffalo Creek protocols, and all such categories except for the shame anxiety, yielded higher proportions.

PATHOGENIC FACTORS

Why and how have the psychological symptoms and character changes of the syndrome become so frequent and so persistent in the survivors of this particular disaster? We can answer questions partly from what we know of the catastrophe—how overwhelming it was, its ongoing nature, the significance of the people's losses, destruction of the sense of communality, and the awareness of human responsibility for the failure of the dam. Given the intensity, the duration and special qualities of the stress on this group of people, we still need to undertstand why so many have been impaired for so long, and why processes of recovery have not taken over in place of processes which have caused entrenchment of the syndrome with permanent effects on the survivors' lives.

Four psychological factors explain the high frequency and persistence of symptoms and deleterious character changes comprising the disaster syndrome.

The Individual's Defensive System

First, the continuing symptoms and the described personality changes resulting from the disaster derive from and are built on a tightly fitting and integrated structure of *first-order* defenses (208) with degrees of rigidity building up in the 3 months to a year after the disaster. This defensive structure consisted of a coordinated group of mechanisms. *Externalization* is used with regard to ego attitudes toward the trauma and its effects: *Others, especially loved ones, are having problems. Projection* is employed with regard to feelings: *Others are angry, hurt, grieving, guilty, or ashamed and often these feelings are directed toward me.* The defense of *denial* was the overall cloak used to hide from awareness the emotional input and significance to the self of the personal experience (410). Denial is the cap, topping the levels of externalization and projection, and it contains the basic, desperately necessary message to the self: *I am as I was before; it happened to all of us and killed some of us, but it is over, and I am the same I that I was before.* This denying message to the self has also been noted by authors reporting studies of auto and industrial accident victims and in clinical work with persons suffering war neurosis (407).

This closely constructed defensive system involving externalization and projection drives preserves symptoms and leads to restricted character formation because it prevents recognition of what happened to the person, i.e., he was severely endangered and felt helpless. The defensive system blunts the significance of total vulnerability and a sense of having been in a state of infantile helplessness. An awareness of these feelings would mean a recognition of the lack of personal omnipotence and invulnerability, in turn forcing a survivor to deal with an altered view of the self. This factor then provides the outer shell for the hardening of the Buffalo Creek syndrome.

The Undoing Process

The second factor is the process of *undoing*. Undoing refers to the work in dreams, fantasy, and reenactment of memories of the disaster in order to erase or gain control of feelings aroused by the traumatic experience.

Guilt and shame feelings about one's wishes, impulses, and behavior during the stress and its long aftermath are the targets of the undoing process. The most direct undoing occurs in dreams in which there is a degree of direct reliving of the traumatic happening up to the point of terrified awakening. As time passes, there is a steady change from the violence of the direct or partially direct reliving to dreams which retain the violence and chaos of the disaster but have an entirely altered manifest content. There is a shift from images of the disaster to images from scenes of other sorts of violence. The aim of undoing is to obscure those aspects of the event that were associated with unacceptable feelings and attitudes toward the self. A man, obsessively recalling his wife slipping from his grasp into the swirling water, used undoing to bury irrational ideas of how he should have behaved. He felt he should have performed far beyond his human capacities, and his retaining these ideas in his unconscious evokes feelings of shame that he had been derelict. The possibility of his enjoying life is hampered by irrational and only partly conscious guilt feelings.

In daily life, undoing was often expressed in violent, dangerous or counterphobic symbolic reenactments of the trauma. Other forms of undoing were observed in complicated religious behavior or in repressive group phenomena. One of the leaders of the litigants was frequently called at night by frightened neighbors who feared another dam would break. He would leave his home at any hour and sit on the slag heap watching it throughout the night, while others would watch him, weapons ready in case there were attacks from "The Company." The dreams, fantasies, and reenactments found in most survivors were aimed at undoing the fears and erasing the irrational guilt and shame incurred by the catastrophe.

Undoing prevents a gradual discharge of anxiety through sharing realistic memories of the disaster in detail with other survivors or counselors. The gradual sharing of realistic memories is different from reliving the catastrophe with all affects emerging at once. The undoing prevents a helpful working through of the irrational guilt and fear by realistic assessment of the disaster. It replaces gaining an increased understanding of the limitations of human beings in such extreme situations (92). In fact, a process of working through over time includes a measure of just how extreme the situation was toward a true picture of the self and others in the context of the total disaster.

Constrictive Behavior

The third factor, *psychological conservatism*, consists of constriction of feelings, interests, ambitions, and enthusiasm. It aims at avoiding excitation and arousal and averts even the slightest chance of dreaded overstimulation and overloading which has been associated with the disaster. Psychological conservatism is analogous to but not the same as the conservation withdrawal syndrome observed in infants by Engel and Reichsmann (108). The conserving aspect of it appears to be aimed at energies needed for survival, so that living becomes solely a matter of survival rather than venturing and seeking stimulations and pleasure. As in persons with war neuroses and accident victims, the tendency to psychological conservation (see discussion on psychic numbing in Chapter 25) spreads into all areas of the person's life as he becomes hypersensitive to any vestiges of stimulation.

Psychological conservation blocks a gradual return to interests, activities, enthusiasm, and ambition. After the shock and disorganization of the mental apparatus by the emotions aroused by trauma, time is needed for ego repair. But time is not enough. These impulses and feelings have to find a mode of discharge, while the conflicts evoked by the trauma need resolution. The manifestations of psychological conservatism indicated that the individual has only partially reconstituted, and his degree of return has been by sacrifice of participation in former interests, activities, and pleasures. It is as though the person has said to himself, "I can afford to return only this far, no further."

Those survivors who do not show psychological conservatism have accepted the time it takes to resume full participation and have gradually permitted themselves stimulation and reaching out. They find from such measured steps that the danger of bringing back the overwhelming experience need not arise.

Disaster as a Dehumanizing Factor

The *dehumanizing effect* of a disaster is the fourth factor contributing to psychopathogenesis. Great physical events like the floods of Hurricane Agnes, tornadoes, and earthquakes cause men to feel puny, helpless, and insignificant in the face of nature's power. In some ways these powerful events change the meaning of the word *human*, since modern men believe they can harness the forces of nature.

When a coal mine explodes or a train is wrecked; when millions are herded into death camps, or when an apparently "illegal" dam breaks, the realization of a lack of concern of men for one another becomes a pathogenic factor contributing to persisting symptoms and long-term character change. Many people in West Virginia believed the dam violated regulations and laws and that its maintenance was a chance the Pittston Company took for its own convenience and advantage. The financial advantages of the mine operating methods used apparently outweighed such consequences as the $13.5 million settlement paid to survivors of the disaster, plus other settlements running into additional millions of dollars. The risk of heaping the slag and impounding the water was taken by the company but borne by the residents of Buffalo Creek Valley. The realization that others apparently acted in that totally callous way toward the self, the family, and the community, and then to have their worst expectations realized, was psychologically devastating. Pride and pleasure in the sense of being human was lost, and in that way the black water's effect on the valley was dehumanizing. This factor underlies the feeling of meaninglessness in character change and also the loss of feelings of basic trust and confidence in human relations. In some ways it is akin to identification with the aggressor in that the evaluation of the self is lowered because one was treated as less than human. The attitude toward the self, in fusion with attitudes of those who seem to take unnecessary risk with thousands of lives, can become ingrained and thereby change character. It replaces a process of reevaluation which would recognize that some men do have little regard for others. An event like Buffalo Creek does much to shake naive, submissive trustfulness. The results of dehumanizing effects lie in finding realistic hopes in more empathic institutions, and in relations with others. Humans working together, as in the litigation, to prevent recurrence of such careless and irresponsible behavior, and giving at least some recompense, may have therapeutic benefit against this pathogenic factor. Such actions tend to reverse the entrenched attitude of resignation, submission, and despair that confirm the sense of subhuman value placed on the self (269).

CONCLUSIONS

Disasters set off an epidemic of traumatic neuroses, the frequency and intensity of which are determined by the nature of the impact, its duration and hazards, the casualties, and the particular context of psychological, political, and sociological forces. In these ways every major disaster is unique. Acute traumatic neurosis is a response to overwhelming overloading of the mental apparatus, leading to psychological disorganization. Reconstitution takes time when the stress has passed. As Horowitz has suggested (Chapter 22) the problem is the hardening of persistent symptoms and character changes.

In our study these manifestations constituting the Buffalo Creek syndrome were found in nearly all the survivors. The clinical studies show that the syndrome is probably similar to the chronic effects of other traumas, including combat and serious accidents, but is an independent entity, not a preexisting and latent psychoneurosis brought out by the stress. It results from the ego damage of the immediate disaster and its ongoing effects. The external stresses acquire significance through the four pathogenic factors which we have described, and the syndrome of symptomatic suffering and character change is maintained and takes shape from the force of these processes.

The forces set in motion when individuals attempt to ward off recurrence of the overwhelming demand and the devastating effect on personality oppose factors which might restore the individual, and thus the family and community, to former strength. If the pathogenic warding-off and defensive factors could be suspended and their consequences delayed while reconstitution takes place, these chronic character changes and symptoms could be prevented or relieved once they have appeared. Our conclusion from the studies of the large number of survivors is that some immediate and short-range therapeutic effort would be effective for the survivors of major disasters.

IMMEDIATE AND SHORT-RANGE INTERVENTION

Immediate and short-range efforts should be *educational,* i.e., finding ways to communicate what can be anticipated as normal reactions such as anxiety, grief, anger, irritability and self-doubt. Information supplied through newspapers, leaflets, television, radio, and personal contact in groups should describe the psychological effects to be expected in the self and in others, in marital relations, in the family, and in children. The four pathogenic factors we have described are reinforced by ignorance, they are attempts to contain feelings which would be better acknowledged. Each of the four factors can be diminished by knowledge and emotional acceptance. Capacity to anticipate changes in the self and in significant relationships will be therapeutic if one knows that these effects may be temporary and that efforts to stifle them are not necessary.

Short-range efforts by mental health teams should be brief and focal, employing individual and group therapy techniques aimed at reintegration and understanding of guilt and shame dynamics. We recommend avoidance of minor tranquilizers and antidepressants, except for hypnotics and sedatives for sleep disturbances, as tranquilizers and antidepressants tend to freeze the character change and symptoms of the chronic traumatic neurosis.

25

DEATH IMPRINT IN BUFFALO CREEK

Robert J. Lifton
Eric Olson

In late 1972 we were asked by lawyers representing the survivors of the Buffalo Creek flood to consult on the psychological effects of this disaster. We subsequently made three trips to Buffalo Creek: April and December 1973, and May 1974. During these three visits, and one additional visit by Olson of the University of Cincinnati team in March 1974, we conducted, together and individually, a total of 41 interviews involving 22 Buffalo Creek survivors. We also talked with several ministers and volunteer workers in the area and read the extensive documentation of the disaster compiled by a variety of observers and recorders; these included psychological statements, legal depositions, journalistic observations, and the University of Cincinnati psychiatric examinations. We have also conferred extensively with Dr. Coles, Dr. Titchener, Professor Erikson, and other professional consultants actively concerned with the Buffalo Creek disaster.

MANIFESTATIONS OF THE SURVIVOR SYNDROME

The effects of the disaster were so extensive that no one exposed to it in Buffalo Creek has escaped them. The overwhelming evidence is that everyone exposed to this disaster experienced some or all of the five manifestations of the survivor syndrome.

For further discussion on the Buffalo Creek disaster *see also* Lifton RJ, Olson E: *The human meaning of total disaster: The Buffalo Creek experience.* Psychiatry 39:1–18, 1976.

Death Imprint and Death Anxiety

The first category is that of the *death imprint* and related *death anxiety*. The death imprint consists of memories and images of the disaster invariably associated with death, dying, and massive destruction. These memories were still extremely vivid during interviews conducted 27 months after the flood, so that one can speak of them as indelible images. The memories of destruction were all encompassing, so that a sense that "it was the end of time" was present in many survivors.

Over the period of our three visits we could observe the extent to which the anxiety and fear associated with these images took on chronic form—fear so strong in many as to constitute permanent inner terror. The fear tended to be associated with flood and disaster, with nature and the elements, and especially with rain and water. As one man related in May 1974:

> When it rained hard last week it was like the past came out again. I took the family down to the cellar and [at times like this] I just know the whole flood is going to come back . . . . It's like you might step out of the trailer and get caught in something. Every time it rains I get the feeling that it's a natural thing for the floods to come.

In other words, what is ordinarily unnatural destruction has become, psychologically speaking, natural—what one expects to happen.

A related symptom, also widespread, is a fear of crowds. Gatherings of large numbers of people become associated with the disaster. One man told me that he avoids crowds because he imagines another disaster and, "if there are 12 people in the crowd only some people would escape and some would be lost. If I was there by myself, I could get away." He was expressing a characteristic feeling that his survival was a matter of luck, perhaps a fluke, and that in the grotesque competition for survival created by such a disaster, he would be better off on his own. Involved here also is the shattering of the survivor's illusion of invulnerability—an illusion we carry with us in both ordinary and dangerous situations—and a resulting feeling of having been rendered precariously vulnerable to the next threat.

Terrifying dreams, still recurring regularly 27 months after the disaster, are especially vivid expressions of death anxiety. One such typical recurrent dream follows:

> I dream I'm in a car on a pier surrounded by muddy water—or else in a pool of muddy water. I feel like I've got to hold on to the side of the pool. If I do I'm all right. I know that I can't get out. I have to stay in it.

The dreamer is threatened by a disaster-related form of death and must struggle desperately to remain alive. The dream suggests being locked in a continuous struggle without being able to leave the lethal environment (the muddy pool).

The tornado warnings of April 1974 were especially traumatic to Buffalo Creek survivors in their intensification of dread. The phenomenon of reactivation contributes greatly to the survivor's sense of permanent vulnerability. As a Baptist minister explained in May 1974:

> I told you [in a previous interview] people had quieted down a bit. But when they announced all those hurricanes, people came to the church and stayed all night. . . . Just let something blow up and they flare up again.

This diffuse, death-related anxiety came to pervade the Buffalo Creek environment to the point of contagion. As in other overwhelming disasters (such as Hiroshima), such outsiders as mental health professionals and clergymen coming in actually experience some of the fear and dread described by people exposed to the disaster. We may sum up this first category by saying that Buffalo Creek survivors remain haunted not just by death but by grotesque and unacceptable forms of death; they feel ever vulnerable to these forms of death, and they perceive their overall environment, including nature itself, as threatening and lethal rather than life-sustaining.

Death Guilt

The second category is that of *death guilt*—the survivor's sense of painful self-condemnation over having lived while others died. Survivors 27 months later were still plagued by the feeling, however irrational, that they could or should have done something to save close relatives who perished. One man, who made a series of desperate efforts to save his wife before she went under, has experienced a mixture of preoccupation with memories of her and his failure to save her, and anger at the coal company because "they killed my wife." Psychologically the two emotions merge, and, like other survivors of extreme situations, he inwardly experiences a certain amount of personal responsibility for having "killed her." Also involved is the survivor's characteristic feeling that his life was purchased at the cost of another's, that the other person's death permitted him to live, that had he died, the other might have lived instead. These feelings, very widespread in Buffalo Creek, are inseparable from the death-related fears already described and are among the most painful emotions known to humankind.

Death guilt is reflected in the preoccupation of survivors with dead relatives—one man's constant thoughts about many dead cousins and still another survivor's brooding over his dead mother, sister, and three brothers. Death guilt is perhaps most vivid in recurrent dreams. Some of these dreams include the reappearance of dead relatives either in everyday situations or uneasy reunions in which it is not clear whether they are or are not actually alive. Much more disturbing and still frequent were dreams in which death guilt was much more direct. The wife of the survivor mentioned earlier, struggling with unanswerable questions, had been unusually close to her husband's dead mother. She relates:

> I dreamed we knew the dam was going to break. In the dream Mrs. T. had a white dress on. She asked me to follow her out in the yard. She just kept going back into a hole that looked like a mine. I don't know why she wanted me to come with her—she held out her hand, but I was afraid.

The dream suggests the dreamer's sense that she should have shared the disturbing fate (the death) of her mother-in-law.

Still more characteristic were recurrent dreams of actual disaster events, or scenes resembling them, in depicting grotesque death, as described by a survivor in May 1974.

> I dreamt about the baby I found with half its face torn off, and the truck full of bodies. Sometimes in those dreams you're running, or trying to get hold of someone to help them out of the mud. Just last week I had that dream. I woke up pulling on my wife. After that you just can't go back to sleep.

In such dreams the survivor experiences an image of ultimate horror—a single image that comes to exemplify his entire disaster experience in the combination of fear, pity, and guilt it evokes in him. Such images are especially likely to include children or women whose grotesque death one witnessed or failed to prevent since in most cultures, ours included, those two groups (children especially) are viewed as particularly helpless and vulnerable.

One survivor contrasted his capacity to absorb his World War II combat experience with his total inability to deal with residual guilt from the flood disaster as expressed in an image of ultimate horror involving a mother pleading with him, while herself drowning, to save her baby:

> When I was on the battlefield in World War II, I was expecting the worst, and it didn't bother me at all like this. When my buddies got killed, I knew I was no part of their getting killed. But when the flood came, I didn't have time to help that lady and her baby who cried for help.

He went on to explain that "feelings about not helping people during the war went away after I came home" but those related to the flood have stayed with him for 27 months, both in his waking life and his dreams.

Although people who have gone through this kind of experience are never quite able to forgive themselves for having survived, another side of them experiences relief and gratitude that it was *they* who had the good fortune to survive in contrast to the fate of those who died, a universal and all-too-human survivor reaction that in turn intensifies their guilt. Since the emotion is so painful, the sense of guilt may be suppressed and covered over by other emotions or patterns such as rage or apathy. But whether suppressed or not, that guilt continues to create in Buffalo Creek survivors a sense of a burden that will not lift. They feel themselves still bound to the dead, living a half-life devoid of pleasure and with limited vitality.

Psychic Numbing

The third category is that of *psychic numbing*—diminished feeling or desensitization, which has persisted over the postdisaster period in the form of various manifestations of apathy, withdrawal, depression, and overall constriction in living. Psychic numbing is perhaps the most universal response to the disaster, and the essence of what has been called the "disaster syndrome." Partly it is an extension of the stunned state experienced at the time of the flood. That state was a defense against feeling the full impact of the overwhelming death immersion. The numbing persists at Buffalo Creek because people still need to defend themselves against the kinds of death anxiety and death guilt discussed earlier. Numbing, then, is an aspect of persistent grief, of the half-life defined by loss, guilt, and close at times to an almost literal identification with the dead. As one of the plaintiffs put it, "I feel dead now. I have no energy. I sit down and I feel numb." Survivors withdraw from groups, from activities of various kinds, from one another. They describe being disinterested in seeing friends or in many cases in doing anything. Even in intimate relationships their capacity for both emotional and physical or sexual feelings tends to be greatly diminished. Their withdrawal may be accompanied by a wide variety of psychosomatic symptoms such as general fatigue, loss of appetite, gastrointestinal difficulties, and aches and pains and dysfunction that can involve just about any organ system. The pattern has been described in other disasters as a breakdown in the ordinary psychosomatic balance or equilibrium, resulting in what used to be called neurasthenia.

Common manifestations of numbing at Buffalo Creek have included memory lapses, general sluggishness and unresponsiveness, confusion about details of one's immediate surroundings and about the passage of time in general. Those lapses, as one survivor makes clear, tend to be specifically associated with the disaster. "I can remember things from 1932 to 1972 better than I can the past 2 years. This past 2 years I can't remember what I do; weeks and months just go by." Numbing or avoidance of feeling can also be expressed in overactivity. Thus one woman said (in May 1974) of her very troubled husband, "He works all the time. He gets himself overtired. He says, 'If I just sit down, I'd die.' "

Numbing is closely related to the psychological defense of denial, and during our interviews people said again and again in a variety of ways, "It's hard to believe that all this happened," or "I still can't accept that it happened." Numbing and denial were sustained because of the survivor's inability to confront or work through the disaster experience. He is thus left psychologically imprisoned in death- and guilt-related conflicts that can neither be dealt with nor eliminated. Feeling stays muted; psychological pain remains silent; and life experience in general is drastically reduced.

In recent years, authorities on disaster have come to recognize that psychic numbing occurs not only in survivors but in observers and evaluators of disaster. Medical and psychological professionals have been shown to experience strong tendencies to ward off anxieties of their own around death and guilt aroused by their contact with survivors, that has in turn led them to deny the existence of these emotions and ignore or underestimate the psychological cost of disaster.

Impaired Human Relationships

A fourth category, *impaired human relationships*, consists especially of *conflict over need or nurturing, as well as strong suspicion of the counterfeit*. So much of their lives having been so suddenly and totally destroyed, survivors feel themselves in great need of love and support but at the same time highly suspicious of any such affection or nurturing that may be offered. While some have been able to help one another, there have also been instances of breakdown of the closest human bonds. One such case is that of a young married couple. Both remember their relationship prior to the flood as "calm and peaceful and loving." Now, according to the wife, her husband is . . . "touchy about everything. Things with me and him are at a kind of halt, a standstill. . . . Something is always bothering him. It's constant. It never seems to stop." They very rarely have sexual relations or even sleep in the same room. The husband's perception is that life in general, since he lost many relatives in the flood, has consisted of one aggravation after another. He says that his wife ". . . has no desire for me. She's hateful and doesn't want to turn toward me." Yet each realized that the other was suffering. They would go through brief periods of slight improvement in their relationship only to find the postdisaster pattern of mutual estrangement and distrust reasserting itself and still predominating.

Since the disaster, the problem of anger and unfocused or unexpressed rage has increased. One woman, talking about the problem, said, "It's like that all over. Everybody is angry and touchy." Often the touchiness is expressed toward fellow survivors in the various forms of envy, jealousy, and resentment that have been frequently observed following disasters and are characteristic of people who feel themselves weakened and victimized.

The hostility tends to be very diffuse. Since the flood, many survivors reported the frequent experience of violent impulses toward anyone who irritated them as well as enormous intensification of whatever difficulty they had experienced in the past in controlling their tempers. One of the survivors put the matter characteristically, "It used to be I could control my temper. Now my temper just goes. I just can't control it. When some little thing happens that seems unfair, I get touchy." And he added a bit later in the interview (May 1974), "Since I lost my wife I can't get what I want. Nothing satisfies me." Thus, anger continues to cover over grief and loss.

Another male survivor said, "I'm 46 years old. I've never been in jail. But if I could have got to some of those officials I probably would have hurt somebody. . . . I still get angry at times. I get all blurry and it flares up real quick. Before the flood, if anything came up, it seems like I could sit down and think and work things out."

The quotation suggests the difficulty survivors have in finding adequate targets for their anger. Many select the former manager of the mining company but seem to sense even as they do so that he as an individual is not an adequate target. Nor is it easy to personify an alternative target. As another man makes clear, "I can't say I feel angry at the people who built the dam, because I've never seen one of them. . . . and I've never seen S.D. (the general manager) since the flood." A good deal of anger is directed toward the mine company, but it too ends in frustration as expressed by one survivor:

> There's a lot of people that's angry. They just don't care because what they worked on for years was completely destroyed. Then Pittston (the coal mining company) offers you just a little for all that. It makes you angrier than hell. To think they could treat old people that way; it makes you want to go out and fight somebody.

This inability to find a satisfying outlet or target tends to lead people either to suppress their anger or express instead their continuous grief. Thus, the survivors are left with diffuse anger they themselves disapprove of, rage they cannot express, an overall sense that everything (and everyone) is suspect, and that life itself has been rendered counterfeit.

Significance of Disaster to the Individual

The fifth category has to do with the *significance or meaning surrounding a disaster*, the capacity of survivors to give their death encounter significant inner form or formulation. At issue here is the survivor's capacity to find sufficient explanation for his experience to be able to resolve the inner conflicts described under the other four categories. Only by finding some such meaning is he able to give meaning to the rest of his life. In many disasters survivors are able to find some comfort, or at least resignation, in the deep conviction that what happened was a matter of God's will or of some larger power that no mortal could influence. No such comfort or resignation could be found among the people of Buffalo Creek. Some of them have attempted to understand the experience within a religious context, and in a church service attended by one of us the minister (not a survivor himself) declared almost boastfully that he had predicted the flood as a punishment for sin in the valley. Survivors we interviewed did not express any such concept but could well be unconsciously affected by a related sense that their own evil or sinfulness had something to do with their miserable fate. That feeling would be consistent with one interpretation of their religion and with inner feelings about disaster and illness prevalent not only in Christian societies but in many non-Western cultures as well. Mostly, however, the Buffalo Creek survivors are left without any acceptable or consoling explanation for the disaster. Instead they expressed a bitter awareness that the disaster was manmade and a conviction that God had nothing to do with it. Those feelings, in our observation, have become increasingly intense and unshakeable over the 27-month period. Some, for instance, make an angry point about terminology in bitter response to public statements that God's will was involved, as the following quotations from three different people in May 1974 suggest:

> *I call this a disaster, not a flood. This wasn't a natural flood.*

> *A few individuals in charge of the coal company are responsible for this. God didn't put the dam up there.*

> *They call it a flood. I call it a dam that Pittston built up there that broke loose . . . . Governor Moore said it was an act of God, but God wasn't up on that slate dump with a bulldozer!*

Similar feelings were expressed to me by a Freewill Baptist minister, "I believe the dam was made by man, not by God, and it collapsed because it was not made right." The same man, able to observe large numbers of survivors closely, concluded that because of the disaster, "People are much more suspicious of God's justice." That last statement is of considerable importance because it suggests the extent to which people can no longer trust in even their Deity to put the moral world back in order. Precisely such a sense of the disruption of the moral universe occurs characteristically in the most severe forms of disaster. It was evident in every single survivor we interviewed. That sense of moral inversion—of wrongdoing going unpunished and responsibility unacknowledged while innocent victims undergo pain and suffering—further prevents psychological resolution and leaves people embittered and confused. They remain locked in their death anxiety, survivor guilt, numbing, and impaired human relationships, bound to the disaster itself and to its destructive psychological influences.

Summary Statement

These five categories of course overlap, and together they constitute Buffalo Creek's particular version of what has been widely described as the *survivor syndrome*. We shall say more shortly about the impressive number of psychiatric conditions found in Buffalo Creek survivors. But we first wish to emphasize that no one exposed to the disaster in Buffalo Creek, whatever his or her diagnosis, could escape from significant psychological suffering associated with the patterns and conflicts described earlier. Indeed, the great majority of people I interviewed, and of those interviewed by the Cincinnati group as well (see also Chapter 24) showed evidence of most or all of the major patterns and conflicts described before. This impressive impact of the Buffalo Creek disaster is related to certain specific characteristics.

UNIQUENESS OF THE BUFFALO CREEK DISASTER

Suddenness of the Flood

More gradual flooding or other kinds of disaster in which there is significant warning does not have the same impact as sudden, unforseen disasters. Twenty-seven months later survivors were still preoccupied with the abruptness of the transition from normal existence to the grotesque scenes of the disaster. They relate that suddenness to their inability, even now, to understand or accept what happened. Commenting on both suddenness and intensity, Harshbarger (Chapter 23) points out that "unlike other flood disasters, this flood more resembled the destruction of a tornado or earthquake than a flood." He reported that workers in the disaster area estimated that during the first 24 hours after the flood 88% of the 4000 persons displaced by the water exhibited shock and incoherent thinking. Leopold and Dillon have recognized that the nature of a disaster, and particularly its suddenness, which gives the ego no time to prepare its defenses, is a significant determinant of the posttraumatic states (245, p. 919). Those findings confirmed an earlier conclusion by Adler (who compared survivors of the Coconut Grove fire in Boston in 1942 with a group of patients who had suffered head injuries) that, "Terrifying events . . . have a higher incidence of neurosis *traceable to the circumstances of the accident* than the everyday head injuries (5)." There is no doubt that the Buffalo Creek disaster qualifies as such a terrifying event. The general principle, in Buffalo Creek and elsewhere, is that the suddenness and terror of a disaster intensify both its immediate and long-range human influences.

Relation of Disaster to Callousness and Irresponsibility of Other Persons

Beyond the confusion and bitterness already noted concerning their recognition that the disaster was caused by other men, the survivors have, over time, expressed their sense of profound humiliation at the low value that neglect seemed to place on their own lives. For they understood not only that the "dam" was manmade but also that it was widely known (for some time prior to the flood) to be dangerous. The inevitable conclusion was that they, the residents of Buffalo Creek, were looked on by the company as less than human. One man who was interviewed in May 1974 told that when it was suggested to the company before the disaster that they put a pipe through the dam to relieve the water pressure, the company's spokesman said that it would not be a good idea to do so because, if they let the water (full of coal waste) out, it would kill the fish in the creek. He then looked up with a bitter smile and said, "Hell, I ain't got nothing against taking care of the environment but there wasn't all that many fish in the creek . . . and besides I reckon one human life was worth the whole batch of them." This kind of perception confirms the feeling on the part of the people of Buffalo Creek that the company cared only about coal and the dollars it brought and viewed the miners and their families, living or dead, as expendable. We want to stress the relationship of this awareness of human callousness to the survivors' specific psychological suffering. This was true in Hiroshima also. Recently Luchterhand, comparing the effects of an ordinary tornado, the Irish famine, and the Nazi holocaust, came to the conclusion that "as the source of stress shifts from indiscriminate violence by nature to the discriminate oppression by man, the damage to human personality becomes less remediable (269, p. 47)." The psychological principle involved, tragic in its effects at Buffalo Creek, is that people who feel their humanity violated and unrecognized by others internalize that diminished sense of themselves in ways that impair their capacity for recovery or even hope.

Continuing Relation of Survivors to the Disaster

We cannot stress too much the psychological significance of the fact that for the most part the people of Buffalo Creek still work in the mines of the company whose policies and actions led to the flood and thereby remain dependent for their livelihood on the agents of the destruction. That continuing situation has created a combination of bitter resentment and unrelieved dependency, a sense of counterfeit nurturance, which the survivors have experienced as demeaning and psychologically painful. Those emotions were intensified by certain actions of the company in getting people to sign agreements for small financial settlements soon after the flood, actions which many Buffalo Creek people, and outside observers as well, perceived as taking advantage of the survivors' numbed, confused, and suggestible postdisaster state. Some thought the company took special advantage of those who were most helpless, such as the elderly. What is of considerable psychological importance (even apart from questions about the accuracy of that perception of the company) is the force of this combination of abuse, resentment, and dependency, in a way that is both specific to the postdisaster period and has roots in the historical past.

Also affecting survivors is the fact that the physical environment has never really been restored or repaired. There are physical reminders of the disaster everywhere. One resident pointed out in May 1974 that everything in the area brought back all the painful memories of the disaster. More than that, the extensive strip mining now taking place is perceived by survivors as further destruction of the land on which they live.

Not only is it felt that the natural surroundings no longer sustain life, but that they have been permanently impaired by the disaster. One man spoke of snakes coming back, many more snakes than before the flood, black snakes and rattlers. Many other survivors had similar impressions, and a number observed that unusual matings between different species of poisonous snakes were taking place. Whatever the actual impact of the flood on the ecology of snakes in the area, the combination of their actual danger and their traditional (Biblical) symbolization of evil contributes to the survivors' sense that the disaster turned nature against them, so that the very land that nurtured them in the past is no more than a disaster area now.

Psychologically speaking, Buffalo Creek survivors feel that they are living under a curse that was initiated by the disaster and now extends indefinitely into the future. This continuing relationship to the disaster not only interferes with renewal but also is largely responsible for the extent and intensity of the fear of recurrence discussed earlier. There is, of course, more than a kernel of reality behind that fear, as there are sludge piles building up that some consider dangerous. What is psychologically more fundamental, however, is the feeling among Buffalo Creek survivors that they have never really emerged from their disaster. Hence the fear of recurrence that accompanies almost all disasters has been unusually strong and sustained in connection with this one. That in turn suggests that

Buffalo Creek survivors, even compared to survivors of most other disasters, feel themselves unusually vulnerable and indefinitely threatened.

Isolation of Area and Community

The Buffalo Creek community has long been rather isolated geographically. It is inbred, strongly attached to its immediate land and surroundings, and has placed enormous significance on home, family, and kin. Thus, after the disaster, it could call upon very limited connections with outside groups, very limited sources of outside support and help, and few possibilities for involvement of a life-enhancing nature that could help the people move beyond the disaster itself. This isolation looms very large in the widespread conflict among survivors over whether to remain in Buffalo Creek or to leave. Many express a strong desire to get away from the area and from its everpresent reminders of the disaster. But powerful emotions hold disaster survivors to the place where they have suffered. These include the complex of psychological ties to people and place that we call "roots," but also the impulse to remain close to the dead.

The nature of the isolation of the people of Buffalo Creek, then, is such that they are trapped in the place of their suffering amidst evidence and reminders of the disaster, held by ties to the living, the dead, and the land that they can neither break from nor find solace in.

Totality of Communal Destruction

The Buffalo Creek disaster was unique in its combination of suddenness, destructive power within a limited circumscribed area, and resulting breakdown of community structure. Harshbarger described Buffalo Creek as a "total loss" disaster (see Chapter 23).

Important factors in creating this totality of impact were the suddenness described earlier, the geography (narrowness of the hollow), and demography (closely bunched nature of the community) of the area. Harshbarger also stated that virtually no one who lived in the valley was untouched by the disaster.

The totality of the Buffalo Creek disaster, then, encompasses this communal breakdown as well as the survivor conflicts described earlier. Both in fact merge in a final common pathway of individual suffering.

SUMMARY

We have made the overall assumption throughout, now well established by extensive observations, that every disaster shares certain common patterns with all other disasters; but that each disaster, in its overall combination of characteristics, becomes unique. Thus, one can find each of the five characteristics listed earlier—suddenness, human callousness in causation, continuing relationship of survivors to the disaster, isolation of the community, and totality of influence—in a number of other disasters. But the occurrence of *all* of them in a single disaster is highly unusual, and helps us understand the extensive human impact of the Buffalo Creek flood.

The Buffalo Creek disaster effects can be considered from the standpoint of causation, trauma, and the preexisting characteristics of the individual or group in terms of inclination (or predisposition) toward certain kinds of reactions. If, for instance, a young man in his twenties undergoes an acute psychotic reaction (including loss of contact with reality) right after being rejected by a girlfriend, we would surmise that the stress or trauma should not ordinarily produce that extreme a reaction and we would look for evidence of predisposition toward psychosis, evidence derived from his individual and family history. On the other hand, where the stress itself is extreme, as in the "massive psychic trauma" of war (204), concentration camps, and severe disasters (244, 245), psychiatrists have regularly observed that psychological impairment can result in virtually anyone, independent of estimates of predisposition. These observations have led a number of authorities to examine closely the nature and impact of massive trauma. Kardiner, for instance, beginning with observations on war, generalizes to explain that "The traumatic event breaks up . . . [the] balance between the ego and the environment by overwhelming the devices which the ego has at its disposal. The anxiety is overwhelming, and the ego shrinkage can be so complete that death can ensue. The entire adaptive equipment is thus disintegrated (204)." Those conclusions concur with many observations made in relation to both world wars, the Korean War, and more recently the Vietnam War as well (257, 417). Hence the insistence of authorities working in these areas on such terms as "traumatic neurosis," "posttraumatic neurosis," or "the traumatic syndrome." Observations on persons surviving Nazi concentration camps as well as the senior author's work on survivors of Hiroshima have strongly confirmed the importance of massive psychic trauma—that is, of extreme stress undergone by large numbers of people involving life and death situations—as always taking precedence over issues of predisposition. Koranyi rightly observes that under such conditions, "Preexisting pathology (predisposition) appeared to be obliterated in the final outcome and become buried under the unvaried likeness and monotony of the survivor syndrome (225).

Putting that observation in simpler words, if the stress is great enough it can produce strikingly similar psychological disturbances in virtually everyone exposed to it, "One can say that the regenerative powers of the ego are not limitless, that the human spirit can be broken beyond repair . . . (343)." Hocking, an Australian, has reviewed a number of situations of extreme stress and concluded that, "There was no correlation between the symptoms of the survivors and the preexisting personality or any other factors in the patients' earlier life," suggesting that, "When the duration and degree of stress are severe, preexisting personality characteristics do little more than determine how long an individual can tolerate the situation before the onset of neurotic symptoms (179)." Brull makes a general statement very relevant to the Buffalo Creek situation: "The conception of trauma really conveys that time which has flowed on without meaning assumes a particular meaning in the sense of burden, pain, disappointment, injury, anxiety, fear, challenge (56). And in a more immediate way with specific reference toward disaster, Leopold and Dillon emphasize the importance of giving "cognizance . . . to the role of the accident itself in producing a discrete illness, which in all likelihood, would not have occurred had there been no accident (245)."

All of these observations have been amply confirmed in Buffalo Creek. For, as this chapter has repeatedly attempted to demonstrate, the trauma there was total and overwhelming. The fact that virtually everyone exposed to it underwent adverse psychological effects makes clear that predisposition can only add to those effects but never be the cause of the posttraumatic states observed. Moreover, the extraordinary percentage of clinical psychiatric syndromes (more than 97%) is further tragic testimony to the causative influence of the trauma—the disaster—itself, since without that trauma there could be no possibility of anything like that percentage of clinically affected individuals. The present major mental health crisis in Buffalo Creek, and the psychological suffering of each individual in association with that crisis, are direct results of the disaster.

26

THE ROLE OF CRISIS INTERVENTION SERVICES IN DISASTER RECOVERY

Richard K. McGee
Edward F. Heffron

Certain aspects of crisis intervention theory which have been discussed by early writers (58, 174, 260, 310, 339), together with the technologies which have emerged from the development of crisis intervention delivery systems in many communities, point clearly to the appropriateness of this type of service in disaster recovery. Some key issues are briefly summarized to set the context for this discussion.

A PHILOSOPHY OF CRISIS INTERVENTION SERVICE

It is not the actual procedures which define crisis intervention activities so much as their underlying philosophy. It is difficult to imagine any problem that would fall outside the scope of appropriate response by a crisis intervention agency. There are no eligibility requirements for clients of a crisis service. The crisis worker is best conceptualized as an ombudsman or facilitator in behalf of people with any type of problem. The need for food, clothing, and shelter can be as much of an emergency to a family as the need for impartial mediating intervention in an angry family dispute. Both types of human problem should receive as much attention as suicide threats and attempts when they are brought to a crisis intervention service.

Attitudes Toward People in Crisis

Crisis intervention services have pioneered new ways of thinking about clients. Successful programs have tended to avoid the sterotyped notions about people usually associated with the delivery of conventional mental health services. The newer attitudes toward clients are summarized in these brief statements.

1. People in crisis are not sick. Crisis intervention is not necessarily a medical or health related service.
2. People can be in crisis and not be mentally ill. Crisis intervention is not necessarily a mental health service.
3. People in crisis need immediate, active, aggressive intervention.
4. People in crisis are the responsibility of the local community. Crisis intervention service is a rightful expectation of every citizen just as is the availability of public education, public health, police and fire protection, and public utilities.

Use of Paraprofessional Personnel

The central role of the volunteer in the development of crisis intervention services (see also Chapter 6) has been discussed in detail in recent literature (101, 282). Paraprofessionals were initially used because of the shortage of professional personnel, but it soon became evident that they had additional attributes which rendered them especially well suited to their role. They now have earned their own place in the delivery of human services.

Taking Emergency Service to the Problem

The earlier crisis intervention services were often restricted to telephone answering and referral mechanisms. While a few programs still confine their interventions to telephone conversations, the majority have taken the assistance to the client when and where it was demanded. Hansell's criterion of good service seems very apt. He argues, "The quality of treatment can be measured by the number of feet of distance it is located from the person's ordinary space of life (164)." The closer the service is rendered to the time and place the client is experiencing the problem, the more effective the service rendered.

Reaching Out Services

Crisis intervention services evolved primarily from the suicide prevention centers that developed across the nation in the last half of the 1960s (282). Such programs were based on the thesis that suicidal behavior is a *cry for help* which may include a substantial component of ambivalence. People often asked for help indirectly or symbolically. Suicide center workers learned to extend a helping relationship despite the fact that people had not asked for it directly. Crisis workers thus identify situations when people are at risk, or in need, and seek them out spontaneously.

These concepts coalesce to form the rationale for extending crisis intervention methodologies into the area of disaster recovery.

THE PENNSYLVANIA FLOOD

Fed by the torrential rains of tropical storm Agnes, on June 23, 1972, the Susquehanna River cascaded over its banks, smashing the "flood proof" dikes and inundating a large portion of both Luzerne and Wyoming Counties. The flood waters, as much as 6 miles across in some areas, forced more than 72,000 people to evacuate their homes, many with less than 30 minutes notice. Two days later, the river crested at 40.6 feet, then slowly began to recede.

Located in the northeastern section of the state, Luzerne County at the time of the flood had a population of 342,000 people, of whom about one quarter were over 55 years of age. Wyoming County was primarily a rural, agricultural area, with about 90% of a population of less than 20,000 operating over 500 individual farms. Nearly 25,000 residences in the two counties were affected, the majority receiving substantial damage. Nearly 3,000 commercial enterprises employing over 11,000 persons curtailed their operations.

During the first few days an estimated 50,000 residents were housed in a variety of evacuation centers extending 20 miles north and south. Thirty days after the flood, only 2500 people were still living in such shelters, but 3000 persons were being fed by recovery agencies.

Like everyone else affected by the flood, the purveyors of mental health and social services were unprepared in the sense of moving equipment and files to "safe" ground. The Mental Health/Mental Retardation (MH/MR) Administration, The Children's Service Center, and the Wilkes-Barre Community Mental Health Center #1 were all inundated. Nevertheless, the MH/MR Administrator, James Lawlor, was able to initiate 24-hour emergency psychiatric service at the unaffected Wilkes-Barre and Nanticoke State General Hospitals the day after the flood, and to arrange emergency communications with several of the federal and state relief units already on the scene. The following day, after assessing projected mental health needs, he was authorized to hire 12 temporary mental health workers for crisis teams.

The teams made contact with emergency shelter and medical unit chiefs and prepared to manage problems of emotional crisis and mental illness encountered in these units. During the next few weeks, the teams visited between 7 and 9 units during each 12-hour working day.

Initially, the crisis teams dealt with depression, anxiety reactions, situational disorders, temporary psychotic episodes, and mentally retarded and disoriented children as they were identified in the shelters.

Two weeks after the flood, 50 volunteer mental health professionals of the Pennsylvania Department of Public Welfare arrived on the scene to assist in a Community Mental Health Center which was serving as focal point of the mental health service delivery system. They remained in the flooded areas for one week. The temporary mental health workers hired by the MH/MR administrator remained only 8 weeks until the emergency funds were depleted. It was evident that a much more durable system was needed—one that could not be supplied by the existing mental health budgets, agencies, and personnel.

The National Institute of Mental Health, in response to requests for assistance from state and local officials, immediately dispatched a mental health team headed by Dr. H.L.P. Resnik, then chief of the newly established Mental Health Emergencies Section. After several days in the flood-stricken areas, the team concluded that the organization of an NIMH-sponsored program should be undertaken at once. During the last 3 weeks of July, a proposal was formulated, coordinated, and funded to commence operations under the title Project Outreach, on August 1, 1972.

PROJECT OUTREACH

The Outreach program was designed to employ 50 paraprofessional workers, referred to as Human Service Counselors. To provide direction and clinical back-up, the staff included six supervisors, two social workers, two casework trainees, a casework supervisor, and a community organization representative.

The basic goal of the program was to prevent occurrence and promote resolution of emotional and psychological disturbances through the provision of crisis intervention services. Services were taken to the clients rather than expecting the clients to come in and ask for them. The procedures of active intervention in the setting where the problem exists, which McGee and Richard (354, 355) discuss as the rationale underlying crisis center teams, were adopted from the beginning of the program planning. The goal was *not* to focus on case finding for existing agencies but rather to provide *direct services* whenever possible to alleviate the crisis.

When the Project Director described the goals and philosophy of the Outreach program at a special interagency meeting, the response was mixed. Some of the agencies expressed concern that 50 paraprofessionals would flood the agencies with referrals and overtax their abilities to respond; some feared that their functions might be eliminated by Outreach workers, and others were annoyed by the amount of funding, indicating that NIMH should have awarded the money to the local agencies so they might hire additional professional staff. However, an interagency inquiry conducted in late March 1973, revealed positive relationships between Outreach and the other agencies in Luzerne–Wyoming Counties, with no evidence that the early fears or apprehensions had materialized.

Responses to the traditional media sources, employment agencies, church bulletins, and community grapevine yielded about 50 applicants, from whom 20 staff members were chosen following personal interviews using hypothetical case studies. The 20 trainees chosen, 13 men and 7 women, ranged in age from 20 to 56 years and in education from 12th grade to Master's degree. The majority were recent college graduates without previous professional experience. Representatives of ethnic groups prominent in the area as well as Viet Nam veterans were included.

Following a 5-day intensive training program, the initial group of workers entered the community on August 28. Efforts during the first week were concentrated on one relatively small area in South Wilkes-Barre that had suffered extensive flood damage, in order to gain knowledge about the community's receptivity to Outreach work, the effectiveness of neighborhood canvassing, the kinds of needs that existed, the nature and speed of the recovery process, and the advisability of assigning the counselors to two-person teams.

On September 18, 1972, an additional 21 counselors joined the Outreach staff, having completed a similar training program. This second group included 11 men and 10 women, aged 19 to 62 years (average age, 30 years). While several were recent college graduates, there was a greater diversity of backgrounds in the second group; it included a recovered alcoholic, a nutritionist, a beautician, a teacher, a former security guard, and several laborers.

Since most service programs were concentrating their efforts on evacuees in temporary trailer sites, it was decided to emphasize services to those evacuees returning to their homes in the Wyoming Valley. The area in which the counselors first worked was characterized by a high proportion of elderly residents with a strong sense of neighborhood identity.

During this early period, the Outreach workers canvassed freely in their assigned area, sometimes meeting people on the street and sometimes knocking on doors to talk to residents. Each day's encounters were reviewed with other counselors and supervisors, thus sharing experiences and gaining advice on difficult matters. It was soon decided that teams composed of paired counselors should work in five geographically defined areas to allow the workers to develop a sense of identification with a locality and responsibility for the people in it. Consideration in team assignments was given not only to whether workers lived in their assigned areas, but also to their personality, sex, age, and education.

Changing Needs in Disaster Recovery Services

By June 1, 1973, Outreach counselors had recorded over 15,000 client contacts. The range of services provided was wide and diversified. Community involvement continually included a focus on present frustrations occasioned by the flood as well as on the failure of community members to receive immediate relief for their needs. As the year progressed, one phase of recovery gave way to the next, and the needs of the citizens reflected the slowly evolving reestablishment of a sense of normality.

Initial Problems. The majority of the problems discovered by the counselors during the late summer of 1972 dealt primarily with concrete needs, most often related to housing. For individuals returning to their flood-damaged residences, Outreach workers were able to eliminate some of the anxiety by providing contacts with craftsmen, contractors, schools, and the myriad of agencies involved in the restoration effort. Many individuals experienced difficulty securing HUD mobile homes or campers, or the necessary utilities (electricity, gas, oil). Intervention by Outreach workers was usually sufficient to resolve the problem, thereby allowing the individual to invest his efforts in recovery-oriented activities.

During late summer and early fall, the flood victims were generally feeling angry, anxious, frustrated, and depressed. For the majority of the victims housed in government-sponsored temporary housing, a new set of problems seemed to develop.

As winter approached, Outreach workers noted an increase in drinking on the part of many flood victims. The Wyoming Valley reportedly had ranked about average in alcohol consumption prior to the flood. There were constant reports of increased tensions within family groups or among individuals housed together as a result of the flood, and increased feelings of isolation among many people residing in both the HUD group sites and the community.

As recovery operations progressed, coordination of all activities became a monumental task exacerbated by lack of experience in coping with disasters and further intensified by manifestations of state and federal rivalries. However, federal and state officials active in flood recovery efforts made an attempt to work together despite bureaucratic complications.

Moving from Everyday to Long-Range Needs. By early December there was a gradual change in the type of problems encountered. The movement was from concrete, tangible needs to expressions of anxiety about the long-range effects of the flood. Up to this time, a majority of the victims had been exceedingly busy with the everyday problems of recovery. By December, most homes had been cleared of debris and boarded up for the winter; Small Business Administration (SBA) applications had been completed and many checks received; children had begun to adjust to new school situations, and Christmas was near. It seemed that this was the first opportunity for many victims to consider their circumstances without the interference of pressing recovery matters.

Wilkes-Barre has been described as "the kind of place people come from." Family reunions and social gatherings were seriously limited by housing and financial considerations. Outreach counselors delivered Christmas trees, with trimming and gifts, and provided an abundance of emotional support, which seemed to be the primary need during this period.

In late December, the Outreach program extended its coverage to include weekends and evenings. Through several in-service training sessions, the counselors learned the techniques of crisis intervention by telephone that have been widely and successfully used elsewhere in preventing suicide. Outreach was the only service providing telephone counseling as well as a crisis team available for immediate response. The extended coverage proved to be an extremely important part of the Outreach program; follow-up service was provided for over 50% of the calls received.

The winter of 1973, although quite mild for northeastern Pennsylvania, was a particularly difficult period of adjustment for many people. After months of frustration in dealing with government agencies, contractors, and other flood-related resources, a feeling of apathy, helplessness, and hopelessness prevailed. Inappropriate response from some agencies had become a part of life. Restoration services were expensive, hard to get, and often of poor quality. Many residents who had hoped to return to their homes by Christmas resigned themselves dejectedly to wait until spring to repair and rebuild.

By the time spring arrived, a sense of loneliness, boredom, and resignation characterized the elderly residents in Wyoming Valley. Living on a fixed income, many had lost the possessions of a lifetime and had to be satisfied with only memories. For most, the reality was—and still is—that they could not ever recover; they simply did not possess the physical and emotional stamina required to begin again.

Classification of Needs and Services

Three days of interviewing nearly 40 workers elicited 60 difficult or challenging case histories. No use was made of recorded data in case files; only worker's impressions of their work were included. From these case descriptions, 8 relatively distinct categories of problem situations emerged. Together, they form a composite of the job description, or the role expectations, of disaster recovery crisis intervention personnel.

Initial Mobilization.   A situation frequently encountered by the crisis workers in their initial canvas in August 1972 involved people who had not yet begun to take any rehabilitative action. They seemed immobilized, as if they did not know what to do first. Some had not yet made the decision to do *anything*. These cases were uncovered in the process of canvassing the flood-damaged neighborhoods. There were a number of deadlines which had been established by the recovery agencies. SBA loan applications had to be processed by a certain date; when approved, the checks had to be cashed by a certain time. Red Cross vouchers for food and clothing expired if they were not used by a given date. Applications for temporary housing had to be made within a given date or the possibility of obtaining a mobile home was eliminated. The crisis workers found many people who were in great need of the benefits provided by these agencies but who had been unable to initiate the contacts. Many were reluctant to be away from their homes due to the fear of looting. Others rationalized that they should not take welfare or charity contributions. Most of them, however, just did not know what to do first; they needed to be led, gently nudged, directed into appropriate action by someone in whom they felt trust and confidence.

> One woman in her mid-60s welcomed the crisis workers and almost immediately began crying. She talked about the things she should be doing, but she had not been able to get herself even to go to the grocery store since her return home 6 weeks earlier. She and her 89-year-old mother had been eating cold canned goods for days since there was no gas or electricity. The mother was confined to bed with a terminal illness and could not care for herself. The daughter badly needed to get away from the house, to reengage with the outside world. The crisis workers developed an action plan to mobilize the woman, one taking her shopping while the other stayed with the mother. Soon she was able to get a friend to stay with the mother while she managed her affairs. She had resources available but unused, because her usual coping methods were nonfunctional. Supportive contacts throughout the project helped her find a job, have her house repaired, and become reestablished to her former level of stability.

The "Given-Up" Syndrome.   Clients who merely need to be mobilized to start their recovery operations may be very depressed, afraid, lonely, or they may be agitated and angry. They may, on first encounter, appear to have serious psychological deficits, but this picture changes rapidly after intervention. Such cases should not be confused with a much more serious postdisaster phenomenon wherein the client has, perhaps consciously and deliberately "thrown in the towel" and quit living. Such reactions may be expected in any disaster area with victims who are elderly or nearing retirement age. For them it is too late to start over. Many of our elderly people had lived through previous disasters—the flood of 1936 hit the same region of Pennsylvania—and were then young enough to reestablish their businesses and homes, rear their children, and save for their years of leisure. Many of these people looked at the destruction of their lives and concluded, "There is no use to try again."

There were a large number of deaths in Luzerne and Wyoming Counties after the flood; these were *not* suicides but were natural deaths. Statistics compiled in the evaluation team's second report (462) showed a dramatic rise in the number of deaths over comparable periods for the past 3 years, primarily due to heart disease. Such data suggest that severe emotional trauma, which carries with it a sense of hopelessness and despair, speeds one's trajectory toward the grave.

When analyzed within the framework of the psychological autopsy (430), such deaths yield convincing evidence that giving up and permitting oneself to die is one form of human response to a major disaster. Crisis intervenors in disaster areas should be prepared to identify and cope with such cases.

Bereavement Crisis Counseling. Victims who suffered loss of a family member experienced complications in their course of recovery due to the need to properly experience a bereavement crisis.

A widow, age 55, whose husband had died 1 month after the flood, explained that although he had been ill with miner's asthma for years, he had been able to manage the family business affairs. She was left alone with the tasks of rebuilding the house and learning how to manage business matters. Intervention with this woman took the form of 1) encouraging her to talk and 2) helping her with constructive planning for her daily activities. She was helped to learn she could cope with seemingly insurmountable tasks. The crisis workers visited her daily at first, then twice a week for a few months, focusing on the full range of feelings and experiences typically faced by the newly bereaved. She soon was able to find a job and start on her financial and social readjustment.

Bereavement counseling is a special form of crisis work. Many of the techniques for intervention are merely logical extensions of the approach taken in any kind of crisis. However, the clients have special needs, hence a particular orientation is necessary for dealing with them effectively. Crisis intervenors in disaster areas should be given special training and consultation in their role as grief counselors. The writings of Parkes (313), Kavanaugh (207), and Hendin (173) provide appropriate resource material for this training.

Multiple Disaster Clients. Clients who suffer a second disaster very soon after the first major one are infrequent, but their emotional plight is such that there is special need for the crisis intervenors. These families have already suffered all of the problems of any other family: loss of possessions, dislocation to temporary housing, loss of employment. Even if they are adapting reasonably well to this first encounter with fate, a second one, such as a fire, resulting in another displacement, may befall them. This second blow becomes very traumatic because it is not shared by many other victims. For example, many families suffered damage or total destruction of their temporary mobile homes by severe winter windstorms. These losses were not considered flood-related, and therefore the resources which they had been conditioned to expect were not available to them. Such cases required even more active and supportive crisis intervention.

Adjustment to Temporary Housing. The department of Housing and Urban Development (HUD) placed over 14,000 families in temporary housing in Luzerne County alone. Most were given mobile homes which they could keep rent-free for 1 year. They were then permitted to continue in the mobile home under certain conditions with rental computed on the basis of their income and expenses. For many, availability of these homes was a help. For others, the difficulties in dealing with HUD constituted a stress which was worse than the flood itself. Harshbarger, (Chapter 23) points this out for Buffalo Creek as well. The emotional and mental cruelty which recovery agencies sometimes impose on people while they are trying to help them is amazing. However, these incidents—unfortunate though they may be—can acquire a significance out of proportion to their real frequency or severity, and as such, may become obstacles to effective interagency cooperation between crisis workers and the HUD program. They must be handled with skill and within a total perspective by mature crisis personnel.

Living away from one's own home and adjusting to strange surroundings, with a sense of temporariness and uncertainty about the future, was a great problem for many.

> The HUD trailer acquired symbolic value to one 50-year-old male. It seemed to relate to his sense of masculine competency and ability to provide for his family. He developed such a severe phobia of the trailer that he became anxious and irritable every evening when he came home. He was able to function well at work, or even while visiting neighbors in their trailers but was unable to sleep in his own trailer. One sleepless night, his wife called the Project Outreach workers. They went immediately, and stayed with him throughout the night. They maintained regular contact with him until he agreed to go to the mental health clinic. However, he kept only two appointments because he did not feel this was helping him. The crisis worker continued to see him twice a week. After six visits, in which they walked around the trailer park, and the client talked freely about himself in relation to the flood and the temporary housing, his

symptoms disappeared. Subsequent contacts revealed no further problems in adjusting to the trailer.

Although many trailer adjustment cases were referred to professional mental health services, they generally did not respond to the traditional psychotherapy and tranquilizer regimen. On the other hand, the creation of a friendship tie with a crisis counselor, who facilitated confrontation and exploration of the situation in which the client found himself, was often successful. The exploration by the paraprofessional did not involve techniques relating to latent personality dynamics, repressed feelings, and developmental experiences. In our experience, the use of these in-depth techniques did not facilitate improvement in crisis situations. It is especially important for crisis workers to feel confident in cases where their own skills are the "treatment of choice" so that unnecessary referrals can be avoided. This may require assistance from supervisory or consultant personnel within the organization.

Especially Helpless Clients. In any community where a crisis intervention program operates, a large number of people will be discovered who are unaware of or fail to use the established service agencies. These cases are likely to be the most difficult ones, often demonstrating chronic problems which are not amenable to solution by routine procedures of any agency. During postdisaster recovery efforts when all of the agencies are strained, it is even more probable that some of these most difficult cases will get lost in the shuffle. The crisis workers in Project Outreach discovered several such clients, and it is apparent that they represent a problem which crisis teams should be prepared to expect.

Cases of Reconstruction Fraud. Following any disaster where there is widespread physical destruction and large amounts of credit for repairs, the honest and legitimate contractors and suppliers are inundated with demands for services. At such times, there are generally a number of less scrupulous people who promise quicker and cheaper repairs for cash in advance. In one area of the Central Region Project Outreach program, the crisis worker found a large number of people who had responded to a dealer advertising wholesale meat at very low prices. It proved to be a version of the standard bait-and-switch game in which people found themselves with low quality meat and long-term promissory notes to pay at high interest rates. In many instances involving sales of food or reconstruction gimmicks, the crisis workers assisted the clients to gain relief through Legal Aid and the Consumer Protection Agency. They also provided necessary emotional support for clients whose experience had left them feeling a general distrust for everyone offering help. In such instances the client's own self-respect had suffered as well, and the understanding crisis worker was called on to play an effective role in this regard.

Exacerbation of Predisaster Problems.   The last problem is an extremely important one for the training of crisis workers. When clients show little response or evidence of successful recovery after intervention, workers are likely to become quite frustrated. In some respects this category cuts across others already discussed, but the problem characteristics are so similar as to merit discussion as a separate group. These people have functioned at a marginal level for years *prior* to the disaster. They may previously have been state hospital patients, borderline mentally retarded persons, chronic alcoholics, permanently nonemployable welfare recipients, or chronic drifters. Generally these persons had over the years gravitated to resources that had sustained their marginal adjustment: family or relatives, neighbors, or a church had been looking after them. In a disaster these support systems are disrupted. Families are relocated; agencies have other pressing concerns. As these chronically dependent members of society lose their support and shelter, they become very visible. The crisis worker's involvement often had little effect.

Occasionally it was possible to assist such people to reestablish their former support systems. However, the client himself did not significantly change his outlook or his motivation to help himself. In every crisis intervention delivery system it is important for the personnel to distinguish between acute crisis cases which will respond to the interventions and the chronically dependent and disabled, lest a heavy toll be taken in the workers' morale and self-confidence.

CONSIDERATIONS FOR THE FUTURE: MECHANISMS FOR THE DELIVERY OF CRISIS SERVICES

The Project Outreach programs have demonstrated that paraprofessional crisis intervention workers can play a vital role in the complex task of recovery from a natural disaster. Their significance in the psychological readjustment of thousands of flood victims has been recorded in private lives and in agency files all along the Susquehanna River basin. A new technology has been added to the armamentarium of recovery and rehabilitation resources, which may be applied wherever natural disasters may strike. Now that the service potential has been demonstrated, the next step is to establish the mechanism whereby it is continually available and ready to function.

Timely Intervention

A foremost consideration is timing, since crisis intervention services are most effective when they are available immediately. In Pennsylvania it was 2 months before the teams were in the field. This was in part due to the natural slowness of bureaucratic state and local governments. Whereas the NIMH was able to respond almost immediately, local agencies often imposed crippling delays while necessary clearances went "through channels." The typical procedures which are difficult enough for the standard mental health programs to surmount are even more paralyzing for emergency crisis intervention procedures.

Connotation of Mental Health

A second consideration relates to the identification of the crisis worker. Immediately upon beginning, nearly all the workers reported that they could not engage their clients if they associated themselves with mental health programs. The concept *mental health,* despite what it means to professionals, means *mental illness* to the general public. People in general do not wish to perceive themselves as needing mental health care. If a worker introduced himself by saying he was with the local mental health program, he was immediately told that the client had no need for his attention and was referred to someone down the street who was observed by the local neighborhood to be "one of those peculiar people." The workers soon learned to avoid such an identity, even to be deliberately vague if they were questioned about it.

One might reasonably ask if the mental health programs should be held responsible for incorrect perceptions on the part of the lay public. An equally reasonable query would be to wonder why crisis intervention services should necessarily be sponsored by mental health systems, especially since there is a high probability for misperception. These questions should be carefully considered in order to establish a crisis intervention delivery system which is most functional and most accessible in disaster areas.

Other Sources for Crisis Services

If one were to survey the attitudes of the general public concerning which agencies were seen as the most prepared to provide immediate assistance in a disaster, were least threatening to the image people have of themselves, and were most understanding of and responsive to the needs of disaster victims, there would probably be near perfect agreement. The American National Red Cross would probably receive top recognition for the greatest efficiency as a disaster recovery unit. Almost certainly it would not be the community mental health center. Therefore, since the Red Cross has established itself worldwide as the agency most capable of moving in with the greatest rapidity and efficiency, with food, clothing, shelter, medical supplies, and first aid for physical problems, why would not the Red Cross be equally appropriate for managing the delivery of *psychological first aid* through crisis intervention services to the disaster victims?

There must be tremendous organizational and logistic difficulties in maintaining the high level of disaster preparedness which the Red Cross currently provides. Most of them probably relate to financial and manpower issues. It is unlikely that the National Chapter, or the Regional Divisions of the Red Cross, could undertake a substantial increment in service delivery without additional money and staff.

However, the federal government, through the NIMH-sponsored Project Outreach, has demonstrated the usefulness of crisis workers in disaster areas. It should be reasonable to expect the availability of funding from appropriate federal sources.

Staffing Programs

The manpower problem might be even more easily conquered. There are currently several sources of volunteer paraprofessional manpower throughout this nation. The National Center for Voluntary Action has established local offices in most American cities. There are local Red Cross and Mental Health Association chapters in most counties of the nation. There are crisis intervention centers which already have groups of trained crisis workers in nearly 300 American cities. These manpower pools have yet to be tapped as part of a national disaster preparedness program. As for training the volunteers for their role prior to a disaster, the task would not be insurmountable. It should, of course, begin in the high-risk areas where disasters may be predicted to occur. The hurricane-prone coastlines of the Southeast and the earthquake areas of the West Coast are two obvious examples.

The Red Cross has been identified for many years as the primary source of high-quality training in first aid, life-saving, water safety, and other important community necessities. Courses in crisis intervention, especially designed for the volunteers in local communities, could, in a period of a few years, prepare large numbers of indigenous citizens to move in immediately and provide services when a disaster strikes. Of course, provisions must be made for them to continue on the job for several weeks, or even months. But with a cadre of trained personnel in the area, the organizational and logistic mechanisms for deploying and compensating them could certainly be arranged as needed. A society which can send a major department of its government into an area and relocate 14,000 families into 8,000 mobile homes and other temporary dwellings can arrange to pay renumeration and expenses of trained crisis intervention personnel, especially if they are already on the scene and ready to function.

The Pennsylvania Flood Recovery program has provided a number of invaluable lessons about the capacity of this society to meet both physical and psychological needs of disaster victims. In building on this experience for the benefit of those who will need similar services later, crisis intervention specialists are constrained to ask how, and under what auspices, their services can be most effectively applied. Perhaps in some areas it will be the mental health system which will prove most feasible. Or perhaps, as in other aspects of disaster relief, it might be the American National Red Cross which is conceptually and organizationally most prepared to sponsor crisis intervention services.

27

THE CORNING FLOOD PROJECT

psychological first aid
following a natural disaster

Ann S. Kliman

ORIGINS OF THE PROJECT

On June 23, 1972, a flood ripped through the city of Corning, New York, killing 18 persons, severely damaging or destroying the homes of 6000 people (out of a total of 20,000), necessitating the emergency evacuation of many thousands more, and crippling trade and industry. Local, state, federal, public, and private resources were immediately mobilized to meet the emergency health, shelter, social, and financial needs of the people. Property damage alone was close to 100 million dollars. The city's major industry, The Corning Glass Works, although badly stricken, was already hard at work to meet the physical needs of the citizens. It also expressed concern about the short- and long-term effects of aftershock following the flood. Dr. Michael Beer, the company's organizational psychologist, contacted Alvin Toffler (409) for advice on how to handle the expected aftershock and was referred to the Situational Crisis Service of The Center For Preventive Psychiatry 180 miles away in White Plains, New York.

Seven days after the flood I was contacted as Director of the Situational Crisis Service. Three days later I went to Corning and met with the Chairman of the Board, Vice-President in charge of personnel, and the organizational psychologist of the Glass Works. Thus the project began under optimal circumstances. Immediately after the disaster a responsible group in the community had recognized potential problems, reached out for professional consultation, and was willing to finance the psychological first-aid efforts of a team experienced in situational crisis intervention.*

At the request of the Corning Corporation, I presented an outline of the predictable postflood psychological problems and a plan of how the community could be mobilized to turn a disaster into an opportunity to promote healthy growth and adaptation. The plan was accepted and immediately implemented. Ms. Maloney, Director of the Corning Family Service Agency, volunteered to be the liaison person and coordinator between the psychological first-aid team and the community.

In considering the results of the project, it is important to understand that the introduction of the situational crisis team under the sponsorship of the Corning Glass Works and the Family Service Agency, both integral to the community, made the team more acceptable than it would have been as a group of unsponsored outsiders.

MODES OF OPERATION

We identified target groups necessary for a cooperative community psychological first-aid effort. They included psychiatrists, psychologists, internists, pediatricians, social agency personnel, nurses, school personnel (prekindergarten through college), industrial and business leaders, clergymen, policemen, firemen, local political leaders, news media personnel, emergency governmental agency personnel (HUD, SBA, IRS, National Guard), camp counselors, Girl Scout and Boy Scout leaders, and all volunteer corps leaders.

A series of workshops and seminars were scheduled with all the target groups. All the groups except the local political leaders and most of the local physicians were receptive and even eager to participate. Since these two groups actively refused to meet with me, I can only surmise some reasons why they were unwilling to participate in the community psychological first-aid effort. The physicians (except the psychiatrists) were accustomed to working within the framework of hospitals and offices and had no experience with community-organized medicine. The politicians were objects of considerable anger in this community and were thought to be responsible for the poor preparation and lateness of the evacuation, as well as for the inadequacy of preflood preparations. Thus, they may have been unwilling to engage themselves in any community activity which encouraged expression of feelings.

About 500 professional and paraprofessional persons were given a brief course, usually consisting of three 90-minute sessions. For workers with heavy case loads, meetings were held 6 hours a month for the first 6

---

* Especially vital in the development of the theoretical framework were Drs. William Niederland, Scientific Advisor, and Gilbert Kliman, Director, The Center for Preventive Psychiatry, White Plains, New York.

months; this group included school personnel, family agency personnel, housing counselors from HUD, and counselors from the Office of Human Development.

The usual curriculum dealt with the following topics:

1. Expected psychological reactions
2. Developmental differences in reactions
3. The importance of verbalizing feelings rather than acting them out
4. Viable alternatives to group psychopathology
5. Preventable and predictable problems, particularly industrial and vehicular accidents

Every meeting was liberally based on actual psychological first-aid problems drawn from the participants' current case loads, whether among defined patients or from the network of persons with whom the counselors were interacting.

The theme of the initial seminars was to share with the community caregivers the concept that in a natural disaster no one escapes completely. Everyone in the disaster area falls into the category of being a direct or indirect victim. Drawing on the work of Lindemann (260), Niederland (303), Lifton (256), and Kliman (221) with people in acute situational crisis, predictions could be made of some reactions of both the direct and indirect victims. Direct victims usually suffer from anxiety reactions: fear that the disaster will recur, feelings of being overwhelmed, feelings of depression and rage, inability to cope, or frenetic coping behavior. Indirect victims often respond with guilt reactions (guilt that they escaped while others didn't) and with increases in guilt-related and stress-induced physical symptoms—accidents, or explosive arguments at home, at school, or on the job. The concept was emphasized that such reactions are *expectable reactions* to acute stress and not necessarily an indication of weakness, mental illness, or inadequacy. Equally important was the concept that by sharing the affects connected with the disaster experience people would learn that they were not alone in their feelings, that their feelings were not abnormal, and that if they shared their feelings, they would not subsequently defend against them in maladaptive ways. Out of these discussions, it became increasingly apparent to the caregivers that feelings of anger, depression, and exhaustion were appropriate after a disaster, and that everyone had choices as to the manner in which these feelings could be expressed.

Among the caregivers directly trained by this minimum curriculum were nurses, teachers, family agency personnel, firemen, policemen, managers, foremen, and government personnel. The training groups consisted of 30 to 300 persons.

In addition to the brief course work, there was a small demonstration program based on my giving direct psychological first-aid service to 4 families. While those family first-aid sessions were conducted, appropriate personnel from local family service agencies were in the room (with consent of the clients), thus learning ways of helping by observation. These same workers carried out the follow-ups and in some instances the continuation of treatment where needed.

Supervisory sessions consisting of personal comment on the first-aid treatments given by the briefly trained caregivers had greater impact than the program of direct demonstrations. About 300 family case studies were presented to me personally by our trained caregivers during the first 6 months, usually in very brief form. These supervisory sessions were mostly for clergymen, teachers, school psychologists, principals, counselors, nurses, family agency personnel, Red Cross workers, and business executives—all of them actively engaged in short-term psychological first aid. Probably several times the 300 families known to me were served by these professionals and paraprofessionals who took the trouble to present a portion of their case load for comment. Thus, well over 1000 families, with several thousand members, were probably served by the trainees. In this way a substantial fraction, perhaps a third, of the community's population of 18,000 citizens was reached.

SOME DISASTER PHENOMENA

During one of the first workshops, Girl Scout camp leaders reported changes in the behavior of the girls compared to that of previous years. The counselors reported a large increase in girls reporting to the nurse with somatic complaints and minor accidents, an increase in arguments in the bunks and at activities, an increase in sleeplessness, nightmares, and inability to concentrate, and a decrease in ability to master skills. Upon careful questioning, it was revealed that most girls who went to the nurse and who precipitated arguments were the girls who were the indirect victims of the flood—those who had suffered only minor inconveniences such as lack of electricity or heat. However, those girls who were fearful, couldn't concentrate or master skills, were sleepless or had nightmares were mostly the direct flood victims—those who were evacuated and whose homes were badly damaged or destroyed.

The Girl Scout camp proved to be a microcosm of the experiences and reactions of the city. Similar reports began pouring in from resource people from all disciplines. A plant manager reported with distress that he didn't know how to handle an employee who had lost his home and who had become *demanding, incompetent,* and *unreasonable* on the job. The manager felt sorry for the employee and didn't want to "kick the man when he was down," but he also felt that the man should get down to work again.

This gave the group an opportunity to discuss, both personally and theoretically, the problems posed when direct and indirect victims work together. The manager realized that while he felt sorry for the direct victim, he did feel that the man was weak and infantile, and so was also angry with him. The appropriateness of both sets of feelings was discussed, which led to more and more members of the group sharing the same type of experiences and reactions. A highly educated scientist who had been flooded out reported with embarrassment that she "just couldn't figure out" how to fill out a simple requisition form and that she was ashamed to ask for help. A store owner who lost his home reported becoming furious with a neighbor (who escaped damage and who put him and his family up in his house) because the bed he slept in was uncomfortable. A social worker expressed increasing irritation with a client whose home had considerable damage because he "wouldn't pull himself together." As each person told his story, others in the group would nod, sigh, and occasionally express the feeling: "I thought it was only me." By sharing experiences and feelings, the group became a mutual support system, and as such, group members were able to reconsider their attitudes, and then to entertain alternative methods of coping with their individual and collective attitudes and feelings. When feelings of guilt about survival and anger directed toward victims were shared, it became less necessary to act out these feelings by accidents or arguments, and the feelings also became less painful. The feelings of helplessness, fearfulness, and anxiety became less shameful after they were shared, and more energy could be directed toward realistic problem solving.

CAREGIVERS: THE HIDDEN VICTIMS

As the groups shared their feelings more freely, it became clearly apparent that a third group of victims was emerging as an entity—the caregivers. The Situational Crisis Service team at the Center for Preventive Psychiatry has long been sensitive to the special burdens it carries in its work to facilitate the adjustment of patients under acute stress. We are aware of feelings of wishing to rescue distressed people, of feeling frustrated because there is so little we can do to change tragic realities, of feeling angry because direct victims can be so demanding and uncooperative, of feeling tired and overburdened. We have learned to acknowledge these feelings and to recognize that we, the caregivers, are often the *hidden victims*. If we did not acknowledge these feelings, they could severely interfere with our therapeutic work. The wish to rescue often leads to doing *for* the victim unnecessarily, to reinforcing the passive, helpless position of the victim rather than facilitating the growth and development of more adaptive coping mechanisms. We can even feel virtuous and proud of "all we are doing for those poor people." However, when "those poor people" are insufficiently grateful, appreciative, or cooperative, we often feel angry and wish to drop the case, telling ourselves it is for good and rational reasons.

A leader can share her burdened feelings with the community caregivers:

Yes, I'm nearly exhausted.

Dammit, there's so much to do I don't know where to start.

Oh, I wish I could take that little boy home with me; he needs a mommy so badly.

You people are so busy fighting with one another you are just making everything worse, and I'm fed up.

Thus, the leader serves as a model and an immediate example that it is possible to have *unacceptable* feelings and not be hurt by them.

It was possible to feel overwhelmed, to acknowledge the feeling, and then to reconsider the priorities and get done what could be done rather than becoming paralyzed. It was possible to express anger at someone and to acknowledge the appropriateness (or inappropriateness) of the feeling verbally rather than acting it out and thus increasing the lack of understanding. It was possible to cope with any feeling and still be able to function. In fact, only by coping with our own feelings could we, as caregivers, do the work that needed to be done.

The author's job as director of the psychological first-aid team was to be a facilitator, to draw on the skill, expertise, and experience of all the caregivers, not to decide for them what they should or should not do. My job was not to give psychological handouts which would serve only to increase the passive, victimized position of the caregivers, but to facilitate their active mastery of the situation. The caregivers, in turn, were able to help people by supporting their ability to cope by *actively* sharing their feelings, by actively reordering priorities according to their needs, and by actively reconsidering their available options.

A TELEPHONE HELP LINE

Out of the workshops, which resensitized the caregivers to the role that affect plays in stressed people, evolved an emergency, 24-hour "help line." The help line was staffed by an interdisciplinary group of caregivers who were supervised by experienced therapists. It was designed to meet urgent or distressing problems in the community by giving callers a chance to talk about how they felt. A staff of trained therapists was available for those who needed more than psychological first aid by phone. Through news media, posters, and the grapevine, the function and purpose of the help line was spread throughout the community. As expected, the majority of calls dealt with practical or physical rather than psychological problems. However, it rapidly became apparent that calls for help on how to fix a fuse, fill out a government form, or where to go for a mobile home were disguised pleas for emotional support. The help line staff was trained to recognize psychological problems behind the practical problems and not to be satisfied by simply solving the practical problem. Staff follow-up calls were encouraged so that particularly vulnerable people would not be lost in the shuffle.

EDUCATING THE PUBLIC

From the onset, educating the public was the foremost priority. Using the network system of the community—schools, clubs, churches, agencies, and organizations—meetings were set up for community members to discuss problems and possible solutions.

Group Meetings

For each meeting the leader of the particular network organization involved issued the invitations and chaired the workshop. The author served as a resource person, encouraging active sharing of facts of the flood experience and of the affective reactions to them. As network members spoke about their feelings, their concrete examples could be used as jumping off points to educate them as to what could be expected in a stressed population, and to facilitate and support tolerance of transient regressions as well as adaptive, productive mastery. The appropriateness and universality of stress reactions was specifically emphasized, as was the unequaled opportunity a crisis situation presents to exercise options for creative change.

Treating the Very Young and the Elderly

These public education workshops also provided an opportunity to explain to the community the specific needs and problems of two particularly vulnerable groups—children under 8 years of age and the aged. Both the very young and the very old are generally treated by society as if they were unable to understand, realize, or cope with what goes on around them. Both groups are usually infantilized, with great efforts made to protect them from unpleasant realities. Many adults *pretend* that the very young and the very old do not see, hear, feel, or know that something difficult, puzzling, or frightening is occurring during a crisis. They are treated as islands of innocence by adults, in part because it is so painful for us to be aware of a child's or an aged person's pain. One result of not sharing realities with children or old people is that we force them into affective isolation just at the time they most need open communication and support. Most children under 8 are developmentally in the stage of magical thinking. They believe that what they wish, think, feel, dream, or dread actually makes things happen. They are not yet mature enough to differentiate accurately between the effect and the action. Thus, in a crisis, young children may feel responsible for the things that are happening, and this sense of responsibility is frightening to a child who is still attempting to master his own controls. Indeed, in a crisis most of us temporarily regress to moments of magical thinking. "If only I had . . ." or "If only I didn't . . ." are cries commonly heard from severely stressed people. Mature adults usually become aware that their guilt is unrealistic, but children need adult support because they do not know their own limitations.

In a crisis, the aged are rarely allowed to exercise their expertise or experience and are treated like young children. This infantilization increases their sense of feeling useless and devalued even more than usual by a society that puts a premium on youth.

One result of this aspect of the public education program has been a shift in attitudes. When the schools opened in September, teachers incorporated flood experiences into the teaching plan. Children were encouraged to play out, draw, or write about their flood experience and the feelings they had about the flood. Rainy days were used as an opportunity to talk about anxious worried feelings. Teachers and parents shared their own feelings with the children, thus giving a vote of confidence to the children that it is safe to have feelings, and that feelings do not make things happen. An attempt was made by several agencies to seek out older persons in the population in order to emotionally support these primarily isolated people and to give them an opportunity to actively engage themselves in community programs. This attempt has been only partially successful, but the community is now more alert to the usefulness as well as the needs of its elderly population.

Automobile Accidents

It was predicted that a rise in auto accidents would follow the disaster. Community attention to the rise in automobile accidents began after about 90 days. From that time, the Corning Police Department made continuously available the statistics on vehicular accidents for the year preceding the flood as well as statistics of reportable accidents after the flood. According to the records, auto accidents normally increased 100% in Corning during the period from December 15 to January 15. It is also recorded that reportable auto accidents had doubled in the first 5 months after the flood, compared to reportable accidents during the same period during the years before the flood. While it might have been assumed that the increase in the number of cars (of the emergency personnel) was a causal factor, this does not take into consideration that Corning has always had a huge influx of summer visitors, and this influx was now absent because of disaster conditions. I encouraged facing rather than avoiding the information that there was a major increase in auto accidents, and that based on police records we could expect an even greater increase during the Christmas to New Year vacation period. Using local radio, newspapers, magazines, house organs, school papers, and industrial bulletins, we actively emphasized safety options which could be implemented. As an apparent result of this preventive public education campaign, the citizens of Corning were able to sharply reduce the number of auto accidents to *below* preflood levels during the historically high accident period between December 15–January 15. From both the humane and economic points of view, this single measure alone indicates that the project was well worth the psychological first-aid team's involvement.

Bereavement

The aid of the Family Service Agency was enlisted to seek out the bereaved family members (221) of the 18 people killed in the flood. Fourteen of the 18 victims were elderly people living alone, with no family in the area. One person, who was out of town when the flood killed his wife and child, refused to return to the city and also refused my offer to go to him. One woman whose husband was killed accepted help from her clergyman (who consulted with me). One family, whose youngest child was drowned in the flood, accepted the offer of crisis intervention. The parents and surviving children entered a course of brief psychotherapy with the specific aim of better dealing with the parents' own grief, and to better help the surviving children deal with the loss of their sibling. With the permission of the family, a staff member of the Family Service Agency sat in on each session in order to learn the techniques necessary for facilitating healthy mourning.

THE GOAL OF BEING DISPENSABLE

The training of local professional and paraprofessional personnel to carry out the techniques of situational crisis intervention and psychological first aid was the most important goal of the team. My job was thus to make myself dispensable by training local personnel to be indispensable. Facilitating the local caregivers' active responsibility enabled me to phase myself out as they became increasingly skilled in performing situational crisis intervention.

Initially, I spent one day a week in Corning, primarily supervising the local caregivers and conducting public education workshops. Six months after the flood my time was reduced to once every 2 weeks, and 9 months after the flood my visits were further reduced to once a month.

COMMUNITY PLANNING

The Corning community, from the first day after the flood disaster, took an active role in planning its own rebuilding. The Glass Works organized a Youth Emergency Service (YES) to rebuild salvageable structures. The young men and women were paid $2 an hour for their work, and they worked hard. Businesses loaned their executives to the city to work with federal agencies as liaison and priority planners. The Corning school system, which suffered 5 million dollars worth of damage, decided to assess its current needs rather than to simply replace its losses. As a result one school was rebuilt with open classrooms because the principal and teachers believed that open rooms would better serve the students. Another school decided to rebuild almost exactly as it had been prior to the flood because the school had met the requirements of its students well. The Fire Department took a look at what they were and were not able to accomplish during and after the flood and then enlisted the aid of community leaders to increase the number of men in the department and to reorganize the working hours more efficiently.

Within a week after the flood, a hot-line was established to counteract rumors that were being spread; it was manned primarily by college faculty and students. People were reassured that the National Guard was not shooting at boys and dogs (indeed the Guard carried no live ammunition); that the Corning Glass Works was continuing operations paying full salary to its employees, and had no intention of moving out of Corning; that all damaged homes would be inspected and no one would have to move back in until the homes were structually safe; that there was no polio or typhoid epidemic in the area; and that looters were not ransacking the city.

Much was not accomplished that might have been. Most strikingly, despite much discussion, no flood control procedures were established. This is unfortunate in view of the fact that Corning is in a high-risk flood area and has flooded three other times since 1900. Moreover, hundreds of people moved back into their homes in particularly high-risk flood areas with little thought that they could be flooded out again.

CONCLUSIONS

To a considerable extent the city of Corning has served as a model of a community that used a disaster as an opportunity to reorder many of its priorities and to reconsider many of its options in a way which promoted growth and healthy adaptation. Some of the success of its rebuilding can be attributed to the availability of its citizens to psychological first aid through the means of caregivers trained for this project under the sponsorship of responsible and respected local groups. Equally essential were the psychological first-aid efforts to facilitate community movement from a passive, victimized, transiently regressed position to an active, healthy mastery.

However, deep repetition–compulsions seem to be at work in Corning, as in many flood communities. More powerful and more profound interventions than those of the current project are needed to overcome the tendency of our species to defy predictable catastrophes.

28

URBAN DISASTER

victims of fire

Alaine Krim

Each year in New York City 25,000 people (approximately 6000 families) are victims of an urban phenomenon—the routing from their homes by devastating fires. The fires, which most often strike in poverty areas where housing has always been inadequate, make displaced persons of the victims. While not constituting a *community* in the usual geographic sense, urban fire victims suffer the same type of psychological stress, disorganization, and dislocation that victims of earthquakes, floods, and tornadoes suffer. The individual catastrophes have little collective impact because of the random nature of the fires that occur in any large urban area. However, if viewed in terms of their effects on a large group of children and on families, urban fires represent a disaster rarely recognized or acknowledged as such. The suddenness yet inevitability, of its recurrence year after year in sections of any city where housing is marginal, must be viewed in the same context as natural disasters.

TRAUMA RESULTING FROM URBAN FIRES

The *stressor event* varies with the damage, danger, and extent of the fire. But for all affected by forced removal from their homes, the trauma of loss and separation prevails. These families must contend with a multiple assault on all that is known to them—the deterioration of their normal

This study was funded by the Agency for Child Development, and the Department of Mental Health and Retardation Services; New York City.

patterns of living. The past becomes unavailable to them and the future unknown.

A disaster has been defined as an "external force" which impinges upon "a structured community, or one of its sections," which can "destroy human life, excite public alarm, disrupt normal patterns of behavior and . . . impair or overload any of the central services necessary to the conduct of normal affairs or to the prevention or alleviation of suffering and loss (156)." When natural catastrophes strike a given area, the private community and government agencies mobilize to provide help and services. Special assistance for a community can be requested from the federal government.

In urban fires there is no such concept of *community*, no marshalling of forces, and little concept of the coordinated services or mental health intervention required by families in acute crisis. In New York City the Red Cross provides one night's emergency funds as a stop-gap measure, and the fire victims are scattered in rundown hotels throughout the city for temporary shelter. The victims are then "wards" of the City's Department of Relocation and Social Services until more permanent housing can be found.

These urban fire disaster families, brought to temporary hotel quarters a few at a time from different areas of the city, have little communality of experience or background other than the experience of fire. They are strangers to each other, facing the immediate requirements of adaptation and response to local government strictures while coping with hotel living in unfamiliar surroundings. Their anxiety-provoking experiences, often part of a long series superimposed on other chronic problems with which the poor struggle, are largely ignored.

The disaster removes the decision-making processes from families. They are placed in crisis within a bureaucratic, controlled structure, slow to respond to personal needs and unable to deal with the traumas the families have suffered. The institutional response is impersonal and operates under laws often applied in a vacuum. Local government personnel may fear making the fire victims too comfortable in their temporary housing, thereby encouraging them to remain indefinitely. Often the victims are blamed for their own plight. Agency regulations make rehousing almost impossible for multiproblem families because of *social desirability criteria*. Ironically, the working poor may also be ineligible for public housing or public assistance due to their income level (468).

Those families who have suffered deaths or severe burns are particularly shattered and distraught, psychologically unable to use concrete help effectively. Complicated city–agency machinery must be negotiated while attempts are made to cope with dislocation and the aftereffects of fire experiences.

In an attempt to alleviate the many problems faced by city fire victims, a special demonstration project has been developed to bring comprehensive on-site services directly to a Manhattan hotel, one of several used by the city to house emergency relocation families. Approximately 75 to 125 families, mostly black or Spanish-speaking, have been living at the hotel at one time. This chapter reviews our project experiences from March 1972 to April 1974.

DEVELOPING AN ON-SITE SERVICES PROGRAM

Under the leadership of an advisory planning board of appointed city officials, a voluntary agency, and a private hospital, this collaborative program reflects the participation of 22 private and government agencies in responding to the psychosocial needs of the disaster victims (231). Included were representatives of the fire and police departments and the Red Cross as auxiliary board members.

Short-Term Intervention

To provide short-term intervention, an on-site staff, including personnel from the Department of Social Services and Relocation, Youth Services Agency, Board of Education, Agency for Child Development, Roosevelt Hospital, and the Jewish Board of Guardians, set up services. Volunteers were enlisted. A day care center (that served more than 600 preschool children during the 2-year project period) was sponsored and administered by the Jewish Board of Guardians Child Development Center, with back-up clinical mental health services. Emergency and short-term psychiatric care for older children and adults, as well as pediatric services, were provided by Roosevelt Hospital.

Housing and financial assistance, emergency funds, school registration, recreation, clothing, child care, physical and mental health—the entire scope of families' needs—was recognized, cutting across professional and nonprofessional roles.

Services and personnel were concentrated on one floor. This central area enabled mothers to bring young children to the day care center, see the relocation manager, meet with a counselor or with a group without taxing their limited time or energies. Some parents acted as helpers and translators for the staff. It is noteworthy that families gravitated to the service floor whenever they had free time—for coffee, an informal talk, a visit. Problems of long standing became evident, and help was offered by those with whom relationships had been established. Only the teenagers' psychological needs were largely unmet. No successful program was devised for them despite numerous attempts. Individual teenagers were seen on an emergency basis only.

An *Information Guide* in English and Spanish listed on-site services as well as neighborhood shops for food, clothing, household equipment, and other necessities. Essential medical and city emergency facilities (with telephone numbers and names of key personnel), names and locations of schools, a street map, and transportation and recreation information were also included in the guide.

Administrative Procedures

The service teams and advisory board met regularly, but interagency differences were not always resolved. Nevertheless, services improved immeasurably during the life of the project. This organized service modality helped to restore many families to effective functioning and to arrange adequate relocation to permanent housing more quickly than in the past.

The service modality was replicated in two other major relocation facilities but without the on-site medical or mental health teams. Although no comparison study has yet been made, indications are that if these services are not readily available, the programs are less effective.

MENTAL HEALTH INTERVENTION: RATIONALE, REACTION PATTERNS, THERAPEUTIC STRATEGIES

As has been emphasized in many disaster studies, the victims' physical needs are met by various relief and government agencies and the communities themselves, but too often psychological shocks suffered by families and children are overlooked. A number of papers have cited the theoretical rationale and practical techniques of crisis intervention that have become increasingly applicable in meeting the mental health needs of a population affected by a disaster (39, 40).

Crisis intervention techniques cannot follow traditional approaches of history-taking and planned appointments, but must allow for quick assessment of personality strengths and needs based on minimal data. To minimize stress, disorganization, acting-out behavior, repression—the range of emotional problems faced by parents and children—intervention on an emergency basis must be offered when and as it is needed. In order to restore the distressed families to a functional equilibrium, the effects of trauma must be addressed at the point of greatest accessibility and vulnerability.

Characteristic Reaction Patterns

Common reactions to disaster have been described in other literature (193, 332, 443, 458), as well as in other chapters of this volume. Outlined here are some characteristic reaction patterns of fire victims observed at the hotel.

Disorientation and Confusion Due to Separation From the Community. All disasters lead to confusion and disorientation, but there are differences between the effects of natural disasters and those of urban fires in New York City. These differences, previously alluded to, include the random nature of the disaster, the removal to a strange area with children now in an "environmentless" neighborhood, and the important fact that few are affected from the same community at any one time and that they are not likely to be able to return to that community.

Before the development of on-site services, adults sometimes were seen in claustrophobic, aimless wanderings around the halls of the hotel. Others sat for days in the cramped rooms, helpless and in shock. Still others were propelled into activity to ward off shock and depression. An indication of their sense of dislocation could be seen in their return to former neighborhoods on weekends, sometimes taking laundry to be done in familiar surroundings.

Shock of Impact. There is rarely a warning period in urban fires. The degrees of danger and injury vary considerably, but for almost all families the suddenness of onset is traumatic in itself. Reactions generally follow two patterns of coping—denial and repression (with a kind of "freezing" of affect), or extreme expressions of anxiety and helplessness (see Chapter 22).

The adults who seem not to show much feeling most often mobilize themselves rapidly to attend to all the reality tasks required for rehousing. For the first 2 or 3 weeks, the external events are met with a flurry of activity. Then comes the waiting period when feelings of helplessness and the difficulties of living in the hotel become overwhelming.

For those whose immediate reactions reflect an inability to cope because of breakdown reactive to the crisis, mental health intervention must address the impact of the disaster with immediate active support, reassurance, and assistance with reality tasks.

Reactions of Guilt, Real or Imagined. Guilt reactions tend to be more extreme if the fire was actually caused by parental neglect or by the children. Some parents neurotically assumed guilt without cause, as did some children.

Reactions to Firemen and Fire-Related Objects. Sirens, smoke, and fire alarm bells often caused severe anxiety. Any sound or smell that reminded them of their previous traumatic experience was met with excessive concern. Many children began to perceive firemen as dangerous. The vapor from a manhole in the street or a broken window often elicited the vision of the fireman dressed in black who "smashes things," "tries to drown people," or "steals them away." Children spoke of *hard* water coming from the fire hose; *soft* water was for play. The stream from the park fountain could drown people and a twig used as a fire hose became an aggressive weapon.

Separation Anxieties and Fears of Abandonment. Many parents and children showed extreme separation anxiety. Children were often concerned about being left behind when the family moved, or expressed fear about where they would go.

Inability to Communicate and Postponement of Grieving and Mourning Period. It was fairly characteristic of parents to avoid discussion of the experiences with their children, although they frequently spoke to others about these experiences when the children were present. Despite the loss of home and personal belongings, and despite what at times appeared to be a family identity crisis triggered by dislocation and exposure to impersonal surroundings, family members found it difficult to share their feelings.

Aggressive and Hostile Reactions. Rage reactions were not unusual. These were frequently expressed by very demanding behavior on the part of adults, sullenness and name-calling by teenagers, destruction of property in the hotel, and abusiveness toward staff, thereby incurring counter-transference reactions.

Sleep Disorders. Sleep disturbances and nightmares were common in both adults and children.

Illness. Psychosomatic symptoms and exacerbation of physical ailments developed, requiring special medical attention.

Regression in Children. Typical of the preschool children was regression in toilet training, thumbsucking, and clinging to both people and possessions. Children followed their older siblings around the hotel or neighborhood, fearful of being alone.

Family Disorganization and Breakups. The fires sometimes resulted in separation of families, creating severe strain on all members. While for some families disorganization may have been a chronic problem, the crisis related to the fire often triggered new episodes of family disorder.

Preoccupation With Moving. A most important reality for all families, preoccupation with moving, sometimes took on obsessive proportions. Mothers spoke constantly of the where, what, and when of relocation, often focusing anxieties and rage on this one issue.

Withdrawal and Isolation of Adults From Their Children. Parents often were emotionally unavailable to their children, a condition that may have predated the crisis but often seemed in response to, or aggravated by, the total impact of the fire experience.

Severe Shock Due to Death or Injury. While incidents of death or injury to family members were not numerous, reactions, as could be anticipated, were extreme. Deaths of neighbors or friends produced recurrent expressions of guilt, obsessive dwelling on events, and hysteria in some children.

One disaster experience illustrates many issues: death, precipitous separation, hospitalization, and disorganization with resultant inability to accept help readily.

The example of Sam shows a degree of catastrophic response not usually seen in a 3-year-old, but in view of the disaster experience, the attending psychiatrist was reluctant to refer to the observable behavior as other than that described by Freud as "a sometimes pathologic mechanism of adaptation." The circumstances were as follows:

CASE REPORT 1

The fire destroyed the apartment totally. Both parents and a 6-month-old infant escaped injury, but a 2-year-old twin girl, Mary, perished. The other twin and Sam, age 3, were hospitalized for smoke inhalation for several days. During that time, their parents were relocated to the hotel, and Mary was buried.

The hospital staff were most attentive to the children and to the mother when she was able to visit. Regular contacts were planned after the release of the children, but the mother did not follow through.

Upon release from the hospital, the children came to the hotel. They kept asking for their sister, Mary. A crisis developed when Sam began tearing up their room, throwing things out the window, finally threatening to throw himself out. He then locked himself into their refrigerator. This aroused the mother sufficiently to request help from the preschool center. Several visits were made to the family's rooms, and it was noted that both children showed extreme vacillation—hysteria, withdrawal, and clinging demands for affection from the visiting staff.

The mother could verbalize very little. Her preoccupation was with Sam's extreme reaction. Her affect was flat, her judgments limited, and she seemed in shock.

A multifaceted approach was developed. The preschool director visited daily, spending some time with the children for whom any attempt at further separation from each other or the mother was clearly inappropriate. The hospital psychiatrist and social worker were asked to visit and continue their contacts "on-site" to avoid further fragmentation of intervention.

With extensive planning and preparation of the family by the mental health team and the preschool staff, arrangements were made for an interim move to an unique family shelter with attendant services and residential staff.

Continued hotel living would have led only to further deterioration and possible catastrophe. The plan meant another move—but one with the prospect of meaningful long-range help. It cannot be claimed that this was more than an emergency plan for an emergency situation, but it is illustrative of one of the more dramatic situations encountered, involving extreme trauma and its manifestations in both mothers and young children.

The Preschool Center

The Jewish Board of Guardians day care center was designed as the primary intervention agent for preschool children and their families. The center inevitably became the focus for family involvement because it had the only fulltime on-site professional team, including the project director, teachers, and a mental health staff of bilingual family counselors (social worker and psychologist).

The initial contact with the parents, the intake interview, began a process of active intervention. The history of the fire trauma was essential to understand how to integrate children into the program and develop a quick psychosocial assessment to determine the special needs of the family group.

The family-centered program established a milieu in which it was possible for reactions, fears, and feelings about the disruption of their lives to be expressed. In this atmosphere parents could, in a short time, describe what they referred to as their *before fire* and *after fire* lives. The availability of the preschool center and counseling, skilled ancillary help with everyday problems, advocacy, and help with health and other unmet needs provided assistance for many who had previously been unserved.

Professionals have long emphasized the importance of adequately preparing children for a move, for entering a new school, or for any change in environment. Children and mothers briefly visited the classroom in advance to talk and snack together with the teachers, but the usual slow introductory process was not possible. During the crisis of relocation, preschool children were thrust into the emergency "revolving door" classroom under great pressure, while their parents went about reconstructing family life. The sense of loss and separation anxieties were eased somewhat by having older brothers and sisters join the group for a few days, thereby accelerating the process of adjustment. Mothers were also able to visit later.

Many children showed symptomatology like that of the adults. Some were repressed, others seemed to be able to cope adequately. As we have said, hyperactivity, aggressive, and regressive reactions were not unusual.

Unfortunately, the concept of *immunizing* (221) young children from psychological effects of emergencies is not possible in a sudden disaster. Therefore, a flexible array of program patterns was devised for the classroom in consideration of individual and group needs. These included subgroupings, one-to-one contacts with teachers or a child therapist, and, when possible, work with mothers and children together in the classroom.

The choice of play materials reflected the emotional needs of the children, as well as their cognitive interests. Projects were designed that could be completed in a short period of time to give an immediate sense of satisfaction and mastery. For example, each child planted quick-sprouting beans, producing plants that could be taken with them when they moved. When needed, a few fire-related toys were introduced to encourage fantasy play and verbalization. For particularly restive children, there was an *active room* with climbing equipment and tricycles and also a *quiet room* with a rocking chair, books, and soft mats.

The program was planned for individualization, calm, and consistency as much as was possible. The staff tried to permit expressions of fears and guilt, to separate reality from fantasy, and to encourage healthy defenses and reparative processes.

In some instances it was necessary to counteract the parental expectation that children ought to behave as though nothing had happened.

CASE REPORT 2

A 5-year-old boy, attractive, energetic, and seemingly ready to enter the group, reacted with great fear when other children used a truck as a fire truck and made the noises of sirens. He ran from the center, screaming, "Not again, not again," and needed much help to calm down. It seems that he had run back into their burning apartment to rescue his dog. His parents thought him brave and lavished much praise on him for being manly. The staff worked with the parents to help them understand that his present reactions did not make him a sissy but were appropriate and necessary for him to work through his grief and fears.

Since these children had already been separated from a life they knew, further separation became a crucial issue. Any change in the group membership reactivated anxieties, despite efforts by staff to help the children anticipate their own moving and the departure of friends. Some children refused to go outdoors. Another wore his snowsuit for 2 weeks to prepare for another abrupt move.

Normally, the ages of 2 to 6 years are characterized by stages of successful weaning, toilet-training, separation, individuation, development of the capacity for interpersonal relationships, and a sense of identity that begins to distinguish self, family, and environment. All young children have death fears and fantasies, questions about survival and annihilation, and separation anxieties with which nursery schools and parents tend to have difficulty in dealing. During the preschool period children make deep attachments to inanimate objects as well as to people (301).

The sudden acute events of the fire disasters interrupted this process for these children. Their fears became their reality. The program was intended to deal with the acute traumatic events and to prevent potential future developmental impairment through special classroom techniques, individual and small group crisis intervention by a trained teacher–therapist, and by work with parents to help them understand their own and their children's reactions.

Individual and Group Counseling

The outreach strategies of mental health staffs from voluntary agencies provided the stimulus for intensive crisis intervention with some families in severe stress. The family counselors and social workers, along with the Department of Relocation and the Department of Social Services, learned about new families as they entered the hotel. Families were invited to visit the preschool center, or to see the psychologist from the hospital to discuss reactions and their own needs or those of their children. Some came individually. Many came to group meetings conducted by a joint team. It was hoped that a feeling of communality could be established.

The impact of the fire experiences—whether totally destructive or peripheral—was influenced by the time of the fire, the weather, how families were rescued, whether they had experienced similar disasters previously, whether any possessions were saved, and worries about looting. Group discussion of these issues helped family members express their feelings of frustration, fear, and grief; many began to acknowledge to themselves the extreme distress they had suffered.

Parents needed not only concrete services and reassurance but help in identifying their feelings and permission to express them. The fragmented reality of life in the hotel, the fatigue that followed total disruption of their lives, their concerns about their children—all these surfaced after brief contacts. Encouraged and supported, they could begin the grieving and mourning process.

Of special significance was the opening up of communication with their children about the disasters, and the recognition that the children's confusions were compounded by the sense of helplessness many parents experienced, or by the feeling that parents could not understand or respond to them in a time of crisis.

Education of on-site personnel from the city agencies to the psychological hazards created by stress constituted an important aspect of the program; this is illustrated dramatically in the following example.

CASE REPORT 3

Mr. & Mrs. Alberto and their 4-year-old daughter, Maria, saw the charred remains of a neighbor's 3 children removed from the burning building. Adults in the building were hysterical with grief. Severe symptoms developed in Maria, whose mother asked for help in handling her child's reactions and her own. Much support and active intervention were required.

Preventing the Department of Relocation from rehousing the Albertos in the *same building* where the disaster had occurred was of primary importance.

Advocacy for this family on the part of the staff was based on successfully communicating to the city agencies the traumatic aftereffects of this experience, and the expectation that a move to the same building would not permit healing but could result in further emotional damage. For the parents, the psychological and environmental supports were intertwined with positive results.

The formal agenda of some parent meetings was devoted entirely to environmental issues. Resource consultants from city agencies and the hotel manager were invited to address these issues and provide information. Inevitably the emotional reactions and distress of the families emerged and exerted a meaningful influence on policies and procedures. The mental health staff usually arranged and conducted these meetings as part of the total strategy of intervention.

For persons whose mental health needs were extreme, the trained clinicians received referrals and provided appropriate help. Follow-up activity was not unusual for both parents and children.

Issues for Preschool Center Staff

The staff's initial attitude was much the same as that of many of the families—active, positive, with concrete plans. But after a while they reacted negatively to the emergency nature of the program—a program constantly in transition. The sheer numbers served in a revolving door center, the strain and anguish of dealing with the turnover of young traumatized children, the constant witnessing of new and fresh tragedy (and at the same time facing the unpredictable changes in city agency policy), all contributed to the staff's feeling "burned out emotionally," a phenomenon analogous to the psychosocial distress suffered by the families.

Since the length of stay in the program varied from a week to several months, and children might be seen regularly or sporadically, teachers and counselors had difficulty in systematically assessing their achievements.

Separation experiences were mutually trying for families and staff. A teacher on a normal vacation was typically referred to as "the teacher who moved." Illnesses and changes of any kind made for problems. Constant regroupings of children, as some left and others arrived, required adaptation in the program as the new group process developed. When a staff member returned from vacation, the group might be totally changed in composition. At one staff meeting a teacher exploded, "Children are not interchangeable parts. We need time to recover from leave-takings and time to absorb new children."

There are other settings where family stresses impinge on staff, e.g., in hospital pediatric services or in children's shelter programs. At the hotel, because living quarters and services were in such close proximity, the pattern of "drop-in" meant not only an overload of work for the staff, but difficulty in maintaining appropriate distance and objectivity.

Identification of special needs of both children and families through a review of each new family's disaster history was attempted during the first few days of entry into the program. This often proved impossible as new crises took precedence. Frequent emergencies in the handling of individual children or a group, or an unexpected change in interagency arrangements often interfered with an orderly, preplanned routine. Thus, urgency of time, crisis, and change were the only constants.

No previous training or experience had prepared staff for the job to be done at the center. While teachers, counselors, aides, and other staff members were hand picked for their empathy, skills, and knowledge, it was difficult to determine beforehand their frustration tolerance. A program of training, consultation, and supervision was attempted, with trainers and consultants on call to help in emergencies. Although the staff support system was impossible to maintain with the consistency essential for optimal functioning, the overall staff training program seemed very effective when judged by the staff's own reactions. Increased self-awareness and recognition of the realities of a short-term, crisis-oriented preschool center led to innovative program approaches. The open sharing of feelings and examination of issues created a sense of community among staff that was reflected in the milieu to which families and children were exposed.

SUMMARY

If the premise of this chapter is accepted—that the recurrent fires in any large city constitute an urban disaster comparable to natural disasters—

then adequate social provisions must be made for the victims.

As noted by Barton, "Chronic forms of collective suffering come to be taken for granted and are largely 'invisible' to many in society (26)." Therefore, when fire disasters occur in any large city, external supports have consisted largely of sporadic, limited, temporary responses by rescue teams. Emergency physical needs are assessed by different agencies, and immediate shelter is arranged with little attention to the traumatic impact of loss and separation on the victims. Their problems are met in a haphazard, uncoordinated manner. Little is heard about their postdisaster problems, for they are victims of invisible isolated disasters, not large enough to command systematic, sustained attention from government agencies and the media.

The basic goal of the 2-year demonstration project described in this chapter has been to implement a program that *a*) helps to coordinate what we know about the needs of poor families who are fire victims; *b*) provides more information about the psychosocial effects of urban fires; *c*) permits assessment of the nature of dislocation and relocation experiences and their impact, and *d*) leads to development of appropriate techniques of intervention.

The demonstration project has emphasized environmental help plus a crisis service that encourages expression of feelings, gives reassurance, and supports such healthy ego defenses as control and mastery. A family-centered milieu has been created by on-site services and a mental health team.

The program has often been at odds with local agency policies requiring conformity and encouraging passive dependence on regulations and repression of independent action. The multiplicity of approaches has included systems analysis and concurrent political activity. The results of the project demonstrated to administrators in the public sector that a comprehensive program of disaster intervention could mobilize families to move more quickly and minimize aftershock.

Recommendations

The Manhattan emergency relocation center is being continued. Although, as yet, efforts to translate the project into an on-going citywide action program have not been successful, we believe the following recommendations have widespread applicability.

1. *An urban disaster unit* should be established in every major city where the threat of fire devastation is likely. This unit or task force should be a permanent ongoing quasigovernmental agency, with funding and representatives from all city departments and voluntary agencies that normally provide services in such emergencies, plus a community mental

health coordinator with specific skills in crisis intervention.

Since city and private agencies now operate independently and in a fragmented way, the task force would need to develop a program design, specific to each area, that can operate on an emergency level. By cutting across all existing bureaucratic procedures and devising new modes of delivering the essential services, a comprehensive program could meet the broad spectrum of psychosocial needs of disaster families.

2. *Community mental health specialists* with special training can help set the guidelines for emergency services that most effectively respond to the impact of disaster. Mental health input can help families to mobilize strengths in order to best use existing or newly developed services (such as mobile disaster teams).

3. *Training for rescue personnel* would be of great value. With the power to redefine approaches and policy, the clinicians within the urban disaster unit could develop mental health training for rescue personnel and other staff involved. Therapeutic work should make use of an interdisciplinary team approach to take advantage of already established relationships, and as a way of building in much needed staff supports.

4. *Family residential disaster shelters*, specially designed, are required to provide families with the appropriate accommodations for adequate living on a temporary basis. The following needs should be considered in the design of such facilities:

a. A residential staff for coordination of assistance, around the clock, 7 days a week

b. On-site personnel to provide comprehensive services for locating housing and financial assistance

c. Mental health teams on call for family disaster intervention

d. On-site crisis intervenors and part-time medical services, e.g., miniclinics, dental offices

e. Day-care center with mental health components

f. Teenage counseling services and recreational facilities

g. Family rooms as a focal point for varied activities to encourage open groups, with family counselors in attendance (Programs for self-help, weekend recreation, communal activities and cooperative babysitting could be arranged here.)

h. On-site educational facilities such as the one-room schoolhouse most hospitals have for children aged 6 through 12

i. Staffs of all on-site services should develop consistent approaches and social network linkages to community services *j.* A follow-up of families relocated to new communities should be established so referrals to needed local services can be made

5. *Research* is of prime importance. While much has been learned from this project, which served over 600 preschool children and provided thousands of client and agency contacts in 2 years (March 1972 to April 1974), systematic evaluation is yet to be done, since, unfortunately, lack of funds prevented us from building-in a formal evaluation design when the project began. We did find, however, that the average length of stay in the hotel for a dislocated family was reduced from about 6 months before the project began to between 3 weeks to 3 months. A comparative study of effectiveness in preventing traumatic aftereffects and developmental damage, with appropriate follow-up studies, is badly needed. A compilation of research studies assembled by the National Academy of Sciences of the National Research Council concentrated only on collective disasters (26). Unanticipated and anticipated responses by communities, medical data, and social behavior in groups were investigated, but insufficient attention was paid to individual and family behavior. And no guidelines have been developed that would apply to specific studies of urban fire disaster families.

Conclusions

Individuals in crisis (308), children in war-time (136), and large-scale disasters have been studied for psychological effects (443). Unexplored issues include how cultural and family structures affect disaster responses, as well as how crisis services affect postdisaster coping. Assumptions are usually made about the predisaster state of personality, family organization, and subsequent coping mechanisms, but systematic research data are lacking.

Research in this specialized area is likely to have direct application to broad aspects of community mental health and particular application to disaster intervention programs required for those catastrophes (such as tenement house fires) that occur only in cities.

29

CRISIS INTERVENTION

the ice cream parlor disaster

John B. Baren

On September 24, 1972, an unusual disaster occurred in Sacramento, California. An F-86 jet fighter of Korean War vintage was participating in a local airshow. The pilot, unable to get the jet airborne at take off, ejected his wing tanks of fuel. The plane hurtled across a busy boulevard and crashed into an ice cream parlor filled with children and adults. In the aftermath of this tragedy 10 adults and 12 children were killed, and approximately 14 were injured. Five seriously injured children and one adult were hospitalized at the Sacramento Medical Center.

This chapter describes the crisis intervention work done by the Center's Crisis Clinic staff with these patients and their families, and the work attempted with the significant others in the lives of all the disaster victims.

None of the psychotherapists involved had any previous experience in treating disaster victims, and in many respects, the treatment described here was a learning experience for staff and patients alike. The basic treatment philosophy employed throughout the period of intervention followed that ordinarily practiced at the Crisis Clinic, namely, family crisis intervention. Silber, Perry, and Bloch (379) point out that children do not react to traumatic life experiences as isolated individuals but in the context of the significant others in their lives.

Therapists found that dealing with the crisis of death on such a massive scale was different from dealing with individual deaths on a case-by-case basis. Drayer, Cameron, and Woodward (100) point out that individuals

involved in disasters are subjected to stresses and trauma rarely encountered in any other life experience, and we found that this applied to
patients and staff alike.

EVOLUTION OF THE
CRISIS INTERVENTION PROGRAM

Initial Contact

The first task, immediately after the disaster, was to care for the medical
needs of the patients as they were brought to the medical center. Our past
experience showed that emotional needs were often overlooked or denied
as the medical needs had priority. Thus, the Crisis Clinic was not at once
involved. The only mental health intervention immediately following the
disaster took place at the county coroner's office where the hospital
chaplain and a local minister began helping families as they came to
identify relatives who had been killed. These activities at the coroner's
office constituted the first stage of crisis intervention. Throughout the
entire course of the intervention, the two ministers worked closely with the
Crisis Clinic therapists and the families involved.

Formulating the Treatment Model

The day after the disaster, the medical center began formulating plans to
meet the emotional needs of the victims who had been hospitalized.
Although less than 24 hours had passed, a variety of hospital services and
personnel were already involved. Therefore, before confusion led to chaos,
the pediatrics unit called a meeting of all personnel thus far involved with
the disaster victims. Five children, ranging in age from 6 to 12 years had
been hospitalized in the pediatrics unit, and 1 woman, age 23, was
hospitalized in the surgery unit. Personnel from the Crisis Clinic and from
pediatrics, surgery, social services, the chaplain's office, the hospital
administration office, and the psychiatric consultation service were present at this meeting. It was decided that the Crisis Clinic would be
responsible for all psychiatric intervention with the patients, their families,
and significant others in the community. Medical treatment of the patients
would be supervised by the chief pediatric and chief surgery residents.
Contact with the news media, attorneys, and investigators would be the
responsibility of hospital administartion personnel. The rationale for
assigning specific roles and treatment responsibility was to minimize the
duplication of services, avoid as much distortion of communication and
subsequent confusion as possible, and alert all treatment personnel to the
total treatment plan. It was the Crisis Clinic's assumption that disasters
create confusion, and if the confusion relating to treatment arrangements

could be kept to a minimum, it would greatly facilitate the success of the intervention.

Each child was assigned an individual psychotherapist who was a specialist in child psychiatry. The therapist's responsibility was to work with the patient, family, and relatives. In anticipation of treating her husband also, the one adult patient (Laura, age 23) was assigned a male and female therapist. Weekly meetings of all treatment staff were held in order to keep all therapists informed of the progress of each case, share experiences, and offer consultation to each other as problems arose.

TREATMENT FOR THE SURVIVORS

The following resumé of each case assigned to the Crisis Clinic staff includes the presenting medical problems of each patient and the losses each suffered in terms of relatives who had been killed in the disaster.

CASE REPORT 1

Anne J., age 11, was hospitalized with blunt abdominal trauma, seromuscular tear of the pylorus, and serosal tears of the ligament of Treitz. Her operation consisted of celiotomy with gastroduodenostomy and repairs of serosal tears. Her mother had been killed in the accident, and she was the sister of Carl J. and the stepsister of Jim L, both of whom were also injured.

CASE REPORT 2

Carl J., age 7, was hospitalized with blunt abdominal trauma. He remained in the hospital for 2 days for observation only.

CASE REPORT 3

Jim L., age 6, was hospitalized with a ruptured spleen and laceration of the small bowel. His operation consisted of diagnostic celiotomy, repair of lacerated small bowel, and removal of the spleen.

CASE REPORT 4

Mark K., age 8, was hospitalized with fractures of his right tibia and fibula, multiple partial amputation fractures of his right hand, and second degree burns to his left and right legs. His operation consisted of debridement and amputation of the right middle finger and closure of the right ring finger. Additionally, the wounds about his legs were dressed, and he was placed in a long leg cast for his fractured tibia. His parents, grandparents, 3 siblings, and 2 cousins were killed in the disaster. He was the nephew of 2 other patients, Ruth S. and Laura M.

CASE REPORT 5

Ruth S., age 12, was hospitalized with burns of both feet and right ankle, minor lacerations, and fracture of the epiphysis of the medial malleolus on the right. Two days after admission, she was given hydrotherapy treatment for her feet. Approximately 2 weeks after admission she underwent extensive debridement and skin grafting to both feet. Her parents, stepsister, brother-in-law, 4 nephews, and 1 niece were killed in the disaster.

CASE REPORT 6

Laura M., age 23, was hospitalized with retroperitoneal hematoma secondary to kidney contusion or liver laceration, nonfunctioning right kidney, fractured ribs, and cerebral concussion. Her 2 sons, parents, stepsister, brother-in-law, niece, and 2 nephews were killed.

APPROACH TO THERAPY

The Children

Initial Contact with Patients.   Following the meeting on the pediatrics unit, all therapists made contact with their assigned patients. Interviews with the children were essentially the same. They were all in a state of emotional shock and confusion, compounded by their drowsiness due to postoperative medications. Collectively, they showed little affect, signs of grief, loss, or severe depression. Their few questions were related primarily to what was physically wrong with them. Contact with them was brief the first day. Therapists essentially wanted to identify themselves to the children and let them know they would continue to see them. They explained they would attempt to help with any difficulties and would be available to talk with them if they were feeling sad or unhappy. It is important to note that, although contact had been minimal the first day and the children were heavily sedated, they remembered that the therapists had talked with them and had planned to return to see them. They did not remember the names of the therapists or why they were there, but they did remember the initial contacts.

Initial Contact with Their Families.   Throughout the first day of intervention, therapists met with the families of the children they were treating. Some family members resisted psychiatric intervention for themselves but did accept therapeutic involvement for the children. The father of Jim L. (stepfather of Anne J. and Carl J.) appeared acutely depressed and in shock although he denied this and refused therapy for himself. He was willing for the therapists to be involved with the children, and the issue of treatment for himself was not pressed. He appeared to be receiving a good deal of emotional support from his extended family, and this met his needs at that time.

In keeping with the basic philosophy of the clinic's approach, family intervention, meetings with the extended family were held at least once a week. This enabled therapists to assess how family members were dealing with their grief, which members needed the most support, and which of them were able to assume leadership roles in helping other family members cope with disaster events. They also shared with the families the overall progress of each child. Bloch, Silber, and Perry (41) point out that in dealing with a disaster at the family level, it is vital to treat the family as a single unit. They feel it enhances open and direct communication of feelings about the disaster and the losses they have suffered. This then helps the child cope with his fears and anxieties, for the adults are not bound up in their need to deny, minimize, or avoid the children's questions. They feel this is an integrative process that helps the family live with the disaster and eventually move on to future goals. The Crisis Clinic found these family meetings to be especially useful in terms of dealing with feelings, particularly about a subject of immediate concern—how to let the children know who had been killed in the disaster.

Continuing Therapy for the Children. Intensive intervention with the children began on the second day of their hospitalization. They were now more alert and began asking questions about the tragedy. Their first questions were concerned with who had been killed. The plan that had been previously decided on at the family meetings was that parents or close relatives would meet with the children initially and let them know who had died. The children shed relatively few tears when their questions were answered as to who had been killed. They showed little affect, appeared to withdraw, and evidenced some degree of denial. Anne J. continued to ask her father and stepfather, "How can you be *sure* Mommy was killed? Did you see her ring? The ring could have been on someone else." Throughout the day, she could not remember being at the ice cream parlor or being in an accident. On the other hand, her natural brother, Carl J., cried openly and showed what we considered to be appropriate affect concerning his mother's death.

Mark K., the 8-year-old boy who lost his parents and 7 other relatives, was told of their deaths by an aunt and uncle. He showed little affect, stoically refused to cry, and stated he remembered nothing of the accident. Throughout the course of his hospitalization, he was rarely observed crying or showing affective signs of grief over his losses.

Ruth S., the 12-year-old girl who was the aunt of Mark K., showed initial grief about her losses, then immediately began to suppress these feelings by stating, "My Mommy told me not to cry if anything like this ever happened."

During the afternoon of the second day, and on the third day, some of the children began experiencing much anxiety about the accident. They became confused about the accident and began having nightmares. Anne J. and her stepbrother, Jim L., experienced nightmares and fantasies about the jet's imagined propellers chopping people up in the disaster. At the same time, they began relating feelings of guilt and anger that they had escaped while friends and relatives had died. The treatment approach was to stress the fact that everyone was thankful they had survived, and everyone cared about them, at the same time minimizing any responsibility they felt for the deaths of others.

Family meetings were held again later that same day, so that therapists and family members could share their evaluations of how the children appeared to be responding. It was at this time that parents and relatives began expressing their own anxieties and the stresses they were feeling. One of the main concerns expressed by some of the adults was whether to let the children observe how upset they felt, particularly in terms of crying in front of them. The therapists suggested that seeing adults upset and tearful demonstrated to the children that it was all right to express their feelings in an open manner, and that stoicism was not expected of them.

During the initial stages of therapy we learned how important it was to keep close watch on the children in order to clarify any distortions in communication they were receiving. This evolved from their having visitors who, out of their own anxieties, said inappropriate things to them. For example, an adult relative of Mark K. and Ruth S. visited them on the third day and his opening statement was, "Well, that's what you get for eating ice cream!" Their therapists heard about this soon after, visited the children, and explained to them how adults often say foolish things out of their own anxiety. Needless to say, therapists tried to keep this type of communication to a minimum.

Reactions to the Funerals.   Four days after their hospitalization, a therapeutic problem arose. The following day was to be the day of funerals, and since the news media would be giving this event extensive coverage, the question arose as to whether or not the children should view or listen to tape recordings of the services. A meeting was held with treatment staff, and later with the families, to discuss this issue. It was decided that since the children appeared to be progressing well, and since the treatment approach had always been direct and honest, this should remain a decision between the children and their families. The children decided either to view the services on the news later in the evening with family members or, in the case of Mark K. and Ruth S., to listen to a tape recording of the memorial service prepared by the minister.

At this specific crisis point, it became clear how important the relationship of the therapist was to each child. Throughout the day, the children sent messages via hospital personnel just to let the therapist know how they were doing, or requesting visits from them. For example, on the day of the funeral, Anne J. asked to see her therapist because she did not understand what being buried meant. After discussing this at length, she decided that this meant her mother was now "in Heaven." It appeared that this was the main resolution of the concept of the funeral for the children.

Returning to Home Situations. After being in the hospital for one week, Anne J. and Jim L. were transferred to a hospital in their own community, 60 miles from Sacramento. Carl J. had been discharged 3 days previously. The children became noticeably more cheerful upon learning of the transfer plans because it meant friends from their own peer group would be able to visit them. The most positive feedback concerning the success of the Crisis Clinic's intervention was the request from the families that the therapists involved with these children be given consultation privileges at their community hospitals so that the work with their children would not be interrupted. This was arranged, and treatment continued on a regular basis. These children and their families were seen on three more occasions during hospitalization and at a termination interview a few days after discharge. At the final family sessions, the children appeared to be doing quite well. Their return to school and support from their peer group aided in their good adjustment. Follow-up at 3- and 5-month intervals indicated continuing good adaptation for 4 of the 5 young patients.

Two of the children, Mark K. and Ruth S., had lost both parents in the disaster. Therefore, the issue of custody was also involved from the outset, and affected the children throughout the course of therapy. The children were placed under the jurisdiction of the juvenile court until legal custody was determined. It appeared that this additional crisis event hindered the grieving process for both children, but particularly for Mark K. A number of relatives wanted custody of him, resulting in family friction and an unpleasant court battle. Because of his anxiety about who would have custody, Mark became withdrawn and unable to deal with his feelings of loss. This continued after his discharge from the hospital and throughout the 2 months he was in outpatient therapy. Once custody for both Mark and Ruth was determined, their adoptive parents, the adult patient Laura and her husband, terminated therapy. Unfortunately, Mark's subsequent emotional adjustment is unknown. Similarly, there was no follow-up work with Ruth, who had apparently been unable to grieve any more openly than Mark.

The Adult Patient

A cotherapy team was assigned to treat Laura M., the 23-year-old patient in the surgical unit. It was felt that since she was married, it would be most beneficial to treat the couple. During the first 3 days of intervention, Laura M. appeared withdrawn, depressed, and was resistant to therapy. On the other hand, her husband welcomed the opportunity of talking with the therapists. He was able to express his feelings in a direct and open manner and vent his grief over the death of their sons.

Even though Laura M. resisted treatment at this time, the therapists visited her regularly and refused to allow her to withdraw into a shell of isolation. They felt it was important to remain aggressive in dealing with her in order to break through her bitterness, anger, and guilt.

By continuing to work with her husband during this period, a positive treatment relationship was formed with him that proved helpful in involving his wife in the therapeutic process. He continued to tell her about the help he got in talking with the therapists, and on the evening of the third day, she asked to see the therapists with her husband. During this session, she was very tearful and verbal. She expressed a wide range of previouly suppressed emotions. She talked at length about her boys, often referring to them in the present tense, yet at the same time reiterating, "They're gone, and I know they're never coming back." She expressed anger at God for their deaths and guilt that she had not been killed rather than them. Therapy was supportive throughout this session, allowing her to ventilate her acute grief, with little interpretations of those feelings, except in a supportive and accepting manner. By the end of the session she was actively involved in the therapeutic process, and asked the therapists to return the following evening.

Now that the treatment relationship had been established, Laura M. became less depressed and more animated in terms of looking toward the future. Over the next 2 weeks, she and her husband were seen every evening. Together with the minister, they made plans for their children's funeral. During the evening of the funeral, she listened to a tape recording of the funeral service prepared by the minister.

During the next 2 weeks, she and her husband began making plans for obtaining legal custody of Laura M.'s sister, Ruth S., and her nephew, Mark K. No problems arose about custody of Ruth S., but other relatives wanted custody of Mark K. Problems around the custody issue seemed to interfere with the couple's ability to continue to work through their grief. Their thoughts and energies were channeled toward getting custody of the children. Although they had much emotional investment in this issue, the therapists began to confront them with their behavior, indicating that they were attempting to deny their losses by bringing home a ready-made family. Laura M. was unable to accept this interpretation. Her husband could accept the interpretation to some degree but would not challenge his wife's wishes. The day before Laura M. was discharged from the hospital, at the final therapeutic session, the couple continued to deny this interpretation. They expressed their feelings that the intervention had been helpful in working through their grief, and even though the therapists felt they should continue to see them, they chose to terminate treatment.

COMMUNITY RESPONSE TO INTERVENTION

Once the treatment plan to meet the needs of the patients in the hospital had been established, the crisis team formulated a plan to meet the needs of the relatives of other victims of the disaster. The patients in the hospital were by no means the only people who had suffered loss; other families had lost children, relatives, and spouses in the disaster. Those crisis team members who were not involved in treating the hospitalized disaster victims were given the task of contacting the families in the community who had encountered losses. Contact was made directly with family members or through clergymen who were working with these families. Therapists let them know that the Crisis Clinic staff was working with families whose relatives had been hospitalized at the Sacramento Medical Center and that if they felt the need for professional help, a staff member would be willing to see them any time at their convenience, either at the Crisis Clinic or at their homes.

A total of 6 families were contacted, and all of them declined service. They felt that the support they were receiving from friends, relatives, and the clergy was sufficient. It appeared to the treatment staff that although this may have been true, the families were resistive to contact and intervention from strangers. It is not known how these families adjusted to the disaster.

The local schools that had been attended by children who had been killed in the disaster were contacted. Principals and teachers were informed that the Crisis Clinic staff would be available for consultation if any classmates of the deceased students appeared to be having difficulty adjusting to the loss. School personnel, although cordial, also appeared resistant to outside intervention. They did not request assistance from the Clinic after our initial contact with them.

A few individuals in the community who heard that the Crisis Clinic was working with disaster victims came to the Clinic seeking help for themselves. These cases involved parents whose children were at the ice cream parlor and had survived the disaster. They were experiencing some anxiety and difficulty in sleeping since the disaster.

CONCLUSIONS

Crisis intervention in a disaster was found by the treatment staff to be a unique and rewarding experience. The modality of crisis intervention was adapted to meet the multiple needs of a major disaster. Family intervention seemed a more effective approach than treating each patient as an isolated individual.

The initial stage of disaster treatment should be developed immediately in an orderly and structured fashion. Formulating a treatment plan where roles and responsibilities are defined and clearly understood by all personnel tends to reduce duplication of services, distorted communication, and general confusion.

Working with all family members proved to be therapeutic for them, and at the same time helped the therapists in their work with the children. Communication was direct and honest; distressing problems and feelings were clarified; and those issues which were assumed to be the most emotionally volatile were handled relatively comfortably by therapists and family members alike.

In this tragedy where many lives were lost the issue of custody of the children who had lost parents appeared to have a deleterious effect on the normal process of resolving grief. These victims extended the process of denial and displaced anger which should have been directed at the disaster and the losses they had suffered.

Aggressive reaching-out, in a therapeutic sense, with victims who were resistant to intervention was beneficial. As the victim's family became involved in the treatment process and reported on the benefits derived from therapy, the resistant victim also became involved in treatment. We thought this was further demonstrated by our inability to involve families in the community who had lost children and spouses in the disaster. Intervention with these victims was not aggressive, and they all resisted involvement.

It has been shown (23) that crisis intervention during a disaster takes an emotional toll on the therapists themselves as well as the victims. We found that the many hours of involvement required to meet the immediate emotional needs of the disaster was physically and emotionally draining for the therapists. The stress of dealing with multiple deaths and the collective anguish of the survivors cannot be denied by the therapists. The chance to meet together regularly, share treatment problems, and ventilate feelings, was thus essential in providing a support system for the staff.

30

RAPID RESPONSE TO DISASTER

the monticello tornado

Don M. Hartsough, Thomas H. Zarle, and Donald R. Ottinger

In the late afternoon of April 3, 1974, a series of severe thunderstorms spawned tornadoes from southern Canada through the midwestern United States to the South. The loss of life and property was unusually high. Small communities in several states were virtually destroyed, and a number of larger towns and cities sustained widespread damage, social disorganization, and personal tragedy. The resort city of Monticello, Indiana, was one of four populated areas in that state to sustain major damage and loss of life. At 5:15 PM, Monticello and surrounding rural areas were struck simultaneously by two and possibly three tornadoes which swept through the downtown area and several residential sections. Considering the estimated 200 million dollars in damages to property, Monticello residents considered it miraculous that only 9 people lost their lives. While some residential sections and a few businesses were not damaged by the tornado, approximately 25 business establishments and 390 homes were completely destroyed. Disaster centers were opened almost immediately, but most residents located housing on that first evening and for the next several weeks with relatives, friends, and other residents whose homes were intact.

This chapter presents a response to the Monticello tornado made by mental health and crisis intervention resources originating from outside the immediate disaster area. The problems unique to formulating a disaster

This project was made possible by the financial and administrative support of Purdue University; the Department of Mental Health; the State Board of Health, Indiana.

recovery plan for a community without its own mental health system are explored, and a systematic approach is demonstrated that takes into account both the needs for planned entry into the community and the desire for as immediate a response as possible. A brief manual for paraprofessional disaster recovery workers is presented, and several types of project work are illustrated. An outreach approach based on crisis intervention, rather than a self-referred "clinical" approach to disasters, is the major focus throughout the chapter.

THE COMMUNITY

Monticello is located on the Tippecanoe River between Lakes Shafer and Freeman in northwestern Indiana. It is a commercial and governmental center for several rural counties which surround it. The population of the city was 5,000 with another 5,000 people residing in the lakes area. During the summer season the population usually increased to 25,000 when cottages and resorts along the lakes are filled to capacity. The major businesses of the community were retail sales, tourism, wood products manufacturing, and other light industry. One senior high school, one junior high school, five elementary schools, and more than 10 churches served the area. The permanent population of Monticello is stable, and many of the extended families in the area are interrelated. It has been predominantly a white, Protestant community since its founding in the middle 1800s.

The near total destruction of the downtown area was the major concern of the community. Approximately 100 downtown buildings were damaged by the tornado; most were of two-story brick construction, built in the late 1800s and the early 1900s. Directly in the path of the tornado as it swept through the area was the White County Court House with its four-faced clock tower, which for 80 years had been a landmark in the state.

RESPONSES TO DISASTER

Professional and Community Elements

Immediately after a major disaster, mental health specialists are likely to feel pressures to provide the benefit of their services to the victims. Pressures to respond may come from responsible citizenry (for example, agency board members) or, perhaps more frequently, from socially conscious professional workers themselves (40). Widespread destruction and loss of life necessitates a desire to "do something," and professionals are not immune. To them, such a situation is often frustrating, if not bewildering. Professional mental health training has typically devoted little if any attention to the needs of disaster victims or their communities. Further, most of the target population is unlikely to be linked with a community's mental health system before a disaster, and equally unlikely to view it as a needed resource after a disaster occurs. As a guide to action, the clinical model is of little assistance because it depends on the initiative of the victim for the provision of services. Crisis theory (63) and crisis intervention techniques seem to offer the most promising points of departure. Even so, problems remain in modifying our typical crisis intervention services and orchestrating them with disaster relief agencies and the dynamics of an affected community. The well meaning mental health worker is then left with a strong desire to provide an undefined service to an unknown clientele through an untried delivery system.

When a disaster strikes a community that lacks organized mental health resources, the foregoing problems are often compounded for those initiating the intervention. "Imported" mental health personnel lack familiarity with the community and its social and political norms. They are likely to be seen as outsiders during the time (immediately after the disaster) when outside intervention may be viewed with ambivalence or outright distrust (26, 332). Further, the professions, services and agencies they represent may be unfamiliar to community residents who, under ordinary circumstances, would require an acceptance period of several months to more than a year for the newcomers. In contrast to these disadvantages is the overriding consideration that "time is of the essence" in disaster recovery intervention as in other forms of crisis intervention (63). The more quickly assistance is afforded disaster victims, the more effective it will be. The intervention plan described here is based on an awareness of these antagonistic elements and is an attempt to map out a balanced strategy which incorporates both dimensions.

Principles of Community Behavior

In formulating our approach to the outlying community of Monticello following the tornado, we used two general observations about communities in disasters as guiding principles. The first was the repeated observation that after a disaster members of a community look first to themselves for relief help and a direction for action (26, 332). As already noted, outsiders and imported programs may be shunted aside in favor of more familiar names and faces. For the present program this meant that if a modified crisis intervention approach were to be used, it should be implemented by community members themselves. While there was a strong temptation to use previously trained crisis center volunteers from a university community 35 miles from the disaster area, we opted instead to train selected citizens from the disaster area itself for the recovery work. The crisis center resource was put to effective use in the training program, but the recovery contacts with Monticello citizens were made exclusively by volunteers from the local community. It may be argued that the extra time (2 weeks) committed to conducting a training program during the immediate postdisaster period would be better spent in direct service to victims. Considering the personal nature of the type of recovery work we envisioned and the advice given to us by key people in the community, we chose to train indigenous personnel from the area affected.

The second general observation used as a guiding principle is based on a view of the community as a dynamic social system (216). Widespread disaster shared by an entire community represents a powerful system input which causes a temporary unsettling of the normal equilibrium. One result of the system interference is less change in the normal restraints. The community is arbitrarily forced to change many of its physical characteristics, and a parallel attitude seems to develop toward changing some of its social action programs as well. This is particularly true if the changes are seen as both aiding the recovery of the community and fulfilling community needs that were recognized before the disaster occurred. In the Monticello project this meant that while considering the short-term goals of disaster recovery, it was also possible to plan for long-term needs of the community with respect to its mental health program and other human services.

A key advantage in initiating the Monticello tornado project was that a professional contact in the community had been maintained by one of the authors for over a year prior to the disaster. A predisaster working relationship that serves as a point of contact is invaluable in initiating a rapid response to an outlying disaster area. As illustrated in the outline of events following, the social worker was able on short notice to gather together key citizens who could give sanction to the project.

The First Fifteen Days

The project staff included 3 psychologists (the authors) and Susan Bowman, MSW, the social worker who served as local coordinator for the disaster recovery program. The following is a sequential account of actions taken by the project staff and its interactions with Monticello residents. It covers a period of 15 days, from the tornado (*T*) to the first volunteer training session for local residents.

T.　　April 3, 1974, was the date of the occurrence of the tornado.

T+1.　Informal discussion was held among project staff members as to response possibilities.

T+2.　Materials related to disaster recovery were gathered, and telephone contacts were made with state and national mental health resources to investigate sources of support for a local project.

T+3. The first communication with the disaster area was through a telephone call from the social worker in Monticello canceling a consultation visit. This call provided the first opportunity to discuss the project with a Monticello resident, as there had been no previous incoming telephone service from the area.

T+5. Planning and tentative formulation of a response strategy was conducted by the project staff. (The disaster area itself was still off-limits to nonresidents; therefore, no on-site visit was possible.)

T+6. A consultation and planning meeting was attended by the authors, who met with representatives of the Indiana State Department of Mental Health, Regional and Federal representatives of the National Institute of Mental Health (NIMH), and staff members of the Comprehensive Community Mental Health Center in Kokomo, Indiana. An overview was provided to participants at this meeting regarding NIMH responses to previous disasters, the needs of disaster communities, and suggested response strategies. A decision was made at this meeting as to responsibilities for coordinating the project. After the meeting, participants visited the Federal Disaster Assistance Center in Monticello to initiate linkage with local resources. (Prior communication with the local social worker greatly facilitated this process.) The visit also provided useful information on Monticello's response to the tornado. As previously noted, most residents did not seek temporary shelter at disaster centers and therefore were scattered around the countryside with relatives and friends. There was a surplus of food and clothing and a severe shortage of storage space for undamaged furniture and equipment. People were preoccupied at this point with clean-up operations and other immediate needs. An evening meeting with the training committee of the Lafayette Crisis Center was held to explain the nature of disaster recovery, and to elicit support for the training of paraprofessional workers for disaster recovery teams in Monticello.

T+7. A morning meeting of the project staff was held to divide duties, share ideas, and plan for subsequent activities in Monticello. (These meetings continued, frequently on a daily basis, throughout the early phases of the project.) A paradigm for the training of paraprofessionals for disaster recovery was formulated. A telephone request was made to the social worker in Monticello to arrange a meeting of local personnel for the following day.

T+8.   The social worker arranged for the project staff to meet with the administrator of the county hospital; the director of nursing from the hospital; the president of the County Mental Health Association, who was also a high school counselor; two local ministers; the director of the Youth Services Bureau; and the director of the Comprehensive Developmental Center. Initially the participants concentrated on the need for a mental health response to the tornado that would be based on a crisis intervention and person-to-person model. Participants from Monticello agreed that the project should be locally based and sanctioned, should have high participation from local residents, and should not emphasize mental illness. A decision was made to have the social worker act as a local coordinator, and efforts began immediately to select residents appropriate for paraprofessional training and, later, disaster recovery work. Decisions were also made regarding subsequent meetings to broaden the sponsorship of the program and to meet with potential volunteers.

T+12.   Contacts were made with university, state, and regional officials to keep them abreast of the progress in Monticello and to explore means of financial support for the project. A meeting was held in Monticello so that official community sanction could be provided the project. The concept of "umbrella sponsorship" by key community groups was accepted, and a letter that listed the sponsoring groups and invited the authors to develop the project was drafted and cosigned by the mayor and the local coordinator. In addition to the Mayor's office, sponsoring groups were the Mental Health Association, the Medical Society, the Bar Association, the Ministerial Association, the School Corporation, the Youth Services Bureau, the County Commissioners, and the Comprehensive Developmental Center. A steering committee was formed whose members included the local coordinator, members of sponsoring groups, and the project staff. The early establishment of local sanction by appropriate governmental units and service agencies was an essential step toward acceptance of the project in the community. The project staff later met with six citizens who had been contacted by the local coordinator as potential disaster workers. This meeting explored the needs of a disaster community and possible resources that could be mobilized. A brief *Manual for Disaster Team Workers* was distributed, and the roles and limits of the project were discussed. It is significant that at this meeting discussion spontaneously evolved into the consideration of long-range mental health goals for the community. Plans were developed for a subsequent orientation meeting for a larger group of volunteer workers.

T+13. An emergency grant request was submitted to Purdue University for funds to cover expenses for the immediate period of intervention and until more complete funding could be obtained. A training staff of 10 experienced paraprofessionals was provided by the Corps of Trainers of the Lafayette Crisis Center. An ancillary meeting was held by the project staff with Extension Homemakers from counties affected by the tornado. Linkage was thus made with the County Homemakers system in White County and Monticello.

T+14. A visit to Monticello was made by the project staff and two Crisis Center trainers to prepare for subsequent training. The Coordinator of the Federal Disaster Assistance Center was informed of the project. Information about disaster relief activities needed by the project volunteers was obtained.

T+15. The first full training session was conducted by the training staff in Monticello for 15 volunteer workers. The needs of disaster communities and the work to be done by volunteers were discussed. A team-building exercise encouraged participants to share their own tornado experiences. Subsequent dates for training sessions were established, as were specific projects to be carried out by the group.

Thus, within the first 15 days following the tornado it was possible to establish a mental health response that was community-based, yet utilized expertise from outside the community. Development and implementation of the project fell into seven sequential and overlapping phases:

1. Discovering the need for a mental health, crisis intervention response
2. Establishing contact with local resources in the disaster area
3. Solidifying contact with local resources and obtaining sanction through an umbrella of sponsoring groups
4. Gathering resources from the disaster area (potential volunteer workers) and also from external sources (crisis intervention trainers and professional consultants)
5. Formulating a training program, a training staff, and training materials

6. Implementing a training program for volunteers living in the local disaster area
7. Planning for follow-up and long-term community goals

A BRIEF MANUAL FOR
DISASTER RECOVERY WORKERS

The following is a summary version of the manual given to disaster recovery workers as part of their training program. This material was designed to orient the worker to the psychological needs of disaster victims, the training program for disaster recovery, and the resources that exist in a community subsequent to a disaster.

There are many reactions that are shared by people in a disaster: shock and disbelief at first; excitement, tension and fatigue as the recovery process takes place; and alternating hopeful and let-down feelings for weeks or months later. These are normal feelings. They happen to most people who endure periods of great stress. In a way, disasters create a test of people's ability to bounce back after a loss and, fortunately, most of us do it well. Experience has shown that we do it better with help—the right kind of help at the right time.

Information and rumor control. Many disasters disrupt communications seriously so that accurate information is hard to find. Perhaps because people want information so badly, there are numerous things passed from one person to another that are not accurate. This adds to the confusion and slows down the recovery process. Where tension is high and little information is available, rumors are likely to spread rapidly. It is important to reduce their effect on people by providing accurate information. The tension and discouragement fostered by false information can be minimized, and citizens saved from needless disappointment. Correct information allows rebuilding to proceed more smoothly and trust in the recovery services to be strengthened.

Expressing feelings about the disaster. Common feelings of people at the time of a sudden disaster are helplessness, fear, and confusion. These feelings are especially strong in people who have no idea of what is happening, such as young children, or in people who can take little action to protect themselves, such as the elderly or infirm. Sometimes, following a disaster, people do not realize that these strong feelings are natural and normal. If this is the case, they may be reluctant to talk about them or to hear others express them. They may feel that admitting to fear or crying is a sign of weakness; or that the feelings, if expressed, will plague them in the future. We know from the experiences of people who have survived very severe disasters that it is better in the long run to let the feelings out than to deny their expression. In the immediate postdisaster period, there is usually shock, disbelief, and dismay at what has happened. For a time we become emotionally numb. As the shock wears off, the emotions that were stirred up by the experience may also return. Things which suddenly remind a person of the disaster may set off a reexperiencing of the dread or fear he felt before. Some people find themselves with a vague sense of uneasiness, some become afraid of doing things they felt safe doing before, and some experience physical distress. It is not uncommon to sleep restlessly or to have nightmares. These are normal behaviors of people who have been through a stressful emotional experience. They represent the healthy process of the emotions trying to work themselves out. We again want to emphasize that it is better in the long run to encourage the normal expression of emotions than to try to keep this process from happening.

Some people will find it quite natural to let their feelings have expression in the aftermath of a disaster experience. However, others may need to keep their emotional reactions to themselves, and their wishes in this regard should be respected. There will be people who need encouragement to share their feelings with someone who will understand and accept them for it. Knowing that someone else appreciates and understands how they feel allows them to be more secure.

Even though some people in a disaster area may not have sustained physical damage or had loved ones killed or injured, they may feel its emotional impact. This is especially true of children, who may need extra reassurance once the immediate danger is past. Any child who can talk should be encouraged to talk about what the experience meant to him.

We usually feel most comfortable expressing ourselves to those we know and trust. On the other hand, a disaster is likely to be shared by all members of the community, so that it may be easier at this time than it would be normally to engage in personal conversations with a person not previously known. This is especially true if the person is understanding and really wants to listen.

Locating places and people with special needs. Major disasters completely disrupt the normal living patterns in a community. Many people suddenly become homeless, and families may be separated or living with strangers. In these circumstances it is difficult to make sure that people's needs are being taken care of. This may be best accomplished by talking informally with people where they are temporarily housed. People vary in being able to recognize their own needs and in feeling comfortable asking for help. In many situations this reluctance can be overcome by personal visits from a recovery worker who has correct information and whose attitude is matter-of-fact and does not convey to the potential recipient that he is weak, helpless, or dependent.

As we have said, children and the elderly are more vulnerable than most people after a disaster, especially if separated from family, familiar surroundings, or prized personal effects. Homeless families in temporary housing should also be given high priority. In crowded housing conditions, special problems may emerge after the immediate impact of the disaster recedes.

Case finding. Some people respond to the stresses of a disaster and are strengthened by them, but for others the stress can be a temporary or even permanently negative influence. Case finding refers to the process of discovering which individuals or families have been adversely affected by the disaster and helping them obtain assistance. In some cases people may be aware that their distress is associated with the disaster, but in some cases they may not make this connection. For example, the incidence of illness or alcoholism may increase during the year following a disaster. Effective case finding can prevent or minimize the delayed effects by providing opportunities for early treatment.

Locating community resources and emerging leadership. A disaster strains a community and its resources. Goods and services which were readily available before the disaster may be much more difficult to locate afterwards. A worker can be of assistance by helping families locate what they need or by directing them to the correct agency or business. The new challenges faced by a community recovering from a disaster may stimulate some people to become leaders who were not leaders before. They can be a vital resource in the rebuilding process and should be identified and encouraged.

One of the most important ingredients in disaster recovery is intangible: a community's belief in its own future. Regardless of the specific task a worker undertakes, a sincere hope for the future will make his work easier and more effective.

THE TRAINING PROGRAM AND PROJECT WORK

Following Richards (354) and our own experience in training crisis intervention workers, we designed the training program to include didactic, experiential, and project foci. The first phase concentrated on an orientation to individual and family needs following a disaster. The second phase focused on the principle of confidentiality and the development of helper skills and community resources. A third phase was devoted to role playing of likely disaster situations in small groups of volunteers and trainers. The fourth phase was devoted to project work conducted by pairs of recovery workers. Finally, the last phase concerned feedback based on the project work and a refinement of helper skills, plus planning for subsequent work. The first volunteer training program was completed 30 days after the tornado occurred.

Volunteers selected the name, "Monticello Neighbor-to-Neighbor Team," for the project. Community work carried out as part of the training program was stimulated through informal and personal contacts the volunteers had with individuals they knew in the community, and by referrals from the local hospital. For example, one of the volunteer workers was assigned to see a hospitalized 59-year-old woman who had sustained a coronary attack during the tornado. She was distraught on finding that, because of her medical condition, she could not return to her apartment and would be placed in a nursing home following discharge from the hospital. The fact that the volunteer could provide her with detailed information about the nursing home and could reassure her that she would not be forgotten helped to alleviate the patient's immediate distress. Subsequently, the volunteer followed her through the nursing home placement. In another instance, a 70-year-old widow was interviewed in a local nursing home. She was placed in the home after her physician found that she had been living for 4 days after the tornado in her damaged apartment without heat or electricity. Since this woman was extremely concerned about her apartment and furnishings, the volunteer visited and checked her home and met with the insurance adjuster. The volunteer continued to visit her periodically in the nursing home to offer reassurance that her possessions were safe and to help her plan for the future.

Another type of project work conducted by the volunteers is illustrated by two situations concerning housing. In one case a family whose home was destroyed did not apply for HUD rental payments because they falsely believed that HUD required repayment of the money. The volunteer obtained accurate information from the HUD office, which led to the family's applying for the rental money. In the second situation an owner of a fishing camp appealed for help for a family housed temporarily and rent-free in one of his lakeside cottages. The family had few resources, claimed lack of success in finding new housing through disaster relief agencies, and refused to move. The owner was reluctant to resort to eviction proceedings, but needed the cottage for business during the approaching resort season. A team of volunteers first established a working relationship with the owner and the family involved; then the volunteers assisted the family in locating permanent housing in a trailer park.

An attempt was also made to relate the project work to broader community needs. A list of relocated businesses and a list indicating the temporary locations of displaced families were developed for possible media publication. The family relocation list also served as a basis for systematic outreach interviewing of those families whose homes were destroyed by the tornado. Finally, volunteers from the project became involved in long-term planning efforts for the purpose of increasing mental health and crisis intervention services for Monticello.

PLANNING FOR A DISASTER RESPONSE

It seems reasonable to conclude that a response from outside mental health specialists to disaster in an outlying area is possible, if attention is given to the entry process into the community. Crisis theory and the techniques used in training crisis workers can be modified to provide an appropriate strategy for intervention. It seems likely that other approaches, e.g., consultation to existing local services, could be adapted to disaster recovery work. In any case, obtaining sanction from the disaster community itself is a crucial step in implementing a recovery program, even under the time pressures to mobilize quickly.

The project described here would have been more effective if planning for a disaster response had taken place *prior* to the tornado. Efforts were expended in locating and digesting relevant material on disasters, discussing alternative responses, and initiating resource contacts—all of which could have been accomplished in less time if a systematic disaster readiness effort had been conducted prior to the actual disaster. In addition, valuable time and energy were spent in negotiating for financial support for the project. This occurred at the very time when such activity diverted resources from the main work of the project itself.

It is strongly recommended that efforts be made to incorporate mental health and crisis intervention approaches to disaster recovery planning on both state and local levels. An outreach (search and find) strategy is much preferred to the customary clinical (wait and treat) approach. Training should be offered to personnel from comprehensive community mental health centers, as well as those from the Federal Disaster Assistance Administration, the Red Cross, and other disaster relief services.

31

POSTDISASTER MOBILIZATION OF A CRISIS INTERVENTION TEAM

the managua experience

Raquel E. Cohen

Increased attention is being focused on mental health intervention potential following catastrophic events that have serious impact on the affected population. Mental health workers are aware of the challenging opportunities for service and prevention which can come about if they are able to mobilize themselves rapidly, gain entry into the mainstream of helping structures, and provide assistance during critical moments following serious disasters (78, 80, 105, 106, 178, 308, 330, 333).

This chapter focuses on the experiences of the first of a series of volunteer teams of the United States–Nicaraguan Emergency Mental Health Project. This team went for 1 month to Managua, Nicaragua, whose population had suffered the effects of a disastrous earthquake 3 months earlier. The following areas will be highlighted:

1. The catastrophic impact of the earthquake on the socioeconomic structures, community services, and mental health of the population.
2. The team's activities, which included direct crisis services plus education and consultation within the human services system of a developing country.
3. A series of crisis intervention projects.
4. Tentative suggestions for further application of crisis intervention techniques and procedures.

NICARAGUA: A QUICK OVERVIEW

Nicaragua is one of the smaller countries of the western hemisphere, although it is the largest of the Central American countries (459). It has an area of 48,000 square miles and a population of around 2½ million people. The official language is Spanish, and the population is 95% Roman Catholic. The climate is tropical. The major causes of death are gastrointestinal and parasitic diseases, infant diseases, and cardiovascular and respiratory ailments.

The society, consisting of a European–Indian ethnic and cultural mix, is homogeneous in comparison to that of other Central American countries. The traditional Hispanic pattern of family life, common to most of Latin America, prevails. The nuclear family forms the basis of family structure, but relationships among kindred are strong and influence many aspects of Nicaraguan life. Because few other institutions in the society have proved as stable and enduring, family and kinship play a dominant role in the social, economic, and political relations of the Nicaraguans. Business loyalties, social prestige, and political alignments generally follow kinship lines.

Like the rest of the Caribbean area, commerce and movement patterns tie Nicaragua principally to Anglo-America and secondarily to Western Europe. Although much less urbanized than many middle latitude countries, there is a significant concentration of urban population. Managua, the capital city, is growing at a rate faster than other urban centers, in spite of its location in an area of seismic instability.

Before the disaster, the Nicaraguan mental health program was underdeveloped; the 14 psychiatrists serving the entire country had had little experience in crisis intervention or community psychiatry. The National Psychiatric Hospital, a 450-bed hospital with only one fulltime psychiatrist on the staff, plus a group of part-time psychiatrists who worked for the Social Assistance Agency, was the main resource of the city. Very little integration of psychiatry into the general medicine programs existed, and little coordination of the efforts to deal with the victims of the earthquake developed.

THE EARTHQUAKE

The Managua earthquake could be catalogued as one of the most catastrophic and bitter events experienced by a population in our recent past. This was due not only to the magnitude of the event and its impact on the city, but also because most of the country's administrative social–supportive structures were centralized in Managua. The timing was also critical in that it occurred 2 days before Christmas when people were

beginning to celebrate the holidays. The heightened expectation of pleasure made that crushing event psychologically more devastating.

The Richter Scale recorded a magnitude of 6.2 with the epicenter in the
heart of the city. There were three strong tremors. After the first one,
around 10:30 PM, many citizens left their homes; some made preparations
to leave in case of stronger tremors; and others went back to sleep, as they
had been accustomed to tremors for many months prior to December. A
second earthquake, at 12:30 AM, destroyed 80% of the homes and
produced the first wave of intense panic, with the exodus of people rushing
through darkness and choking clouds of dust, tripping on bricks and
cement scattered by the tumbling houses. Many persons were injured or
killed by falling debris. The last earthquake occurred around 3:00 AM,
razing the few houses that had not been damaged. Fires raged uncontrolled
due to the interruption of water flow and the destruction of fire engines
within their stations.

Within 4 to 6 hours after the earthquake, world aid supplies began
arriving in planes which continued landing every 20 minutes for several
days. Supplies included field hospitals (as the hospitals of Managua had
been damaged or destroyed) plus milk, water, food, medication, and
disinfectants for the water supply reservoirs. The destruction was of a
magnitude that appeared overwhelming. Besides the immediate human
and property losses, there remained the problems of the wounded, the
displaced, and the unemployed. The following human statistics provide a
framework for the magnitude of the reconstruction needs: 10,000 killed,
20,000 wounded, 250,000 displaced, 50,000 homes destroyed and 24,000
badly damaged, 14 industrial plants leveled, and 95% of the shops
destroyed.

MENTAL HEALTH TEAM FORMATION

Two of the future team members, community psychiatrists who were
aware of the potential for intervention and interested in the country by
language and affective ties, immediately contacted the National Institute
of Mental Health (NIMH) to organize a crisis team for Managua. The
organizational problems included: 1) no previous demand for this type of
help to a foreign country; 2) lack of a central coordinating structure within
NIMH; 3) the fact that NIMH is a national institution, and 4) the priority
given by international agencies to physical aid. Negotiation and planning
had to be completed, first within NIMH and then between NIMH and the
Nicaraguan government. Thus, it took 3 months to assemble the volunteer
team, obtain funding for basic expenses (food, shelter, and transportation),
and establish relations with the Nicaraguan government to gain sanction
for the entrance of the team and provide some shared economic support.

Two days of meetings were arranged (funded by NIMH) to acquaint team members with each other, develop a conceptual model for the crisis intervention program, and establish guidelines for the interrelationship with the Managuan institutions.

Information Gathering

Answers were sought to the following questions:

1. What information was available to give the team a description of: *a*) the extent of the catastrophe, *b*) the manner in which the population sustained the impact, *c*) the immediate measures taken to develop the human support systems to direct the emergency programs?
2. What were the characteristics of the population's environment both before and after the event: *a*) physical, *b*) political, *c*) cultural, and *d*) economic?
3. What organized public and private structures were there at the time of planning to assist the population's functioning? (We learned that the Public Health Ministry, the National Assistance and Welfare Board, and the Social Security Institute provided the main support services in the country. The Committee on Emergency, which was instituted after the earthquake, gave direction and coordination to broad human services in the City of Managua.)
4. Who would be giving the supporting sanction for team member activities?
5. What conceptual principles and guidelines would we use to design crisis intervention activities within the native human services structure in Managua?

Conceptual Model for Intervention

Theoretical formulations used to develop our procedures and methods were drawn from: *a*) open system theory (14, 15), *b*) psychosocial findings reported by Cassel (67, 68), and *c*) principles and practices of community psychiatry (63, 64, 79, 217).

Intra-team organization was essential to divide responsibilities, develop linkages with key individuals in the Managuan community, and delineate specific activities and goals for each team member and for the team as a whole.

Philosophical and practical approaches included the following:

1. All our activities would be directed toward developing procedures that would be found useful by the individuals with whom we would be working within the crisis intervention projects.
2. We would start with feasible and salient limited activities, working

within the disaster aid network and then enlarge our scope as more knowledge and familiarity with the situation developed. To implement this we would identify patterns of service and link into them.

3. As we became familiar with the service structures in the city, we would try to collaborate and cooperate with the established organizations that had been set up to offer direct help to individuals traumatized by the earthquake, while also offering indirect services (consultation and education) to the caregivers.

4. We would continue to scan for further opportunities to participate in the broader areas of health, education, and welfare.

5. We would continue to develop relationships broadly at every level of organization and leadership in these systems.

6. We would accumulate and organize data emerging from our activities to be used as continuous feedback to keep the team's activity focused on the main objectives.

To implement these aims, we would have to develop a proactive and supportive stance. The design of the organization within the mental health team had to be structured *a priori*, but it would be flexible, balancing immediate needs with clear direction and defined boundaries. We would present our area of expertise, and ask native caregivers to select their priorities and options from defined and clearly verbalized team positions. We did not ask what we could do to "help," but gave them a definite inventory of our skills and asked them to fit it to the postdisaster situation.

What emerged, in broad terms, were two categories of project objectives: *a*) aid to individuals affected by the earthquake, and *b*) support to caregivers through role modeling, education, consultation, and catalytic activities within community agencies, including linking of systems to integrate their efforts in the crisis intervention projects.

TEAM OPERATIONS

On arrival of the full team complement, the first few days were used for orientation and for meeting key people in agency leadership and administrative roles. The fact that the team members were bilingual and bicultural facilitated rapid establishment of relationships. Mindful of the leadership group's wishes and priorities, we identified the most practical areas for the beginning activities of team intervention. The *match and mix* between the small team of United States mental health workers and the enormity of needs that had gone unheeded until we arrived, and which would continue after our departure, was the primary task to which we addressed ourselves. By matching some of our interests and knowledge with the array of choices, we eventually developed several clearly defined areas of intervention. The team then set up six specific projects.

Children's Project

The children's project consisted of ambulatory services for parents and children ranging from 2½ to 16 years of age who presented symptoms of "post-earthquake traumatic neurosis." Interventive techniques were applied, using individual and group therapy as well as medication.

Lecture Series for Caregivers

A series of lectures in Spanish were developed on the techniques of crisis intervention, community psychiatry, and short-term psychotherapy for mental health practitioners. This course offered both intellectual and emotional support to a group of workers who had been called on to be supportive to others while themselves experiencing trauma. Many of them showed symptoms of delayed mourning reaction.

Aid to Professional Groups

Consultation and education were provided to the following groups: *a*) counselors at the National University, *b*) faculty of the Universities Central America, *c*) members of the Health and Welfare Council, *d*) students from behavioral science disciplines, *e*) educators from the Public Health Department, *f*) clergymen, and *g*) members of private community institutions.

Instruction for Nursing Personnel

We offered consultation and a series of presentations on crisis intervention to public health nursing supervisors and special nursing personnel. Services were also provided to the 16 neighborhood health centers in Managua. Seminars, small-group presentations, role playing, and individual supervision were offered throughout the month.

Mental Health Clinic

A mental health clinic was established in The Camp America #2, a development of 1000 houses built in 3 days by Aid for International Development (AID) for displaced families. (Five similar camps were built around the city.) Using one of the houses as a base, three mental health workers participated in outreach programs. A psychologist provided back-up services. This group also linked to several other organized supportive groups that had established themselves in this camp, and together they began to develop some educational and preventive programs. This clinic later became a major training setting for nurses and psychology professionals working with the governmental agencies of the City. Services offered at the clinic were screening, emergency treatment, individual supportive treatment, chemotherapy when necessary, and group interaction.

Plans for the Future

A planning project for "Emergency Help through Human Services" was offered to the Managuan government. The model provided for development of a human services support system within the already structured organizations of the Ministry of Health Education, the JNAPS (National Council of Assistance and Provision Services), and the OCIP, a joint group of 12 to 14 national and foreign private service organizations in Managua. The project was based on the principle that outside consultants could help establish an emergency project but that responsibility for maintaining an ongoing operation should be carried out by a native director chosen by governmental and private agency units. The plan as established contained the following proposals:

1. Mobilizing a group of individuals already employed by the public institutions to be "loaned" to work in the project
2. Using the team of mental health workers from the United States as consultants, educators, and project demonstrators, linked to their professional counterparts in Managua
3. Coordinating the efforts of public and private groups to attain the objectives of intervention; existing community activities were not organizing supportive processes effectively to meet individual needs
4. These groups could follow up the emergency mobilization with long-term planning for future needs.

This blueprint was implemented by subsequent teams from the United States. Ten crisis centers were developed, manned by 30 Nicaraguan graduate students in psychology, nursing, and social work under the supervision of Nicaraguan mental health professionals. The centers were funded by the private agencies.

Other projects were developed, but the plans described here illustrate the types of activities started by the first team. As of this writing, three teams have gone to Managua and have followed through with these projects as well as establishing new ones.

INTERVENTION PHENOMENOLOGY

The team was able to observe the problems faced by a population suffering from the aftereffects of a dislocated human systems network. The people we were seeing seemed to be still in the recoil stage or beginning of the adaptive phase as described by Tyhurst (413). It appeared puzzling to us initially that there were still much data to document this phase 3 months after the disaster, but it became understandable as we realized that the people continued to experience the shaking of the earth's crust and learned of other earthquakes in Costa Rica and Hawaii. Another stimulus that threatened adaptive mechanisms was that newspaper headlines continued to describe dire effects of earthquakes and portend potential disasters for Managua. The lack of supportive human systems with trained manpower tended to prevent positive adaptation to trauma, and the real hardships such as lack of jobs, disrupted daily activities, and inadequate housing added to the stress.

There were similar responses from many people, although there were differences in such factors as impact of stress, strength of personality and health at time of event, extent of property and human loss, distress and discomfort in living following the earthquake, extent of empathic identification with the trauma of the population, loss of socioeconomic status, need to move out of the neighborhood or city, age, sex, and social network affiliations. The intensity of the emotional tonality, the manner of narrating the individual experiences to us 3 months after the earthquake, and the feelings of crisis of a large number of persons were very similar. This pointed to the need for providing help not only to the citizens but also to the professional caregivers. Our intervention techniques with professionals were adapted to their individual coping styles. Some asked for help in an overt manner, others within the setting of an egalitarian collegial situation. Unique group techniques, adaptations of traditional crisis intervention, were developed. The focus of the group intervention was on both the cognitive and affective level of the individual's functioning. Our objective was to support and enhance coping endeavors that had been inoperative. A clear message had to be signaled that the individual professional or caregiver was not a patient but was reacting to extreme conditions of stress. A small fraction of our intervention was directed to individuals clearly diagnosed as suffering from different varieties of classic mental disturbance.

RESULTS OBTAINED BY THE TEAMS

The combined efforts of the American and Managuan mental health workers, sustained by the interest and sanction of the governmental and health leaders, led to the following results:

1. Implementation of a crisis intervention program to directly assist individuals traumatized by the earthquake.
2. Collaborative linking with human services structures.
3. Beginning consultative relations with health planners for long-term construction of new health institutions.

4. Development of ongoing projects to be continued by the second team of professionals from the United States.
5. Development of direct services for caregivers, for phobic children and their parents, and for adults.
6. Instituting catalytic activities to develop multidisciplinary integrated planning programs in several institutions within the health and welfare structures.
7. Developing a multilevel educational program for public and private institutions.

SUMMARY

This chapter has focused on the activities of an American mental health team working on a volunteer basis in Managua, 3 months after a devastating earthquake. The activities of the team were based on guidelines and principles learned from previous studies in crisis intervention following disasters. These efforts exemplify Caplan's point: "By deploying helping services to deal with individuals in crisis, a small amount of effort leads to a maximum amount of lasting response (62)." By using the main criterion of *utility* in providing relevant and efficacious intervention efforts to meet the special needs of the population affected by the catastrophe, the team was able to achieve some of their objectives and leave a group of ongoing projects for the incoming team. The feedback received since then from a large number of Nicaraguan individuals has substantiated and verified many of the results observed.

32

COMMUNITY RESOURCES FOR DISASTER AID

an annotated inventory

Don M. Hartsough, H.L.P. Resnik, and Howard J. Parad

A community disaster brings about the temporary coalescence of organizations that under ordinary circumstances may have little or no interaction. A one-stop disaster relief center, for example, may house personnel from 20 or more local, state, and national agencies.* Some, such as the American Red Cross, are readily identified as primarily disaster relief organizations, while for others the disaster work is incidental to their ongoing operations. If mental health and related personnel intend to contribute to disaster aid, it would be advisable to develop an understanding of the functions other organizations serve in times of disaster. The ideal time for this interagency understanding is *during the early phases of a community disaster aid preparedness program.* Unfortunately, massive community denial mechanisms (It can't happen here!), in the face of frequent disasters induced by fire, flood, tornado, or earthquake, all too often prevent the establishment of viable disaster aid preparedness programs.

AGENCIES AVAILABLE FOR DISASTER RELIEF

Some of the human services organizations found at the scene of a community disaster are discussed briefly in the following paragraphs. Specifically, they are the ones likely to be encountered by mental health personnel in a federally coordinated Disaster Assistance Center. The specific cluster of agencies will vary according to the type of disaster and

---

* See Chapter 28 for a detailed discussion of the optimal components for an urban disaster aid unit for dealing with fire victims.

the resources of the local community because, as Dynes states, "In the United States, responsibility for [disaster] activity rests primarily with local governmental units (103)." Thus, the purpose of the list is to orient the new disaster worker to the variety of services provided; it is not intended as a definitive set of relief and recovery organizations.

American Red Cross

The Red Cross is specifically chartered as a national disaster relief organization with local chapters. It is found at all major disasters and may be activated before predictable disasters such as hurricanes. It provides emergency relief to anyone in apparent need through direct financial assistance (not loans), food, clothing, temporary housing, household goods, occupational supplies and equipment, medical care, and other basic services. It may also be involved in postemergency recovery operations such as family relocation and casework. It is in the process of developing training programs in crisis intervention for its field workers.

Agricultural Stabilization and Conservation Service

The Agricultural Stabilization and Conservation Service is a field service unit of the United States Department of Agriculture. Following a disaster, it provides assistance to farmers whose property has sustained structural damage. It will assist in fence building and livestock maintenance and will pay a major portion of the costs incurred for removing debris from the farm when using hired equipment and labor.

Administrative Building Council

A state agency, the Administrative Building Council or similar unit, assists local government in inspecting commercial, public, and industrial buildings which are damaged or destroyed in a disaster. It may also inspect family dwellings and farm buildings on request. During the recovery process, it will review building plans and certify them regarding building compliances.

Army Corps of Engineers

Personnel and equipment from regular Army Corps of Engineers projects can be transferred to disaster areas for clean-up work, debris removal, and demolition of damaged or unsafe buildings. These services are provided free of charge to disaster victims.

Community Action Program

If the locality struck by disaster has a Community Action Program or other programs sponsored by the federal Office of Economic Opportunity, there may be services available for disaster victims through these programs.

These include assistance to families for food, clothing, legal services, medical care, emergency funds, and employment.

County Agent and County Extension Homemaker

The County Agent and the County Extension Homemaker are often excellent sources of direct assistance to farmers and their families during the early postdisaster period. They are frequently known to rural and small town disaster victims through their regular agricultural extension services. The County Agent can offer clean-up assistance, debris removal, and information on farm rehabilitation. The County Extension Homemaker is a coordinator of Homemaker Extension and 4-H Clubs and thus is in direct communication with a network of families in impact areas.

Crisis Centers and Hot-Lines

As indicated by several authors in the present volume, crisis centers and hot-lines are potential disaster relief organizations. While they typically are not included in disaster planning, their personnel are already trained to work with people in emotionally stressful situations. Crisis center volunteers could be mobilized quickly to work in emergency shelters, relocation centers, and with uninjured relatives of disaster victims in hospitals. When telephone facilities remain intact in disaster situations, the 24-hour telephone services of these organizations could be used for information, referral, and telephone counseling. Many crisis centers have excellent training programs for volunteer crisis workers; these programs might well be mobilized to train large numbers of disaster aid workers during the postdisaster mobilization and recovery periods.

Employment Security Division

A state agency, the Employment Security Division provides unemployment benefits to persons left jobless as a result of the disaster and aids in seeking employment for persons who will not be returning to work for their former employer because of the disaster.

Farmers Home Administration

The Farmers Home Administration can make emergency loans to farmers to replace, restore, or repair damaged or destroyed farm property. It can also loan money for the purchase of essential personal possessions and make emergency loans to replace farm machinery and livestock.

Federal Disaster Assistance Administration

The Federal Disaster Assistance Administration (FDAA) assumes a role as the official coordinating and information-giving agency for disaster relief activities. It establishes a one-stop Disaster Relief Center in all major disasters to house under one roof personnel from federal, state, and local governmental units, plus most of the voluntary organizations providing services to victims. State and federal coordinators assigned to the local FDAA Center meet daily at a prearranged time with leaders of the other organizations to facilitate liaison and cooperation. Literature and press releases regarding locally available services are provided by the FDAA Center.

Food Stamps

The Food Stamp Program, administered through the local Department of Public Welfare, provides essential commodities at reduced prices for citizens who qualify. After a disaster, the Food Stamp Program is made available to disaster victims in addition to predisaster recipients.

Housing and Urban Development

A federal agency, the Department of Housing and Urban Development (HUD), provides temporary housing and a variety of other housing assistance to all people whose shelter has been affected by the disaster, including both renters and homeowners. It is a major relief agency in any disaster causing widespread property damage. HUD will provide apartments and homes, where available, and its own mobile homes as temporary housing for at least 1 year; and it will assist owners in obtaining repairs to make homes livable. Disaster victims must establish eligibility for one of the HUD programs by meeting personally with an HUD representative, usually at the FDAA Center.

Internal Revenue Service

Disaster victims may be given special consideration by the Internal Revenue Service (IRS) such as income tax deductions for property losses 1 year earlier than would ordinarily apply. The IRS can also be consulted regarding lost records, delayed income tax reporting, and assessment of property losses.

Legal Aid

Legal Aid is a locally sponsored program oriented primarily to matters of civil law. It offers free legal services in solving disaster-caused problems for individuals who qualify.

Mental Health Programs

Until recently, mental health facilities have been unlikely to be represented at an FDAA Disaster Relief Center. During the recent past, however, several projects have demonstrated viable roles for mental health personnel in disaster recovery, including short-term crisis intervention services for victims, hot-line consultation for parents regarding children upset by the disaster, and training of paraprofessional outreach workers. While much mental health work is done following the immediate emergency period, being included in the FDAA Center would provide linkage with other community caregivers as well as with victims at a time of great stress. This would increase the accessibility and probably the effectiveness of services for populations at risk. Planning with established relief agencies before a disaster strikes is a first step toward being included in the FDAA Center. It is urgently important that community mental health centers participate in this process *before* disaster strikes.

Mental health agencies can provide individual, family, and group postdisaster counseling services for the depressed and the disturbed, and long-term ombudsman and support services for those who still need special resources or have been unable to adapt to the changes imposed by the disaster. The local family service agency will often accept referrals of those needing personal or family counseling.

Specific recognition of the necessity for encouraging the development of counseling resources in disaster planning has been advocated by the Mental Emergencies Section of NIMH.

The Disaster Relief Act of 1974 contains a small but potentially powerful section for mental health professionals. Under the Crisis Counseling Assistance and Training section (42 USC 5183) of this Act, the National Institute of Mental Health may provide services to victims of disasters and training to disaster workers. This legislation followed on the heels of The Emergency Medical Services System Act of 1973 (PL 93-154) which, for the first time, legitimized mental health crises as a proper concern of the emergency health care delivery system. Now, it remains to be seen whether sufficient funds will be appropriated and applied so that people in crisis will encounter professionals and other mental health workers who are adequately trained in crisis intervention.

Information about the services currently available may be obtained by writing to the Mental Health Disaster Assistance Programs, National Institute of Mental Health, 5600 Fishers Lane, Rockville, Maryland, 20852.

Mennonite Disaster Service

Manpower to help in repairing homes is often provided free of charge by the Mennonite Disaster Service.

National Guard

In addition to the protection of property and the emergency rescue of victims, the National Guard provides trucks and labor for assistance in moving and other services during the immediate postdisaster period. In many communities the National Guard armory is also a likely location for the FDAA Center.

Public Health Service

The Public Health Service, in cooperation with state and local health officers, provides emergency medical care and preventive health services. (Further information on programs available may be obtained by writing the Public Health Service, 5600 Fishers Lane, Rockville, Maryland, 20852.)

Religious Organizations

Religious organizations such as the Christian Relief Fund and the Pentacostal Disaster Relief Service provide a variety of direct support services to disaster victims. These include food, clothing, household furnishings, and financial aid. Some religious groups have well-developed relief supply capabilities located regionally throughout the country, while others gather supplies after the disaster and implement relief through local leaders.

Salvation Army

The Salvation Army is a religiously based, emergency relief organization that is involved mostly during the emergency period of a disaster. It supplies food, clothing, and shelter until housing can be found, and in addition gives spiritual aid to victims and their relatives. Its most visible function is the mobile canteen service, frequently called to major emergencies (e.g., fires, train wrecks) in addition to community disasters. It often serves as a gathering point for donated supplies for disaster victims.

Small Business Administration

The Small Business Administration (SBA), like HUD, is a major relief agency in disasters which cause widespread property damage. Its primary vehicle of assistance is the low-interest, long-term loan to rebuild or repair homes, or to maintain or replace businesses. SBA funds, less insurance recovered, are available to help restore property to its pre-disaster condition. The application and qualification procedures can be complex and may require sustained effort by the applicant.

Social Security Administration

Disaster victims who are Social Security recipients may qualify for increased benefits due to their altered financial conditions.

State Board of Health

The State Board of Health maintains free inspection and advisory services regarding environmental health problems, such as polluted water supplies, damaged septic and sewage disposal systems, and food handling or manufacturing locations suspected of contamination. With the Public

Health Service, it is also a coordinating unit for the control of infectious diseases which may follow in the wake of a disaster.

State Department of Insurance

The State Department of Insurance or similar state-level office will investigate complaints of a disaster victim who states that his insurance settlement is not being fairly or promptly managed by his insurance company.

State Police, State Fire Marshall, Local Fire Department

Inspection of damaged buildings and official documentation of property loss are required for building reoccupancy and insurance settlements. These tasks will be assigned to one or more official emergency organizations, among them the state police, the state fire marshall, and the local fire department.

IV

Preventive Programming for Effective Crisis Coping

The critical reader may justifiably contend that this section on prevention may have been more appropriately located at the beginning of the book. After all, isn't the best way to begin a preventive one, through programs that show promise of averting mental health emergencies?

As Caplan has clearly indicated in his Foreword, life opportunities and community programs that enhance the individual's social surroundings (including such significant others as family, friends, neighbors, formal and informal caregivers) offer great potential for promoting successful crisis coping. The chapters in this section demonstrate primary, early secondary, and tertiary preventive programs aimed at this goal by reaching different populations-at-risk.

Beatt's Family Development Project, based on the conceptual framework developed by Reuben Hill and his colleagues at the University of Minnesota Family Study Center, is guided by a life-cycle crisis mastery model: as families deal adaptively with the tasks of one developmental stage, it is postulated that they are likely to cope successfully with the subsequent normal transitional crises that beset all individuals and families. The demand for this growth-oriented educational service reflects the public's increasing awareness of and receptivity to primary preventive programs aimed at marital and family well-being, not at pathology.

Similarly, the low-budget Warm-Line Project instituted by Brown and Reid represents a promising, highly replicable effort in the prevention of early childhood developmental problems and parent-child relationship disorders. Programs modeled on the Warm-Line are already under way in

Sycamore, New York, El Paso, Texas, and communities in California and New Jersey. If undetected and unattended, how often do these incipient parent-child problems erupt into mental health emergencies, later requiring extensive and expensive remedial therapy?

All too often the preventive possibilities of mental health consultation—with its opportunities for averting maladaptive coping by individuals and institutions—are the subject of speculation rather than action. A happy exception is the project inaugurated by Rose and Paulson who, avoiding the role of "emergency fixer," go beyond mental health treatment of problem children to involve classroom teachers and school administrators in programs that appear to stimulate a more growth-producing social surrounding for all concerned.

Separation and divorce have been much studied by social scientists, yet the potential for preventive intervention inherent in these transitional crises has received relatively little attention. Utilizing the concept of "crisis matrix," Jacobson and Portuges suggest critical points of emotional hazard at which brief, economical, early secondary prevention may well forestall serious psychological problems from occurring in the growing, at-risk populations of persons whose marriages are undergoing separation or dissolution. While work with the parents at this time may be at an early secondary level, we think that outreaching intervention efforts with the children may well be a type of primary *prevention if the children are seen prior to the onset of certain expectable problems attending the trauma of separation and divorce.*

Since the publication of Lindemann's classic study of the crisis of bereavement (260), researchers and clinicians alike have advocated experimentally controlled studies to find out what happens when mental health professionals do or don't intervene when death suddenly strikes a family. Polak and his colleagues present us with a candid (and sobering!) interim report of just such a research experiment. Along with his insight into what makes for healthy coping with bereavement, Polak speculates that currently available intrapersonal and interpersonal interventive strategies are perhaps not powerful enough to offset certain environmental forces impinging on the bereaved family.

In our Preface *and earlier* Introductory Notes *we mentioned our concern about the impact of deinstitutionalization programs on the mentally ill. One poignant example is the board-and-care facility—too often an inadequate or marginal substitute for mental hospitalization. Using novel techniques of experiential research, Reynolds and Farberow give us a vivid image of the social environment of typical board-and-care facilities. From the perspective of tertiary prevention they offer specific guidelines for destigmatizing the board-and-care resident—at the very best improving his rehabilitation potential for independent living, at the very least enhancing his self worth; but in either event significantly reducing the likelihood of rehospitalization.*

33

THE FAMILY DEVELOPMENT APPROACH

a program for coping with transitional crises

Earl J. Beatt

The program described in this chapter is based on a postulate of crisis theory which states that the opportunity derived through the mobilization of individual and family resources challenges a person toward mastery of future life situations. Erikson and Rapoport (111, 341) refer to "normal" or "maturational" transitional crises that all human beings experience in the process of growing up. They contend that if appropriate task training is provided during normal transitional crises, such crises can be successfully mediated and that the next maturational stage is more likely to yield its full potential for further growth and development.

BACKGROUND

The concept of a Family Life Center emerged in 1964 from a meeting of the executives of five midwest family service agencies concerning future directions for effective service. Such centers would promote the fulfillment of maximum family potentials by offering diversified programs of treatment, social provision, and prevention. Research to evaluate services and stimulate new modes of practice was seen as an integral component.

In collaboration with Reuben Hill and the Family Study Center of the University of Minnesota, the Minneapolis Family and Children's Service began to explore conceptual frameworks for implementing a Family Life

Center. The guiding perspective was a developmental approach as described by Hill (7):

> The day of taking the family for granted should be drawn to a close. Family specialists must consider what concerted effort they can make to help all families in a program of family development, which in a democratic society can be seen as a progressive upgrading of families comparable to urban development. Such a program is intended to be in contrast to the concepts of family adjustment or preservation of families which implies some restoration of the status quo. Families should be viewed as more than an accommodating and adapting unit: indeed, they should be seen as capable of transcending their present dimensions in realizing their goals and objectives, in growing and developing over time.

Such an approach provided a new dimension to agency service by enhancing growth as well as dealing with dysfunction. It opened up the community of clients to normal families as well as to malfunctioning families.

Hill identifies four distinct concepts of the family developmental framework:

1. The family is viewed as a totality, a relatively closed boundary-maintaining system.
2. The study of family structure includes attention to position, role, norms, role cluster, and role complexes.
3. The study of family functioning involves assessment of direction, goal, purpose, and the phenomena of equilibrium-seeking.
4. Attention to the family time continuum means dealing with orderly sequences, the sequential regularities observable in the family over its life history, such as role sequences, careers of family positions, intercontingencies of careers, and stages of development (176).

The usefulness of these concepts is more easily understood when the family's development is charted in terms of stages. These stages provide a convenient framework for examining the properties and processes interacting within the family at a particular time in its development—that is, as it is *becoming established* (childless young married couple); *expanding* (from the addition of the first child to the addition of the last child, *stabilizing* (period of child-rearing until the first child leaves the home); and *contracting* (period when children are emancipated until the last child leaves home). Merging into one another, these stages are characterized by changes in family size, age, composition, and roles.

Throughout these stages of the family life cycle, each family member has his own developmental tasks, the accomplishment of which is dependent on and contributory to the successful task achievement by other family members. In addition, of course, there are basic tasks or functions that society expects the family to perform, e.g., reproduction, physical maintenance, socialization, affection-giving. "When these basic tasks are particularized by the sequences in which they must be performed and the hierarchy of importance which they have at different points in time, they become family developmental tasks" (72).

A primary assumption of the family developmental approach is that as families master the tasks of one stage, they are likely to move more successfully through the stages of each succeeding normal transitional crisis.

While it is the ultimate goal in Family and Children's Service to identify family developmental tasks at each stage of the family life span and to develop and organize training programs to assist normal families in mastering these tasks (224), the longitudinal research aspects require some years of examination and experimentation before the agency will be able to provide programs throughout the total family span. We now provide programs of developmental training for premarital couples and for parents with children between the ages of 2 and 5.

The program for premarital couples described here was designed to reduce the impact of the normal transitional crisis of moving from single status to the dyadic relationship in marriage.

PREMARITAL COMMUNICATIONS TRAINING PROGRAM FOR COUPLES*

How can a person who has never married, experience marriage? How can a person prepare for the transition from a single to a married state before the transition occurs? What can be done to facilitate an effective transition?

Professionals exhibit a wide range of attitudes toward this normal transitional crisis. Some attempt to prepare the couple by identifying potential areas of conflict, for example, attitudinal and value differences. They often try to confront a couple with the problems they think the couple will encounter after marriage. However, this confrontation is often premature since couples are not experiencing what is being anticipated; and, fortunately, many couples never do encounter the problems they are "supposed to." Other professionals prefer to supply pertinent information to create informed and refined attitudes and values. Few programs have

* The Communications Training Program For Couples was developed by Sherod Miller and Elam W. Nunnally, University of Minnesota Family Study Center, with the assistance of the Minneapolis Family and Children's Service, and supported by a grant from the National Institute of Mental Health to the University of Minnesota Family Study Center: *Problem-Solving Behavior of Family Groups*. (5R01MH 15521-05, National Institute of Mental Health).

attempted to teach specific behaviors which engaging* couples can use during and after their transition into marriage.

Formal methods for achieving these ends traditionally include individual and conjoint premarital counseling services, functional marriage classes, topical lecture series, and small group discussions. Review of the literature showed little agreement about specific topical information (such as financial planning and budgeting, family planning, housing) that couples should know in order to successfully launch their marital careers.

Some literature did suggest that certain developmental tasks must be accomplished by couples if they are to achieve a satisfactory transition into marriage and subsequent marital adjustment. These included the establishment of mutually satisfactory sexual adjustment, a communications system, problem-solving skills, and relationships with friends and relatives (341, 344, 363). However, we were unable to find material which was theoretically sound and systematically designed to teach couples how (behaviorally) they might go about accomplishing the tasks believed to be essential to successful initiation into the first phase of family life.

Rationale

In our search for concepts which could be practically applied to facilitate engaging couples' behavioral preparation for marriage, the study team became intrigued with Foote and Cottrell's (128) concept of "interpersonal competence." These authors suggested that interpersonal competence can be learned since it is not a trait or state but rather involves capabilities to meet and deal with a changing world. Foote also made a crucial theoretical distinction between two concepts. The concept of *matchmaking* is a static notion, emphasizing the initial choice and maximum fit between partners. On the other hand, the concept of *continual matching over time* acknowledges that, although couples may initially enjoy extensive convergence in attitudes, values, and interests, people and things around them are continually in the process of changing. Consequently, Foote emphasized the importance of developing interpersonal competence to accommodate and even create change in order to keep the marital relationship viable over time. Rather than assuming a passive, patient (matchmaking) orientation toward getting married, Foote encouraged mates to become their own active "agents in mutual development" throughout their marital career (127).

The study team recognized that endorsing the creation of interpersonal competence as preparation for marital career development was one thing but translating this perspective into a practical educational program was another. We were also acutely aware of the inadequacy of attempting to

---

* We prefer the term *engaging* to *engaged* because the former connotes a dynamic active process of relating.

teach couples marital role behavior. Such a program would assume that there are correct marital behaviors to learn and specific, agreed on, normative standards to meet. We recognized that this type of program would fail to equip couples with interpersonal competence for creating their own marital script. It would not teach a higher order set of principles which could be applied at different times and in different situations to invent roles and relationships that would be satisfying and fulfilling to both partners.

We believed that attempts to forecast the problems which engaging couples could encounter after marriage or to teach normative role behaviors would not necessarily help couples become interpersonally competent. Consequently, the team decided to focus on the nature of interpersonal relationships.

Theoretical Framework

Our next step was to examine how marriage counselors discover ways in which couples relate and how they go about helping couples change their interaction. We reasoned that, if engaged couples could learn some principles and skills for understanding and modifying relationships, they could more effectively direct their own lives together. To learn more about the theoretical dynamics of relationships the team turned to modern systems and communication theory.

In systems theory, families are characterized as "rule governed systems" (426). These rules delimit how the system interacts and have a powerful impact on how effectively it functions. The process of communication between members of a system may be viewed both as an index for understanding the system and as a vehicle for altering the system. In ongoing relationships, the nature of the relationship cannot be endlessly fluctuating and unstable. Such a condition is characteristic of dysfunctional relationships. On the other hand, relationships which are defined and confirmed too quickly and which do not possess procedures for reordering themselves are limited in their capacity to meet internal and external system demands for modification over time.

The type of social system which functions most effectively appears to be one in which rules both define interaction patterns to establish some degree of stability and, at the same time, provide procedures for changing patterns to maintain flexibility (386). Thus, in order to provide for both stability and change within the system, we believed that couples needed to learn two sets of skills: *awareness* skills to enable them to understand their rules and interaction patterns, and *communication* skills to enable them to constructively change the rules and interaction patterns.

It is, of course, very difficult for members of a social system to simultaneously participate in and monitor the system. Nevertheless, humans are able to step outside the circle of their own ongoing interaction with another person and temporarily talk about "how we talk," "how we make decisions," or "how we deal with tension between us." And people can be taught to do so—to "meta-communicate," that is, to communicate about their communication (426). In the process of learning how to meta-communicate effectively, couples establish procedures for self-monitoring, regulating, and directing the *rules* of the relationship, and consequently, the relationship itself.

Principal Goals and Objectives

With this overall purpose in mind, the following goals were selected for use in the program: First, increase each couple's ability to reflect on and accurately perceive their own dyadic processes by *a*) refining each member's private self awareness; *b*) heightening each partner's awareness of his own contribution to interaction; and *c*) helping couples to explore their own rules of relationship, particularly their rules for conflict situations and their patterns of maintaining esteem for themselves and others. Second, increase each couple's capacity for clear, direct, open meta-communication, especially communication about their relationship.

Translating these goals into a behaviorally focused practice program was not a smooth or orderly process. As we began recruiting couples and experimenting with various ways of heightening awareness and teaching open communication skills, we found ourselves frequently retreating to strategies outside the model we were attempting to develop. When we wore our "counseling goggles," we saw many problems to resolve to "really prepare couples for marriage." The struggle to separate ourselves from this comfortable and familiar perspective in order to create an alternative set of developmental lenses to help us look at relationships differently was both a stressful and an exhilarating experience. In time, we were able to identify a set of dimensions which yielded a new model. We also quickly discovered that when trouble arose, one or more of these dimensions was being violated.

DIMENSIONS UNDERLYING THE MODEL

The following dimensions combined to form an interrelated network of principles for effectively conducting our couples communication program, which we called UNITE.

An Educational–Developmental Orientation

Equipping versus Repairing. This dimension is the pivotal point of the entire program. Typically, therapy models are built on efforts to repair relationships after trouble has set in. UNITE is designed to equip couples with perspective and skills to enable them to direct the course of their relationship in day-to-day decisions. It is designed to upgrade the communications and negotiations skills of many average couples, as opposed to investing heavily in efforts to mend the relationships of a few couples.

Learning Procedures and Principles for Effective Communication. It is important that couples possess a mutually understood and accepted set of communication procedures (390). With a common set of procedures for talking constructively about their relationships, couples can integrate and use the cognitive, emotive, and behavioral aspects of their life more successfully. They can reduce false assumptions and misunderstandings (235) that interfere with their growth. In the process of developing procedural consensus, couples learn how to learn together (29).

Focus on System

Dyad versus Individual or Group. Effective communication training for dyads (engaging, married, or considering remarriage) must include both partners similtaneously and focus on their interaction together. This is important in order to a) provide *common* "mental maps" to help a couple heighten their awareness of their typical communications while learning methods of altering their interaction in directions they choose; and b) avoid or minimize one-sided, unequal inputs of awareness and communication skills into the couple's system. When one partner is excluded, both partners are often disadvantaged. This condition frequently prevents adaptive changes in the system because fresh input is usually met by attempts to limit and govern the effects of the new input on the system (426).

Focus on How Rather Than Why. We assume that *how* a message is sent (style) is just as important as *why* it is sent. In closed mechanical (nonsocial) systems, the initial circumstances determine the final state. As a result, search for causes of malfunctioning is important. However, in open social systems, the initial state of the system can be totally independent of the current state. As Watzlawick and associates put it, ". . . the *system is then its own best explanation*, and the study of its present organization the appropriate methodology (426)."

The operation of this dimension can have a liberating effect; when couples learn *how* to *describe* the things they see and hear, and link their sensory data with the alternative meanings they have constructed, they are learning to examine how they relate to each other without getting sidetracked on trying to determine *why* (cause) they said or did something.

Increased Flexibility. A number of distinctive styles of communication are presented in UNITE. Possession of a complete repertory of interactional styles within a relationship suggests flexibility and potential adaptability to a variety of internal and external constraints encountered by the system. However, in our work we have found that very few couples possess a full repertoire of interactional styles. Couples most often lack what we call a "high-information" and "-risk" style of communicating. Thus, in order to expand most couples' interactional alternatives, we spend considerable time refining skills which yield a sustained sequential pattern of this style of communication during serious discussions.

System Autonomy.   When members of an engaging pair share perspectives and skills requisite to interpersonal competence, their choices are increased, both inside their relationship and outside the relationship as they encounter other systems. UNITE attempts to enhance a couple's autonomy and ability to cope by increasing their internal resources, thus reducing dependency on external resources, such as professional counselors or chance circumstances.

Skill Orientation

Expanded versus Limited Couple Awareness.   To be aware of oneself and others, and conscious of one's behavior and its multiple meanings to self and others, is uniquely human. We assumed that by equipping each member with skills for heightening awareness of self, others, situation, and system, we were taking the first step toward adding more variety and more useful information to the relationship.

Heightened Awareness is a Two-Edged Sword.   To be aware of interpersonal discomfort, and not be able to alter the feeling if you want to do so, can be exasperating. To perceive something untoward in your relationship, yet not be able to express it and move to alleviate it, can be worse than no recognition at all. On the other hand, knowing how to both recognize self-information (thoughts, feelings, intentions) and express it effectively can be very satisfying and productive.

This expression involves certain communication skills. Couples who do not exercise these communications skills depend heavily on guesswork. But individuals who can effectively express important self-information, and know how to elicit this information from their partner, interact differently than couples who do not do these things. Our exploratory research indicates that the ingredients of effective communication can be discovered, taught, and used by couples to improve their ability to communicate directly, congruently, and supportively.

It is particularly in this respect that UNITE is different from many sensitivity training or encounter experiences. Most programs of this type do not identify and teach specific skills. They depend heavily on experience alone, without integrating conceptual frameworks and associated behavioral dimensions to assist the participants in the transfer of what they learn to other social contexts outside the isolated group experience.

Presentation of Conceptual Frameworks

In UNITE a variety of conceptual frameworks are presented for the following reasons. *First*, they eliminate some of the mystery surrounding relationships by helping couples systematically understand predictable properties of relationships. *Second*, they serve as "advance organizers" for learning specific skills and making sense out of their experience in the program (11). *Third*, they provide common bases from which couples can amplify awareness of their own communication patterns and negotiate their own changes. *Fourth*, they provide structure for evaluating the effects of the program.

Voluntarism and Participant Choice

Maxicontract. We assume that learning is most effective when an individual takes the initiative for his own learning. Before joining a group, each couple meets with an instructor to discover what the program is designed to teach and express what they as a couple are looking for. If the program does not match their interest, we help them find an appropriate alternative resource (e.g., sex counseling, a lecture series).

The purpose of this interview is to set a "maxicontract" with each member of the couple to insure conjoint participation of the couple in the program. Any couple may join the program if both members want:

1. To *identify* (with help from the program) communication skills which they wish to improve
2. To *practice* these skills during the group session
3. To *transfer and experiment* with these skills outside the group session and report back to the group on their experiences
4. To *attend* all six sessions together

Minicontract. Once the program has begun, participation remains voluntary. At any point during a group session, one or both members of a couple may choose not to participate in an exercise or receive group feedback on their interaction process. We have discovered that pushing a couple may prohibit rather than encourage the couple to learn about themselves. Group norms to perform and group pursuit of the couple with intent to help can prevent learning. When a couple establishes their own "minicontract" in the group—expressing their intention to work, explore, and discover—at that moment in that situation, the iron is hot, and learning occurs.

Group Context as Learning Environment

In UNITE, the group is viewed as a significant social context (243). The group becomes a short-term structure in which trust can grow and from which support can be drawn. Although the life of the group is important, it is not an end in itself. The function of the group is to create a safe learning environment where couples can discover that exploring and experimenting with their own relationship patterns can be interesting and rewarding. Here they learn skills for discovering and directing their own relationship rather than directives from authorities about how they should relate.

A number of distinct advantages accrue to participants when they join this type of group program which maximizes reflectivity and visibility. In a group, as opposed to a couple meeting alone with one counselor, there are more sources for feedback—more observers, more points of view. A couple's interaction pattern is less likely to be labeled quickly, thereby lessening the destructive impact labeling can have on future behavior. But when a group develops consensus, the weight of the collective is usually taken seriously.

Furthermore, within a group of couples, each couple has multiple models immediately available to watch and question. Various styles of relating are usually accessible—a wide range of behaviors to emulate or avoid. As a consequence of exposure to different interaction styles (observing other couples and practicing behavior introduced during the sessions), pressure generated to consider alternatives *comes largely from within the dyad itself.*

The group context is especially salient with respect to engaging couples. Often, family and friends take a hands-off attitude concerning the couple's relationship. Thus, engaging couples are often sealed off from reflective feedback, which could be very useful to them during this period of critical role transition.

Besides being insulated from feedback, engaging couples are usually isolated. Groups of engaging couples do not typically run around together. Differential timing of falling in love within friendship groups, and geographic mobility, reduce the availability of reference groups. Consequently a time-bounded, group learning experience may afford a rare opportunity for many engaging couples to obtain constructive feedback from peers and to observe alternative patterns of dyadic relationship development prior to marriage. These dimensions also summarize our view of man; we assume he is not saturated with problems of sickness. He can learn how to maintain or change himself and his significant relationships as he chooses, by using his unique capacities to be aware of himself and to verbally express his awareness.

Groups are composed of five to seven couples. They meet with one or two instructors in 3-hour sessions, one night per week, for six consecutive weeks. Each session builds on the experience of previous exercises, simulations, discussions, and reading of the couple's communication handbook. The handbook supplements the lectures and provides a number of exercises to help couples practice at home and transfer their learning to the relationship outside the group context.

FOCUS OF THE SIX SESSIONS ON CONCEPTUAL FRAMEWORKS

During the *first session*, couples are introduced to *The Awareness Wheel*, a framework for understanding complete and congruent, as well as incomplete and incongruent, self-awareness. Along with the basic dimensions of self-awareness, participants are taught skills for verbally expressing their awareness.

In the *second session*, the focus shifts to learning how to accurately exchange important information with your partner. New behavioral skills are introduced, along with the *Shared Meaning Framework* for matching messages sent with messages received.

The *third session* is built around the *Communication Styles framework*. Here, several styles are identified which have differential impact. Each style fits different content and intentions. In the process of becoming more aware of alternative styles, couples become more aware of their choices; *what* they can communicate and *how* they can communicate.

In the *last three sessions*, attention centers on heightening each partner's awareness of his intentions to build, maintain, or diminish his self-esteem and that of his partner, particularly as they openly deal with such conflict issues in their relationship as sexual adjustment, financial matters, or in-law relationships. Finally, a fourth *Integrating Framework* is presented to help pull together the material previously covered.

SUMMARY AND CONCLUSIONS

In the past 5 years, over 300 groups have been conducted. The following advantages have emerged from this experience. First, the program offers a meaningful supplement or alternative to traditional methods of preparation for marriage. Second, groups have been conducted in a number of different settings—churches, university continuing education divisions, community centers—since the program's educational orientation frees it from exclusive use in therapeutic settings. Third, as experience was gained with premarital groups, the UNITE program was extended to couples at other stages (during marriage or in anticipation of remarriage) and found to be beneficial.

The developmental model operates best when groups are formed from couples looking for an educational rather than a therapeutic experience. When couples are experiencing interpersonal tension (such as couples seeking marriage counseling), their relationships are insufficiently flexible for the couple to monitor themselves and experiment with alternative modes of interacting. Their preoccupation with survival is best accommodated with a counseling relationship. We found that such couples may later be ready to experiment with and elaborate their interaction patterns and can then contract for improving communication skills. However, some recent research (325) indicates that systematic training in communications skills can significantly improve interpersonal skills and the ability to elicit self-exploration from the spouse in deteriorated marriages.

We have found the optimal size of the groups to be five to seven couples. Although this results in a higher than desirable cost per participant, the size limitation is necessary to avoid incomplete training experiences.

UNITE is a structured, educational program for couples which attempts to do three things: first, increase each partner's awareness of self and his contribution to interaction within significant relationships; second, increase each partner's skill in effectively expressing his own self-information—that is, making this self-awareness available to his or her partner; and third, enhance each partner's sense of choice within the relationship for maintaining or changing ways of relating in mutually satisfying ways.

It has been our contention that the successful resolution of normal transitional crises makes it possible to master future vicissitudes with less anxiety and vulnerability (309), and it is our hope that our program for dealing with the normative crises of premarital couples may be viewed as one way to prevent emergency mental health problems.

34

THE WARM-LINE

a primary preventive service for parents of young children

Saul L. Brown
Helen Reid

THE WARM-LINE SERVICE DEFINED

Just as the name suggests, the *Warm-Line* is something less than a *hot-line*. Worried parents who call in receive a return call, but not always immediately; they *are* called within 24 hours. The aim is to help parents with ordinary worries that inevitably arise in the everyday experience of parenting babies, toddlers, and children up to the age of 5 years.

The line is referred to as *warm* because our telephone response is warm. Also, parents are given something fairly specific: suggestions, alternatives, information about child development, as well as reassurance and warm, sensitive interest. Psychodynamic formulations or clarifications may be offered, but our staff is cautious and selective about these. We carefully avoid giving pediatric-medical advice.

PRESCHOOL–INFANT PARENTING SERVICE (PIPS)

The Warm-Line is one element of the Preschool and Infant Parenting Service (PIPS), an early prevention program in the Child and Family Psychiatry Division of the Department of Psychiatry at Cedars-Sinai Medical Center. Other elements in the PIPS are a Mother and Toddler Drop-In Service and a Brief Service for Parents of Young Children.

The Mother-Toddler Service is organized as an informal once-a-week group experience to which mothers come, bringing their babies up to age 2½. During the course of the group sessions, interactions with the babies

407

occur, and staff are able to help mothers become aware of and work out normal developmental problems. Group process interchanges with individual interventions.

The Brief Service for Parents consists of a series of 6 group sessions, held weekly. This is a more formal arrangement than the drop-in program. A diagnostic interview is held for each family before the group series begins and a family summary interview takes place at the end of the series.

These three elements of the PIPS constitute a series of services ranging from a *primary prevention* focus on normal problems of early parenting in the Warm-Line, and the Drop-In Service, to a more clinical focus in the Brief Service Parent Groups.

Additional services for young children and their parents beyond those in PIPS are provided by the Division of Child and Family Psychiatry. A major service is the *therapeutic nursery school*. Another service, related to the therapeutic nursery school, is the *Mother-Infant Unit* (MIU) program which provides conjoint treatment to mothers and very young children when atypical ego development is occurring. These services, together with the extensive services available in the Division of Family and Child Psychiatry, lend clinical depth to the PIPS.

BEHIND THE WARM-LINE

A Warm-Line telephone consultation service evokes the image of a fairly simple process. In fact, however, it derives from a complex of theoretical notions and clinical experiences, and it requires a carefully organized administrative process.

While the clinical experiences and the administrative know-how are largely our own, we have drawn on the theoretical contributions of many others whose writings are in the mental health literature of the past 15 years. Papers gathered in the volumes edited by Gerald Caplan (62) and Howard Parad (308) elucidate most of the theory and a considerable amount of the clinical experience that underlie our work. Brody's paper, *Preventive Intervention in Current Problems of Early Childhood* (53), has particular pertinence for us. While she cautions against overly facile theorizing about problems in the mother-infant relationship as inevitable predisposers to later psychopathology, she nevertheless appeals to mental health professionals to stop "pussyfooting" with parents and to provide firm and active guidance about those aspects of psychosexual development that we understand well. Brody also offers valuable clinical examples of how she has helped parents of infants less than 2 years old, using psychodynamic insight together with directly educative interventions.

The theoretical base underlying our way of working includes not only Brody's notions but also those of Ackerman who, in his paper, *Preventive*

Implications of Family Research (2), introduces the concept of *family development* as a way of comprehending child-parent relationships. He outlines such items as the nature of the family organization, the role functions of each member and the changes occurring over time, the quality of the intergenerational ties, and the dynamics of the parental relationship. He emphasizes how all of these interlace with the ongoing development of the individual child. One of the present authors has elaborated further on some of these concepts, placing particular emphasis on the sequential developmental phases within a family group and the complex ways in which these affect not only the mother-infant unit but all of the family relationships (55).

The concept of transitional crisis follows naturally on the theory of family development. In their paper, *A Framework for Studying Families in Crisis* (310), Parad and Caplan develop this theme and offer three ways of classifying family response to crises of transition: 1) family life style, 2) intermediate problem-solving mechanisms, and 3) need-response pattern. While each of these has its importance for clinical work with a family crisis, the ways in which our staff responds to Warm-Line calls fall most readily into the areas of "intermediate problem-solving" and "need-response patterns." A call into the Warm-Line does not always mean that a transitional crisis exists in a family. But the staff respondent does listen for what the need-response patterns may be as they occur between mother and infant, and enters into a problem-solving effort with the parent. This becomes both an educative and an interpretive effort.

A broad theoretical base for the PIPS program and the Warm-Line derives from the encyclopedic studies of attachment and separation processes between infants and parents described by Bowlby (49). His emphasis on origins of anxiety through poorly monitored separation experience has influenced our understanding.

The particular range of developmental problems that come to the Warm-Line and that are met in the PIPS program reflect many of the issues of separation and individuation that have been so carefully and usefully described by Mahler (273).

WARM-LINE STATISTICS AND STAFF

In the first 11 months of the Warm-Line's existence there were 401 call-ins. In the most recent period there have been an average of 6 to 8 calls each day. A secretary receives these and relays them to one of 10 professionals who have volunteered their services to the Warm-Line. Most of the volunteer professionals hold a Master's degree in social work. Each gives an average of 10 hours per week to the PIPS program. Members of the volunteer staff, even though they are all Master's-level mental health professionals, require several months of training to achieve a sense of competence in each of the services that make up the total program. We believe participation in each subunit of the PIPS is important for all of the PIPS staff members in order to develop overall feeling of involvement, competence, and effectiveness. However, a particular kind of challenge occurs in the Warm-Line where the staff member needs to call on knowledge of early development, diagnostic acumen, and clear communicative skills—all in a short period of time.

THE WARM-LINE AT WORK

Following are 4 examples from the Warm-Line, illustrating progressively more complex problems and circumstances. The fourth example shows how the Warm-Line serves a case-finding function in instances where serious psychopathology has already developed.

CASE REPORT 1

Problem: Mother said her 18-month-old son seemed to know when he had to make a BM, and he accepted being placed on the toilet, but each time he would retain the BM and make it in his diaper after it was replaced. Because the family was to move in a month she felt some pressure to get him trained quickly, but she also felt in doubt about this.

Staff Response: Mother was given reassurance that her child was progressing appropriately in view of his ability to let her know when he needed to go to the toilet. Suggestion was offered that the next step would be for him to be placed in training pants. However, staff person advised mother to consider delaying since it seemed unwise to introduce a major change just before the family was to move.

Mother's Response: She was relieved with the recommendation since she felt pressured in preparing for the move and didn't really feel ready to carry out the training in a consistent and calm way. All of this led to further exchange with the staff person about how a child reacts to change of home. She was responsive to suggestions that she involve her child in the packing, and that she show him the house to which they would be moving.

Discussion: Mother was helped to avoid the rising anxiety that occurs with uncertainty about whether or not to toilet train at a given time. The child was relieved from being placed under undue pressure. Also mother's sensitivity about her child's reactions to moving was increased, and she was better able to help master an event that is often disruptive and may have lingering effects.

CASE REPORT 2

Problem: Mother said that her 16-month-old son had been hospitalized 2 nights because of a hernia repair. Since then he would not sleep the night through, and she was taking him into her bed when he cried. She was troubled about this because it had gone on for 2 weeks.

Staff Response: It was suggested that she set up a cot next to his crib and that when he awakened she should lie there, patting him until he fell asleep again. She was also advised to talk to him about the hospital experience whenever it seemed timely, even if she had doubts about how much he understood her words.

Mother's Response: Mother carried out the recommendation and a week later reported that after the third night her child no longer awakened nor needed her in the room.

Discussion: Following traumatic experiences such as a hospitalization or other similar events, a child and one parent may become entangled in a mutually regressive tie which is increasingly difficult to dissolve and may affect other family members as well. In this case case the phone contact helped mother bring the child's appropriate anxieties and regression to a peaceful end without becoming a source for family disruption.

CASE REPORT 3

Problem: Mother said that since she had weaned her 14-month-old daughter at age 12 months, the child had become very irritable and clinging, crying often. In the phone discussion it came out that mother had restricted the child to 3 meals a day, plus one snack. She believed a tight feeding schedule was desirable since she didn't want her daughter to repeat her own childhood weight problems. Mother reported also that the child's body seemed extremely tense.

Staff Response: With considerable caution, mother's commitment to the 3 meals only was challenged. It was suggested that she experiment with letting the child eat healthy foods at will throughout the day and do this for several days. Food was to be within the child's independent reach. She was urged to call in every couple of days to talk about it.

Mother's Response: Mother followed the suggestion. She reported that for about 2 days the child seemed to eat almost continuously and then slacked off. She shared her anxiety about this and received support. By the end of the week the child's irritability and clinging had lessened. The free eating schedule was continued along with regular meals.

Mother responded to invitation to the Mother-Toddler Drop-In group for additional contact. In those sessions she shared facts about the family— that because of her husband's profession there had been several moves in the 1 year of her daughter's life. Staff observed mother's tendency to keep the child close to her and to discourage appropriate independent explorations. Mother accepted these observations and various suggestions that were offered about alternative behavior. Specifically, she was told to do something at home 4 times a day for 15 minutes each time, during which she was not to let her child interrupt her.

Discussion: Mother's identification with her 1-year-old included projection of her own unresolved childhood trauma onto the child. Both seemed on the edge of a pathologic symbiotic entanglement related to oral and regressive attachment experience. Mother's reaction to her own experience, now replayed with her child, threatened to establish a perpetual controlling and angry-distrustful attitude in the child toward her "depriving" mother. The Warm-Line, plus follow-up clinical intervention, produced a dramatic reversal. By the end of the third Drop-In meeting, child was leaving mother more easily, and her body was noticeably relaxed. The child became free to play with toys and to engage with other toddlers in the group meetings. (The question about whether mother might need additional clinical help was not resolved at time of this writing. She continued to come to weekly Drop-In meetings over a 3-month period.)

CASE REPORT 4

Problem: Mother called about her 1-year-old boy who awakened her at 5 AM each day. She was exhausted. She accepted suggestion that she leave him to play with toys in his crib and also with a bottle.

A few days later mother called again to say her problem with her son was better, but she was concerned about her 2½-year-old daughter who had frequent tantrums, was terrified to have her diaper removed, would not take a bath without wearing it, and even resisted being cleaned after BMs. She would not wear training pants. Also, she would gorge herself on sugar.

Staff Response: A family diagnostic interview was suggested. Father was away so mother and the 2 children were seen. Mother revealed her great anxiety at the time of her first pregnancy and the birth of her daughter. She herself had been an insecure child and felt "unwanted."

Mother was invited to attend a six-session mothers' group. Following this another family session was held with father present. In this, parents were advised that their daughter needed fairly intensive psychotherapy and that they should attend a series of group meetings for parents. They cooperated with both recommendations. An experienced staff member worked with the child twice a week for the next 6 months with a successful resolution of the phobia and the rage reactions. Parents continued in a long-term weekly parents' group. Mother has also been seen for weekly psychotherapy.

Discussion: In this case, mother's first phone call about her 1-year-old was almost in the nature of a "testing" before she revealed her much more serious problem with her 2½-year-old daughter. The latter's phobic reaction to exposing the anal-genital area of her body reflected a breakdown of her developmental progression and an incapacity to master normal castration anxiety. Her mother's profound uncertainty about parenting and about her own inner child-self, coupled with uncertainties in her husband, were contributing to the child's confusion about the intactness of her body. The presence of a baby brother compounded this.

Parents were able to accept the need for extended clinical intervention for the child and for themselves.

DISCUSSION

The Warm-Line techniques we have described are familiar to mental health professionals who are knowledgeable about crisis intervention. Those who have been involved in crisis intervention and who have theorized about it have also had much to say about early prevention and primary prevention (10, 62, 63, 308). Le Masters in his paper, *Parenthood As Crisis*, reviews the growing realization that parenting in the first 2 or 3 years constitutes a critical period in the family life (242). In spite of this the mental health profession has not shown outstanding leadership in using its skills and knowledge to help parents with infants and very young children to evolve through this phase of life in a way that is productive of genuine emotional growth and mental health (470). Generally, mental health professionals have tended to leave the job to physicians and pediatricians. Ironically, one often observes highly trained mental health professionals seeking advice and counsel about *their own* small children from pediatricians or physicians. This, even though it is well known that medical training usually gives only limited attention to psychodynamics and the origins of emotional conflict. Most physicians have only a minimal comprehension of how to work with such problems as ambivalence, anxiety, and guilt. Our own experience with a large number of worried parents suggests that pediatricians and physicians do not meet the primary prevention challenge very well. Their responses and advice tend to be "canned," and lacking in sensitivity to the particular anxieties of a particular parent. Educational pamphlets for parents from such sources as the U.S. Office of Education have also not had much effect since they tend to be general and didactic. Articles in popular magazines about child rearing may, indeed, have more influence than we are able to estimate in reducing parental anxiety. Parent effectiveness classes also are constructive resources for parents but often fail to meet the specific anxieties that arise.

Withal, it is our conviction that person-to-person contact is by far the most desirable way to meet the needs of young parents as they move into their new roles. For many this contact can be very effectively carried out on the telephone. For about half of those parents who have called in, the telephone discussion seems to be enough. Ventilation of feelings and a review of facts about child development, plus suggestions about possible ways that a particular problem might be resolved, seem to be what the parent needs. For the other half of those who call in, more specific clinical interventions are indicated. As previously indicated, we now have in our Child and Family Psychiatry Division a progression of clinical services available to be used for different types of need. However, defensiveness and sensitivity of most parents of very young children make the introduction of specific clinical measures or "secondary prevention" a most delicate matter. Staff persons need to be very skillful in supporting and working with the ego defenses of parents. Diagnostic acumen about family systems and how the dynamics of relationships in the family may be affecting a particular child is a prerequisite, but only the beginning. The difficult challenge is in finding a way to engage the parents, usually the mother at the outset, in a clinical effort. The Drop-In Service, with its informality and open-endedness, seems to be a highly effective mechanism.

In general, group techniques with young parents appear to us to be the most productive. Troubled parents can hear from each other with much less transference overloading than from a therapist.

In spite of parental sensitivity, we believe that we should not be too hesitant nor wait too long in pressing parents to use clinical help when we conclude that it is necessary. Indeed, parents often seem relieved once told in a clear and noncritical way that they need such help. One of the most dismaying findings in the therapeutic nursery school in our Division as well as in our parenting services has been that parents have often been told to "wait and see" by professionals to whom they had turned for help.

We have come to realize how difficult it is to bring the availability of our services to the awareness of young parents. In addition to finding ways to provide appropriate publicity, resistances to using mental health facilities need to be circumvented. Indeed, a number of parents who call in are determined to keep their identity hidden, presumably out of shame or embarrassment. This confirms for us the belief that for many parents, a telephone Warm-Line, with its built in anonymity, is the only way that many parents would be able to make contact with mental health resources.

Aside from resistances to using mental health help, the problem of publicizing the existence of service is a formidable one. We have used public service radio announcements and have arranged for periodic newspaper releases and even small newspaper ads. In each of these we have placed heavy emphasis on the idea that our service is for "normal worries" of parents in relation to their *normal* babies, toddlers, and preschool age children. The greatest numbers of phone-ins have resulted from articles that include the fact that we are also doing *research* on the usefulness of telephone help. Resistance to calling seems lessened if parents feel part of a research program.

We realized from these experiences that distribution of a "mental health checklist" which parents can use as a guide for deciding whether they ought to call in on the Warm-Line could be useful. The checklist we have devised is appended to this chapter. We have distributed it in various ways—through nursery schools, physicians' offices, and supermarket handouts. Response in just a few months of its distribution is promising. Disseminating a mental health checklist in this way means that we are placing the responsibility for helping parents with early prevention of emotional and psychological problems where it belongs, namely, on the mental health profession.

FOLLOW-UP AND ASSESSMENT

To date, we have not had opportunity to carry out detailed follow-up of more than a few of our Warm-Line cases. At the 1973 meeting of the American Orthopsychiatric Association we presented a follow-up study related to the brief services for parents of preschool children and infants provided by our Division of Child Psychiatry (347).

In that study 26 families were contacted for follow-up, and we learned that the brief clinical intervention was felt to be of positive significance by 80% of the parents. More data need to be reviewed relative to how the Warm-Line callers feel about their experience.

SUMMARY

We have described a telephone "Warm-Line" for parents of children under the age of 5 years as an example of a primary prevention unit in a Division of Child and Family Psychiatry in a Mental Health Center. We have reviewed its origin and staffing and have provided some case examples. We have made some assertions about the optimal surrounding clinical services in which a primary prevention unit such as Warm-Line should function. Knowledge about early development, skill in providing supportive help to parents, and competence in family diagnosis are essential staff prerequisites. We have noted the value of having a progression of clinical services available for parents of young children. Given such a progression, the Warm-Line functions as both a direct service and a case finding resource. For about half of the parents who call, further service is not indicated. For the others the additional clinical programs are necessary. We have also included an example of a mental health checklist for parents and asserted our belief that it is time that mental health professionals take responsibility for guiding parents of very young children. We believe that such preventive services as the Warm-Line can play a significant role in avoiding the mental health emergencies that often occur when immediate help is not available to deal with crises in child development and parent-child relationships.

THALIANS FAMILY AND CHILD GUIDANCE UNIT
P. O. Box 48750
Los Angeles, CA   90048

Parenting Research Checklist for Children from Birth to Age 5

It is not uncommon for parents of infants and young children to be concerned about their child's growth and development, both physically and emotionally, and about their roles as parents. We are conducting a research program on how parents can be helped over the telephone by professionals who are experts in CHILD and FAMILY DEVELOPMENT. By responding to this checklist you will be assisting our research, and, in turn, find we may be of some assistance to you. If you call, or request a call from us, you will be able to consult by telephone, in confidence, with a trained professional in the field of Child Development. (We do *not* answer medical questions.) We are a nonprofit organization; there is no fee or obligation to you.

Please check those boxes that apply to you:

I worry about my child's	Never	Sometimes	Often	Very Much
Crying	___	___	___	___
Sleeping habits	___	___	___	___
Eating	___	___	___	___
Toilet habits	___	___	___	___
Intelligence	___	___	___	___
Obedience	___	___	___	___
Nervousness	___	___	___	___
Anger	___	___	___	___
Tantrums	___	___	___	___
Moodiness	___	___	___	___
Ability to have fun	___	___	___	___
Motor coordination (rolling over, sitting, crawling, walking)	___	___	___	___
Overactivity	___	___	___	___
Getting sick often	___	___	___	___
Relationships with other children or siblings	___	___	___	___
Jealousy	___	___	___	___
Other (please specify)				

At some time or another, parents may find themselves checking an item(s) in the last two columns. If you have, you may want to call us. (Of course, you may call at any time for any reason.) We are the **WARM-LINE**, and our number is *652-3122*. When you do call, or mail this request for a call from us, let us know the most convenient time for you to talk, day or evening.

PARENTS' NAME_____ TELEPHONE_____

CHILD'S BIRTHDATE_____SEX_____

BEST TIME TO CALL BACK_____

35

REDEFINING AND PREVENTING MENTAL HEALTH EMERGENCIES IN THE SCHOOLS

Elaine Rose
Terry L. Paulson

Mental health crises always occur within a context, and one of the most far-reaching contexts for crisis is our school system. The crisis extends beyond the "identified problem students" to the institution itself—to the community pressures, demand for accountability, and widespread budget and personnel cutbacks. One of the goals of a mental health consultant is to help educators facilitate growth in light of such crises. Prevention of mental health emergencies occurs when individuals and institutional systems are able to cope with crisis constructively. Each decision point can be seen as a crisis, one that admittedly varies in importance and scope. The process of institutional growth through crisis occurs when participants recognize and respond to the communication of felt needs. The parallel process of personal growth through crisis can be seen as getting in touch with, owning, and acting on one's thoughts, feelings, and opinions. Frequently, this process, whether institutional or individual, necessitates the development of new alternatives for crisis resolution. Helping educators to use their own resources and expertise to explore such alternatives and to expand their ability for that utilization is the concern of this chapter.

In spite of the many referrals for mental health treatment, the majority of "problem children" in the schools remain divorced from mental health contact until, in the moment of crisis, community inconvenience and pressure brings them to the attention of mental health agencies. The mental health consultant is most often viewed as an "emergency fixer."

Educators are often quick to refer in time of crisis, overlooking the potential of their natural rapport with, and emotional significance for, their students.

A PILOT PROJECT

The pilot project discussed in this chapter was designed to help the school staff define the singular problem they were facing as an example from a category of problems. The "acting-out," 8-year-old bully terrorizing his classmates represents a certain type of developmental configuration which every elementary teacher can expect to meet at some time in her classroom. Likewise, the underachieving gifted high school student who withdraws from the school milieu is one expression of predictable adolescent conflict. This conflict, when redefined through the consultation process, identifies the student's flight as one part of his struggle with emerging adulthood. Educators then can either use already acquired skills to identify and resolve such problems or learn additional and alternative skills through the use of the consultant's expertise.

With this approach, school personnel are taught to identify and assess individual behavior in a framework they can comprehend. In summary, the organizing principle of the consultations discussed has a twofold thrust. The necessary first step is to develop an awareness of student mental health needs and possible crisis experiences. Based on this awareness, the staff is encouraged to recognize their potential as positive change agents for the prevention of emergencies.

The authors' consultations in secondary and elementary school settings occurred in the Los Angeles area. All consultations were approached in light of the felt crises as perceived by the teachers, counselors, and administrators involved. The first two examples given here deal with distinct yet complementary therapeutic approaches implemented in one elementary school consultation.

DEVELOPING AN APPROACH TO SPECIFIC PROBLEMS

The question, "How do you get these kids to talk?" is a common one shared by all elementary school teachers faced with silent classrooms when discussion is called for. In an attempt to confront just such a problem, teachers participating in an ongoing consultation with the authors developed total classroom contingencies designed to increase student verbalizations in discussion. The consultation structure provided a weekly seminar at the school; teachers who were interested and who committed themselves to the program received unit credit for their involvement (59). The goal of the technique presented was to facilitate and direct teacher attempts to train students to own their own thoughts, feelings, and opinions, and to judge the value of their statements without reference to how their statements compared to those of the teacher. The importance of positive and negative feedback by teachers was accepted; it does have an impact on student behavior, whether by chance or design. Overloaded teachers often provide immediate negative feedback for disruptive and inappropriate behavior; for example, "How many times do I have to tell you to pay attention, Michael?" "Will you sit still!" "We're waiting for you, John!" But they fail to respond as dramatically to the positive comments and questions. There is a tendency to pass off appropriate behavior with an "OK," a "Go on," or an "It's about time!" In the technique presented, teachers were asked to use a blue–red grading pencil and a pad of paper with paired verbal statements to provide immediate positive and negative feedback during an open-ended classroom rap session, in an effort to structure and redirect the teacher feedback and facilitate student expression of opinions and feelings.

An Elementary Class "Rap Group"

Members of Mrs. S's sixth grade class, when given the opportunity to engage in group discussion, often remained silent for long periods. Many students would lower their heads or look to other peers in hopes that they would begin. Mrs. S. had been taught to carry the ball, pressing students for answers, commenting on her feelings and opinions, making side suggestions for possible avenues of inquiry, and summing up each statement. Mrs. S., though popular with her students, was not pleased with her students' passivity and apathy during group discussion. She volunteered to try the blue–red pencil "gimmick" in an effort to facilitate their interaction. She was instructed to set the stage for the session by informing them of her expectations and rules of the game. She contracted with her students for an additional music appreciation period (where they would bring music of their own choice), the length of which would be determined by the number of blue marks over and above the red marks received. She was instructed to use an open-ended question to start the interaction and to avoid contributing her input. The scene she asked them to visualize was, "You're at home alone; there's a knock at the door; a man enters and with a smile informs you that you are the fortunate recipient of one million dollars. What would you do?" This dialogue ensued:

Mark: "A whole million dollars?" (Teacher makes a blue mark on the pad.)

Teacher: "Yes, a million dollars."

Mike: "Why'd you give him a blue mark?" (She gives another blue mark.)

Teacher: "For the same reason I gave you one; you asked for a statement of clarification. You wanted to make sure you had things straight."

Mark: "I'd buy a bike for me, a car for mom, and a bike for all my friends." (Teacher gives a blue mark for statement of opinion.)

Tom: "Not me. I wouldn't tell anybody,'cause they'd all be running after me for money. I'd buy a few things, but save most of it." (Teacher gives another blue mark for his opinion as presented.)

Teacher: "That's one way to handle it. I'm glad you expressed that."

Mike: "That's stupid! You always do dumb things!" (Teacher makes a red mark for an insulting aggressive statement without making a statement.)

Mark: "Quiet! Mike, you got a red mark!"

Mike: "What did I do?" (He receives a blue mark for a question of clarification.)

Teacher: "You were insulting Tom. You both have a right to your opinions, but to be different does not mean that one is right or wrong or stupid. The blue mark was for asking for clarification." (She turns to the rest of the class.) "How could Mike have handled it differently?"

Beverly: "He could have told us what he would do." (She receives a blue mark.)

Mike: "You know what I would do, I'd quit school. (Other kids laugh and the teacher makes a blue mark for the appropriate expression of an opinion.) With all that money I wouldn't have to go."

Beverly: "I'd still go, because I wouldn't have anything else to do. All my friends would be at school." (A blue mark was given.)

Teacher: "I think that's a good point."

John: (whispering to Jerry) "I'm captain today, do you want to be up second?" (Teacher quietly makes a red mark, then makes a second one before they are confronted by another member of the class.)

Tom: "John! Cut it out."

The conversation continued for 20 minutes. The class received 32 blue marks and 7 red ones, contributing ten minutes toward their music appreciation time on Friday. The teacher was pleased by the students' positive response and decided to make the program an ongoing part of her classroom schedule.

Dialogue with the Younger Child

Early on Tuesday morning the kindergarten children bounced into class with the usual amount of enthusiasm. Five minutes later, they were sitting on their rugs when Mrs. W. introduced her red and blue pencil. She showed the class a picture depicting a playground confrontation over access to some play equipment and asked for comment. She began by putting a blue mark on her paper as soon as the first child raised his hand and began to speak in reaction.

Mark: "I don't like that!" (Teacher makes a blue mark visible to the children.)

Teacher: "I like the way Mark raised his hand and shared his idea."

Bill: "I don't either." (Another blue mark is made.)

Teacher: "Neither one of you likes the picture; what is it that you don't like?"

Mark: "She was gonna play, 'n' they wouldn't let her!" (Blue mark)

Bill: "They were gonna hit her!" (Blue mark)

Teacher: "If that were you and they wouldn't let you play, how would you feel?" (She saw Judy's hand raised.) "Judy, how would you feel?"

Judy: "Very sad, 'cause I want to play." (Blue mark)

The discussion continued with the teacher giving blue marks for statements of feelings and opinions until Jeff interrupted the discussion.

Audrey: "I like playing—"

Jeff: (Loudly and defiantly in reaction to being hit by a distant neighbor with long arms) "My brother's gonna get you!"

Teacher: "I don't like that, Jeff; I'm going to have to make a red mark." (She calmly makes a red mark.) "You interrupted Audrey and threatened Bill. We don't threaten or interrupt; we listen and then let others know what we think and feel."

Jeff: "He hit me; he started it!" (He receives another red mark.)

She then asked the children to tell her what the red and blue marks stood for. The children's suggestions again resulted in blue marks. The young children were not involved with any contract for additional incentives; the immediate feedback of the visible blue and red marks indicating teacher approval was enough to maintain the children's interaction for an extended discussion period.

DISCUSSION

The mechanics of the program were quite simple and easily implemented by a teacher in a normal elementary classroom setting. The blue–red grading pencil was used to provide visible feedback to students involved in the rap group discussion. A blue mark by the teacher indicated an appropriate expression of a student's thoughts, feelings, or opinions concerning the subject under discussion. It might have been an expression of like or dislike, a suggestion, a statement of active disagreement, a question of clarification, or a statement of feeling. The teacher was asked to pair the giving of a blue mark with a positive statement of acceptance or understanding on her part. A red mark by the teacher indicated an inappropriate statement or outburst. During a discussion, the child might threaten, make a sarcastic statement, insult another child or the teacher, blame, call another names, interrupt while another was speaking, or carry on a side conversation. The teacher was asked to minimize verbal lectures for such inappropriate behavior to increase the probability of peer and self control, thus lightening some of the teacher's load.

The marks, besides providing individual feedback, were redeemable at a later time by the whole class for an activity reinforcer contracted for earlier. Teachers used a variety of reinforcers, all of which were desired by the students and within the acceptable limits set by the teachers. Examples of the contracted activities included additional music appreciation time, additional physical education time, and additional special arts and crafts time. Red marks were totaled and subtracted from the total of blue marks to determine the amount of reinforcer earned by the class during the discussion. The response–cost design was used to increase the probability of developing individual and group accountability, thus transferring some teacher-assumed responsibilities to the students.

It was equally important for teachers to set the stage for the classroom rap groups. This was divided into three aspects: a clear statement of the desired goal and rules of the game, a prior contract for a back-up activity reinforcer, and choice of an open-ended content area for discussion. Teachers were asked to make the rules of the game clear and to explain the meaning of the red and blue marks as well as giving examples of the behavior that would warrant them. It was stressed that a clear explanation of expectancies fosters the early learning of new behaviors. It was felt that students would have a tendency to find and express the "right" answer that they felt the teacher wanted to hear unless it was made clear that *any positive* student expression would be welcome. This clarification would indicate that new rules were operating in their discussion. Contracting for the back-up activity reinforcer was conducted with the entire class prior to the discussion; acceptable suggestions by the class were narrowed by student choice. The contract was written on the board and signed by the teacher and a student representative (for example, "I, Mrs. W., promise to provide 1 minute of additional music appreciation time on Friday afternoon for every three blue points earned over red marks earned during our class discussion. The students will choose the music for the additional time earned.") Finally, teachers were asked to choose an open-ended topic, one that indicated no one right or wrong answer. Any question, topic, picture, or saying that was open to a wide range of reactions was acceptable.

Teachers involved in the consultation seminar were given great latitude in making the technique their own. Teachers were asked to adapt the structure to their own strengths and styles while keeping in mind the importance of immediate differential feedback and the necessity of setting the stage for discussion. Many of the teachers' suggestions were incorporated in the program as applied in the classroom setting. Many of the skills required for this structured discussion experience were already available to the teachers involved. The consultants' task was to redirect and support the use of those very skills in the class discussion.

The program, although growing out of a need to facilitate classroom interaction, was designed to expand the decision-making potential of all the students involved. It was hoped that the growth achieved within the group discussion context would increase the possibility of functional coping on the part of those same students in response to crises arising outside the confines of the group. The prevention of mental health emergencies begins when individuals learn to cope constructively with even the smallest of crises.

Learning theory and its derivative techniques are often rejected on the grounds that they are dehumanizing and manipulative; the criticism is that man is approached as an "it," avoiding the unique human qualities of his existence. At one time or another we all have experienced ourselves as spontaneously sensing, feeling, thinking, choosing people. We like to affirm such a reality for our children. The thought of manipulating the context and consequences of our children's behavior in an effort to bring about a desired change creates an uncomfortable dissonance. Learning theory has little to say about the goals or direction of change desired; it does have much to say about facilitating movement in a chosen direction. To deny the responsibility of determining the consequences and contexts for a child's behavior does not alter the fact that such variables will have an impact on that behavior. The authors have presented what they feel was a creative integration of a learning theory approach with a humanistic mental health goal, that of increasing the ability for self-expression.

PSYCHODRAMATIC TECHNIQUES IN THE CLASSROOM

During the same elementary school consultation, the authors used psychodramatic techniques in an effort to increase the number of growth-enhancing options available to the teachers. Psychodrama was used for two purposes: conflict resolution and appropriate role rehearsal. The techniques were implemented at the kindergarten and third grade levels.

In the consultation seminar a kindergarten teacher expressed concern over the difficulty some of the children were having waiting in line to use the play equipment and her own discomfort with the techniques she was using to settle the ensuing squabbles. Psychodrama was discussed as a possible alternative approach in handling conflict resolution and in developing social sensitivity. Two sessions of the consultation were given over to psychodrama demonstration and experience. The consultant was then invited to demonstrate psychodrama in the kindergarten classroom. The consultant used a large picture, already in the classroom, showing children on a playground. The children were asked to act out the picture, first in pantomime and then with words, and then to talk about it. The entire procedure took about ten minutes.

The psychodramatic techniques allowed the children to identify with both the winner and loser in the picture without being in the heat of the battle. Alternative behaviors were explored and rehearsed in two sessions in the classroom. The teacher was later able to use simplified techniques (role rehearsal and role reversal) out on the playground and relate them back to the classroom experience. She found that an already provided picture series lent itself well to further use within the psychodramatic framework.

Psychodrama and the Problem Child

The third grade teacher, Mrs. B., brought the case of Andy to the attention of the consultation seminar. Andy was a bully on the playground, disrupting games and assaulting other children. He was large for his age and was an only child of middle-aged parents. He was well known to the other teachers and was increasingly becoming a problem child at the school. The possibility of using psychodrama was discussed and tried out in the seminar, with teachers enacting roles of the children involved in one of Andy's latest altercations. The focus again was placed on facilitating conflict resolution. After the role playing in the seminar, the teacher and the consultant agreed to try it in the classroom with Andy.

Using a classroom picture, the third grade class enacted a scene of a coach congratulating a winner, with two losers looking on. Volunteers spoke for the feelings of both the winner and losers. Suddenly Andy spoke out, "I'm such a loser!" This comment elicited much feeling from his classmates and set the stage for the rehearsal and reversal of the winner–loser roles, accompanied by exploration of feelings related to each role. The class was able to identify with the feelings of both. After the experience the teacher expressed to the consultant and to the other teachers her surprise that Andy was experiencing himself as a "loser" and her admiration that he was able to express that feeling. She felt her new attitude toward Andy was demonstrated in the course of their daily classroom interactions.

Discussion

Psychodrama has been insufficiently explored as a modality for working with children in nonclinical settings. The *in situ* reversal of roles allows children in conflict to experience each other's feelings and thus increase their social sensitivity. With increased sensitivity, children may practice and acquire more appropriate social skills through repeated role rehearsal. Practicing of alternative problem solutions allows children to broaden their awareness of options and to fit the situation with their personalities. Because all of this takes place in the context of play involving their peer group rather than an interviewing, teacher-to-child relationship, the entire group is able to see and empathize with both the protagonist and antagonist. All the children in the group are freed to experience a closer identification with each other, an initial step toward future closeness in relationships. Teachers who understand the prevalence of competitive feelings can use the individual immediate conflict situation to help students accept winner and loser roles. Teachers who already have experience in directing children's activities need minimal training to utilize these two psychodrama techniques and can do so within the normal classroom setting.

COMBINING PRIMARY AND SECONDARY PREVENTION AT THE HIGH SCHOOL LEVEL

A "leadership lab" for under-achieving "gifted" students was organized and led jointly by the school counselor and the mental health consultant. The twofold purpose of the program was: first, to train the counselor to conduct problem-oriented, communication-based groups; second, to help gifted students who volunteered to participate to identify and verbalize their concerns and difficulties within the school system, in an effort to match student needs and program offerings.

A new and harassed high school counselor, charged by the administration of one San Fernando Valley high school with "keeping kids in school" *and* keeping those qualified in the "gifted sequence," asked for consultation. He had been confronted by students, on the one hand, who found no "relevance" in any course work, and by teachers, on the other, who retreated to their most authoritarian stance under the students' attacks. All the participants in this almost daily occurrence experienced crisis.

In the process of a traditional mental health consultation,* the consultant and the counselor/consultee jointly worked out a proposal for a "leadership lab" for students identified as gifted; the lab was approved by the administration on an experimental and voluntary basis.

The counselor invited ten students who had declined to participate in "gifted" courses, and had instead enrolled in courses labeled "basic," to join the leadership lab that met weekly during the school day on a noncredit basis. These students were attending school sporadically and were involved in other acting-out behavior. The purpose described to the students was to help them develop their communication skills and to air their school concerns. An additional goal, as defined by the consultant and the consultee, was to train the latter to lead a problem-solving, communication-based group.

An Experience with Psychodrama

Led by the consultant and the consultee, the lab met for one semester. One of the main techniques used in the lab was psychodrama, through which students reenacted their difficult experiences with both administrators and teachers.

Tom: "Yesterday me and my buddy got sent to Mr. Clang for cutting again. Man, he's weird."

Barry: "Right on, man. Stay away from him!"

Consultant (C): "You've all had experiences with him, huh?"

Tom: "Yeah, you know he always has to be right, and ya can't say anything to him or he gets worse. But I know how to handle him so he knows what I think of him but he can't come back at me—so he just gets madder and madder. Mike argued back with him, but I just gave him hard looks."

C: "Would you be willing to show us how that went? It would be easier than explaining it."

Tom: "Whadda ya mean?"

C: "Well, how about picking someone to be Mr. Clang and someone to be Mike and you be you, and we'll do the whole scene as if it's just now happening. Then maybe we can either learn ways to be with Mr. Clang from your experience or figure out some other ways."

---

* Consultation was conducted under the auspices of the Los Angeles County Olive View Medical Center—Community Mental Health Adult Outpatient Clinic.

Barry: "Can I be ole Mr. Clang? I could really dig it."

Ray: "Yeah, and I'll be Mike, 'cause he and I do just the same."

Lisa: "What about us?"

C: "Well in this kind of scene we'll need some people who might think they know what somebody's feeling but not saying, so if you get that idea anytime while this is going on, you just get up and stand behind the person and say what you think as if you were them. Then if it fits, you can stay with them, but if it doesn't, they have the right to tell you so and you have to sit down. We call that doubling. Let's start; you'll see how it works. Tom, where did all this happen?"

Tom: "Where it always happens, in the V.P.'s (vice principal) office."

C: "OK, let's fix this up to look like the office. You take charge. What was there? Desk, chairs, what?"

Tom: "Well, let's see. Yeah, desk here." (C pushes table over to be desk in designated spot.) "Chairs here and here. OK."

C: "And where were you?"

Tom: "Me and Mike was waiting out in the waiting room for over half an hour."

C: "OK, we're starting when he comes out to get you, right?"

Tom: "Yeah."

C: (To Barry) "You know how he acts?"

Barry: "Watch this!" (In assumed voice) "So it's you again! I'm certainly getting tired of seeing you—and you, too! What is it this time? Come in here. Well, come on—I haven't got all day to spend with you jokers, what have you done now?"

C: (Interrupting as boys get up) "Tom, is that the right feeling? I don't care about the words, but does he have the right feeling?"

Tom: "Sure, but the words are important 'cause the first thing he said after we got in was—" (C interrupts.)

C: "OK, you show Barry, change places. Barry, you be Tom. Now, Tom, you'll be Mr. Clang." (Boys change places.)

Tom: (As Mr. Clang) "Look at you! Dirty pants—hair down to here." (Gesturing broadly) "If you'd dress right and cut your hair, you could stay out of trouble." (Out of character) "Now he don't have no right to—"

C: "OK, wait now; you're not being Mr. Clang. Let's see what you and

Mike did. Change back. Did you get the idea, Barry?" (Boys exchange.)

Barry: "Know it by heart." (Repeats Tom's words, adding own variations.)

Tom: (Sits, looks at Mr. Clang—says nothing, but stares.)

Barry: (As Mr. Clang, hesitates, goes on more rigidly.) "What can we expect from someone who looks like you? I'm going to have to give you a week's suspension."

Tom: (Sits—glares silently.)

Barry: (As Mr. Clang) "Maybe 2 weeks suspension." (Shifting in seat) "Kids like you don't appreciate what we do for you."

C: "Barry, are you having some feelings while this is going on?"

Barry: "Hey, yeah."

C: "OK, let's back up to where you started with the hair bit. Only this time say what you're feeling, and, Tom, are you having some feelings while you're sitting there?"

Tom: "Sure, but ya can't let him know."

C: "Well, he's not here now, so would you be willing to let us know? I'm not saying you have to ever let him know."

Tom: "Well (pause), I dunno."

C: "OK, you do just what you did before, and, Barry, this time you give us your feelings and (to group) if anyone thinks of some now, get up and help Barry."

Barry: (Repeats words.)

Tom: (Sits and stares.)

Barry: "Why don't you answer me? You're making a fool out of me. You can't do that to me. I'll show you, I'll threaten you with worse stuff."

Tom: (Sits and stares.)

Barry: "I've got to get to you. I feel like my power's being challenged."

Gail: (Raising hand) "I think he feels—"

C: "Go on up, Gail. He'll tell you if you're right."

Gail: (Stands by Barry.) "You're making me feel helpless, and that makes me mad."

Barry: "Wow! Yeah!"

Tom: (Exploding) "But I feel helpless all the time here. What am I supposed to do! That Goddamn motherfucker gets you for one thing and brings everything else in."

C: "OK, so that's it, then. It seems like everyone in this scene feels helpless. Now is there any way to deal with Mr. Clang or is it also hopeless?"

Barry: "Hey, you know, I never knew how Mr. Clang felt or why, but I think I've got an idea. But, Tom, you can't just sit and stare; boy, that really gets to me!"

Tom: (Grinning) "Yeah, see, that's why I do it."

The group went on for the rest of the hour exploring feelings that precipitate behaviors and behaviors that evoke feelings. They decided to spend the next session trying some of the alternative ways of interacting with Mr. Clang that they had thought of.

Discussion

Psychodrama's action orientation fit the needs of this antiestablishment adolescent group. Students who were reluctant to "talk about" enthusiastically "acted about" their feelings and conflicts with adult authority as personified in particular administrators.

In the wrap-up period of the psychodrama, the students were able to begin to form relationships with their new counselor based on their newly acquired perceptions of her as a person, rather than stereotyping her by role. When the counselor first entered the group she experienced a loss of role identification, with a resulting high degree of anxiety, that centered on the issues of performance and self-expectation. She experienced herself as a student rather than a teacher in front of her students. Her wish that students would not see her outside of her role was countered by the students' positive response to her very real person.

From the beginning of the semester, all students who attended (8 of the 10 completed the sessions) expressed surprise that the administration would offer such a "class." At the end of the semester, half the group signed up for new course offerings in the "gifted" program for the following school year. Some of these new courses were developed from the proposals made by the group. One of the students accepted a referral for therapy in the consultant's clinic. All wanted to continue with the lab another semester.

As a result of this experimental, voluntary project, the school administration decided to offer three leadership lab courses for credit in the following school year to those students identified by counselors as both able and willing to participate in such a group. It was further decided to enlarge the project to include students outside the "gifted" program. The proposal was presented and accepted as a vehicle for exploring student age-appropriate issues with those in authority. The course instructors were to be counselor–consultant teams; all teams were to meet for group consultation. The purpose of the experimental group and of the credit course model was to make possible the training of school personnel to take over entirely the role of group leader in an ongoing, school-validated group, offering educators and students a place to examine and resolve the students' school-related problems.

SUMMARY

While counselors in this school had formerly spent their time and ability focusing only on curriculum-advising and programing, they were constantly discomfited by student demands which revealed needs for other kinds of services. They passed this discomfiture on to the mental health consultant by making "crisis referrals" of troublesome pupils. Concurrently, the administration was searching for the most expedient and efficient use of counselor time in a system which was suffering personnel cutbacks. The administration proposed a series of fragmented assignments (counseling combined with curriculum programing) that were unacceptable to the counselors. The use of counselor time for more "holistic" counseling was finally seen as viable by all concerned.

By initially addressing the need of an individual counselor's request for emergency mental health consultation, the consultant stimulated and became involved in a pilot project which resulted in a gradual shift in the system. The single emergency, redefined by the consultant, was now viewed as an example of a class of problems in the school system.

In a beleaguered atmosphere, identifying a specific crisis as an example of a class of recurring predicaments helps participants to examine their own skills and seek new skills for the resolution of the crisis. Whether dealing with the individual or the institutional system, efforts were made by the consultation project to move beyond the crisis situation in order to facilitate growth through the discussion of viable alternatives. In all the examples presented, educators were able to expand their role expectations to include human relations and mental health functions as defined in the course of ongoing consultation. Specific techniques for the development of communication skills, social sensitivity, and conflict resolution were added to their professional repertoires. Discrete aspects of learning theory and psychodrama were transposed from the clinical to the educational setting through the collaborative work of the consultants and the consultees.

Both mental health and school professionals involved in this pilot project believe that further development and extension of this preventive consultation program shows promise of reducing the incidence of school system crises as well as crisis referrals of individual pupils to local mental health clinics.

36

MARITAL SEPARATION
AND DIVORCE

assessment of and preventive considerations for crisis intervention

Gerald F. Jacobson
Stephen H. Portuges

Crisis theory teaches us that crisis follows a hazard which represents a significant loss or threat of loss (60, 260, 339). We therefore expect, and indeed we find, that the impending or actual dissolution of a marriage and its sequelae account for a significant number of the individuals who use the services of a crisis intervention clinic. In the context of this discussion, the term *separation* refers to a separation from a marital partner, rather than to that involved in any other type of relationship. The experiences described here involved individuals undergoing various stages of marital separation and divorce who received crisis help at the Benjamin Rush Centers for Problems of Living in Los Angeles (193, 194, 195), and at the Southern California Center for Problems of Living in Santa Barbara. Clinical experiences and some formulations regarding marital disruption are discussed, as are some of the preventive treatment techniques that were found helpful in its management. This information has also led to the development of a more formal research project, now in progress, that will attempt to differentiate between adaptive and maladaptive ways of resolving various aspects of the separation-divorce process, with special emphasis on suicide potential.

BACKGROUND OF THE PROBLEM

There is a striking tendency in psychiatric literature to treat divorce as a homogeneous status variable and to overlook the *process* whereby persons

NIMH Grant 5 RO1 MH21863-02, *Relation of Suicide to Marital Separation and Divorce.*

terminate a marital relationship. This oversight is reflected in a number of ways; research articles suggest that psychiatric morbidity is higher among separated and divorced persons (43, 54, 274, 299, 305), and many clinical publications regard divorce as a reflection of underlying neurotic problems (34). Neither of these trends takes into account what we consider to be a critical factor in adjustment to divorce: the *quality* of such adjustment is related to the *process* by which the marital relationship is ended, that is, the more adaptive the resolution of marital dissolution dilemmas, the better the subsequent psychosocial performance.

There is ample evidence to indicate that the process of separation and divorce is highly stressful; Goode's study of 426 divorced women revealed that distress was reported highest at the time of the actual separation (151). That such stress has a major impact on subsequent functioning is shown in the work of Holmes and Rahe (186), and Rahe, et al. (336). These investigators have scaled several significant life events according to their degree of impact and amount of required readjustment. Among the items on their life change scale, divorce ranks second only to the loss of a spouse through death. Subsequent studies have confirmed this relationship between such life events and psychiatric impairment (3, 74, 172, 186, 384, 388, 414), and while this underscores the potential impact of marital dissolution, it tells us little about why some persons do *not* suffer depressed psychological performance, even though divorced. Our contention is that the variation in outcomes is understandable only by observing persons as they move through the transition from being separated to being divorced, and to note the quality of the resolution of the separation-divorce process. These observations can then be related to adjustment after divorce.

In our work at the Benjamin Rush Center, we have learned to regard each of several naturally occurring events in the marital dissolution process as potential emotional hazards. These events include *a*) the first serious mention of a marital separation, *b*) the actual separation, and *c*) receiving the final decree. The occurrence of any of these marriage-threatening events may precipitate a crisis; that one or more of them always occurs when a marriage ends renders the marital dissolution process a veritable matrix of potential crises. While poor resolution of any one of these crises may well lead to psychiatric impairment, adaptive resolutions may result in improved functioning. The role of the intervenor is clearly to aid persons in finding adaptive resolutions to the problems posed by a dissolving marriage or by one threatened with termination.

THE THREAT OF MARITAL DISSOLUTION

Persons frequently enter treatment as a result of active marital conflict, and treatment begins by focusing on the most recent event which led the person to seek help. In a number of instances, this event involves a threat to the continuation of the marriage. When such a threat exists, it becomes the focus of the intervention. While this seems an obvious point for crisis intervenors, it is often overlooked. The person in crisis may, for example, present the reason for seeking aid as one which involves long-term difficulties in the marriage. He or she may ask for marriage counseling. By presenting the issue in this manner, the person in crisis avoids the more urgent immediate issue of the threat to the marriage. Therapists may also fall into the same trap. Technically, one can avoid this pitfall by responding to the recital of long-term problems with the question, "Why now?" Why is help sought when the long-term problems have been coped with more or less successfully for years? Putting the matter in these terms will then elicit the marital threat when it exists.

Once having identified the event which brings the person in at this time, we ascertain whether there are antecedents that give special meaning to the threatening event. Typically, two types of antecedents turn up: those which are located outside of the marital dyad, and those which are centered in the marital relationship itself.

An External Threat

Changes in the relationship to one's children illustrate antecedents external to the marital dyad. In long marriages one finds that marital balance may be upset when children grow up and leave home. In other instances, serious illness, injury, or death of a child may result in a threat to the marriage.

In younger couples we look above all to changes in the relationship with members of the original family as possible antecedents of marital breakup. One of the key elements in a marriage is the renegotiation of one's earlier family relations with concomitant reawakening of earlier conflicts. Unresolved separation problems from parents may exist and may be intensified by significant changes in the life of the younger couple, e.g., the birth of a child. Becoming a mother may intensify the need of a young wife for her own mother; under such circumstances failure of the wife's mother to respond may result in increased demands on the husband with resulting marital strain if he is unable to meet these demands, perhaps due to unresolved separation problems of his own.

In other cases, changes in one or both of the parents of the young couple may precipitate marital conflict. For example, a couple came to a crisis intervention center with nonspecific complaints about each other that did not appear to explain their serious consideration of divorce. Exploration of any recent changes in the dyadic relationship yielded no results. However, it became apparent that marital stress had immediately followed the announcement by the wife's widowed mother that she would remarry. This event stirred up unresolved emotional issues in the young wife in regard to the mother and to the death of the father, which she in turn expressed in the form of marital dissatisfaction. The intervenor clarified this sequence of events to the young couple, and gave them an opportunity to express their feelings about the remarriage of the wife's mother, and to differentiate their response to that event from matters relating to one another. By the end of the intervention, that couple had decided not to separate.

An Internal Threat

Sometimes, however, despite rigorous pursuit of a recent event signaling change, one finds only gradual deterioration of the marriage. This deterioration does not represent the immediate hazard for which people come to a crisis intervention center, but rather the impending separation itself. The couple realizes that the situation as it exists is no longer tolerable, but the threat of no longer having the partner is a major hazard in that it presents a situation for which coping mechanisms are not available. Accordingly, it is subsequent to this hazard that a crisis develops.

Potential Outcomes

The crisis intervenor should be aware of the possible outcomes of the situation involving potential marital separation and divorce. We consider that there are three of these: 1) a continuation of the marriage with a return to the previous level of equilibrium, or possibly a better one; 2) a "clean" separation, and 3) a "stable-unstable" equilibrium. The first two of these are self-explanatory. The third is a frequently seen and sometimes maladaptive resolution. The couple neither commits itself to separation nor to reconciliation; rather, the relationship remains in limbo while both maneuver for coping mechanisms which will enable them to come to more definite resolutions. Such a situation can be stable over a period of several weeks to months but is often unstable in the long run.

A typical stable-unstable equilibrium was seen in an older married couple who had divorced then remarried, and had also had numerous separations. While this couple was being seen in a crisis clinic, the wife moved out of the house into a nearby apartment, leaving the husband with the children. Neither filed for divorce nor, despite the pleadings of the husband, did the family reunite. Through the aid of the intervenor a somewhat more stable situation was attained where all concerned accepted that the situation would be as it was at least for the immediate future.

In other instances the interaction during the stable-unstable period is more destructive. Frequently, one or both partners continue to provoke each other for a period of several months. Such provocation may represent an attempt to escape the responsibility of being the one who takes the final step toward separation and divorce, a need to continue neurotic gratification in the relationship, or a wish to avoid the pain of separation. In one such case the husband stated to the wife that he was agreeable to a separation but that she would have to leave the house and leave him with the children. She replied that while she did not love him she would not take such a step and would therefore continue in the marriage.

Approaches to Management

Management of the situation of impending marital separation and divorce makes use of the usual crisis intervention techniques for clarifying to the person what his previous coping had been and why it had failed. In cases of the slowly deteriorating marriage, the needs that the marriage has met are pointed out, as well as the manner in which it is now failing to meet the needs. The advantages and disadvantages of separation or reconciliation should be identified. The intervenor must discuss the need to face and work through grief if a separation should occur. The opportunity must be afforded the person in crisis to explore these highly charged matters in a nonjudgmental and supportive setting.

In situations where events external to the marital couple were involved in precipitating the potential breakup, these events should be outlined by the therapist and their impact on the marriage delineated. This clarification will help determine the extent to which issues outside of the marriage, such as children or parents, contribute to current problems. When this *is* the case, resolution of the external issues may under some circumstances be more adaptive than marital breakup.

We find it helpful to share with the patient at a proper time the three possible alternatives outlined previously. This is particularly true when there is a stable-unstable situation and when the individual may not be aware of that fact. We must recognize, however, that many couples may elect the stable-unstable solution, and that the major contribution of the crisis consultant lies in allowing people to face honestly what they are doing. In addition, there is significant preventive work that can be done in relation to the children, particularly in instances where children feel guilty about the possible separation and divorce or become involved as pawns between the parents. Under these circumstances one can clarify how the children are being used, and the parents can be helped to deal with the problem without scapegoating or otherwise displacing the marital conflict onto the children.

It should go without saying that advice as to whether or not a separation is indicated is *not* the task of the crisis intervenor. The individual may well come to the crisis intervenor with that expectation, and it is often hard to know whether he or she consciously or unconsciously wishes permission to stay in the marriage or to leave it. Often some game that is being played with an actual or imaginary parent is repeated with a crisis consultant. It is important to be aware of this and to make it very clear that the responsibility for actual decision about the separation lies with the individual.

It is similarly important that professionals look at prejudices that they themselves may have regarding either marriage or divorce. Until recently divorce was not socially respectable, and some therapists in crisis clinics did poorly with people in the throes of possible separation and divorce because they did not recognize that divorce could be a constructive solution for some individuals. Aiding the person in finding the most adaptive level of coping of which he or she is capable is our task, whether this involves the maintenance or termination of the marriage.

RECENT SEPARATION AND/OR DIVORCE

The events immediately following a separation are highly meaningful and account for a significant number of persons seen in crisis intervention centers. The more sudden a separation is and/or the more its possibility was denied by one or both of the partners, the more intense the crisis that follows the separation is likely to be. An example is that of a woman who precipitously left her husband with whom she had been living on the East Coast without any preceding discussion of separation or divorce. She traveled across the country to California where she experienced a brief psychotic episode during which she was seen at a crisis intervention center. The intervenor related her acute disturbance to the intense conflict around the sudden change in her marital relationship. Her psychosis cleared, and she chose not to return to her husband, at least for the time being.

Potential Outcomes

The potential outcomes of recent separation and divorce are exactly the same as those of potential separation and divorce. One must be very careful to determine if one is dealing with a separation that is likely to be permanent, or a temporary one that might result in reconciliation. In many cases, intervenors have made the error of assuming that a separation is final when actually a state of vacillation between separation and reconciliation exists. We differentiate between these possibilities by a careful examination of the relationship. During the first and each subsequent interview, the frequency and nature of the contacts between the spouses should be carefully elicited. When indicated, the contacts are reviewed day by day, and even hour by hour. We inquire into contacts in person, by phone, by mail, and through intermediaries such as children or friends. Parenthetically, we find that mental health professionals tend to be reluctant to ask about such matters in detail. This reluctance may be due to a concern about being too active, but in our view seems more likely to indicate a tendency to join the person in crisis in avoiding the painful issue of separation.

In the event that the separation is likely to be permanent, management is similar to that of bereavement and of other separations: recognition and expression of appropriate grief, elicitation and acceptance of the anger at the lost partner, and careful work on new coping mechanisms which can lead to the establishment of other significant relationships. Support of family members is often helpful under these circumstances, and family consultations in the service of obtaining such support are sometimes appropriate.

If there is a situation of intermittent separation, we may diagnose a stable-unstable balance and deal with the individual in terms of the possibilities, hopes, or fears of reconciliation, as well as the possibilities, hopes, and fears of a separation. It is important to note that working through of grief cannot occur so long as there is considerable interaction between the spouses and/or significant hope of reconciliation. However, other affects, such as fear or anger, may be intense. The intervenor should provide an atmosphere in the therapeutic setting which is conducive to the expression of these feelings, without encouraging their indiscriminate expression elsewhere.

Special Points of Consideration

There is one topic which the intervenor should avoid–review of what went wrong with the marriage. Such a review is often very tempting to both the client and the intervenor alike because it avoids the painful issues which attend separation and divorce. Moreover, emphasis on what has gone wrong often tends to lower the already impaired self-esteem of a person in a marital separation-divorce crisis and may exacerbate depression. Marriage counseling is indicated if, and only if, there is a commitment by both partners to "make a go" of the marriage. Marriage counseling is a separate treatment modality from crisis intervention during separation and divorce.

The highly important possibility of suicide in situations involving marital separation and divorce must always be kept in mind. The indicators of suicidal outcome are of special concern in the previously mentioned research.

CRISES FOLLOWING DIVORCE

Statistics indicate that more than one half of all divorced individuals eventually remarry. During the interim there are several characteristic points where new crises may occur. The first of these occurs when the decree of divorce is granted. There is clinical evidence that the granting of a final decree is an important psychological event. Conscious or unconscious hopes for reconciliation are dashed, and the realization that the marriage is finally over hits with renewed force. Consequently, reactions seen at the original separation may again be observed.

Once divorce has occurred, the most typical adjustment involves repeopling one's world. Such activity includes renewing familiar ties, renegotiating friendships, and reestablishing sexual relations. Social organizations may also be an important factor for the formerly married. Especially in urban areas, commercial and noncommercial groups offer social activities which provide coping resources. Crises may occur when previously available supports of this nature are no longer available. Such crises are more likely to occur if the grief over the original separation is not worked through sufficiently. In these cases, the consultant must point out that the unresolved issues involving the earlier separation have made the current matter more hazardous. An illustrative example is the middle-aged man who entered treatment after the termination of a relationship with a woman that had lasted only 3 weeks. His severe depression reflected his previous denial of the significance of the loss of his 23-year marital relationship.

REMARRIAGE

The issue of remarriage is a very broad one and can be mentioned only briefly here. As with other forms of heterosexual involvement, remarriage involves a working through of the loss of previous marriage with all of its old themes, as well as the infantile themes that involve both the original marriage and the remarriage. A factor greatly complicating both dating and remarriage involves relationships with children. Oedipal conflicts that can be handled with varying degrees of difficulty in the original family become greatly exacerbated in the presence of stepparents and stepchildren. For remarriage to be successful, considerable maturation on the part of both partners is involved, and meaningful working through of the original separation and divorce is a necessity.

The handling of marital conflicts in remarriage has many of the elements of the handling of marital conflicts at any time. However, events relating to the former marriage should always be considered. For example, it is not at all uncommon for problems with children from a former marriage to become acute at the time of remarriage of one of the parents. The intervenor should consider that disturbances in the children could be related to either their reaction to the remarriage of one of the parents, and/or to the reaction of the other spouse who uses the children to express his or her response to the spouse's remarriage. Clarification of such a series of events can often be very helpful.

SUMMARY

This synopsis of preventive intervention strategies with persons in the process of marital dissolution and in the period after divorce underscores the manner in which unresolved issues of the former are reflected in the problems of the latter. It should also serve to focus the efforts of crisis consultants in assessing the echoes of past events as they are manifest in current crises.

37

CRISIS INTERVENTION IN ACUTE BEREAVEMENT

a controlled study of primary prevention

Paul R. Polak, Donald J. Egan,
Richard L. VandenBergh, Vail Williams

Community mental health programs have placed an increasing emphasis on prevention, and crisis intervention has played a key role in these preventive programs. In spite of this important direction in clinical practice, little controlled research has been carried out to test either the efficacy of crisis intervention techniques or the ability of preventive programs to actually prevent psychiatric problems. An overview is given here of a 4-year random assignment study in Denver, Colorado, of families experiencing the sudden death of a family member and treated with crisis intervention techniques. Follow-up data are compared with those from two untreated control groups. Treatment was provided by an intervention team, and outcome was measured by an independent research assessment team.

Crisis states have often been pinpointed as opportune points of focus for preventive mental health programs (63). A number of researchers have found that individuals experience a significant increase in the risk of morbidity and mortality within the first year after the death of a family member (315, 346). The present study provided preventive crisis services to families after a sudden death to test the hypothesis that such intervention would decrease the incidence of psychiatric or physical illness, and social disturbance.

Research supported by NIMH Grant ROI MH 15867.

CRISIS INTERVENTION IN ACUTE GRIEF

Intervention began when intervention team members accompanied the medical examiner of the Denver County Coroner's Office to the home of the surviving family members, usually within 1 to 2 hours after the death. The first meeting with the family lasted from 1 to 6 hours, and intervention techniques varied from arranging supervision for children to assisting in notification of relatives and facilitating grief work.

The natural process of grief experienced by individuals during the initial hours after a sudden death was fluctuating and cyclical. Periods during which a recently bereaved widow would withdraw to lie down and rest, for example, alternated with intense hysterical sobbing when deep feelings of grief, guilt, and anger might be open for discussion.

Families were seen for 2 to 6 sessions over a period of 1 to 10 weeks; the intervenors used crisis intervention techniques within a social systems framework (326). Treatment focused on increasing the effectiveness of the family in coping with feelings, decisions, and problems of adjustment related to the death (260). Intervention took place within the boundaries and values of the social system in its natural setting rather than by following a formal psychotherapeutic format. Therapeutic telephone interactions were employed regularly and frequently.

Patterns of Relationship

The intervention team observed three patterns of relationship among families coping with sudden death and societal values (421). The first type of family incorporated the societal values of middle America whereby death, like aging, is viewed with suspicion and fear; the body is not to be touched; decorum is to be maintained, and an aseptic approach is definitely preferred. These families deferred to morticians, ministers, physicians, and other experts in keeping with implicit mass media messages that families are unqualified to deal with death, and that outside experts should be consulted. In place of the closely knit, extended family of 50 years ago, these independent nuclear families had social club and professional memberships. Being so accustomed to experts and professionals, they tended to accept crisis services at the time of bereavement, and in the opinion of the crisis intervention team, treatment seemed most effective with this group.

A second type of family dealt with death according to its own values, regardless of the values of society as a whole. These families tended to be surrounded by clearly competent friends and neighbors, and functioned with ease and grace at the time of a death. The body was often touched and wept over freely. Children were not shunted aside, but encouraged to cry, laugh, and play in their usual manner. With these families the intervenors, although welcome, seemed superfluous, and intervention did not seem to make any major constructive contribution.

A third type of family had few or no contacts with either the extended family, social networks of friends and neighbors, or with clubs, ministers, or agencies. These socially isolated families often needed help the most but usually displayed great resistance to accepting it.

Effect of Decedent's Role On the Family

Members of the intervention team felt that the single most important factor in the reorganization of a family following a death was the role played by the decedent prior to the death (421). Instrumental roles, such as that of the breadwinner, for instance, became difficult to reallocate if the needed skills were lacking among surviving family members. On the other hand, expressive roles of the decedent that camouflaged or kept in balance an important family conflict, especially if such expressive roles were deviant or symptomatic, frequently led to a destructive family outcome after the death. Finally, when the role of the decedent placed a significant financial, social, or interpersonal burden on the family, but did not symbolize an important and otherwise unexpressed family conflict, the family often seemed to function better after the death.

RESEARCH EVALUATION

Design

The research design involved three subject groups: 1) an experimental group (E) made up of families receiving crisis intervention after a recent sudden death within the family; 2) a control group (C_1) of persons who received no crisis intervention following a recent sudden death; and 3) a control group (C_2) of families having no recent death and receiving no intervention. Each of these groups was assessed for outcome measures, at 6 and at 18 months after the death, by a research team independent from the intervention team. The families who experienced a recent sudden death within the family were randomly assigned into either E or the C_1 group. The C_2 group consisted of randomly selected families who had not experienced a sudden death within a 2-year period of time prior to contact. All groups were matched for age, socioeconomic status, education, and residential location (437).

Measurements

Outcome dimensions which were measured at 6 to 18 months after the death, were as follows:

1. *Medical illness*, measured by a health questionnaire consisting of the Cornell Medical Index (52), questions adapted from the Boston Bereavement Project (13), and overall health ratings made by a physician on the basis of direct interviews.

2. *Psychiatric illness*, measured by the MMPI (170), the Stirling County Questionnaire (12), and Beck's Depression Scale (31), as well as overall psychiatric illness ratings made by a psychiatrist after direct interviews with family members.

3. *Family functioning*, measured by the Winter and Ferriera unrevealed difference technique (120), as well as by the Bodin free drawing technique (44).

4. *Crisis-coping behavior*, measured by a questionnaire developed by the project staff to obtain stress levels relating to specific bereavement adjustment problems.

5. *Social cost*, estimated from knowledge of income before and after the death, expenses, and indirect costs.

In addition to these outcome measurements, a field approach was used to obtain qualitative and process-oriented data. Descriptions of the crisis intervention efforts were obtained by having the intervention staff report observations and fill out various Likert (258) and semantic differential scales about the treatment intervention. These scales were limited to the E group only. Finally, qualitative data were collected by the research psychiatrist and other research staff through interviews with each family in all three groups at the 6- and 18-month follow-up periods.

Data Analyses

Two major data analyses were used. An analysis of variance was conducted on the measures of outcome which allowed each individual and each family to be treated as a unit of measure. Comparison analyses were made between the E and C_1 groups, and between the combined E and C_1 groups and the C_2 group. This permitted comparison of the treated group with untreated controls as well as study of the impact of death itself by comparing the two groups in which death occurred (E and C_1) with the control group in which death did not occur (C_2). The C_2 group provided "base rates" for various incidences of medical and psychiatric illnesses as well as crisis-coping behavior. Results of this analysis are reported in Table 37.1.

The second major analysis conducted was a multivariate analysis designed to determine those variables which best distinguished individuals or families who experienced significant changes in social, physical, or mental functioning as a result of the death from those who did not. Three general clusters were hypothesized *a priori*: environmental variables, family or social system variables, and individual variables. It was hypothesized that environmental, social system, and individual clusters, either singly or in combination, would predict poor outcome. Preliminary work has been carried out in which individual items such as ratings of unexpressed feelings of hopelessness and despair, poor crisis-coping ability, and a history of somatization were used as predictors of poor outcome. Of the 13 subjects who developed a serious physical or emotional illness within 6 months of the death, 7 were predicted to do so ($P < .01$). It is anticipated that predictive accuracy will be improved when environmental and social system items are integrated with individual items in a combined predictive scale. Finally, detailed analyses are presently being made on the process and qualitative data in order to determine the impact of the present project on the bereavement system or subsystem.

RESULTS

The results reported here focus on 6-month outcome data in two areas: first, data which bear on the efficacy of crisis intervention as a technique for primary prevention; second, the effects of the crisis of sudden death on subsequent physical, mental, and social functioning.

Refusal Rates at Follow-Up

A total of 54 E cases were eligible for 6-month follow-up assessment, but of these, 10 families were dropped from the sample because they could not be contacted or had moved out of state. Of the 44 remaining cases, 7 (16%) refused to continue participation; thus, 37 (84%) were evaluated. In the C_1 group, a total of 122 cases were identified for assessment; 25 of these were dropped from the sample because they could not be contacted. Of the 97 that could be contacted, 65 (67%) agreed to be evaluated; 32 (33%) refused to participate. Finally, in the C_2 group, a total of 158 cases were selected for assessment. Forty-four of these families were dropped, either due to a death in the family within the 2-year period before contact, or due to inability to contact them, leaving a total of 114 cases that could be contacted. Of these, 57 (50%) were evaluated and 57 (50%) refused evaluation. A chi-square test revealed a significant difference ($X^2 = 17.6$; $P < .01$) between the groups on acceptance rates for follow-up evaluation. Families who experienced a severe crisis were more willing and open to sharing their experiences than the project staff initially expected.

Efficacy of Crisis Intervention in Primary Prevention

Preliminary data analysis of the 6-month follow-up evaluation strongly suggested that there were few differences between the bereaved families who received treatment and those who did not on the standard outcome measures of coping behavior, medical and psychiatric illness, and social functioning. The treatment group did tend to have a slightly lower depression score (Table 37.1).

TABLE 37.1. Analysis of Variance Comparisons of the 6-Month Outcome Follow-Up Data for Treatment and Nontreatment Groups

Outcome measurement	E group (mean)	C_1 group (mean)	F (ratio)	P value	Descriptive comments
Health questionnaires					
Cornell Medical Index	27.2	25.6	0.20		No significant difference between the groups in general physical health; E group reported more general illnesses and higher hospitalization rate for emotional disturbances
Medical rating					
before the death	1.21	1.17	0.02		
after the death	1.47	1.47	0.00		
Illness	1.36	1.13	9.13	<.01	
More frequent	1.22	1.10	3.99	<.05	
hospitalization for					
emotional illness	1.20	1.00	8.03	<.01	
Psychiatric					
MMPI (abnormal— normal)	1.51	1.70	3.90	<.05	MMPI showed the E group to be more socially withdrawn, worried, and depressed than the C_1 group (8–7 profile), a relatively significant number of more abnormal profiles, and generally poorer health
Sterling County	68.91	72.49	0.87		
Mood inventory	9.61	7.76	1.49		
Ten Best Questions	12.93	12.86	0.03		
Psychiatric ratings:					
before the death	2.02	1.57	3.43		
after the death	2.26	2.04	0.61		
W&F* spontaneous agreement					W&F* showed greater *spontaneous agreement* individually or as a family, and a higher *choice fulfillment* rate on an individual basis in the E group
individual	23.4	16.6	18.8	<.01	
family	63.1	22.6	24.8	<.01	
W&F* choice fulfillment					
individual	35.4	34.3	0.44		
family	127.8	95.1	10.25	<.01	

TABLE 37.1. *(continued)*

Bodin					
Family closeness perception	1.50	1.13	6.76	<.01	The E group exhibited a significantly greater distance in relations with individual family members, the family unit, and the decedent. The E group drawings revealed a wish to be more central to the family
Individual closeness perception	1.51	1.13	5.81	<.05	
Closeness to decedent	1.42	1.01	4.47	<.05	
Subject central figure	1.25	1.43	4.32	<.05	
Crisis coping at death					The E group experienced greater difficulty in dealing with family-related and social-oriented problems at the time of death relative to their *importance*; problems involving socializing produced greater *stress* and remained a problem after the death
Family					
import	22.7	15.7	5.06	<.05	
strain	17.8	12.8	3.18		
Social					
import	19.5	11.4	8.52	<.01	
strain	13.4	7.5	5.92	<.05	
Crisis coping at 6 months					
Social	16.9	11.3	4.23	<.05	
Social cost					At 6 months E group had higher living expenses than C_1 group (both before and after the death); the E group also had more indirect economic losses, although the cost of these losses did *not* differ significantly between groups
Gross income					
before the death	963.40	787.40	1.60		
after the death	701.8	605.0	0.85		
Expenses at 6 months					
before the death	2385.9	1456.7	8.85	<.01	
after the death	1842.7	1241.8	6.54	<.05	
Economic losses					
import	1.04	0.57	5.49	<.05	
cost	0.97	0.65	1.65		

* W&F = Winter and Ferriera

Effects of Sudden Death on
Surviving Family Members

We compared those families who experienced a sudden death (E and C_1) with families who had no death within a 2-year period before participation in the project (C_2). Results clearly show (Table 37.2) that the death of a family member has a strong negative impact on the physical and emotional health as well as social functioning of surviving family members when compared to family members who did not experience a recent sudden death in the family. The experience of sudden death in a family, a striking environmental event which often produced major interpersonal and intra-psychic reverberations, seemed to have far-reaching impact on the lives of the survivors. The application of a short-term interventive technique focused on strengthening interpersonal and intrapsychic adaptation to the death apparently did not.

At the 6- and 18-month follow-up interviews, the research assessment team reported some clinical observations on the interaction among environmental, social systems, and individual variables that may help lay the groundwork for the initial interpretation of these challenging 6-month follow-up results.

ASSESSMENT TEAM OBSERVATIONS ON DEATH

In the course of interviewing families who experienced the sudden death of a family member, the evaluation staff observed a number of consistent patterns involving environmental, social systems, and individual variables that seemed to be associated with bereavement outcome. The relationship between each observed pattern and subsequent outcome is being subjected to statistical analysis. If these observations prove valid, they raise questions about important facets of existing conceptual frameworks of bereavement processes.

Environmental Factors

Tragic circumstances around the death seemed to correlate highly with poor outcome as measured by the development of physical or mental illness or serious social disruption in the family. The more sudden and unexpected the death was, the more violent it was, and the more it involved dismemberment and disfiguration of the decedent, the more likely the family was to experience high rates of medical illness, psychiatric illness, and social disturbance. If the death was directly observed by surviving family members and occurred in the home, it seemed more likely to lead to poor outcome than did unobserved deaths occurring away from the home. Death by suicide and deaths involving a child under 12 also seemed associated with poor outcome. Finally, when family members directly or indirectly contributed to the death such as through parental negligence or direct facilitation of suicide, poor outcome often resulted.

In some instances, death seemed to alleviate environmental stresses and improve adjustment of family members. This happened when death provided relief from a heavy nursing burden in a chronic debilitating illness, or when death provided relief from chronic economic and social burdens such as those imposed on a family by a socially disruptive, chronically ill alcoholic.

Certain environmental factors tended to promote externalization. Family members who belonged to fundamentalist religious groups had incorporated highly structured explanations of the causes of death and of man's fate after death. These families attributed the death to God's will and refused to discuss any facet of their realistic involvement in the death or to elaborate on the specific grief reactions of family members. These families would, in psychiatric terms, be considered to be using denial quite extensively, and at times, pathologically. Yet, by all measurements up to 2 years after the death, they appeared to maintain good physical and mental health ratings and appeared to be benefiting from this defense.

Social Systems Factors

In observing the reactions of a number of families to a sudden death, it was our impression that a family must be able to carry out a number of organizational tasks in order to adjust to the death. One of the most important of these tasks is role reallocation. In order to accomplish this, family members must first be able to realistically appraise the role carried out by the decedent. They must then be able to define which of these roles can be assumed by surviving family members. Finally, the roles must be reallocated when appropriate within the reconstituted family group. The roles referred to include not only instrumental roles, such as breadwinner and disciplinarian, but also expressive roles such as communications facilitator and mediator.

In view of the complexity of role reallocation and other organizational tasks after the death, the familial characteristics that we observed to be associated with good outcome are not surprising. Families with a high degree of effective communication and flexibility tended not to develop physical or mental illness or disturbed social functioning. The same was true of families who had previously exhibited a high degree of problem-solving capacity and families who could call on an effective network of formal and informal social resources outside the family. Families who exhibited the opposite characteristics, such as poor communication and problem-solving capacity and social isolation, tended to experience poor outcome.

TABLE 37.2 Determination of the Impact of Death Based on 6-Month Outcome Data

Outcome measurement	E and C_1 (means)	C_2 (means)	F (ratio)	P value	Descriptive comments
Health questionnaires					
Cornell Medical Index	26.2	24.1	0.54		CMI showed higher depression scores, more fears and worries in the death group
Medical rating					
before the death	1.19	1.27	0.13		
after the death	1.47	1.19	1.45		
Depression	0.91	0.26	13.80	<.01	
Fears and worries	1.34	0.71	8.20	<.01	
Psychiatric					
MMPI					MMPI tended to show an elevated paranoia scale for the death group, but showed no difference in MMPI normality profiles of the 2 groups. The death group showed greater psychiatric dysfunction and depression, had a higher predictor score for abnormal grieving, and at 6 months had worse psychiatric ratings
Pa Scale	11.6	10.3	8.65	<.01	
Abnormal–normal	1.62	1.61	0.01		
Sterling County	71.06	78.41	7.90	<.01	
Mood Inventory	8.5	5.4	9.80	<.01	
Ten Best Questions	12.9	12.14	5.61	<.05	
Psychiatric ratings					
before the death	1.76	1.41	2.60		
after the death	2.12	1.47	9.02	<.01	
Family functioning					
W&F* spontaneous agreement					W&F*—showed more spontaneous agreement, both individually and as a family on family interaction by the death group. They also had a higher choice fulfillment score as a family, although the non-death group scored higher as individuals
individual	19.8	17.2	5.60	<.05	
family	41.45	20.85	23.30	<.01	
W&F* choice fulfillment					
individual	34.8	38.25	8.60	<.01	
family	110.3	91.94	12.50	<.01	

TABLE 37.2 (continued)

Crisis coping at death					
Intrapersonal					The death group felt and experienced greater stress around intrapersonal family and social problems, both at the time of death and 6 months later when compared to the non-death group
import	18.51	7.5	25.30	<.01	
stress	16.0	6.1	22.00	<.01	
Family					
import	18.2	9.1	19.70	<.01	
stress	14.5	6.8	17.70	<.01	
Social					
import	14.3	9.2	7.70	<.01	
stress	9.6	5.4	7.20	<.01	
Crisis coping at 6 months					
Intrapersonal	15.0	4.9	25.40	<.01	
Family	16.2	8.8	13.99	<.01	
Social	13.3	6.6	15.70	<.01	
Social cost					
Gross income	638.7	841.3	8.23	<.01	The death group had a lower gross income and experienced greater indirect losses on a cost basis than did the non-death group
Expenses at 6 months	1451.7	1673.2	1.76		
Economic losses					
import	0.74	0.30	11.90	<.01	
cost	0.76	0.30	9.40	<.01	

*W&F = Winter and Ferriera

The role played by the decedent prior to death also tended to be predictive of outcome. When the decedent played an expressive role in relation to an ongoing family conflict, and at the same time served to keep the conflict in balance, death often resulted in mental and physical illness and social disruption for family members. Scapegoat, delinquent, and mental patient are examples of such expressive roles. The negative effects were magnified when the circumstances of the death itself served to intensify and potentiate the unresolved family conflict.

Individual Factors

As previously described, preliminary data suggest that a subject's degree of unexpressed feelings of hopelessness and despair, combined with poor crisis-coping ability and tendency to discharge emotional conflicts through somatic dysfunction rather than behavioral dysfunction, were predictive of the development of serious physical and emotional illnesses. These results support the findings of previous retrospective studies (13, 154, 215, 367).

Interview data suggested that additional variables might also be predictive of subsequent serious illness. It was our impression that individuals who were able to maintain a healthy level of denial had better outcome. Individuals who had lost a favorite child or an only child through death tended to have poor outcome. When an individual in fact or fantasy felt that he had contributed significantly to the death of the family member, he was more likely to experience physical or psychiatric illness.

Finally, as earlier indicated, we believed that the predictive value of individual variables would be enhanced when they were considered in combination with environmental, family, and social systems variables.

Interaction Among Environmental, Social System, and Individual Factors

Perhaps the most important observation was the crucial interaction among environmental, social systems, and individual variables in determining outcome. In reviewing our case notes, it seemed that families rated comparably on social systems variables who experienced deaths with large differences in environmental stress showed significant differences in bereavement outcome. When environmental factors seemed comparable, the family with negative social systems patterns tended to experience poorer outcome. Finally, in those instances where the environmental characteristics of the death, the family variables, and the characteristics of the individual all predisposed toward a poor outcome, the risk of illness and social disturbance was very high.

Conversely, it often seemed that the effects of particularly negative environmental variables around a death could be counteracted by a flexible family system with impressive communication and problem-solving skills, while the same tragic circumstances occurring in a fragmented, uncommunicative family might lead to poor physical and mental health after the death. These interaction effects are best illustrated by the following case examples.

CASE REPORT 1

The family consisted of a mother and father in their late 50s, 3 married daughters, and an 18-year-old son who lived at home and whose death is reported here. The son had clearly become the father's favorite but in a significantly pathologic way. He was physically small but was pushed by the father into athletic activities that required extensive training and exaggerated aggressiveness on the son's part to overcome his small size. The son had considerable success as a wrestler in high school. He was also an accomplished artist, but his father had strongly discouraged and rejected his artistic aspirations.

The family communication among the siblings and mother was good but the father, a manufacturer's representative who went on frequent business trips, used his excessive work schedule to exclude himself from the family and from family communications. The relationship between the father and mother was poor. Sexual intercourse took place only once every 6 months, and this was a major source of irritation and tension in the marriage. The wife had several times considered either a divorce or an affair, and the father felt at times that the son was the only thing holding the marriage together.

One year before his death, the son made a suicide attempt, a gunshot wound to the chest, narrowly missing his heart. He was placed in psychiatric therapy, but the parents were never extensively involved. Three years prior to his death, at age 15, he had begun using marijuana, LSD, and other psychedelic drugs. One year later he was arrested for dealing in drugs and spent 3 months in a federal correctional institution for youth. In the 2 years prior to his death he began using heroin intravenously, and his heroin intake was probably at a preaddiction level just before his death. Although the family knew of his involvement with drugs, the parents underestimated the extent and seriousness of his use of heroin.

At the time of the son's death the parents had been planning to leave on vacation in 1 or 2 days. The son often asked his father for money which the father suspected he used to buy drugs. On the evening before the son's death, the father gave his son $35.00, which he may have used to buy the dose of street methadone which proved fatal. His body was discovered the next morning in his bedroom at home by two friends.

After the death, the father withdrew quite excessively and for a year visited the son's grave daily. At the 2-year evaluation point he was still stopping by the son's grave 3 times a week. He continued to insist that his son had died of a heart attack. Communication between mother and daughters continued to be good after the death, but the mother and father became increasingly estranged.

The father was mildly diabetic prior to his son's death. He gained 25 pounds in the first year after the death. For the first time in his life he began smoking cigarettes and at 18 months was up to two packs a day.

CASE REPORT 2

A second family experienced a death that involved comparably stressful environmental factors. The mother and father, in their late 40s, had a 15-year-old son and a 13-year-old daughter. The son plugged an electrical appliance with faulty wiring into an outside wall socket at home while standing on wet grass in his bare feet and was instantly electrocuted. The father, an electrician, had been repairing the faulty wiring of the appliance on the day before the death, but the mother interrupted his work to ask him to do another chore and he never completed the repair.

The family was quite open in their grief. The father wished that he had completed the repair but after prompting by the interviewer stated that he had trained the son in the basic precautions to be followed when using electrical devices. If the son had followed these, they probably would have saved his life.

The son was popular, successful, independent, and quite civic-minded. The daughter appeared to be developing in the same fashion. The parents had a long and happy relationship, were strongly religious, and both actively participated in family affairs with the children. The family openly supported and comforted each other after the death and continued in much the same fashion as before the tragedy. Health and mental health ratings and family functioning measures remained positive 6 and 18 months after the death.

DISCUSSION

If the trends observed in the 6-month data remain consistent, they might be interpreted in a number of different ways:

1. The specific type of crisis therapy used was not effective as a preventive strategy, but other types of crisis intervention might have been more successful.
2. Longer term types of therapy than crisis therapy might be necessary for intervention to be effective in acute bereavement.
3. The therapy used was successful, but it requires more than 6 months for its impact to become evident.
4. Neither the therapy used, nor other types of existing short-term and long-term intervention are effective interventive strategies for acute bereavement.*

---

* *Editors' Note:* Still another possibility is that the E and C samples were not matched on certain crucial variables.

We would speculate that the conceptual frameworks and interventive strategies now available are inadequate to make a significant impact on the major forces surrounding bereavement that we observed in the present study. Both the outcome data and our clinical observations strongly suggest that environmental forces are immensely powerful determinants of outcome. Yet, existing mental health conceptual frameworks are derived primarily from intrapsychic and interpersonal factors.

We know a great deal about the relationship between guilt and the superego, but we know very little about the guilt that stems from a father's direct contribution to his son's death. It is difficult to conceptualize how the external environmental forces involved in a tragic death lead to ill health and social disturbance, and even more difficult to construct interventive strategies that might constructively counteract these forces.

The effects of some tragic environmental circumstances observed in the present study seemed to have been ameliorated when bereaved individuals were members of a strong, openly communicative family system with significant problem-solving resources. This would suggest that our attempt to use interventive strategies based on a social systems framework was a step in the right direction. But while social systems may be the appropriate locus for intervention, we have the strong impression that the available techniques of social systems intervention are not adequate to produce effective social systems change. Even if effective social systems intervention techniques were available, they might not change the ultimate outcome unless they were combined with an understanding of the environmental forces involved in sudden bereavement and the application of effective interventive techniques for modifying these forces. We hope our continued studies will lead to more information about these environmental forces and how they interact with families and individuals who are faced with the difficult prospect of coping with sudden death.

38

EXPERIENTIAL RESEARCH IN A
BOARD-AND-ROOM SETTING

David K. Reynolds
Norman L. Farberow

Suicide rates among Veterans Administration (VA) psychiatric patients are about ten times those for all males in the population of the United States (116). We became interested in the possible contribution of the social system within the hospital to this high suicide rate. Suicide has been recognized as a social–psychological problem, but investigation of the social factors contributing to the event has been primarily in the examination of demographic aspects and their covariation, age, sex, race, socioeconomic status, rural–urban location, and neighborhood characteristics. Investigations of the content of the social problems *per se* have been few.

The study of the society of a mental hospital or after-care facility, in our thinking, is crucial in relation to its contribution to the alleviation or continuation of psychological states. The factors within such societies need to be studied in intensive detail.

After considering several ways to gather information concerning the effects of the social systems in hospitals or after-care facilities on personality functioning, we decided that a useful tactic might be to immerse a trained observer in the system and allow him to experience its effects. He could then report his observations of his social world, his

Research supported by NIMH Grant MH 22800. The authors also wish to thank Mrs. Helen Sonier Sullivan, M.A., for her contributions to the study.

psychological functioning, and their interaction. To this end, in the summer of 1971 the senior author, an anthropologist, was admitted to a VA psychiatric facility and lived on the ward as a depressed, suicidal patient for 2 weeks. An account of his experience and analysis can be found elsewhere (352, 353).

Close examination of the statistical data on suicides reveals that most suicides of neuropsychiatric patients occur during the period *following release* from a psychiatric facility (117). Why should this be so? Presumably the patient has improved sufficiently to be discharged or placed on some after-care status. Confinement within the hospital is no longer deemed necessary. Seemingly, his prognosis is more positive than during hospitalization, but the likelihood of his killing himself increases.

We suspect there is something about the *change* of life circumstance that precipitates suicidal behavior. But what? Our experiential research within the psychiatric hospital caused us to take note of the loss of comrades and positive personal identity associated with discharge. The patient is pulled out of a restricted but secure social world in which he has been perceived as increasingly knowledgeable and psychiatrically "well." But into what sort of social milieu is he thrust? What social–personal rewards does he find in exchange for the losses he has incurred?

RESEARCH PLAN

In order to examine the psychosocial effects of the critical posthospital period the senior author arranged to conduct experiential research in several after-care facilities. In all, he lived as a resident in four facilities, ranging in size from a family care unit housing three residents to a board-and-care home with over 100 residents. In the largest facility we were able to place another experiential researcher at the same time. A female graduate student in clinical psychology assumed the role of an improved formerly depressed suicidal patient in order to obtain a measure of reliability in the reporting, i.e., to "calibrate" our researcher–instrument. Again, we were interested in the conditions that evoke suicidal behavior—only this time the focus was on the posthospital care period. The research from the largest board-and-care facility provides the major data base for this report.

Permission had been obtained from all the facilities to conduct the research. They clearly understood that the conditions of the research required that it be without their knowledge of who we were or when we would enter. We attempt here to provide an inside account of an expatient's experience in a large board-and-care facility, to give our readers some "feel" for what it's like to live in such a place. We must caution the reader about the difficulties in generalizing from these personal experiences. True, the two researchers had some remarkably similar experiences, and we were able to confirm our impressions that *some* of our fellow residents shared *some* of these experiences. However, we recognize that the impact of a social system is mediated by the psychological state of the individual—his phenomenologic world is *his* alone, and those elements of his phenomenologic world that are shared with others should be discovered by investigation and not simply assumed.

The first part of this report deals with what we call the "career" of the board-and-care resident. It is essentially a chronologically ordered account of the stages passed through in our entry, acceptance, and departure from the board-and-care community. The second section describes some of the ways in which self-esteem and self-trust are nurtured or destroyed within the board-and-care setting.

CAREER OF THE BOARD-AND-CARE RESIDENT

The board-and-care facility in which we lived consisted of a large apartment building and two satellite buildings housing a total of about 150 residents. It was located in a racially mixed neighborhood near a community college. Approximately 90% of the residents were veterans and the remaining 10% were nonveterans on welfare programs. The facility boasted a relatively large staff, good food, a swimming pool, and a reputation of being one of the better board-and-care homes in the Los Angeles area.

Newcomer Status

A prospective resident may or may not be taken to visit a board-and-care facility before going there to live. "Helen Summers" (our female researcher's alternate identity) was given a tour a few days before entering. Excerpts from her journal give an account of the orientation tour and her first day as a resident.

> This afternoon Sharon, my social worker, took me out to the house to look around and to be introduced as a prospective member. The first impression is of a somewhat complex maze of areas and rooms with stairs connecting various places. Although the patients seemed friendly and anxious to greet us, the faces were mostly a blur and didn't stick.
>
> Once in the office, the woman at the desk put us in the charge of a man who, I later found out, is the administrator. First we went on a tour of the house-patio, music room and library, TV room, dining room, canteen, occupational therapy (OT) shop, and a couple of apartments.
>
> With a few exceptions the administrator was careful to give me a sense of being included, of being a part of the decision about what was going to happen to me. For the most part he did this by physically including me in

the circle when we would stop some place, addressing me personally, asking me if I had any questions and then *waiting* to hear my answers. I think this is very important—mostly because of how it felt on the few occasions when it didn't happen. A couple of times my social worker and the administrator took off ahead, laughing and joking—they had known each other before. At those times I felt very much in the way—kind of like a hapless third wheel trailing along behind.

Then our guide started telling my social worker about one of the girls, and he used the word "crazy" in reference to her. I'm sure that I wouldn't even have noticed if he hadn't become so embarrassed and started apologizing. Small as this incident was, it created a distance between us, reinforcing our respective roles, me as patient, him as non-patient.

There were also subtle changes in voice pitch and vocabulary when this man spoke to me as opposed to when he spoke to Sharon. I was speaking very quietly and he seemed to respond to that by speaking quietly in return. Actually, it felt quite nice. I was feeling bombarded on all sides by new impressions and so the softness of his voice felt very reassuring.

By the time we got back to his office I was totally confused as to how one place connected to another; I couldn't remember the name of anyone I had met and faces had all become a blur. At that point he wanted to know if I had any questions, but my mind wouldn't work and I couldn't think of a single thing. I was grateful when he didn't push too hard, and Sharon filled in the gap by asking some questions of her own while I tried to collect myself. At some point the administrator was showing something to Sharon, and he suddenly brought out a brochure of the facility and gave it to me. Something about the spontaneity of his gesture suggested that this wasn't usual procedure. But if it isn't, I think it should be. While I was here my head was too jumbled up to think clearly of any questions I wanted to ask. But the brochure gave me something to mull over in a quiet place by myself later, and it really helped allay some of the anxiety about moving into a strange place. . . .

Arrived at the house at about 3 o'clock yesterday afternoon. The woman at the desk was very pleasant, but I got the impression that either I was unexpected or that it was inconvenient for me to be there at that time. For about the first ten minutes she spoke about me in the third person, talking with Sharon about forms, arrangements, medication, etc. I was already feeling rather anxious and scared, and this only added a feeling of insignificance to the rest of what I was feeling. When she spoke to me, though, she was warm and welcoming. However, this only made the total message more confusing because at the same time she retained that distracted air, periodically calling on the intercom for someone—to do something with me, I supposed. Then she had me sign a card, took the money and gave me a key, explaining that it was also to be used for opening the back doors. By that time a man came into the office, introduced himself, and said he would show us to the room. He struck me as a somewhat brusque, perhaps efficient, sort of person. He asked if we had been there before and when Sharon said we had, he proceeded straight to the room although Sharon said I might need to see it again. In the room he showed me my bed, put his hands on my shoulders, told me that he hoped I would be happy there and to come and see him if I wanted to talk about anything. Although he said nice things, they didn't feel particularly genuine to me—like he had a job to do. After telling me that he would see me at dinner, he left.

My room is on the second floor across from the TV room. It is actually an apartment except that the kitchen isn't equipped as a kitchen and the living room functions as another bedroom. The rooms are fairly spacious and there is an uncrowded feeling about them, although there is the usual female array of toilet articles and clothes. There is a certain aura of impersonality about it as if there were little overlapping of the individuals involved. Each person has the right to half of whatever space is in his room. I found half of the bureau top, closet and dresser draws cleared for me. Contrary to what I had expected I had no sense whatsoever of moving into someone else's room.

I stayed in my room until dinner, feeling mildly stranded. The other woman came and went in her room a few times, but she didn't say anything to me. My roommate didn't come in at all, and from the few things scattered on her side of the room it was impossible to make any guesses about her age or anything about her.

At 5 o'clock the other woman told me I could go to dinner if I wanted. She asked me my name and told me what hers was. I was feeling quite apprehensive about facing so many new people at dinner and would have preferred to walk with her except that she bolted ahead.

I found the walk alone from my room to the dining room a hideous interminable ordeal, and I would never have left what I already regarded as the isolated security of my room except that I felt that I should find out what dinner time was like. I felt extraordinary gratitude to the staff member I met earlier for appearing from nowhere to rescue me. He brought me in to introduce me to the housefather, but I still found it impossible to remember names or faces; and when he was gone, I wasn't sure that I'd ever be able to recognize him again.

As the dining room was already full, I went to the TV room to wait for the second dinner serving. A young man with a sombrero came over to talk to me. It was my first formal introduction to any of the other patients there. He asked me a lot of questions and I had the impression that I was being hustled to a certain degree, but just as I was beginning to feel too invaded we were called into dinner. I was struck by the almost total lack of conversation at our table. People would ask or signal for what they wanted, then eat quickly and silently and leave.

The woman in charge of the serving—I think she might be the housemother—struck me as an exceptionally warm and motherly sort of person. She kind of bustled around, mopping up spills, handing out food, clucking over people as if we were her family. Although I had never been introduced to her, she seemed to know my name and made me feel very welcome.

After dinner I went to sit outside for a little while. I found that while I hadn't noticed any social pressure to leave my room that afternoon, there was certainly a lot more pressure to socialize once you got outside. Besides the man I met earlier, several other men came over to talk. Pretty soon I started feeling too hassled and I wanted to be alone. So I said I was going upstairs and I left. No explanations were necessary. In fact, I could have said nothing at all. No one would have said anything to stop me.

I stayed in my room reading for the rest of the evening, partly because I really wanted to be alone and partly because I wanted to see if there would be any effort to get me out. No one said anything and I went to bed early.

At about 12:30 AM I was awakened by the sound of someone in the room. At about the same time there was a sound, as of a fire hydrant bursting outside of the window. When I sat up, there was a woman in her fifties standing right next to my bed looking out of the window. When I asked her what the noise was, she said they were trying to put out a fire, and then she continued into something about a fire burning up the whole world and Christ being burned by fire and men after her, etc. She continued on like this for sometime. I was already feeling somewhat disoriented, and when she began talking like this I started feeling really frightened. I didn't know what to expect next. Although I kept trying to go back to sleep, I periodically would feel her presence and would start up to find her leaning over me, looking for a cigarette, staring at the clock, or just looking at me. It's hard to describe the terror I felt mingled with a kind of free-floating anxiety. I wasn't thinking rationally. When she wasn't standing over me, she was rummaging through closets and drawers, taking things out, putting them back again. I don't think she ever sat down for more than 5 minutes, and she certainly never lay down. By 4:30 AM I gave up all hope of sleep, got up and started to get dressed. With my contact lenses in I felt better able to face any crisis, and I set about retrieving my possessions that this woman had scattered about the room. Meanwhile the woman came back, told me her name was M, and helped me find my things. By this time I was beginning to think more rationally, and we talked off and on for the next couple of hours while I crocheted. It occurred to me that M might have been as unnerved by my presence as I was by hers. Although she continued to drift off into some personal fantasies at times, she was quite coherent in other instances, even exhibiting a gentle caring for me, concern that I might be crying when I was rubbing my eyes, or touching my face or worrying about my breakfast.

Actually, I found myself becoming quite fond of M during those early morning hours. Still, I was aware of a persistent trembling sensation that has continued through much of this day. Part of it is a product of lack of sleep, I know, but part of it is from the intense terror I felt, however unfounded. I wonder if a new resident in that situation might not have found it equally frightening. It is a new place, the apartments are relatively isolated and even the two people in the next room seem strange and distant.

"Mr. Kent's" (the author's alternate identity) experience on arrival was quite similar. He was in the first stage of the resident's career (we call it *newcomer status*). During this stage the new resident was noticed, greeted, and made welcome. Among the "15 commandments" posted around the facility was one encouraging the residents to welcome newcomers, introduce themselves, and be helpful to them. He learned quickly that the question "Where are you from?" most often meant not "What state were you born in?" or "Where did you used to live?" but "What *hospital* were you discharged from?" This, and even more specifically, the *ward* from which one came was an important basis for determining a connection, a shared base of experiences with others.

As in most settings, special privileges are permitted newcomers. Some of the criticism for inappropriate and thoughtless behavior was suspended while a person got adjusted. There was a great deal of information a new resident needed about the routine of the facility, so he was allowed to ask many questions of his fellows, who generally answered patiently.

Interim Phase

The newcomer status wore off. And the next interim period is considered to be one of the most dangerous for the potentially suicidal patient. During this interim phase, several upsetting experiences converged to make Kent question the wisdom of continuing such a low-quality existence. Fewer people made less effort to express concern for him as the novelty of his arrival declined—and understandably so, since he'd been absorbing his fellows' concern without returning appropriate responses that would have built sustaining friendships. He began to note jealously the greetings expressed to other newcomers, and the stereotypic quality of these initial interactions somehow sapped their genuineness. These people didn't really care about him, he felt, they were merely carrying out formalities. Simultaneously, he envisioned himself as facing the prospect of living in this facility for the rest of his life. And with that realization came the fear that living here might make him into the same sort of apathetic, artificial creature he could see all around. It was like a preview of things to come. He overheard one resident being asked how old he was. "Thirty-seven," was the response. Suddenly it struck Kent that in 6 years he, too, could be in the same condition this fellow was in.

At this point, just a few days after entering for Kent (but perhaps longer for other residents), he was no longer a newcomer but he hadn't yet learned the individual lifeways possible in a board-and-care home, nor even the names of most of his companions. His relationships with his friends back on the psychiatric hospital ward were curtailed, and new close friendships were yet to develop in this setting. No one had begun talking of moving beyond the board-and-care home as a presumed step on his return to society as they had on his first day in the mental hospital. He was expected to stay. The conflict between the functions of a board-and-care home as a stepping stone to the community on the one hand and a warehouse, an extension of the hospital ward, on the other, will be important to keep in mind as we continue.

Not only did comparisons with those in this milieu who were sicker than Kent make him despondent, but also comparisons with those who appeared to be in better shape than he produced the same effect. Those who seemed to interact confidently with the female residents underscored his own shyness and hesitation in this area. On the psychiatric ward from which he came there had been no women. Of course, there were female nurses assistants. But they are so closely bound to their roles that they aren't perceived as socially accessible companions. Suddenly he found himself in a small society that included women, some young and pretty. And though they were spatially accessible they were unreachable. In his journal he wrote:

> As I withdraw a bit this morning, lying in bed, the sounds of activity outside my room mock me and emphasize the difference between me and the others. How can they go on with their lives, uncaring, while I am sad—not even wondering why I'm not among them? Such is the selfishness of the depressed.

Membership Status

If the resident survives this interim period, however, he progresses to a real membership in the community of the after-care setting. He begins to know individuals, and to have expectations and a sense of what is just and unjust within the accepted norms of the facility. Here we offer a few examples of the sense of being drawn into the web of interrelationships among the residents. At breakfast one morning Kent noticed that one man rushed into the dining room and quickly exchanged the box of dry cereal in his bowl with that of his neighbor's. At breakfast the next morning Kent tried to switch cereals, too, but the resident who arrived shortly afterward claimed his own cereal back and so Kent gave it to him. To get even, Kent passed the milk pitcher away from him to the other end of the table. The resident had to ask Kent to pass the milk. This kind of petty childishness was a clue that Kent was being drawn into social relationships of sufficient depth to pull affective reactions from him.

In another more significant set of encounters with two roommates Kent recorded in his journal these experiences:

> Found a roach in the bathroom. It's hard to describe the feeling of impotence and anger. All I can do is ask for help and all I get are reassurances. I slept with angry fantasies on my mind.

At 3 AM my roommate (A) lit a cigarette. "You shouldn't do that," I told him sleepily. We had an agreement that he could smoke in the room all day but not at night. A few minutes later he lit another. I felt he was trying to "get to" me. "That does it!" I jumped up and hastily threw on my clothes. "I'll raise hell and see if you keep this up." I stalked over to the houseparents' apartment, rang the bell, and woke the housefather, whose response was "You tell him I'll report this to the administrator in the morning."

But then I began to wonder, "How angry is A? If anything is going to happen, it will be in the first hour while he's upset." I lay with one eye open. It took well over an hour to get back to sleep. I learned later that A had gone after a previous roommate with a razor blade. Glad I didn't know that *then*.

The next day I was transferred to a new room. One of my new roommates had entered the facility that same day.

The new guy (C) rang the apartment bell. He'd forgotten his key. He seemed to be a pretty far out, quiet, soft-spoken youth. He started to leave again without his key. I reminded him and he took it. A few minutes later he was back ringing the bell. I opened it and he was standing there, key in hand. We talked about his being new here and getting used to the place after awhile.

I went to bed and he came to the side of my bed in jockey shorts and stood there for a moment then went back to bed. A few minutes later there he was by the side of my bed again. In a flat voice he asked, "Want a blow job?"

"No thanks," I replied trying to act as if he'd offered a stick of gum. "Go back to bed, man." Soon he was up wandering around. "Look, man, we can't have you wandering. Some of us have to go to work in the morning." He muttered that he wasn't "set right," and I said we'd try to help him get well.

Then he lit a cigarette in bed and I showed him the posted rules about that. "I don't want to sound like I'm laying a lot of rules on you, but you'd better just adapt yourself to them once and for all and then you'll fit in fine."

The recognition of how completely Kent had become identified with his fellow residents came one night at a local public park. A group of residents went expecting a dance, but instead there was a community water carnival at the park that night. As they waited for the carnival to begin, some began playing volleyball and Kent wandered over to play basketball. A young man who was playing basketball asked him what all those people were doing over there. Kent hesitated, then realized that the question wasn't in reference to the strange people playing volleyball, but to the crowd that had gathered to view the water carnival. Kent was so sensitive to being a part of what he felt to be a conspicuous group that he misinterpreted the young man's question at first. Apparently his association with those disturbed people wasn't as obvious as he had felt. He was both embarrassed to be a part of this group and even more upset to realize that he depended on and needed them for his own sense of belongingness and security. To be dependent on a socially stigmatized group can be very disquieting.

The resident who has adapted to life in a board-and-care facility has a number of options or niches into which he can fit himself. For example, there is the gamester who is expert at all sorts of games from chess and checkers to bridge, pinochle, tennis, ping-pong, and pool. His day is spent playing or organizing games. Another resident spends a great deal of time at a local doughnut shop where he has established informal relations with the counterman so that at times he exchanges light clean-up work or entertainment for free coffee and doughnuts. Another, the hustler, arranges dinner dates and other activities with residents of the opposite sex. Escapists of several sorts utilize television, sleep, reading, hallucinations, alcohol, movies, and even church activities to keep them psychologically if not bodily away from the facility for much of the day. Helen, for example, found herself drawn to the patient-operated canteen.

> More than any other area around here the canteen is changeable, with people coming and going, having fun in different ways. More and more I find myself wandering in there, and I see other people gravitating there as well, enjoying the distraction in a kind of vicarious way. Yet, in the end I think it's the *vicariousness* that's the problem and realization of that fact can make you even more depressed than before. At this point the most satisfied people here seem to me to be the ones who have found a niche in which they can *do* something as opposed to being *done to* continually— whether it is working in the kitchen, emptying ash cans, or, in one woman's case, working her own garden.

Exit Phase

For many residents in board-and-care homes the exit phases of their career are never experienced. Reflecting back on the experience we had, we have some understanding of why it is an end point, a catchment, a cul-de-sac for many residents. The rewards of the life are simple but reasonable; the demands are very few. It is a sheltered world of acquaintance–peers with whom the resident need not compete. There is a benevolent authority to whom he can appeal in case of trouble—and then hope for action. Within very broad limits (including financial and medical) a resident's freedom of movement is unrestricted. There are irritations, to be sure—disturbing fellow residents, occasionally insensitive management, limited personal space, and an erratic schedule of activities. But these are relatively minor provided one is able to shrink his aspirations and potential to fit the rewards offered by the system. It's not a *bad* place to live, only a terribly, terribly *limiting* one. Helen also was becoming more aware of a certain dead-end atmosphere to the place that was frightening. She wrote:

For even if you accept the fact that some of the people here have everything they want and are quite happy, "Helen Summers" and Helen Sonier Sullivan (the researcher) have in common the fact that they have both known other ways of life that they have found more fulfilling even though they have been disappointed at times. They still have places to go. The feeling that most of the people here are at the end of the road already is kind of scary. So far, I have only heard two people even talk vaguely about leaving. Few people have asked me how long I plan to stay (which would imply that I will be leaving); rather, the question is, "Do you think you're going to like it here?" It is as if we live in a minisociety in which each person's past is a private trust and only identical futures exist. We just *live* here.

Perhaps one answer lies in a series of graded facilities, each a step closer to independent living. The expatient would be assigned to each step for a prescribed limited period of time with the expectation that he'd move on. One thing is certain: although limiting in some ways, the unhurried community life of a board-and-care facility offers a comfortable alternative to the loneliness, meaninglessness, and competitive hassle of independent living on many levels of our society. It would be easier to pull people away from stagnation in an after-care facility if the larger society were more attractive.

Those who do decide to leave the facility can be expected to have doubts about their ability to "make it" on the outside. There is a kind of temporary stardom or prestige that attaches to one who is about to move out on his own. But there is disengagement, too, as people realize that he isn't likely to return again—unless he fails. His thoughts begin to turn toward his new life situation, the prospective change fills his conversations, and the social world of his resident peers begins to mend the hole in the social fabric that his absence will cause, even before he goes. On the day Kent left he felt a heavy sense of anticlimax. Few people seemed to acknowledge or even notice his going. The one bright spot was his recollection that earlier in the week two staff members had given him their *home* phone numbers should he have trouble and need someone to talk to. As he left, there was a clear understanding (even perhaps an expectation) that he was welcome should he decide to return.

Helen felt this way:

> Am still feeling somewhat unsettled and agitated at my inability to sort out my feelings. I'm sure that my partial reluctance to leave stems to some degree from the relative involvement I've achieved this last week. I wonder about those for whom this has been their only home for several years, or who, like S, for example, have adopted family substitutes from available other members. I wonder if the sense of security and sureness might not outweigh the inconveniences of living here and make it terribly difficult to leave if there is no strong internal or external motivation.

> Also, while I *know* I can make it on the outside, I am aware of a tiny
> scared feeling inside of me. If I let myself play with the feeling, I realize
> that it takes strength to live outside, but it really does not require that
> much in here.

Another route for leaving the board-and-care home was to head back to
the hospital. Several of our residents asked to return to the protected
haven of their former psychiatric ward. Several others wanted to go back
sufficiently to cause enough trouble to require rehospitalization.

The career cycle may be renewed when a resident who left on his own
comes back to the board-and-care facility. The fact that welfare payments
were cut back when one left the board-and-care home presented the newly
independent exresident with an immediate problem. Understandably,
some persons saw this as punishment for leaving. Compound this
economic problem with the undeveloped skills necessary for living
alone—skills such as cooking, budgeting time, finding and holding a job,
handling money, dealing with physical illness—and life on the outside was
frequently considered more trouble than it was worth. And of equal
importance was the unbearable loneliness on the outside. As one fellow
who came back put it, "You start talking to strangers in the park, and they
have other people to talk to and other things to talk about."

DISCUSSION

Attitude of Professionals

Why is it important to be aware of the resident's career cycle? We think it's
possible for mental health professionals to practice a kind of psychological
"vaccination" or "inoculation." Part of the impact of the loss of newcomer
status or the fear of leaving a facility lies in the unexpectedness and lack of
understanding of what's being experienced. If we could forewarn expatients that they might have these experiences and give them a conceptual
framework for handling them—that these upsets are to be viewed as
natural steps in the progressive pull toward return to community life—we
can prevent their becoming serious setbacks. What is perceived to be
expected and natural becomes more controllable and less traumatic.
Furthermore, that we can foresee what the resident is likely to encounter
makes our future predictions and suggestions more weighty. Among most
patients and expatients there is the strong feeling that the professionals
have no real sense of what they're going through. Our approach demands
that we listen to residents' accounts of their experiences and use their
expert knowledge to build our understanding and our credibility with them.
The senior author has seen this tactic used quite effectively by Morita
psychotherapists in Japan (4).

Self-Esteem in the Board-and-Care Facility

There are processes of tearing down and building up self-esteem and self-trust among board-and-care residents. The analysis isn't particularly deep or profound; it is little more than saying that psychiatric patients and expatients are human beings, not unlike the rest of us. They are hurt by slights and gratified by positive gestures just as we would be in their circumstances. Some of the reasons why staff members in psychiatric hospitals and after-care facilities keep patients in a subservient, powerless role may be this very recognition that patients aren't so different from the rest of us. Some staff members, particularly those who feel unqualified to occupy their positions because of lack of education, training, and experience, seem to need to emphasize the differences between themselves and their wards. Their feelings of inadequacy and inferiority are projected on the residents of these facilities who are seen to be scarcely capable of doing anything for themselves.

It has also been suggested that if one keeps patients/residents powerless, they are more controllable. The staff can trade back some minor freedoms and rewards in exchange for cooperation and help in getting the facility's work done. One of the most upsetting qualities that we have observed in residents is their lack of indignation, their passive acceptance of the slings and arrows of outrageous staff members and other authority figures. In one case, for example, a resident had an abscessed tooth and was experiencing a great deal of pain. Her family dentist for 12 years wouldn't treat her without medical stamps. Her medical stamps, like her monthly welfare checks, hadn't been arriving with any regularity. But her unquestioning acceptance of the lack of control over her life resulted in continued pain. It didn't occur to her to cause a disturbance. Her welfare contact person neither involved the resident in the process of getting her check and stamps, nor even let her know how things were progressing when there was a mixup. In turn, the resident didn't want to "bother" her contact person more than once a month. As Helen put it, "All she knows is that she has no money, no stickers, and a tooth that's probably getting worse. . . ." The resident had accepted her status as a second-class human being.

There is a fear, largely unfounded, that if mentally ill persons are given much personal freedom, it will be dangerous for themselves and society. Our feelings, on the contrary, are that patient powerlessness breeds a great deal of unnecessary trouble for hospital and after-care staff. There may be some hostility and a sense of injustice on the part of staff members that results in keeping patients down. Some staff members feel that the mental hospital has become a "last resort" in both senses of the word. The life in a board-and-care home *is* a soft one in a number of respects. The hard-working staff member may compensate for the fact that he has to work by exerting his authority.

Reinforcement of Staff–Resident Roles

How does one go about strangling a person's sense of self-worth? One of the most effective techniques is to disbelieve and mistrust him. The following incidents may serve to give the reader some understanding of both unintended and malicious "putting down" of residents. One day a number of residents were waiting for the facility minibus to take us to our work assignments. The staff person backed the bus out of the garage carefully. We called to him that he was swinging the bus around enough to miss the pole that stood in his way. Although we stood within a few feet of the pole he didn't consider our judgment sound enough to rely on because he pulled the vehicle forward and backed out again. Then he brought the bus to a stop about 20 feet ahead of the place where we had lined up to board so that we would have to walk up to the bus. He was roundly cursed by several residents, but in whispers.

On another occasion a group of patients boarded a chartered bus for a special event. One resident in the front of the bus counted all the riders as they climbed aboard. When the recreation director arrived she wondered aloud how many people were on the bus. The resident told her. However, she proceeded to count again (an act that seemed reasonable in the light of her responsibility to see that everyone was on the bus and would return on the bus later), but when she arrived at the same figure that she had been told, she gave no acknowledgment that the resident had been right. It was as if the resident's counting hadn't counted.

Persons who are stigmatized often aren't considered to be worthy of explanations. A number of times an event we residents were looking forward to was canceled with no reason offered. In other instances we were required to wait for unusually long periods (beyond the waiting expected in institutional living) without an explanation.

Residents themselves, though on the whole supportive of one another, can unwittingly undermine the self-esteem of their fellows. They, too, share the same attitudes of stigma regarding mental illness that we find in the general population. For example, when two residents were arguing one day, the worst insult that was hurled involved calling the other resident "crazy" and imitating his uncontrolled facial grimace. In another case, one man complimented his companion's dress by saying he looked so good he looked like he didn't belong in "this hospital."

Given that staff and fellow residents have the capability to chip away at a person's self-esteem, what is the payoff for more positive action? Contrary to general belief, there is *less* trouble when persons are treated as if they are responsible, worthwhile individuals. "Bedlam bingo" erupted on one psychiatric ward whenever a volunteer group of condescending old ladies who ostensibly arrived to play bingo, but instead converged on the ward to "help out the poor, unfortunate patients." Residents became confused, wandered around, and generally created disturbances whenever this group appeared, although the disturbances didn't occur when other groups came to sponsor bingo games. Another chaotic evening in a board-and-care home resulted when a communication mixup brought together a number of residents who were expecting to be entertained by a visiting group, and a tightly knit group of hospital patients on an outing who expected merely to use the facility's piano to entertain themselves. Initial expressions of disgruntlement by both groups were put down somewhat hastily and without genuine regard for those who expressed their legitimate disappointment. The night proceeded with two persons being shoved fully clothed into the pool, a nude young lady sailing nymph-like along the balcony pursued by an irate manager, and a runaway attempt to avoid being returned to the mental hospital. The timing of these disruptions was not coincidental.

But not only is there less trouble on the whole, there is also the reward of watching progress toward responsible, independent living. Powerlessness breeds not only disruption but also withdrawal and apathy. An effort to pull a person out of his isolation, only to set him in a reality situation in which he will be kept helpless and dependent, is sheer folly.

Restructuring Staff–Resident Roles

How then does one go about building self-esteem? One simple way is by knowing the residents' names. Another way is by being polite, thanking them for their exertions. One day several residents helped our bus driver carry some boxes of personal effects up the stairs to the psychiatric ward on which a former resident was then living. The boxes were heavy and bulky. After we deposited them the nurse turned to our driver and thanked him, but said nothing to us. Contrast her behavior with a handyman at the facility who expressed genuine gratitude when a resident helped out with the work. One incident illustrates this handyman's attitude toward the residents. A resident had forgotten his medication at mealtime. The handyman called across the patio to remind the resident of his omission. "I'll be right over," the man called. He began to descend the stairs, cross the patio, and climb the stairs to the handyman who called back, "I'll meet you halfway." And he did, nearly always.

Meeting residents halfway is an excellent way of demonstrating their worth. Including them in conversations is another. It is amazing that staff members seem to assume that patients and residents see and hear only those communications that are directed at them. It is as foolish as thinking that children learn in school only what they are *formally* taught. Staff members who hold exclusive conversations, sometimes about a patient in his own presence, are perpetuating a nonperson image for that individual.

Trusting residents with keys, for example, is a communication that the resident is considered responsible.

Learning a resident's point of view is not only a fascinating undertaking but also sound in a practical sense. A resident is a kind of expert on the facility in which he lives. *Listening* to him can result in suggestions for improvements and can forestall potential problems before they become inflamed. Particularly whenever a patient was upset, one wise manager found it useful to sit down with the person over a cup of coffee and talk about what was bothering him. That's one way for two *adults* to work on a problem together. Also, taking residents' complaints and suggestions seriously indicates their worth. Kent felt dispirited and rebellious when his complaints about roaches appeared to be ignored and then doubted by some staff people.

Offering residents choices at meals, letting them choose the television programs they prefer to watch, providing a phonograph on which they can play their own records, giving them some choice of rooms, offering a variety of work and play opportunities—all these are communications that management considers residents capable of making reasonable decisions among several available choices.

The staff member who stays after working hours in any facility shows genuine concern for his clients. Residents noticed staff members who showed up on their days off or stayed later than they had to. Such staff members generally show a number of the other esteem-supporting traits listed, as well.

Working alongside a resident is a way of minimizing the status distinction between management and client. Effective conversations between staff members and residents were held while lawns were watered, soft-drink machines refilled, and rooms cleaned. Calling a patient into an office may be perceived as the beginning of a ritualized "put-down."

A sensitive staff member recognizes and acknowledges a resident's successes and strengths. Kent was heartened by praise of his beard. However, *over-praising* is a mistake. Taking for granted an appropriate adult behavior is a kind of praise, too. One resident complained privately when a staff member "made a big fuss" over a simple crocheting project of hers. She was capable of crocheting much more complex patterns, had actually done so, and felt the praise to be patronizing.

Some of the simple, practical ways people tell other people what they consider they're worth have been discussed. As after-care facilities become more "human" places in which to live, increased self-esteem develops among the residents. For the stigmatized former mental patient, and particularly for the potentially suicidal former mental patient, self-esteem fosters a meaningful, continuing existence.

REFERENCES

1. Abrahams RB: Mutual help for the widowed. Social Work 17:55, 1972

2. Ackerman N: Preventive implications of family research. *In* Prevention of Mental Disorders in Children. Edited by G Caplan. New York City, Basic Books, 1961

3. Adamson JD, Schmale AH: Object loss, giving up, and the onset of psychiatric disease. Psychosom Med 27:6, 1965

4. Addams J: Democracy and Social Ethics. New York City, Macmillan, 1902

5. Adler A: Two different types of post-traumatic neuroses. Am J Psychiatry 102:237, 1945

6. Alberti RE, Emmons ML: Your Perfect Right: A Guide to Assertive Behavior. San Luis Obispo, Calif, Impact, 1970

7. Alfaro R: A group therapy approach to suicide prevention. Bull Suicidology 6:56, 1970

8. Allport GW: The limits of social service. *In* National Policies for Education, Health and Social Services. Edited by JE Russell. New York City, Russell and Russell, 1961

9. Aronfreed J: The socialization of altruistic and sympathetic behavior. *In* Altruism and Helping Behavior. Edited by JR Macaulay, L Berkowitz. New York City, Academic Press, 1970

10. Augenbraun B, Reid H, Friedman D: Brief intervention as a preventive force in disorders of early childhood. *In* Children and Their Parents in Brief Therapy. Edited by H Barten, S Barten. New York City, Behavioral Publications, 1973

11. Ausubel DP: The Psychology of Meaningful Verbal Learning. New York City, Grune and Stratton, 1963

12. Azrin NH, Hutchinson RR, Hake DF: Extinction-induced aggression. J Exp Anal Behav 9:191, 1966

13. Bahnson CB, Bahnson MB: Role of the ego defenses: Denial and repression in the etiology of malignant neoplasm: Ann NY Acad Sci 125:825, 1966

14. Baker F: Organizational Systems: General Systems Approaches to Complex Organizations. Homewood, Ill, Dorsey Press, 1973

15. Baker F: Review of general systems concepts and their relevance for medical care. Systematics 7:209, 1969

16. Balson PM: The use of behavior therapy techniques in crisis intervention: A case report. J Behav Ther Exp Psychiatry 2:297, 1971

17. Bandura A: Principles of Behavior Modification. New York City, Holt, Rinehart, and Winston, 1969

18. Bandura A: Psychotherapy based on modeling principles. *In* Handbook of Psychotherapy and Behavior Change: An Empirical Analysis. Edited by AE Bergen, SL Garfield. New York City, Wiley, 1971

19. Bard M: Alternatives to traditional law enforcement. *In* Psychology and the Problems of Society. Edited by EF Korten, et al. Washington, DC, American Psychological Association, 1970

20. Bard M: The price of survival for cancer victims. *In* Where Medicine Fails. Edited by AL Strauss. Chicago, Trans-action Books, Aldine Publishing Co, 1970

21. Bard M: Training Police as Specialists in Family Crisis Intervention. Washington, DC, US Department of Justice, Law Enforcement Assistance Administration, National Institute of Law Enforcement and Criminal Justice, May, 1970

22. Bard M, Zacker J, Rutter E: Family Crisis and Conflict Management. Washington, DC, US Department of Justice, Law Enforcement Assistance Administration, National Institute of Law Enforcement and Criminal Justice, 1972

23. Baren JB: Crisis intervention: The ice-cream parlor tragedy, ex Change 4:28, 1973

24. Barish H: Self-help groups. *In* Encyclopedia of Social Work. Edited by R Morris. New York City, National Association of Social Workers, 1971

25. Barten HH, Barten SH (eds): Children and Their Parents in Brief Therapy. New York City, Behavioral Publications, 1973

26. Barton A: Communities in Disaster: A Sociological Analysis of Collective Stress Situations. New York City, Doubleday, 1969

27. Batchelor IR, Napier MB: The sequelae and short-term prognosis of attempted suicide. J Neurol Neurosurg Psychiatry 17:261, 1954

28. Bates FL, et al: The social and psychological consequences of a natural disaster. Washington, DC, National Academy of Sciences—National Research Council, 1963

29. Bateson G: Social planning and the concept of deutero-learning. Sci Philos Relig 2:81, 1942

30. Beabeau EC: Development and validation of a scale to assess treatment effectiveness in psychotherapy. Paper read at the Rocky Mountain Psychological Association, 1971

31. Beck AT: Depression: Clinical, Experimental, and Theoretical Aspects. New York City, Harper & Row, 1968

32. Becker W: Parents Are Teachers. Champaign, Ill, Research Press, 1971

33. Behen L, Dunen H, Resnik HLP: Evolution of a coordinated emergency psychiatric service. Hosp Community Psychiatry 22:7, 1971

34. Bergler E: Divorce Won't Help. New York City, Harper and Brothers, 1948

35. Berkowitz BP, Graziano AM: Training parents as behavior therapists: A review, Behav Res Ther 10:297, 1972

36. Berkowitz L: The self, selfishness and altruism. *In* Altruism and Helping Behavior. Edited by JR Macauley, L Berkowitz. New York City, Academic Press, 1970

37. Bernal ME: Behavioral feedback in the modification of brat behaviors. J Nerv Ment Dis 148:375, 1969

38. Bernard J: The sociological study of conflict. *In* The Nature of Conflict: Studies on the Sociological Aspects of International Tension. Published by the International Sociological Association, Paris, 1957

39. Birnbaum F, Coplon J, Scharff I: Crisis intervention after a natural disaster. Social Casework 54:545, 1973

40. Blaufarb H, Levine J: Crisis intervention in an earthquake, Social Work 17:16, 1972

41. Bloch DA, Silber E, Perry SE: Some factors in the emotional reaction of children to disaster. Am J Psychiatry 113:416, 1956

42. Bloch HS: An open-ended crisis-oriented group for the poor who are sick. Arch Gen Psychiatry 18:178, 1968

43. Blumenthal MD: Mental health among the divorced. Arch Gen Psychiatry 16:603, 1967

44. Bodin AM: Conjoint family assessment: An evolving field. *In* Advances in Clinical Assessment. Edited by PW McReynolds. Palo Alto, Calif, Science and Behavior Books, 1967

45. Boulding KE: Conflict and Defense: A General Theory. New York City, Harper & Row, 1962

46. Bourne PG: Men, Stress and Vietnam. Boston, Little, Brown and Co, 1970

47. Bowen PR, Masotti LH: Civil violence: A theoretical overview. *In* Riots and Rebellion: Civil Violence in the Urban Community. Beverly Hills, Calif, Sage, 1968

48. Bowers MK, Mullan H, Berkowitz B: Observations on suicide occurring during group psychotherapy. Am J Psychother 13:93, 1959

49. Bowlby J: Attachment and Loss. Vols I, II. New York City, Basic Books, Inc, 1973

50. Brauer LD, Gilman ED, Klerman GL: Psychiatric treatment ideologies among university faculty. Psychiatric Opinion 10:25, 1973

51. Breuer J, Freud S: Studies on Hysteria. London, Hogarth Press, 1955

52. Brodman K, Erdmann Jr AJ, Wolff HG: Cornell Medical Index. New York City, Cornell University Medical College, 1949

53. Brody S: Preventive intervention in current problems of early childhood. *In* Prevention of Mental Disorders in Children. Edited by G Caplan. New York City, Basic Books, 1961

54. Broscoe CW, et al: Divorce and psychiatric disease. Arch Gen Psychiatry 29:119, 1973

55. Brown S: Family experience and change. *In* Family Roots of School Learning and Behavior Disorders. Edited by R Friedman. Springfield, Ill, Charles C Thomas, 1973

56. Brull F: The trauma: Theoretical considerations. Isr Ann Psychiatry 7-8:96, 1967-1970

57. Burgess AW, Holmstrom LL: Rape: Victims of crisis. Bowie, Md, Robert J Brady Co, 1974

58. Cadden V: Crisis in the family. *In* Principles of Preventive Psychiatry. Edited by G Caplan. New York City, Basic Books, 1964

59. Canter L, Paulson T: A class-credit model of in-school consultation: A functional-behavioral approach. Paper read at the Western Psychological Association Convention. Anaheim, Calif, April 13, 1973

60. Caplan G: An Approach to Community Mental Health. New York City, Grune & Stratton, 1961

61. Caplan G: Patterns of parental response to the crisis of premature birth. Psychiatry 23:365, 1960

62. Caplan G (ed): Prevention of Mental Disorders in Children. New York City, Basic Books, 1961

63. Caplan G: Principles of Preventive Psychiatry. New York City, Basic Books, 1964

64. Caplan G: Support Systems and Community Mental Health: Lectures in Concept Development. New York City, Behavioral Publications, 1973

65. Caplan G: The Theory and Practice of Mental Health Consultation. New York City, Basic Books, 1970

66. Carlton MG: The pre-admission period and precare programs for the mentally ill: A review of the literature. *In* Perspectives in Community Mental Health. Edited by AJ Bindman, AD Spiegel. Chicago, Aldine Publishing Co, 1969

67. Cassel J: An epidemiological perspective of psycho-social factors in disease etiology. Report undated

68. Cassel J: Health consequences of population density and crowding. *In* Rapid Population Growth. Prepared by the National Academy of Sciences. Baltimore, Johns Hopkins Press 12:462, 1971

69. Cassel J: Social science theory as a source of hypotheses in epidemiological research. Paper read at the Conference on the Relation of Social Factors to the Etiology of Disease. November 28 - December 2, 1962

70. Caudill W: The Psychiatric Hospital as a Small Society. Cambridge, Mass, Harvard University Press, 1958

71. Chafetz ME, Blane HT, Hill MJ: Frontiers of Alcoholism. New York City, Science House, 1970

72. Christensen HG: Handbook of Marriage and the Family. Chicago, Rand McNally & Co, 1964

73. Claiborne WL: Tragedy averted by talks. The Washington Post, October 13, 1972

74. Cline DW, Chosy JJ: A prospective study of life changes and subsequent health changes. Arch Gen Psychiatry 27:51, 1972

75. Coelho GU, et al: Coping & Adaptation. Washington, DC, A Behavioral Sciences Bibliography. PHS Publication No. 2087, 1970

76. Coelho GU, et al: Coping strategies in a new learning environment. Arch Gen Psychiatry 101:141, 1944

77. Cohen A, Laue J (eds): Intervenor roles: I. The mediators and intervenor roles; II. The community advocates. *In* Crisis and Change. Community Crisis Intervention Project, Social Science Institute. St. Louis, Mo, Washington University Press 2:1-2, 1972

78. Cohen RE: Community organizational aspects of establishing and maintaining a local program. *In* American Handbook of Psychiatry. Edited by S Arieti, G Caplan. New York City, Basic Books, 1974

79. Cohen RE: Crisis in educational systems: Threat or challenge? Timely Issues in Education 4:13, 1973

80. Cohen RE: Intervention at a critical moment of crisis: A cooperative venture. Existential Psychiatry J (In press)

81. Coleman JV, Errera P: The general hospital emergency room and its psychiatric problems. Am J Public Health 53:1294, 1963

82. Collins AC: Natural delivery systems. Am J Orthopsychiatry 43:46, 1973

83. Coser LA: The Function of Social Conflict. New York City, Free Press, 1964

84. Cowan EL: Social and community interventions. Ann Rev Psychol 24:423, 1973

85. Croog SH, Lipson A, Levine S: Help patterns in severe illness: The roles of kin network, non-family resources and institutions. J Marriage Fam 34:23, 1972

86. Cumming J, Cumming E: Ego and Milieu: Theory and Practice of Environmental Therapy. New York City, Altherton Press, 1966

87. Danzig E, et al: The Effects of a Threatening Rumor on a Disaster-Stricken Community. Washington, DC, Nat Acad Sci, 1958

88. Darbonne A: Crisis: A review of theory, practice and research. Psychotherapy 4:49, 1967

89. Darley JM, Latane B: Norms and normative behavior: Field studies of social interdependence. *In* Altruism and Helping Behavior. Edited by JR Macauley, L Berkowitz. New York City, Academic Press, 1970

90. Davidian H: Aspects of Anxiety in Iran. Aust NZ J Psychiatry 3:3A:254, 1969

91. Decker JB, Stubblebine JM: Crisis intervention and prevention of psychiatric disability: A follow-up study. Am J Psychiatry 129:725, 1972

92. Des Pres T: The survivor. Encounter 37:3, 1971

93. Deutsch M: Toward an understanding of conflict. Int J Group Tensions 1:42, 1971

94. Diggory JC: Calculation of some costs of suicide prevention using certain predictors of suicidal behavior. Psychol Bull 71:5, 1969

95. Dohrnwend BP, Dohrnwend BS: Social Status and Psychological Disorder. New York City, Wiley-Interscience, 1969

96. Drabek T: Social processes in disaster: Family evacuation. Social Problems 16:336, 1969

97. Drabek T, Boggs K: Families in disaster: Reactions and relatives. J Marriage Fam 30:443, 1968

98. Drabek T, Quarantelli EL: Scapegoats, villains and disasters, Transaction 4:12, 1967

99. Drabek T, Stephenson J: When disaster strikes. J Appl Soc Psychol 1:187, 1970

100. Drayer CS, Cameron DC, Woodward WD: Psychological first aid in community disasters. JAMA 156:36, 1954

101. Dublin LI: Suicide prevention. *In* On the Nature of Suicide. Edited by ES Shneidman. San Francisco, Jossey-Bass, 1969

102. Durkheim E: Suicide. Glencoe, Ill, Free Press, 1951

103. Dynes RR: Organized Behavior in Disaster. Lexington, Mass, DC Heath, 1970

104. Dynes RR, Quarantelli EL: Editors' introduction, Am Behav Sci 13:325, 1970

105. Dynes RR, Quarantelli EL: Effects of disaster on community life. *In* Proceedings of Seminar on Family Agencies' Role in Disaster. Canadian Department of National Health and Welfare. November 14-17, 1966

106. Dynes RR, Warheit G: Organizations in disasters, EMO National Digest 9:12, 1969

107. Eisler RM, Harsen M: Behavioral techniques in family-oriented crisis intervention, Arch Gen Psychiatry 28:111, 1973

108. Engel GL: Anxiety and drepressive withdrawal, Int J Psychoanal 43:89, 1962

109. Epstein LJ, Simon A: Alternatives to state hospitalization for the geriatric mentally ill. Am J Psychiatry 124:955, 1968

110. Epstein N: Brief group therapy in a child guidance clinic. Social Work 15:33, 1970

111. Erikson EH: Identity and the life cycle. Psychol Issues 1:1, 1959

112. Erikson EH: Insight and Responsibility. New York City, Norton, 1964

113. Errera P, Wyshak G, Jarecki H: Psychiatric care in a general hospital emergency room. Arch Gen Psychiatry 9:105, 1963

114. Fairweather G, et al: Community Life for the Mentally Ill: An Alternative to Institutional Care. Chicago, Aldine Publishing Co, 1969

115. Farberow NL: Group therapy with suicidal persons. *In* Suicidal Behaviors. Edited by HLP Resnik. Boston, Little, Brown & Co, 1968

116. Farberow NL, Cutter F, MacKinnon D: Status of Suicide in the Veterans Administration, Report III. (Unpublished report to Veterans Administration), 1973

117. Farberow NL, et al: An eight-year survey of hospital suicides. Life-Threatening Behavior 1:184, 1971

118. Farberow NL, Shneidman ES: The Cry for Help. New York City, McGraw-Hill Book Co, 1961

119. Fernsterheim M: Behavior therapy: Assertive training in groups. *In* Progress in Group and Family Therapy. Edited by CJ Sayer, HS Kaplan. New York City, Brunner/Mazel, 1972

120. Ferriera AJ, Winter WD: Family interaction and decision making. Arch Gen Psychiatry 13:214, 1965

121. Fink CF: Conflict management strategies implied by expected utility models of behavior. Am Behav Sci 15:837, 1972

122. Firestone JM: Theory of the riot process. Am Behav Sci 15:859, 1972

123. Fish L: Using social systems treatment techniques on a crisis unit. Hosp Community Psychiatry 22:8, 1971

124. Fisher RJ: Third party consultation: A method for the study and resolution of conflict. J Conflict Resolution 16:67, 1972

125. Flomenhaft K, Langsley DG: After the crisis. Ment Hgy 55:473, 1971

126. Fogleman CW, Parenton VJ: Disaster and aftermath: Selected aspects of individual and group behavior in critical situations. Social Forces 38:129, 1959

127. Foote NN: Matching of husband and wife in phases of development. *In* Source Book in Marriage and the Family. Edited by MB Sussman. Boston, Houghton Mifflin Co, 1963

128. Foote NN, Cottrell Jr LS: Identity and Interpersonal Competence: A New Direction in Family Research. Chicago, University of Chicago Press, 1955

129. Form W, Nosow S: Community in Disaster. New York City, Harper & Row, 1958

130. Fox R: The Samaritan contribution to suicide prevention. Proceedings of the Sixth International Conference for Suicide Prevention. Los Angeles Suicide Prevention Center, 1972

131. Foxman J: The psychiatric emergency team in community mental health. LAC Mental Health J 1:29, 1972

132. Framo J: Rationale and techniques of intensive family therapy, *In* Intensive Family Therapy. Edited by I Boszormenyi-Nagy, J Framo. New York City, Brunner/Mazel, 1972

133. Frank J: Persuasion and Healing. Baltimore, Johns Hopkins University Press, 1973

134. Frankel FH, Chafetz ME, Blane HT: Treatment of psychosocial crises in the emergency service of a general hospital. JAMA 195:114, 1966

135. Frederick CJ, Farberow NL: Group psychotherapy with suicidal persons: A comparison with standard group methods. Int J Soc Psychiatry 16:103, 1970

136. Freud A, Burlingham D: War and Children. London, Medical War Books, 1943

137. Freud S: Beyond the Pleasure Principle. London, Hogarth Press, 1953

138. Fried M: Grieving for a lost home. *In* The Urban Condition. Edited by LJ Duhl. New York City, Basic Books, 1963

139. Fried M: The World of the Urban Working Class. Cambridge, Mass, Harvard University Press, 1973

140. Friedman T, et al: The psychiatric home treatment service: Preliminary report of five years of treatment experience. Am J Psychiatry 120:8, 1964

141. Frisch E: An Historical Survey of Jewish Philanthropy. New York City, Macmillan, 1924

142. Fritz C: Disaster. *In* Contemporary Social Problems. Edited by RK Merton, RA Nisbet. New York City, Harcourt, Brace and World, 1961

143. Fritz C, Marks E: The NORC studies of human behavior in disaster. J Soc Issues 10:33, 1954

144. Furst SS: Psychic Trauma: A Survey. New York City, Basic Books, 1967

145. Gans HJ: The Urban Villagers. Glencoe, Ill, Free Press, 1962

146. Glass A: Principles of combat psychiatry. Milit Med 117:27, 1955

147. Goffman E: Asylums. New York City, Doubleday & Co, 1961

148. Golann SE, Eisdorfer C (eds): Handbook of Community Mental Health. New York City, Appleton-Century-Crofts, 1972

149. Goldberg M, Mudd EH: Suicide: The effects of suicidal behavior upon marriage and the family. *In* Suicidal Behaviors. Edited by HLP Resnik. Boston, Little, Brown & Co, 1968

150. Goode WJ: The theoretical limits of professionalization. *In* The Semi-Professions and Their Organization. Edited by A Etzioni. New York City, Free Press, 1969

151. Goode WJ: Women in Divorce. (Originally published as *After Divorce.*) New York City, Free Press, 1956

152. Gotschalk LA, Gleser GC: The Measurement of Psychological States Through the Content Analysis of Verbal Behavior. Berkeley, University of California Press, 1969

153. Grant H, Murray R: Emergency Care. Bowie, Md, Robert J Brady Co, 1971

154. Greene W, Young LE, Swishen SN: Psychological factors and reticuloen-dothelial disease. Psychosom Med 18:284, 1956

155. Grinker RR, Spiegel JP: Men Under Stress. New York City, Blakiston Co, 1945

156. Grosser GH, Wechsler H, Greenblatt M (eds): The Threat of Impending Disaster. Cambridge, Mass, MIT Press, 1964

157. Gruenberg EM, Huxley J: Mental health services can be organized to prevent chronic disability. Community Mental Health J 6:431, 1970

158. Hadlik J: Group psychotherapy for adolescents following a suicide attempt. Proceedings of the Fifth International Conference for Suicide Prevention. Edited by R Fox. Vienna, International Association for Suicide Prevention, April, 1970

159. Haley J: Strategies of Psychotherapy. New York City, Grune & Stratton, 1963

160. Hall RV, et al: Modification of behavior problems in the home with a parent as observer and experimenter. J Appl Behav Anal 5:53, 1972

161. Halmos P: The Personal Service Society. London, Constable Press, 1970

162. Hamburg DA, Adams JE: A perspective on coping behavior, seeking and utilizing information in major transitions. Arch Gen Psychiatry 17:277, 1967

163. Hansell N: A system: Patient predicament and clinical service. Arch Gen Psychiatry 17:204, 1967

164. Hansell N: Casualty management method: An aspect of mental health technology in transition. Arch Gen Psychiatry 19:281, 1968

165. Hansell N: Elements of a local service system. *In* American Handbook of Psychiatry. Edited by S Arieti, G Caplan. New York City, Basic Books, 1974

166. Hansell N, Benson ML: Interrupting prolonged patienthood. Arch Gen Psychiatry 24:238, 1971

167. Hansell N, et al: Decision counseling method: Expanding coping at crisis-in-transit. Arch Gen Psychiatry 22:462, 1970

168. Hansell N, et al: The mental health expediter. Arch Gen Psychiatry 18:392, 1968

169. Harshbarger D: Some ecological implications for the organization of human intervention throughout the life-span. *In* Life-Span Developmental Psychology: Personality and Socialization. Edited by KW Schale, PB Baltes. New York City, Academic Press, 1973.

170. Hathaway SR, McKinley JC: MMPI. New York City, Psychological Corporation, 1951

171. Haughton A: Suicide prevention programs in the U.S.—An overview. Bull Suicidology, Vol 24. July, 1968

172. Heisel JS: Life changes as etiologic factors in juvenile rheumatoid arthirtis, J Psychosom Res 16:411, 1972

173. Hendin D: Death as a Fact of Life. New York, W W Norton, 1973

174. Hill R: Generic features of families under stress. *In* Crisis Intervention: Selected Readings. Edited by HJ Parad. New York City, Family Service Association of America, 1965

175. Hill R, Hansen D: Families in disaster. *In* Man and Society in Disaster. Edited by GW Baker, D Chapman. New York City, Basic Books, 1962

176. Hill R, Rodger RH: Sociological frameworks appropriate for family-oriented psychiatry. Voices 5:69, 1969.

177. Hinsie LE, Campbell RJ: Psychiatric Dictionary. New York City, Oxford University Press, 1960

178. Hirschowitz RG: Crisis Theory. Proceedings of the National Multi-Professional Conference: Psychopathology and Mental Health of the Family. Johannesburg, South Africa, June 27-30, 1972

179. Hocking F: Psychiatric aspects of extreme environmental stress. Dis Nerv Syst 31:542, 1970

180. Hollingshead AB, Redlich FD: Social Class and Mental Illness. New York City, Wiley and Sons, 1958

181. Holmes TH, Rahe RH: The social readjustment rating scale. J Psychosom Res II: 213, 1967

182. Horowitz MJ: Image Formation and Cognition. New York City, Appleton-Century-Crofts, 1970

183. Horowitz MJ: Phase-oriented treatment of stress response syndromes. Am J Psychother 27: 506, 1973

184. Horowitz MJ: Psychic trauma: Return of images after a stress film. Arch Gen Psychiatry 20:552, 1969

185. Horowitz MJ, Becker SS: Cognitive response to stress: Experimental studies of a compulsion to repeat trauma. *In* Psychoanalysis and Contemporary Science. Vol I. Edited by RR Holt, E Peterfreund. New York City, Macmillan, 1972

186. Horowitz MJ, Solomon GF: A prediction of stress response syndromes in

Vietnam veterans: Observations and suggestions for treatment. J Social Issues (In press)

187. Hurvitz N: The characteristics of peer self-help psychotherapy groups. Psychotherapy 7:41, 1970

188. Indin BM: The crisis club: A group experience for suicidal patients. Ment Hyg 50:280, 1966

189. Jackson DD: Family interaction, family homeostasis and some implications for conjoint family psychotherapy. *In* Individual and Family Dynamics. Edited by JH Masserman. New York City, Grune & Stratton, 1959

190. Jackson DD: Family rules: Marital *quid pro quo*. Arch Gen Psychiatry 12:589, 1965

191. Jacobs J: Adolescent Suicide. New York City, Wiley-Interscience, 1971

192. Jacobson GF: Crisis theory and treatment strategy: Some sociocultural and psychodynamic considerations. J Nerv Ment Dis 141:2, 1965

193. Jacobson GF: Emergency services in community mental health. Am J Public Health 64:124, 1974

194. Jacobson GF, Strickler M, Morley W: Generic and individual approaches to crisis intervention. Am J Public Health 58:338, 1968

195. Jacobson GF, et al: The scope and practice of an early-access brief treatment psychiatric center. Am J Psychiatry 121:12, 1965

196. James M, Jongeward D: Born to Win. Menlo Park, Calif, Addison-Wesley, 1971

197. Janis IL: Psychological Stress: Psychoanalytic and Behavioral Studies of Surgical Patients. New York City, Wiley & Sons, 1958

198. Janis IL: Stress and Frustration. New York City, Harcourt-Brace-Jovanovich, 1969

199. Jellinek EM: The Disease Concept of Alcoholism. New Haven, College and University Press, 1960

200. Kalis BL: Crisis theory: Its relevance for community psychology and directions for development. *In* Community Psychology and Mental Health. Edited by D Adelson, BL Kalis. Scranton, Pa, Chandler Publishing Co, 1970

201. Kanfer FH, Phillips JS: Learning Foundations of Behavior Therapy. New York City, Wiley, 1970

202. Kaplan DM: Observations on crisis theory and practice. Social Casework 49:51, 1968

203. Kaplan DM, Mason E: Maternal reactions to premature birth viewed as an acute emotional disorder. *In* Crisis intervention: Selected Readings. Edited by HJ Parad. New York City, Family Service Association of America, 1965

204. Kardiner A: Traumatic Neuroses of War. *In* American Handbook of Psychiatry. Edited by S Arieti. New York City, Basic Books, 1959

205. Katz A: Self-help organizations and volunteer participation in social welfare. Social Work 15:51, 1970

206. Kaufman H: Aggression and Altruism. New York City, Holt, Rinehart & Winston, 1970

207. Kavanaugh RE: Facing Death. Los Angeles, Nash Publishing Co, 1972

208. Kernberg O: A psychoanalytic classification of character pathology. J Am Psychoanal Assoc 18:800, 1970

209. Kibel HD: A group member's suicide: Treating collective trauma. Int J Group Psychother 23:42, 1973

210. Killian L: The significance of multiple group membership in disaster. Am J Sociol 57:309, 1952

211. Kincannon KC: Prediction of the standard MMPI scale. J Consult Clin Psychol 32:3, 1968

212. Kirkbride TS: Construction, organization and general arrangements of hospitals for the insane. Ment Hosp 6:14, 1955

213. Kirkbride TS: Description of the pleasure grounds and farm of the Pennsylvania hospital for the insane. Am J Insanity 4:347, 1848

214. Kirtley DD, Sacks JM: Reactions of a psychotherapy group to ambiguous circumstances surrounding the death of a group member. J Consult Clin Psychol 33:195, 1969

215. Kissen DM, Eysenck HJ: Personality in male lung cancer patients. J Psychosom Res 6:213, 1962

216. Klein DC: Community Dynamics and Mental Health. New York City, Wiley, 1968

217. Klein DC, Lindemann E: Preventive intervention in individual family crisis situations. *In* Prevention of Mental Disorders in Children. Edited by G Caplan. New York City, Basic Books, 1961

218. Klein DC, Ross A: Kindergarten entry: A study of role transition. *In* Crisis Intervention: Selected Readings. Edited by HJ Parad. New York City, Family Service Association of America, 1965

219. Klerman GL: Mental health and the urban crisis. Am J Orthopsychiatry 39:818, 1969

220. Klerman GL, Missett JR, Thomas P: Shift in utilization of mental health services. (Unpublished manuscript), 1971

221. Kliman G: Psychological Emergencies of Childhood. New York City, Grune & Stratton, 1968

222. Kluckhohn C, Leighton D: The Navajo. Cambridge, Mass, Harvard University Press, 1946

223. Kluckhohn F, Spiegel J: Value orientations in varying cultures. Group for the Advancement of Psychiatry, Report #1, 1954

224. Koch L: Facilitating program development by staff study. Social Casework 53:224, 1972

225. Koranyi E: Psychodynamic theories of the "survivor syndrome." Can Psychiatr J 14:165, 1969

226. Knox DH: Marriage Happiness: A Behavioral Approach to Counseling. Champaign, Ill, Research Press, 1971

227. Kramer M: Application of Mental Health Statistics. Geneva, World Health Organization, 1969

228. Kramer M: Some Implications of Trends in the Usage of Psychiatric Facilities

for Community Mental Health Programs and Related Research. Washington, DC, PHS Publication #1434, 1967

229. Krebs DL: Altruism—An examination of the concept and a review of the literature. Psychol Bull 73:258, 1970

230. Krebs DL, Whitten P: Guilt-edged giving, the shame of it all. Psychology Today 5:50, 1972

231. Krim A: Families in crisis. Children Today 3:2, 1974

232. Kropotkin P: Mutual Aid. Boston, Extending Horizon Books, 1955

233. Krystal H: Massive Psychic Trauma. New York City, International Universities Press, 1968

234. Krystal H, Niederland WG: Clinical observations on the survivor syndrome. *In* Massive Psychic Trauma. Edited by H Krystal. New York City, International Universities Press, 1968

235. Laing RD, Phillipson H, Lee AR: Interpersonal Perception: A Theory and Method of Research. New York City, Springer Pub Co, 1966

236. Langsley DG, Kaplan DM: The Treatment of Families in Crisis. New York City, Grune & Stratton, 1968

237. Langsley DG, et al: Family crisis therapy—Results and implications. Family Process 7:145, 1968

238. Langsley DG, et al: Avoiding mental hospital admission: A follow-up study. Am J Psychiatry 127:1391, 1971

239. Lazare A, Eisenthal S, Wasserman L: The customer approach to patienthood: Attending to patient requests in a walk-in clinic. Arch Gen Psychiatry 32:553, 1975

240. Lazarus RS: Psychological Stress and the Coping Process. New York City, McGraw-Hill, 1966

241. Lebow MD: Behavior Modification for the Family. *In* Family Therapy: An Introduction to Theory and Technique. Edited by GD Erickson, TP Hogan. Monterey, Calif, Brooks/Cole, 1972

242. LeMasters EE: Parenthood as crisis. *In* Crisis Intervention: Selected Readings. Edited by HJ Parad. New York City, Family Service Association of America, 1965

243. Lennard HL, Bernstein A: Patterns in Human Interaction: An Introduction to Clinical Sociology. San Francisco, Jossey-Bass, 1969

244. Leopold RL: Management of a post-traumatic neurosis. *In* Psychosomatic Medicine. Edited by JH Nodine. Philadelphia, Lea & Febiger, 1962

245. Leopold RL, Dillon H: Psycho-anatomy of a disaster: A long-term study of post-traumatic neuroses in survivors of a marine explosion. Am J Psychiatry 120:913, 1963

246. Lettieri DJ: A suicidal death prediction scale. Proceedings of the Sixth International Conference for Suicide Prevention. Los Angeles, Suicide Prevention Center, 1972

247. Leventhal T: Evaluation of a brief therapy program for children. Children's Psychiatric Center, Eatontown, NJ. (Unpublished manuscript), 1970

248. Levy L, Rowitz L: Ecological attributes of high and low rate mental hospital utilization areas in Chicago. Social Psychiatry 6:20, 1971

249. Lewinsohn PM, Weinstein MS, Shaw DA: Depression: A clinical-research approach. *In* Advances in Behavior Therapy. Edited by R Rubin, C Franks. New York City, Academic Press, 1969

250. Lewis GH: Role differentiation. Am Sociol Rev 37:424, 1972

251. Liberman RP: Behavioral approaches to family and couple therapy. Am J Orthopsychiatry 40:106, 1970

252. Liberman RP, DeRisi W, King LW: Behavioral interventions with families. *In* Current Psychiatric Therapies. Edited by J Masserman. New York City, Grune & Stratton, 1973

253. Liberman RP, Raskin DE: Depression: A behavioral formulation. Arch Gen Psychiatry 24:515, 1971

254. Libet JM, Lewinsohn PM: Concept of social skill with reference to the behavior of depressed persons. J Consult Clin Psychol 40:304, 1973

255. Lidz T: Psychiatric casualties from Guadalcanal: A study of reactions to extreme stress. Psychiatry 9:193, 1946

256. Lifton RJ: Death in Life: Survivors of Hiroshima. New York City, Random House, 1967

257. Lifton R: Home From the War. New York City, Simon & Schuster, 1973

258. Likert RA: Techniques for the measurement of attitudes. Arch Psychol, Vol 140. 1932

259. Lindemann E: Science and philosophy: Sources of humanitarian faith. *In* Social Work as Human Relations. New York City, Columbia University Press, 1949

260. Lindemann E: Symptomatology and management of acute grief. *In* Crisis Intervention: Selected Readings. Edited by HJ Parad. New York City, Family Service Association of America, 1965

261. Linn MW, et al: A social dysfunction rating scale. J Psychiatr Res 6:299, 1969

262. Lisansky ET: The avoided diagnosis—alcoholism. Bull Am Coll Physicians, March, 1974

263. Litman RE: Models for predicting suicidal lethality. Proceedings of the Sixth International Conference for Suicide Prevention. Los Angeles Suicide Prevention Center, 1972

264. Litman RE: Suicide prevention center patients: Follow-up study. Bull Suicidology 6:12, 1970

265. Litman RE: The management of suicidal patients in medical practice. *In* The Psychology of Suicide. Edited by ES Schneidman, NL Farberow, RE Litman. New York City, Science House, 1972

266. Litman RE, et al: Prediction models of suicidal behaviors. *In* the Prediction of Suicide. Edited by AT Beck, et al. Bowie, Md, Charles Press, 1974

267. Loya F: Suicide rates among Chicano youth in Denver, Colorado. Paper read at the AAS meeting in Houston, Texas, April, 1973

268. Luborski L, Todd TC, Katcher EH: A self-administered social assets scale for

predicting physical and psychological illness and health. J Psychosom Res 17:109, 1973

269. Luchterhand EG: Sociological approaches to massive stress in natural and man-made disaster. Int Psychiatr Clin 8:29, 1971

270. Ludwig AM, Farrelly F: The code of chronicity. Arch Gen Psychiatry 15:562, 1966

271. Macaulay JR, Berkowitz L: Overview. *In* Altruism and Helping Behavior. Edited by JR Macaulay, L Berkowitz. New York City, Academic Press, 1970

272. MacMillan AM: The health opinion survey. Psychol Rep 3:325, 1957

273. Mahler MS, Pine F, Bergman A: The mother's reaction to the toddler's drive for individuation. *In* Parenthood, Its Psychology and Psychopathology. Edited by EJ Anthony, T Benedee. Boston, Little, Brown & Co, 1970

274. Maltzberg B: Mental status and the incidence of mental disease, Int J Soc Psychiatry 10:19, 1964

275. Maris RE: Social Forces in Urban Suicide. Homewood, Ill, The Dorsey Press, 1969

276. Marks E, et al: Human reactions in disaster situations. National Opinion Research Center, University of Chicago. (Unpublished report), 1954

277. Markus GB, Tanter R: A conflict model for strategists and managers. Am Behav Sci 15:809, 1972

278. May R: Love and Will. New York City, Norton, 1969

279. Mayeroff M: On Caring. New York City, Harper & Row, 1972

280. McCartney JL: Suicide as a complication to group psychotherapy. Milit Med 126:895, 1961

281. McFall RM, Twentyman CT: Four experiments on the relative contributions of rehearsal, modeling and coaching to assertion training. J Abnorm Psychol 81:199, 1973

282. McGee RK: Crisis Intervention in the Community. Baltimore, University Park Press, 1974

283. McGee TF: Some basic considerations in crisis intervention. Community Mental Health J 4:319, 1968

284. McInnes RS, et al: An analysis of the service relationships between state mental hospitals and one local mental health program. California Department of Mental Hygiene Biostatistics Bulletin 23. Sacramento, Calif, 1962

285. McParttand TS, Hickart RH: Social and clinical outcomes of psychiatric treatment. Arch Gen Psychiatry 14:179, 1966

286. Mendel WM: Effect of length of hospitalization on rate and quality of remission from acute psychotic episodes. J Nerv Ment Dis 143:226, 1966

287. Michels T, Cunningham J, Kilpatrick M: An exploratory study of group treatment for suicidal people. (Unpublished thesis) University of Southern California, Los Angeles, 1973

288. Miller EJ, Rice AK: Systems of Organization. London, Tavistock Publications, 1967

289. Miller ER, Shaskan DA: A note on the group management of a disgruntled, suicidal patient. Int J Group Psychother 13:216, 1963

290. Minuchin S: Conflict resolution family therapy. Psychiatry 28:278, 1965

291. Miskimins W, et al: Prediction of suicide in a psychiatric hospital. J Clin Psychol 23:296, 1967

292. Moore BE, Fine BD: A Glossary of Psychoanalytic Terms and Concepts. New York City, The American Psychoanalytic Association, 1968

293. Moore HE: Tornadoes Over Texas. Austin, University of Texas Press, 1958

294. Moore HE, Friedsam HJ: Reported emotional stress following a disaster. Social Forces 38:135, 1959-1960

295. Moore HE, et al: Before the Wind: A Study of the Response to Hurricane Carla. Washington, National Academy of Sciences, 1963

296. Morley WE: Treatment of the patient in crisis. West Med 77:77, 1965

297. Morely WE, Brown VB: The crisis-intervention group: A natural mating or a marriage of convenience? Psychother Theory, Res Pract 6:1, 1969

298. Motto JA: Contact as a suicide prevention influence: A method and a preliminary report. Proc Sixth Int Conf Suicide Prev. Los Angeles Suicide Prevention Center, 1972

299. Myers JK, Lindenthal JJ, Pepper MP: Life events and psychiatric impairment, J Nerv Ment Dis 152:149, 1971

300. Nelson LD: The helping role in disaster. Paper read at American Sociological Association Meetings, Annual Proceedings, American Sociological Association, 1972

301. Neubauer PB (ed): Concepts of Development in Early Childhood Education. Springfield, Ill, Charles C Thomas, 1965

302. Nieberg HL: Agonistics—Rituals of Conflict. *In* Collective Violence. Edited by JF Short, ME Wolfgang. Chicago, Aldine Press, 1972

303. Niederland WG: Clinical observations on the 'survivors syndrome.' Int J Psychiatry 49:313, 1968

304. Nugent T: Death at Buffalo Creek. New York City, WW Norton & Co. 1973

305. Odegard O: Marriage and mental health. Acta Psychiatr Neurol Scand 80:153, 1952

306. Osnos P: Guards air grievances: Jail is calm. The Washington Post, October 13, 1972

307. Ottenberg DJ, Rosen A, Fox V: Acute alcoholic emergencies. *In* Emergency Psychiatric Care. Edited by HLP Resnik, HL Reuben. Bowie, Md, Charles Press, 1975

308. Parad HJ (ed): Crisis Intervention: Selected Readings. New York, Family Service Association of America, 1965

309. Parad HJ: Crisis intervention. *In* Encyclopedia of Social Work. Edited by R Morris. New York City, National Association of Social Workers, 1971

310. Parad HJ, Caplan C: A framework for studying families in crisis. *In* Crisis Intervention: Selected Readings. Edited by HJ Parad. New York City, Family Service Association of America, 1965

311. Parad HJ, Parad LG: A study of crisis-oriented planned short-term treatment. Social Casework 49:346, 418, 1968

312. Parad LG: Short-term treatment: An overview of historical trends, issues and potentials. Smith Coll Stud Soc Work 41:119, 1971

313. Parkes CM: Bereavement: Studies of Grief in Adult Life. New York City, International Universities Press, 1972

314. Parkes CM: The first year of bereavement: A longitudinal study of the reaction of London widows to the death of their husbands. Psychiatry 33:444, 1970

315. Parkes CM, Brown JR: Health after bereavement. Psychosom Med 34:5, 1972

316. Parloff MB, Kelman HC, Frank JD: Comfort, effectiveness and self-awareness as criteria of improvement in psychotherapy. Am J Psychiatry 111:343, 1954

317. Parsons T: The Social System. Glencoe, Ill, Free Press, 1951

318. Pasamanick B, Scarpitti F, Dintz S: Schizophrenics in the Community: An Experimental Study in the Prevention of Hospitalization. New York City, Appleton-Century-Crofts, 1967

319. Patterson GR: Families: Applications of Social Learning to Family Life. Champaign, Ill, Research Press, 1971

320. Patterson GR, Cobb J, Ray R: A social engineering technology for retraining aggressive boys. *In* Georgia Symposium in Experimental Clinical Psychology. Vol 2. Edited by H Adams, L Unikel. Springfield, Ill, Charles C Thomas, 1972

321. Patterson GR, Gullion MD: Living With Children: New Methods for Parents and Teachers. Revised edition. Champaign, Ill, Research Press, 1971

322. Patterson GR, Reid JB: Reciprocity and coercion: Two facets of social systems. *In* Behavior Modification in Clinical Psychology. Edited by C Neuringer, J Michael. New York City, Appleton-Century-Crofts, 1970

323. Peck HB, Kaplan S: Crisis theory and therapeutic change in small groups: Some implications for community mental health program. Int J Group Psychother 16:2, 1966

324. Perls FS: Gestalt Therapy Verbatim. Lafayette, Calif, Real People Press, 1969

325. Pierce RM: Training and interpersonal communication skills with the partners of deteriorated marriages. The Family Coordinator 22:223, 1973

326. Polak P: Social systems intervention. Arch Gen Psychiatry 25:110, 1971

327. Polak P, Laycob L: Rapid tranquilization. Am J Psychiatry 128:640, 1971

328. Quarantelli EL: A note on the protective function of the family in disaster. Marriage and Family Living 22:263, 1960

329. Quarantelli EL: Images of withdrawal behavior. Soc Prob 8:68, 1960

330. Quarantelli EL: Organization under stress. *In* Symposium on Emergency Operations. Edited by R Brictson. Santa Monica, Calif, Systems Development Corporation, 1966

331. Quarantelli EL: The nature and conditions of panic. Am J Sociol 60:267, 1954

332. Quarantelli EL, Dynes RR: Images of Disaster Behavior: Myths and Consequences. Columbus, Disaster Research Center, Ohio State University, 1973

333. Quarantelli EL: Operational problems of organizations in disasters. *In* 1967 Emergency Operations Symposium. Edited by R Brictson. Santa Monica, Calif, Systems Development Corporation, 1967

334. Quarantelli EL: When disaster strikes. Psychology Today 5:66, 1972

335. Rahe RH, Holmes TH: Life crisis and disease onset: A prospective study of life crises and health changes. (Unpublished manuscript) Seattle, University of Washington School of Medicine, 1972

336. Rahe RH, McKean Jr JE, Arthur RJ: A longitudinal study of life-change and illness patterns. J Psychosom Res 10:355, 1967

337. Rankin RM, Foxman J: The effect of a psychiatric emergency team on the community and the clinic. LAC Ment Health J 2:7, 1973

338. Rapoport L: Crisis intervention as a mode of brief treatment. *In* Theories of Social Casework. Edited by RW Roberts, RH Nee. Chicago, University of Chicago Press, 1970

339. Rapoport L: The state of crisis: Some theoretical considerations. *In* Crisis Intervention: Selected Readings. Edited by HJ Parad. New York City, Family Service Association of America, 1965

340. Rapoport L: Working with families in crisis: An exploration in preventive intervention. *In* Crisis Intervention: Selected Readings. *Idem.*

341. Rapoport R: Normal crises, family structure and mental health. *In* Crisis Intervention: Selected Readings. *Idem.*

342. Rapoport R, Rapoport RN: New light on the honeymoon. Human Relations 17:33, 1964

343. Rappaport EA: Beyond traumatic neurosis. Int J Psychoanal 49:719, 1968

344. Rausch HL, Wells G, Campbell J: Adaptation to the first years of marriage. Psychiatry 26:368, 1963

345. Redlich FC, et al: The Connecticut Mental Health Center: A joint venture of state and university in community psychiatry. Conn Med 30:656, 1966

346. Rees WD, Lutkins SG: Mortality of bereavement. Br Med J 4:13, 1967

347. Reid H, et al: Preventative interventions for the very young: An infant consultation service interweaves service, training and research. Paper read at The American Orthopsychiatric Association Meeting, May 29-June 1, 1973, New York

348. Reid WJ, Shyne AW: Brief and Extended Casework. New York City, Columbia University Press, 1969

349. Reidel DC, et al: Developing a system for utliization, review and evaluation in community mental health centers. Hosp Community Psychiatry 22:229, 1971

350. Reiss D: The suicide six: Observations on suicidal behavior and group function. Int J Soc Psychiatry 14:201, 1968

351. Resnik HLP, Ruben HL: Emergency Psychiatric Care: The Management of Mental Health Crises. Bowie, Md, Charles Press, 1975

352. Reynolds DK: Directed behavior change. (Unpublished dissertation) University of California, Los Angeles, 1969

353. Reynolds DK, Farberow NL: Experiential research: An inside perspective on suicide and social systems. Life-Threatening Behaviors 3:261, 1974

354. Richard WC: Crisis intervention services following a natural disaster: The Pennsylvania recovery project. J Community Psychol, Vol 2, 1974

355. Richard WC, McGee RK: The CARE team: An answer to the need for a suicide prevention center outreach program. *In* Crisis Intervention and Counseling by Telephone. Edited by D Lester, GW Brockopp. Springfield, Ill, Charles C Thomas, 1973

356. Richman J, Rosenbaum M: Suicide: The role of hostility and death wishes from the family and significant others. Am J Psychiatry 126:1652, 1970

357. Richmond M: Friendly Visiting Among the Poor. New York City, Macmillan, 1899

358. Rittenhouse JD: Endurance of effect: Family unit treatment compared to identified patient treatment. Reprinted from the Proceedings, 78th Annual Convention, American Psychological Association, 1970

359. Roen SR, Gottesfeld H: Strategies and tactics in community mental health services. *In* Progress in Community Mental Health. Vol II. Edited by HH Barten, L. Bellak. New York City, Grune & Stratton, 1972

360. Rosenthal AJ, Levine SV: Brief psychotherapy with children: Process of therapy. Am J Psychiatry 128:141, 1971

361. Rosenthal AM: Thirty-Eight Witnesses. New York City, McGraw-Hill, 1964

362. Rotter JB: External control and internal control. Psychology Today 5:37, 1971

363. Rutledge AL: Premarital Counseling. Cambridge, Mass, Schenkman Publishing Co, Inc, 1966

364. Ryan TJ, Watson P: Frustrative nonreward theory applied to children's behavior. Psychol Bull 69:111, 1968

365. Ryan W: Preventive services in the social context: Power, pathology, and prevention. *In* Preventive Services in Mental Health Programs. Edited by BL Bloom, DP Buck. Boulder, Western Interstate Commission for Higher Education, 1967

366. Satir V: Conjoint Family Therapy. Palo Alto, Calif, Science & Behavior Books, 1967

367. Schmale Jr AH, Ikey HP: The effect of hopelessness in the development of cancer. Psychosom Med 26:634, 1964

368. Schofield W: Psychotherapy: The Purchase of Friendship. Englewood Cliffs, Prentice-Hall, 1964

369. Schur E: Radical Nonintervention. Englewood Cliffs. Prentice-Hall, 1973

370. Schur M: The Id and the Regulatory Process of the Ego. New York City, International Universities Press, 1966

371. Schwartz DA: A non-hospital in a hospital. Am J Public Health 61:2376, 1971

372. Schwartz MD, Errera P: Psychiatric care in a general hospital emergency room. Arch Gen Psychiatry 9:113, 1968

373. Schwartz SL: A review of crisis intervention programs. Psychiatr Q 45:498, 1971

374. Selkin J, Morris J: Some behavioral factors which influence the recovery rate of suicide attempters. Bull Suicidology 8:29, 1971

375. Selye H: The Physiology and Pathology of Exposure to Stress. Montreal, Acta, Inc, 1950

376. Selye H, et al: Stress. Psychology Today 3:24, 1969

377. Sennett R; The Uses of Disorder. New York City, Vintage, 1970

378. Shaw R, Blumenfeld H, Senf R: A short-term treatment program in a child guidance clinic. Social Work 13:81, 1968

379. Silber E, Perry SE, Bloch DA: Patterns of parent-child interaction in a disaster. Psychiatry 21:159, 1958

380. Silber E, et al: Adaptive behavior in competent adolescents. Arch Gen Psychiatry 5:354, 1961

381. Silverman P: Services to the widowed: First steps in a program of preventive intervention. Community Ment Health J 3:37, 1967

382. Siporin M: Disaster aid. *In* Encyclopedia of Social Work. Edited by R Morris. New York City, National Association of Social Workers, 1971

383. Siporin M: Situational assessment and intervention. Social Casework 53:91, 1972

384. Smith WG: Critical life events and prevention strategies in mental health, Arch Gen Psychiatry 25:103, 1971

385. Sorokin P: Forms and Techniques of Altruism and Spiritual Growth. Boston, Beacon Press, 1954

386. Speer DC: Family Systems: Morphostasis and morphogenesis, or is homeostasis enough? Family Process 9:259, 1970

387. Spiegel JP: Theories of violence: An integrated approach. Int J Group Tensions 1:77, 1971

388. Spilken AZ, Jacobs MA: Prediction of illness behavior from measures of life crisis, manifest distress and maladaptive coping. Psychosom Med 33:251, 1971

389. Spitzer RL, et al: The psychiatric status schedule. Arch Gen Psychiatry 23:41, 1970

390. Sprey J: The family as a system in conflict. J Marriage Fam 31:699, 1966

391. Starr D: The night the Blue Bird burned. Can Nurse 68:7, 1972

392. Stein K: A challenge to the role of the crisis concept in emergency psychotherapy. (Unpublished dissertation) University of Oregon, 1969

393. Stoddard ER: Some latent consequences of bureaucratic efficiency in disaster relief. Hum Organ 28:117, 1969

394. Straus R: Alcohol and alcoholism. *In* Contemporary Social Problems. Edited by RK Merton, RA Nisbet. New York City, Harcourt Brace, 1971

395. Strickler M: Applying crisis theory in a community clinic. Social Casework 46:150, 1965

396. Strickler M, Allgeyer J: The crisis group: A new application of crisis theory. Social Work 12:28, 1967

397. Strickler M, LaSor B: The concept of loss in crisis intervention. Ment Hyg 54:301, 1970

398. Stuart RB: Behavioral contracting within the families of delinquents. J Behav Ther Exp Psychiatry 2:1, 1971

399. Stuart RB: Operant interpersonal treatment for marital discord. J Consult Clin Psychol 33:675, 1969

400. Stubblebine JM, Decker JB: Are urban mental health centers worth it? Am J Psychiatry, (Part I) 127:908; (Part II) 128:480, 1971

401. Taplin JR: Crisis theory: Critique and reformulation. Community Ment Health J 7:13, 1971

402. Taylor JB, Zurcher LA, Key WH: Tornado. Seattle, University of Washington Press, 1970

403. Tharp RG, Wetzel RJ: Behavior Modification in the Natural Environment. New York City, Academic Press, 1969

404. Thomas EJ, Carter RD, Gambrill ED: Some possibilities of behavioral modification with marital problems using "SAM" (signal system for the assessment and modification of behavior). *In* Advances in Behavior Therapy—1969. Edited by RD Rubin, H Fensterheim, AA Lazarus, CM Franks. New York City, Academic Press, 1969

405. Tillich P: The philosophy of social work. Soc Serv Rev 36:13, 1962

406. Tischler G: Decision-making process in the emergency room. Arch Gen Psychiatry 14:69, 1966

407. Titchener JL, Ross WD: Acute or chronic stress as determinants of behavior, character and neurosis. *In* American Handbook of Psychiatry. Edited by S Arieti, E Brody. New York City, Basic Books, 1974

408. Titmuss RM: The Gift Relationship. London, George Allen and Unwin, 1970

409. Toffler A: Future Shock. New York City, Random House, 1970

410. Trunnell E, Holt W: The concept of denial or disavowal. J Am Psychoanal Assoc 22:767, 1974

411. Tuckman J, Youngman WF: A scale for assessing suicide risk of attempted suicide. J Clin Psychol 24:17, 1968

412. Tyhurst JS: Individual reactions to community disaster: The natural history of psychiatric phenomena. Am J Psychiatry 107:764, 1951

413. Tyhurst JS: The role of transition states—including disasters—in mental illness. *In* Symposium on Preventive and Social Psychiatry. Washington, DC, Walter Reed Army Institue of Research, 1957

414. Uhlenhuth EH, Paykel ES: Symptom intensity and life events. Arch Gen Psychiatry 28:473, 1973

415. Ullman M: A unifying concept linking therapeutic and community process. *In* General Systems Theory and Psychiatry. Edited by W Gray, FJ Duhl, ND Rizzo. Boston, Little, Brown and Co, 1969

416. Underhill R: The Navajos. Norman, Okla, University of Oklahoma Press, 1959

417. Vanputten T, Emory WH: Traumatic neuroses in Vietnam returnees. Arch Gen Psychiatry 29:695, 1973

418. Varley BK: Are social workers dedicated to service? Social Work 11:84, 1966

419. Vattano AJ: Power to the people: Self-help groups. Social Work 17:7, 1972

420. Visotsky HM, et al: Coping behavior under extreme stress. Arch Gen Psychiatry 5:423, 1961

421. Vollman RR, et al: The reactions of family systems to sudden and unexpected death. Omega 2:101, 1971

422. Wahler RG: Oppositional children: A quest for parental reinforcement control. J Appl Behav Anal 2:159, 1969

423. Walder LO, et al: Parents as agents of behavior change. *In* Handbook of Community Mental Health. Edited by SE Golann, C Eisdorfer. New York City, Appleton-Century-Crofts, 1972

424. Wallace AFC: Mazeway disintegration: The individual's perception of socio-cultural disorganization. Hum Organ 16:23, 1957

425. Walton M, Reeves GD, Shannon RF: Crisis team intervention in school-community unrest. Social Casework 52:1, 1971

426. Watzlawick P, Beavin JH, Jackson DD: Pragmatics of Human Communication: A Study of Interaction Patterns, Pathologies, and Paradoxes. New York City, WW Norton & Co, 1967

427. Weil RJ, Dunsworth FA: Psychiatric aspects of disaster—A case history: Some experiences during the Spring Hill, Nova Scotia mining disaster. Can Psychiatr Assoc J 3:11, 1958

428. Weinberger G: Brief therapy with children and parents. *In* Brief Therapies. Edited by H Barten. New York City, Behavioral Publications, 1971

429. Weinberger G: Some common assumptions underlying traditional child psychotherapy: Fallacy and reformulation. Psychotherapy 9:149, 1972

430. Weisman AD, Kastenbaum R: The psychological autopsy. Community Ment Health J (Monograph Series) No. 4, 1968

431. Weissman M, Fox K, Klerman GL: Hostility and depression associated with suicide attempts. Am J Psychiatry 130:450, 1973

432. Weitz WA: Experiencing the role of a hospitalized psychiatric patient: A professional's view from the other side. Prof Psychol 3:151, 1972

433. Westman JC, et al: Role of child psychiatry and divorce. Arch Gen Psychiatry 23:416, 1970

434. Whyte WF: Street-Corner Society. Chicago, University of Chicago Press, 1942

435. Wilensky HL: The professionalization of everyone? AM J Sociol 70:137, 1964

436. Wilkins J: A follow-up study of those who called a suicide prevention center. Am J Psychiatry 127:2, 1970

437. Williams WV, Polak PR, Vollman RR: Crisis intervention in acute grief. Paper presented at the 22nd Institute of Hospital and Community Psychiatry, Philadelphia, September 21-24, 1970

438. Winget CM, Kramer M, Whitman RM: Dreams and demography. Can Psychiatr Assoc J 17:203, 1972

439. Wold CI: A two-year follow-up of suicide prevention center patients. Life-Threatening Behavior 3:3, 1973

440. Wold CI: Characteristics of 26,000 suicide prevention center patients. Bull Suicidology Vol 24, Spring, 1970

441. Wold CI: Sub-groupings of suicidal people. Omega 2:19, 1971

442. Wold CI, Litman RE: Suicide after contact with a suicide prevention center. Arch Gen Psychiatry 28:735, 1973

443. Wolfenstein M: Disaster: A Psychological Essay. New York City, Free Press, 1957

444. Wolpe J: The instigation of assertive behavior: Transcripts from two cases. J Behav Ther Exp Psychiatry 1:145, 1970

445. Wolpe J: The Practice of Behavior Therapy. New York City, Pergamon Press, 1969

446. Wright D: The Psychology of Moral Behavior. Baltimore, Penguin Books, 1971

447. Yalom ID: The Theory and Practice of Group Psychotherapy. New York City, Basic Books, 1970

448. Young OR: Intermediaries: Additional thoughts on third parties, J Conflict Resolution 16:51, 1972

449. Young R: The Role of the Navajo in the Southwestern Drama. Gallup, NM, Independent Press, 1968

450. Zacker J, Bard M: The effects of conflict management training on police performance. J Appl Psychol 58:202, 1973

451. Zeilberger J, Sampen S, Sloane H: Modification of a child's behavior in the home with the mother as the therapist. J Appl Behav Anal 1:47, 1968

452. Zolik ES, Levin I, Hubek P: Comprehensive community care and patient re-hospitalization. Reprinted from the Proceedings, 78th Annual Convention, American Psychological Association, 1970

453. Zonana H, Henisz JE, Levine M: Psychiatric emergency services: A decade later. Psychiatry in Medicine, 1972

454. Zonana H, Klerman GL: Resistances to becoming accessible. *In* The Outpatient: Consumer and Client. Edited by A Tulipan, A Cutting. Oil City, Penn, Psychiatric Outpatient Clinics of America (POCA), 1972

455. Zuk G: Family Therapy. Arch Gen Psychiatry 16:71, 1967

456. Alcohol and Health, First Special Report to the U.S. Congress. US Department of HEW, December, 1971

457. American National Red Cross: First Aid. Fourth edition. Garden City, NY, Doubleday, 1957

458. American Psychiatric Association's Committee on Civil Defense: First Aid for Psychological Reactions in Disasters. Second edition. Washington, DC, American Psychiatric Association, 1966

459. Area Handbook for Nicaragua. Superintendent of Documents, US Government Printing Office, Washington, DC

460. California Bureau of Criminal Statistics: Crime and Delinquency in California. 1969

461. Committee on Injuries, American Academy of Orthopaedic Surgeons: Emergency Care and Transportation of the Sick and Injured. Chicago, AAOS, 1971

462. Community Mental Health Research and Development Corporation: Project Outreach Progress, Report No. 2, February 15, 1973. Buffalo, NY, State University of New York, Department of Psychiatry, 1973

463. Lemberg Center for the Study of Violence: Race-Related Civil Disorders, 1967-1969. Report No. 1. Waltham, Mass, Brandeis University, 1971

464. Lemberg Center for the Study of Violence: The Long, Hot Summer? Report No. 2. Waltham, Mass, Brandeis University, 1972

465. National Center for Health Statistics: Socioeconomic Characteristics of Diseased Persons, US, 1962-1963 Deaths. Serial 22, #9. Washington, DC, HEW, 1969

466. National Vital Statistics Division, Public Health Service: Vital Statistics of the United States, 1968. Washington, DC, US Government Printing Office, 1969

467. Office of Emergency Preparedness, Executive Office of the President. Disaster Preparedness: Report to the Congress. Washington, DC, US Government Printing Office, 1972

468. Office of Special Housing Services: First Annual Report. New York City, Human Resources Administration, March 1973-March 1974

469. President's Commission on Law Enforcement and Administration of Justice: The Challenge of Crime in a Free Society. Washington, DC, 1967

470. Report of the Joint Commission on Mental Health of Children: Crisis in Child Mental Health, Challenge for the 1970's. New York City, Harper & Row, 1969